THE AMERICAN VICE PRESIDENCY

The

AMERICAN VICE PRESIDENCY

From Irrelevance to Power

JULES WITCOVER

 Smithsonian Books

WASHINGTON, DC

This book may be purchased for educational, business, or sales promotional use. For information, please write: Special Markets Department, Smithsonian Books, P. O. Box 37012, MRC 513, Washington, DC 20013

Published by Smithsonian Books
Director: Carolyn Gleason
Production Editor: Christina Wiginton

Edited by Robin Whitaker
Designed by Mary Parsons

Library of Congress Cataloging-in-Publication Data
  Witcover, Jules.
  The American Vice Presidency : From Irrelevance to Power / Jules Witcover.
    pages   cm
  Includes bibliographical references.
  ISBN 978-1-58834-471-7
  1. Vice-Presidents—United States—Biography. 2. Vice-Presidents—United States—History. 3. United States—Politics and government. I. Title.
  E176.49.W58 2014
  352.23'90922—dc23
  2014004242

Manufactured in the United States of America
18 17 16 15 14   5 4 3 2 1

For permission to reproduce illustrations appearing in this book, please correspond directly with the owners of the works as seen below. Smithsonian Books does not retain reproduction rights for these images individually, or maintain a file of addresses for sources.

Unless indicated below all photos are from the Smithsonian Institution.
Courtesy of the Library of Congress: pgs. 57; 96 © Colonial Press, NY; 114; 122; 164; 174; 182; 204; 210 © Moffet Studio, Chicago; 219; 239; 246; 253; 290; 337; 348; 391; 416; 429; 444; 455; 468; 479; 495

CONTENTS

*To Walter Mondale, who first made a reality
of the assistant presidency*

INTRODUCTION

hrough most of the history of the American vice presidency, the office had little significance or utility in governing the nation's affairs. Most often it was awarded purely on the basis of political considerations of home state or region or as a reward for past service. The office was chronically subject to lame jokes and its occupant to ridicule, often with reason. When the first vice president, John Adams, took office in 1789, he acknowledged regarding his role as a presidential standby: "In this I am nothing, but I may be everything."[1]

That dismal appraisal no longer holds. Over the past four decades, vice presidents as never before have helped shape and implement domestic and foreign policies in the administrations in which they've served. In particular, four of the last six occupants of the office—Walter Mondale, Al Gore, Dick Cheney, and Joe Biden—have performed tasks far beyond the old ceremonial and political chores of the vice presidency. They have become genuine partners in governance with their presidents. In the process, not only have they enhanced their own prominence and utility; they have also elevated the public stature of the office, to the point that it is not too much to say that the American vice president has for all practical purposes come to be the de facto assistant president. The days when public figures of stature routinely shunned the position are over.

But this transformation of the vice presidency did not occur overnight. For nearly two hundred years, its occupants generally toiled in obscurity and irrelevance until circumstances and enlightened presidential leadership gave the office its current prominence. No statute empowers the vice president; only the sitting president can do so by delegating authority and responsibilities, and even now there is no assurance it will be done.

When the founding fathers of the American Republic gathered in Philadelphia in 1787 to write the new nation's constitution, the vice presidency was a mere afterthought in the discussion of how to choose the president. In the first election, there was never any doubt that General George Washington, hero of the Revolution and presiding officer of the Constitutional Convention, would be selected overwhelmingly. But the founders feared that following Washington's service an indecisive scramble to succeed him would occur. So many states might put forward favorite sons that no one candidate would acquire the majority required to elect a widely acceptable president.

To avoid that outcome, Delegate Hugh Williamson of North Carolina proposed that each state appoint "electors" who would cast three ballots for the position—prominent citizens voting rather than legislators, to minimize improper influence. Only one of the three ballots could be given to a state's favorite son, presumably producing a broader-based choice. Another delegate, Gouverneur Morris of New York, suggested that two votes per elector would serve the same purpose, and it was so decided.

This "double-balloting" for the presidency, it was reasoned, would arrive at the two most deserving candidates, so why not make the runner-up vice president? Then both offices would be filled by individuals presumably worthy of holding the higher office. At the same time, beyond being a standby for the presidency, the otherwise idle vice president would serve as president of the Senate, chairing it but voting only to break a tie. The scheme ensured, however, that from the vice presidency's first years and most of them thereafter, the office would be regarded as a mere appendage to the machinery of national governance, and its occupant would be airily dismissed as such. If there was any approximate model, it was the lightly regarded office of lieutenant governor in several of the original states.

The very notion of a vice presidency triggered a contentious debate among the founders over the necessity, utility, and wisdom of including the office, the manner in which its holder would be chosen, and what that person's functions and duties would be. The idea that a vice president was needed at all gained credibility and support only when the complicated method for selecting the president conveniently and simultaneously also provided for a spare president-in-waiting.

Even placing the executive power in the hands of a single individual worried some delegates, mindful that rebellion against a monarch in England was what had led to the creation of the new nation in the New World. Once that concern was overcome, the core of the discussion became the need to give the small states in the new union an equitable voice in the presidential selection. Delegate Charles Pinckney of South Carolina expressed fear: "The most populous states by combining in favor of the same individual will be able to carry their points."[2] The same would be true if the election of the president were decided by a direct vote based on population, as favored by Morris, by James Wilson of Pennsylvania, and by James Madison of Virginia.

When Roger Sherman of Connecticut argued that the president "ought to be appointed by and accountable to the legislature only,"[3] which was the depository of the supreme will of the society, Morris raised a cautionary flag. Having the legislature pick the president, he warned, "would give birth to intrigue and corruption" between the two branches "previous to election and to partiality in the executive afterwards to friends who promoted him." Madison agreed, saying that under this process "tyrannical laws may be made" that would "be executed in a tyrannical manner."[4] So some formula also had to be found to protect the rights and influence of the smaller states in choosing the chief executive, a formula in which the president would not be indebted to particular legislators who had voted for him. It was from this quest that creation of the vice presidency emerged.

To sidestep the direct voting for president by members of the national legislature, Wilson proposed that each state legislature choose as the presidential electors private citizens equal to the number of its congressional delegation—two senators plus the number of legislators in the House of Representatives as determined by population. From this so-called electoral college, which would meet in the individual states to minimize collusion among them, the candidate achieving a majority would be elected president, and the runner-up, vice president.

When Madison reported this solution to the convention, he offered only a mild caution. "The only objection which occurred," he wrote, "was that each Citizen after having given his vote for his fellow Citizen [from his own state] would throw away his second on some obscure Citizen of another state, in order to ensure the object of his first choice." Then he added, too optimistically as history would show, "But it could hardly be supposed that the Citizens of many States would be so sanguine of having their favorite selected, as not to give their second vote [for vice president] with sincerity to the next object of their choice."[5]

Indeed, the so-called double balloting was greeted with some optimism. Delaware's John Dickinson decided that each state's "partiality" for its own favorite son would work to the advantage of all. "Let the people of each State choose its best Citizen," he said. "The people will know the most eminent characters of their own State, and the people of a different State will feel an emulation in selecting those of which they have the greatest reason to be proud" for the two top executive posts.[6]

In a moment of prescience, Nathaniel Gorham of Massachusetts urged that the Senate be required to confirm the plurality of the vice president, but he was ignored. Madison subsequently wrote, "As the regulation stands, a very obscure man with a very few votes may arrive at the appointment."[7] That outcome did not occur under the double-balloting system, but in due time under a subsequent and different method of choosing the vice president, Madison's warning would echo in regrettable vice presidential selections.

At a time that political parties did not yet exist in the young nation, there was no anticipation that this arrangement might produce a president and vice president of sharply differing political loyalties. Indeed, the notion of factions was widely disparaged as the new country generally demonstrated strong unity in the task of creating a new self-government distinct from the one in England, from which it had just achieved independence.

Hugh Williamson of North Carolina, a member of the convention's Committee of Eleven, assigned to draft the Constitution, sounded a sour postmortem on the creation of the presidential standby. "Such an office as vice president was not wanted," he said. "It was introduced only for the sake of a valuable mode of election which required two be chosen at the same time."[8]

When a vice presidency was first proposed, many delegates to the Constitutional Convention pondered what the officeholder would do while he stood by to take over the duties and powers of the presidency of a deceased or disabled chief executive. Thus came the patchwork of having the vice president simultaneously serve as president of the Senate, with a single right and assignment—to cast the deciding vote in case of a tie.

This idea also had its opponents, who cited an apparent breach of the separation of executive and legislative powers, with the vice president having a foot in each branch. One who objected was Elbridge Gerry of Massachusetts, later himself the fifth vice president. "We might as well put the President himself at the head of the legislature," he warned. "The close intimacy that must subsist between the President and Vice President makes it absolutely improper." Gouverneur Morris quipped about that expected kinship: "The vice president will be the first heir apparent that ever loved his father." But Roger Sherman saw the practical utility of making the vice president the presiding officer of the Senate. Without it, he noted, the man "would be without employment."[9]

In point of fact, presiding would not be much employment at all, inasmuch as the man in the chair would not really be a senator and would have no other function than breaking a tie. He would have no explicit power to join in debate on the issue at hand or any other business on the floor of the Senate. Delegate Luther Martin of Maryland ridiculed the proposed vice president as "that great officer of government." With the candidate needing only to finish second in the presidential balloting, he said, it would be "very possible, and not improbable, that he may be appointed by the electors of a single large state," conceivably his own. An apparently disgusted Martin later reported to his state legislature, "Every part of the system which relates to the Vice President, as well as the present mode of electing the President, was introduced and agreed upon after I left Philadelphia."[10]

On the other hand, William R. Davie of North Carolina saw particular advantage in having the relatively unoccupied vice president available to break Senate tie votes. "From the nature of his election and office," Davie said, he "represents no one state in particular, but all the states." Therefore, he reasoned, "it is impossible that any officer could be chosen more impartially. He is, in consequence of his election, the creature of no particular district or state, but the office and representation of the Union. He must possess the confidence of the states in a very great degree, and consequently be the most proper person to decide in cases of this kind."[11]

Another prominent delegate, George Mason of Virginia, argued instead for a "Council of State" acting as an advisory body to the president, chaired by a "Vice President of the United States pro tempore," who would succeed the president "upon any vacancy or disability of the chief magistrate."

Having one individual serve as both vice president and president of the Senate, Mason feared, would be "a fatal defect . . . dangerously blending" the executive and legislative branches.[12]

In all this, the drafters seemed to be more worried about having the vice president take on the limited role of president of the Senate than themselves clarifying how and under what circumstances he would succeed to the presidency if destiny were to require it. They also left ambiguous whether in such an event the vice president would actually become president, or would merely assume the functions and responsibilities of the office as an acting president until another person was elected or until a surviving incumbent could resume them.

Alexander Hamilton of New York, discussing the vice presidency in terms of presidential succession, made clear his belief that a vice president would take over only temporarily. It would happen, Hamilton proposed, only in case of "the death, resignation, impeachment, removal from office or absence from the United States of the President." Then, the vice president would "exercise all the powers of this Constitution vested in the President until another shall be appointed, or until he shall return to the United States if his absence was with the Consent of the Senate and Assembly."[13]

The Committee of Eleven, charged with drafting the final language on succession, deleted the reference to a president's physical absence from the country. Considering the possibility that the vice president might die first or be disabled, or that both the president and vice president might perish at the same time, Delegate Edmund Randolph of Virginia won approval of another resolution providing in such an event "the Legislature may declare by law what officer of the United States shall act as President . . . until such disability be removed or a president shall be elected."[14]

Surprisingly, considering the criticality of the matter in presidential succession, the convention's Committee on Style, which wrote the final language, left unspecified the means whereby Congress would identify and choose that officer to "act as President" in such circumstances. Eventually, Article II, Section 1, read that in the case of a vacancy in the presidency, "the Powers and Duties . . . of the Same" were to "devolve on the Vice President," creating confusion later as to whether "the Same" referred to transferring the powers and functions only or to the office itself.

In such manner did the matter rest. The U.S. Constitution was adopted by the convention in Philadelphia on September 17, 1787, and was presented to twelve of the thirteen original states for ratification, absent only Rhode Island. The document was signed by thirty-nine of the forty-two delegates present, with George Washington of Virginia presiding. Nine months later, on June 21, 1788, the Constitution became effective with the ratification of the ninth state, New Hampshire.

In September, the Congress under the expiring Articles of Confederation, which had called the Constitutional Convention, set late 1788 and early 1789 for the election of the first president and vice president of the United States and their inauguration on April 21, 1789. Of the thirteen original states, only ten chose electors under the newly adopted procedure; North Carolina and Rhode Island had not yet ratified the Constitution, and a factional split in the two houses of the New York State Assembly resulted in no electors selected. The choices were made in January by members of the legislature in four states, by popular vote in four others, and the rest by a combination thereof.

As noted, the first national election took place in the absence of political parties of the sort that later came to be an integral and divisive aspect of the system. Factions based on a rough combination of personal relations among the politically engaged and general philosophies held by region, social standing, and means of employment, however, soon emerged. Those who advocated a strong central government came to be known as Federalists; their critics bore no special name and were referred to at first simply as Anti-Federalists.

Some of the loyal followers of Washington also possessed strains of personal ambition that would in the future disturb the harmony of the new and expanding nation. Notably Hamilton, one of Washington's principal lieutenants and allies, harbored these. He was given to political intrigue that in time was to plague another Federalist and arguably the second most highly regarded man in the newly formed union, the lawyer-farmer John Adams of Massachusetts. In this climate of intrigue the election of the first American president and vice president proceeded; the only question about the outcome concerned which worthy patriot would be chosen to stand in the wings when the icon George Washington was officially crowned as the young nation's supreme leader.

CHAPTER 1

JOHN ADAMS
OF MASSACHUSETTS

I n the first presidential election in American history, neither George Washington, nor John Adams, nor any of the other candidates waged open campaigns. They all considered any overt effort to pursue the highest office demeaning, and in any event the outcome was a foregone conclusion. Washington expressed little interest, to the point that Alexander Hamilton felt compelled to write to him: "On your acceptance of the office of President, the success of the new government may materially depend."[1]

Adams readily recognized that the presidency should and would go to Washington as the young country's unchallenged leader in peace as well as war. At the same time, he allowed himself to believe, in light of his own record during and after the Revolution, that he was entitled to be vice president and that the vote would clearly indicate so. Neither in appearance nor demeanor did Adams command great approval or warmth; he was short, portly, and balding and often given to irascibility. But his intelligence, loyalty, and persistence were unchallenged, except by bitter political foes, among whom Hamilton was in the forefront.

In advance of the actual presidential balloting, Hamilton, as a man of ambition and cunning, saw Adams as a challenge to him in the Federalist ranks and took steps to reduce the New Englander's vote. He urged electors in several northern states to deny their second ballots to Adams, lest he somehow edge out Washington for the presidency or at least see himself as the successor to Washington, a role Hamilton himself coveted.

In New York, a serious effort for the vice presidency was made in behalf of Governor George Clinton, a brigadier general in the revolutionary army, charged with defending the state's Hudson Highlands, and a close friend of Washington. From Virginia, the revolutionary hero Patrick Henry was said to be behind it.

James Madison, regarding the prospects of a New York–Virginia coalition in behalf of Clinton, turned to Hamilton for clarification. "I cannot . . . believe that the plan will succeed," Hamilton replied. "Nor indeed do I think that Clinton would be disposed to exchange his present appointment [as governor of New York] for that office [of the vice presidency] or to risk his popularity by holding both." Nevertheless, he wrote, the notion "merits attention and ought not to be neglected as chimerical or impracticable."[2]

In fact, in late 1788 an Anti-Federalist committee that had formed in New York wrote a circular to like-minded political figures elsewhere advocating "a person who will be zealously engaged in promoting such amendments to the new constitution as will render the Liberties of the Country secure under it" for election as the vice president. The committee expected that all of the New York electors would vote for Clinton as well. If the recipients of the circular would join Virginia and New York, it would be "highly probable . . . that Governor Clinton would be elected." Such an election would be of monumental importance because of "the influence that the Vice President will have in the administration of the new Government."[3]

But the circular aroused the Federalist *Gazette* in Philadelphia to write that Clinton's candidacy constituted a "last shift of the opposers of the constitution, to destroy it in *embryo*," warning that the farmer–turned–military man possessed "neither dignity nor understanding fit for that important station," another premature assessment of the office's importance. "After inflaming the state of New York by false jealousies, he now calls for a new convention, to *quiet the minds of the people.*"[4]

Madison, alarmed over the perceived threat to the Constitution, of which he was a principal architect, wrote to Thomas Jefferson, "The enemies to the Government, at the head & the most inveterate of whom is Mr. [Patrick] Henry, are laying a train for the election of Governour Clinton." If so, the

Gazette promised, "Clinton's chance of being appointed vice-president will be as bad as Paddy Henry's prospect of being chosen president."[5]

Hamilton was said also to have urged General Henry Knox of Massachusetts to persuade Adams that he was too august an American himself to serve under Washington,[6] another early indication of the low esteem the vice presidency was to have. Ultimately satisfied that Washington's election as president was secure, however, Hamilton finally backed Adams for vice president as a supporter of the new constitution who preferred to delay amending it until experience could provide more wisdom in approaching the effort.

If Adams was inactive in the election process, he was not indifferent to it. He recognized that for all the shortcomings of the vice presidency, being elected to it would confirm his stature as second only to Washington in the ranks of the revolutionary patriots. At the same time, he wrote to his daughter Abigail, called Nabby: "I am willing to serve the public on manly conditions, but not on childish ones." Adams's wife, Abigail, conveyed her view that any office less than the vice presidency would be "beneath him," though certainly a cabinet post in the Washington administration would have been more demanding of his experience and intellect,[7] considering the sparse duties carved out for the vice president.

Voting for the electors was generally light, and in early February those chosen met in the separate states, cast their ballots, and forwarded the results to the capital in New York in accordance with the procedures laid out in Article II at the Constitutional Convention. In early March the votes of the ten participating states were tallied, and to no one's surprise Washington was overwhelmingly elected president, with sixty-nine votes, receiving one of the two cast by each elector. As the commander-in-chief of the army of the Revolution and then president of the Constitutional Convention, he had achieved iconic status and undisputed acclaim throughout the states.

The electors' second votes were scattered among a host of candidates, and although Adams did receive the second-highest total and was thereby was elected vice president, his thirty-four votes were fewer than half of Washington's. Adams was disappointed at his own total, especially when he learned of Hamilton's mischief. He said later that the election was, "in the scurvy manner in which it was done, a curse rather than a blessing."[8] The experience did little to assuage Adams's reservations about popular elections and his musings that the president should be appointed for life, which fueled the allegations that he was a "monarchist" opposed to popular will.

Inasmuch as Washington as president would have all executive power under the new constitution, and Adams as vice president none at all, Adams's influence would be conditioned solely on Washington's health and survival. It was in this context that Adams memorably observed his situation as vice president: "Gentlemen, I feel a great difficulty how to act," he said. "I am Vice President. In this I am nothing, but I may be everything."[9] Later, in a letter to Abigail, he also wrote, "My country in its wisdom has contrived for me the most insignificant office that ever the invention of man contrived or his imagination conceived."[10]

In the eight years that followed, Adams found ample reason for that judgment. Yet he remained in the public eye and loyal to Washington while the American Republic struggled to survive as the most intriguing experiment yet undertaken in the exercise of self-government anywhere in the world. He could console himself in the thought that even if destiny had not elevated him to the presidency, he could still seek the highest office by election upon Washington's retirement and, if successful, go finally from nothing to everything.

The election of John Adams as the first American vice president came only nine months after his return from Europe, where he had spent most of the previous decade as his country's minister to Great Britain. Born in Braintree, Massachusetts, in 1735, as a youth Adams often attended New England's famed town meetings, graduated from Harvard in 1755, and taught school while studying nights for the law. Admitted to the Boston bar in 1758, he played a critical role in the repeal of the despised Stamp Act and emerged as one of the colonists' most prominent legal defenders against British oppression. In 1761, upon the death of his father, the elder John Adams, he inherited the family farm and looked forward to the agricultural life, while as a Braintree freeholder he also engaged himself in the local politics.

In 1774, he was elected to the Continental Congress and was part of the committee that helped Thomas Jefferson draft the Declaration of Independence. At the outbreak of the American Revolution, he chaired the board charged with recruitment, provisioning, and dispatch of the Continental army. In 1777 the Congress sent him to represent it at the Court of Paris, where he developed a close and strong friendship with Jefferson, also in diplomatic service there.

Upon return, Adams drafted the Massachusetts State Constitution, adopted in 1780, calling for three branches of government with a strong executive. The Congress next appointed him minister to London, and in 1782 he negotiated a treaty with the Netherlands recognizing American independence. By the time he returned home in 1788, speculation was rife that with Washington certain to be elected the first president under the new constitution, Adams, as the most celebrated New Englander, was most likely to run second to him and become vice president.

Prior to the balloting, many fellows-in-arms from the Revolution and the Constitutional Convention flocked to urge Adams's availability. Although he remained aloof to the entreaties, he indicated to Abigail that he believed that, after Washington, no other leader of the Revolution deserved to stand next in line. Accordingly, as she wrote to their daughter Nabby, he was open only to the vice presidency of the new government, but he also offered evidence that he did not warm to the very limited duties that would fall to him in the second office.[11]

Pondering the role of presiding officer of the Senate and its mandate to vote only to break a tie, he wondered as he made the slow trek from Braintree to New York how he would fit in. "Not wholly without experience in public assemblies," he wrote, "I have been more accustomed to take a share in their debates than to preside in their deliberations."[12] Some months later, after one of the most unfortunate passages in a long public life, he acknowledged succinctly to John Quincy that, in truth, the office he held was "not quite adapted to my character," that it was too "mechanical," and that mistakenly he was inclined to think he must "throw a little light on the subject when need be."[13]

But in his initial observations to the Senate as vice president, Adams addressed a major concern to him. "But I am President also of the Senate. When the President [Washington] comes into the Senate," he asked the body, "what shall I be?" The question launched the first debate in the chamber, one in which the new vice president's ability to hold his tongue would immediately be tested and found wanting. Senator Oliver Ellsworth of

Connecticut, a constitutional expert, rose and assured Adams, "Whenever the Senate are to be there, sir, you must be at the head of them." Ellsworth, however, added, "But further, sir, I shall not pretend to say."[14]

Ensuing debate only deepened Adams's dilemma as presiding officer of the Senate with that limited mandate. When the House voted that the chief executive be known simply as "George Washington, President of the United States," the Senate took up the argument, with Adams weighing in more than some senators appreciated.[15] When Senator Ralph Izard of South Carolina proposed that Washington be addressed as "Excellency," Senator Ellsworth commented that "President" was surely too bland, and Adams agreed, noting fire company and cricket club leaders were so described.[16]

When a Senate committee was named to consider the matter further, it came up with "His Highness the President of the United States of America and Protector of the Rights of the Same." Adams jumped in to offer others, and the debate went on for nearly a month. Adams insisted he was merely responding to senators' call for advice. He later wrote in response to being asked, "Whether I should say, 'Mr. Washington,' 'Mr. President,' 'Sir,' 'May it please your Excellency,' or what else? I observed that it had been common while Washington commanded the army to call him 'His Excellency,' but I was free to own it would appear to me better to give him no title but 'Sir' or 'Mr. President,' than to put him on a level with a governor of Bermuda."[17]

Yet at the same time, Adams suggested that the elected leader of the nation warranted special esteem and recognition for the great sacrifices and burdens the office imposed and as a lure to the country's best and brightest to seek the highest public office. While he himself insisted that he wasn't interested in any lofty title, he indicated at one point that something like "His Majesty the President" might be fitting. One who clearly disagreed was James Madison, who told the House, "The more simple, the more republican we are in our manners, the more dignity we shall acquire."[18]

Adams, for all his trouble in joining the debate despite the formal stricture against doing so, invited sharp verbal abuse from the Anti-Federalist senator William Maclay of Pennsylvania, who fueled criticism of the first vice president as a "monarchist" at heart. Maclay urged the Senate to amend the Constitution to read, "No title of nobility shall be granted by the United States."

Maclay's views of Adams were clearly colored by personal animosity, as when he wrote mockingly of him presiding over the Senate: "I cannot help thinking of a monkey put into breeches."[19] Others joined in the ridicule over the fuss Adams made over Washington's title. Senator Izard offered that the portly vice president himself be called "His Rotundity," and in the end the Senate agreed with the House decision that the first officer be called simply "the President of the United States."

The new vice president was particularly disturbed by the talk that he favored hereditary leadership by a king of some sort. However, in correspondence with his friend Benjamin Rush of Philadelphia he did indicate it was conceivable that the young country might some future day have to turn to a monarchy as "an asylum against discord, seditions and civil war" to keep the peace. Subsequently, in reassurance to Rush of his fealty to revolutionary objectives, he wrote, "I am a mortal and irreconcilable enemy to monarchy. I am no friend to hereditary limited monarchy in America. Do not, therefore, my friend, misunderstand me and misrepresent me to posterity."[20]

Adams as vice president was also plagued by heavy pressures from friends and other job seekers urging his sponsorship for positions in the new government temporarily headquartered in New York. He took refuge in saying, correctly, that his own job gave him no patronage to dispense and that power was in the hands of the president alone. These and other frustrations were compounded during in his first days in office by his separation from his closest confidante, wife Abigail, who did not arrive in New York until the start of summer, with their son Charles, now a student at Harvard.

Adams's first serious engagement despite the constitutional limitations on him occurred that first summer when his old Senate antagonist, the Anti-Federalist Maclay, offered a proposal to give the Senate a voice in the removal of officers of the cabinet. Federalists saw the bill as a raid on presidential power in their hands, saying only the chief executive could so decide. Adams lobbied energetically against the bill, and a tie vote resulted, which he dutifully broke in the Federalists' favor—his first substantive action as vice president. Before he left the office, he cast twenty-nine such votes, never surpassed by any subsequent presidential standby.

In September, the new administration and the country at large were jolted by the news of revolution in France. No one rejoiced more than Maclay, who not only proclaimed France's delivery from "royalty, nobility and vile pageantry, by which a few of the human race lord it over and tread on the necks of their fellow mortals," but also took advantage of it to vilify Adams as a monarchist. "Ye Gods," he wrote, "with what indignation do I review the late attempt of some creatures among us to revive the vile machinery. Oh Adams, Adams, what a wretch thou art!"[21]

For his own part, the American vice president felt compelled in a series of essays, later known as *Discourses on Davila,* to reaffirm his conviction that free-wheeling passions could imperil democracy.[22] In the process, however, he again fed suspicions of monarchist inclinations of his own. The essays also conveyed his appreciation for the causes of the French Revolution while expressing his fears of the ultimate outcome. He predicted that the choice of only one legislative body, as opposed to his own preference for two, as in the new American government, could only result in "great and lasting calamities," and he feared "a republic of thirty million atheists,"with all institutions, including the church, shattered.[23]

Adams's views on the political explosion in France inevitably put him in conflict with Jefferson, as was expressed in written exchanges over a year's time. When Adams wrote somewhat skeptically in *Discourses on Davila* of the possible negative ramifications of the French Revolution and of "the monarchical principle," Jefferson penned a reference to "the political heresies that have sprung up amongst us."[24] It caused a public furor over an apparent rift between them. Jefferson, insisting he had intended the reference to be private, subsequently wrote to Washington that he was "mortified," adding that he had "cordial esteem" for Adams despite "his apostasy to hereditary monarchy." There again was that allusion to the alleged affection toward royal regimes.[25]

When Congress addressed two significant problems, the vice president was again shunted to the sidelines by the limits imposed on the presiding officer of the Senate. The first was the debate over locating the permanent capital of the country. New Yorkers and many New Englanders wanted it to stay at its temporary home. Pennsylvania argued for the more centrally located Philadelphia. Southerners and particularly Virginians lobbied for the construction of a new capital city on the banks of the Potomac River as the gateway to their region.

One morning in June outside Washington's house in New York, when Hamilton encountered Jefferson, now back from France and serving as secretary of state, the treasury secretary suggested they join in a compromise. For Jefferson's support of the bill, Hamilton said he would urge the Pennsylvania congressional delegation to vote for the Potomac site for the permanent capital, with the proviso that the temporary site be moved to Philadelphia.[26]

When the compromise came before the Senate on a motion to keep the capital at New York for two more years, a tie vote resulted. Adams broke the tie, casting in the negative, and in July both houses of Congress voted to shift the capital to Philadelphia for ten years, after which it would be moved to the banks of the Potomac, where no city yet existed.

The second problem was how to cope with the huge public debt accumulated in the War of Independence. Hamilton, as Washington's secretary of the treasury and a zealous advocate of a strong central state, proposed that the federal government assume the debts of all of the states along with its own. But southerners particularly feared their interests would be undermined by the debt assumption, and, led by Madison, they defeated the proposal in April 1790.

Although the original intent of the founders was that the new nation could be governed without its elected officials breaking into "factions," the party system was already emerging. Washington and Hamilton, and nominally Adams, were seen in the Federalist camp of centralized, business orientation; the rest, mostly rural and agricultural-based, were at first lumped together simply as Anti-Federalists, with the Virginians Jefferson and Madison in the forefront against Hamilton's proposed national bank.

From the Senate president's chair, Adams professed to be presiding with "no party virulence or personal reflections."[27] In general, he observed, "There is nothing I dread so much as the division of the Republic into two great parties, each under its leader. . . . This, in my humble opinion, is to be feared as the greatest political evil under our Constitution."[28] But all members of Washington's cabinet were Federalists except Jefferson, as secretary of state, leading an eminent historian later to observe, "Federalists thought of themselves as a government, not as a party."[29]

In May 1792, as the second presidential election approached, Washington was still telling colleagues he wanted to retire. But in the face of continued pleas that he seek a second term, he had not yet made a decision. Adams therefore was in limbo about his own future and returned home to

Massachusetts for the summer. Clinton and Senator Aaron Burr also were contenders for the vice presidency, with Burr particularly dismissed as "an embryo Caesar in the United States" by his fellow New Yorker Hamilton in letters to friends.[30]

It was not until November that Washington agreed to run for a second term, at which time Adams returned to Philadelphia. Again there was no active campaigning by any of those on the presidential ballot, and Washington was reelected unanimously with Adams as vice president, having received seventy-seven of the second votes to fifty for Clinton, four for Jefferson, and one for Aaron Burr. John Adams was back in the isolation of his office of low public regard, but with less than the resounding margin of victory for which he had hoped and believed was his due.

Throughout the second term, Abigail chose to remain at the farm in Quincy, the new name taken for their town after it was split off from Braintree. Her health was part of the reason for passing up the arduous journey by carriage to Philadelphia, but family finances were also a factor. The vice president's annual salary of only five thousand dollars would be stretched hard, and Congress would be in session only for six months. The decision ensured that the couple's remarkable correspondence would continue, a bonus to the written history of the time.

Of Adams's placid if humdrum routine, he wrote to Abigail, "I go to the Senate every day, read the newspapers before I go and the public papers afterward, see a few friends once a week, go to church on Sundays; write now and then a line to you and Nabby, and oftener to Charles than to his brothers to see if I can fix his attention and excite some ambition"—the latter a reference to his son's unfocused path.[31]

Washington's second term was dominated by foreign-policy crises, in which his vice president played little role. Although Adams had served as an American minister in both Paris and London, the president made no notable use of him in dealing with the war between England and France. When Paris sent the young and impetuous Edmond Genet to Philadelphia to rally support for the French side, Washington turned to Jefferson, as his secretary of state, not Adams, in weighing whether to lay out a red carpet at the risk of offending London. Jefferson enthusiastically embraced "Citizen" Genet and urged Washington to do likewise. The president, however, was determined to remain neutral, aware of British protests against

French privateer seizures of English ships in U.S. ports and enlistments of American sailors to man the French vessels. Genet's brazen intrusions into American policies eventually embarrassed Jefferson and weakened his hand with Washington, without appreciably strengthening that of Adams in the debate over how to deal with the war between the British and the French.

Meanwhile, expectations that the first president would not stand for a third term also fanned the embers of growing factionalism between Hamilton Federalists and their critics rallying behind Jefferson. On the last day of 1793, Jefferson resigned as secretary of state. Adams, who had remained on friendly terms with the man while disagreeing with him, particularly on his ardor for France and his rejoicing in its revolution, wrote Abigail that he regretted his resignation. "But his want of candor," he confessed to her, "his obstinate prejudices of both aversion and attachment, his real partiality in spite of all his pretensions, his low notions about many things, have so utterly reconciled me to [his departure] . . . that I will not weep." Adams concluded on Jefferson's return to Monticello, "Jefferson went off yesterday, and a good riddance to bad ware."[32]

With the arrival of spring, however, Adams reconnected with Jefferson, sending him a book and sharing with him their mutual pleasure in rural life and desire for peace with England, the United States now threatened by British seizures of American merchant ships and sailors. As president of the Senate, Adams blocked a suspension of trade with Great Britain by breaking a tie vote in opposition, and he informed Jefferson of Washington's decision to send Chief Justice John Jay to London to try to avert war. The exchanges of correspondence continued for two years, sustaining the personal friendship, without enhancing Adams's role.[33]

Jay in London got no assurances that the British would open their ports to American ships or guarantee American sailors' protection against seizure; they agreed only to pull out remaining troops in forts in the American western outposts. In June 1795, Washington invited Adams to dinner and the next day presented the Jay Treaty to the Senate for ratification. With Adams presiding but taking no other part, the Senate bitterly debated the treaty behind closed doors for thirteen days, before ratifying it by the required two-thirds majority, with the vice president not called upon to vote. When the news broke, Washington and Jay were roundly castigated in the opposition press. But Adams stood solidly behind the president, even as he was left out of the administration's foreign-policy strategy, for all his diplomatic experience in London. He wrote to Abigail, "My own Situation is of such compleat Insignificance that I have scarcely the Power to do good or Evil."[34]

As the next presidential election approached in 1796, Adams could say or do nothing about his own ambitions or plans to reach for the presidency until Washington announced he would not stand for a third term. As vice president, Adams was a logical replacement for the Federalists, and he did indeed regard himself as the "heir apparent," as he told Abigail. As far as she was concerned, he had to seek the presidency, because, according to her, he had declared at one point, "I will be second under no man but Washington."[35]

Adams himself expressed concern whether he could physically handle the pressures of the presidency, though he regularly walked up to five miles daily. But his eyes were growing weak, and he had lately been experiencing trembling in his hands, observing it was "painful to the vanity of an old man to acknowledge the decays of nature."[36] He confided to John Quincy, "A pen is as terrible to me as a sword to a coward, or as a rod to a child," even as he was spending hours writing long letters and essays.[37]

Early in the election year, he told Abigail, "I am weary of the game. Yet I don't know how I would live out of it." Serving as president, she warned, would not be easy. "You know what is before you—the whips, the scorpions, the thorns without roses, the dangers, anxieties, the weight of empire."[38] Yet there was little doubt he would seek the office.

Not until mid-September, with the electoral college due to meet in December, did Washington finally say he would retire, and Adams as the Federalist and Jefferson as the Anti-Federalist became the leading opposing candidates to succeed him. Two others, the Federalist Thomas Pinckney and the Anti-Federalist Burr, were also running ostensibly for the vice presidency, although all four would be on the presidential ballot. Each presidential elector again would cast two ballots for president, with the winner becoming the chief executive, the vice president his standby. Fisher Ames of Massachusetts, one of the Federalists' prime orators, called Washington's much-awaited announcement "a signal, like dropping a hat, for the party pacers to start."[39]

Jefferson, who by now was using his free time in retirement to build his loose faction into a party, continued to stay at Monticello. Not satisfied with their being known as the Anti-Federalists, Jefferson, in a 1792 letter to Washington, first referred to his movement as Republican, later changing it to Democratic-Republican and then simply Democratic. Whatever the name, Jefferson earlier had famously said, "If I could not go to heaven but with a party, I would not go at all." Two centuries later, the historian Arthur M. Schlesinger Jr. was moved to observe, "The quadrennial presidential contest served, after Washington's retirement, both as an inescapable focus for national party competition and as a powerful incentive to national party organization. Even Jefferson soon decided that, with the right party, he would be willing to go, if not to heaven, at least to the White House."[40]

Although Jefferson did not overtly campaign for the presidency, his vigorous organizational efforts for the new party amounted to running for the office. Adams, in Quincy, and Jefferson, at Monticello, remained at home while their backers launched fierce verbal and written attacks on the other. Hamilton, as he had done before in 1792, plotted secretively, lobbying for electors' votes for Thomas Pinckney to win the presidency and Jefferson the vice presidency, hoping to leave Adams in the cold. Of the declared candidates, only Burr took to the road courting electors in New England, raising questions among Republicans in the South whether he sought to undercut their native son, Jefferson.

In the leading Republican paper of the day, the *Aurora,* Adams was castigated again as a defender of monarchy, while Jefferson was praised as "the friend of the people."[41] The Federalists meanwhile hammered at Jefferson as a "Jacobin" apologist for the French and as an atheist. The shape of party politics was emerging more clearly now: the Federalists behind Hamilton, identified as sympathetic to the British, were referred to as "the English party"; Jefferson and his Republican cohorts, as "the French party."

Adams, returning to Philadelphia in early December to await the results, wrote to Abigail of his agonizing and the possibility of losing: "I can pronounce Thomas Jefferson to be chosen P of US with firmness and a good grace that I don't fear. But here alone abed, by my fireside, nobody to speak to, pouring upon my disgrace and future prospects—this is ugly."[42]

The next week, however, as word trickled in from the various states whose electors had voted, Adams was able to write his wife much more brightly of reports that he would be elected. Jefferson, at Monticello, meanwhile was advised by Madison that he probably would finish second and that he ought to accept the vice presidency. He responded, not entirely believably, that he would have no problem serving under Adams's presidency, explaining, "He had always been my senior, from the commencement of my public life." Also before the results were announced, Jefferson wrote Adams a note in which he said he hadn't doubted for "one single moment" that his principal opponent would win. He also wrote to Madison authorizing him, if a tie resulted, sending the election to the House of Representatives for resolution, to "solicit on my behalf that Mr. Adams be preferred."[43]

In February, when all the electoral votes had been tallied by Adams as president of the Senate, he announced his own election to the presidency, by a mere three votes over Jefferson. He had received seventy-one ballots to sixty-eight for the man from Monticello, fifty-nine for Pinckney, thirty for Burr, and eleven for Samuel Adams. The double-balloting scheme had proved to be an electoral monster, producing a president and vice president of opposing factions and objectives. New England electors, aware of Hamilton's latest plot against native son Adams, gave him all thirty-nine of their first presidential votes and gave only twenty-two of their second votes to Pinckney. Jefferson meanwhile picked up enough electors in the South and elsewhere to beat out Pinckney for the vice presidency. Hamilton thus lost both efforts to keep Adams and Jefferson out of the next administration.[44]

Adams's margin of only three electoral votes over Jefferson emphatically announced the arrival of the Republicans and the beginning of the end for the Federalists. Without Washington, their pro-British inclinations, resolutely trumpeted by pro-French Jefferson and Madison, played on the negative sentiments of much of formerly colonial America.

Shortly before Adams and Jefferson were inaugurated, the vice president elect wrote a letter to Adams conveying his support in even more extravagant terms than before. He wrote to Adams, "I have no ambition to govern men. It is a painful and thankless office. . . . I devoutly wish you may be able to shun for us this war by which our agriculture, commerce and credit will be destroyed. If you are, the glory will be all your own; and that your administration may be filled with glory and happiness to yourself and advantage to us is the sincere wish of one who, though, in the course of our voyage through life, various little incidents have happened or been contrived to separate us, retains still for you the solid esteem of the moments when we were working for our independence, and sentiments of respect and affectionate attachment."[45]

Before mailing the letter, however, Jefferson sent it to Madison, in Philadelphia, unsealed, to read, so that if anything in it "should render the delivery of it ineligible in your opinion, you may return it to me."[46] Madison was aghast at the contents. He held on to the letter and never mailed it. He advised Jefferson that while the expressions of comradeship were well intentioned, he needed to consider how they might read in the event of Adams's presidency running afoul and prove an embarrassment or politically damaging to the writer in the future. Jefferson revised the letter, limiting himself to extending his good wishes for the new presidency and repeating his view that he could not play an active role in the Adams administration as a member of the legislative branch as president of the Senate.

And so, on March 4, 1797, in Philadelphia, John Adams, Federalist, and Thomas Jefferson, Republican, were sworn in as the second president and vice president of the United States, a pair of political strange bedfellows in the infancy of party strife never contemplated, or at least not desired, by the young nation's founding fathers.

CHAPTER 2

THOMAS JEFFERSON
OF VIRGINIA

T he vice presidency of Thomas Jefferson was the consolation prize for having been beaten by John Adams for the presidency by a mere three electoral votes. But Jefferson was not going to be content to stand idly by, as Adams had done as President Washington's vice president, awaiting and expecting his ascendancy as a loyal Federalist. As the leader of the already emerging rival ideological faction, Jefferson would spend much of his next years nurturing that faction, with a mind to winning control of the new government in the next national election.

The man who was to be called the founder of the Democratic Party was born on April 13, 1743, in the family-built home called Shadwell on the Rivanna River in what is now Albemarle County, Virginia. He was the third child and first son of the successful surveyor, planter, and slave owner Peter Jefferson and his wife, Jane Randolph, of a prominent Virginia family. He took to his studies early under local clergymen. When his father died at forty-nine, young Tom at fourteen assumed the role of male head of the household. Two years later he went off to Williamsburg to attend the College of William and Mary, where he was said to have wasted most of his first year in revelry in the first real town he had ever visited. Thereafter, however, he came under the tutelage of two prominent classical scholars and buckled down. A year later one of them brought Jefferson into his law office there.[1]

Though he was a shy and reluctant speaker, young Jefferson soon won recognition as an accomplished writer marked for esteem as a public man. He graduated from William and Mary at age nineteen, and after a five-year apprenticeship he was admitted to the Virginia bar in 1767. A year later, with funds inherited from his father, Jefferson began building his hilltop home eventually called Monticello.[2]

In 1769, Jefferson took a seat in the Virginia House of Burgesses. In 1774, he was assigned to write a paper of guidance for the Virginia delegation to the First Continental Congress, called "A Summary View of the Rights of British America," an eloquent indictment of the British Parliament's treatment of the colonies. The next year, when Jefferson was sent to Philadelphia as a replacement in the Virginia delegation to the Second Continental Congress, his pen was called on again. With the American Revolution already started in Lexington and Concord, he was assigned to draft the "Declaration of the Causes and Necessity for Taking Up Arms against the British Crown." Both documents presaged Jefferson's historic 1776 Declaration of Independence in its direct and bitter attack not only on the British Parliament but also on King George III himself. As the historian Joseph J. Ellis observed in his Jefferson biography *American Sphinx,* one could readily recognize in Jefferson's "Summary" and "Causes of Necessity" "a preview of coming attractions" and "a dress rehearsal" of the bill of indictment against the English monarch justifying the colonies' breaking away from his rule.[3]

The composition of the final document declaring the independence of "the United States of America" was assigned to John Adams and Jefferson, with Adams readily leaving the actual composition to his admired younger friend from Virginia, while he prepared for the Continental Congress debate on its adoption. From mid-May to early July 1776, while working on drafts for a new Virginia constitution, Jefferson spent only a few days composing America's most famous document.[4]

In 1779 he was elected governor, and in 1781, when turncoat General Benedict Arnold invaded the state and torched Richmond just as Jefferson's term was ending, Jefferson was forced to flee the capital. Amid allegations that he had failed to provide adequate defense for the city, the legislature launched an inquiry, but Jefferson was exonerated.[5] Adding to his despondency over the fate of Richmond, in 1782 his wife, Martha, died several months after giving birth for the seventh time in their ten-year marriage. Jefferson was distraught. It is said that on her deathbed she asked him to promise never to remarry, and he never did.[6]

In 1784, Jefferson went to France as the American minister, to negotiate commercial contracts with European states and seek loans to pay off Revolutionary War debts. During the Constitutional Convention in 1787 he kept in touch with his friend James Madison, urging him to have a bill of rights incorporated. After witnessing the outbreak of the French Revolution in 1789, he returned home and on arrival became Washington's first secretary of state. At the end of 1793, as previously noted, Jefferson resigned his cabinet post and returned to Monticello.[7]

By this time, Jefferson was concentrating on the development of the new party that was first designated as the Anti-Federalist faction but was soon to be called Republican and eventually Democratic. In 1796 under its aegis, he ran for the presidency against the Federalist vice president Adams, narrowly losing in the electoral college, as we know, which placed him in the vice presidency under Adams in 1797.

In the wake of the now-ratified Jay Treaty, which seemed so favorable to Britain and hostile to France, there was much anticipation as to what role Adams might have Jefferson, as a prime American admirer of the French, play toward healing the breach. Adams had not forgotten some of Jefferson's past slights and criticisms, telling a friend, Tristram Dalton, "His entanglements with characters and politics which have been pernicious are and have been a source of inquietude and anxiety to me."[8]

A day before the inaugurations of the two men, Jefferson called on Adams at the St. Francis Hotel in Philadelphia, where both would be staying. It was their first meeting in about three years and was sufficiently amiable that Adams returned the call the next morning. As Jefferson recalled and wrote much later, Adams plunged at once into discussing the French crisis, expressing his desire that Jefferson play a leading role in settling it. The Directory of the new French Republic viewed the Jay Treaty as a decidedly pro-British pact, and as a result the American minister there, James Monroe of Virginia, had been recalled, replaced by General Charles Cotesworth Pinckney of South Carolina, a strong Federalist. Now Adams, as Jefferson remembered, said it was "the first wish of his heart" to dispatch the prospective vice president to Paris but that "it did not seem justifiable for him to send away the person destined to take his place in case of an accident to himself, nor decent to remove from consideration one who was a rival for public favor."[9]

Jefferson wrote that he agreed with that thinking and in any event was tired of living in Europe and hoped never to return. He also reminded Adams, as he well knew, that as president of the Senate, the vice president was a constitutional officer of the legislative branch; hence it would be improper for him to undertake executive branch functions.

The episode made clear to both sides that that there would be little party comity in the new administration. Adams, looking back on the affair, wrote, "We parted as good friends as we had always lived; but we consulted very little together afterwards. Party violence soon rendered it impracticable, or at least useless."[10] And Jefferson noted that henceforth Adams never spoke of a role for him regarding French policy or ever consulted with him concerning any aspects of the government.

With Jefferson out of that loop within the Adams administration, the crisis with France deepened. The French Directory forced Pinckney to leave Paris and take temporary haven in Amsterdam, even as more American shipping in the Caribbean was seized by the French in what was becoming an undeclared war against the United States. At the same time, Jefferson did not hesitate to fire partisan barbs at the rival Federalists and, at least by implication, at their president. A letter Jefferson had written a year earlier to an Italian friend, Philip Mazzei, surfaced in a Federalist newspaper, charging that the United States had fallen to "timid men who prefer the calm of despotism to the boisterous sea of liberty." It was an obvious allegation that Adams preferred accommodation with England over friendship with France.[11]

Adams countered Jefferson's harsh words with renewed efforts to achieve peace through negotiations with France, while urging Congress to build up America's defenses, particularly against attacks and plunder of American shipping at sea. The equipping of three new navy frigates was authorized to put some muscle behind Adams's words. Meanwhile, the armies of the young French general Napoleon Bonaparte were attacking Austria and Italy and reportedly contemplating an invasion of Britain, increasing the Adams's urgency to avoid outright war with France.

Jefferson, assuming more political direction of the pro-French Republicans than ever before, privately intervened, calling on the French representative in Philadelphia to prolong the negotiations with the new American team. The French diplomat noted later that the vice president had reminded him of Adams's situation: "He only became President by three votes, and the system of the United States will change along with him." In other words, the trouble would be resolved with Jefferson's election to the presidency the next time the American people went to the ballot box.[12]

In any event, the French Directory eventually refused to see the new American mission, and injury was added to insult when three secret agents known only as X, Y, and Z made outrageous stipulations as representatives of the French foreign minister Charles-Maurice de Talleyrand-Perigord. They reported that negotiations could proceed only with the payment of $250,000 to Talleyrand, as well as a $1 million loan to France to make up for what the agents said were insults by Adams to their country.

The American negotiators flatly refused, and Adams pressed on in his further military buildup of fortifications at home and more warships at sea to confront marauding French vessels. While calling for these defensive measures, Adams kept the dispatches relating to the XYZ bribery effort secret. Jefferson thereupon accused Adams of warmongering and demanded that the papers be opened to congressional scrutiny. In what proved to be a major political blunder on Jefferson's part, the Federalists responded by pushing a resolution through Congress ordering publication and wide distribution of the XYZ Papers.[13]

Their disclosure electrified the American public and greatly dampened the pro-French ardor that had been born of the French assistance to the American Revolution and heightened by the French Revolution. Federalist pressure for war against France soared, and in May 1798 Congress suspended the 1778 treaty with France. At Adams's urging, it created the Navy Department to oversee shipbuilding and attacks on armed French ships. Adams called for tripling the size of the provisional army and the taxes to pay for it. Congress also approved an enlarged provisional army, and Adams persuaded General Washington to come out of retirement to lead it with the authority to choose his own staff.

As public furor over the XYZ Papers spilled out into street protests in Philadelphia and New York, Vice President Jefferson also was vexed by the notion of a standing army used to suppress domestic dissent. He was disturbed, too, when Adams surprisingly emerged as a reborn national hero while steadfastly insisting he still sought a peaceful settlement with France. Shunted to the sidelines in the administration in which he marginally served, Jefferson filled the vacuum by working to subvert Adams's initiatives, obviously with an eye on achieving victory over him in the 1800 presidential election, which had so narrowly eluded him in 1796.

The Federalist newspapers, meanwhile, jumped on Jefferson, one intoning editorially, "The Vice President—May his heart be purged of Gallicism in the pure fire of Federalism or be lost in the furnace," and "John Adams —May he like Samson slay thousands of Frenchmen with the jawbone of Jefferson."[14]

Also in the summer of 1798, news reached the president that his three-man commission to Paris had broken up, a disturbing development to Adams. Amid clamors in some quarters for a declaration of war, Adams diplomatically informed Paris, "I will never send another minister to France without assurances that he will be received, respected and honored as the representative of a great, free, powerful and independent nation."[15]

With Adams subsequently drawing an assurance from Paris that his next envoy would be so welcomed, the clouds of war blew over, and in the next presidential election Jefferson was able to argue that the Federalists had favored war with France as the only way to retain control of the government. And then, on December 1, 1799, the sudden death of Washington at sixty-seven put aside all else in respectful mourning.

Meanwhile, in the summer of 1798, the high-riding Federalists had committed a major political blunder. They had pushed through Congress the infamous Alien and Sedition and Naturalization Acts, to which Adams had yielded. The first two laws empowered the president to deport any "dangerous" foreigner and to fine and imprison anyone for writing "false, scandalous and malicious" observations or for stirring up disorder or rebellion among the people and against the government. The third extended the residence requirement for citizenship from five to fourteen years, and the acts taken together were read by the Republicans as another Federalist effort to kill their infant party in its crib.[16]

The Jeffersonians were confident that the Naturalization Act, with its bias against British, Irish, and French Americans in direct contravention of the Bill of Rights, would drive immigrants into their new party, as would the Alien and Sedition Acts. Jefferson predicted that such assaults on basic constitutional guarantees of freedom would eventually backfire on their proponents. "A little patience," he counseled, "and we shall see the reign of witches pass over, their spells dissolved, and the people recovering their true sight, restoring their government to its true principles."[17]

Jefferson as a champion of the First Amendment's guarantee of free speech was obviously appalled and retreated to Monticello to plot how to make the most of the Federalist actions. He condemned these blatant efforts to stifle political dissent, using them to recruit more support for the new party and to broadcast that the Federalists, with Hamilton still pulling the strings, were as determined as ever to impose a monarchical rule on the country.

Amid spreading domestic fears of disloyalty at home and objections to the new legislative acts of repression, Jefferson spent much of the next six months drafting and refining what came to be known as the Kentucky Resolutions, counters to the Alien and Sedition Acts. The resolutions insisted on the right of each state to nullify any act of the federal government it considered to be a violation of the Constitution. Madison at the same time authored the Virginia Resolutions to the same general purpose. In a letter to Madison, Jefferson almost sounded on the verge of leading a secession, warning that unless the public joined them in their stand, he was "determined, were we to be disappointed in this, to sever ourselves from the union we so much value, rather than give up the rights of self-government."[18]

The legislatures in Kentucky and Virginia passed the respective resolutions restating that powers not granted to the federal government were reserved to the states, which could reject laws passed by Congress if those legislatures deemed them unconstitutional. They became cornerstones of the Republicans' creed as the party moved to wrest national power from the fading Federalists in the 1800 election.

About a month later, news reached America of another significant death—of the French Republic, with Napoleon Bonaparte declaring himself first consul at the age of thirty-three. The end of the French Revolution was a particular blow to Jefferson, its prime American champion, but Napoleon by now wanted no part of a distracting war with America. Jefferson was able to focus more intently now on a matter of even greater concern and importance to him—his bid in the 1800 election to replace Adams in the president's chair.

After years of partisan sparring between the Federalists and the Republicans, the battle lines were drawn. Adams, despite his cantankerous personality, generally eschewed direct public appeals and was not particularly known as a political brawler. Many of the oratorical punches he threw at rivals were in otherwise loving written exchanges with his highly political wife, Abigail, in perhaps American politics' most engaging, long-running correspondence. Jefferson by contrast was notorious for waging verbal combat through others, such as the like-minded and cooperative political associate James Madison and the hired-gun propagandist James Callender, a vitriolic Britain-hater.

When Callender was out of work, Jefferson sent him money to carry him over, later deviously writing to James Monroe that his generosity had exceeded his good judgment. "As to myself, no man wished more to see his pen stopped; but I considered him still as a proper object of benevolence," he told Monroe, adding about Callender's view of the payments, "He considers these as proofs of my approbation of his writings, when they were mere charities, yielded under a strong conviction that he was injuring us by his writings." At the same time, Jefferson urged Madison and Monroe to circulate pamphlets espousing the Republican cause, cautioning Monroe, "Do not let my name be connected with the business."[19]

While ever professing his friendship toward Adams, Jefferson continued to bankroll Callender's writing against the president whose office Jefferson now sought. He brushed aside Adams's continued commitment to peace with France, encouraging Callender to cast the choice in the 1800 presidential campaign as either Adams and war or Jefferson and peace. Callender stooped to the vilest personal descriptions of Adams as "a gross hypocrite" and a "hideous hermaphroditical character which has neither the force and firmness of a man nor the gentleness and sensibility of a woman." Jefferson, shown the galley proofs of Callender's handiwork, told him they could "not fail to produce the best effects."[20] For his trouble, Jefferson's hired gun was arrested in May of the election year for sedition, for inciting the public against the president, and received a sentence of seven months in jail.

Callender for his part, dissatisfied at one point with Jefferson's payments, later wrote in a Federalist newspaper in Richmond that Jefferson, then president, had for many years kept one of his slaves as a concubine. "By this wench Sally, our President has had several children. There is not an individual in the neighborhood of Charlottesville who does not believe the story, and not a few who know it. . . . The AFRICAN VENUS is said to officiate as housekeeper at Monticello."[21] The reference was to Sally Hemings, and the story spread, with Jefferson neither confirming nor denying it.

From the Federalist side, meanwhile, came a heavy assault on Jefferson for pro-French allegiance and allegations of atheism or of deism—accepting the existence of God without accepting his authority over all things. The Reverend William Linn of New York warned that Jefferson's election would "destroy religion, introduce immorality, and loosen all the bonds of society. . . . The voice of the nation in calling a deist to the first office must be construed into no less than rebellion against God."[22]

For a young nation that was said to have been born absent of parties, the affliction now was rampant once the unifying or at least the restraining of partisan passions by the dominant presence of George Washington had passed. As Abigail Adams observed, not only was the country's politics in the grip of rival philosophical differences, but also a schism within the Federalist ranks threatened to bring about the first electoral defeat of an incumbent president. With sixteen states choosing presidential electors in 1800, state legislatures selected them in eleven and popular vote chose them in the other five. Again the double-balloting scheme that had been invented to frustrate voting for favorite sons in the several states enabled Hamilton to participate in another electoral fiasco of unintended consequences.

Southern party leaders decided on another Pinckney from South Carolina, Charles Cotesworth Pinckney, recently the American minister to France, to run with Adams, ostensibly but not necessarily for vice president. Hamilton urged the Federalist electors in South Carolina, who would naturally cast one of their two presidential votes for Pinckney, to withhold the other from Adams and presumably give it to the fellow southerner Jefferson. If Federalists elsewhere voted for both Adams and Pinckney, Pinckney rather than Adams might be elected president.

While Hamilton thus went about his machinations, Jefferson was the clear choice of the Republicans, with Senator Aaron Burr of New York running with him for vice president. Burr, a New Jersey–born colonel of distinction in the Revolutionary War, was chosen on the basis of his masterful political organizing work in New York City, which had assured the Empire State's presidential electors for the Republicans. Adams had won New York in 1796, and the Jeffersonians knew they had to carry it this time around. When Hamilton, leading the Federalist effort for state legislative seats, ran a slate of loyal but lesser-known figures, Burr trumped him, recruiting such prominent Republicans as Governor George Clinton to run from New York City districts. Burr swept all city seats and the state's electoral votes for Jefferson, all but assuring the Virginian's election.

Subsequently, when the Republicans were to meet to determine their national ticket, there was no question Jefferson was to be the presidential nominee. Clinton was sounded out to be the vice presidential candidate but declined, recommending Burr, who was placed on the party's ticket with the clear understanding he was to be its nominee for the second office.

Hamilton meanwhile remained determined that regardless of party fealty, Adams would not be returned to public office, preferring Jefferson to his fellow Federalist from Massachusetts. "If we must have an enemy at the head of government," he wrote to party stalwart Thomas Sedgwick, "let it be one who we can oppose, and for whom we are not responsible, who will not involve our party in the disgrace and foolish and bad measures. Under Adams, as under Jefferson, the government will sink."[23]

Jefferson for his part was perfectly willing to leave it to Hamilton to divide the ranks of his own party. Abigail Adams wrote to son John Quincy: "The Jacobins are so gratified to see the Federalist split to pieces that they enjoy in Silence the game, whilst in the Southern States they combine to bring Mr. Jefferson in as president."[24] When Hamilton undertook a New England tour supposedly to say good-bye to members of the disbanding provisional army, he pressed Federalist leaders to get behind Pinckney's candidacy. Abigail was not deceived, calling the trip "merely an electioneering business to feel the pulse of the New England states, and impress upon those upon whom he could have any influence to vote for Pinckney." She predicted it would backfire on "the little cock sparrow general" and was right regarding the loyalty to Adams at home.[25]

But once again the double balloting for the presidency resulted in confusion and drove Adams from the White House. While Hamilton's latest conspiracy did contribute to Adams's departure, it ultimately landed his other archenemy, Jefferson, in the presidency. In critical South Carolina and across the South, Jefferson and Burr swept nearly all the electoral votes. But when the electors in their states forwarded the results to the new capital at Washington for the final tally, Jefferson and Burr astonishingly finished in a tie, each winning seventy-three votes. Adams finished third with sixty-five and found himself out of office. So the election was not over; the Constitution specified that in case of a tie, the issue would go to the House of Representatives for resolution.

The Republicans' clear intention had been that if their camp won, their leader, Jefferson, was to be president and Burr vice president. Burr himself well understood that expectation, but in a colossal blunder, the Republicans had failed to take the precaution of casting one fewer vote for Burr than for Jefferson. It didn't happen, as Jefferson and Burr together swept all the electoral votes in both South Carolina and Georgia.

Burr, for his part, was not ready to step aside and settle for the vice presidency. He was still feeling used over the short shrift he had been given in the 1796 election, when he had received only one electoral vote from Virginia. He told John Taylor of the Old Dominion, "After what happened at the last election . . . I was really averse to have my name in question . . . but being so, it is most obvious that I should not choose to be trifled with." Apparently in response to those remarks, Jefferson said later he "had taken some measures" to assure that Virginia's Republican electors' second votes went unanimously for Burr.[26]

In any event, while the Republicans in the 1800 election had just won a majority in the new House of Representatives, the presidential outcome would be decided by the old House, in which the Federalists had the majority. The Constitution required, however, that the vote be taken by state delegation, with each state having a single vote. On that basis, neither party had a majority as also was required to declare the winner. Jefferson wrote to Madison: "The Feds in the legislature have expressed dispositions to make all they can of the embarrassment, so after the most energetic efforts, crowned with success, we remain in the hands of our enemies for want of foresight in the original arrangement."[27]

At first, the Federalists in Congress schemed to find ways to throw out the indecisive election and hold another. Jefferson meanwhile, in the most diplomatic language he could muster, suggested rather naively to Burr that as vice president he would deprive the Jefferson administration of his service in a cabinet position, hinting that if he turned down the powerless vice presidency there would be a major place for him in the cabinet. "I feel most sensibly the loss we sustain of your aid in our new administration," Jefferson wrote, dismissing Burr's equal claim on the presidency as the votes stood.[28]

To Jefferson's transparently ludicrous proposition, Burr's reply suggested complete acquiescence to Jefferson's desires. He said he himself had expected that Rhode Island would have withheld one of its two votes from him, adding, "I do not however apprehend any embarrassment even in Case the Votes should come out alike for us—my personal friends are perfectly informed of my wishes on the subject and can never think of diverting a single vote from you—on the Contrary, they will be found among your most zealous adherents. I see no reason to doubt of your having at least nine States [the required majority] if the business should come before the H. of Reps."[29]

Regarding Jefferson's notion of putting Burr in his cabinet, Burr wrote he was certain Jefferson, if elected, would have many good Republicans from which to choose, but he added improbably, "I will cheerfully abandon the office of V.P. if it is thought that I can be more useful in any Active Station. In short, my whole time and attention shall be unceasingly employed to render your Administration grateful and honorable to our Country and to yourself."[30]

In a letter to the Maryland congressman Samuel Smith, Burr wrote that it was highly improbable that he would have an equal number of votes to those of Jefferson, adding, "But if such should be the result, every man who knows me ought to know that I would utterly disclaim all competition. Be assured that the federal party can entertain no wish for such an exchange. As to my friends, they would dishonor my views and insult my feelings by a suspicion that I would submit to be instrumental in counteracting the wishes and expectations of the people of the United States. And I now constitute you my proxy to declare these sentiments if the occasion shall require."[31] Either Burr later had second thoughts or he was shamelessly pulling Jefferson's leg over his preposterous suggestion about giving up a chance to be president or at least vice president. James Bayard, a Federalist congressman from Delaware, insisted that Burr would accept Federalist support if it came his way.

When the House convened in February 1801, the Federalist caucus decided to back Burr, on the grounds that dealing with an ambitious op- portunist would be better than dealing with Jefferson, a deeply committed ideologue opposed to the core of Federalist doctrine. But Hamilton fired off a flood of letters to fellow Federalists condemning Burr as a "voluptu- ary . . . without probity."[32] At least Jefferson could be counted on, he went on, to sustain the Hamilton bank, avoid war in Europe, and retain some Federalists in lower government positions.

But Hamilton's grip on his party was fading, the Federalists having lost both houses of Congress for the first time, and their overtures to Burr were well underway. At first Burr insisted he was not interested in entertaining them. In advance of the tie vote, apparently under the impression that Jefferson would be elected to the first office, he had written to a Jefferson lieutenant, Samuel Smith, "Every man who knows me ought to know that I would utterly disclaim all competition," referring to Jefferson.[33]

Soon thereafter, however, he had a change of heart. Prior to the voting, he had been told that one elector in Vermont was going to vote for Pinck- ney rather than Burr to assure Jefferson's victory. Now he learned that the elector had failed to do so and that Burr had received all four of Vermont's second votes under the double-balloting scheme, creating his tie with Jef- ferson. Burr was advised to say no more about stepping aside for Jefferson and await further developments. Burr suddenly realized that an unexpected opportunity was knocking at his door, and he decided to invite it to enter.

But Hamilton was on hand to spread further venom against the fellow New Yorker who had bested him in the critical fight for their state's political control. He called Burr a dangerous man "of a temper bold enough to think no enterprise too hazardous and to think none too difficult,"[34] altogether "the most unfit man in the U.S. for the office of President."[35]

Hamilton called on Federalists to make a deal with Jefferson with four conditions: that he would support the present fiscal system of which Ham- ilton was the principal architect; that he would adhere to neutrality in foreign policy; that he would preserve and gradually increase the navy; that he would retain on the federal payroll all Federalists then serving, with the exception of cabinet members. The deal, he argued, would not only preserve most of the Federalist agenda but also lay seeds of division between Jefferson as president and Burr as vice president. Indeed, on Sunday, sometime after Bayard and Nicholas had talked, Jefferson wrote to Governor Monroe, "Many attempts have been made to obtain terms and promises from me. I have declared to them unequivocally that I would not receive the government on capitulation, that I would not go into it with my hands tied."[36]

On February 11, a cold and snowy day in Washington, the Congress finally convened to vote as crowds jammed the galleries to witness the historic event. The first order of business was to tabulate the vote and officially announce the tie. As president of the Senate, Jefferson presided, and he called for the state delegation votes. On the first ballot Jefferson won eight states, one short of the majority needed, Burr won six, and two, Vermont and Maryland, were deadlocked and cast blank ballots. Burr actually won more individual House members, fifty-five to Jefferson's fifty-one, but the state delegation votes were what mattered.

The roll call continued through the afternoon, night, and early the next morning with no change. One ill member was carried on a stretcher through the snow to the Capitol to cast his vote for Jefferson and maintain the stalemate. A Sunday hiatus gave birth to a host of rumors, from threats of force from Virginia and mobilizations in Pennsylvania and among Republicans in the mid-Atlantic states. Governor Monroe, in Virginia, ordered state militia to guard an arsenal lest Federalists try to arm themselves, and Jefferson himself warned of Federalist talk of a "dissolution" of the Union. At one point he called on Adams, who subsequently expressed fears that the two parties had come to a "precipice" and that "civil war was expected."

During this fearful time, Delaware's Bayard, who had been voting for Burr as the lesser of two evils, proposed a bargain whereby he would abstain from voting on the next roll call, reducing the majority of states required to eight, which Jefferson already had. He sought to have the Virginian John Nicholas, a close Jefferson friend, approach the candidate on the acceptability of the Hamilton terms. Nicholas said he considered the terms reasonable and would vouch for Jefferson's acceptance but balked on approaching him. Bayard told Speaker Sedgwick what he was up to and meanwhile conferred with five other Federalists, four from Maryland and one from Vermont, about breaking the impasse. Nicholas said later that he had passed the proposal to a Jefferson adviser who told him Jefferson had authorized him to say it "corresponded with his views and intentions," but Jefferson later denied in the most strenuous terms that he had struck any deal.

At the time Bayard made his decision, he provided an altogether different reason for his behavior: "Burr has acted a miserable paultry part. The election was in his power, but he was determined to come in as a Democrat." At the time, Bayard told his wife that Burr had declined to meet the terms that the Federalists demanded. Bayard also confided to Hamilton that Burr "was determined not to shackle himself with federal principles."[37] After six days of roll calls and thirty-six ballots, on February 17 the Federalists caved in. The pivotal Vermont member absented himself, throwing the state to Jefferson, and four Marylanders cast blank ballots, giving their state to him. Bayard also abstained, as did the South Carolina delegation. Jefferson was elected with ten states to four for Burr and two not voting. The Republicans also wound up with a thirty-three-seat majority in the House, ending the Federalist reign and putting the newly formed opposition party in power.

Jefferson's vice presidency was not quite a stepping-stone to the presidency, as the office came to be advertised. Rather, he got there as the prime architect of the new rival party built as he occupied the second office. Accordingly, he had a stronger claim to the presidency than did Burr, whose place on the Republican ticket was more a reward for his efforts in carrying New York for the party, and for Jefferson, than for playing any broader strategic or policy role in it.

It remained a mystery, however, why the transparently ambitious Burr didn't take the deal that the Federalists had apparently offered him for making him president, just as they had Jefferson. His insistence that he could not and would not act against the principles of his own party might have been more expected from Jefferson, who despite his denials appeared to have done just that. And so Aaron Burr of New York prepared to take office as part of the Jefferson administration but in the context of the bitter postcampaign fight that he had lost. Neither was it a propitious premise for a productive or rewarding Burr vice presidency, nor did it hopefully augur what was to come.

CHAPTER 3

AARON BURR

OF NEW YORK

From the moment Aaron Burr took the oath of office as vice president on March 4, 1801, it was clear he would be on the outside of the Jefferson presidency looking in. His demeanor in dealing with the electoral college vote that had left him in a tie with Jefferson and with the poisonous aftermath in its resolution in the House of Representatives killed any possibilities of partnership between the two contenders, though both were members of the lately emerged Jeffersonian Party.

At their inauguration, much was made of Burr's gesture in yielding his seat as presiding officer of the Senate to the new president upon his entry to take his oath of office. Behind the symbolism, however, there was little substance of cooperation as the business of the Jefferson administration got underway.[1]

One of Jefferson's first tasks was the appointment of the five top members of his cabinet, and in making them he never consulted with Burr. When the time came to hand out federal patronage in the several states, and Burr submitted the names of five New Yorkers in behalf of himself and the other Republicans of the state congressional delegation, Jefferson at first hired only two. He pointedly ignored the one for which Burr pushed hardest, his close friend Matthew Livingston Davis.[2] The politically astute Albert Gallatin quickly grasped the implication of the rejection of Burr's appeal—that there would be no second vice presidential term for his friend

Burr. "I wish the Republicans would make up their mind," Gallatin wrote to Jefferson. "Do they eventually mean not to support Burr as your successor when you shall see fit to retire? Do they mean not to support him at next election for Vice-President?"[3]

Gallatin by this time was aware that Jefferson wanted James Madison, his Virginian compatriot and the secretary of state, as his presidential successor in 1809. But it would not do to have the president and vice president both from Virginia in Jefferson's second term, so the president had to figure a way to have someone other than Burr in the second post who would not be seen as the heir apparent.[4]

Two direct letters from Burr to Jefferson in Davis's behalf went ignored, and after a third in November, Jefferson finally sent Burr an icy reply: "These letters all relating to office, fall within a general rule . . . of not answering letters on office specifically, but leaving the answer to be found in what is done or not done on them."[5] Instead of discussing the matter with Burr, whose work in New York in his behalf in 1800 had been critical to Jefferson's election, the president turned to the state's aging governor, George Clinton, for guidance in a pointed snub of his vice president.

Indeed, the governor and his politically ambitious nephew DeWitt Clinton soon moved in on Burr's patronage role, DeWitt becoming Burr's prime rival in New York. Eventually, the position Burr sought for Davis went to DeWitt's father-in-law, the same Samuel Osgood who had warned Jefferson that Davis was a Burr loyalist.

Burr in the meantime was not going to be a willing tool for Jefferson. As president of the Senate, he declined to rubber-stamp the president's efforts to repeal Adams's Judiciary Act of 1801. The law had created additional federal courts and a host of new federal judges, and Adams, just before leaving office, had made many midnight appointments of Federalists. Jefferson was determined to break the rival party's hold on its one remaining federal branch by replacing these judges with fellow Republicans, in contradiction of his famous inaugural conciliatory declaration: "We are all Republicans; we are all Federalists."

On one tie vote, Burr did cast the deciding ballot with the administration to keep the prospect of appeal alive. But on a subsequent ballot, he voted to recommit the bill to tone down the partisan sting he perceived in it. This even-handed treatment did not please Jefferson and was not overlooked by some Federalists who were beginning to cast a favorable eye on Burr, now increasingly a man without a party.[6]

Jefferson's vice president demonstrated his apostasy in other ways as well. At a Federalist dinner celebrating Washington's birthday in the new capital city in 1802, Burr showed up unannounced and offered a simple toast, to a "*union* of all *honest* men!"[7] The remark was taken by Jeffersonians as a brazen slap at the president and by many Federalists as a statement of independence and availability. Burr, referring to his icy relationship with Jefferson, sarcastically informed his son-in-law John Alston, "I dine with the president about once a fortnight, and now and then meet the ministers in the street. They are all very busy: quite men of business. The Senate and the vice-president are content with each other, and move on with courtesy."[8]

James Cheetham, the editor of the *New York American Citizen* and a conspicuous Burr hater, told Jefferson of Burr's frequent criticism. "The end is obvious," he wrote. "It is to bring the present administration to disrepute, and thereby to place Mr. Burr in the Presidential Chair."[9] At this same time, a handbill was circulated calling the vice president a "Cataline" (traitor) and a man of "abandoned profligacy" in his affairs with women, reinforcing a reputation that clung to him as a widower now perceived as a possible presidential heir.[10]

Later in 1802, when Burr supporters decided to start a newspaper, the *Morning Chronicle,* Cheetham attacked its editor, Dr. Peter Irving, as a "young man of handsome talents," implying a sexual relationship with Burr. He said of the vice president, "There is a softness, an insinuating deceitfulness about him admirably calculated to fascinate youth." He referred to Irving as a "beau," as "Miss Irving," and "Her Ladyship." Burr declared Cheetham's slurs and innuendoes "false and groundless" and initiated libel charges against him.[11]

Burr, as clear evidence that he realized he would not be offered a second term in the second office, launched a quest for the governorship of New York. In it, he was challenged by a moderate, Morgan Lewis, and supporters of Governor Clinton, who continued to have presidential ambitions, saw the opportunity to end Burr's similar aspirations. In the summer of 1802, Senator John Armstrong wrote to DeWitt Clinton, "Can we look to any circumstances more auspicious to ourselves than the present? I think not. The cards are with us. . . . An unbroken vote from this State does not merely disappoint Mr. B—it prostrates him and his ambition forever, and will be a useful admonition to future schismatics."[12]

A Burr loyalist, John Swartwout, accused Clinton of trying to destroy Burr's reputation for his own political ends, and Clinton replied by calling him "a liar, a scoundrel and a villain." At this, Swartwout challenged Clinton to a duel, in which Swartwout suffered two leg wounds but recovered. Clinton offered to shake hands with his foe but added he would rather have had a shot at Burr himself.[13]

Burr's reputation, however, was of little concern to Jefferson at this point. A development in Europe was unfolding that eventually would bring him into further conflict with his dissident vice president. Upon the signing of the third Treaty of San Ildefonso, in 1800, Spain had granted France the rights to the Louisiana Territory, but France did not take immediate possession. In late 1802, the Spanish administrator of the port of New Orleans disclosed that the new French owners intended to restrict the port's access.

Concerned, Jefferson wrote his minister in Paris, Robert Livingston, that access to the port was imperative because three-eighths of the territory's produce passed through that market. He warned, "The day France takes possession of New Orleans" the United States would be compelled to "marry ourselves to the British fleet and nation" to deal with the commercial threat that would occur.[14] Jefferson alerted Congress to "the danger to which our peace would be perpetually exposed whilst so important a key to the commerce of the Western country remained under foreign power."[15]

Jefferson therefore obtained an appropriation of two million dollars from Congress to initiate negotiations with Napoleon to buy a small portion of the Louisiana Territory that would include New Orleans and the territories of west and east Florida only. He instructed Livingston to make the offer and dispatched Monroe to Paris in April 1803. Livingston meanwhile was astounded when Talleyrand inquired whether the United States would be interested in buying the entire Louisiana Territory! The deal was negotiated at the bargain price of fifteen million dollars, along with a promise, as the French required, to extend American citizenship and religious freedom to all Catholics living in that vast expanse. Talleyrand, in the understatement of the young century, told the two American negotiators, "You have made a noble bargain for yourselves, and I suppose you will make the most of it."[16] Jefferson submitted the deal to the Senate, which easily ratified it.

The Louisiana Purchase provided a rationale for Jefferson to change his mind about seeking a second term in 1804, after he had said it was his "decided purpose" not to do so but to return to Monticello instead. The only question was the identity of his running mate, since Burr's conduct before and since becoming vice president had made him unacceptable to the president and other Republican stalwarts. In January of the presidential year, Burr met with Jefferson and indicated his willingness to remove himself from the picture if Jefferson would extend some gesture to advance his ambition to become governor of New York, but Jefferson offered none.

The one positive development that had come from that fiasco was congressional approval but not yet Senate ratification of the Twelfth Amendment to the Constitution, which soon would require the separate election of president and vice president, discarding the double-balloting fiasco. With the party system and the Jeffersonian Party barely out of the cradle, the Republican caucus in Congress in conversations with state party leaders met to choose the national ticket for 1804. They unanimously endorsed Jefferson for a second term and then cast ballots for his running mate. The Philadelphia *Aurora* reported afterward, "It is worthy of notice that the name of Mr. Burr was not introduced in the meeting or in a single vote."[17]

Governor Clinton, who had now decided he would not seek another term in Albany, was named on sixty-seven ballots, more than the majority required. The choice of Clinton sat well with Jefferson, inasmuch as the New Yorker's advanced age indicated he would not seek the presidency in 1808, when the path would be clear in Republican ranks for Madison to succeed Jefferson. As for Burr, he looked to New York to salvage his political career. Hamilton immediately warned that Burr's election as governor would fuel a scheme by New England Federalists to bring about the breakup of the Union, achieved at such great cost in the Revolution, with a defecting Burr in command.

Concerned about the possibility of additional agrarian states being carved out of the Louisiana Purchase, Federalists in Massachusetts formed the Essex Junto. Timothy Pickering, secretary of state under Washington and Adams, wrote in late 1803, "Although the end of all our Revolutionary labors and expectations is disappointed, I rather anticipate a new confederacy exempt from the corrupt and corrupting influences and oppression of the aristocratic Democrats of the South." He predicted, "There will be a separation [and] the British provinces, even with the assent of Britain, will become members of the Northern Confederacy."[18]

The Essex Junto first approached Hamilton with a scheme of electing him rather than Burr to the New York governorship, then having New York and New Jersey secede from the Union and join Nova Scotia and other Canadian provinces in the prophesied northern confederacy. But Hamilton, for all his hostility toward Jefferson, wanted no part of breaking up the Union. So the Essex Junto turned to the discontented Burr as a prospective co-conspirator, military leader, and even president of the new continental power.

The very notion of breaking up the Union met strong editorial opposition. *Mirror of the Times* of Wilmington, Delaware, reported of one Fourth of July toast in Philadelphia: "The advocates of Burrism and third party principles—May they be speedily shipped on Board a British prison ship, and exported to the congenial regions of Nova Scotia."[19] Jefferson, learning of the conspiracy, wrote a friend, "It will be found in this, as in all similar cases, that crooked schemes will end by overwhelming their authors and coadjutors in disgrace."[20]

When approached with the scheme, Burr wanted no part of it either. While he said he agreed with the northern Federalists' concern that the "Northern states must be governed by Virginia or govern Virginia, and that there was no middle course," he said he felt he "must go on democratically" to achieve a better power arrangement with the southern states within the Union.[21]

So Burr pressed on in his pursuit of the New York governorship. By running an effective reformer's campaign against the political machine of DeWitt Clinton in New York City, he hoped to restore his own political reputation in the state and nationally. But Jefferson's pointed unwillingness even to say a favorable word about him did Burr no good, and Hamilton's earlier assaults on Burr in their 1800 fight over control of the state were picked up and greatly embroidered by Cheetham. He resumed his earlier allegations against Burr as an inveterate womanizer who consorted not only with white and black prostitutes but also homosexuals and preyed on young boys.

At the same time, Cheetham, the major political provocateur, taunted Hamilton by writing in the *American Citizen:* "I dare assert that you attributed to Aaron Burr one of the most atrocious and unprincipled of crimes. He has not called upon you. . . . Either he is guilty or he is the most mean and despicable bastard in the universe." And he asked Burr in print whether he was "so degraded as to permit even General Hamilton to slander him with impunity?"[22] In behaving like a boxing promoter trying to build a big gate for a fight between two prominent heavyweights, Cheetham was playing with fire.

Through all this, Burr sought to brush off the whole barrage, at one point telling his daughter, Theodosia, he might send her "some new and amusing libels against the vice president."[23] But on Election Day the various attacks took their toll, and he lost to Lewis. Hamilton's role in the defeat of Burr in New York soon was repaid in measure far beyond its significance.

In March 1804, a New Yorker, Dr. Charles Cooper, in a letter to a friend that found its way into print, said he had heard Hamilton at a dinner party in Albany harshly criticize Burr "as a dangerous man and one who ought not to be trusted with the reins of government." When Hamilton's father-in-law, Philip Schuyler, wrote in protest to the *New-York Post,* the irate Cooper's reply to him was printed in the *Albany Register:* "I could detail to you a still more despicable opinion which General Hamilton has expressed of Mr. Burr."[24]

Two months later, Burr wrote Hamilton calling on him to explain or retract the use of the word *despicable.* Hamilton sloughed Burr off, saying the word *despicable* was too ambiguous for him to confirm or deny its use. He parsed words to squirm out of the bind. "'Tis evident," he shamelessly argued, "that the phrase 'still more despicable' admits to infinite shades, from very light to very dark." Then he asked, "How am I to judge of the degree intended? Or how shall I annex any precise idea to language so indefinite?" Remarkably, Hamilton concluded by seeming to minimize the whole matter: "I trust, on more reflection, you will see the matter in the same light as me. If not, I can only regret the circumstance, and abide the consequence."[25] But Burr would not let the matter go. He wrote back about the evasion, "I regret to find in it nothing of that sincerity and delicacy which you profess to Value," lecturing Hamilton that "political opposition can never absolve Gentlemen from the necessity of a rigid adherence to the laws of honor and the rules of decorum."[26]

But now Burr had enough of Hamilton's word games and dodges. He pressed for Hamilton's apology. Still, Burr was not mollified with an apology. Apparently determined to humiliate Hamilton further, he demanded a flat retraction, to which Hamilton replied he could not be held responsible for any "*rumours* which may be afloat" over their long acquaintanceship. Going on the offensive, he now accused Burr of "premeditated hostility." Burr finally ended the verbal duel by challenging Hamilton to a real one, with weapons of Hamilton's choice.[27]

Another two weeks went by before they physically faced off. In that time, surprisingly, Hamilton and Burr both attended a Society of the Cincinnati dinner, at which Hamilton mounted a table and sang a lusty military ditty while Burr sat by morosely, listening. In the week before the duel, Hamilton showed no sign of concern, even hosting seventy guests at a lavish ball in a wooded site in which unseen musicians were hidden to serenade strolling couples.[28]

In anticipation of the worst, however, he wrote an "apologia" for later publication in which he again engaged in slippery semantic games, saying basically he hadn't said anything against Burr that many others had not often said. Although he was strongly opposed to dueling, Hamilton said he felt obliged to accept the challenge to maintain his "ability to be in the future useful," ostensibly to preserve his own honor but practically to save his political life. Of his intentions regarding the challenge, he wrote, "My religious and moral principles are strongly opposed to the practice of duelling. . . . As well because it is possible I have injured Col. Burr . . . as from my general principles and temper. . . . I have resolved to . . . *reserve and throw away* my first fire, and *I have thoughts* even of *reserving* my second fire—and thus give a double opportunity to Col. Burr to pause and reflect."[29]

Burr in advance of the duel wrote no similar rationale or indication of intent, instead penning letters to daughter, Theodosia, and son-in-law, Joseph Alston, on the prospective settling of his financial and property affairs, which were in disorder.

According to the extant code of honor, Hamilton selected a pair of old family pistols for the duel and gave Burr his choice of the two. On the morning of July 11, on a cliff overlooking the Hudson River at Weehawken, New Jersey, the two heroes of the American Revolution paced off the required distance and on the signal fired the pistols. Hamilton's shot went into the air, splitting an overhead branch; Burr's shot hit Hamilton's right hip and lodged in his spleen. He was taken by boat back across the Hudson to New York, where he died of his wounds the next day.[30]

The precise words of Doctor Cooper's that had precipitated the duel were never reported, but Hamilton over the years had repeatedly slandered Burr without inciting a deadly confrontation. At the site of the duel, as Hamilton fell, Burr's second (i.e., his assistant and witness) hustled him away, leaving in the wake of the sensational event a torrent of attacks on the sitting vice president as both a coward and an assassin. Hamilton received the equivalent of a state funeral three days after the duel, while Burr remained in his Richmond Hill mansion.

After eleven days, as a coroner's inquest was held in New Jersey, bearing the threat of a murder charge against Burr, he fled, taking refuge in the Philadelphia home of his friend Charles Biddle. Subsequently he was indicted in New York for violating the law against dueling and by a New Jersey grand jury for murder. Again he joked of his dilemma with his daughter, writing her that the neighboring states were fighting over "which of them shall have the honor of hanging the vice-president!"[31] In Philadelphia he met a favorite mistress, Celeste, about whom he whimsically confided to daughter Theodosia: "If a male friend of yours should be dying of ennui, recommend him to engage in a duel and a courtship at the same time."[32]

Meanwhile, little had been said about removing Burr from being a heartbeat away from the presidency. He soon moved south to Georgia and Florida. Eventually he headed north, avoiding both New Jersey and New York, where indictments hung over him. The man who shot Alexander Hamilton to death was, however, still the vice president of the United States, and so, incredibly, he took refuge in Washington, where there was no law against dueling. After his arrival, Burr dined with a suddenly cordial Jefferson and was warmly welcomed by Madison and Gallatin. And when Congress convened on November 4, he took his chair as president of the Senate. Federalist senator William Plumber observed of the scene,

"It certainly is the first time—and God grant that it may be the last—that ever a man so justly charged with such an infamous crime, presided in the American Senate. We are, indeed, fallen on evil times."[33]

In his final task as president of the Senate, Burr chaired a sensational trial of impeachment against the Supreme Court justice Samuel Chase, accused by Jefferson through congressional allies of making "a seditious and official attack on the principles of our Constitution and on the proceedings of [the] State."[34] Burr, still under indictment himself, imposed strict rules of decorum in the chamber as he presided even-handedly and was widely commended for his role. Chase was acquitted on all eight articles, and Burr, in his final official appearance as vice president, delivered a farewell speech to the Senate that was so unexpected and emotionally overwhelming that many of the listening senators were reduced to tears.

Over the next three years as a fugitive, Burr became involved in a series of bizarre adventures that included leading an attempted secession of the western part of the country being expanded by the Louisiana Purchase and the creation of a buffer state between Louisiana and Mexico with himself as president. In 1806 he led a force of about sixty men on flatboard boats down the Ohio and Mississippi Rivers on a mysterious mission. When a confederate informed Jefferson that Burr was intent on committing treason, Jefferson ordered him captured, and in 1807 he was indicted. In his trial, presided over by longtime adversary John Marshall, Burr won acquittal on the grounds that the prosecution had failed to produce the two witnesses constitutionally required to commit him of treason. He moved to Europe for a time but returned to practice law, discredited and destitute when he died at age eighty.

Unlike the tenures of Adams and Jefferson before him, Burr's vice presidency did not lead him to the presidency. Instead, like both of them, he occupied the office mostly devoid of official responsibilities and opportunities to shape and carry out the policies of the administration to which he was elected. His place in history was shaped not by the office he held but by a common political feud and the deadly resolution he insisted on, still honored at the time.

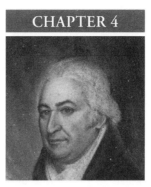

CHAPTER 4

GEORGE CLINTON
OF NEW YORK

With Aaron Burr banished from the Republican national ticket in 1804, another New Yorker, Governor George Clinton, was drafted to be Jefferson's running mate, and upon election it fell to Burr as the departing president of the Senate to administer the vice presidential oath to Clinton as his replacement. The Jefferson-Clinton team was easily elected over the eroding Federalist Party slate of Charles Cotesworth Pinckney of South Carolina and Rufus King of New York. With the demise of presidential double balloting in the adoption of the Twelfth Amendment to the Constitution, victory delivered both the presidency and the vice presidency to the same party. The general prosperity in Jefferson's first term and national pride in the Louisiana Purchase assured the Virginian's landslide reelection, carrying Clinton with him. Jefferson obviously had needed no help from the aging New Yorker, and over the next four years he treated his vice president accordingly.

The stand-alone election of the vice president, rather than the presidential runner-up being awarded the office, was a significant development. While it in no way increased the influence of the office unless the president so decided, it did set up the vice presidential nomination as a vehicle for barter by the presidential nominees in quest of electoral college support from certain states and regions of the country.

Clinton's succeeding of Burr in the second office had its ironies. In

1800, Burr, as a leading political operative in the Empire State, had persuaded Clinton to join other state party luminaries to run as presidential electors. Their listing was widely credited with swinging New York and the election and had earned Burr his place on the winning ticket. Four years later, with Burr discredited, Jefferson was well pleased to have Clinton as vice president. Not only was he a fellow critic of the Federalist philosophy and someone on whom Jefferson had relied for political counsel on politics in the Empire State; at the age of sixty-five and overtly looking to retire from public life, Clinton also seemed unlikely to seek the presidency in 1808, when Jefferson hoped his friend and fellow Virginian James Madison would succeed him as president.

Like all three previous vice presidents—Adams, Jefferson, and Burr—Clinton soon learned that he would not make or influence policy in the administration in which he served. Despite his more than two decades of executive leadership in New York, during which he was accustomed to making high-level decisions, he was unfamiliar with the legislative branch in which he now would function, as well as with the city of Washington itself. Though he looked the part of a senator—silver-haired and distinguished—he had neither the legislative skills of his predecessor Burr nor Burr's youthful enthusiasm.

John Quincy Adams of Massachusetts, son of the former president, offered a harsh judgment of the man: "Mr. Clinton is totally ignorant of all the most common forms of proceeding in the Senate, and yet by the rules he is to decide every question or order without debate and without appeal. His judgment is neither quick nor strong: so there is no more dependence upon the correctness of his determinations from his understanding than from his experience. As the only duty of a Vice-President, under our Constitution, is to preside in Senate, it ought be considered what his qualifications for the office are at his election. In this respect a worse choice an Mr. Clinton could scarcely have been made."[1]

The seven-term governor of New York and three-time loser of the presidency or vice presidency before replacing Burr on the Republican ticket in 1804, George Clinton was no aristocrat. A farmer-lawyer from rural Ulster County, in the Hudson River valley, he shared Jefferson's commitment to agrarian interests and his wariness of federal encroachment on states' rights and individual liberties. But he, too, was a Revolutionary War hero, rising under Washington to the rank of brigadier general after an early political career in the colonial assembly and later as a member of the Second Continental Congress. First elected governor of New York in 1777, he succeeded wealthy Philip Schuyler, later the son-in-law of Hamilton and eventually a bitter political foe. At eighteen Clinton served on a privateer ship in the Caribbean in the French and Indian War, and after studying law in New York he returned to Ulster as county surrogate. He was elected to the Second Continental Congress in 1775, where he met Washington. After a few months in Philadelphia, Clinton returned to New York as the commander of the four county militias responsible for defense of the Hudson River highlands. Under his direction two forts were built, and he eventually recruited enlistments for the Continental army under Washington's command. "The forts," he reported, "are in so respectable a state of defense, as to promise us security against any attack on that quarter."[2]

In April 1777, a New York convention drafted and adopted the state's first constitution, and Clinton was among four men put forward for governor. A flurry of votes in secret ballot from members of the military under his command and farmers surprisingly elected him over the aristocratic Federalist Schuyler. Clinton's election ushered in a new era of the "yeoman" influence of small farmers in the state's politics.[3]

Clinton notified Washington that "with a Degree of Pain" he was requesting to leave his military post when "the Designs of the Enemy are not fully known." He added, "I will most cheerfully return to the army until the Fate of the present campaign is determined" if the obligations of his new position should permit it. Hamilton, as a lieutenant-general and Washington's chief aide, wrote to Major General Israel Putnam, Clinton's superior officer: "It is regretted that so useful an officer is obliged to leave the posts under his superintendency at a time like this," a sentiment in which Washington joined while extending good wishes to Clinton as governor.[4]

Clinton's early optimism about the security of the Hudson Highlands was soon dashed. In September, after the British occupied Philadelphia, a large flotilla of ships laden with British and Hessian troops sailed up the Hudson, causing Washington to order his generals to call out the militias in Connecticut and New York. He urgently requested that Clinton take personal direction of Forts Clinton and Montgomery in guarding the New York Highlands against the assaults of the British general John Burgoyne.

In a fight between more than four thousand invaders and six hundred American militiamen, many unarmed, the defenders inflicted heavy casualties but eventually surrendered the forts. Clinton barely evaded capture and resumed direction of the resistance, which ultimately prevented the British forces in northern New York from joining up and relieving Burgoyne's beleaguered forces, which eventually surrendered.

After the war, Clinton resumed his full-time responsibilities as the governor of New York, by this time sufficiently entrenched to repel easily another challenge from the aristocratic Schuyler. During the war, with much of the southern part of New York State under British occupation, Clinton had been a strong advocate for increasing the power of Congress to prosecute the war and achieve a greater sense of nationhood at home. Afterward, as governor he became more concerned about the rights and liberties of his state and of fellow New Yorkers within the developing and expanding federal government and about the state's heavy financial burden to it. His earlier flirtations with national office, including brief Anti-Federalist campaigns in New York and Virginia to elect him president or vice president in 1789 and vice president in 1792, did not divert him from his prime allegiance and defense of the interests of his home state.

But in early 1804, with Burr summarily dismissed for a second vice presidential term and Clinton fixed on retiring from the New York governorship, his selection to be Jefferson's reelection running mate became obvious. With his long service in Albany, his war experience, and his solid Anti-Federalist credentials, Clinton at sixty-five was just right as one who would not pose a serious challenge to the younger Madison for the presidency in 1808.

Jefferson accordingly paid little attention to Clinton, disregarding him on patronage matters in New York and turning a deaf ear to his urgings for more protection of American shipping, critical to the port of New York, amid turmoil in Europe. Clinton deplored as inadequate the ultimate appropriation of one million dollars to defend the entire east coast, about which he was not consulted.

As John Quincy Adams so uncharitably observed after Clinton took the chair as presiding officer of the Senate, he was a fish out of water after so many years of swimming in familiar political waters in Albany. He returned often to his home in Poughkeepsie and, unlike Burr, usually absented himself from the Washington social circuit, seldom entertaining colleagues and living mostly in boardinghouses, his wife, Cornelia, having died in 1800.

After so many years in power in New York and with an abundance of free time as the vice president, Clinton tried to keep his hand in his state's politics. In 1807, in desperation to reestablish Republican control in New York, some of the vice president's loyalists called on him to return and seek yet another gubernatorial nomination. Irritated, he asked his friends not to force him to make an "absolute refusal" of any such nomination.

Meanwhile, as the so-called Burr Conspiracy in the West spread, Clinton applauded Jefferson's disavowal of any administration involvement and warned his nephew DeWitt Clinton to steer clear of it. He expressed strong doubts that Burr's activities reflected only interest in land speculation.

At the same time, the national party that Jefferson had constructed was suffering divisions over his successor in 1808. Publicly he remained silent while clearly preferring Madison. But because Clinton, increasingly out of the loop of the Jefferson inner circle, had reservations about the administration's foreign policies, his name again began to surface for the next presidential nomination, although he now was in his late sixties. His New York base could appeal to many voters, especially elsewhere in the North, who felt that sixteen years of the last twenty of a Virginian in the presidency was enough. Also being injected into the speculation was another Virginian, James Monroe, who along with William Pinckney had negotiated the treaty with Great Britain in 1806, which Jefferson found so unsatisfactory.

The Republican congressional caucuses that had emerged in 1800 and were continued in 1804 were essentially to select the vice presidential nominees, since in both years Jefferson was the agreed presidential choice. In 1808, for the first time the party presidential nomination involved real competition. Madison's strong support in Congress made the caucus his favored device, whereas Monroe's and Clinton's chances seemed better in a process of broader representation. Both hoped that at the least the caucus would be delayed, preventing an early Madison nomination. But it was called for in January, long before adjournment, because a movement for Monroe was growing in the Virginia legislature and the Madison backers hoped to undercut it.

On January 23, 1808, Senator Stephen Bradley of Vermont as the previous Republican caucus chairman, summoned party members of Congress to the Senate chamber to nominate the Republican ticket. His right to call the caucus was challenged by a New York Republican, but eighty-nine members showed up, of whom eighty-three voted to nominate Secretary of State Madison for the presidency. The caucus then voted on the vice presidential nomination, and seventy-nine went for Clinton for a second term.

Most Clinton and Monroe supporters in Congress declined to attend, but Madison still had a majority of the party legislators. In Virginia, backers of Monroe refused to recognize the result of the caucus or of another by the party members in the state legislature that nominated Madison electors. They formed a rival faction that nominated electors pledged to Monroe. Clinton meanwhile, still considering himself a candidate for the presidency, complained that he had not been told of the congressional caucus or its purpose, and he never formally accepted its vice presidential nomination.[5]

Clinton told New York senator Samuel Mitchell he thought himself "treated with great disrespect and cruelty" by the caucus goers, apparently to be cavalierly dismissed as a serious presidential prospect.[6] Some of the Clintonians complained that Virginia's pride in the presidencies of Washington and Jefferson had "stimulated the people of that state to believe that Virginia geese are all swans."[7]

Mitchell wrote his wife about Madison's and Clinton's prospects: "There does not appear the remotest probability of [Clinton's] success as President. The former gives dinners and makes generous displays to the members. The latter lives snug at his lodgings, and keeps aloof from such captivating exhibitions. The Secretary of State has a wife to aid his pretensions. The Vice-President has nothing of female succor on his side."[8]

Clinton meanwhile, demonstrating what he now thought of Jefferson's conduct of foreign policy and how its continuance under Madison would imperil the country, wrote to DeWitt Clinton: "It is in my Opinion impossible that the Cause of Republicanism can exist much longer under the present visionary Feeble and I might add Corrupt Management of our National Affairs. It is calculated to disgust our best Friends and is fast doing so."[9]

John Randolph of Virginia undertook to rally his state's "Tertium Quids"—a third faction of the Republican Party—to Clinton as a way to detour Madison, but Clinton's unusual behavior hampered the effort. He continued to ignore and say nothing of the Republican caucus endorsement of him for another term as vice president, generating a belief in some quarters that he had left the party. He denied it and refused to withdraw his presidential candidacy.

Meanwhile, in August of the election year, some two dozen or so prominent Federalists from seven New England and mid-Atlantic states, plus South Carolina, caucused to consider nominating the party's ticket. But when some of the New York and Pennsylvania delegates balked at Clinton, the Federalist caucus settled on Pinckney of South Carolina and Rufus King of New York.

Clinton's advanced age—he as now sixty-nine and in declining physical condition—also was raised against him as a presidential nominee. But if he was too old, his defenders asked, why had the Republican congressional caucus chosen him to continue as vice president, first in line of succession for the presidency? At the same time, they challenged the legitimacy of the congressional caucus to nominate the Republican ticket, since the Constitution specifically provided for electors to decide the election, taking it out of the hands of Congress.

Some Pennsylvania Republicans favored Clinton for president and Monroe for vice president but on reflection concluded that Clinton could prevail only in league with Federalists, an unacceptable circumstance. In the end, they gave all their twenty electoral votes to Madison. In Clinton's own New York, fears of being out in the cold in a Madison administration produced a split in the state's electoral votes, with thirteen for Madison and six for their former governor.

In Virginia, bad feelings remained over Clinton's stubbornness in refusing to say whether he accepted the vice presidential nomination again. Later, Monroe's supporters, recognizing he trailed Madison, contrived the notion of running Clinton for president and Monroe for vice president as a means of bringing Monroe decisive support from New York. Unsaid was the prospect that Clinton, if elected president, might not live out his term or seek a second term, leaving Monroe well positioned to ascend to the presidency. Randolph, a veteran Anti-Federalist but a fierce foe of Jefferson in Virginia, endorsed the Clinton-Monroe ticket but now carried little weight in the Old Dominion.

Once again Clinton was disappointed at the prospect of another four years as vice president. He had had enough of presiding over the Senate and enough of the foreign policy of Jefferson and Madison. But he had no alternative and quietly went along for the ride into the general election, in which the Republican ticket of Madison and Clinton easily prevailed.

In the new Madison administration, inaugurated on March 4, 1809, Clinton didn't bother to put in an appearance until weeks later, when the first congressional session began. While there, he was as isolated from power as he had been in the last four years of the Jefferson administration. But by this time Clinton neither had the vigor nor the inclination to take any significant task. Dutifully he continued to preside over the Senate when he was in Washington, but ill health and his desire to be back home in New York diminished that time. Why he agreed to serve another term as vice president under another president with whom he had major differences, in a position he long before had grown tired of, remained a mystery.

Clinton's last significant action as vice president came in 1811, three years after election to his second term, when he cast the deciding vote breaking a 17–17 tie in the Senate on rechartering the Bank of the United States, sought by Madison and Gallatin. Clinton, siding with the seventeen old Republicans and against the seven Federalists and ten Republicans for rechartering, killed the bank with only the eleventh vote he cast in his two vice presidential terms.[10]

In doing so, he weighed in as the champion of government of limited, proscribed powers. Questioning the constitutionality of creating such a national bank not expressly mentioned by the founders, he wrote that were it needed, "the Constitution happily furnishes the means for remedying the evil by amendment." The aging vice president was true to his old Anti-Federalist moorings. "In the course of a long life," he concluded, "I have found that Government is not to be strengthened by an assumption of doubtful powers, but by a wise and energetic execution of those which are incontestable; the former never fails to produce suspicion and distrust, while the latter inspires respect and confidence."[11]

Two months later, George Clinton died at age seventy-three. Gouverneur Morris in his eulogy frankly declared that although Clinton had regularly presided over the Senate, "to share in the measures of administration was not his part. To influence them was not in his power," and the man's sense of duty and propriety "induced him to be silent."[12] The observations, which could have been taken as an indictment of Jefferson and Madison for not making better use of this upright and committed fellow Republican, were no more than a description of what little was expected of the American vice president in those first years of the Republic and for many years thereafter.

For the first time, the American vice presidency was vacant and would remain so for the remaining eleven months of Clinton's second term. There existed no provision for a replacement, either by election or appointment, and few seemed to care or even notice. The circumstance was yet another commentary on the continuing insignificant regard for the office. The vacancy left Senator Pro Tem William H. Crawford of Georgia, who was in the Senate for only five years and little known in the country, next in the line of presidential succession until the inauguration of the next elected vice president.

CHAPTER 5

ELBRIDGE GERRY

OF MASSACHUSETTS

With the vice presidency remaining vacant for nearly a year after the death of George Clinton, predictably a northern Republican would be sought as Madison's running mate in 1812, in order to bring the strength of New England to the Virginian's bid for presidential reelection.

The Republican congressional caucus first turned to John Langdon of New Hampshire, giving him sixty-four votes to only sixteen for Elbridge Gerry of Massachusetts. But when Langdon declined the nomination, the caucus held a second vote, and Gerry, an enthusiastic backer of Madison on the prosecution of the War of 1812, which had just begun in response to British interference with American shipping and commerce, won seventy-four of the seventy-seven ballots cast.

After two terms as governor of Massachusetts, Gerry had just been defeated for a third term, in part for his support of Madison's foreign policies, unpopular in New England. But like Clinton, his vice presidential predecessor, Gerry had a long and distinguished history as a son of the American Revolution—a signer of the Declaration of Independence, a member of the Continental and Confederation Congresses, a delegate to the Constitutional Convention, and a member of the first U.S. House of Representatives.

He was the son of a successful prominent Marblehead trader, shipowner, and merchant whose vessels carried fish, whale oil, and lumber products to the West Indies, returning with rum, sugar, and molasses. The father, Thomas Gerry, a member of what was called "the codfish aristocracy" in New England, also sent his ship to ports in Spain for choice wines. Then he sold them in his general store on the family wharf in Marblehead, eventually the prime fishing harbor among the North American colonies under British rule.[1]

The town had a reputation for rugged independence. A minister in neighboring Salem, William Bentley, once described its denizens "as profane, intemperate and ungoverned as any people on the Continent."[2] Elbridge Gerry, named after a favored uncle, John Elbridge, was committed to the family business, enrolled at Harvard at the age of fourteen, and later moved to Cambridge. On a business trip to New York he met Thomas Jefferson and eventually married a New York woman but in his demeanor remained a Marblehead elitist, like his father, and a fierce patriot of the soon-to-be American Republic. Early on, when the British Parliament began to impose taxes detrimental to the town's prosperity, Elbridge's voice could be heard in loud dissent in local councils and town meetings.

The Boston Massacre of 1770, in which British troops fired into a crowd of angry protesters, triggered Gerry's entry into full-throated opposition to British occupation. He initiated a boycott on the sale or use of imported tea, which remained a subject of British taxation. Eventually, after joining with Samuel Adams in a Boston-Marblehead campaign of resistance to British edicts, he gained new prominence in New England politics. When in 1772 Adams created a Boston committee of correspondence to show solidarity against the English, Gerry helped organize one in Marblehead. His further outspoken protests against British taxation and other impositions finally led to Gerry's election as Marblehead's representative to the Massachusetts legislature.

Subsequently, however, a local fight over the construction of a hospital in Marblehead to cope with a smallpox epidemic led to a mob burning it down, demonstrating to Gerry that the British were not the only inhibitions to local rule. He resigned from the Marblehead committee of correspondence for a time, rejoining when a British edict closed Boston Harbor to commerce after the destruction caused by the Boston Tea Party. By 1775, he was a member of the Massachusetts Provincial Congress, formed in defiance of the British after a new governor, General Thomas Gage, had dissolved the old legislature. Gerry quickly served on key committees, including one considering means of self-defense, presumably against growing British oppression, and another against colonial taxes in an act of open revolt.[3]

At the same time, he proposed to Adams that other steps be taken to put the colony on a war footing, foreseeing a threat not only to political but also to religious freedom. "I understand that Soldiers are attended to their Graves with Mass," he wrote, "and I expect that popery [Catholicism] will be soon not only tolerated but established in Boston." And in Marblehead, Gerry was elected at a town meeting to direct extra pay for local "minutemen" to train "in the arts of war, on which alone . . . depends the Salvation of the Country from Slavery."[4]

As a result of such preparations, Marblehead came close to replacing Lexington and Concord as the places where "the shots heard 'round the world" announcing the start of the American Revolutionary War were fired. On the night of April 18, 1775, as Gerry and his colleagues were asleep in the Black Horse Tavern after discussing the movement of armaments to avoid British detection, they were awakened by the sound of marching British troops on their way to Concord. They fled, and troops entered the tavern but found only empty beds. The war could have begun right there but for the flight of Gerry and his party.[5]

Once the fighting started, Gerry took a leading role in acquiring arms from the other colonies and from overseas for a Massachusetts army in the making. He plunged deeply into financial and currency matters to pay for the war and was among the first to propose Washington as commander-in-chief of what became the Continental army. After holding out for a time for a conciliation with the British, Gerry became a strong voice in the Continental Congress for declaring American independence and was a signer of the Declaration, penned by Jefferson. Originally favoring the creation of a new central government to prosecute the war, he also defended states' rights and sovereignty and opposed the extension of powers to a central entity, in line with Anti-Federalist principles in debates over the Articles of Confederation in 1777, which in the end he also signed.[6]

After enactment of the Paris Peace Treaty, officially ending the Revolutionary War in 1783, Gerry reverted to an earlier fear not only of a return to monarchy but also of a military aristocracy, opposing a standing peacetime army and favoring state militias. A congressional debate the next year ended in disbanding most of the Continental army for reliance chiefly on the militias.

At the Constitutional Convention in Philadelphia in 1787, Gerry set out to restructure the Articles of Confederation to strengthen the central government in dealing with civil unrest, as in the Shays Rebellion, the protests against farm mortgage foreclosures. At the same time, however, he insisted on dual powers in the states, putting him on a middle course between extreme nationalists like Hamilton and Madison, in favor of reducing the role of the states. In the end, Gerry successfully argued for equal small-state representation in the Senate. Interesting in light of later developments, Gerry also protested the very creation of the office of the vice presidency and the notion of making him the president of the Senate with power only to break a tie. "We might as well put the President himself at the head of the Legislature," he complained, citing the separation of powers doctrine.[7]

Unhappy with various other proposals that he deemed would put too much power in the hands of the executive, Gerry finally resorted to stalling tactics, calling for more debate on issues already voted on and for a second constitutional convention to consider amendments. At last, he moved for the incorporation of a national bill of citizen rights that would assure trial by jury and freedom of the press, and he declined to sign the Constitution without one, fighting ratification in Massachusetts. Eventually, however, he declared his support.

In the administration of John Adams, Gerry served as minister to France during the notorious XYZ Affair. As one of three Adams negotiators with France to avert a looming war, he was victimized in the scandalous effort by the French agents of Talleyrand who tried but failed to bribe the negotiators to achieve a favorable peace treaty but nevertheless tarnished Gerry's reputation in the process. When the other two American negotiators returned home, however, Gerry stayed on and was able finally to report a more conciliatory French attitude. He remained in Adams's confidence and one of his closest friends over the years.[8]

Back home and back in politics as a member of Congress, Gerry at first embraced Federalist policies but soon broke away over the faction's pro-British inclinations, siding with the pro-French leanings of the Anti-Federalists. He later lost four bids for governor of Massachusetts before finally winning election in 1810. In his first term, he functioned as a moderate and conciliatory figure, striving to unite Federalists and Republicans as he had sought to do as a state legislator. In his second term, however, with the advent of the war that divided pro-British Federalists and pro-French Republicans, Gerry himself became fiercely partisan, using his office and an inventive scheme to maximize Republican and minimize Federalist strengths.

After a long history of Federalist dominance in Massachusetts, the Republicans began to take hold, gaining control of the executive, legislative, and judicial branches in the Bay State in 1811. Under Gerry, they first focused on the state Senate, passing a bill abandoning old county lines and dividing Massachusetts into senatorial districts and drawing the borders in a way to assure more and stronger Republican election results. They did the same for congressional districts, and in Gerry's home Essex County they elected three Republicans where the Federalists previously had swept all five seats. A little-known Federalist artist drew a map of the new voting district whose shape resembled a salamander. A wit renamed it "gerrymander," and the label quickly entered into the political lexicon and has never left.[9] The practice actually goes back to colonial times but has been memorialized by Gerry's usage, although pronounced with a soft *g* as in *jerry*, rather than the hard *g* as in his name.

In 1812, Gerry was an odd choice of a running mate for Madison, having just been defeated for a third term as governor of Massachusetts, but coming from a northern state he provided the regional balance that had been honored on all the previous winning tickets. Also, because New England was strongly against war with England, Gerry's selection as representing the pro-war position was considered a means of softening the prevailing sentiment.[10] And like his predecessor George Clinton of New York, he was in his late sixties and not considered likely to seek the presidency when his term ended, facilitating the selection of the successor the sitting president wanted. Gerry also was another revolutionary-era hero, though not in uniform.

As was the custom, in the 1812 campaign neither Madison and Gerry nor their challengers running as Federalists, New York mayor DeWitt Clinton and Jared Ingersoll of Philadelphia, spoke in their own behalf, letting rival newspapers in each camp joust among themselves. Gerry was quoted as later telling a friend who urged him to speak out: "I cannot alter the method which brought me to high political office and make a direct appeal to the voters."[11] In the electoral college, Madison and Gerry won easily, picking up three additional Federalist electors from New England. They carried all states except Clinton's New York and the neighboring New Jersey but won the popular vote by only 2.8 percent.

Gerry's deportment in national office resembled his service as governor, originally seeking comity with the opposing Federalists as he presided over the Senate but soon shifting to sharp partisanship. Amid his increasing concerns about Federalist intentions to somehow restore British and even monarchical influence in America, Gerry came into the vice presidency in 1813 as a strong supporter of Madison's decision to go to war against the British in defense of American shipping rights. Upon Jefferson's 1809 enactment of the embargo against the British and French, Gerry had envisioned Federalist secession plots to extract New England from the infant Union or a civil war and had written to Jefferson of his fears.[12] Now his suspicions of Federalist disloyalty made him particularly partisan and ever more strongly supportive of Madison, though like previous vice presidents he had little voice in the administration's deliberations.

Indeed, Gerry seemed to welcome the War of 1812 as a way to revive the patriotic fervor of the Revolution in defense of American freedom. "We have been long enough at peace," he wrote. "We are losing our spirit, our character, and our independence. We are degenerating into a mere nation of traders, and forgetting the honour of our ancestors and the interest of posterity. We must be aroused by some great event that may stir up the ancient patriotism of the people."[13]

Gerry was a popular figure on the Washington social scene, more cordial in such circumstances than he was in the heat of political debate as a wary and suspicious enemy of wayward Federalists. When he reached the age of seventy, however, the strain began to show itself. On the morning of November 23, 1814, he arose complaining of chest pains. After breakfast he took a carriage to the Senate, but as the pains increased he returned to his boardinghouse, where he stretched out on his bed and died. He thus was the second vice president in a row to succumb while in office, four months before completion of his term. Again the vice presidency was vacant, to remain so until the next national election.

Elbridge Gerry was another northern enabler of the Virginia domination of the presidency, providing the regional ticket balance as Madison joined Washington and Jefferson in occupying the presidency for nearly eighteen of its first twenty-two years. But not even Gerry's staunch championing of Madison's War of 1812 earned him permanent approbation. Rather, he is best identified in the history books as the creator of "gerrymandering," as the term took its place in the American political lexicon.

CHAPTER 6

DANIEL D. TOMPKINS
OF NEW YORK

I n 1816, the Virginia dynasty continued with the presidential election of James Monroe, Madison's secretary of state, the only break in its rule having been the 1796 election of John Adams of Massachusetts, succeeding Washington's two terms. And in that brief four-year hiatus, another Virginian, Thomas Jefferson, had served as vice president before achieving the presidency himself in 1800.

Along with the continuing dominance of the Jeffersonian Party, the practice of regional balance on the national ticket also continued, with a New Yorker becoming vice president for the third time. In 1808 and 1812 Madison had survived the diminishing Federalists' lament of "too many Virginians," but it was heard again in 1816, when another New Yorker, Governor Daniel D. Tompkins, and a Georgian, William H. Crawford, challenged Monroe, who was Madison's thinly veiled choice to succeed him.

The Virginia dynasty at first was thought in some quarters to be in jeopardy, because eight years earlier Monroe himself briefly had bucked it by seeking the presidential nomination in competition with Madison. He left some ill will in the Virginia party caucus in the futile effort to hook up with George Clinton of New York against the dynasty. With Madison in his corner this time, Monroe managed to prevail in the Virginia caucus, but the prospects of another Virginia–New York alliance seemed dimmed by the presidential ambitions of Governor Tompkins.

The *Albany Argus* unhesitatingly put forward the name of the Empire State's governor, editorializing, "If private worth—if public service—if fervent patriotism and practical talents are to be regarded in selecting a President, then Governor Tompkins stands forth to the nation with unrivalled pretensions."[1] Tompkins, however, was not as well known among congressional caucusers from other states as either Monroe or Crawford, a veteran senator and former cabinet member. Nor was Tompkins a Revolutionary War veteran or a founding father, like all the previous presidents and vice presidents, having been born in 1774, two years before the publication of the Declaration of Independence.

He was one of eleven children of a tenant farmer eventually involved in local and state politics. Educated at Columbia, where he had finished first in his class in 1792, the genial young Daniel, known as the "Farmer's Boy," married into the family of a politically minded member of the Tammany Society and became an active "Bucktail" Republican, challenging the Clinton domination of the state party. In 1804 he was elected to Congress, but prior to its convening he resigned to accept an appointment to the state supreme court.

In 1807 at only thirty-three, Daniel Tompkins won the governorship with the backing of New York mayor DeWitt Clinton, unseating Morgan Lewis, the establishment candidate. Soon he distanced himself from Clinton and aligned more with the foreign policies of Jefferson, supporting his secretary of state, Madison, in the presidential run in 1808. Tompkins was reelected governor in 1810 and became a staunch backer of the War of 1812, throwing himself enthusiastically into helping the recruitment of New York militia and armaments. In the process he contributed considerable sums of his own money and endorsed local bank loans that put him personally in debt, with major consequences long afterward.

As the wartime governor of New York, Tompkins became the chief disbursing officer of military expenses for both the state and the United States, authorized to spend a million dollars in behalf of New York and three million for the federal government. Much of it was done at his own responsibility at a time when the credit of the United States was in dire straits. The commingling of funds would eventually lead to a huge burden on him and questions of his handling of all the money.

In 1814, Madison offered Tompkins a cabinet post, but he turned it down on the grounds that he could be more helpful to the administration as governor of New York. He later explained one of the real reasons for doing so: "[It] was the inadequacy of my circumstances to remove to Washington & support so large and expensive family as mine is, on the salary of that office."[2]

Financial matters seemed always to be occupying Tompkins, busy mobilizing resources for the late war while lacking discipline in handling his private funds. When the war ended, he continued to concern himself with military fortifications and other preparedness out of a belief that the 1814 Treaty of Ghent, with the British, would bring only a hiatus. In a debate in the legislature over the construction of a great canal linking Lake Erie and New York waterways to the east, Tompkins opposed it on grounds that military works had to take precedence. "England will never forgive us for our victories on the land, and on the ocean and the lakes," he declared, "and take my word for it we shall have another war with her within two years."[3]

His early coolness to the canal system, embraced by DeWitt Clinton to his everlasting credit in the state, later was regarded by some as Tompkins's greatest mistake as governor and central to his quarrels with Clinton. Nevertheless, Tompkins's popularity remained very high in the New York legislature, which in 1816 nominated him for president. But in a Republican congressional caucus in Washington, Monroe prevailed over Crawford and was nominated. Then, restoring the Virginia–New York alliance, the caucus chose Tompkins for the vice presidential nomination.[4]

The New Yorker agreed to take the second spot, to the surprise of some colleagues who regarded the governorship of the increasingly important Empire State as much more influential. But at the same time, Tompkins acceded to local party leaders to seek simultaneously another term as governor, and he won handily. The Federalists, increasingly in eclipse, didn't bother to run a full presidential ticket, and Monroe and Tompkins were elected easily.[5] The rising leader of the New York Republicans, Martin Van Buren, was said to have wanted Tompkins to serve as both governor and vice president to block the gubernatorial ambitions of DeWitt Clinton, but Tompkins declined.[6] The very notion of such dual service was a commentary on the continuing low regard of the second national office and on its demands on the time and energies of its occupants.

In his first months as vice president, Tompkins conscientiously presided over the Senate, but his heart was never in Washington. He spent much of the summer and fall of his first year in office back home on Staten Island. Although Tompkins was only forty-three years old at the time, he was unwell. In early September 1817, he wrote a letter to his friend Smith Thompson in a despondent vein: "You will be less surprised at my delay in attending to the contents of your letters, when I inform you that the injuries I received by the fall from my horse at Fort Greene during the War have increased upon me for several years till finally, for the last six weeks, they have confined me to my house and a few rods around it and sometimes to my bed. I am thereby deprived of the power of visiting the City or riding or walking abroad or attending to my extensive outdoor concerns." Accordingly, he wrote, "I shall probably resign the office of Vice President at the next session, if not sooner, as there is very little hope of my ever being able to perform its duties thereafter."[7]

Beyond his physical state, Tompkins was plagued now by various financial obligations over real estate dealings on Staten Island and Manhattan, forcing him to absent himself from presiding over the Senate and return to New York for the remainder of the session. New York historian Jabez Hammond wrote later of Tompkins: "He was irregular and unmethodical in business; not systematical in keeping his accounts; employed too many agents; mingled his own private funds with those of the public; was naturally careless about money, and sometimes profuse in his expenses." Even so, Hammond noted, "No candid man charged him with intentional dishonesty in his pecuniary transactions."[8]

As the wartime governor of New York, Tompkins's handling of public money had produced an official allegation that he had spent $120,000 of unaccounted-for funds. A very public, and to Tompkins painful, feud ensued that left him distraught. Fortunately during this period, demands on Tompkins in Washington were light. Seldom was he called upon to break a tie vote in the Senate. Van Buren visited him and wrote, "I found him, in comparison with what he had been, exceedingly helpless . . . his resolution [not] strong enough to enable him to bear up against the injustice and the calumny of which he was now made the victim." Tompkins's son-in-law Gilbert Thompson told Van Buren that the man was drinking too much, attributing the malaise to the financial pressures on him.[9]

Even so, while continuing as vice president Tompkins was nominated in New York for another term as governor but lost a close race against DeWitt

Clinton. He won some solace when the state legislature authorized a final settlement to his advantage in the money dispute. Returning to Washington after the gubernatorial election, Tompkins was called upon to preside over the critical Senate debate on the Missouri Compromise. Missouri was admitted to the Union as a slave state, and Maine as free, maintaining a balance of eleven states in each category.

As the presider for the debate, Tompkins's conduct was widely criticized as disorderly. He eventually returned to New York, and the Missouri Compromise eventually went forward without him. His absence angered many anti-slavery northern senators, who felt, in the event of a tie vote on the compromise, he might have been able to break it in favor of their side. Although no tie ensued, the Federalist Rufus King for one criticized Tompkins for having "fled the field on the day of battle."[10] For all his bad feelings about being rejected by the voters of New York and his obvious dissatisfaction with serving in the Senate, Tompkins nevertheless clung to the vice presidency. His defeat in New York seemed to matter little in the Era of Good Feelings, of the Monroe presidency, nor did his deep financial difficulties deny his renomination, in such low significance was the office held.

The Monroe-Tompkins team was easily reelected in 1820, as the Federalist Party continued to disintegrate. A Republican caucus call to nominate the party's ticket drew so few participants that no nominations were made, and the state electors simply voted for the incumbents. Senator William Plumer of New Hampshire declined to vote for Tompkins because, he said, the vice president was absent from the Senate "nearly three fourths of the time," adding, "He has not that weight of character which his office requires—the fact is he is grossly intemperate."[11]

Tompkins began his second vice presidential term by skipping his and Monroe's inaugurations in Washington and taking his oath of office in New York. Though he wanted the vice presidency as a badge, his continued interest in New York politics kept his focus and his presence there. In 1821 a third state constitutional convention was held in Albany, and Tompkins was elected its president, which one delegate described as the result of "the madness of party" and Tompkins as "degenerated into a degraded sot."[12] For seventy-five days from August into November, he remained there, debating with the Clinton faction over such issues as voter qualifications, the appointment of judges, and the pace of racial emancipation in the state.

Upon adjournment of the convention, the vice president retreated to his home on Staten Island in an effort to regain his failing health. In January 1822 he returned to Washington to preside over the Senate but soon absented himself again. A Washington observer wrote to Andrew Jackson, "The Vice President left this city yesterday. I don't think he was perfectly sober during his stay here. He was several times so drunk in the chair that he could with difficulty put the question. I understand he will never return here."[13]

Tompkins now was only forty-eight years old. Hounded by creditors who had obtained state supreme court judgments against him of more than forty-two thousand dollars, he desperately attempted to realize some money from his home and land on Staten Island. He was forced to move to a cheap boardinghouse in lower Manhattan while he continued to struggle with the federal government's claims against him and with his counterclaims. To make matters even worse, an appropriations bill now came before the Senate calling for withholding the salaries of government officials who had outstanding accounts owed the U.S. Treasury. Had he been presiding, he would have heard his friend Van Buren making a plea in behalf of "gallant and heroic men, who had sustained the honor of their country in the hour of danger," and whether they "should be kept out of their just dues."[14]

The appropriations provision passed, making Tompkins destitute and leading him to invite a federal suit against him so that he could publicly defend himself. He called witnesses who testified to his tireless efforts to pay troops and arm them in the War of 1812. In closing, this broken man urged the jury to let neither partisanship nor pity govern their judgment. "Could I believe that your verdict on this occasion was to be guided by your sympathy, I should despise both it and you. I demand of you justice only."[15] After several hours of deliberating, the jury ruled in his favor, saying the government owed him nearly $137,000, but further disputes continued. Finally Monroe stepped in, informing Congress that the Treasury Department had concluded it owed Tompkins about thirty-five thousand dollars and, at Monroe's recommendation, had authorized that the vice president be paid as "an essential accommodation."[16]

On January 21, 1824, Tompkins came to the Senate a final time, leaving on May 20 with a low-key farewell. A week later the Senate agreed to a last Monroe request to approve another sixty thousand dollars to Tompkins to settle all claims. He continued, however, to drink heavily and, without a will, died as a private citizen on June 11, 1825. His estate on Staten Island was sold off to satisfy unsettled debts left to his wife, Hannah, who outlived him by nearly four years. In 1847, Congress finally voted to give fifty thousand dollars to his heirs.

The first postrevolutionary figure to aspire to the presidency, Daniel D. Tompkins reached a sorrowful early end at age fifty, which belied his great promise as a young governor and vice president. Like the holders of the second office before him, his marginal involvement in the administration in which he served denied him much opportunity to make his mark on the national stage. It might have been too much to say upon his death, as the former New York mayor and diarist Philip Hone did later, that "there was a time when no man in the state dared to compete with him for any office in the gift of the people; and his habits of intemperance alone prevented him from being President of the United States."[17] But Tompkins's life story was certainly one of leadership potential derailed, by either personal weakness or misfortune or both.

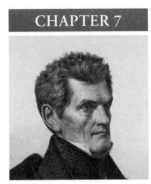

CHAPTER 7

JOHN C. CALHOUN

OF SOUTH CAROLINA

For the first time in the young Republic, a vice president was elected on one party ticket in 1824 and four years later was reelected on the ticket of another. Politics, personal animosities, and the quirks of the electoral system contrived to make John C. Calhoun of South Carolina the running mate of the National Republican nominee, John Quincy Adams, in the first election, and in 1828 Calhoun was elected again, this time with the Democratic president Andrew Jackson.

At the core of this unusual phenomenon was the manner of the second Adams's victory in the 1824 election, in which Jackson surpassed the son of the former president in both the popular vote and the electoral college but failed to achieve the required electoral majority. The election thus was thrown into the House of Representatives, and Adams finally prevailed when one of the losing candidates, House Speaker Henry Clay, was said to have steered to Adams the electors he had won in three states. Calhoun meanwhile was easily elected vice president on his own.

When Adams subsequently named Clay to be his secretary of state, Jackson supporters loudly accused them of a "corrupt bargain," and Calhoun shared the view. Nearly halfway through his term, Calhoun struck up an alliance with Jackson and joined him as his running mate in 1828, when they defeated Adams and his new running mate, Richard Rush of Pennsylvania.

Another twist of fate had placed Calhoun on the path to the vice presidency in the first place. In 1824, the South Carolina General Assembly chose William Lowndes as its nominee for president, but he died at sea. The assembly filled the vacancy with Calhoun, another native son, who was then President James Monroe's secretary of war.[1]

Another presidential hopeful, the former senator William H. Crawford of Georgia, attacked Calhoun's stewardship of the armed forces, citing allegations of waste and fraud in the War Department. But Calhoun's stout defense of his role in mobilizing the military in the War of 1812 propelled him to national prominence and to the vice presidential nomination as Adams's running mate. In the end, however, it was Calhoun's fervent advocacy of the states' right to nullify federal law and secede from the Union that led to the Civil War and his contentious place in American history.

The son of a Scots-Irish farmer who had emigrated from Virginia to the backcountry of South Carolina and become a fighter of Indians and lawless frontiersmen, John Caldwell Calhoun was raised with a strong sense of independence coupled with community responsibility, emulating his parents in local church and colonial politics. He had three brothers and one sister, and the family owned a dozen or more slaves, whose children became his playmates in youth, while also being deferential to him in keeping with the social imperatives of the time. Patrick Calhoun, the father, served a term in the House of Representatives, then in the South Carolina General Assembly, and later the state Senate. He led the way in the development of the back country and, not incidentally, in the expansion of slavery in the region.[2]

John Calhoun was only thirteen years old when his father died. Young Calhoun and his older brothers were required to work the farm diligently, often alongside the slave children. He also became an avid reader, and upon his father's death and his brothers' departure he assumed management of the twelve-hundred-acre plantation and its thirty slaves. When he was eighteen, his brothers urged him to go back to school, taking over the plantation and financing his education for the betterment of the whole family.

After studying at Yale and Litchfield Law School, in Connecticut, Calhoun was admitted to the South Carolina bar in late 1807. That year, the British frigate *Leopard* attacked the American warship *Chesapeake* after being refused permission to board and search for deserters. He wrote a resolution of protest that won him local praise and notoriety, leading to his election to the South Carolina House of Representatives.[3]

As chairman of the Committee on Claims, Calhoun encountered obligations dealing with the South's "peculiar institution" of slavery that later would dominate his time, energies, and reputation in the history books. More than half a century earlier the General Assembly had stipulated that to make sure owners of slaves would "not be tempted to conceal the crimes of their slaves to the prejudice of the public," owners of executed slaves could be compensated up to two hundred dollars each. Calhoun recommended that the owners of eight such slaves be paid $120.40 each. The situation was handled as a simple case of restitution for the destruction of private property.[4]

In 1810, Calhoun was elected to the U.S. House of Representatives at age twenty-nine. Now married with an infant son, he declared himself a nationalist, involved with the concerns of the whole country. He joined in confronting Great Britain over its intrusions into American shipping and the impressment of American seamen on English vessels, which led to the War of 1812. The new House Speaker, Henry Clay of Kentucky, invited Calhoun to join what was known as the "War Mess" of westerners of nationalist bent dining at a boardinghouse near the Capitol. In 1812 Calhoun was among those who accompanied Clay in urging Madison to call for a declaration of war.

The War of 1812, ill-conceived and for much of the time ill-conducted by the Madison administration, came perilously close to an American defeat. In 1814 it suffered the humiliation of the burning of the capital city, including the White House and both chambers of Congress. But Calhoun's stolid support of the war effort earned him the reputation as the nation's "young Hercules who carried the war on his shoulders," as proclaimed by a Philadelphia lawyer.[5] When the peace treaty was signed in 1815, Calhoun declared, "I feel pleasure and pride in being able to say that I am of a party which drew the sword . . . and succeeded in the contest."[6]

His determined focus on maintaining the defense of the nation recommended Calhoun as war secretary in the new Madison administration. Resigning from the House in 1817 after seven years and accepting the post, Calhoun soon found himself on a collision course with the hero of the War of 1812, General Jackson. In 1816, while Calhoun was still in Congress,

Jackson, as commander of the army's Southern Division, had sent a military surveyor into Indian country along the Mississippi River to examine lands where uprisings might occur. Without Jackson's knowledge, President Madison's war department ordered the surveyor to New York, where he finished and published his report on the Mississippi area survey. Jackson was livid at the intrusion and complained to Calhoun's deputy, who curtly told Jackson that department orders superseded those of commanders in the field.

Still outraged, Jackson awaited the inaugural of James Monroe, the new president in 1817, and protested again, while commanding his troops that no orders were to be obeyed unless transmitted through appropriate military channels—meaning through him. Monroe chose to treat the matter as a misunderstanding, writing to the renowned hero of New Orleans: "The principal is clear, that every order from the dept. of war, to whomever directed, must be obeyed. I cannot think that you are of a different opinion." But he warned, "Should the alternative be presented, I will not hesitate to do my duty."[7]

In November 1817, an incident in what was still Spanish Florida added fuel to the dispute. The region was a weakly policed haven for escaped slaves and assorted criminals. Seminole Indians there now killed more than fifty American soldiers, women, and children near the Georgia border. Calhoun ordered the general in command in Georgia to pursue the Indians across the Florida line unless they took shelter under Spanish authorities. Ten days later, Calhoun ordered Jackson to relieve the general and "adopt the necessary measures to terminate" the incident.[8]

But Jackson took the orders as an invitation to invade and take over Florida. He wrote directly to Monroe, not Calhoun, warning of leaving the American troops idle outside some Spanish post, and offered to seize Florida while he was there. "Let it be signified to me through any channel . . . that the position of the Floridas would be desirable to the United States," he suggested, "and in sixty days it will be accomplished."[9] In a subsequent letter to Calhoun, however, Jackson gave no indication of his grandiose intent.

In March 1818 Jackson moved his army into the Spanish territory, killing Seminoles, destroying their villages, pushing them into west Florida, and occupying the Spanish post of St. Mark's. Monroe and Calhoun wanted

Jackson to calm things down in a way that Florida could be acquired by peaceful negotiations, but the hot-blooded general had his own ideas. Jackson biographer Irving Bartlett wrote later that by sending Jackson, "instead of a fox they sent a lion."[10]

Unknown to Calhoun, Jackson pressed on to Pensacola in west Florida, surrounded Fort Barancas, where the Spanish governor and garrison were housed, and in two days achieved their surrender, along with that of the Seminoles who had sought refuge there. Two British men, accused of being foreign agents in prodding the Indians, were summarily court-martialed by Jackson and executed, complicating the American diplomatic case.

In all this, Monroe seemed unwilling to challenge Jackson as insubordinate, other than to tell the complaining British minister that the general had acted without authorization. A cabinet meeting concluded that Jackson had disregarded Monroe's instructions and had engaged in an unauthorized war against Spain.[11] Meanwhile, Jackson's already immense popularity at home grew even greater.

Calhoun pointed out the obvious—that Jackson of all people should have accepted the imperative of observing the chain of command—and wanted an investigation of the general's actions, including the possibility of a court-martial. But Monroe had no interest in a confrontation with Jackson. He settled for returning his Florida conquests to Spain as prerequisite to guarantees of peaceful border maintenance, and several months later he purchased Florida from Spain for five million dollars.

In Calhoun's remaining time as war secretary, he made efforts to get along with Jackson, but not to the point of looking the other way on further acts of insubordination. Jackson finally retired from the army in June 1821, by which time his military feats had made him a serious prospect for the presidency in 1824. Calhoun likewise saw himself as a legitimate "Republican" candidate, along with Monroe's treasury secretary, William Crawford, Secretary of State John Quincy Adams, and Speaker Henry Clay. By now the rival Federalists of the immediate post–revolutionary era had shrunk to near invisibility or vanished altogether.

Crawford won a sparsely attended congressional caucus victory but was soon hampered by a paralytic stroke. Calhoun's entry surprised and angered Adams, but early support for Calhoun in Pennsylvania faded with the political emergence of Jackson, so Calhoun withdrew. Pennsylvania backers of Adams and Jackson in the state endorsed Calhoun for the vice presidency, assuring his election.

But in the electoral college the tie vote between Adams and Jackson for president and the "corrupt bargain" that saw Henry Clay's electors go to Adams disturbed Calhoun. He wrote a friend, "Mr. Clay has made the Prest [sic] against the voice of his constituents, and . . . has been rewarded by the man elevated by him by the first office in his gift, the most dangerous stab, which the liberty of this country has ever received. I will not be on that side. I am with the people, and shall remain so."[12]

Calhoun found himself in an administration in which he would have little opportunity or inclination to play a major policy role. As presiding officer of the Senate, however, he was circumspect, not believing it was his prerogative to interrupt a senator as he spoke in debate, to limit his time to orate, or to call him to order for some perceived indiscretion. But of fifteen standing committees of the Senate, Calhoun gave chairmanships to eight administration men and seven to those somewhat or very hostile to the incumbent president.

Adams, however, didn't want fairness or neutrality; he wanted his men heading all the committees. And Clay, displeased with Calhoun's complaints about the "corrupt bargain," recognized Calhoun as a threat to his own continuing presidential ambitions and to the Adams agenda, which in its pursuit of internal improvements would advance Clay's own concept of the American System.

In 1825, when Adams sought Senate confirmation to send observers to a meeting of Central and South American ministers in Panama, Calhoun opposed the initiative. He viewed it as a step toward recognition of Haiti, which would be sending a delegation of former slaves and would disturb the American South. Van Buren saw the clash as an opportunity to recruit Calhoun for the next Jackson presidential bid.

Adams and Calhoun also clashed over Senate resolutions that would change electing the president and vice president to "a direct vote of the People, in districts." It was to be done "without the intervention of the Senate or House of Representatives" and would prohibit "the appointment of any Member of Congress to any office of honor or trust under the United

States during the term for which the member had been elected."[13] The latter proposal was a direct assault on Clay, who had resigned from the House to become Adams's secretary of state.

On March 30, 1826, John Randolph of Virginia tested Calhoun's patience and endurance in the chair when he unleashed a tirade against Adams and Clay. A high administration official, believed by many to be Adams himself, then proceeded to castigate Calhoun in print for not halting the Randolph assault. The Senate later authorized its presiding officer to call any senator to order for offensive words uttered in debate. But Calhoun insisted that as president of the Senate he had not been elected by the senators and therefore had no power to silence any of them or to call them out of order for partisan remarks.[14] The principal tangible outcome of Randolph's verbal assault was a duel with Clay, who saw himself as insulted, and in April they exchanged fire on the southern shore of the Potomac. Neither man was hurt, and the irrepressible Randolph continued his obnoxious ways.[15]

In any event, the spectacle of a president or close associate publicly dressing down his vice president cemented the hostility between Adams and Calhoun. It inevitably drove Calhoun into the Jackson camp as his best vehicle for removing Adams from the presidency in the 1828 election. Knowing now he would not be offered a second term in the Adams administration nor wanting one, an alliance with Jackson was the surest way to keep alive his own political ambitions.

Adams and Calhoun had maintained a proper if cool relationship up to then. Upon Calhoun's return to the Senate at the end of 1826, he found himself the subject of renewed accusations of profiteering by a chief aide when he was Monroe's war secretary. He immediately called on the House of Representatives to investigate the allegations, saying meanwhile he would desist from presiding over the Senate. After six weeks of hearings Calhoun was exonerated, but the investigation threatened his aspirations to higher office.

By now Calhoun clearly had no political future in the Adams administration. Calhoun wrote Jackson of his disaffection from Adams over the "corrupt bargain" and indicated his interest in an alliance with Jackson to undo that wrong in the 1828 election. The issue, he said, was "between power and liberty, and it must be determined in the next three years." Jackson responded cordially, "I trust that my name will always be found on the side of the people, and that we shall march hand in hand in their cause." Calhoun thereupon signed on, writing confidently, "Every indication is in our favor, or rather I should say in favor of the country's cause."[16] Calhoun doubtless was attracted to the alliance by Jackson's assertion that if elected he would serve only a single term, so Calhoun would be content running for another vice presidential term on the Jackson ticket, then seeking the presidency again in 1832 with greatly enhanced prospects of success.[17]

Van Buren saw Calhoun as the right fit for ousting Adams by wedding the "planters of the South and the plain Republicans of the North." He described the alliance as "the most natural and beneficial," observing, "The country has once flourished under a party thus constituted and may again."[18] In another observation toward the creation of a Jacksonian Democratic Party, Van Buren wrote, "If Gen Jackson and his friends will put his election on old party grounds, preserve the old systems, avoid if not condemn the practices of the last campaign, we can by adding his personal popularity to the yet remaining force of old party feeling, not only succeed in electing him but our success will be worth something."[19]

Calhoun sealed his place on the Jackson ticket with a string of unanimous nominations in Pennsylvania, Ohio, New Jersey, and Kentucky, as well as support in New York and Virginia, the old North-South alliance. A potential conflict with Van Buren came in the spring of 1828 with the New Yorker's role in the Senate passage of what soon was known as "the Tariff of Abominations." It was hated in Calhoun's home state for imposing greater hardships on the cotton and other agricultural interests of the South. Calhoun suggested to South Carolinians that tariff relief would come from the election of Jackson.

In the first election under a new party system, neither presidential nominee was spared personal vitriol. A scandal involving Jackson and his wife, Rachel, who had still been married though in the process of divorce when they first ran off together, was resurrected; Adams was still pummeled for the "corrupt bargain" that made Clay his secretary of state. Their running mates, Calhoun and Richard Rush of Pennsylvania, Adams's minister to London, remained, however, essentially unmentioned as another commentary on the general importance of their positions of the day. Under the Democratic Party banner or simply the Democratic Party, Jackson and Calhoun won easily.

Not having to campaign in person in 1828, Calhoun spent much of the preelection period at his Pendleton, South Carolina, home, preparing an analysis of the hated tariff at the request of the state legislature. The legislature in late 1827 had declared the tariff unconstitutional and called on Calhoun to lay out the case. Thereupon he wrote what came to be called the South Carolina Exposition and Protest, in which he revisited the same rights argument that Jefferson had mustered to challenge the Alien and Sedition Acts, enacted under Adams.

Calhoun contended again that in forming the Union the several states had entered into a compact with a federal government with limited powers but had not surrendered their sovereignty in the process. Therefore, he argued, the people of any state could elect delegates to a state convention, determine if they wished to declare a federal law unconstitutional, and declare it to be null and void within the state's boundaries. Congress then would be faced with the option of accepting the nullification or passing a constitutional amendment bestowing power on the federal government to enact the law, subject to ratification by three-fourths of the states. Calhoun saw this reasoning as the remedy to the oppressive tariff that his and other southern states might take, short of outright secession from the Union.

Not wishing to begin his tenure in the Jackson administration with such a challenge to the federal government, of which he was now a part, Calhoun did not claim or disclose his role in writing the exposition. But Jackson and Van Buren, now as secretary of state, clearly had their suspicions.[20]

As Calhoun remained in the vice presidency, he almost at once ran into conflict with Van Buren, his earlier collaborator, called the "Little Magician" for his canny political skills. After resigning as governor of New York and relocating to Washington, Van Buren became a constant companion to the new president, whose wife had died shortly before the election, and set out to become the most influential member of the Jackson inner circle. From the protectionist North, Van Buren was on a collision course with Calhoun, who had spent much of his first year under Jackson back in South Carolina, crafting his case for states' nullification of the tariff.

The situation disintegrated even more when a social scandal hit official

Washington, sparked not by Calhoun but by his wife, Floride. With Jackson a widower, much of the social entertaining fell to her as the mate of the vice president, including receiving courtesy visits from members of the president's cabinet and their wives. It so happened that the wife of Secretary of War John Eaton, the former Margaret (Peggy) O'Neale Timberlake, the attractive daughter of a saloonkeeper, had what was known as a shady past. While her former husband, a naval purser, was away from home, she had been seen around town with Eaton, and after the husband's death in a rumored suicide she and Eaton were married in January 1829. Eaton now was a close Jackson friend and Peggy a favorite of the president.

When Floride Calhoun refused to admit Peggy to the Jackson administration social circle on the basis of the rampant gossip, Calhoun supported her action, to the ire of the president. Other cabinet wives nervously followed Floride's lead at first, causing more social turmoil, until Van Buren stepped in, included the Eatons in his own diplomatic entertaining, and arranged for the foreign ministers of England and Russia to invite them to their dinner parties.[21] His actions thereby won even greater gratitude from Jackson while heightening his feud with Calhoun.

In the Senate in January 1830, Calhoun presided over a heated debate on the sale of public lands in the West, which turned into an argument over nullification. With Senate rules prohibiting his direct participation, the vice president sent coaching notes from the chair to his fellow South Carolinian senator Robert Hayne when Hayne was engaged on the issue by Senator Daniel Webster of Massachusetts. Hayne reminded New England senators that they had considered nullification themselves and even the possibility of secession during the War of 1812. Webster countered that the federal government was not a mere agent of the states but an agent of the Union and that the arbiter of federal law was the U.S. Supreme Court, not any state. Any state attempting to put itself above the Union, Webster charged, would be committing an act of treason that could precipitate civil war. He closed with the memorable defense of "liberty and Union, now and forever, one and inseparable," destined to enter the history books.[22]

Other southern states at this juncture shied away from backing nullification. But soon after, at a dinner celebrating Jefferson's birthday, with Jackson, Calhoun, and Van Buren in attendance, the president and vice president engaged in a dramatic moment that cryptically defined their positions. Van Buren had reminded Jackson in advance that his own toast would be taken as a signal of the stand he intended the Democratic Party to support and a hush fell over the crowd as the president rose and held up his glass. Looking directly at Calhoun, Jackson toasted: "Our Federal Union—it must be preserved!" Calhoun then rose and replied with his own glass aloft: "The Union—next to our liberty the most dear. May we all remember that it can only be preserved by respecting the rights of the states and distributing equally the benefits and burdens of the Union!"[23]

Van Buren diplomatically rose with a toast of his own, calling for "mutual forbearance and reciprocal concessions," yet was satisfied that Jackson had put the vice president in his place. A few days later Jackson left no doubt about where he stood. He told a South Carolina congressman, "Give my compliments to my friends in your state, and say to them, that if a single drop of blood shall be shed there in opposition to the laws of the United States, I will hang the first man I can lay my hand on engaged in such treasonable conduct, upon the first tree I can reach."[24]

The Jackson-Calhoun relationship further soured in May 1830, when Crawford, as Jackson's treasury secretary, sent Jackson a letter offering proof that Calhoun, as President Monroe's secretary of war, had sought to have the general arrested and tried for invading Spanish Florida on his own authority during the suppression of the Seminole Indians. When Jackson demanded an explanation of Calhoun, he replied, "I cannot recognize the right on your part to call in question my conduct," alluding to his position as Jackson's civilian superior at the time. Calhoun dismissed the revival of the old argument as nothing more than politics, whereupon Jackson broke off the exchange, signaling a low point in their relations.[25]

In December 1831, circumstances conspired to give Calhoun an opportunity to repay Van Buren for his rebuff to Floride. Encouraged by Van Buren, a shake-up of Jackson's cabinet occurred in the wake of the Peggy Eaton affair, also known now as the "Petticoat War." As part of the cabinet changes, Jackson nominated Van Buren to be his ambassador to London, and Calhoun was in the chair as presiding officer of the Senate considering confirmation of the appointment.

The process predictably was a stormy one, with all manner of unsettled scores against Van Buren raised by offended senators. Again Calhoun was kept out of the debate by the rules, but he got his chance to express his feelings when the vote on confirmation ended in a tie—contrived, many believed, to give Calhoun satisfaction. Van Buren had already gone to London, and when the vice president voted against confirmation, the secretary of state was forced to return to Washington. According to Thomas Hart Benton, a U.S. senator from Missouri, Calhoun had gloated, "It will kill him, sir, kill him dead. He will never kick, sir, never kick." But if he meant the rejection would undermine Van Buren's chances to replace him as Jackson's running mate in 1832, he was sorely mistaken. "You have broken a minister," Benton accurately prophesied, "and elected a Vice President."[26]

Jackson regarded Calhoun's vote as a petty and mean act. "I have no hesitation," he wrote at the time, to say "that Calhoun is one of the most base hypocritical and principled villains in the United States. His course of secret session, and vote in the case of Mr. Van Buren, has displayed a want of every sense of honor, justice and magnanimity. His vote has dam'd him by all honest men in the Senate, and when laid before the nation, and laid it will be, will not only dam him and his associates, but astonish the American people."[27]

There could be no doubt now about Jackson's intentions, seeing Calhoun's public actions as a slap not only at Van Buren but also at himself. "The people will resent the insult offered to the Executive and the wound inflicted on our national character," he wrote to his secretary of state, "and the injury intended to our foreign relations, in your rejection, by placing you in the chair of the very man whose casting vote rejected you."[28] It would be Calhoun out as Jackson's running mate in 1832 and Van Buren in.

Jackson meanwhile, with Van Buren as his political organizer, remained in solid control of the newly identified Democratic Party. Well into the presidential election year, the Democrats met in Baltimore, where the National Republicans had already nominated Clay for president, and simply confirmed Jackson's renomination by a host of state party conventions, anointing Van Buren as his handpicked choice for vice president.

With the candidates themselves still not openly campaigning, much of the contest was played out in the partisan newspapers, with political cartoons increasingly coming to the fore. The National Republicans sought to make much of Jackson's handpicking of his running mate, one cartoon showing Jackson with baby Martin in his arms and another picturing Van Buren handing Jackson a crown as the devil was giving him a scepter.

Jackson, striving to divert the nullification threat in the approaching election, proposed a new, reduced tariff bill designed more to raise revenue than to shelter northern industries, warning manufacturers not to expect voters to "continue permanently to pay high taxes for their benefit."[29] But Calhoun was not placated. He declared he would seek nullification of the bill by South Carolina, and in October the state legislature called for a state convention. It voted overwhelmingly to declare the tariffs of 1828 and 1832 "unauthorized by the Constitution" and accordingly "null, void and no law, nor binding on this state, its officers or citizens."[30]

On Election Day, Jackson was easily reelected with Van Buren as his vice president, evidence that the manner of the latter's nomination by King Andrew didn't seem to bother the voters. Starting in February 1833 in South Carolina, enforcement of the tariffs would be banned by the nullification edict, as well as any appeals to federal courts, and any federal attempts to interfere would result in the state's secession from the Union. Robert Hayne resigned from the Senate to become governor, and four days before the end of 1832 Calhoun resigned the vice presidency—the first time anyone had done so—and accepted appointment to Hayne's Senate seat to lead the nullification fight from the Senate floor.

Jackson quickly responded. Declaring he was ready to "die with the Union," he dispatched a warship and other vessels to Charleston Harbor, said he was ready to lead a Union army there himself, and threatened to have Calhoun hanged for treason. In a proclamation to the people of South Carolina, he called "the power to annul a law of the United States, assumed by one State, incompatible with the existence of the Union, contradicted by the letter of the Constitution, unauthorized by its spirit, inconsistent with every principle on which it was founded, and destructive of the great object for which it was formed."[31]

The state legislature defiantly labeled Jackson's views "erroneous and dangerous, leading not only to the establishment of a consolidated government" but also to "the concentration of all powers in the chief executive."[32] Thereupon he asked Congress for a "force bill" authorizing use of the military to achieve compliance. The state, finding itself isolated, sought a compromise through Calhoun and Clay that would reduce the onerous tariff. Two weeks later, the state convention withdrew the nullification ordinance while still insisting the force bill was itself null and void. Jackson was satisfied and, no doubt, relieved to have Calhoun out of his administration, if only a few weeks earlier than would otherwise have been the case.

For the third time in the country's brief history, the vice presidency was vacant, but only through the transition period ending on March 4, 1833. Calhoun remained in the Senate, still nurturing dim hopes for a future presidency. In 1843, he resigned with the notion of running for the White House as an independent but soon abandoned the idea and returned to South Carolina to attend to his struggling farm. In 1844, he accepted an appointment as secretary of state under President John Tyler to fill an unexpected vacancy and participated in negotiations on the annexation of Texas until his abbreviated term expired a year later. Again later in 1845, he returned to the U.S. Senate from South Carolina and remained there until his death in 1850, to the end an advocate of withdrawal from the Union.

Calhoun's vice presidencies under Adams and then Jackson had been marked by basic policy disagreements and often personal animosities that magnified the difficulty of serving effectively in an ultimately powerless position. Still, as a willful and determined man, Calhoun was able to stretch the possibilities of the vice presidency to its limits in ways that might have encouraged other ambitious politicians to seek the much-abused office. Rather than laboring in behalf of the president under whom he served, Calhoun made the vice presidency a base for opposition, mischief, and eventually disloyalty. Yet he remained true to his convictions on positions that broke him both physically and politically in the end.

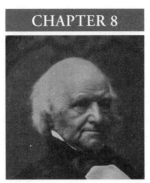

CHAPTER 8

MARTIN VAN BUREN
OF NEW YORK

After the vice presidential resignation of John C. Calhoun, Martin Van Buren was now poised to fill the void in the election of 1832, with President Andrew Jackson solidly behind him. Unlike previous vice presidents who had acquired the office with at most the sufferance of the presidents under whom they served, Van Buren was the explicit choice of Jackson, who had come to depend heavily on his counsel, particularly regarding political strategy.

Unlike Jackson, Van Buren learned and honed his skills not on the field of arms but on the political battlegrounds of rural New York. He was the son of a farmer–tavern keeper in the Dutch community of Kinderhook, in the Hudson River valley south of Albany, born there in 1782 as the American Revolution approached its formal end through the peace treaty with the English. His was the sixth generation of Van Burens in the Dutch-speaking community, where men married late but then fathered large broods. Martin was one of six siblings ranging from age four to twenty-four and living over the family tavern, and early in life he learned how to hold his own through goodwill and accommodation. Small in stature but from an early age fastidious in his appearance, he eventually acquired the reputation of a dandy, which never left him.[1]

Young Martin was schooled in the village and had none of the formal education, including writing skills, that many of his contemporaries acquired. In this strong Federalist area, he became the law apprentice of a local son of a Federalist state senator, Peter Silvester. Martin's father, Abraham, however, was an ardent Jeffersonian, whose tavern became a gathering place for prominent Republicans.

Resisting the Federalist views of the Silvester clan, Van Buren eventually became friendly with the Van Ness family, Kinderhook Republican leaders. Not yet twenty, he was a delegate to the Republican Party caucus in Troy and helped one of them, John Peter Van Ness, win a seat in the U.S. House of Representatives. Within a year he was able to leave Kinderhook for the first time for New York City, where he was given a job in the law office of another Van Ness kin, William.

William Van Ness had influential Republican connections, one of his eventual claims to fame being Burr's second in his fateful duel with Hamilton, and he provided young Van Buren with entry into the turbulent Republican world of the city. After gaining admission to the bar, Van Buren returned to Kinderhook in 1803 and joined a half brother, James Van Alen, the town clerk, as his law partner. But the next year, when the Van Nesses pleaded with their protégé to back Burr for governor, Martin stuck with the regular Republican organization candidate Morgan Lewis. He chose party loyalty over friendship and gratitude, an early evidence of his commitment to party solidarity.[2] He made his living as a lawyer, without the experiences of military service or foreign travel, but politics became more than his avocation.

Soon after that election, William Van Ness was indicted as an accessory to murder for his role in Burr's duel with Hamilton. Van Buren defended his old benefactor in court and won his release. At age twenty-four Van Buren was appointed surrogate in his home county, Columbia, and four years later, now married to Hannah Hoes, a distant relative, was elected to the state Senate. He strongly supported the War of 1812 against Federalist opposition and later broke with DeWitt Clinton over the mayor's pursuit of Federalist backing in his failed 1812 bid for the presidency.[3]

In 1815, Van Buren became state attorney general and in Albany soon emerged as the leader of the Republican "Bucktail" faction, which revised the New York Constitution and ended the Clinton hold on the party. He then created the powerful Albany Regency, which long thereafter maintained power through strict party discipline, equitable award of patronage, and the organization of local clubs around the state. In 1818, Van Buren's wife died of tuberculosis, leaving him with five sons, and he never married again.

In 1821, Van Buren was elected to the U.S. Senate, where he similarly organized the large New York congressional delegation. Looking beyond his New York base, he helped elect Philip Barbour of Virginia as Speaker of the House, replacing John Taylor of New York, a Clinton man, and in the process signaled his interest in restoring the North-South alliance of the early years of the Virginia dynasty.

As a gregarious and fashionably dressed widower new to Washington, New York's "Little Magician" joined the social whirl with great success. He acquired a reputation as both a pursuer and a target of attractive young women, including a granddaughter of Jefferson, meanwhile broadening his contacts with fellow congressmen of influence from other sections of the country. A new southern friend was Calhoun, then the secretary of war, who would eventually play a leading role with Van Buren in Andrew Jackson's political climb, as noted previously.

While maintaining the leadership of the Albany Regency back home, Van Buren also focused on national issues in his plan to build a national party. As a U.S. senator he took care to adopt cautious positions on the tariff, internal improvements, banking, and slavery, thus accommodating his plans to revive the Old Republican North-South alliance.

Still the loyal party man, Van Buren supported William Crawford as the winner of the Republican congressional caucus for the presidency in 1824, even after the Georgian's serious illness had compromised his chances as a serious contender. Van Buren believed Crawford could still win and would be the most receptive to the Old Republican alliance Van Buren hoped to reestablish.[4] He warned Regency members of the high stakes beyond the election if New York didn't go for Crawford. What he really was after was extending the power of the Regency nationwide through his revived party structure. Crawford was nominated in a low turnout of the Republican congressional caucus, but Van Buren failed in the end to deliver the New York electors for him, and Crawford was finished.

As already noted, the 1824 election was now in Clay's hands, and in giving his electors to John Quincy Adams and winding up as Adams's secretary of state, the alleged infamous "corrupt bargain" was struck. The outcome was a colossal blunder for Van Buren, the supposed political genius. Why he had stuck with the stricken Crawford when he could have switched to either Jackson or Clay was puzzling. In his later autobiography, he wrote, "I left Albany for Washington as completely broken down a politician as my bitterest enemies could desire."[5] Biographer Donald B. Cole later speculated that Van Buren's "determination to place national goals ahead of state goals, and to create a political party based upon Old Republican principles and an alliance of New York and Virginia, North and South, was the reason." Cole suggested that Van Buren needed an acceptable Old Republican who represented the South, and only Crawford of the other candidates filled the bill. "In trying to revive the old contest throughout the United States," Cole concluded, "he had weakened his hold on New York."[6]

In the wake of the failure to deny New York's electors to Adams, Van Buren worked to maintain his influence in the Albany Regency. Although he was dismayed at the election of Adams and how it was achieved, he largely held his tongue for some time. But eventually some of Adams's domestic plans and particularly his involvement in the Panama conference of South and Central American nations drove Van Buren to seek an alliance with Calhoun, who shared Van Buren's opposition to Adams's plans to send a delegation to the conference. They found common ground in what was a larger mutual undertaking—replacing Adams in the White House with Jackson. Applying his Regency organizational skills to that end, Van Buren made a substantial start on building what came to be called the Jacksonian Democracy in the pattern of the Old Republicanism of Jefferson.

Van Buren had to walk a tightrope in accommodating both the North and the South. While supportive of DeWitt Clinton's successful Erie Canal, he had to bear in mind the Old Republican opposition to federally planned and financed internal improvements. In reaching out to the South, he had to strike a centrist course in light of strong protectionist support for northern manufacture and bitter southern opposition to high tariffs on the region's agricultural livelihood. And regarding slavery, he opposed it in harmony with fellow northerners while placating southerners by defending its continuation where it already existed.

Eventually Van Buren became Jackson's chief political strategist and adviser. But in time he split with Vice President Calhoun over the South Carolinian's threat to nullify the Tariff of Abominations, seen in the South as throttling the region's agriculture. Van Buren was sympathetic both with the southern farmers, who hated the tariff, and the northern manufacturers, who desired it, and with the Jeffersonian defense of states' rights. At the same time, he shared Jackson's opposition to nullification, insisting that the Union had to be preserved at all costs. As for Calhoun, it was clear by now that he would not be Adams's running mate in 1828 and hoped Jackson would offer him a second vice presidential term in the new administration the old general anticipated would be his.

Before Van Buren could concentrate on his ambitious national party building, he had to focus on reelection to the Senate. He mended fences with the Albany Regency and with DeWitt Clinton, just reelected governor, and won easily. Now both Calhoun and Clinton had their eyes on the second federal office. In January 1928, the New York legislature nominated Jackson for president and dodged controversy by nominating no one for vice president. Two weeks later, DeWitt Clinton dropped dead, and the path seemed clear for Calhoun.

Just as significant for Van Buren, the valued patronage plums in New York now fell under his direction as he grew in importance in Jackson's eyes and attentions. Jackson himself was seen increasingly by the Little Magician as a man in the Old Republican mold of Jefferson. He was not a Revolutionary War hero to be sure, but a hero of the next generation in the second war against the British, who would manifest immense personal appeal along with advancing the cause of party that Van Buren so ardently pursued.

For all that, Clinton's death left a gaping vacuum in the political leadership of New York State. The lieutenant governor who succeeded him, Nathaniel Pitcher, was a minor political figure, and the Regency decided he would not be strong enough to hold the seat in the next election. He was persuaded to step aside after serving a few months as acting governor, and the organization turned to Van Buren to seek the governorship, even though he just been reelected to the U.S. Senate, with high aspirations of continuing to play a major role in Jackson's second term. But he agreed to run for governor and was elected in January 1829. Barely a month later, however, President Jackson asked Van Buren to return to Washington as secretary of state in his new administration.

The new governor of New York was once again confronted with the choice of whether to restore and maintain what he had built there or go on to pursue his ambitions for a national party. He realized, however, that as secretary of state, a presidential candidacy of his own after Jackson's retirement would become a possibility. He finally agreed to return to Washington, turning over the governorship to his lieutenant governor.

As the ranking member of the Jackson cabinet, Van Buren had Jackson's strong confidence but was by no means running things. Jackson asserted his own will in the other cabinet appointments, and inevitably an internal power struggle developed between the two earlier allies, Van Buren and Calhoun, now vice president. As secretary of state, Van Buren proved to be surprisingly effective, considering his sparse foreign policy experience. Trade in the West Indies was cleared along with the opening of American ports to the British, and the settlement of twenty-five million francs in French debts in return for a reduction in tariffs on imported wine was also achieved. Also, during this time, the Peggy Eaton scandal was gripping Washington. As noted earlier, much of Van Buren's diplomacy was devoted to smoothing ruptured feelings by providing social engagements for her among the diplomatic corps, to the gratitude of her friend Jackson.

Regarding Calhoun, Van Buren took on the role of mediator with Jackson in their headlong clash over nullification, coaching the president on his famous dinner toast at the Jefferson birthday celebration, "The Union: It must be preserved," and offering his own toast for "mutual forbearance and reciprocal concessions."[7]

That fall, with Van Buren as Jackson's secretary of state, the president suddenly proposed a plan to him designed explicitly to make him his successor in the White House. Aging and tiring, Jackson had been saying he would serve only a single term. But now he informed Van Buren that he had decided to run again after all in 1832, with Van Buren as his running mate. Then, he told Van Buren privately, after their election and inauguration, he would resign the presidency, elevating his friend to the first office. Van Buren rejected the scheme,[8] perhaps as too transparent and likely to undermine the credibility of such a presidency from the start.

Rather, some months later during their morning ride on horseback along the Potomac, the Little Magician told Jackson in a scheme of his own that he wanted to resign from the cabinet. The president immediately replied that he could not afford to lose him but listened as Van Buren explained what he had in mind. Jackson, he said, could use Van Buren's resignation as a rationale for breaking up the whole cabinet, which then included three troublesome Calhoun supporters. Van Buren proposed that the president then appoint him ambassador to London and appoint Secretary of War John Eaton to another overseas post, bringing all Van Buren men into the cabinet.[9] Unspoken was the scheme of sending Van Buren to London, which would take him out of the line of political fire during a time of internal turmoil and dissention prior to the 1832 campaign, in which he would indeed be Jackson's chosen running mate.

Jackson followed through on the Van Buren strategy, breaking up his cabinet and sending the Little Magician to London, writing him that he hoped to retire from the presidency soon to "open the door" for a successor, adding knowingly that Van Buren would "understand" him. Shortly afterward came another letter in the same vein, saying Jackson wanted to arrange "the selection of a vice president" to his satisfaction, enabling him to retire "to the peaceful shades of the Hermitage," his mansion in Tennessee.[10]

In the meantime, however, Van Buren was basking in the luxury of being an ambassador, writing so glowingly to Jackson about his new circumstance that the president began to wonder whether his preferred successor had changed his mind. But when Louis McLane, who had become Jackson's treasury secretary in the cabinet shake-up, began to indicate vice presidential ambitions of his own, Van Buren dropped the coyness. In response to a suggestion that he return to the Senate rather than seek the second office, he wrote Jackson that he had a "strong repugnance" to the idea and was ready to be his vice presidential running mate. He would remain abroad to avoid the approaching Democratic convention, leaving his "friends" to decide his future.[11]

Reports of other Jackson supporters considering a challenge to Van Buren soon faded. At the convention in Baltimore in May, Jackson was renominated by acclamation, and the only real business was endorsing his choice of running mate. To assure a unified party, the convention adopted a rule requiring a two-thirds vote for nomination of both president and vice president, and Van Buren cleared the hurdle with 260 of the 326 votes cast.[12]

On Van Buren's return in early July, he went to the White House and was shocked by Jackson's emaciated appearance and concerned by his distress. Congress had just passed a bill pushed by Clay to recharter the Bank of the United States. The president greeted him with "The bank, Mr. Van Buren, is trying to kill me, but I will kill it!"[13] Whereupon Jackson vetoed the bill, only to be confronted a few days later with passage of a new tariff bill, both issues on which Van Buren would have to take positions as the campaign unfolded.

The opposition to the Democrats in the 1832 election was split between the National Republican ticket headed by Henry Clay and the new Anti-Mason third party, which chose as its presidential nominee the former attorney general William Wirt of Maryland, himself a former Mason. Together they railed against "King Andrew I" for his use of the veto against the bank, and they began to call themselves "Whigs," after the British who opposed their monarch in the eighteenth century.

The Democrats happily focused not on Clay but on the return of the national bank and particularly its banker champion, Nicholas Biddle, who played into Jackson's hands by saying, "This worthy President thinks that because he has scalped Indians and imprisoned judges he is to have his way with the Bank. He is mistaken."[14] But it was Biddle who was wrong, because the Democratic strategy trumpeted the election as a battle of the "real people" against the huge moneyed interests in an early version of American class warfare.

Jackson assured Van Buren that his veto of the bank bill would turn out to be a political masterstroke. "The veto works well," he enthused. "Instead of crushing me as was expected and intended, it will crush the Bank." Van Buren agreed: "The veto is popular beyond my most sanguine expectations."[15]

On this and other issues, he sought not so much to drive Jackson's decision making as to be a cautionary voice of moderation, as he continued to maintain his goal of cementing the North-South alliance as the bedrock of the Jacksonian Democratic Party. On the whole nullification matter, Van Buren preached understanding of the South's position on states' rights and slavery without succumbing to or apologizing for it. When Jackson issued a proclamation condemning nullification as "incompatible with the existence of the Union," he subsequently wrote Van Buren that he intended to charge nullifiers with "acts of treason," calling on Congress for "the power to call upon volunteers" to quash "this wicked faction in its bud."[16] Van Buren counseled Jackson to cool off and, in dealing with Virginia, to allow for "honest differences of opinion." Typically, he wrote, "You will say, I am on my old track—caution—caution." Jackson continued to talk tough, while promising Van Buren that he would act with "forbearance."[17]

The Democratic ticket of Jackson and Van Buren—wedding the old Jeffersonian planters of the South and "the plain Republicans" of the North—was easily elected. Once sworn in as vice president, Van Buren as presiding officer of the Senate had to contend with a torrent of abuse against Jackson, particularly from the old foe Clay, over killing the second national bank and the rate of transferred deposits to state banks. In one such tirade, Clay compared Jackson to the "the worst of the Roman emperors" and demanded that Van Buren tell the president of the "tears of helpless widows . . . and of unclad and unfed orphans" who had suffered at Jackson's hands.

Van Buren sat calmly through the abuse, but when it was over he rose from his chair and walked threateningly over to Clay on the Senate floor. As other senators stared in anticipation of a brawl, Van Buren politely asked of Clay, "Mr. Senator, allow me to be indebted to you for another pinch of your aromatic Maccoboy." He then took the snuff, inhaled it, and returned to his chair, deflating Clay.[18]

As president of the Senate, Van Buren also had to find accommodating ground on the slavery issue. As a northerner who favored emancipation but was cool to abolitionists, he believed questions related to the issue should be left to the states. Required to break a tie vote on a Calhoun resolution authorizing local postal officials to confiscate abolitionist mailings barred by state law, he cast his ballot with the South—apparently a nod to the preservation of his cherished North-South party alliance.[19]

As the congressional argument over the bank dragged on, including a Senate resolution to censure Jackson, Van Buren continued to counsel the president to soften his responses, and the legislative session ended with the Second Bank of the United States still interred and the fight over. Jacksonian Democracy was firmly established, but the strong sentiment against Jackson himself among the splintered opposition led to the coalescence of what came to be called the Whig Party. As Jackson had fully intended, Van Buren would use the vice presidency as a stepping-stone to the Democratic presidential nomination in 1836 and then election.

But for all the knowledge and experience he gained from being at

Jackson's elbow as his lieutenant as well as his standby, Van Buren as president was soon the victim of an economic depression and what came to be called the panic of 1837. In the process, he acquired a new nickname: "Martin Van Ruin." In *The National Experience: A History of the United States,* it is said of him that he "was a pale copy of his chief" and had none of Jackson's talents to deal with the collapse of the economy.[20] In 1840, he lost his bid for reelection to the Whig nominee, General William Henry Harrison, another War of 1812 hero, as the Whigs chanted, "Van, Van, he's a used-up man."

Van Buren retired to his Kinderhook estate to contemplate a possible comeback and, in the spring of 1842, made an extensive southern and western swing to assess his prospects. But he lost the party nomination in 1844 to the dark horse governor James K. Polk of Tennessee at a wild convention at which Polk first sought only the vice presidential nomination. Van Buren tried again as the nominee of the new Free Soil Party but lost to still another military hero, General Zachary Taylor, the Whig candidate, and lived long enough to witness the secession of the southern states and the start of the Civil War. He died at his home in New York's Hudson Valley on July 24, 1862, at age seventy-nine.

Van Buren probably came closer than any previous vice president in playing key administrative roles in both domestic and foreign affairs. Upon assuming the presidency, however, the earlier access to and close association with his predecessor were not enough to make his single term a success. Rather, his greatest political contribution was his prime role in building Jacksonian Democracy and the Democratic Party itself.

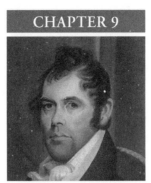

CHAPTER 9

RICHARD MENTOR JOHNSON
OF KENTUCKY

As the presidential election year of 1836 approached, the lame-duck president Jackson had already resolved that his handpicked vice president, Martin Van Buren, would be the presidential nominee of the Jacksonian Democratic Party, of which he had been the principal architect. As for a running mate, Jackson and others concluded that it would be best to nominate a westerner to balance the New Yorker, who, while highly regarded for his political acumen, aroused reservations elsewhere in the country. For the first time under the Twelfth Amendment, however, the choice would fall to the United States Senate.

In Tennessee, some original Jackson men who were cool to Van Buren pushed the rival presidential candidacy of Senator Hugh Lawson White of their state, and Jackson felt White's strength also signaled the need for a Van Buren running mate from the West, particularly someone who had been loyal to Jackson. With Jackson's own pending retirement, another hero of the War of 1812, but of considerably less luster, emerged in Congressman Richard Mentor Johnson of Kentucky. As an army colonel in 1813, he claimed to have killed the feared Shawnee Indian chief Tecumseh, allied with the British, in the Battle of the Thames, in Ontario, Canada, northeast of Detroit.[1]

The claim was never verified beyond a report that Tecumseh, in the course of a tomahawk charge, had fallen from a bullet fired by an American officer on horseback, Johnson having been mounted at the time. When the war broke out, Johnson had formed two mounted regiments under the governor of the Indiana Territory, General William Henry Harrison. Under Harrison's command, Johnson and his troops had crossed into Canada in pursuit of the British general Henry Proctor and the Shawnee Indians accompanying him, who had been attacking American settlements. Johnson's reported encounter with Tecumseh, given the fame it brought him, proved to be the pivotal event of his life.[2]

But aside from that, Johnson had compiled an impressive record in the Kentucky legislature before the war and also did so as a thirty-year member of the U.S. Congress, serving at different times in the House and Senate between 1807 and 1837. He was one of the "War Hawks" led by House Speaker Henry Clay, who pushed President Madison to take up arms against the British for attacks on American shipping and frontier settlements and who voted to declare war in 1812. Much wounded in the frontier warfare, Johnson returned to Congress in 1814 and as a senator became an ardent Jackson supporter. As a frontiersman, he was a defender of the farmer and distrustful of bankers and speculators and, as a military man, a champion of veterans, their wives or widows, and their children.

In 1819, when Jackson faced the censure sought by Clay for the execution of two British citizens as spies during the Seminole Indian war, Johnson was among the general's defenders in Congress. He voted for Jackson in 1824, when the presidential election against John Quincy Adams was thrown into the House. He was also said to have been the one to inform Jackson of Adams's appointment of Clay as secretary of state in the "corrupt bargain," which sealed Jackson's commitment to Johnson thereafter.

Johnson at first was touted among western supporters as a presidential candidate, a natural successor to Jackson, a fellow frontiersman and warrior against the Indians. Circulation of pamphlets casting him as the next Jackson spread through the West along with a biography and even a play, *Tecumseh, or the Battle of the Thames,* featuring the Johnson character as hero.[3]

Van Buren himself was not thrilled over the prospects of Johnson as his running mate. He would have preferred the former senator William C. Rives of Virginia, Jackson's minister to Paris in his first term, in furthering restoration of the alliance between the two bedrock states of the Jeffersonian era. At the same time Van Buren was peeved over the constant southern complaints about him, accusing him of abolitionist sentiments, despite all his efforts to accommodate the South. "God knows I have suffered enough for my Southern partialities," he wrote to Rives's wife. "Since I was a boy I have been stigmatized as the apologist of Southern institutions, & now forsooth you good people will have it . . . that I am an abolitionist."[4] Rives felt his service to Jackson had been brushed aside and with it the special tie between New York and Virginia, but Jackson felt strongly about having a westerner on the ticket and could not be ignored.

Van Buren also was concerned about Johnson's reputation for some shady deals involving his kin and even more so about his more immediate family life. Despite later accounts that he had had a log-cabin boyhood, his father became one of Kentucky's largest landowners, and his mother was said to have broken off his early engagement with a young woman because she felt the bride-to-be was unworthy. Supposedly out of revenge after his father's death, young Johnson took a mulatto slave girl named Julia Chinn, left to him by his father, and treated her as his common-law wife.[5] He gave her control over his business affairs and educated their two children. When she died, the story went, he took up with another slave girl, and when she left him for another man, Johnson had her sold at auction and began a relationship with her sister.

Somehow all this did not derail his rise in Kentucky politics, although it drew wide condemnation of him later as a prospective vice president. Chief Justice John Catron of the Tennessee Supreme Court complained that Johnson was "not only positively unpopular with that class who give tone to a public man, but affirmatively odious" in Tennessee.[6] He warned Jackson, "The very moment Col. J. is announced [as Van Buren's running mate], the newspapers will open upon him with facts, that he had endeavored often to force his daughters into society, that the mother in her life time, and they now, rode in carriages, and claimed equality."[7] The judge also observed of Johnson's abilities that he wanted "capacity, a fact generally known and universally admitted." He urged Jackson, "Assure our friends that the humblest of us do not believe that a lucky random shot, even if it did kill Tecumseh, qualifies a man for the Vice Presidency."[8]

But with Jackson headed for retirement after his two terms, the

Democratic ticket lacked the glamour of the Hero of New Orleans. So perhaps giving Van Buren, who had never served in the military and lacked Jackson's personal popularity, another old war hero as his running mate would add luster. Playing on Johnson's image as a frontiersman rather than on his long service in Congress, the Democratic operatives unabashedly started peddling him with the ludicrous campaign rhyme: "Rumpsey, Dumpsey; Colonel Johnson killed Tecumseh!"[9]

When the Democrats held a national convention in Baltimore on May 20, 1835, it was done so merely to ratify Jackson's choice of Van Buren to run for president. Van Buren was unopposed, but the Virginians insisted on Rives as his running mate instead of the Jackson-anointed Johnson, splitting the convention. Tennessee had no delegates present, whereupon the Jackson–Van Buren forces drafted an unknown Tennessean named Edmund Rucker, who was visiting the convention, to cast the state's fifteen votes needed to give Johnson the vice presidential nomination. Johnson was chosen on the first ballot.[10]

The rival Whigs held no national convention in 1836, instead using a combination of state legislative caucuses, conventions, and local meetings that resulted in multiple nominations by this yet-to-be-consolidated party. A Whig convention in Pennsylvania successfully put forward Johnson's superior officer in the War of 1812, General William Henry Harrison, the hero of the Battle of Tippecanoe. For vice president, the anti–Van Buren forces were offered a choice between to a former Democrat from Virginia, John Tyler, and an Anti-Mason from New York, Francis Granger. The multiplicity of candidates doomed the Whigs' chances, who sought to win support on the basis of opposition to King Andrew's handpicking of his heir.

In a way, Johnson's political ambitions were a factor in Harrison's decision to seek the presidency himself. The attention coming Johnson's way in the political exploitation of Tecumseh's death inspired western followers of Harrison to advertise his own military record as more deserving of the Jackson mantle than that of the man who had served under Harrison. Johnson's boosters had been glorifying him at commemorative celebrations at the site of the battle, apparently to Harrison's irritation. When the general was invited to attend one of the commemorations, he publicly chastised Johnson for posing as the hero of the battle in which Harrison was the American commander. Harrison enthusiasts then began to generate a groundswell for a candidacy of his own.

In the fall campaign, Johnson became a Whig target as a "great amalgamator" who had "habitually and practically" demonstrated his personal commitment to "abolitionist principles in his own home."[11] Johnson proved to be poison to the ticket in the slave states, and even his home state of Kentucky went for Harrison and Granger. As a champion of the working man Johnson gained some labor support, especially as an aggressive congressional foe of imprisonment for nonpayment of debt. But the Democratic strategy was to deemphasize personality other than to cast Van Buren as the vehicle for continuing the Jacksonian era. It sought to shape the election as between one solid political party grounded in Jeffersonian principles and a disorganized and discontented collection of national bank diehards and other anti-Jackson critics. Johnson characterized the campaign of 1836 as "the great . . . and final battle against 35 millions of money, against nullification, against a scheme of protection and of its correlative, waste by internal improvements."[12]

On Election Day, Van Buren won with only 50.9 percent of the popular vote to 49.1 percent for the Whig candidates combined, but his margin in the electoral college was much wider. In the vice presidential race, however, Johnson fell one vote short of a majority, Virginia champing over the snub to William Rives and withholding its twenty-three votes. Thus, the choice fell to the Senate, with the choice between the top finishers, Johnson and Granger. The states, each casting one vote along party lines, easily elected Johnson.

He embarked on the vice presidency with little prospect of playing any significant role in the administration of Van Buren. As a former vice president who had been heavily engaged in the Jackson administration, Van Buren might have been expected to involve the second officer in his own. But Johnson, for all his many years in Congress, was essentially devoid of administrative experience, and beyond that he was well aware that he had been a drag on the Democratic ticket. So he was reduced largely to his office's only active responsibility, as president of the Senate, which he addressed with the humility of a newcomer to Capitol Hill, which he was not.

In taking the chair, Johnson told the senators what he was hoping for to offset his diffidence: "The intelligence of the Senate will guard the country from any injury that might result from the imperfections of the presiding officer."[13]

In his four years as presiding officer, Johnson was required to cast a tiebreaker fourteen times, more than any predecessor save Adams and Calhoun. Most of the time he obediently voted to sustain the administration's policies and desires. Coming into office weighed down with considerable personal debt, Johnson, by obligation or preference, devoted a considerable amount of his time in tending to various personal enterprises, including the maintenance of a hotel and saloon back in Kentucky.

Amos Kendall, a New Hampshire transplant to Kentucky and an eventual Van Buren cabinet member, sent the president a letter from a Kentucky friend reporting his visit to "Col. Johnson's Watering establishment," where the sitting vice president was seen "happy in the inglorious pursuit of tavern keeping—even giving his personal superintendence to the chicken and egg purchasing and water-melon selling department." Kendall also reported that Johnson was consorting with "a young Delilah of about the complexion of Shakespears [sic] swarthy Othello . . . said to be his third wife; his second, which he sold for her infidelity, having been the sister of the present lady."[14]

As Van Buren struggled with a severe economic downturn at home and the tightening of credit under his continuation of Jackson's hard-money policies, Johnson endured his own personal deterioration. He had never been a challenge to Van Buren's dandified appearance and stylish dress, and his own casualness did nothing to enhance his esteem in Washington. He even began to take on a somewhat comic visage, wearing as a trademark a bright red vest that was ill-fitted to the Senate's customary sober mien.

It was soon obvious that neither Van Buren nor the party hierarchy wanted to offer the distinctly unimpressive Johnson a second term as vice president. Former president Jackson, who had championed him as a fellow frontiersman and a War of 1812 hero, appraised Johnson now as a dead weight on the Democratic ticket. He urged the nomination of fellow Tennessean James K. Polk, who had just won the governorship impressively and was modestly seeking the vice presidency.[15] Jackson wrote the Democratic editor Francis P. Blair, "I like Col. Johnson but I like my country more,"[16] and he threatened to abandon Van Buren unless Polk was nominated in place of Johnson.

At the party's convention in Baltimore in May 1840, Van Buren's renomination was not in question, but the opposition to Johnson was strong and vocal. Van Buren nevertheless held firm on Johnson, not wanting a convention out of control. Even so, the convention delegates could not agree on nominating Johnson and finally voted to nominate no one but to leave the vice presidential nomination to the state party organizations, which finally settled for Johnson again. While Van Buren returned to New York to shore up his somewhat neglected political base, Johnson took to the stump, in vain urging the president to do the same. He took to retelling tales of his adventures on the frontier, but he was not the charismatic Jackson.[17]

Harrison and his managers had learned much about politics in 1836, and they appropriated many of the successful trappings of Old Hickory to refashion the true hero of the Battles of Tippecanoe and the Thames into another Andy Jackson. When a Democratic editor in Baltimore mocked Harrison as the product of an aristocratic Virginia family who had become a country squire in Ohio, the Whigs turned the tables. They started casting Old Tippecanoe has a hard cider–drinking Indian fighter of the log-cabin wilderness, contrasting him with Van Buren as a diminutive preening and perfumed New Yorker. They even got Harrison to take a swig or two from the jug in public, joining the competition for "the common man" with a vengeance.[18] As his running mate, the Whigs chose the former senator Tyler, an aristocratic Virginia Democrat and strong states-righter, as an obvious contrast to Johnson.

The 1840 presidential contest was soon being called the Log Cabin Campaign, with the polished Harrison mischaracterized as a genuine backwoodsman. Meanwhile Old Dick Johnson, in the fashion of a rough-and-tumble man of the Kentucky frontier, sought to be a sort of surrogate Jackson in behalf of the gentrified Little Magician, the son of a rural New York tavern keeper. The Harrison campaign, masterminded by cigar-puffing Thurlow Weed of New York, beat Van Buren at his own game of political organizing, with an added dose of showmanship. Soon the campaign was flooded with signs and trinkets of the rugged West, and Johnson was reduced to an oft-ridiculed sideshow.

In the end the Jacksonian era came to a halt with the blossoming of the Whig Party, after its strong if disorganized entry into national politics only four years earlier. Although Harrison's popular-vote victory was modest, he won in a landslide in the electoral college. As president of the Senate, Johnson had to suffer through a final task of tallying the electoral votes that made John Tyler of Virginia his successor. He went back to Kentucky and two years later sought to return to the Senate but lost. In 1844 and again in 1848 he tried for the Senate, but to no one's surprise he was bypassed by the Kentucky legislature. Finally his old supporters in Scott County voted him a seat in the state legislature in 1850, but eleven days later he died of a stroke at age seventy.

Of the nine men who had held the vice presidency up to this time, Richard Mentor Johnson unquestionably had the most unusual, and unlikely, political résumé. But like the other vice presidents before him, except Van Buren, Johnson held the office with little political influence. That fate, however, was not to fall for very long to the man he swore in on his own last day as president of the Senate, John Tyler.

CHAPTER 10

JOHN TYLER
OF VIRGINIA

The tenth vice president of the United States and the first Whig to hold the office was a former Democrat who served the shortest period of any occupant up to that time: only thirty-three days. Yet the decisions he made in unexpectedly leaving the vice presidency were of the highest significance, both constitutionally and politically, of any occupant up to his time.

John Tyler of Virginia, upon being sworn in with President William Henry Harrison on March 4, 1841, performed his duty as president of the Senate for less than two hours, then skipped the lavish inaugural facilities and went home to Williamsburg. Such had the minimal responsibilities of the vice president required of him. Barely a month later, however, at sunrise on April 5, Tyler was awakened by Fletcher Webster, the son of Secretary of State Daniel Webster, and Robert Beale, the assistant doorkeeper of the Senate, arriving on horseback. They delivered to him a letter from the Harrison cabinet informing him that the night before, Harrison had died, the first president to perish in office.[1]

The news apparently did not come as a complete surprise to Tyler, who at only fifty-one now became the youngest president to serve up to that time. He had learned earlier that the sixty-eight-year-old Harrison, speaking for ninety minutes at his inauguration on a chilly winter day in neither hat nor overcoat, had contracted pneumonia. According to the Democratic senator Thomas Hart Benton of Missouri, Tyler had remained in Williamsburg because he "would feel it indelicate to repair to the seat of government, of his own will, on hearing of the report of the president's illness."[2] In any event, the vice president had had some time to consider the ramifications of such an outcome and how to deal with it.

As the first presidential standby to ascend to the highest office by constitutional mandate, Tyler had no precedents to help determine his actions. The first steps he took were to notify his family members of the news at breakfast and to consult with a Williamsburg neighbor and friend, Nathaniel Beverly Tucker, a law professor at the College of William and Mary. Tucker, remembering that Harrison in the 1840 campaign had pledged to serve only a single term, now urged Tyler to make the same declaration and not seek a term in his own right in 1844. Tyler, offering no comment, rushed off to Washington, taking a steamboat up the James River to Richmond and then catching a train to the capital, a trip of 230 miles made in twenty-one hours.[3]

On arrival he went to Brown's Indian Queen Hotel, where he met with the members of the Harrison cabinet he had inherited. The senior member, Secretary of State Daniel Webster, informed Tyler that under Harrison, all administrative decisions were made "before the Cabinet, and their settlement was decided by the majority, each member of the Cabinet and the president having one vote." Tyler was having none of it. "I am the President," he declared, "and I shall be held responsible for my administration. I shall be pleased to avail myself of your counsel and advice. But I can never consent to being dictated to as to what I shall do or not do. When you think otherwise, your resignations will be accepted."[4] They all agreed to stay on under those conditions.

Then Tyler took preemptive action in their presence. The chief justice of the U.S. Circuit Court for the District of Columbia was brought to the hotel, where he administered the oath of office of the president of the United States to Tyler. The judge signed an affidavit verifying that Tyler had asserted he was qualified to assume the presidency without taking a second oath but had asked that it be administered again, anticipating that "doubts may arise and for greater caution."[5] Tyler took the position that this second oath taking had not been imperative, inasmuch as in the vice presidential oath he had already taken he had sworn to uphold the Constitution. But he wanted to leave no question that he was assuming the presidency and not simply its powers in an acting capacity.

The language on succession was quite ambiguous. Article II, Section 1, read: "In case of the removal of the President from office, or of his death, resignation or inability to discharge the powers and duties of the said office, the same shall devolve on the Vice-President." But did the words *the same* refer to the office itself or to the powers and duties of it? The rest of the sentence fed the uncertainty, leaving open the interpretation that the successor was merely to serve as a stand-in: "And the Congress may by law provide for the case of removal, death, resignation or inability, both of the President and Vice-President, declaring what officer shall then act as President; and such officer shall act accordingly until the disability be removed, or a President shall be elected." By seizing the office so unambiguously and decisively, Tyler removed doubt that a successor was empowered merely to "act as president," but was to be the actual chief executive in all the office's manifestations.

The question was hardly academic. Former president John Quincy Adams, despairing at the ascendancy of the southern states-rights champion, argued that Tyler should be identified as "Vice-President Acting as President."[6] He wrote, "Tyler is a political sectarian, of the slave-driving, Virginian, Jeffersonian school, principled against all improvement, with all the interests and passions and vices of slavery rooted in his moral and political constitution—with talents not above mediocrity, and a spirit incapable of expansion to the dimensions of the station upon which he has been cast by the hand of Providence, unseen through the apparent agency of chance. No one ever thought of his being placed in the executive chair."[7]

The question of Tyler's legitimacy, or at least credibility, as president was reduced to the chiding identification "His Accidency." Meanwhile, all this debate raised a hypothetical question in the Senate: if a vice president assumed the presidency, would the Senate president pro tem assume the vice presidency? No ruling was in place for this circumstance. As the country had done since its inception, the Senate president pro tem might take over an absent or deceased vice president's Senate duties, but the office itself would remain vacant until the next election.

John Tyler had come to the vice presidency as the son of a governor of Virginia from the revolutionary generation who opposed the Constitution at the state's ratifying convention. Born in 1790 on his father's estate in southern Virginia, which he later inherited, Tyler graduated from William and Mary, studied law under his father and also Edmund Randolph, the young country's first attorney general. But he disagreed with Randolph's advocacy of a strong central government, becoming in the Jefferson tradition a staunch defender of states' rights and an opponent of the concept of the national bank. At twenty-one he was elected to the Virginia House of Delegates, married into more wealth and greater slave ownership than in his own family, and had seven children before his wife, Letitia, suffered a paralytic stroke and died in 1842.[8]

Young Tyler served five years in the state legislature and at age twenty-seven was elected to the U.S. House of Representatives. There he served two terms, opposing a strong national bank, protective tariffs for northern industry, and a federal transportation network, all of which he thought detrimental to southern agrarian interests. In all this, he remained a Jeffersonian Democrat and was elected as governor in 1825 and then as a U.S. senator from Virginia. He supported Jackson for the presidency in 1828 and 1832, joining with Jackson in opposition to rechartering the national bank but breaking with him over both his removal of federal deposits and some of his cabinet appointments. In 1833 Tyler was the only Senate Democrat to vote against Jackson's Force Bill, which overrode a South Carolina ordinance of nullification of the tariff of 1832 and authorized sending federal troops into Charleston Harbor.[9]

Tyler pointedly distinguished his opposition: it was not to a state's right to secede from the Union but to South Carolina's attempt at nullification: "I disclaim the policy adopted by her; all here know I did not approve of her course. I will not join in the denunciations which have been so loudly thundered against her, nor will I deny that she has much cause of complaint." Rather, he said of Jackson's response, "His proclamation has swept away all the barriers of the Constitution and given us in place of the Federal government, under which we had fondly believed we were living, a consolidated military despotism."[10]

Thereafter Tyler became a political ally of the Whig leader Henry Clay in opposing Jackson, voting with the Senate majority in 1834 to censure the president over his refusal to inform Congress about his removal of federal deposits from the national bank. Striking the King Andrew lament, Tyler declared, "The presidential office swallows up all power, and the president becomes every inch a king."[11] When the Virginia legislature "instructed" Tyler to withdraw his censure vote, he refused but decided he had to resign from the Senate.

While still a Democrat, Tyler now found himself in league with the emerging Whig Party, with Clay as its most prominent presidential aspirant. In 1836, the still disorganized Whigs decided not to hold a national nominating convention and instead left the participating states to choose their own methods to select a standard-bearer. In the resulting hodge-podge, four separate Whig candidates ran against Jackson's handpicked choice to succeed him, Vice President Martin Van Buren, in a strategy designed to deny Van Buren an electoral college majority and to put the election into the House of Representatives.

For vice president, Tyler was offered as a running mate with one or the other of the Whigs, but Democrat Van Buren was elected, and in the separate race for vice president Tyler finished third behind the Democrat Richard M. Johnson and the Whig Francis Granger. None of the three, however, received a majority, throwing the choice to the Senate between the top two finishers, leaving Tyler out. Johnson won easily over Granger on the first ballot.[12]

Out of all public office now, Tyler was elected president of the Virginia Colonization Society, an organization to rid the state of freed former slaves by encouraging their emigration to a colony on the west coast of Africa. He saw the scheme as "a dream of philanthropy" creating all-Negro colonies that would "be to Africa what Jamestown and Plymouth have been to America."[13]

In 1838, when Tyler was again seeking a seat in the Virginia House of Delegates, he ran as a Whig, was elected and chosen unanimously to be its Speaker, but was stymied in a subsequent bid to return to the U.S. Senate. Tyler's political career soon took a surprising and unexpected turn, however, at the Whig nominating convention at Harrisburg in December 1839, when Clay entered with a clear plurality of the delegates but short of the majority needed. In opposition to Clay, the party leaders Thurlow Weed of New York and Thaddeus Stevens of Pennsylvania engineered approval of a unit rule for voting whereby each state would cast all its votes for its leading candidate. They argued that Clay could not carry their key states and others critical to winning the 1840 presidential election. At the end of the day, Clay was overtaken by William Henry Harrison and lost the nomination to him. The convention strategists believed that as a military hero with no particularly objectionable political views, Harrison could beat Van Buren this time by simply tapping into the broad anti-incumbent sentiment in a land gripped by deep economic woes.

Turning to the matter of Harrison's running mate, Weed and Stevens agreed the position should go to a prominent Clay supporter from the South. After three others had rejected the nomination, it was finally offered to Tyler, as a sop to Clay and as a slaveholder in a pitch to the South.[14] It seemed to have been done without much thought to whether this former Jacksonian Democrat had really bought into the Whig philosophy and agenda of nationalism.

Tyler's nomination inevitably stirred speculation of promises made or deals struck on his part. Then and later he stoutly denied any. Daniel Webster, for one, came to his defense. "When Harrison and Tyler were nominated," he declared later, "their opinions on public questions were generally known." Subsequently, Tyler himself said, "I have no recollection of having opened my lips in that body on any subject whatever."[15] As for Harrison, all he offered was a flat statement that if elected he would "under no circumstances" consent to be a candidate for a second term.[16] If Tyler had any thoughts of the presidency in his future, this statement was probably what gave him hope of that prospect, as it still did for Clay.

In the 1840 campaign, Tyler was pretty much in the shadows as the now more organized Whigs, seizing on Harrison's credentials as an old Indian fighter, greatly embellished his image as a rough-hewn man of the frontier, belying his history and actual status as a wealthy country gentleman in Ohio. In all this, Tyler was reduced to an appendage and found a place in history as part of one of the most famous and oft-repeated campaign slogans: "Tippecanoe and Tyler too." His stature as a nonentity was also immortalized in a Whig campaign rhyme: "We will vote for Tyler therefore, without a why or wherefore," which in turn led Philip Hone to observe, "There was rhyme but no reason in it."[17]

Pressured repeatedly to take a position on the bank question, Tyler artfully dodged, taking safe ground and giving no offense, despite his earlier open opposition to a national bank. When asked where he stood on the subject of the protective tariff, he replied, "I am in favor of what General Harrison and Mr. Clay are in favor of; I am in favor of preserving the compromise bill as it now stands; between General Harrison, Mr. Clay and myself, there is no difference of opinion on this subject."[18]

With little surprise, Harrison won overwhelmingly in the electoral college and brought Tyler in with him, although the popular vote was much closer—only six percentage points separating the old general from the former Democratic president, who struggled under the campaign taunts "Martin Van Ruin" and "Van, Van, he's a used-up man."

Harrison's death only a month into his presidency and Tyler's sudden elevation to the office after having just recently been sworn in as vice president shocked Whig regulars. So did his swift action in taking the presidential oath and his flat declaration to his cabinet that he meant to be the nation's chief executive in both title and reality. If Clay had expected he would have a free hand in implementing the major features of his American System—restoration of a national bank, protective tariffs, and internal transportation projects linking the states into a more homogeneous federal entity—he was soon disappointed. Tyler revealed himself as devoted as ever to the defense and protection of states' rights and to the sovereignty he had held prior to quitting the Democratic Party of Jackson and Van Buren. Clay furthermore now saw Tyler as another barrier to his own crumbling presidential ambitions.

When Congress met in a special session in late May 1841, Representative John McKeon of New York questioned whether Tyler was entitled to be addressed as president. A resolution of affirmation was quickly passed without a formal vote. While Tyler was now recognized as the legal president, he did not automatically become the head of the Whig Party. Henry Clay remained the recognized leader, and he had no intention of surrendering that role in advancing his view of the Whig agenda, especially to a former Jacksonian. When in the special session Clay pressed Tyler to seek another national bank, a prime Whig objective, the new president told him he would wait until the next regular session starting in December.

Finally Clay offered a compromise on a bank bill, but Tyler vetoed it, and still another passed by Congress, on the grounds that it was an unconstitutional infringement on the rights of the individual states. As the special session was winding up, Clay, in the hope of forcing Tyler out, led a protest in which all members of the cabinet resigned, with the exception of Secretary of State Daniel Webster. Tyler responded by sending the Senate new cabinet nominations, which the senators quickly confirmed and then adjourned until the next regular session.

Later that day, about sixty Whigs gathered on the Capitol plaza and adopted a statement dissociating themselves from Tyler, leaving him without a party. A drawn-out battle between the president and the Senate ensued, in which many of Tyler's subsequent other appointments requiring confirmation were rejected.[19]

Clay, more determined now than ever to wrest the presidency from "His Accidency," resigned from the Senate in March 1842 to prepare for his candidacy in 1844. Meanwhile, Tyler continued to wield his veto pen against the Whig majority in Congress, using it ten times in his four years as president. As presidents often have done, Tyler looked to foreign policy to make his mark, achieving the Webster-Ashburton Treaty, which settled certain land and territorial disputes with the British, and executing the historic annexation of Texas into the Union. He justified the latter in part as a vehicle for providing more living space for slaves and thereby preserving the "peculiar institution."

Tyler became the first president not to seek a second term. Long widowed, he remarried in 1845, with Julia Gardiner, in the first White House wedding, and had another seven children with her. As a former president, in 1861 he was the chairman of a Washington conference that sought but failed to avert the Civil War. He subsequently served at the Virginia convention that voted to secede from the Union and was elected to the provisional Congress of the Confederacy. But he died in 1862 before he could take his seat. Nevertheless, on the basis of that election, *The Smithsonian Book of Presidential Trivia* mentions Tyler as "the only president to commit a public act of treason against the U.S. government," the Confederacy at the time of his death being at war with the Union he had once led.[20]

The unanticipated presidency of John Tyler was riddled from its start to its end with controversy and strife. This one-time staunch Jeffersonian Democrat sought to sustain his Virginia countryman's "republican principles" in the Whig Party, which chose him to be its vice president and lived to regret it. In the end, nothing so became John Tyler as the manner in which he embarked on his presidency. By swiftly and resolutely declaring its legitimacy and firmly using the power bestowed by it, he cemented a peaceful, orderly, and constitutional succession that has stood the test of time.

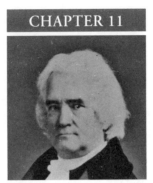

CHAPTER 11

GEORGE M. DALLAS
OF PENNSYLVANIA

U nusual circumstances in the political careers of President James K. Polk and his vice president, George Mifflin Dallas, saw the one who actively sought the second office in 1844 winding up in the first, and the man who showed little interest in the second nonetheless landing it. Polk, a former governor of Tennessee twice defeated for reelection, calculated that his chances for the presidency were over and the best he could hope to achieve was the vice presidency. Dallas, much less distinguished as a Philadelphia party leader and an appointed U.S. senator with little ambition for national office, nevertheless found himself elected as vice president.

The man who became the eleventh vice president of the United States was born in Philadelphia on July 10, 1792. He was the second of the six children of Alexander Dallas, a local lawyer and later a secretary of the Commonwealth of Pennsylvania, a recorder of U.S. Supreme Court opinions, President James Madison's secretary of the treasury in 1814, and subsequently an acting secretary of war, before dying at the age of fifty-nine.

The son, George, graduated with highest honors from the College of New Jersey (Princeton) in 1810 and was admitted to the Pennsylvania bar three years later at age twenty. He became the personal secretary to the former treasury secretary Albert Gallatin and traveled with him on diplomatic missions to St. Petersburg and London. In August 1814, when the British were setting fire to the U.S. Capitol and the White House, young Dallas brought a draft of British peace terms in the War of 1812 to Washington.

In 1816 he moved back to Philadelphia, where he married the daughter of a prominent Federalist family and had eight children with her. Taking to an aristocratic lifestyle and dress, he acquired expensive tastes that kept him constantly in debt, a circumstance that obliged him to reject a number of government posts, though he did become counsel to the Second Bank of the United States. He also wrote poetry and spoke fluent French, which left a surface impression of erudition.

In 1817 Dallas became deputy attorney general of Philadelphia, but he lacked the drive of the ambitious politician and a willingness to engage in the competitive world of elective politics. His one term in the U.S. Senate was by appointment of the state legislature, as were all his other government offices, until in 1844 he was elected as vice president.

The developments that produced this outcome were among the more bizarre in national election annals. Polk was a disciple and favorite of Andrew Jackson, the former president and a fellow Tennessean. Dallas saw in Polk a vehicle to help restore the Jacksonian Democracy by making him the running mate of the Democratic front-runner former president Van Buren, seeking to regain the White House. The Little Magician first needed to claim the nomination in a large field in order to take on his old nemesis, Henry Clay, the Whig nominee, in the November election. But he was well ahead in delegates pledged to him. Early in April, Polk visited Jackson at his Hermitage mansion to discuss the strategy to team himself with Van Buren.

Several days later, in separate newspapers and apparently without collusion, Van Buren and Clay each declared his strong opposition to the annexation of the recently independent Republic of Texas. Rather than thus removing the issue from the campaign, their comments proved to destroy the presidential aspirations of both men. Public opinion for bringing Texas into the Union was very strong; Van Buren's impolitic statement would soon cost him the Democratic nomination and ignite a Jackson plan to put "Young Hickory" Polk on a path to the presidency.

Other circumstances that would provide Polk a more direct and immediate route were at work, however. Jackson told Polk the plan had to be revised with Polk replacing Van Buren as the Jacksonian nominee. With

Clay so openly and categorically opposed to the annexation, the Democrats now clearly needed and wanted a pro-annexation nominee. Jackson earlier had embraced pro-annexation, saying, "The god of the universe . . . intended this great valley [Texas] to belong to one nation,"[1] and he immediately recognized that Van Buren had committed political suicide with his statement. He wrote Van Buren a sharply candid letter telling him that in his judgment his old political strategist had about as much chance of being elected president again as there was "to turn the current of the Mississippi."[2]

Only five days before Van Buren wrote his anti-annexation declaration, Polk had written to a Democratic club in Cincinnati saying he was "in favor of the immediate re-annexation of Texas to the territory and Government of the United States," believing he was simply following the party line. Learning how he had put himself in disagreement with Van Buren no doubt caused him temporary concern, but in the end this arrangement would work to his advantage.[3]

In an utterly self-serving report, Polk told the Tennessee congressman Cave Johnson, an ally: "Gen. J says the candidate for the first office should be an annexation man, and from the Southwest, and he and other friends here urge that my friends should insist upon that point. I tell them, and it is true, that I have never aspired so high and that in all probability the attempt to place me in the first position would be utterly abortive. In the confusion that will prevail . . . there is no telling what will occur." Then he added that in any event the development would leave him in a favorable position for the vice presidential nomination, declaring, "I aspire to the 2nd office."[4]

Van Buren meanwhile counted his delegates to the approaching Democratic convention in Baltimore, hoping the nomination would still be his. When the Whigs met in the same city, Clay was unanimously nominated with little stir over his own anti-annexation statement. President Tyler, abandoned by his adopted party, meanwhile held a rump convention of his own there, vainly holding out hope of running on the slogan "Tyler and Texas." Elsewhere in Baltimore, the Jackson Democrats prepared to decide Van Buren's fate, with Polk and friends now implementing a revised strategy. Van Buren suffered a severe setback when the convention voted to require a two-thirds margin for nomination, which killed his chances.

In competition with Michigan's Lewis Cass for the presidential nomination, Van Buren led but fell thirty-one votes short of the two-thirds majority. Cass and five other candidates received votes, but none of them was for Polk. On the fourth roll call Cass moved ahead but also fell short of the needed majority, and after an overnight recess Polk for the first time got forty-four votes and the flood gates opened for him, gaining the nomination by acclamation—arguably making him the first truly dark-horse nominee.

Then the convention turned to nominating Polk's running mate. Nothing was heard of George Dallas of Pennsylvania. The convention, also by acclamation, nominated Senator Silas Wright of New York, leader of the Van Buren forces, in a conciliatory gesture. But Wright declined, whereupon the offer was extended to James Buchanan, Dallas's bitter rival for leadership of the Pennsylvania Democrats, who also declined. Five more men turned it down, until the Pennsylvania delegation rallied to Dallas and gained his nomination. Dallas's backing of Texas annexation as well as his Pennsylvania connection brought a mostly positive response at the convention and in important quarters in the South. Calhoun was reported as praising the nomination because there would be no New Yorker on the ticket.[5]

The Whigs, not surprisingly, were lulled by the prospect of running against the Democratic ticket of a twice-defeated Tennessee governor and a Pennsylvania political leader of little national experience. The Philadelphia Whig leader Sidney George Fisher wrote, "Polk is a fourth rate partizan [sic] politician, of ordinary abilities, no eminence or reputation and chiefly distinguished for being a successful stump orator in Tennessee." He called Dallas "a reckless partizan totally devoid of principle and capable of upholding or relinquishing any opinions whenever his own or his party's interests require it."[6] A surprised Dallas made a request of Polk if at any time he was to become a burden in the campaign: "Pray cut me loose instantly and resolutely. Personally I have not the slightest wish to quit the pursuits of private life." Aware of the functional shortcomings of the vice presidency, he described himself as "a bobtail annexed to a great kite."[7]

To make his best contribution to the Democratic ticket during in the 1844 campaign, Dallas concentrated on bringing home Pennsylvania's electoral votes. The question of the protective tariff that continued to divide the northern and southern states posed his diciest challenge. As a Tennessee congressman, Polk had voted against the Tariff of Abominations of 1828 and for reducing its rates in 1832, positions sharply opposed in industrial Pennsylvania and by Dallas at the time. Polk was warned that to carry Pennsylvania he would have to offer at least a nod to the needs of northern manufacture. Dallas therefore had to put party before state and region and also take a softer position on the tariff question in harmony with the presidential nominee.

Under pressure from Dallas and other Pennsylvanians, Polk wrote a letter saying while he opposed the tariff for the purpose of industrial protection only, he supported it to raise needed revenue, at the same time offering reasonable shelter to domestic industries dependent on the making of iron and steel. A relieved Dallas replied, "I think your doctrine on the tariff will impair your strength here very little if at all, and perhaps it is the matter on which brevity would be the soul of wit."[8]

Dallas also counseled Polk to tread lightly on the discussion of immigration policies that were stirring up considerable talk in Philadelphia and elsewhere in southeastern Pennsylvania. He warned of coalitions of Whigs, abolitionists, and nativists imperiling a Democratic victory in the state and raised the specter of abolition further dividing North and South, urging Polk, "Postpone the tariff question until the country is secured against the alarming strides of abolition."[9] In the end, all such fears were swept aside as the two centerpieces of the Democratic strategy, New York and Pennsylvania, went for Polk and Dallas, beating Clay and Theodore Frelinghuysen of New Jersey, though only 1.5 percent separated the two parties in the popular vote.

Even before Dallas's election as vice president, he had reason to consider that the presidency itself was not out of his reach. Less than five months before the election, Polk had announced that, if elected, he would "enter upon the discharge of the high and solemn duties, with the settled purpose of not being a candidate for reelection."[10] He kept that pledge, but other subsequent circumstances made Dallas's musings first unlikely and later impossible.

For one thing, his political fight with James Buchanan, which occupied much of Dallas's time and energies in Pennsylvania, followed them to Washington. Polk, over the strenuous objections of his vice president, appointed Buchanan as his secretary of state and as such the first among equals in the Polk cabinet. Dallas himself was not a member, but from the outset Polk listened to him in dealing with heavy patronage demands from the politically important Keystone State.

Both Dallas and Buchanan, as the leaders of the major factions in the Pennsylvania Democracy, vied for Polk's ear and largesse in distributing lucrative and influential federal offices in the state and desirable diplomatic posts abroad. Shortly after the election, Dallas himself unwittingly paved the way for Buchanan's appointment to the State Department, proposing that Polk dismiss all Tyler men, particularly John C. Calhoun as his secretary of state, blaming him for the Senate's defeat of the Texas annexation treaty Tyler had sought.

Buchanan's friends in Pennsylvania, meanwhile, sought the State Department for him. They got the state's presidential electors to urge the appointment in casting their electoral votes for Polk, a move that outraged Dallas. He wrote, "A more grotesque and humiliating movement could not well be made," and he denounced them "for their precipitous meddling." Dallas said he did not intend to stand idly by in his new eminence. "I have become vice president willy-nilly," he said, "and anticipate the necessity of enduring heavy and painful and protracted sacrifices, as the consequence. Well! I am not, in the bargain, disposed to be considered a cypher! On the contrary, I am resolved that no one shall be taken from Pennsylvania in a cabinet office who is notoriously hostile to the vice president. If such a choice be made, my relations with the administration are at once at an end."[11]

In light of Polk's pledged retirement after a single term, Dallas already seemed to be anticipating a drag-out fight with Buchanan for the 1848 Democratic presidential nomination. He insisted that Pennsylvania's Democrats would never accept as their voice in the Polk administration "the distinguished gentleman so prematurely and arrantly foisted upon Mr. Polk."[12] He fervently hoped that Senator Robert J. Walker of Mississippi, married to his niece, would become secretary of state instead of Buchanan. But Polk had no intention of letting his vice president, essentially a stranger to him, pick his cabinet for him.

Walker meanwhile told Dallas in January that he expected Polk to keep Calhoun at State for at least a time, and therefore he was pursuing the top job at the Treasury, but Dallas continued to pitch Walker for secretary of state. In late February, when Polk's selection of Buchanan became known, Dallas called it "a most dangerous choice" and groused about trouble ahead that could have been avoided had Walker gotten the State appointment.

Dallas, nonetheless, continued to press for an influential position for

Walker. Polk finally gave him the Treasury Department to make peace with his vice president and with the South. But Jackson, for one, warned Polk that the Dallas-Walker alliance could cause trouble, as the struggle for Pennsylvania dominance between Dallas and Buchanan was certain to go on.

Polk for his part made clear to his cabinet appointees that he intended to be in charge and expected loyalty. "I desire to select men who agree with me," he pointedly told Buchanan on his appointment, "and who will cordially cooperate with me in carrying out my principles and policy." He warned at the same time that any cabinet member who pursued the next presidential nomination while serving would be told to resign.[13] Nevertheless, Polk found himself repeatedly enmeshed in refereeing the patronage wars between Dallas and Buchanan, finally promising to pay more attention to his vice president.

One vote Dallas cast to break a Senate tie proved to be his own biggest challenge. In 1846, after Polk's decision to seek tariff reductions, the balloting on doing so ended in a tie. After much soul-searching Dallas supported it, against the interests of his state's iron and steel industry.[14] To make the choice more palatable to Dallas, Richard Rush, a Pennsylvania ally of his, wrote to him: "Pennsylvanians are small men. . . . You are not of their race and they left you. The *union* put you where you are, and can keep you there and do more. . . . Pennsylvania cannot lead, she can only follow and bellow. You cannot repudiate the state, you must love her openly, and your notion of elevating her in the scale of the union is noble, and may *begin* to come about, but at present the union is your element and platform."[15]

To his Pennsylvania constituents, Dallas rationalized, "An officer, elected by the suffrage of all twenty-eight states, and bound by his oath and every constitutional obligation, faithfully and fairly to represent, in the execution of his high trust, all the citizens of the Union [could not] narrow his great sphere and act with reference only to [his own state's] interest."[16]

Dallas was so concerned about the negative reaction back home that he had the Senate sergeant-at-arms deliver a handwritten message to his wife, Sophy, that at the slightest indication of riot in the city of Philadelphia because of passage of the tariff bills, she should "pack up and bring the whole brood to Washington."[17] His fears were well-founded. When news of the tariff's passage and Dallas's tie-breaking role in it reached the City of Brotherly Love, he was hanged in effigy from telegraph wires on a main street.

Diarist Philip Hone castigated a "faithless, corrupt administration" that had destroyed Pennsylvania's domestic industry, declaring that the names of Polk and Dallas "be recorded on the same page with those scourges of mankind, war . . . small pox, cholera and yellow fever."[18]

While voting for the tariff gave Dallas hope for southern support if he were to seek the presidency in 1848, his strong assertions of Manifest Destiny—the expansion into Oregon, the annexation of Texas, and support of the coming war against Mexico—ran counter to that objective. An argument with Great Britain over the dividing line between Canada and the United States in the Northwest, along with reports of British mischief making in Mexico, fed Dallas's concern of English interference with Polk's hopes of complete American dominance on the continent. What Dallas most feared was fighting two wars at one time if the row with the British was not peacefully resolved. In the end, however, the British accepted the 49th parallel as the northern border with Canada.

By now war had begun with Mexico, and Dallas embraced it completely, even advocating the annexation of the northern Mexican states, when the endgame of the war became the subject of competition among the prospective 1848 presidential candidates. Buchanan said that if an honorable peace could not be reached with Mexico, the United States should "fulfill that destiny which Providence may have in store for both countries." Dallas also weighed in, saying that nothing in the Constitution inhibited America from accepting "the vast task which may be assigned to it by the resistless force of events—guardianship of a crowded and confederated continent."[19]

Polk, however, was tired of war after nearly two years of it. When an American negotiator brought a peace offer from the Mexicans that included their surrender of any claims to California and New Mexico, the American purchase of them for fifteen million dollars, and the resolution of three million dollars in American claims on Mexico, Polk agreed. The Senate ratified the peace treaty in March 1848, and with it went Dallas's rationale for a presidential candidacy based on further continental expansion.[20]

Undaunted, in an effort to strike a middle ground on the slavery issue at home, Dallas adopted the concept of popular sovereignty in determining whether slavery would be permitted or prohibited in the western territories. But this position only drew animosity from both sides on the slavery issue and further buried his sinking presidential aspirations. Nevertheless, he challenged Buchanan for Pennsylvania's designation as its favorite son. Dallas's only hope was running overwhelmingly in Philadelphia, where supporters held a large rally for him in advance of the state party convention. In the fight for Philadelphia's eighty-five delegates, Dallas won forty-seven to Buchanan's thirty-eight, but the margin was insufficient to overcome Buchanan's strength elsewhere in the state.

Soon after, a caucus of the Democrats in the state legislature endorsed Buchanan, and the state party convention followed suit. But the convention rejected Buchanan's support of extending the Missouri Compromise to other states, pairing free and slave states in admission to the Union, damaging his chances at the national convention in Baltimore in May. In the end, the demoralized Democrats rejected both Buchanan and Dallas, and after a flirtation with General Zachary Taylor, hero of the Mexican War who eventually threw in with the Whig Party, they nominated Senator Lewis Cass of Michigan on the fourth ballot.

Dallas's relations with Polk had disintegrated to such a degree by now that the two barely spoke. After the election, in which Taylor and his running mate, Millard Fillmore of New York, were easily elected, Dallas returned to the Senate. But by this time he had grown weary of the routine and looked forward to his retirement. There was some talk of a second presidential bid in 1852, but he observed in his diary: "The Presidency is fast getting out of my head, and I don't want my mind diverted from a steady and exclusive pursuit of professional practice," meaning making money.[21]

Seven years later, Dallas was called back into public service by President Franklin Pierce as his minister to Great Britain. He replaced, of all people, his old and bitter Pennsylvania rival, James Buchanan, who had resigned to challenge Pierce for the presidency. Also surprisingly, after Buchanan was elected, he kept Dallas in the London post until he resigned in May 1861 and returned home, where three and a half years later Dallas died at the age of seventy-two.

George Mifflin Dallas left behind perhaps the bitterest assessment of the vice presidency of any occupant up to that time. He wrote that with the exception of the obligation to serve as president of the Senate, the vice president "forms no part of the government—he enters into no administrative sphere—he has practically no legislative, executive or judicial functions:—while the Senate sits, he presides, that's all—he doesn't debate or vote (except to end a tie); he merely preserves the order and courtesy of business." Referring to when Congress was in recess, he asked, "Where is he to go? What has he to do?—nowhere, nothing! He might, to be sure, meddle with affairs of state, rummage through the departments, devote his leisure to the study of public questions and interests, holding himself in readiness to counsel to help at every emergency in the great onward movement of the vast machine:—But, then, recollect, that this course would sometimes be esteemed intrusive, sometimes factious, sometimes vain and arrogant, and, as it is prescribed by no law, it could not fail to be treated lightly because guaranteed by no responsibility."[22]

The harshness of this little-regarded vice president's appraisal aside, his description of the job summed up its significance and utilization about as well as it then warranted and deserved. Dallas's words were an indictment of the office, of the haphazard process that had placed him in it, and of the president under whom he served, for failure to make more of its potential for constructive public service. It was an indictment that would remain valid for most vice presidencies well into the next century.

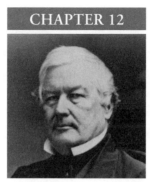

CHAPTER 12

MILLARD FILLMORE

OF NEW YORK

Afer more than half a century of American presidencies serving their full four-year terms, for the second time in eight years a vice president was elevated to the first office in 1850. President Zachary Taylor, in the White House only sixteen months, contracted acute gastro-enteritis and died, making Millard Fillmore of Buffalo the chief executive.

Fillmore's highest public offices prior to obtaining the vice presidency had been as a member of the U.S. House of Representatives and as the state comptroller of New York. Born in the upstate farm town of Locke in 1800, the second of nine children of Nathaniel and Phoebe Fillmore was given his mother's maiden name for his odd first name.[1]

Growing up, young Millard worked his father's land with little formal schooling. Up to the age of seventeen he could barely read, although he carried a dictionary with him. At nineteen he attended a small academy in New Hope and, with the aid of his future father-in-law, undertook some legal training while becoming a local teacher and subsequently a law clerk in Aurora, eighteen miles from Buffalo. He was admitted to the New York bar in 1824, two years later he married the judge's daughter Abigail, and in 1830 they settled in Buffalo, where his law practice flourished and they became socially prominent.[2]

The city was at the western end of the Erie Canal, and not surprisingly

Fillmore became a supporter of Henry Clay's American System and its emphasis on internal transportation improvements. He caught the eye of the Whig leader Thurlow Weed, who helped him win a seat in the state assembly in 1828, after which Fillmore himself soon became a party leader in the western end of the state. Four years later, when National Republicans and Anti-Masons linked, he was elected to Congress from the Buffalo district, where after a one-term break, taken to deal with the merging of these two factions into the Whig Party, Fillmore served for six more years in the House.

When the Whigs won the White House and took control of both houses of Congress in 1841, Fillmore became chairman of the powerful Ways and Means Committee, in which he helped engineer passage of the protective Tariff of 1842 over the stiff opposition of President John Tyler. At the end of his latest term, tired of Washington life, he returned to Buffalo again, indicating little ambition for a greater political role. Nevertheless, in the summer of 1843 former president John Quincy Adams visited him and urged him to return to public service. He was thus spurred to pursue the Whig nomination for vice president, but boss Weed favored his close friend and former New York governor William Seward, a bitter Fillmore rival. When Seward expressed no interest in the second national office, Weed urged Fillmore to seek the governorship, opening the way for a draft of Seward for the vice presidential nomination. Fillmore balked, writing a friend, "I need not tell you that I have no desire to run for governor. . . . I am not willing to be treacherously killed by this pretended kindness."[3]

In 1844, when Henry Clay captured the Whig nomination for president and the vice presidential nomination went to Theodore Frelinghuysen of New Jersey, Fillmore yielded to Weed's pressure and agreed to stand for governor. But he lost to Democrat Silas Wright, a defeat that also cost Clay the state and, his allies claimed, the presidency. In the process, however, Fillmore emerged as a rival to the Weed-Seward partnership for Whig leadership in New York, and the vice presidency remained in his mind.

Prior to the 1848 election, General Taylor, a lifelong soldier, insisted he had never entertained the idea of a political career until his Mexican War exploits made him the target of both major parties. "Such an idea never entered my head," he said, "nor is it likely to enter the head of any sane person." He declined to take any overt steps to high political office, observing, "If I ever occupy the White House it must be by the spontaneous move of the people."[4]

For some time while he was being courted, Taylor declined even to declare a party preference, finally owning up only that had he voted in the last presidential election (he never had cast a vote in such an election), "it would have been for Mr. Clay." The man from Kentucky, oft frustrated in his presidential ambitions, wryly commented of Taylor's seeming qualification for the office, "I wish I could slay a Mexican."[5]

After some regular Whigs champed at his distance from party celebrations and commitments, Taylor finally relented to the point of writing a letter to his son-in-law, Captain John Allison, in April 1848, in which he declared that he would have none of the campaign shenanigans, though admitted, "I AM A WHIG, *but not an ultra Whig.*" Then he added, "I trust I will not be again called on to make further explanations."[6]

At the Whig convention in May, Clay's hopes of finally achieving the presidency were dashed by the reluctant political warrior Taylor, who led Clay on the first ballot and widened the lead until he won the nomination over Clay and Winfield Scott on the fourth roll call. Clay, disappointed again, petulantly washed his hands of the whole matter. "Self-respect, the consistency of my character, and my true fame," he loftily said, "require that I should take no active or partisan agency in the ensuing contest." With a jibe at the political novice and hero of the Mexican War, he added, "The Whig party has been overthrown by a mere personal party."[7]

With Taylor's positions on critical Whig issues unspoken, the party leaders wanted his running mate to be a dependable Whig. Fillmore, having run once for the vice presidential nomination in 1844, was a good fit for the profile the party leaders believed was needed to complement Taylor, a warrior much favored in the South and also a longtime Louisiana slave owner. The New Yorker Fillmore deftly walked the line on slavery, declaring it an evil but saying it wasn't the business of the federal government to say where it could or could not exist in the nation. His embrace of popular sovereignty—leaving slavery's existence to the choice of each state—was designed to assuage hostile feelings on both sides of the argument, in North and South. Accordingly, Fillmore soon emerged as a northern counterbalance to Taylor the Louisiana slaveholder.

Taylor's history on slavery gave the ticket sufficient evidence of where he stood; Fillmore, in his artful dodging on the issue, hoped to mollify the North. Taylor's complete lack of experience in domestic national issues seemed not to matter at all. If Taylor was to be elected, others of experience would be at his side. The first step was to win the White House, and Fillmore, a demonstrated statewide vote-getter in becoming the comptroller of New York, seemed the right man to help Taylor get there. Furthermore, Fillmore could be offered to the convention as a consolation prize to the disappointed supporters of Clay, as a devotee of the Kentuckian's American System.

Neither Taylor nor Fillmore was much engaged in the fall campaign against the Democratic nominee, Senator Lewis Cass of Michigan, and former president Van Buren, who was running on a new Free Soil Party ticket. Those two split the customary Democratic vote and thereby gave the election to the Whigs. Neither Whig nominee partook in the raucous rallies and parades that had come to mark pursuit of the presidency. Fillmore basically hitched a ride to national prominence on the coattails of the popular hero of the Mexican War, who to the end pointedly disavowed any partisanship in accepting the Whig nomination.

Fillmore embarked on the vice presidency with the hope that his experience in Washington and Taylor's lack of it would give him a more substantive role in the new administration than most of his predecessors had enjoyed. Thurlow Weed reported that Taylor had said of the vice president he barely knew, "I wish Mr. Fillmore would take all of the business in his own hands."[8] Incorrectly, Taylor came to the presidency believing the vice president would be a member of his cabinet.

Fillmore's hope that Taylor would be true to his word soon crumbled. When the New Yorkers Weed and Seward made a recommendation on a key federal appointment in the Empire State and Taylor accepted it, an angry vice president asked him to withdraw it. Weed thereupon rushed to Washington, urging Taylor to avoid further patronage disputes by placing recommendations from the state in the hands of Governor Hamilton Fish. Weed represented Fish as impartial, when in fact he was a close ally of Weed and Seward, and Taylor naively agreed. Matters got worse for Fillmore when the job of collector of the port of Buffalo, in the vice president's backyard, also went to a Weed-Seward man. Further complaints by

Fillmore brought a Taylor promise to treat him better, but it didn't happen. Fillmore was on notice that despite the president's earlier observation that he wished his vice president would take all of the business in his own hands, Taylor had no intention of letting that occur.

In Fillmore's sole active function in the second office, as president of the Senate, he, like all those who had served before him, was charged by the Constitution with overseeing but not entering into the debates on all issues, great and small. They included all aspects of the slavery question, which critically included the issue of whether it would be extended into the western territories, particularly when the admission of new states was contemplated. The 1848 treaty ending the Mexican War expanded those territories to include California and New Mexico, which in 1849 Taylor proposed apply at once for statehood. Under Mexican rule, slavery already had been banned, and in October 1849 Californians held a convention and drafted a constitution barring slavery. In New Mexico, the same process went forward more slowly, but an impatient Taylor didn't wait with his statehood proposal.

Southern members of Congress, led by Calhoun talking darkly of secession, balked. Assuming all along that Taylor as a slaveholder was an ally, Calhoun felt he had betrayed them by advocating admission of California as a free state and potentially New Mexico as well.

The intense North-South conflict gave rise to the Compromise of 1850, fashioned by Clay with the help of the Democratic senator Stephen A. Douglas of Illinois, who debated ferociously in the Senate with Fillmore in the chair. Under the compromise, California would enter the Union as a free state, and territorial governments would be established in the remaining former Mexican lands with the slavery question left to the settlers there. Texas would abandon a boundary claim against New Mexico in return for the United States' assumption of Texas's national debt incurred before joining the Union. Slavery in the District of Columbia would be abolished with compensation to slave owners and with the adoption of a tough fugitive slave law.[9]

Clay opened the debate in January 1850 with seriously ill Calhoun sitting silently on the Senate floor, listening to the aging Kentuckian's case for the compromise as the best way to preserve the Union. Shortly afterward, Calhoun offered his rebuttal to Clay, though too weak to present it, so listening as a colleague read it for him. He pleaded for the North to yield in what he characterized as the restoration of the South's equal rights in determining the fate of slavery in the territories. If the North could not do so, he said, "say so; and let the States we both represent agree to separate and go in peace." Then he added, "If you are unwilling we should part in peace, tell us so; and we shall know what to do, when you reduce the question to submission or resistance."[10] Calhoun never got his answer; on March 31 he died, with the fate of the Union still undecided.

Two days later Fillmore presided over the funeral service for Calhoun in the Senate chamber. Aware of the rising furor over the slavery issue and the peril facing the Union, the next day he took the unusual step of addressing the Senate on his role as the keeper of civility in the hallowed chamber and his "powers and duties to preserve order."[11] According to the rules in place during the first days of the Senate, only the presiding officer could call an offending or unruly senator to order, but a revision in 1828 empowered any senator to do so as well. Fillmore observed that senators were not inclined "to appear as volunteers in the discharge of such an invidious duty," so the obligation fell to him when required. At the risk of being accused of interfering with freedom of speech, he said, he intended to call out any senator whose remarks he felt might imperil proper discourse.

Weeks later, a bitter clash on the Senate floor validated his worry. Henry Foote of Mississippi launched a sharp personal attack on Thomas Hart Benton of Missouri, which ended in Benton advancing on Foote and the latter drawing a pistol on the Senate floor. As the two foes exchanged more invectives, Fillmore quickly recognized another senator who called for adjournment, and the presiding officer quickly complied.[12]

Through all this, Fillmore supported Clay on the basic compromise in spite of Taylor's opposition to it. He told the president that in the event of a tie vote in the Senate, he would vote for passage. But before the debate reached that stage, fate intervened. At a Fourth of July celebration in the hot sun, Taylor drank a quantity of iced drinks, then suffered cramps and an attack of gastroenteritis that killed him five days later. Fillmore was notified the night of Taylor's death and took the presidential oath of office in the House of Representatives the next day at noon. No one seemed worried that overnight the country was without a sworn-in president, the line of succession clearly established and recognized by now. With Fillmore already in support of the Clay compromise, its enactment was assured, making California a free state, making New Mexico and Utah territories with the slavery issue decided by popular sovereignty, and settling the other issues as well.

Fillmore's abbreviated presidency was rife with political mistakes and miscalculations from the very start. On his first day in office, all members of the Taylor cabinet submitted what they thought were pro forma resignations in keeping with the usual custom in a sudden change in administrations. To their surprise and in some cases anger, Fillmore accepted the lot of them, all loyal Whigs, leaving himself devoid of experience in key departments, even though he himself had little of it. He added insult to injury by asking them to stay on for a while until he could find suitable replacements, and they all declined. So little had Fillmore contemplated the possibility of his ascension that it took him months to assemble his own cabinet, with a number of men invited to service also begging off. Fillmore's one obvious selection was his mentor, Daniel Webster, to be his secretary of state and closest adviser.

But Fillmore had no grip on the Whig Party, whose leadership he had just inherited, giving the aging and tired Clay another opportunity to assert himself, though apparently without the energy to make an effective attempt. In the worked-over Clay compromise on the extension of slavery into the western territory, the South got the bulk of what it wanted, with Fillmore focusing on enforcing the Fugitive Slave Act, which was part of the extension package. Fillmore defended the seizure of fugitive slaves in the North and payments to captors under the law, which eventually left a stain on the Fillmore legacy.

As early as 1851 the latest "accidental president" declared that he would not seek a presidential term in his own right, though he advocated another try by the increasingly frail Webster. Fillmore finally agreed to oppose the Whig nomination of General Winfield Scott, the preferred candidate of his old New York rival, Seward. Again Fillmore counted heavily on his courtship of the South to sustain him. At the Whig convention in Baltimore in June 1852, the forces of Fillmore and Scott labored on a relatively even scale through more than forty ballots until on the forty-third Scott was nominated.

Out of office at last, Fillmore ran again in 1856 as the nominee of the

American Party, more popularly known as the Know-Nothings, winning 44 percent in the slave states but only eight electoral votes. During the Civil War, he organized a volunteer home guard of elderly men in Buffalo and helped raise money for wounded soldier relief, and not surprisingly he opposed the emancipation of American blacks and their enlistment in the Union army. He died in Buffalo in 1874 at age seventy-four. His presidential tenure was little recommendation for the elevation of the vice president to the highest office.

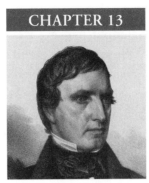

CHAPTER 13

WILLIAM R. KING
OF ALABAMA

A man who arguably may have been the most qualified vice president to carry out the office's sole active constitutional responsibility, as president of the Senate, never had the opportunity to do so. Senator William R. King of Alabama, elected as the running mate of Senator Franklin Pierce of New Hampshire in 1852, had been sworn into the vice presidency for only twenty-five days when a severe case of tuberculosis took his life on April 18, 1853.

For many years in the Senate, King had been regularly chosen by his colleagues as temporary Senate president pro tem, to occupy the chair in the very frequent absences of the vice president of either party. In his nearly twenty-nine years in the Senate, his peers had elected him eleven times to function as the stand-in, presiding over some of the most tumultuous debates in Senate history. His selection was a tribute to his customary calm and even-handed manners. Nevertheless, the few mentions of King in later history books mostly record his challenge to the famous Whig leader Henry Clay to a duel, after a sharp exchange of words on the Senate floor in 1841. The notoriously proud Clay finally backed down and apologized.

Whether King's tenure would follow the precedent of denying the vice president a voice in the decision making in the administration to which he was elected, let alone other significant functions, never came to be tested. Shortly after his election with Pierce, King's worsening illness forced him to resign his Senate seat prematurely and find a warmer climate in hope of a quick recovery.

On January 17, 1853, he sailed to Havana, Cuba, but soon realized he would be physically unable to return to Washington for the prescribed March 4 inauguration. He won approval of Congress to be sworn in as vice president abroad and on March 24 took the oath in the seaport town of Matanzas, sixty miles east of Havana. Gamely trying to return, he sailed to Mobile, Alabama, reached his plantation eleven trying days later, and died the next day at age sixty-seven. Again the vice presidency was left vacant, this time for nearly the next four years.

King's long-established demeanor of fairness and collegiality in the Senate, rather than his views on the major issues of the day, was what had brought him to the brink of national power. At a time of increasing regional conflict over slavery and other threats to the preservation of the Union, King became a voice of mediation and conciliation, even as a Jacksonian Democrat he clashed with Clay and other advocates of the American System.

Born in North Carolina on April 7, 1786, William Rufus Devane King was the son of a wealthy planter and jurist who had fought in the Revolutionary War. The father, a slave owner, had been a delegate to the North Carolina convention to ratify the Constitution and later served in the state assembly. As a young man, William attended local academies and the University of North Carolina through his junior year. After continuing legal training under a leading lawyer in the state, he was admitted to the bar in 1805. Five years later, a few months short of the required age of twenty-five, King was elected to the U.S. House of Representatives from Wilmington, where he joined the band of young "war hawks" with Calhoun behind Clay, pushing hard for military confrontation with Great Britain in what became the War of 1812.

In 1816, King resigned from the House to become secretary to William Pinkney, appointed U.S. minister to Russia. He served a year in St. Petersburg before moving to the Alabama Territory, where he later organized a land company. He founded the town of Selma, which nearly two centuries later became a milestone in the fight for the civil rights of black Americans as the site of a major racial clash. In 1819, King was a delegate to the constitutional convention that brought statehood to Alabama and subsequently became one of its first United States senators. In 1825, when the House chose John Quincy Adams over Andrew Jackson in their rancorous contest for the presidency, King helped deliver the state's electoral votes for Jackson. Meanwhile, he continued his Senate association with Calhoun, whose clash with Jackson brought the issue of state nullification of federal law to the political forefront of the era.

King disagreed, however, with Calhoun's argument that the 1828 Tariff of Abominations, providing for high protective tariffs for northern industry, warranted the South's right to disregard it. Of nullification, King declared, "I view it as neither peaceful nor constitutional, but clearly revolutionary in its character, and if persevered, it must, in the nature of things, result in the severance of the Union. . . . From such a calamity," he said, "may God in his mercy deliver us."[1] As for Calhoun, King said he was "a dead cock in the pit," predicting, "The father of nullification under no circumstances can ever receive the support of the Southern States."[2]

This and other issues brought King increasingly into conflict with Clay. However, always striving to conciliate on matters of regional disagreement, he subsequently supported Clay's compromise tariff, which chagrined Jackson as well as southern foes of protectionism. But once again in opposition to Clay, King resisted Clay's efforts to recharter the national bank and became entangled in Jackson's order to remove federal funds from it, which led to a Senate censure of the president. When King and Thomas Hart Benton of Missouri, another Jackson supporter, fought to have the censure expunged, King, as an expert on Senate rules, stoutly defended the president. Of Clay's effort to force Jackson to produce a pertinent document, King declared, "The Senate was in no danger; it had never been so strong or so saucy as it was at the present moment."[3]

It was from the context of this ill feeling that King's challenge to Clay to a duel emerged in 1841. The Whigs behind Clay had won control of the Senate for the first time, and he clashed with Democrats over the Senate's printing of the contract held by Francis P. Blair, editor of the *Washington Globe,* a Democratic organ. At last holding a majority in the chamber, the irascible Clay was moved to greater heights of temper than ever. When Senator Albert Cuthbert of Georgia had the temerity to break in on one of Clay's harangues, the Kentuckian told him, "I will not, I cannot, be interrupted. I will not permit an interruption. The practice is much too common . . . and I trust it will not be continued here." As Cuthbert started to offer a reply,

Clay irately asked if "the senator applies to me? If he does, I will call him to order." Cuthbert replied that when Clay showed "proper courtesies towards his opponents," he could expect courtesy from Cuthbert "and not till then."[4]

Another Democrat wrote of the Kentuckian: "Clay's insolence is insufferable, and it will not be borne. Never have I seen power so tyrannically used as the new Senate are now using it, and every federal [Whig] senator bows servilely to the arrogant dictation of Clay."[5]

Concerning the *Globe* and Blair, Clay said he believed it "to be an infamous paper, and its chief editor an infamous man." When King in his moderate way replied that Blair's character would "compare gloriously" with Clay's own, Clay rose and shot back, "That is false, it is a slanderous base and cowardly declaration and the senator knows it to be so!" King in his mild manner responded simply and tersely to the chair, "Mr. President, I have no reply to make—none whatever. But Mr. Clay deserves a response."[6]

In the code of the day, the meaning was clear. King sat down and scribbled on a piece of paper his challenge to a duel. Then he left the chamber, handing the paper to Lewis Linn of Missouri, who gave it to Clay. The die was cast. Each side appointed a second for the affair, and as the law then required, the Senate sergeant-at-arms arrested the two senators. Clay now thought better of his rashness and posted a bond of five thousand dollars specifying he would take no hostile action against King. The placid Alabamian insisted on "an unequivocal apology" from Clay, who gave it with the acknowledgment that it would have been wiser to keep his views on Blair to himself. King then apologized in turn, after which Clay walked over to King's desk and, perhaps in his manner of showing goodwill, asked King for a pinch of his snuff.[7] They shook hands as applause broke out in the fascinated gallery.

King's own courtesy and benign manner was not lost on Jacksonian Democratic leaders. They well remembered with embarrassment their previous vice president from Kentucky, Richard Johnson, whose personal marital history and unkempt visage often reflected poorly on the party. King was the opposite. When the 1840 campaign neared, he came quickly to mind as a vice presidential nominee from the South to replace Johnson as President Van Buren's running mate. After all, King had often filled in for the truant Johnson as the Senate president pro tem. Johnson, however, stayed on the Democratic ticket with Van Buren, and King's fans looked ahead to the 1844 campaign.

In Washington, King was a close friend and roommate of James Buchanan of Pennsylvania, a presidential hopeful, and they often discussed their mutual national ambitions. Some Alabamians had been mentioning King also as a possible presidential candidate, but he told Buchanan that in return for Buchanan's support for the Democratic vice presidential nomination King would not compete with him. Calhoun, also seeking the presidency, pointed out to King that only one southerner could be on the ticket. With Polk of Tennessee the presidential nominee, a northerner, Dallas of Pennsylvania, got the vice presidential nod.

In 1844, when Van Buren scuttled his own chances for reelection by declaring his opposition to the annexation of Texas, King wanted the Democratic presidential nomination to go to Buchanan, hoping his friend would advocate him as his southern, ticket-balancing running mate; instead Lewis Cass was nominated. Meanwhile President Tyler, who was tired of having his appointments rejected by the Senate, turned to one of its most popular members and nominated King to be his minister to France.

King had a successful tenure in Paris, being instrumental in neutralizing French objections to the U.S. annexation of Texas. But his heart remained in the Senate, and he wrote Buchanan, who was now secretary of state: "Most sincerely do I wish that we had both remained in the Senate."[8] Accordingly, he decided to seek his old seat in the next election through the Alabama State Legislature. But running as a Union supporter against the incumbent Dixon Lewis, who was a states' rights defender, King suffered the only election defeat in his career. Seven months later, however, President Polk named the other Alabama senator, Arthur Bagby, minister to Russia, and Alabama's governor appointed King to fill the vacancy. Later in 1848, King ran for and won a full term, beating the Whig leader Arthur Hopkins.

Meanwhile, King had continued to keep his eye on the vice presidency, whose function as presiding officer of the Senate often fell his way. At the Democratic National Convention of 1848, his name was among those offered for the second office, but the nomination to be Lewis Cass's running mate went to General William O. Butler of Kentucky, another veteran of the War of 1812 and the Mexican War. The electoral appeal of military leaders continued to hold sway.

That outcome left King in a front seat in the Senate during a most contentious time. At this point, his feelings about remaining in the Senate seem to have changed. He wrote to Buchanan: "A seat in the Senate is, I assure you far from being desirable to me; bringing with it as it does at this particular time especially, great responsibility, great labor, and no little anxiety."[9] The bitter argument over the expansion of slavery into the western territories reached its height with Clay's proposal of the Compromise of 1850, whose amendment was the subject of heated and extended controversy. King, as was his custom, urged that northern and southern colleagues find middle ground.

While King agreed with Clay's general quest for compromise, he opposed the direct admission of California to statehood, preferring that it first retain territorial status for a time during this troubled period. Congress, he insisted, had "about as much constitutional power to prohibit slavery from going into the Territories of the United States as [it had] power to pass an act carrying slavery there." But while he said the abolition of slavery in the District of Columbia would unfairly impede the interest of slave owners in neighboring Virginia, he believed the trading of slaves there ought to be prohibited.[10]

As modifications to Clay's compromise were being considered, King joined a majority view of the select Senate Committee of Thirteen: that state legislatures had a right to take action on slavery in their jurisdictions, but territorial legislatures did not until they became states. Many southerners were critical of the Alabamian while others applauded his conciliatory efforts. At the same time, he warned northern abolitionists that if they sought to undercut the South's legitimate rights, its sons would "hurl defiance at the fanatical crew, and unitedly determine to defend their rights at every hazard and every sacrifice."[11]

When the sudden death of President Zachary Taylor in July 1850 raised Vice President Millard Fillmore to the Oval Office, King was unanimously chosen as the Senate president pro tem to assume the presiding duties for the remainder of Fillmore's unexpired term, another tribute to his fair-mindedness.

In 1852, the Alabama Democratic convention, in endorsing the amended Compromise of 1850, also directed the state's delegates to the national party convention to back King for either the presidential or vice presidential nomination. A marathon forty-nine-ballot contest for the first office ensued. Those initially involved—Lewis Cass, James Buchanan, William Marcy of New York, and Stephen A. Douglas of Illinois—were all set aside in favor of Franklin Pierce, another Mexican War general. As a consolation prize to the defeated Buchanan, the Pierce camp permitted him to select the vice presidential nominee, and he put forward his friend King, easily selected on the second ballot. At last King had within his grasp the office whose main duties he had so often performed as Senate president pro tem in the absence of elected vice presidents.

The Pierce-King ticket easily prevailed over the weak Whig entry of Winfield Scott and William A. Graham of North Carolina. But King's deteriorating physical condition from tuberculosis limited his participation. Despite resigning his Senate several weeks after the selection in order to repair to the tropical climes of Cuba in the hope of a recuperation, one never occurred.

Upon King's death, Pierce, who had paid little notice to him in his brief tenure as vice president, respectfully observed that his illness "was watched by the nation with painful solicitation" and "his loss to the country, under all circumstances, [was] justly regarded as irreparable."[12] But Pierce had given no evidence of consulting with or involving his vice president in the formation of his administration. It was considered likely in any event that, had King lived, he would have remained primarily occupied as president over the Senate. It was a task for which he was eminently well-suited, and he had fulfilled it with great bipartisan approval during all his years in Washington. But the vice presidency itself warranted greater employment, not yet granted by any president under whom King had served.

CHAPTER 14

JOHN C. BRECKINRIDGE
OF KENTUCKY

The man elected to the vice presidency as running mate to James Buchanan in 1856 was destined to become one of the most divisive and controversial figures in the Civil War, soon to follow. The thirty-six-year-old John Cabell Breckinridge, the youngest vice president ever to serve, was another veteran of the Mexican War, having spent six months as a volunteer infantry officer. Becoming a member of the Kentucky legislature at age twenty-eight, he had started in politics as a Jacksonian Democrat, but as a strong supporter of slavery he took a course that ultimately found him fighting against the Union he had vowed to defend.

The namesake of his grandfather and father, the third John C. was born on January 16, 1821, into a prominent political family. His grandfather was an Anti-Federalist ally of Jefferson who had served in the Senate and as Jefferson's attorney general. The youngest John C. earned a bachelor's degree at Centre College, in Danville, Kentucky, and studied law at Princeton and at Transylvania, in Lexington. Winning a seat in Congress soon after passage of the Compromise of 1850, involving slavery's expansion into the western territories, Breckinridge became an outspoken voice for southern Democrats arguing that the federal government could not bar the peculiar institution anywhere in the territories.[1]

Despite his views on slavery, Breckinridge was a defender of the Union, a position that cast him as a moderate in many southern eyes. During his time in the Kentucky legislature he supported the Kentucky Colonization Society, which as a branch of a national organization advocated the resettlement of black slaves abroad. It was a view shared by Abraham Lincoln for a time. Breckinridge was not a cotton planter or a major slaveholder, but he did own some household servants and comfortably embraced the exploitation of slaves that was at the heart of southern society.

When in 1854 the Missouri Compromise was repealed by the Kansas-Nebraska Act on the basis of the concept of popular sovereignty, individual territories were left to decide whether they would accept or outlaw slavery. Settlers in the territories, Breckinridge argued, should be "free to form their own institutions, and enter the Union with or without slavery, as their constitutions should prescribe."[2]

The clash over the Kansas-Nebraska Act further ignited northern animosity toward slavery and its southern proponents, feeding the disintegration of the Whig Party. Its remnants gave rise to the new Republican Party, as well as the anti-immigrant, anti-Catholic American Party, which came to be known as the Know-Nothings. The spread of the latter helped persuade Breckinridge that his reelection to the Senate as a Democrat was so imperiled that he did not seek a third term. Still in his mid-thirties, he returned to Kentucky and focused on land speculation in the western territories to restore his financial health.

Breckinridge's loyalty to the Union while clinging to the peculiar institution made him an attractive prospect for the Democratic vice presidential nomination in 1856. Seeking reelection, President Franklin Pierce, soiled politically in the Kansas-Nebraska row, was challenged by Douglas and Buchanan. The latter, most recently minister to Great Britain, was thereby out of the line of fire in the heated dispute over Kansas and Nebraska. Douglas fell behind in the voting and withdrew in the cause of unity, making Buchanan the nominee as a less divisive figure in the slavery conversation.

As nominations for vice president began, the Kentucky delegation appeared to be throwing a monkey wrench into the prospects of native son Breckinridge by nominating a fellow Kentuckian, the former House Speaker Linn Boyd. Breckinridge rose and said he would not run against him, making a speech that so captured the convention that the delegates insisted on him, and he was nominated on the second ballot.

The Buchanan-Breckinridge ticket faced a new lineup in the fall. With the Whig Party in shreds, many of its leaders, including William Seward, threw in with the new national alignment calling itself the Republican Party, which convened in Philadelphia in June 1856. There it wrote a strong free-soil, anti-slavery expansion platform without condemning the practice where it already existed, and it nominated John Charles Fremont, a soldier and explorer, for the presidency. Meanwhile the Know-Nothings, another refuge for the fallen-away Whigs, having gained support in the latest state and congressional elections, nominated former president Fillmore.

While Buchanan dodged the slavery controversy as best he could, Breckinridge pitched for southern votes as a staunch defender of the right of (white) citizens in the territories to write their own laws. On a speaking tour through Ohio, Indiana, Michigan, and Pennsylvania, he accused the Republican Party of threatening the existence of the Union, declaring, "He must be blind indeed, and given over to fatal delusion, who does not see that the Union of the States is in imminent peril." He charged northern Whigs with "hurling every epithet of hate and ignominy against their brethren of the South," fostering "sectional hostility . . . fed by misrepresentations of the opinions and feelings of the Southern people." He warned that the Republican Party's ulterior purpose regarding slavery was "to combine public opinion and public action in such a form as to abolish the institution wherever it exists."[3]

In November the Democrats behind Buchanan and Breckinridge carried all of the slaveholding states except Maryland, which voted for the Know-Nothings, and won Kentucky for the first time in a presidential election, to Breckinridge's gratification.[4] But he soon realized that he was to suffer the same fate of isolation in the new administration that had fallen to most of his predecessors.

On one early occasion, when Breckinridge sought an interview with Buchanan, he was referred to the president's niece and hostess, Harriet Lane, Buchanan being a bachelor. Insulted at the rude dismissal, Breckinridge left town without contacting her. When word of the apparent rebuff reached Buchanan, he had three of his aides write his vice president pleading a misunderstanding. Breckinridge was told that the instruction to contact Miss Lane was some kind of password to gain admission to the presidential presence. Still, Breckinridge never met with Buchanan privately over the next three years.

Breckinridge's pro-slavery views found him in the middle of intensifying hostility between Buchanan and Stephen Douglas over Kansas, where rival groups split on slavery. Breckinridge sided with the president on admitting Kansas to the Union as a slave state but quietly favored Douglas's reelection to the Senate, which Buchanan fiercely opposed. Invited by the Illinois Democratic Committee to speak in behalf of Douglas during his famous debates with Lincoln, Breckinridge politely declined. But he added he had "often in conversation expressed the wish that Mr. Douglas may succeed over his Republican competitor."[5]

As president of the Senate, Breckinridge was in the chair on January 4, 1859, when the body met for the last time in its small chamber before moving to the new, larger Senate. Despite his stout defense of slavery, he remained at this time opposed to secession over it. He liked to tell of a dinner party conversation with a South Carolina congressman about meeting a state militiaman in South Carolina who said of the possibility of war over secession, "I tell you, sah, we cannot stand it any longer. We intend to fight." Breckinridge said he asked, "And from what are you suffering?" The man replied, "Why, sah, we are suffering from the oppression of the Federal Government. We have suffered under it for thirty years, and will stand it no more." Breckinridge suggested to his host that he invite some of his constituents to visit the North "if only for the purpose of teaching them what an almighty big country they will have to whip before they get through!"[6]

With the Buchanan administration in disarray and Breckinridge's own prospects diminishing for a second term, another opportunity suddenly arose when Senator Linn Boyd of Kentucky died. Kentucky Democrats thereupon nominated Breckinridge for the Senate seat upon completion of his vice presidency, a welcome prospect to salve his uncertainty. Meanwhile, the presidential election year of 1860 approached with the controversy over slavery and its boiling point growing ever closer.

In February 1860, Senator Jefferson Davis of Mississippi introduced a series of resolutions laying out the demands of the most extreme southern senators. They called for a national slave code protecting the peculiar institution in the territories, reaffirming personal liberty laws on slave ownership, and declaring attacks on it unconstitutional. Davis offered them on the floor but sought adoption only in the Senate Democratic caucus, to undermine Douglas and his advocacy of popular sovereignty in advance of the Democratic National Convention in Charleston in April.

There, Davis submitted his resolutions as a campaign plank endorsed by a majority of the platform committee, obliging the Douglas forces to fight for a rival minority report. One Ohio delegate warned the southerners, "You cannot expect one northern electoral vote, or one sympathizing member of Congress from the free states," both of which were needed to put another Democrat in the White House.[7] After several days of heated debate, a compromise was struck but was boycotted by the Deep South delegates, who walked out. An effort by the remaining delegates to nominate Douglas was defeated, and they decided to adjourn and meet again in June.

In the meantime, the Republicans convened in Chicago, where Lincoln, arguing that slavery had to be contained and that Congress had a right to exclude slavery from the territories, was the surprise choice over William Seward of New York. Hannibal Hamlin of Maine was picked as Lincoln's running mate. Also in June, border-state and other remnants of the shattered Whigs met in Baltimore as the Constitutional Union Party and, hoping to head off secession, nominated John Bell of Tennessee for president and Edward Everett of Massachusetts for vice president.

In Baltimore as well, the mostly northern Democratic delegates reconvened in June and nominated Douglas, adhering to his support of popular sovereignty on slavery expansion, with Senator Herschel V. Johnson of Georgia as his running mate. The southern Democrats met separately in Baltimore and nominated Breckinridge for president and Joseph Lane as his running mate, an Oregon Democrat who was originally from Kentucky and shared southern sentiments. The divisions set up an unprecedented four-way general election for the Oval Office in November, with the fate of slavery at stake.

Breckinridge considered long about accepting the nomination of a splintered segment of his party, with fewer than half the Kentucky delegates to the original Democratic convention in Baltimore attending the subsequent gathering of the southerners. "When I discovered, though with regret, that my name had been presented to the country," he said later, "it did not take me long to determine that I would not meanly abandon those with whom I was determined to act." Long afterward, Jefferson Davis's wife wrote that Breckinridge had told her on accepting the nomination, "I trust that I have the courage to lead a forlorn hope."[8]

The southern Democratic nominee vowed to campaign little before the November election, but charges from Douglas and other foes against his loyalty and consistency persuaded him to answer them. At a large barbecue in Kentucky, he delivered a three-hour defense, denying that he had ever petitioned for the pardon of abolitionist John Brown, or that he had supported the Whig Zachary Taylor against the Democrat Lewis Cass in 1848, or that he had once backed the emancipation of blacks in Kentucky or favored the admissibility of a territory to bar slavery. The last stance put him in conflict with Douglas, who charged that the southern Democrats were out to break up the Union. Breckinridge insisted he had never made "an utterance to reveal a thought of mine hostile to the Constitution and union of the States." Douglas responded that while he was not saying "all the Breckinridge men" were "disunionists," there was "not a disunionist in America who [was] not a Breckinridge man."[9]

The Kentuckian, fearing that the Democratic split would put the Republican Party in power for the first time, initially considered bowing out but was persuaded by Jefferson Davis to stay in the race. As the prospect of a Lincoln victory loomed larger, Davis next proposed that all three Democrats—Douglas, Breckinridge, and Bell—withdraw and back a compromise candidate. Breckinridge and Bell agreed, but Douglas refused, arguing that northern Democrats would never support the choice endorsed by the southern Democrats and would take their chances with Lincoln.

He was right. Lincoln won only 40 percent of the popular vote but the majority required in the electoral college, where Breckinridge finished second, all his electoral votes coming from the South. After the election Breckinridge returned to the Senate to finish out his service as presiding officer. In December, four southern states—South Carolina, Alabama, Mississippi, and Florida—took the fateful step out of the Union, and in January he watched as his friend Davis led a group of other southern senators as part of the exodus. In March, one of Breckinridge's last duties in the second office was to swear in Hamlin as his successor, who then gave the Senate oath to the Kentuckian, who had been sent back by his state to his old seat.

In the early morning of April 12, South Carolina Guard troops fired on

Fort Sumter, and the Civil War was on. On July 4, Lincoln called a special session of Congress to pass legislation raising more soldiers and money for the conduct of the war. Breckinridge returned to Washington to lead remaining Senate Democrats in what was for him indeed a forlorn exercise, trying to limit the powers of the federal government as he perceived the Constitution to do. He called on the Senate to urge Lincoln to withdraw all federal troops from the seceded states and warned that the border states would join with the Deep South states if federal force was used against them.

As for his own Kentucky, he said, "She will exhaust all honorable means to reunite these States [into the Union], but if that fails . . . turning to her southern sisters, with whom she is identified by geographic position and by the ties of friendship, of intercourse, of commerce, and of common wrongs, she will unite with them to found a noble Republic, and invite beneath its stainless banner such other states as know how . . . to respect constitutional obligations and the comity of a confederacy."[10]

As the special session continued on August 1, Breckinridge spoke on the Senate floor against Lincoln's order to expand martial law. The Oregon Republican senator Edward D. Baker entered the chamber wearing a Union blue uniform and took issue with him. "These speeches of his, soon broadcast over the land, what meaning have they?" he asked. "Are they not intended for disorganization in our very midst? Sir, are they not words of brilliant, polished treason, even in the very Capitol?"[11]

Asked by Baker what he would do about the dire situation, Breckinridge said he would "have us stop the war," adding, "I would prefer to see these States all reunited upon true constitutional principles to any other object that could be offered me in life. . . . But I definitely prefer to see a peaceful restoration of these States, than to see endless, devastating war, at the end of which I see the grave of public liberty and of personal freedom."[12] Soon after, Colonel Baker was killed leading his militia in the Battle of Ball's Bluff, along the banks of the Potomac. Breckinridge returned to Kentucky after the special session, speaking for peace and saying if Kentucky went to war against the Confederacy he could no longer represent the state in the Senate. Pro-Union forces subsequently won the state legislative elections, and on September 21, the legislature sent troops to break up another large peace rally and arrest Breckinridge. But he fled to Virginia, where he joined the Confederate army in Richmond, observing that he was proudly exchanging his "term of six years in the Senate of the United States for the musket of a soldier."[13] On December 4 the Senate expelled him by a vote of thirty-six to zero, declaring him a traitor who had "joined the enemies of the country."[14]

Commissioned a brigadier general and later a major general, Breckinridge fought in the major western battles of Shiloh, Stone's River, Chickamauga, and Chattanooga and then in the southeastern slaughter at Cold Harbor, before leading a raid on Washington in July 1864. His troops got as close as Silver Spring, Maryland, on the northeast outskirts, and they sacked the home of Francis Blair, where Breckinridge had often dined as a friend. Before they could enter the capital city, however, Union troops forced them to retreat west to Winchester, Virginia, in the Shenandoah Valley, where they were defeated by General Philip H. Sheridan.

Near the end of the war, Confederate president Davis appointed Breckinridge his secretary of war. When General Robert E. Lee finally surrendered at Appomattox and Davis wanted to keep fighting, Breckinridge told him, "This has been a magnificent epic; in God's name let it not terminate in farce."[15] Davis, fleeing Richmond with his cabinet, was captured, but Breckinridge got away to Florida, then Cuba and England, and eventually settled with his family in Toronto.[16]

On Christmas Day 1868, President Andrew Johnson issued a blanket pardon to all Confederate soldiers, and Breckinridge soon after returned to Kentucky, where he resumed the practice of law and began building railroads. At only age fifty-four, his health rapidly declined, and he died on May 17, 1875. Having gone to the brink of the American presidency, both as vice president and as a presidential candidate, he left the American scene with a checkered record: beloved in the South, castigated in the North, but still wed to the idea of national union.

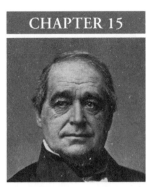

CHAPTER 15

HANNIBAL HAMLIN

OF MAINE

A s the United States struggled through the last painful throes of the Civil War, Vice President Hannibal Hamlin, a strong advocate for an end to slavery, was frustrated by his limited role in trying to achieve that goal and, indeed, in any aspect of Abraham Lincoln's efforts to save the American Union. Despite early promises from Lincoln to involve him, the president essentially followed the traditional course of shunting his standby aside.

As Lincoln's reelection campaign of 1864 approached, Hamlin hoped his engagement would broaden, anticipating a second vice presidential term. But Lincoln's political calculations determined otherwise, and it was Hamlin's fate to be dropped from the Republican ticket as the war neared a conclusion. Less than six weeks after leaving the vice presidency, upon the assassination of Lincoln, Hamlin saw his replacement become president and commander in chief of the Union armies. One can only surmise, had the man from Maine still been in the second office on that fateful night, how postwar America would have emerged and what Hamlin's place in history would have been.

Hamlin, the grandson of an officer in General George Washington's army in 1775 and the son of the practicing physician Cyrus Hamlin, sheriff of Oxford County, Maine, was exposed at an early age to books of biography, history, and politics that helped prepared him for public responsibility.

Although his forebears in New England were Federalists and later Whigs, young Hannibal, named after an uncle as well as for the great Carthaginian general, soon became a Jacksonian Democrat.[1]

After early public schooling, the boy was enrolled at Hebron Academy, in Maine. His father's sudden death of pneumonia ended Hannibal's hopes of college. In 1830, he and a friend bought the local weekly newspaper, the *Oxford Jeffersonian,* where he picked up printing skills while giving the paper a faithful Jeffersonian editorial line. Eventually he moved to Portland to read law at a prestigious firm and, after admission to the bar, won his first case against a prominent local judge, subsequently marrying the judge's daughter. In 1835, he was elected to the Maine House of Representatives and became an advocate for ending the death penalty in the state and for the eventual emancipation of black slaves, while not embracing the militancy of the abolitionist movement.

Young Hamlin was a tall and strapping fellow after years of farmwork and had a notably swarthy complexion, which later fanned reports that he was a mulatto. In one debate, an older, red-faced legislator made an insensitive remark about his complexion, to which Hamlin replied, "If the gentleman chooses to find fault with me on account of my complexion, what has he to say about himself? I take my complexion from nature; he gets his from the brandy bottle. Which is more honorable?" The older man apologized, and Hamlin thereafter was nicknamed the "Carthaginian of Maine."[2] In 1837, he was elected Speaker of the House in the Maine legislature, lost the position after the panic of that year, but regained it the next year. In 1843 he was elected to the U.S. Congress, where he encountered another racial jibe when referred to as "that black Penobscot Indian."[3]

When a gag rule barring anti-slavery petitions was debated in the House, Hamlin argued forcefully for accepting them all and letting the House decide to adopt them or not: "Let this committee report to us what are the duties we owe—not to the South, but to the Union, the whole Union, and nothing but the Union."[4]

On the annexation of Texas, he said he favored it as an expansion of the Union, not for the purpose of extending slavery, and he argued for notifying the British that the United States intended to terminate the joint occupation of the Oregon Territory. North and South should join, he urged, "to plant our stars and stripes, and they should float over Texas forever, and march on until they should wave on the shores of the Pacific in the distant Oregon."[5]

In the House, Hamlin was instrumental in shaping the Wilmot Proviso, which would bar slavery in any territory taken from Mexico in the recent war, to the ire of President Polk. The proviso was twice rejected in the Senate, but Hamlin's hand in it underscored his anti-slavery view. The slavery fight went on, with Polk advocating extension ever westward of the Missouri Compromise of 1820, whose line separated free and slave territory obtained in the Louisiana Purchase, casting it as protection of free white labor. But anti-slavery forces saw it a vehicle for keeping black slaves out.

During his second term in the House, Hamlin decided to run for the Senate. After a narrow defeat by a legislative vote on his first try, the death of an incumbent opened a seat, and he won it in 1848 with the support of Free Soil members in a clear anti-slavery test. Hamlin agreed with their anti-slavery position but remained a loyal Democrat.

In the Senate, Hamlin became disturbed by the unruliness and intemperance he often encountered there. He argued often with Senator Jefferson Davis over slavery issues, to the point that Hamlin for a time carried a handgun. He was present in 1848 when Senator Henry Foote of Mississippi drew a pistol on Senator Thomas Hart Benton of Missouri in their row over slavery. Himself not much of a drinker, Hamlin talked of the heavy tippling in the Senate cloakroom and even on the floor.[6] He wrote to one friend, "Brawling billingsgate seems to assume the place of wisdom in an American statesman, backed up by the weapons of the highwayman and the assassain [sic]." He lamented that the Senate had "turned into an arena for political blackguards."[7]

For all that, Hamlin flourished in the Senate, and from the outset he left no doubt of his strong view that, both morally and constitutionally, slavery was wrong. In his maiden speech, he said he was amazed that "in this model Republic—with the sun of liberty shining upon us—we have been gravely discussing the proposition whether we will not create by law the institution of human slavery in territories now free."[8]

With Polk's departure from the White House and the inauguration of the Whig Zachary Taylor, Hamlin found himself with an anti-slavery ally in the Oval Office. For openers, the new president was strong for the swift admission of California as a free state. Californians had already drafted a constitution and applied for entry into the Union, and Taylor urged the territories of New Mexico and Utah to do the same. Also, at the end of January 1850, the old Whig conciliator Henry Clay offered a series of resolutions that included California statehood and constituted the Compromise of 1850. Hamlin readily agreed that the state should be admitted but had reservations about some of the other Clay resolutions. After months of debate and negotiation, California was admitted as a free state, the territories of New Mexico and Utah were left without restriction on slavery, and the Oregon Territory, where slavery was not an issue, was left free.

But the slavery issue continued to confound Hamlin. In January 1854, when Stephen Douglas proposed that popular sovereignty be applied to the so-called Indian Territory west of Missouri, splitting it into the two states of Kansas and Nebraska, an irate Hamlin asked: Should the 1820 Missouri Compromise be repealed "and let Kansas be made a slave country? Where will this spirit end? Shall we repeal freedom and make slavery? It comes to that."[9] He voted against the Kansas-Nebraska Bill, one of four Democrats to stand up to their party, but it passed easily. A result was agitation for a new anti-slavery party that could drive the last stake into the heart of the Whigs, a lure for many defecting Democrats.

In June 1854, a group calling itself the Independent Democrats of Maine nominated and elected Anson P. Morrill for governor, after which they began to call themselves Republicans. The next spring, Morrill wrote Hamlin and urged him to join, reporting, "They are looking to you for direction and advice more than to any one man at this time. You have a host of good friends in our Republican party, & so far as I know, no enemies. . . . Has the time not come when you can act openly with us?"[10]

But Hamlin was not one to make such a decision precipitously. He continued to support the Democratic Party on most issues unrelated to slavery, in order to hold on to his influential Senate committee chairmanships. In 1855 when his wife, Sarah, became ill, he considered resigning from the Senate but was dissuaded by political friends. After she passed away the next year, he married Sarah's younger half-sister, with whom he would have three more children.

Politically as well as personally, 1856 was a pivotal year in Hamlin's life. On June 12, he rose in the Senate and resigned as the chairman of a key committee, explaining, "I love my country more than I love my party," and he could not accept the calamity of "Bleeding Kansas" upon the introduction of slavery there.[11] But principle might not have been the whole story. His prospects for renomination were far from certain.

Maine Republicans moved swiftly to bring Hamlin into their fold. They proposed that he run for the governorship as a Republican, assuring him he would win. But Hamlin had no interest in leaving the U.S. Senate to be governor. A scheme was hatched in which the Republican legislature, by prearrangement, would vote him back into the Senate after his election as governor. An old friend told him, "This is the only way in which we can keep you there, for if you refuse what is so universally desired, it will be said you are not with us, and thus you will be defeated."[12] In the end, Hamlin agreed to run for the governorship as a Republican.

Hamlin won a sweeping victory and became somewhat of a national celebrity. In keeping with the strange agreement, Hamlin was inaugurated as governor in Augusta, and five days later, the Republican state legislators, holding the majority, caucused and nominated him to be the next U.S. senator from Maine. He then resigned the governorship and returned to Washington to begin his third term in the Senate.

There, the slavery question continued to dominate. In 1858, as the Senate debated the admission of Kansas under a state constitution permitting slavery, the Democratic Party split wide open on sectional lines. Hamlin accurately wrote about his former party: "Most of the northern Dems affirm that they will not force upon the people of Kansas a Const. which establishes slavery. If they succeed in remanding the Const. for a vote on it, the South will bolt. If they succeed in forcing the Constitution on the people of Kansas, then the Dems feel that it will utterly destroy them in all the North."[13] In cold political terms, he concluded, it all boded well for his new Republican Party.

As the 1860 election approached, some Maine Republicans urged Hamlin to seek the Republican presidential nomination. But Hamlin favored Abraham Lincoln of Illinois. In mid-May, the convention met at the new Wigwam, in Chicago, and on the third ballot chose Lincoln over William Seward. In a gesture to the losing camp, the party agreed that Lincoln's running mate should come from the East. The Sewardites readily agreed, one of them noting that Hamlin was "a good friend of Mr. Seward," was "geographically distant from Lincoln and was once a Democrat. It was deemed judicious to pretend to patronize the Democratic element."[14]

Hamlin was shocked at the news. The next day he wrote to his wife, Ellen: "I neither expected or desired it. But it has been made and as a faithful man to the cause, it leaves me no alternative but to accept it." He said he took consolation that if the Lincoln-Hamlin ticket won, his duties would "not be hard or unpleasant."[15] In June, as already noted, the Democrats split badly, with Douglas, John C. Breckinridge, and John Bell chosen on separate tickets, to the obvious benefit of the Republican ticket.

In this national campaign in which race had become a central issue over the expansion of slavery into the West, the notably swarthy Hamlin again had to endure vicious rumors, especially in the South, that he was a black man. Robert Barnwell Rhett, the editor of the *Charleston Mercury* in South Carolina, charged at a Breckinridge rally in Charleston, "Hamlin is what we call a mulatto. . . . He has black blood in him." He said the "Black Republicans" had put "a renegade Sothernor *[sic]* on one side for President, for Lincoln is a native Kentuckian, and they put a man of colored blood on the other side of the ticket for Vice President of the United States."[16]

A campaigner for the Constitutional Union ticket in Tennessee, William G. Brownlow, observed that Hamlin looked, acted, and thought so much like a black man that if he dressed as a field hand he could be sold in the South.[17] Other similar allegations and slurs were heard across the Deep South. In November, the Lincoln-Hamlin ticket swept eighteen northern states and won the election with 180 electoral votes, compared with 72 for Breckinridge, 39 for Bell, and only 12 for Douglas, who was shut out in the South.

Soon after, Lincoln wrote Hamlin, "I am anxious for a personal interview with you as early a date as possible. Can you, without much inconvenience, meet me in Chicago?"[18] They met there and had a warm and convivial conversation that encouraged Hamlin to think he would be more than the traditional vice presidential standby.

At the end of several meetings, according to Hamlin, Lincoln told him, "I shall accept and shall always be willing to accept, in the very best spirit, any advice that you, the Vice-President, may give me."[19] Hamlin must have thought: so far so good. In fact, one of his cabinet recommendations,

Gideon Welles of Connecticut, ultimately was nominated as secretary of the navy.

Meanwhile, the election of Lincoln, seen in much of the South as an anti-slavery rebuke of the region, triggered the flight to secession. On December 20 the South Carolina legislature voted to leave the Union, followed in the next six weeks by Mississippi, Florida, Alabama, Georgia, Louisiana, and Texas. Delegates from each of these states met in Montgomery and on February 7 adopted a constitution for the new Confederate States of America, with Jefferson Davis as its president.

In Lincoln's inaugural address on March 4, he concluded by striking a sober but hopeful tone. "I am loath to close," he said. "We are not enemies but friends. We must not be enemies. The mystic chords of memory, stretching from every battlefield and patriot grave, to every living heart and hearthstone, all over this broad land, will yet swell the chorus of the Union, when again touched, as surely they will be, by the better angels of our nature."[20] But Vice President Hamlin began the chore of presiding over a special session of the Senate with a heavy heart. He told a Bangor friend, Colonel James Dunning, "There's going to be a war, and a terrible one, just as sure as the sun will shine tomorrow. Those Southerners mean [to] fight, and I know they do. We ought to lose no time in getting ready."[21]

Some thirty Deep South congressmen had already informed their constituents, "The argument is exhausted," and most of the bloc left Washington. Buchanan, after denying the right of South Carolina to secede but saying he didn't have the power to stop it, finally told Congress the Union was "a sacred trust," and he would continue to collect federal taxes in all the states and to protect federal property in them, which included Fort Sumter, in the Charleston Harbor.[22]

With the special congressional session over, Hamlin headed home and arrived in Bangor on April 4. Eight days later, after Lincoln had ordered more provisions to Fort Sumter, Confederate forces in South Carolina fired on Sumter under orders from President Davis, and the Civil War was on. Hamlin set out at once to do what he could to mobilize Maine volunteers for the war, then went to New York to continue the effort nationally. Hamlin, after his early involvements with Lincoln, could not have been faulted for assuming these would continue and even intensify with the advent of the terrible war that had now descended on the administration and the Union. But as time went on and he was not brought more significantly into the administration's deliberations and actions, his frustration grew. In 1862, he confided to a correspondent that had he known in Chicago how being vice president would be, he would rather have stayed in the Senate, adding, "But as it was there was no choice left me."[23]

The same summer, when the wife of General John Fremont asked for his help in getting her husband a new command, Hamlin forlornly replied, "What can I do? The slow and unsatisfactory movements of the Government do not meet with my approbation, and that is known, and of course I am not consulted at all, nor do I think there is much disposition in any quarter to regard my counsel I may give much if at all."[24]

Also, one day when a New York congressman, William A. Wheeler, dropped by Hamlin's office on the Senate side of the Capitol to invite him to lunch, he found the vice president snoozing behind his desk after a long and windy debate on the floor. Aroused by Wheeler, Hamlin told him, "I will take lunch with you on condition that you promise me you will never be vice president. I am only a fifth wheel of a coach and can do little for my friends."[25] (If Wheeler made such a promise, he broke it seventeen years later by occupying the second office in the Rutherford B. Hayes administration.)

Presiding over the Senate during the war had to be particularly frustrating for Hamlin, inasmuch as he could neither speak nor vote on the many critical issues brought before the Senate, including raising money for the maintenance of the Union troops and other wartime matters. His torpor was disturbed on January 27, 1863, however, during a debate on a bill to exempt Lincoln from damages involved in his suspension of habeas corpus, one of his most controversial actions of the war. A bitter administration critic, Senator Willard Saulsbury of Delaware, obviously drunk, struggled to his feet to declare sarcastically that the president should not be so fined. He said, after having seen and conversed with Lincoln, "I say here, in my place in the Senate of the United States, that I never did see or converse with so weak and so imbecile a man as Abraham Lincoln, President of the United States."[26]

Senator James Grimes of Iowa jumped to his feet, asking Hamlin whether such arch remarks were in order under Senate rules. Hamlin aroused himself and blithely replied, "The Chair was not listening to what the Senator from Delaware was saying and did not hear the words." Sauls-bury shot back, "That is the fault of the Chair." When Senator James Bayard of Delaware rose to complain that the president should be referred to only by title, not name, on the Senate floor, Saulsbury declared, "I do not intend to be deterred from the expression of my opinion by any black-guardism" from the floor. Hamlin declared Saulsbury out of order and told him to sit down, but the man continued his tirade against Lincoln, saying, "The voice of freedom is out of order in the councils of the nation!" Whereupon Hamlin ordered the Senate sergeant-at-arms to remove Saulsbury from the chamber. (Related to this episode or not, one of Hamlin's only initiatives as president of the Senate was to bar the sale of liquor in the Senate restaurant.)[27]

Through all this, a much more notable lament of Hamlin's was Lincoln's reluctance to use his war powers to arm the slaves to fight on the Union's side and free them thereafter. Hamlin reminisced much later about Lincoln: "He was slow to move, much slower than it seemed to us he should have been; much slower than I wanted him to be. . . . I urged him over and over again to act; but the time had not come, in his judgment."[28] Hamlin must have been surprised then when, according to one account, he called on Lincoln at the White House on June 18, 1862, at which time the president asked Hamlin to accompany him to Lincoln's residence at the Soldier's Home in Washington, where the president showed Hamlin his draft of the Emancipation Proclamation and asked him for suggestions. For all Hamlin's frustrations about not being in the loop on key wartime decisions, he had to have been warmed by this gesture.

Hamlin now urged Lincoln to take the next step and permit enlistment of black volunteers into the military. He told a Bangor rally, "We want to save, as much as possible, our men, [even] if it is done by men a little blacker than myself."[29] When his son Cyrus delivered ten white officers willing to lead black troops, Hamlin brought them to the White House, where Lincoln interviewed them and agreed. In October, Hamlin had an opportunity to discuss military matters with the president and took the occasion to press for more aggression on the part of General George McClellan, prior to Lincoln's decision to relieve McClellan as commander of the Army of the Potomac. But Hamlin remained unhappy with the progress of the war and in time learned to hold his tongue. He wrote to wife, Ellen,

"I suppose military men know best, and as my opinions are not asked at all, I keep my silence, as I have nothing to say. I have learned to give my opinion when asked for."[30]

In the meantime, he visited soldiers from Maine, including the wounded at military hospitals, and kept close track of his two sons in uniform. The vice president himself had enlisted as a private in the Maine Coast Guard, and when his unit was called to active duty in the summer of 1864 he turned down the exemption to which he was entitled and went along. But when he tried to gain a promotion for a Maine general, nothing came of it, in what was a diminution of his role in patronage for the state. As for Lincoln, he was growing weary of Hamlin's patronage pleadings. On one letter from his vice president, Lincoln scribbled, "The Vice-President says I promised to make this appointment, & I suppose I must make it."[31]

Lincoln's regard for Hamlin, considered more radical than the president, may have been reflected in a derogatory remark attributed to him. He was said to have asked whether "the Richmond people [at the Confederate capital] would like to have Hannibal Hamlin here any better than myself? In that one alternative I have an insurance on my life worth half the prairie land in Illinois."[32]

For all of Hamlin's professed yearnings to return to the Senate, as the 1864 national election approached he was willing to stand for reelection as vice president. There was no clear path for regaining entry to his old stamping ground, with Senator William Pitt Fessenden entrenched there and as leader of the Maine Republican Party as well. In January, the *Bangor Jeffersonian* called for Hamlin's renomination, and in March the Maine State Legislature passed a resolution backing another term for the Lincoln-Hamlin ticket. In June, when the Republicans, now calling themselves the Union Party for reasons of patriotic fervor, held their convention in Baltimore, the general surmise was that the man from Maine would again be Lincoln's running mate. There was no question that the war president would be renominated, and he was, unanimously, on the first ballot.

But when the roll call of the states began for the vice presidential nomination, names other than Hamlin's were entered. New York proposed its own senator Daniel D. Dickinson, and Indiana nominated the Tennessee military governor Andrew Johnson, a "War Democrat" who was a firm champion of the preservation of the Union. President Lincoln professed his neutrality, and the Maine delegation was expected to be solid for Hamlin in leading the New England states for his renomination. Instead, Connecticut gave all of its twelve votes to Johnson, Massachusetts gave only three to Hamlin, and the rest of the Yankee states scattered. The count after the first ballot was 200 for Johnson, 150 for Hamlin, and 108 for Dickinson. What was going on?

Before the second roll call began, Kentucky switched its twenty-one votes to Johnson, Oregon and Kansas joined in, then Pennsylvania, with its fifty-two shifting from Hamlin to the Tennessean. Secretary of State William Seward and the New York Republican boss Thurlow Weed, concerned about Dickinson's strength and fearing a challenge from him for party dominance in New York, also switched the votes under their control to Johnson.[33] Seeing that occur, even Maine switched to Johnson, and he was nominated with 494 votes to 27 for Dickinson and only 9 for Hamlin. What had happened?

Lincoln had not been neutral at all. Convinced that his reelection was imperative for the Union to complete its military mission and for its preservation, he concluded that he needed a War Democrat as his second-term running mate. He much preferred Johnson over the other War Democrat under consideration, General Benjamin F. Butler, who was personally obnoxious to Lincoln and when sounded out declined, disparaging the vice presidency in the process.[34] Lincoln apparently had nothing against Hamlin, but Hamlin came from what was now considered a safe Republican state and was judged to bring little politically to the ticket. The president had decided to remain silent about dumping Hamlin to avoid causing resentment and possible loss of support in New England. So Lincoln, without endorsing Johnson, quietly had the word passed to key Republican operatives in the states.

One old Lincoln friend, Judge S. Newton Pettis, a Pennsylvania delegate to the Republican National Convention, said later he had called on the president at the White House on the morning of the convention and asked him whom he wanted as his running mate. Pettis reported that Lincoln replied softly, "Governor Johnson of Tennessee."[35] This version of what had happened was later disputed by Hamlin's grandson Charles. He cited Lincoln's secretary, John J. Nicolay, as asserting that Lincoln had deliberately adopted a hands-off position on his running mate for 1864.[36]

Apparently at the time, Hamlin was unaware of any Lincoln role in the decision to drop him from the ticket. A quarter of a century later, he ran into Judge Pettis at the inauguration of President Benjamin Harrison, and Pettis told him of Lincoln's statement in the White House that he wanted Johnson as his second-term running mate. "Judge Pettis," Hamlin replied, "I am sorry you told me that." Later, Hamlin wrote to Pettis, "Mr. L evidently became alarmed about his re-election and changed his position. That is all I care to say. If we shall meet again I may say something more to you. I will write no more."[37]

When Maine Republican committees called on Hamlin in the fall to campaign for the Lincoln-Johnson ticket, he complied while telling Ellen, "I had hoped sincerely that they would let me off, but as they do not I am unwilling to refuse, as they would attribute it to my disappointment, which is not the fact. . . . Hence I shall once more make some stump speeches." At a victory rally in Bangor on Election Night, he even called for three cheers for Johnson, an indication that he might not yet be ready to retire from elective politics.[38]

Lincoln himself observed, "Hamlin has the Senate on his brain and nothing more or less will cure him,"[39] and in part to facilitate Hamlin's return to Congress the president persuaded Maine's senator Fessenden to become his treasury secretary. Meanwhile, Hamlin urged Lincoln to appoint Fessenden to the Supreme Court, but Fessenden preferred to go back to the Senate, and the state legislature in the end voted to keep him there, in another rebuke of Hamlin. The former vice president again said he had "really no particular desire to go back to the Senate," except for the opportunity he would have had to dispense patronage to his friends in Maine.[40]

When Fessenden left the treasury to seek his old Senate seat, Lincoln considered offering the post to Hamlin, but Fessenden strongly objected. In the end, Lincoln told Hamlin rather disingenuously, "You have not been treated right. It is too bad, too bad. But what can I do? I am tied hand and foot."[41] As for Hamlin, he told his wife he would not "ask favor of the Administration to prevent me from going to the poor house. So you see I have some pride."[42] In his final duties as president of the Senate, Hamlin tallied the election results and announced the Lincoln-Johnson ticket the winner, and on Inauguration Day he accompanied his successor to the ceremony, with ramifications to be related in the next chapter.

Two days after paying a farewell call on Lincoln, Hamlin headed home to Maine. The *New York Herald* reported that he did so "thoroughly disgusted with every thing and almost everybody in public life, excepting the President. He complains that almost every one with whom he has had anything to do has played him false."[43]

On the night of April 14, Hamlin's daughter Sarah, her husband, George, her brother Charles and his wife, Sallie, were attending the comedy *Our American Cousin* at Ford's Theater when she heard "the crack of a pistol" and saw a man fleeing across the stage as Lincoln lay wounded in the presidential box. Early the next morning in Bangor, her father learned of the president's assassination. He boarded a steamer for Washington and arrived for the funeral moments before it began, standing near the casket in the East Room of the White House at the side of Andrew Johnson, his successor and now president of the United States in an ironic coda to Hamlin's long national service in Washington.[44]

After returning to Maine and relaxing and farming for a few months, in August 1865 Hamlin was appointed collector of the Port of Boston for a year, until resigning in disagreement with the reconstruction agenda of the man who had succeeded him as the Republican vice presidential nominee. But the next year the Maine State Legislature sent Hamlin back to the United States Senate, where he served two more full terms.

By this time Hamlin was the grand old man of the Senate and ready for retirement. President James Garfield, in one of his last official acts before an assassin's bullet ended his presidency, nominated Hamlin to be the American minister to Spain, which was swiftly confirmed by the Senate. He served for two years before retiring to Maine to farm, fish, and reflect on his long political career, until his death at age eighty-one.

Lincoln's decision to drop Hamlin as his vice president after a single term deprived the country of a champion of slave emancipation who, had he been elevated to the presidency upon Lincoln's assassination, might have changed the nature and outcome of the Reconstruction era after the Civil War. The circumstance remains one of the more intriguing speculations of that most critical postwar period.

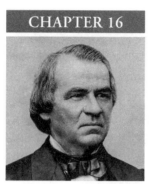

CHAPTER 16

ANDREW JOHNSON
OF TENNESSEE

I n 1865, for the third time in twenty-four years, a vice president succeeded a deceased president in the Oval Office, this time only forty-one days after taking the second office and as the nation just emerged from a calamitous civil war. Only five days before, the Confederate commander General Robert E. Lee had surrendered to the Union commander General Ulysses S. Grant at Appomattox Courthouse, delivering to President Abraham Lincoln the Union-preserving victory he had so long sought. With huge ramifications for that preservation, his assassination on the night of April 14, at the hands of the Confederate zealot John Wilkes Booth as Lincoln was attending a play at Ford's Theater, in Washington, elevated Andrew Johnson of Tennessee to the presidency.

Johnson's arrival at that august position was a product of Lincoln's determination to achieve a second term and an end to the Civil War. To assure that outcome, Lincoln, when nearing completion of his first presidential term, had concluded that he needed to choose a new running mate. This decision related less to dissatisfaction with Hamlin than to the desire to fortify the ticket with a prominent member of the War Democrats, who supported the Union. Johnson filled the bill, as a former governor and U.S. senator from Tennessee, Lincoln's military governor of the state at the time, and a loyalist to the Union even after his state had seceded from it.

Johnson, however, was not the only man considered. Another War

Democrat, the Union major general Benjamin F. Butler, commander at Fort Monroe, in Hampton, Virginia, not only turned down an overture from Lincoln but did it with uncommon disdain and arrogance. When Lincoln sent a secret emissary, Simon Cameron of Pennsylvania, to Butler to sound him out on his availability, Butler, who held a high opinion of himself unshared by many others, asserted he'd rather continue his military career in wartime. He gave Cameron this caustic and irreverent reply to his commander-in-chief, providing his assessment of the proposal:

"Please say to Mr. Lincoln, that while I appreciate with the fullest sensibility this act of friendship and the compliment he pays me, yet I must decline. Tell him with the prospects of the campaign, I would not quit the field to be Vice-President, even with himself as President, unless he will give me bond with sureties, that he will die or resign within three months after his inauguration. Ask him what he thinks I have done to deserve the punishment, at forty-six years of age, of being made to sit as presiding office over the Senate, to listen to debates, more or less stupid, in which I can take no part nor say a word, nor even be allowed a vote upon any subject which concerns the welfare of my country, except when my enemies might think my vote would injure me in the estimate of the people, and therefore, by some parliamentary trick, make a tie on such question, so I should be compelled to vote; and then at the end of four years (as nowadays no Vice-President is ever elected President), and because of the dignity of the position I had held, not to be permitted to go on with my profession, and therefore with nothing left for me to do save to ornament my lot in the cemetery tastefully and get into it gracefully and respectably, as a Vice-President should do."[1]

Johnson had no such contemptuous attitude toward the office or toward the new president's call to service, and the vice presidency was another step in a long-held ambition for high public office from his humblest beginnings. An unschooled country boy, he literally was born in a log cabin in Raleigh, North Carolina, on December 29, 1808. When he was only three years old, his father, Jacob Johnson, a bank porter and local constable who could not read, died, leaving his mother, Mary, called Polly, a seamstress and laundress, to raise him and a brother. When she remarried, she managed to get the two boys placed as apprentices in a Raleigh tailor shop, from which they fled after an altercation with a neighbor. Next Andrew went to Lauren, South Carolina, to another tailor shop, where his proposal of marriage to a local girl was rejected by her mother. Dejected, he returned to Tennessee, found yet another tailor shop and another girl, and in 1827 married Eliza McCardle, the daughter of a shoemaker in Greenville. Self-educated with help from her, he built a thriving tailor shop of his own, invested in real estate, and started a family. Interested in politics and an enthusiast for Andrew Jackson, he joined a local debating society and was elected an alderman in Greenville in 1829 and mayor in 1834.[2]

Young Johnson was a rising star, elected as a Whig to the state legislature the next year, where he introduced homesteading legislation designed to give poor men land to work if they lived on it. In 1837, however, he voted against bringing railroad service to eastern Tennessee and lost his seat. Switching to the Democratic Party, he won the seat back, and in 1840, the party's state convention appointed him as one of the two Tennessee presidential electors and sent him around the state speaking for President Van Buren and local Democratic candidates.

Johnson prospered as a tailor in Greenville and bought a large house opposite his shop and a farm on which he settled his mother and stepfather. For service in the militia he came to be called Colonel Johnson and for the first time became the owner of a few slaves.[3] In 1843 he was elected to the U.S. House of Representatives, where he was now a strong proponent of Jacksonian policies and an opponent of Whig protectionism, federal expenditures for internal improvements, and all manner of other projects. In the House, Johnson also spoke against anti-slavery petitions and denied the authority of either the federal government or an individual right to abolish slavery.[4]

In 1844, he was reelected to the House, where he supported the annexation and statehood of Texas and the Mexican War. In 1846, he introduced his homestead bill giving "every poor man in the United States who is the head of a family" 160 acres of public land to farm "without money and without price." It got nowhere, but Johnson persevered to its enactment years later.[5] In 1852, faced with his House seat being gerrymandered against him, he ran for and won the governorship of Tennessee, with emphasis on his populist roots, and was reelected in 1854. In 1857, the state legislature elected him to the United States Senate, where he again pushed his homesteading bill, finally passing it in 1860, only to have it vetoed by President James Buchanan. His efforts to override fell three votes short.[6]

Meanwhile, committed as ever to the preservation of the Union, Johnson was determined to discourage Tennessee's secession. At a Democratic convention in Charleston in April 1860, the Tennessee delegation was instructed to vote for Johnson as the state's favorite son for president, and its newspapers joined the call. The *Nashville Union and American* praised him unabashedly as "a people's man . . . unafflicted with crude learning of schools . . . real homemade man, standing head and shoulders taller than those who have rubbed their backs against a college wall."[7] But Carl Schurz, a German writer and later a U.S. senator, subsequently described Johnson as "sullen . . . betokening a strong will inspired by bitter feelings" and with a face having "no genial sunlight in it."[8]

At the convention, the Tennessee delegation cast all its votes for Johnson through twenty-six rounds before he dropped out, and Douglas was nominated as the choice of the northern Democrats. In a separate convention, the southern Democrats picked Vice President John C. Breckinridge of Kentucky, and on Election Day, Johnson voted for him as the best alternative for preserving the Union while opposing him on secession. "The blood of secession at the Charleston convention," he told friends, "is not on my head."[9] The day before the election, predicting a Lincoln victory, he told friends, "When the crisis comes, I will be found standing by the Union."[10]

Back in the Senate, Johnson took on the basic concept of secession. "I am unwilling, of my own volition, to walk outside of the Union which has been the result of a Constitution made by the patriots of the Revolution," he said. "I believe I may speak with some degree of confidence for the people of my State; we intend to fight that battle inside and not outside of the Union, and if anybody must go out of the Union, it must be those who violate it."[11] He declared that Tennessee did not intend to go out. "It is our Constitution; it is our Union, . . . and we do not intend to be driven from it." He got down to cases: "The Constitution declares and defines what is treason. Let us talk about things by their right name! . . . If anything be treason . . . is not levying war upon the United States treason? Is not attempt to take its property treason? . . . It is treason and nothing but treason. . . . Then let us stand by the Constitution; and in saving the Union, save this, the greatest government on earth."[12]

The very next day, South Carolina gave its answer. The state declared its secession from the Union, and four days later Governor Francis Pickens proclaimed the state a sovereign and independent entity. In rapid order over the next six weeks, Mississippi, Florida, Alabama, Georgia, Louisiana, and Texas followed suit. Then, five days after Confederate forces fired on Fort Sumter, on April 12, Virginia joined the exodus, followed the next month by Arkansas and North Carolina.

Alexander H. Stephens, soon to be vice president of the Confederate States of America, said of Johnson's oration, "I know of no instance in history when one speech effected such results, immediate and remote, as this one did."[13] The Tennessean was hanged and burned in effigy in Memphis, Nashville, and other cities in his own state. Still, when a state convention was called to consider secession, it was roundly rejected. A spectator in the visitors' gallery rose and called for "three cheers for the Union!" and "three cheers for Andy Johnson!" Finally the Senate sergeant-at-arms was ordered to clear the gallery.

In Tennessee, a Lincoln order to dispatch Union troops to the state finally fired up secessionist sentiment in the middle and western counties, to the point that when Johnson responded to pleas from Tennessee Unionists to return home, he was jeered by crowds. At the town of Liberty a mob boarded his train, with one man threatening him until Johnson pulled a pistol from his coat.[14]

In Nashville, the legislature authorized Governor Isham Harris to raise fifty-five thousand troops for the Confederate army. Harris also set June 8 for a statewide vote on secession, against which Johnson barnstormed in his native east Tennessee. While that area sided with him for staying in the Union, middle and west Tennessee voted heavily to get out, and the statewide secession carried. With threats to assassinate Johnson spreading and Confederate forces occupying most of Tennessee, he left the state by open carriage for neutral Kentucky. Eventually he returned to Washington as a senator from a seceded state. When the Union forces suffered a defeat in the battle of Bull Run, at Manassas, Virginia, Johnson supported Lincoln's war aims, saying, "I have hitherto warred against traitors and treason, and in behalf of the government which was constructed by our fathers, I intend to continue to the end."[15]

In March 1862, with much of Tennessee now occupied by Northern forces, Lincoln sent Johnson back as a military governor with the rank of brigadier general and with sweeping powers to restore Union authority and return the state to the fold. Johnson rationalized his own authority by holding that Tennessee was still part of the Union and that repression of the secessionists was wholly legitimate. He went to Nashville and issued a proclamation of assurance that he came not on a mission of vengeance but to restore civil order. While promising to "punish intelligent and conscious treason in high places," he said he was empowered to offer "full and complete amnesty" even to those citizens who had "assumed an attitude of hostility to the government."[16]

Still, allegiance to the Confederacy in east Tennessee nagged at Johnson as he attempted to administer the state. Nashville's social circle cold-shouldered him, and threats to his life abounded against this "traitor to the South." When the mayor and city council refused to take the oath of allegiance to the Union, he had them arrested and appointed replacements. Preachers who agitated for rebellion were jailed. He instructed the local Union general, "There must be a vigorous and efficient prosecution of this war. The burdens and penalties resulting from it must be made to rest upon the rebels, and they to feel it. Treason must be made odious, traitors punished and impoverished."[17]

When a siege of Nashville was expected, Johnson refused to leave. His wife, Eliza, and other family members, harassed by Confederates at home in Greenville, managed to get to Nashville, where they all survived the threat. Not until late November 1863 was Tennessee cleared of Confederate forces, and as the presidential election year of 1864 began, state political leaders decided to send a delegation to the Republican National Convention in Baltimore in June, to be drawn from Tennessee's three geographical divisions. They decided also that the ten delegates would recommend Johnson for the vice presidential nomination to run with Lincoln, with Johnson neither seeking nor rejecting the possibility.

By now, Lincoln had decided to find a running mate other than Hannibal Hamlin to bolster his chances for a second term. He wanted, obviously, a Union loyalist but also someone who might strengthen the Republican ticket, now carrying the label of the National Union Party. Johnson, as both a Democrat and a southerner, seemed the obvious choice, but rumors of Johnson's overbearing manner and excessive drinking obliged Lincoln to check them out. He sent an aide, Charles A. Dana, to call on Johnson at the state Capitol, where Johnson greeted him with a bottle of whiskey and glasses for both of them. After several days of inquiry, Dana concluded that while Johnson drank a fair amount he found nothing to indicate that the military governor exceeded the imbibing of a normal southern gentleman of sober and responsible demeanor.[18]

Within the new National Union Party, many radicals were unhappy with Lincoln's prosecution of the war and what they feared was a too conciliatory posture toward the South in considering postwar reconstruction of the Union. His Proclamation of Amnesty on Reconstruction, issued in December 1863, offered a full pardon and the return of all property except slaves to Southerners who would repudiate rebellion and pledge allegiance to the Union. It provided that any state in which 10 percent of its citizens took the pledge could form a government and be readmitted. And in April 1864 the Senate approved the Thirteenth Amendment to end slavery everywhere in the country.

In May, the Radical Republicans held a convention of their own and nominated the 1856 standard bearer, General Fremont, but could not draw any significant support for a challenge to the incumbent president.[19] At the regular Republican convention in June, Thaddeus Stevens of Pennsylvania denied the right of Tennessee to send delegates, because Southerners had no right in the Union, which they had now deserted. "Can't you get a candidate for Vice President without going down to a damned rebel province for one?" he thundered.[20] But the Tennessee delegation was seated and nominated Lincoln and Johnson for the two top positions in the National Union Party.

The *New York World,* bitterly opposed, declared in its lead editorial, "The age of statesmen is gone; the age of rail-splitters and tailors, of buffoons, boors and fanatics, has succeeded. . . . A rail-splitting buffoon and a boorish tailor, both from the backwoods, both growing up in uncouth ignorance, they afford a grotesque sight for a satiric poet." Butler, in whose vast contempt the vice presidency was beneath, wrote his wife, "Hurrah for Lincoln and Johnson! That's the ticket! This country has more vitality than any other on earth if it can stand this sort of administration for another four years!"[21]

Johnson himself preferred to see the result of the Baltimore convention as confirmation of "a principle not to be disregarded. It was that the right of secession, and the power of a State to place itself out of the Union, are not recognized." He explained his party's choice of a Southerner for vice president: "The Union party declared its belief that the rebellious States are still in the Union, that their loyal citizens are still citizens of the United States."[22]

The convention's platform called for defeat of the Confederate rebellion, restoration of the Union, and ratification of the Thirteenth Amendment, ending slavery, but it did not satisfy many radicals. In July, they pushed their own tougher reconstruction plan, called the Wade-Davis Bill, advocating readmission only when 50 percent of the citizens of a state had signed an "iron-clad oath" that they had never voluntarily supported the Confederacy and that freedmen would be assured of their rights in federal courts. Lincoln killed it with a pocket veto as a means of ruling out retribution that would undercut the desire of Southerners to want to rejoin the Union, and Johnson commended him for his action. Johnson's support suggested that he was onboard with Lincoln's approach.[23]

In August, the Democrats convened in Chicago and adopted a platform of a negotiated peace and a return to the prewar Union. They nominated the former general George B. McClellan for president and Senator George H. Pendleton of Ohio for vice president. The Democrats deplored anti-slavery issues, including the Emancipation Proclamation, and labeled Lincoln a dictator.

Meanwhile Johnson, returning to Nashville, declared an end to clemency toward foes of the Union. In September, a state party convention discussed reconstruction and bringing Tennessee back into the Union in time to vote in that year's presidential election. Voters had to swear allegiance not only to the Union but also to state opposition to all armistices or negotiations for peace with rebel forces.

At the request of the Republican campaign manager, Henry Raymond, Johnson agreed to make campaign speeches for the ticket in several Northern states. In Logansport, Indiana, he pointedly declared his legitimacy despite coming from a state that had seceded. "Fellow citizens," he began, "and I trust I shall be permitted to call you such, notwithstanding I reside in a state that was said to have rebelled and separated itself from the United States, for I hold to the doctrine that a State cannot secede."[24] He then proceeded to explain revealingly how as a son of the South he could embrace emancipation of the slaves. He argued that more whites than blacks were being freed, because blacks were thus given the opportunity to find their own place in what he vowed was still a "white man's government."[25] The conservative Nashville *Daily Press* editorialized, "Whoever thinks a nigger as good as a poor white man" ought to vote for Lincoln and Johnson.[26]

On October 24, after a large torchlight parade of blacks before the Tennessee Capitol, Johnson lashed out at white slaveholders who consorted with their female slaves in conduct "compared to which polygamy is a virtue." He mockingly challenged anyone to "pass by their dwellings, and you will see as many mulatto as Negro children, the former bearing an unmistakable resemblance to their aristocratic owners!"[27]

The blacks had suffered so much, he said, it "almost induced a wish that, as in the days of old, a Moses might arise who should lead them safely to their promised land of freedom and happiness." When a cry of "You be our Moses!" rose from the crowd, Johnson, carried away, replied, "God no doubt has prepared somewhere an instrument for the great work He designs to perform in behalf of the outraged people, and in due time your leader will come forth, your Moses will be revealed to you." Again the shout was heard: "We want no Moses but you!" Johnson responded, "Well, then, humble and unworthy as I am, if no better shall be found, I will indeed be your Moses, and lead you through the Red Sea of war and bondage to a fairer future of liberty and peace!"[28]

On Election Day, the ticket of Lincoln and Johnson won 55 percent of the popular vote to 45 percent for McClellan and Pendleton, with many Northern soldiers voting from the field, and the Republicans trounced the Democrats in the electoral college, 212 to 21. Meanwhile, the war went on, with a rebel thrust into Tennessee led by General Breckinridge, the former vice president, which was finally turned back at Nashville in mid-December, sending Confederate forces into retreat toward Alabama.

On February 22, 1865, under the guidance of Johnson, Tennessee held a statewide vote ratifying state constitutional amendments abolishing slavery for all time, annulling the previous secession and all of the legislation passed during it, and repudiating all debts incurred by the rebel government. Retiring as military governor, Johnson proclaimed, "A new era dawns upon the people of Tennessee."[29]

The new civilian administration in Tennessee was to be inaugurated on March 4, the same day as the national inauguration of Lincoln and Johnson. The vice president elect hoped he could be in Nashville for the auspicious occasion toward which he had labored so long and hard. But on January 14 he received a telegram from Lincoln: "When do you expect to be here? Would be glad to have your suggestions as to supplying your place as military governor." And then another: "It is our unanimous conclusion that it is unsafe for you not to be here on the 4th of March. Be sure to reach here by that time."[30]

So Johnson had no choice but to head for Washington on February 25 in order to arrive in time. As his train rolled through Kentucky with the war still on, there were warnings of a possible attack on him, and he arrived looking haggard and ill. On the night before the swearing in, Johnson attended a reception in his honor and awoke the next morning with a hangover. He was also recovering from an attack of typhoid that would have kept him from the inauguration ceremony but for Lincoln's insistence.

The retiring vice president, Hamlin, rode with Johnson by carriage to the Capitol, where they went to Hamlin's office. En route, Johnson confided to him, "I am now very weak and enervated, and I require all the strength I can get. Can you give me some good whiskey?" Hamlin told him he was not a drinker and didn't keep any liquor in the office. At just that moment the caterer arrived, and a bottle was produced, from which Johnson poured himself a large drink and downed it. Shortly afterward, as he and Hamlin started to leave for the inauguration, Johnson poured himself another glassful and drank it neat.[31]

At the ceremony in a crowded and hot Senate chamber, Hamlin delivered a brief thanks and introduced Johnson. Obviously affected by what probably was a combination of his fever, a hangover, and the two stiff drinks, he proceeded to deliver the most startling and embarrassing inaugural remarks on record. Unleashing an old-fashioned country harangue, he began, "I am a-goin' for to tell you here today; yes, I'm a-goin' for to tell you all, that I'm a plebian! I glory in it; I am a plebian! The people, yes the people of the United States have made me what I am; and I am a-goin for a to tell you here today, yes, today, in this place, that the people are everything."[32]

Johnson then called out to the cabinet members William Seward, Edwin Stanton, "and you too, Mr. ———," forgetting the name of cabinet member Gideon Welles and asking John Forney, the secretary of the Senate, for it. He reminded all of them that their power, as his own, came from the people, not from Lincoln, which was not precisely correct. Hamlin was seen tugging on the new vice president's coattail in a vain effort to get him to desist. Finally Johnson took the oath of office, placing his hand on a Bible.[33] When it came time for him as the new president of the Senate to swear in the new members, he completely botched the job, finally turning to a clerk and telling him, "Here, you swear them in. You know it better than I do."[34]

After Lincoln had taken his oath and delivered his second inaugural address with its historic line, "with malice toward none, with charity for all," Hamlin took Johnson by the arm and led him from the chamber. For days afterward, Washington was abuzz over Johnson's remarks and behavior. But Lincoln himself told his secretary of the treasury, Hugh McCulloch, "I have known Andy for many years; he made a bad slip the other day, but you needn't be scared. Andy ain't a drunkard."[35]

The *New York World* said that journalistic obligation required the report of Johnson's conduct. It went on: "The pity of it is that the life of this chief magistrate [Lincoln] should be made precious to us by the thought that he at least excludes from the most august station in the land the person who defiled our chief council chamber with the spewing of a drunken boor." The next day, the same newspaper added that compared to Johnson, "even Caligula's horse was respectable."[36] For the next two weeks, Johnson remained closeted in the suburban home of two friends. Fortunately the Senate was not then in session. Senator Charles Sumner of Massachusetts composed a resolution calling for Johnson's resignation, but the Republican caucus did not adopt it.

The storm over Johnson's faux pas soon was engulfed by climactic developments in the war. At Five Forks, Virginia, the last great battle was fought when General Philip Sheridan drove the forces of General Robert E. Lee from Richmond, together with Confederate president Jefferson Davis, and four days later Lincoln walked victoriously through the abandoned Confederate capital. In Washington, a suddenly resuscitated Johnson joined the wild street demonstrations.

On the night of Friday, April 14, Johnson had dinner at the Kirkland House, where the former governor Leonard Farwell of Wisconsin invited Johnson to join him at Ford's Theater, a few blocks away, to see Laura Keene in *Our American Cousin,* which Lincoln and Grant would also be attending. Johnson declined, saying he never went to the theater and wanted to read a bit before turning in, and did so. The next thing he knew, Farwell was urgently rapping at his door, informing him that Lincoln had been shot. Johnson brushed aside the protecting troops already outside his door and rushed to the Petersen house across from the theater, where Lincoln now lay diagonally across a bed too small for his gangling f igure.[37]

The next morning church bells began to chime, announcing Lincoln's death, and a few hours later Chief Justice of the United States Salmon P. Chase administered the presidential oath of office to Johnson in the hotel parlor in the presence of the assembled cabinet members and a few friends. The new president spoke briefly, commenting, "The only assurance that I can now give of the future is reference to the past. The course which I have taken in connection with this rebellion must be regarded as a guarantee for the future. . . . I shall ask and rely upon you and others in carrying the government through its present perils."[38] He then held his first cabinet meeting and asked all members to stay in their posts. In the assassination plot that claimed Lincoln's life and severely wounded Secretary of State Seward, Johnson himself had been targeted to be killed by one George Atzerodt, who was captured with three other conspirators, tried, convicted, and executed.[39]

The hope and expectation of the Radical Republicans was that Johnson, who had dealt harshly with slaveholders in Tennessee as military governor and had talked of being Moses to that black rally in Nashville before the election, would govern as a prodder of fellow southerners to accept the new order. Instead, he bent over backward to assist in the restoration of much of what had been the Old South, dealing with reconstruction as in the purview of the executive branch, not the legislative, in keeping with this "presidential reconstruction." Only a month into his accidental presidency, he issued a proclamation granting amnesty to Confederates who would take an oath of loyalty to the Constitution, with their seized property, except for previous slaves, restored to them. Then he laid out the steps for North Carolina, and presumably other Confederate states, to rejoin the Union by having an appointed provisional governor call a state convention to amend its constitution, again with seized property returned to pliant Confederates. This return of property was seen by abolitionists and freedmen as an abrogation of the functions of the Freedmen's Bureau to allocate farmland to former slaves.

Before long, prominent white political figures of the South were returning as members of Congress, governors, and other state officials, many bent on maintaining as much of the prewar social order as possible. South Carolina simply "repealed" its secession rather than acknowledging that the act was unconstitutional. At the same time, Johnson was granting pardons willy-nilly to ranking Confederate officers and officials who were rapidly getting themselves elected to state posts. Many who didn't bother to seek pardons were granted clemency in order to assume office, including the Confederate vice president Alexander Stephens, elected to Congress from Georgia. Soon the leniency extended to southerners evolved into their arrogance and often a return of hatred toward their benefactors and the freedmen.

Radical Republicans were outraged at Johnson. Thaddeus Stevens wrote Charles Sumner: "Is it possible to devise any plan to arrest the government in its ruinous career? When will you be in Washington? Can't we collect bold men enough to lay the foundation for a party to take the helm of this government, and keep it off the rocks?" And a few days later: "Is there no way to arrest the insane course of the President in Washington?"[40] When Congress reconvened in December 1865, the Republican majority created the Joint Committee on Reconstruction to rival Johnson's "presidential" version. Radical Republicans and moderates joined in February 1866 and enacted two bills, extending the life and increasing the powers of the Freedmen's Bureau and passing the Civil Rights Act providing legal protection for the freed blacks. Johnson promptly opposed both as unconstitutional. He vetoed the first, and the veto was narrowly sustained by Congress.

Many other similar actions by moderates to advance legislative reconstruction or to counter Johnson's efforts to restore aspects of the old order marked his accidental presidency. In June 1866, the Fourteenth Amendment to the Constitution passed, categorically prohibiting the deprivation of "life, liberty, or property without due process of law" or denial of "the equal protection of the laws." Almost a year later, Congress passed the Reconstruction Act of 1867, establishing five military districts embracing ten Confederate states, where state constitutional conventions were held as a prelude to readmission to the Union. Again Johnson vetoed the legislation, and again Congress overrode the veto. Fearful that this president would use his power as commander in chief of the armed forces to further disrupt its reconstruction plan, Congress passed the Army Appropriations Act, requiring the president to function through the military governors in the Confederate states, and the Tenure of Office Act, which kept him from firing cabinet members opposed to his program.

Johnson had retained Lincoln's secretary of war, Edwin Stanton, as the only member sympathetic to the Radical Republicans. While Congress was in recess, he fired Stanton and appointed General Grant as his replacement, but upon return the legislators refused to agree to Stanton's removal. Grant left the War Department, and Stanton returned to his old office and barricaded himself inside, in consultation with this Radical Republican friends.

On February 24, the House of Representatives' majority voted unanimously to impeach Johnson for "high crimes and misdemeanors in office" in his ignoring the Tenure of Office Act and attempting to bring Congress into contempt and reproach. In the ensuing Senate trial, his lawyers argued in his absence that Johnson had not broken the law, because Stanton had been appointed by Lincoln and had served beyond Lincoln's tenure. Johnson was saved by a single Senate vote.

Afterward, Stanton resigned, and Johnson completed his term. His hope of shaping a party of Union preservationists, War Democrats, and a grateful recovering white South with which to win a second term in 1868 proved wildly illusionary. Out of office for the first time in thirty years, he ran for the Senate again that fall but was defeated. He ran again in 1875 and won, returning to the scene of his impeachment and his near miss of conviction. At the end of the short winter session, Johnson went back to Tennessee, where four months later he suffered a stroke and died at age sixty-six.

Johnson's passage from the scene was marked in his home state with customary honors, but his presidency consigned him to a starkly negative place in his country's history. His vice presidency, far from being a stepping-stone to greater esteem in the White House, was more a gateway to condemnation for his repressive treatment of the freedmen of the South. His impeachment was the first such presidential censure; his greater repudiation was in the wide condemnation of his reconstruction policies that violated Lincoln's second inaugural pledge of a presidency committed to "malice toward none, with charity for all."

CHAPTER 17

SCHUYLER COLFAX

OF INDIANA

T he calamitous presidency of Andrew Johnson, which shook the Republican Party over Reconstruction, assured that he would not be offered a term of his own in 1868. Nor was there, as a result of his early ascendancy to the first office, any incumbent vice president waiting in the wings to claim it. Still, the party did not have to look far for its nominee, as General U. S. Grant, the Northern hero of the Civil War, was riding high in public acclaim. Among those prominently mentioned as his running mate was the Speaker of the House Schuyler Colfax of Indiana, who had played a significant role in the congressional resistance and eventual challenge to Johnson's assumption of presidential reconstruction of the war-torn Union.

Colfax was born in New York City on March 23, 1823, a descendant of General William Colfax, who had fought in the Revolutionary War, from the Battle of Bunker Hill to Yorktown. The general was a member of George Washington's Life Guard and became its commander near the end of the war. Afterward he married Hester Schuyler, a cousin of another revolutionary general, Philip Schuyler. Their son, the first Schuyler Colfax, married in 1820 but died two years later, four months before his own namesake son was born. Young Schuyler attended school until his teens, when he had to drop out to help his mother. They moved to Brooklyn, where in 1834 she was remarried, to George W. Matthews, who was then only fourteen years older than his new stepson, and they became close friends.[1]

The family moved in 1836 to New Castle, Indiana, a frontier town far removed from the city life with which the boy had become familiar. He clerked in the family store, which shared space with the village post office, and also worked on neighboring farms. In 1841 the family moved to South Bend, another village of fewer than a thousand souls, which remained Colfax's home the rest of his life. Matthews was elected a county auditor as a Whig and made his stepson a deputy. Schuyler was a small lad of medium height with a genial disposition, which may have brought him the nickname "Smiler." From an early age, he developed an inordinate interest in newspapers, particularly political news. By sixteen he was writing articles for the *Indiana State Journal* on the state legislature and at nineteen was hired by the local Whigs to edit the South Bend *Free Press.* Eventually he wrote to the editor of the *New-York Tribune,* Horace Greeley, inquiring whether he might submit articles about his section of the country. The prominent Whig editor wrote back, "I shall be happy to hear from you on the terms so generously proposed by you as often as you think proper. . . . Let me hear what you see and learn about Politics, Business, Crops, etc."[2]

Young Colfax and Greeley remained lifetime friends, as the young man wrote long and fluidly about local political figures, especially about his early Whig and western hero, Henry Clay of Kentucky. He also joined a temperance society in South Bend, took a teetotaler's oath, and stuck to it all his life. He wrote his fiancée of the pledge: "Thus far I have kept it strictly, and in all my gayety and blithesomeness no temptation shall ever lead me to pollute my lips with the liquid fire."[3] In due time, however, he found other routes off the straight and narrow.

In 1844, Colfax got married and the next year purchased the local paper, renaming it the *St. Joseph Valley Register.* Now a confirmed Whig, he became a delegate to the party's national convention in 1848 and to its state convention in the following year to write a new Indiana constitution. There he led an effort against a provision barring blacks from settling in the state and those already there from buying land. His labors failed, but the passage of the Thirteenth Amendment in 1865 finally achieved the same end.[4]

In 1851, as the Whig candidate for Congress from his district, he narrowly lost to the incumbent Democrat. Then in 1854, with the Whigs in disintegration, he ran again and won, but this time as an anti-slavery Know-Nothing, an emerging new nativist party that more prominently opposed alcohol, immigrants, and Catholics. The first Know-Nothing lodge was opened in the state that year, and Colfax specified he would remain in the ranks only for its anti-slavery plank. The Know-Nothings, a hodge-podge of disaffected Republicans, Democrats, and Whigs, split over the Kansas-Nebraska Act and quickly fell apart, and in 1856 Colfax retained his seat as a Republican.

As the threat of secession over the slavery issue grew, his voice in the House and in the party against its extension into the West became more prominent, and he traveled widely, speaking in support of preservation of the Union. When the war came and the Southern states did pull out, the House Republicans took over the majority, and his chairmanship of the House Post Offices and Post Roads Committee positioned him as a major dispenser of patronage within the House. In 1863 he was elected Speaker, and with his power to appoint committee chairmen, his popularity and support climbed.

As Speaker, Colfax proved to be a fair and cordial arbiter of the House rules, with an occasional flair for the dramatic, and he frequently directly counseled President Lincoln on matters of state. As the war's end approached, Colfax discussed Lincoln's plans with him for reconciliation with the South and for its reconstruction. On April 14, 1865, with the armed conflict over, Lincoln invited the Speaker to join his party that night at Ford's Theater. Colfax declined, but when he was awakened later and told of the tragedy, he rushed to the president's bedside, across the street from the theater.[5]

After Lincoln's funeral, Colfax was soon obliged to confront the reconstruction plans of the new president, Andrew Johnson, which did not square with his own understanding of what Lincoln had been considering and with what Colfax himself favored. In his campaign for reelection in 1864, he had been happy to have the support of Johnson, who had just been made Lincoln's running mate for his second term. Colfax had praised him then as "that loyal, Jackson-like and heroic Senator from Tennessee," and in April 1865 in eulogizing Lincoln he had said of Johnson, "Andrew Johnson, to whom the public confidence was so quickly and worthily transferred, is cast in a sterner mold than he whose place he fills. He has warred on traitors in his mountain home as they have warred on him; and he insists, with this crowning infamy filling up their cup of wickedness, that treason should be made odious, and that mercy to the leaders who engendered it is cruelty to the nation."[6]

But Colfax was not encouraged subsequently when Johnson proceeded during the summer and fall of 1865 to undertake presidential reconstruction with no regard to the congressional leadership. The Speaker later said that prior to the assassination he had tried to convince both Lincoln and Johnson of the wisdom of calling a special session of Congress to consider how best to bring the rebel states back into the Union. Before that happened, he wrote a friend, "I want to be very certain that a majority of their voters are—not merely whopped back into the Union, as they say—but heartily devoted to the Union & ready to fight with us agst. all its enemies at home or abroad, now & in the future."[7]

In November 1865 Colfax made a major speech in Washington that was among the first serious cautions about presidential reconstruction at the hands of Johnson. He warned that Southerners who only months earlier were "struggling to blast this nation from the map of the world" were proposing to enter Congress in the next session "to resume their former business of governing the country they struggled so earnestly to ruin." He noted that the Constitution gave each house of Congress the exclusive right to judge the qualifications of elected members, adding, "And I apprehend they will exercise that right." While commending conditions laid down by Johnson as "eminently wise and patriotic," he called for ratification of new Southern state constitutions that would protect the personal and property rights of black freedmen. He expressed confidence that when the executive and legislative branches compared their views, they "would cordially cooperate."[8]

According to an entry in the diary of Gideon Welles, Johnson's inherited navy secretary, the new president referred to Colfax in conversation with several cabinet members as "this little fellow . . . shoved in here to make a speech in advance of [Johnson's] message, and to give out that the principle enunciated in his speech was the true policy of the country." Radical Republicans were quick to praise Colfax for arguing that black suffrage and other rights be part of Reconstruction, but the conservative *Chicago Times* editorially commented that the Republicans had "conspired to defeat the work of restoration already done and happily carried forward by the president, and Schuyler Colfax was a leading conspirator among them for that purpose."[9]

When the Thirty-Eighth Congress convened that fall, the reelection of Colfax as Speaker of the House was considered a test of his Reconstruction views. If so, he passed it easily, defeating James Brooks of New York. Applauded as he took the chair, he told the members, "It is for you, Representatives, to do our work as faithfully and as well as did the fearless saviors of the Union on their more dangerous arena of duty. Then we may hope to see these vacant and once abandoned seats around us gradually filling, until this Hall shall contain Representatives from every State and district."[10]

Colfax then appointed a joint House-Senate committee to "inquire into the condition of the States which formed the so-called Confederate States of America" as to their eligibility to send representatives to either house, with none seated until this was done. Some aspirants who perhaps optimistically came to the chamber were sent away. Despite Colfax's hope for harmony with the White House on Reconstruction, he eventually had to face reality with Johnson's veto of the Freedmen's Bureau Bill and other vetoes. He predicted that Congress would override the veto of the Civil Rights Bill passed afterward in 1866, and he was right. Soon after, he told some Indiana callers that they had to look to Congress, not to the executive, for "legalized reconstruction." And he condensed his position thus: "Loyal men shall govern a preserved Republic."[11]

Johnson's vetoes and the general aspect of his reconstruction policy of lenience to the South, particularly to political figures who had supported the Confederate side and sought readmission to Congress, were intolerable to Colfax and to many other Radical Republicans and moderates in the Republican Party. Along with these actions was evidence that the president was considering the creation of a new party that could be the vehicle for his election to another term in his own right. In June he invited delegates from all thirty-six states to the District of Columbia, and supporters called for a National Union convention in Philadelphia for the same purpose, the first of four such gatherings elsewhere over the summer and fall.[12]

By the spring of 1866, talk of impeaching Johnson spread rapidly among the Radical Republicans. As Speaker, Colfax was sympathetic but took no leadership role. The obvious grounds for action against Johnson were his reconstruction plans, but many in Congress believed that impeachment could be sought only for specific illegal, indictable acts, which he was careful not to commit.

The congressional elections of 1866 went badly for Johnson. He fared well in the South, but the congressional Republicans built their strength in the North and won a two-thirds majority in both houses, enabling them to override any subsequent presidential veto. When Congress returned in December 1866, the emboldened Radicals introduced a resolution creating a committee to investigate possible impeachment, but it failed the necessary two-thirds vote. In January 1867, another motion, this one charging the president with high crimes and misdemeanors, including abuse of power, corruption in making appointments and granting pardons, and election tampering, passed and was sent to the House Judiciary Committee. But it was shelved there.

Meanwhile, Congress had passed the Tenure of Office Act, curbing the president's power to remove postmasters and others from positions of patronage. A provision was added stipulating that cabinet officials were to hold their offices for the duration of the term of the president who had appointed them, plus one month, subject to removal by and with the advice and consent of the Senate.

Johnson quickly vetoed the act and the latest reconstruction legislation written by Congress but was overridden. He seemed to acquiesce, not wanting to give his critics legitimate grounds for impeachment, and the threat seemed to fade for a time. Then, on July 29, 1867, when Johnson fired Secretary of War Edwin Stanton without Senate approval, in violation of the Tenure of Office Act, Colfax was convinced the president had to be impeached, an action now devoutly desired by the Radical Republicans. It fell to the genial "Smiler" Colfax to bring the moderates along as well while demonstrating fairness in the chair.

On February 24, 1868, the House voted overwhelmingly for the impeachment resolution, with every Republican in favor. Despite the subsequent Senate acquittal of Johnson, there was no possibility that the Republicans would nominate him in the next presidential election, so he pursued, hopelessly, a nomination by his old Democratic Party. The immense popularity of the Civil War hero U. S. Grant assured his Republican nomination for the presidency, and Colfax was one of several men considered as his running mate. He resisted overtures to run for governor of Indiana or for the U.S. Senate, but he was clearly interested in the Republican vice presidential nomination.

The main prospect at the outset was Senator Benjamin F. Wade, the president pro tem of the Senate, but at the party convention in Chicago, Colfax was nominated on the sixth ballot. As a teetotaler, some delegates saw him as a ticket balancer, offsetting Grant's notable propensity for hard liquor. The social Smiler Colfax, now a widower who taught Sunday School and spoke at temperance meetings, was a popular choice. In the Democratic Party, which bypassed the only recently acquitted Johnson of impeachment charges, Governor Horatio Seymour of New York was nominated.

With Grant resisting speech making, Colfax pitched in against Seymour, and in defense of the Civil War he did not hesitate to "wave the bloody shirt" against unrepentant rebels, "murderous traitors with their shirts and their hands red with the blood of murdered Union men." In Detroit, Colfax told prospective Democratic voters, "When you go to the ballot box and drop in that ballot by which you and other millions of our country rule this land and control its destinies, you are going side by side, if not in actual proximity yet in the spirit, in principle and in soul with the men on the battlefield who sought to kill you for our adherence to the flag. . . . they drew the bead upon you; they aimed at your heart because you were faithful to the allegiance which they themselves repudiated. God's providence turned aside that bullet, but if the men with whom you are going to vote could have led the way you would have been bleeding in your graves. Now go and vote with them if you want to."[13]

Many Democrats struggled against allegations of being on the wrong side of the war and in return played the race card by questioning black suffrage and other Reconstruction policies. But Grant and Colfax won comfortably, with Grant's stature as the North's hero of the war dominant. A fellow congressman, Godlove S. Orth, wrote the vice president elect: "I believe your chances to succeed Grant are at this time better than those of any living man. To keep them in this condition will require the constant action of yourself & friends."[14]

Only weeks after the election, Colfax married a second time, at age forty-five. His bride, Ellen Wade, about fifteen years his junior, was the niece of Senator Ben Wade. She presided over the Colfax home, which was open to many of her husband's political associates, including a host of journalists he befriended as former colleagues of the press. But after ruling over the House for fourteen years as Speaker, Colfax found presiding over the Senate as vice president a letdown. In that post he had no patronage, a severe disappointment for the former Speaker who had made a career, and a host of friends, in dispensing it.

He was in demand as a speaker around the country, however, often addressing religious and temperance meetings. Although he was known for receiving and keeping gifts in office, he insisted he did not speak for money, writing in 1871 that he had not "spoken at all" at any event where admission was charged.[15] But in 1868 Colfax, always deeply interested in railroads in connection with expansion of the American West, had acquired some steeply discounted railroad stock from a colleague, Congressman Oakes Ames of Massachusetts, about which he later would have much regret.[16]

During the 1870 congressional elections, he pointedly announced that at only age fifty he would not be seeking reelection to the vice presidency in 1872. The announcement immediately launched speculation as to why and what he would be doing thereafter. Railroad magnate Jay Cooke, then planning construction of the Northern Pacific Railroad, sounded him out about a job in Washington looking after interests in acquiring land grants, federal appropriations for advance construction, and protection for workers in the Indian territories. Cooke later wrote that he thought "Mr. Colfax would combine his editorial, political and oratorical talents" to help achieve the project, for which he would be paid twenty-five thousand dollars a year. The offer was attractive to Colfax, who had never made much money, but he turned it down, noting he would otherwise have to resign the vice presidency.

Cooke then offered to hire Colfax after he was to leave office, and the vice president said nothing would please him more at that time. Cooke tried again, asking Colfax whether he might accept a temporary position with no government activities at all, but again the answer was no. He told Cooke he would be as helpful to him as he could "without any remuneration whatever," and that was the end of the offer.[17] It turned out, however, that earlier Colfax had taken advantage of a Cooke offer to buy original stock at very favorable price, separate from the stock he had acquired from Ames.[18]

In August 1871, Colfax was surprised to receive a letter from Grant. The secretary of state, Hamilton Fish, was ailing and wanted to resign. "In plain English," Grant asked, "will you give up the Vice-Presidency to be Secretary of State for the balance of my term of office? . . . In all my heart I hope you will say yes, though I confess the sacrifice you will be making."[19]

Nothing came of this strange request, when Fish acceded to a petition from Colfax and forty-four senators to stay in office.

One of the vice president's last notable official duties came in 1872 when he cast a tie-breaking vote for an amendment to an amnesty bill providing equal rights for blacks on public conveyances, in railroad stations, theaters, churches, and schools, and on juries. The proposal, which later was dropped from the bill, was ahead of its time, and Colfax observed of it: "We should either acknowledge that the Constitution is a nullity or should insist on that obedience to it by all, and protection under it to all."[20]

In 1872, Grant remained popular and was assured of renomination. But a stock market crash resulting from wild gold speculation in 1869, dissatisfaction with the conduct of the administration and corruption within it, and the emergence of the new Liberal Republican faction all clouded the election outcome. In May, the Liberal Republicans called their own national convention in Cincinnati and nominated the New York publisher Horace Greeley for president. The immobilized Democrats threw in with them, holding no convention of their own.

Meanwhile, Colfax's original declaration that he would not run again had inspired Senator Henry Wilson of Massachusetts and friends to jump in. But Colfax suddenly changed his mind. When Wilson was asked by the *New-York Tribune* how Colfax's change of heart had affected his own position, he replied, "The revocation of the Vice President and his declination was to me a surprise. It placed me in an unpleasant position, and my first impulse was to withdraw from the contest, but by the advice of some of the best Republicans of the land—East, West and South—I leave the question to personal and political friends." But upon the advice of leading Republicans, Wilson decided to leave the matter in the party's hands.[21] At the Republican convention in Philadelphia in June, with Grant remaining aloof and neutral, Wilson was chosen on the first ballot as his 1872 running mate.

More than two months after the convention, Colfax was implicated in a questionable stock deal in which a finance company called Credit Mobilier, established by the directors of the Union Pacific Railroad in 1867 to underwrite its construction, was investigated on charges of lining the pockets of certain members of Congress. Representative Oakes Ames had been recruited to offer stock to them, including Speaker Colfax; Senator Wilson; Congressmen James A. Garfield, a future president; James Brooks;

and James G. Blaine, a future presidential nominee. Some paid ridiculously low prices for the stock, some did not have to put any money down, and all reaped large dividends. The charges against Colfax had not been aired at the time of his defeat for renomination and hence were not a factor in that outcome.

In January 1873, however, the House investigating committee called Colfax to testify. He had already said he had never owned any of the stock that he had not paid for, but Ames testified that because the retiring vice president lacked the money needed to buy the stock, it had been bought with its rising dividends. Notes produced by Ames indicated that Colfax had received another twelve hundred dollars in dividends, but he denied ever having received the dividend check. When it was turned up in the files of the House sergeant-at-arms and recorded on a bank deposit slip in Colfax's handwriting, he insisted the money had come from a completely unrelated source. Further, the committee produced evidence that Colfax, as chairman of the House Post Offices and Post Roads Committee, had taken payments for post office contracts.

A resolution to impeach him was introduced in the House but failed to pass on an essentially party-line vote, with members willing to let Colfax off with only weeks left in his term. He remained, however, a disgraced symbol of congressional and Wall Street corruption. Of all the other members of Congress involved, only Ames and Brooks were formally censured by the House. The once highly admired Colfax retired to his home in South Bend. After being asked to deliver remarks at the unveiling of a Lincoln statue in Springfield, Illinois, he embarked on a lucrative turn as a Lincoln lecturer. En route to a speech engagement in Iowa on January 13, 1885, he suffered a heart attack at a railroad station in Mankato, Minnesota, and died, identified only by the papers he carried.

Schuyler Colfax thus left the scene as little more than an asterisk in the history books. He was a foot soldier in the ranks of Radical Republicans and toiled constructively in the cause of congressional reconstruction as Speaker of the House. As such he was widely regarded as a man of genial rectitude. But as vice president in the Grant administration he was a man without a serious mission. Left to the temptations of ill gain, in the end Colfax would be remembered most for the corruption to which he himself contributed. And in his hands, the second office, already held in low regard by many if not most Americans, was further diminished.

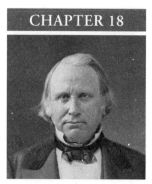

CHAPTER 18

HENRY WILSON

OF MASSACHUSETTS

ew men who rose to the doorstep of the American presidency had a more unlikely road to that prominence than the man who became President Grant's vice president in his second term, Henry Wilson. Actually he was born Jeremiah Jones Colbath in the village of Farmington, New Hampshire, on February 16, 1812. For the most pecuniary of reasons, his father, Winthrop Colbath, a poor, unkempt, and hard-drinking ne'er-do-well, named his first child after a wealthy bachelor neighbor in the hope, unfulfilled, that the man would leave his namesake a substantial amount of money if he died childless. The callous act may have contributed in time to the boy's alienation from the New England aristocracy and fierce identification with the plight of the poor and disadvantaged, a plight that he shared as a youth and an identification that he maintained through his life.

Growing up uneducated in either scholarship or manners, he developed into a rough-hewn troublemaker with a profane tongue, which his mother, Abigail, sought to combat by urging him to read. When he was ten years old, his father placed him as a field hand with a local farmer, committing him to live, work, and obey his "master" until he reached the age of twenty-one. He was not to leave without permission, not to "play at cards, dice, or any other unlawful games . . . not haunt or frequent taverns, playhouses or alehouses . . . not commit fornication [or] contract matrimony." At the end of this indentured servitude, he would be given "one yoke of likely working cattle" and "one good suit for everyday wear."[1]

Rather than rebelling, the young man sold his hard-earned livestock and enrolled briefly in three private academies, eventually becoming a part-time teacher. At age nineteen he took a vow against drinking, including advocating temperance in general. And on his twenty-first birthday he changed his name to Henry Wilson to make a clean break from his unsatisfactory past. He moved to Natick, Massachusetts, where he found a master cobbler to teach him the trade. In time he built a thriving business, making shoes himself and later taking on others to help with that work. On a trip to Washington, D.C., he observed things that set him on his life's course, scenes ranging from Congress at work to black servitude at its most brutal, featuring the auctioning off of men herded into slave pens. On the way back to New England, he witnessed many of them toiling under close supervision in tobacco fields in Maryland. He vowed to do what he could to combat the glaring evil.

In 1837, while he was teaching school on the side in Natick, a young girl named Harriet Howe caught his eye, and after three years, when she was still only sixteen years old, he married her, bringing more stability to his life. In 1840 as a Whig, he won a seat in the Massachusetts General Court.[2] He was reelected in 1842 and then to the state Senate in 1844, at age twenty-eight.

The Whig Party in Massachusetts at the time was split between the economy-driven "Cotton Whigs," who supported the textile mills in New England and the mills' link to the cotton plantations of the South, and the moralistic "Conscience Whigs," whose politics were motivated by opposition to slavery and the economic power it bestowed on the South. As part of the latter group, Wilson argued that if anti-slavery forces in the Whig and Democratic Parties could unite into a party of their own, the Whig Party in the North could become the vehicle to wrest from the South its hold on slavery and its power over the country's economy. But in time he fell out with the Whigs, and after a flirtation with the new Free Soil and then the Know-Nothing Party, he found a home in the emerging Republican Party.

In 1854, the Know-Nothings in Massachusetts elected Wilson to the U.S. Senate, but he took the seat as a Republican, to some party distress, teaming with the Republican Charles Sumner as the fiercest of anti-slavery warriors. When in 1855, during the fight over the Kansas-Nebraska Bill, Sumner delivered a blistering assault on "the crime against Kansas," Congressman Preston Brooks of South Carolina walked onto the Senate floor and broke a cane over Sumner's head. Wilson denounced the "brutal, murderous and cowardly assault," whereupon Senator Andrew Butler of South Carolina, Brooks's uncle, called Wilson "a liar!" as the president of the Senate called for order.[3] Wilson told a friend he feared the same fate as a result of his outspoken anti-slavery views. Newspapers reported that Wilson carried revolvers and a rifle disguised as a walking cane as he came and left the Senate. He wrote a friend asking him to look after his family if anything happened to him.[4]

Later in the month, when Wilson took a train to Trenton for a Republican organizational meeting, he was accompanied by a bodyguard of armed friends, and he told his audience that "the same power that spilled the blood of the freemen of Kansas had used the bludgeon against Senator Sumner." And back in Washington when a friend confided his fear to Wilson that the senator would be murdered, Wilson pulled a pair of revolvers from his coat, remarking, "Then two will be killed; I am a pretty strong man."[5]

Brooks, meanwhile, portraying the aggrieved party, challenged Wilson to a duel. Wilson refused, saying he would not engage in "the lingering relic of barbarous civilization, which the law of the country has branded as a crime," nor would he retract his accusation against Brooks for brutal and cowardly behavior. Then he wired his wife: "Have declined to fight a duel, shall do my duty and leave the result to God. If assailed, shall defend my life, if possible, at any cost. Be calm."[6]

Across Massachusetts and beyond, Wilson was lauded for his conduct. As a Republican, he was still guided by his commitment to the fight against human bondage but did not seek to eradicate slavery where it already existed in the South. He was more interested in loosening the economic stranglehold that slavery had on the prosperity of the country. In 1859, Wilson was jolted by the raid of abolitionist John Brown on a federal arsenal at Harper's Ferry, still within Virginia at the time, as part of an attempt to spark a slave insurrection. He feared that the Republican Party would be blamed for encouraging violence in the quest for an end to slavery and would doom the chances to put one of its own in the White House in 1860.

But the threat passed with the nomination of Abraham Lincoln and Hannibal Hamlin of Maine as his running mate and the politically serendipitous three-way split in the Democratic constituency that brought victory to the Republican team.

Wilson saw the victory as the culmination of his long effort to crush the power of the South, and in his exuberance he sent an unwise signal. At a tumultuous victory celebration in Boston, he exulted, "Tonight, thanks be to God, we stand with the Slave Power beneath our feet. That haughty power which corrupted the Whig party, strangled the American party, and used the Democratic party as a tool, lies crushed in the dust tonight, and our heel is upon it." And to the southern slaveholders threatening to secede, he challenged, "Go on if you dare! We intend to stand by the Union, come what may."[7] But the South wasn't listening, didn't hear, or didn't care. South Carolina seceded on December 20, ten sister states soon followed, along with the firing on Fort Sumter and the outbreak of the Civil War.

With the Republicans in the Senate majority, Wilson became chairman of the Military Affairs Committee. For a time he served as an aide-de-camp to General George McClellan, later agreeing with the criticism of the general's cautious leadership. Back in the Senate, Wilson was among the Radical Republicans who pushed for ending the slave trade in the District of Columbia, for taking blacks into the Union army, for equal pay for them there, and for Lincoln to issue an early emancipation proclamation. When the Emancipation Proclamation was finally made public in January 1863, it was accompanied by authorization to take the freedmen into the armed forces.

In 1865, as the war ground mercifully toward an end and Grant accepted Lee's surrender at Appomattox, Wilson joined other public figures of the North on a steamer trip to Charleston for a celebratory flag-raising ceremony at Fort Sumter on April 14. Two days later he boarded again for the party's next stop in Florida when he received a telegram on deck. He went to his cabin to read it and suddenly reappeared in a state of shock. "Good God! The President is killed!" he wailed to his companions. The ship turned northward for Washington amid its passengers' despair and confusion about what the future would bring.[8]

Wilson himself realized that the end of armed combat did not mean the end of the quest for restoring the Union and extending its liberties to the newly freed slaves. Speaking to the Boston chapter of the American Antislavery Society later in May, he warned that "the dark spirits of slavery still live," and the group's duty to wipe out its injustices remained "as clear as the track of the sun across the heavens, that is, to enfranchise every black man in the Republic."[9] At the same time, he opposed meting out the death penalty or lengthy prison terms to most Confederate officials, including the Confederate president Jefferson Davis, saying he deserved a speedy trial for treason or quick release.

In this sense, Wilson initially seemed to be in harmony with the first reconstruction steps of the new president, Andrew Johnson. But Johnson, in his determination to bring the rebel states back into the Union, soon exhibited what the Radical Republicans saw as excessive and even unjust leniency toward the South. Wilson soon was in the forefront of the Republican drive to derail presidential reconstruction and replace it with a congressional agenda laden with devices to combat continued southern white repression of the newly freed black slaves. In a July 4 speech to a black crowd in Washington, he promised to introduce in the first postwar session of Congress a civil rights bill outlawing racial discrimination and giving blacks the vote. He did so, but it won support only from the Radical Republicans and ultimately failed.

Later, however, as Johnson vetoed other legislative proposals to the same purpose, including extension of the Freedmen's Bureau, moderate Republicans joined the Radicals in a direct clash with Lincoln's successor, whose abiding hostility toward blacks became abundantly apparent. Wilson continued to insist that black suffrage was the key to breaking the white stranglehold on the South; he wanted to make it a condition by which southerners could again hold office in the Union, but Johnson would have none of it.

Prior to the 1866 congressional elections, Wilson attacked the National Union Convention in Philadelphia designed to rally support for Johnson, condemning it as "a conglomeration of pardoned and unpardoned rebels, copperheads and the flunkies of the Whig party."[10] He campaigned aggressively through the North and as far west as Chicago, traveling more than three thousand miles in opposition to Johnson's presidential reconstruction. In the fall elections, rejection of Johnson's agenda was overwhelming, with the coalition of moderate Republicans and the Radical Republicans capturing a clear two-thirds majority in the next Congress.

Wilson interpreted the result as a mandate from northern voters for black suffrage. He pushed particularly for the franchise in the District of Columbia and embarked on a tour of the South to assuage whites and bring them back into the Union as Republican voters. He took pains at the same time to persuade the black freedmen to eschew any thought of racial conflict: "See to it that while you are pulling yourself up, you don't pull others down." And he warned them that it would not be possible to "legislate you into any man's parlor." Laws could protect their civil rights, he said, "but your own brains, heart, conscience and life must fix your social position."[11]

Still, his message was a hard sell to the defeated white South. Wilson shared Johnson's desire to bring the region back into the Union, but he also wanted greater consideration for the freedmen than the president proposed. In statewide elections in 1867, Wilson's efforts to advance universal suffrage were rebuffed. In February 1868, when Johnson was impeached by the House but acquitted in the Senate in his firing of Secretary of War Edwin Stanton, the Radical Republicans saw their chance to seize the executive branch. Wilson entertained personal ambitions to gain a place on the Republican ticket with U. S. Grant, as a unifying leader.

In late May, with the Senate debating the readmission of seven southern states to the Union, Wilson rose and impatiently called on the Republican majority to allow the readmission as soon as the states ratified the Fourteenth Amendment, as required. "I would welcome back these states with their reform constitutions with a glad heart, with bonfires, with illuminations," he said, openly noting that doing so would "give more than one hundred thousand majority for General Grant."

In advance of the Republican National Convention, the Massachusetts state party advocated Wilson for the vice presidency, but he lacked wider support even in New England, and House Speaker Schuyler Colfax was nominated. The Democrats meanwhile brushed aside incumbent Johnson and chose New York governor Horatio Seymour with General Frank P. Blair Jr. as his running mate. Throughout the fall, Wilson toured eight states speaking for the Grant-Colfax ticket, unabashedly waving "the bloody shirt," charging at one New York rally that no Union soldier killed "was sent to his account by a Republican bullet. Let the mothers, wives and sisters of the North remember this. . . . There are over four hundred thousand heroes beneath the sod. Who sent them there? Democrats!"[12] On Election Night, the Republican victory in the popular vote was lower than expected, but Grant and Colfax won easily in the electoral college.

During Grant's first term, Wilson remained dissatisfied with the protection of blacks in the South. He appealed specifically for federal action against the rising Ku Klux Klan, for construction of more public schools in the South, and for an end to school segregation in the District of Columbia. Although the work of Reconstruction was far from completed, the issue lost much of its intensity. Wilson began to focus less on "slave power" and more on "money power" in the hands of corporate America and the ramifications for the working man. He called for a "new departure" for the Republican Party in supporting shorter working hours, protections against imported labor, and civil service reform. He also resumed his long interest in temperance and women's rights, broadening his reputation as a champion of the underdog.

In September 1870, when Vice President Colfax suddenly announced that he would not seek a second term in 1872, Wilson rekindled his ambition for the office. Considerable dissatisfaction with Grant was being heard within the Republican Party over his annexation of the Caribbean island of Santo Domingo through a treaty, which was then rejected by the Senate. When Colfax then changed his mind and said if chosen again he would run, Wilson at first considered withdrawing but agreed to stay in the race and was nominated.

In early September, the New York *Sun* broke the story of the Credit Mobilier scandal, listing Wilson along with Colfax as members of Congress who had received railroad stock for their support in the building of the Union Pacific Railroad. Wilson was reported at first to have flatly denied it. Questioned by a House investigating committee, he acknowledged that he had bought the stock in his wife's name but later returned it and got his money back. The committee finally cleared him of wrongdoing other than first calculating to create "an erroneous impression" to the public.

In the fall, Grant left the active campaigning to Wilson, who traveled ten thousand miles and made ninety-six speeches in behalf of the Republican ticket, against the Democratic presidential nominee, the New York editor Horace Greeley. Playing on the working-class backgrounds of the Republican candidates, a campaign banner showed Grant as "the Galena tanner," whose father indeed ran a leather tannery, and Wilson as the Natick shoemaker, both in workers' aprons.[13] The Republican ticket easily won the popular vote and all 286 electoral votes, because two weeks after the election Greeley died, before the electoral college met.

Wilson's campaign exertions took a heavy toll, incapacitating him for most of his vice presidency. In May 1873, barely two months after being inaugurated, he suffered a stroke at age sixty-one, leaving him without control of his facial muscles and unable to talk when fatigued. Disregarding doctors after a brief summer convalescence, he returned to Washington to preside over the Senate but had to return home to Massachusetts a month later. There he spent his time writing a long history of the slave power and his role in combating it during the Civil War and the Reconstruction era.[14]

Wilson heaped blame on Grant for the failures of Reconstruction, diminishing his own role in the Credit Mobilier scandal and that of other scandals involving the administration. He told Congressman James Garfield that Grant was "more unpopular than Andrew Johnson was in his darkest days" by virtue of terrible appointments, was "still struggling for a third term," and was "the millstone around the neck of [the Republican] party that would sink it out of sight."[15]

In early 1875, Wilson undertook a six-week tour of the South, creating suspicions that he might try for the presidency himself the next year, but that fall he went to his doctor complaining of head pain, soon suffered another stroke, and on November 22 died in his Senate president's office at age sixty-three. Henry Wilson had served in the vice presidency less than three years, and for most of that time he had been incapacitated, in disagreement with the president under whom he served, and was essentially disregarded by him.

Once again, a vice president had neither sought nor been accorded any significant share of executive power. And once again the second office would remain vacant for more than a year, to little evident public concern. Yet in the station Henry Wilson did reach in public life, he could claim considerable achievement in defending and improving the lot of the working class from which he had climbed, of whatever race and economic stature.

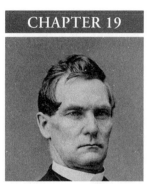

CHAPTER 19

WILLIAM A. WHEELER

OF NEW YORK

From the earliest years of the vice presidency, one of its only attractions for the ambitious politician was the possibility of ascension to the presidency, but no occupant aspired to that objective less than William Almon Wheeler of New York. Wheeler was content to remain a U.S. congressman from the upstate small town of Malone, which his speech accepting the Republican vice presidential nomination in 1876 made clear: "It is an honor which comes to me unexpectedly, which I did not seek, and which I say in all frankness I did not desire. So long as I might remain in the public service my preference was to remain in the House of Representatives."[1]

William Wheeler seemed an unlikely figure to have any political future at all. Born in Malone near the Canadian border on June 30, 1819, his father, Almon Wheeler, died in debt and in ill health at age thirty-seven, when the boy was only eight years old, leaving his destitute mother, Eliza, to raise him and a brother. She took in boarders from a nearby academy, and he performed farming chores to help while attending local public schools. He scraped up enough money by age nineteen to attend the University of Vermont for two years but had to quit with eye trouble. He then studied law under a local attorney for four years and was admitted to the New York bar. But he again became ill with a throat ailment that forced him to abandon his profession in 1851.[2] In fact, ill health plagued Wheeler throughout his life, limiting his engagement as a political speaker.

Turning to politics, he became the Malone town clerk at an annual salary of thirty dollars and taught in a neighboring town school for ten dollars a month. He wrote much later of the time, "I built many air castles in those days, but this [vice presidential] nomination was not among the structures."[3]

In 1867, he was elected a delegate at large to a state constitutional convention and was chosen its presiding officer. In unanticipated preparation for fulfilling his later responsibility as president of the U.S. Senate, he could not participate in the convention's debates, causing a colleague, Erastus Brooks, to call the limitation "a severe ordeal for a man of ability, literally putting a padlock upon his mind." He made committee appointments without regard to party, saying at the time, "I came to the chair with the single purpose of administering its duties fairly and impartially; remembering that the trust confided in us was neither for majorities nor minority, but for all alike as citizens of a common State."[4] Subsequently elected to the state Senate, he was chosen its speaker pro tem on the strength of that earlier service. Thereafter, during his five terms in the U.S. Congress, Wheeler was judged by one observer to be "a kind of legislative conscience" to other members who looked to his rare comments on the floor and to his votes for guidance.[5]

In 1871, a fierce political power struggle erupted between rival Republican factions in Louisiana, catching President Ulysses S. Grant in the middle, with Wheeler ultimately drawn in to arbitrate as chairman of the House Committee on Southern Affairs. The factions conducted separate conventions, nominated candidates for the governorship and other offices, and vied for control of the state. In a highly irregular military involvement in politics, Grant sent federal troops to protect the radical faction's convention in a federal building. The battle threw the state into chaos as, in effect, the two governors and two state legislatures clashed, with Grant vacillating on the role of federal troops and making a hash of his reconstruction efforts in the state. He tried to kick the ball to Congress while having to send federal troops to New Orleans to quell street violence.

The turmoil continued through 1874 and into 1875, until Wheeler led a committee investigation into the fiasco in New Orleans, where he encountered local abuse, was threatened with assassination, and on one occasion was fired on.[6] He eventually negotiated a truce between the factions, which was endorsed by the House and known as the Wheeler Compromise. It basically recognized William Pitt Kellogg of the radical faction as governor and seated enough Democrats in the lower house of the state legislature to gain control, while the state Senate remained Republican.

The deal subsequently was violated by the state's Democrats, including a failed effort to impeach Kellogg, and Grant essentially was content to be rid of the mess.[7] Wheeler took from the experience the sense that it was folly for the North after the war to try to impose its will on the South, including enforcement of the new constitutional guarantees to the freedmen, with the continued presence of federal troops.

In 1876, Wheeler was chosen by the rival Democratic caucus in the House to serve on a special committee to investigate Grant's war secretary, William Belknap, a Civil War general, on impeachment charges of corruption. Belknap was accused of accepting large kickbacks in the award of military contracts in Indian Territory, with his first wife a collaborator. Despite his government salary of only eight thousand dollars, he and his wife staged extravagant parties, which eventually raised eyebrows and brought about articles of impeachment against him. With the House committee poised to vote on those articles, Belknap sped to the White House and gave his resignation to the president, bursting into tears. Nevertheless the House voted unanimously to send the articles to the Senate, where a majority approved all charges but not the two-thirds required, so Belknap was acquitted.

In contrast, a Wheeler colleague, Robert H. Ellis, wrote of Wheeler later, "Other men have not accounted it an offense to use knowledge obtained by them as legislators as a basis for investments and business transactions. . . . With simple tastes, [Wheeler] has never been greedy of gain either for its own sake or the luxury it would buy. As a legislator, the thought never occurred to him that his influence could bring riches, and not the shadow of a stain rests on his name."[8] And when Congress voted a raise for itself, castigated by critics as "the salary grab," Wheeler wrote to the secretary of treasury, "As this measure was opposed by my vote in all its stages, it does not comport with my views of consistency or propriety to take the above sum to my personal use. I desire, therefore, without giving publicity to the act, to return it to the treasury, which I do by enclosing herewith five-twenty bonds of the United States, purchased with said funds and assigned by me to you for the sole purpose of cancellation."[9]

If the self-effacing congressman Wheeler ever had any further political ambition, it had been to become Speaker of the House. In 1872, when James G. Blaine of Maine ran for the office, Blaine's archrival, Senator Roscoe Conkling of New York, proposed to back Wheeler against him. Wheeler would have no part of it and supported Blaine. Now, in 1876, Conkling and Blaine were both vying for the Republican presidential nomination along with two favorite-son governors, Rutherford B. Hayes of Ohio and John F. Hartranft of Pennsylvania. Wheeler also was nominated as a long shot. Conkling again was bent on stopping Blaine, and when it became clear that Conkling could not be nominated himself, he and allies threw the Empire State's support to Hayes.

When the first roll call of the states began on June 16, Blaine finished first but well short of the required majority. Hayes was far behind in the pack, and Wheeler was at the bottom with only three votes. As Blaine slipped and Hayes climbed slowly, votes seesawed in several states until New York withdrew Conkling's name on the seventh ballot, and Hayes was nominated. Wheeler subsequently was proposed for vice president among other more well-known Republicans and was nominated. Hayes, on hearing of his name, asked his wife, "Who is Wheeler?"[10]

Many years later, Wheeler was memorialized in historian Allan Nevins's foreword to John F. Kennedy's Pulitzer prize-winning *Profiles in Courage,* offering an exchange between Conkling and then congressman Wheeler. Conkling was said to have proposed, "Wheeler, if you will act with us, there is nothing in the gift of the State of New York to which you may not reasonably aspire." Wheeler is said to have replied, "Mr. Conkling, there is nothing in the gift of the State of New York which will compensate me for the forfeiture of my self-respect."[11]

In the campaign between Hayes and the Democrat Samuel Tilden, one of the most tumultuous and contentious presidential campaigns up to that time, Wheeler was asked to address some mass meetings in his state, but he begged off pleading weariness and ill health, adding, "I regret I was nominated. You know I did not want the place. I should have gone back to the House, and into a Republican majority. I should have almost to a certainty, been its Speaker, which I would greatly prefer to being *laid away*."[12] In saying this, he left no doubt that he considered presiding over the Senate if elected vice president comparable to being put in the ground.

Democratic speakers focused on the many tales of scandal and corruption in the Grant years, and through it all Wheeler emerged with his reputation intact as a man of incorruptible integrity, unsusceptible to the temptations of personal ambition or wealth.

Tilden and his running mate, Thomas Hendricks of Indiana, won 51 percent of the popular vote to 48 percent for Hayes-Wheeler, but neither side had the required majority in the electoral college, throwing the election into the House of Representatives. The votes in three southern states still under federal occupation—South Carolina, Florida, and Louisiana—were contested, and finally a joint bipartisan commission of House, Senate, and Supreme Court members awarded all the disputed electors to Hayes and Wheeler in a 8–7 vote, declaring them elected by a single electoral vote. Ironically, one of those three states that made Wheeler vice president was Louisiana, where a year earlier his adjudication of its gubernatorial and legislative elections had resulted in a compromise that seemed to please no one and was later violated by the state's Democratic leaders.

In presiding over the Senate, Wheeler cast only six tie-breaking votes in four years, one of which helped seat William Pitt Kellogg, from Louisiana, in the Senate. This was the same man who had become governor of the state in the compromise struck by Wheeler in his thankless arbitration mission handed to him by Grant.

As vice president, Wheeler had little influence in the Hayes administration, but the president did occasionally sound him out on personalities in the cabinet. For example, about his secretary of state, William Evarts, Hayes wrote in his diary: "Mr. Vice President does not like Mr. Evarts. He thinks E. is not frank to those who speak about appointments. He does not say so, but by an equivocal, noncommittal way of talking allows them to hope. When there is no hope tell the man so. He will be disappointed at the time, but it is the best way. Mr. Wheeler is right. Prompt and square talk is in the long run safest and is just to the parties concerned. I must also bear this in mind."[13]

But Hayes excluded Wheeler from cabinet meetings and party caucuses, to Wheeler's consternation, and the vice president generally felt he was a lost soul, even to the point of remarking about attending church: "I hear the minister praying for the president, his Cabinet, both Houses of Congress, the Supreme Court, the governors and legislatures of all the states and every individual heathen . . . and find myself wholly left out."[14]

Wheeler, an old-fashioned homebody, was, however, often invited to the White House for social occasions, such as they were. As a widower in his sixties, he was a frequent Sunday night visitor, leading psalm singing in the library, with Secretary of the Interior Carl Schurz at the piano.

Hayes's failure to admit Wheeler to his inner circle was somewhat surprising, because well before the 1880 election, when the president let it be known he would not be seeking a second term, he mused in his diary about his successor: "If New York could with a fair degree of unity present a man like say the vice president . . . he probably could be nominated." But considering the turmoil among the state's Republicans, the chances of their putting forward someone like Wheeler, who was at such odds with Conkling, did not seem likely.[15] If Hayes, in considering who might best take his place in the Oval Office upon his own retirement, really thought of Wheeler, one might have expected he would have made much greater use of him, rather than allowing him to wallow in customary vice presidential isolation and boredom. But Wheeler seems to have suffered in silence, satisfied that it was customary and proper that the man sentenced to the office be required to wait in the wings.

After leaving the vice presidency, Wheeler ran for the U.S. Senate despite his unhappy tenure as its presiding officer, but lost and retired from public life. On June 4, 1887, days short of his sixty-eighth birthday, he died in his hometown of Malone. Apparently no American vice president sought less from the office and received less from it than this decent and unpretentious country lawyer.

CHAPTER 20

CHESTER A. ARTHUR
OF NEW YORK

O ne of the least likely men ever to become vice president became as well one of the least likely men ever to become president. Chester Alan Arthur, a little-known customhouse collector of the Port of New York, ousted from that position earlier on allegations of corruption, was chosen as the running mate of the 1880 Republican presidential nominee, James A. Garfield. Only four months after they took office, Garfield was assassinated by a man who, although unknown to Arthur, proclaimed on committing the foul deed that he had done it to put Arthur in the White House.

Nothing in Chester Arthur's beginnings or early years warranted such an event propelling him to national awareness and prominence. "Chet," as he was known as a boy, was born on October 5, 1829, into placid and nonpolitical circumstances in North Fairfield, Vermont, the son of a Baptist minister who preached in various churches in Vermont and neighboring upstate New York, until the family settled in Schenectady. Arthur attended Union College and graduated from it as a Phi Beta Kappa in 1848, then taught school, studied law, and was admitted to the bar in 1854 in New York City, where he started a small law firm. Sympathetic to abolition, he helped gain the right of black men to ride New York streetcars and the freedom of eight slaves brought into New York by a Virginia owner.[1]

During the Civil War, Arthur became a judge advocate general and later quartermaster general of the New York militia, giving him a military credential helpful when he entered politics, as well as the right to be called "General," although he never served in combat. Originally considering himself a Whig, Arthur was exposed early to the rough-and-tumble tactics of boss Thurlow Weed and joined the conservative wing of the Republican Party.[2] In 1867 at the party's state convention he hooked up with the man who soon would be both ally and rival on the state and national stages, the charismatic but tempestuous Roscoe Conkling. Arthur quickly became a loyal lieutenant in the Conkling organization, and after Conkling helped elect General Ulysses S. Grant as president in 1868, the grateful Grant rewarded him by appointing his friend Arthur to the lucrative job of New York customhouse collector.[3]

Grant was reelected in 1872 and toyed with seeking a third term in 1876 but was rebuffed, whereupon Conkling sought the Republican presidential nomination himself, with Arthur's loyal support. At the party's national convention in Cincinnati in June, Conkling, after trailing badly, threw his support to the eventual nominee, Governor Rutherford B. Hayes of Ohio, with Arthur dutifully falling in line. Arthur raised money and rallied New York voters for Hayes, hoping to keep his job at the customhouse if the Ohioan was elected over the Democrat Samuel J. Tilden.

But upon election, the reform-minded Hayes, well aware of allegations of payroll padding and other corruption at the customhouse, ordered an investigation of it. Among the allegations against Arthur and other "spoilsmen" were demands of salary kickbacks of from 2 to 6 percent to the Republican Party and as much as fifty thousand dollars a year in port fees siphoned off for the collector himself, about as much as the president's annual salary at the time.[4] The *New York Times,* however, at first defended Arthur, saying that while the customhouse was "the most investigated place in the country," it had "come out from each ordeal without a single breath of allegation against its head."[5]

Hayes instituted a civil-service merit system that angered both Arthur and Conkling, and Arthur was obliged to testify before a commission created by Hayes. He repeatedly insisted that although he was under great pressure to hire political friends he had given jobs only to qualified applicants. Hayes meanwhile forbade all federal workers from participating in political campaigns and other activities, a blow aimed at the heart of the Conkling organization.

Hayes eventually called for the resignations of Arthur and two Conkling men, and when Hayes nominated two replacements for them, Conkling led the Senate in refusing to confirm the men. Ultimately, however, they were replaced in what the editor E. L. Godkin called "an effective blow struck at what [was] worst in the present system" and at Conkling and his machine.[6] The bitterness continued through Hayes's presidency, and when Hayes decided not to seek a second term, and Grant, fresh from a long European tour, expressed interest again in a third presidential term, Conkling immediately took charge, along with Arthur.

At the Republican National Convention in Chicago, they stood firm through thirty-four ballots, until a longshot, the freshman senator James A. Garfield, made a stirring speech, and some New York delegates, in defiance of Conkling, switched to him on the thirty-fifth ballot, securing his nomination. As a gesture of conciliation, Conkling was offered the right to name Garfield's running mate. Arthur, learning of the offer, approached Conkling, who told him Garfield was certain to lose and advised him to forget about it. Arthur was overheard by a reporter replying, "The office of vice president is a greater honor than I ever dreamed of attaining. A barren nomination would be a great honor. In a calmer moment you will look at this differently." But Conkling snapped back, "If you wish for my favor and respect, you will contemptuously decline it." Arthur's reply, according to another bystander, was: "Such an honor and opportunity comes to very few of the millions of Americans, and to that man but once. No man can refuse it, and I will not." Whereupon Conkling turned and stalked from the room.[7]

Garfield meanwhile had just offered the vice presidential nomination to another New Yorker and friend, Congressman Levi P. Morton, a wealthy and prominent banker. Morton also consulted with Conkling and decided he would turn down the offer, easing the dilemma. Arthur's name went before the convention, and he was nominated on the first ballot, so little did the delegates think of his troubles at the New York customhouse.

On the Democratic side, the former Union general Winfield S. Scott was nominated for the presidency with the former congressman William H.

English of Indiana as his running mate. In August, Garfield swallowed his pride and went to New York to make peace with Conkling, but the New York Republican boss would not meet with him. Many reformers in the state also held their noses at having Arthur on the ticket. E. L. Godkin, the editor of the *Nation* magazine, wrote derisively of Arthur's nomination: "There is no place in which his powers of mischief will be so small as in the vice presidency." With Garfield only forty-eight years old and in robust health, Godkin added that the chances of Arthur being called to the presidency was a "too unlikely contingency to be making extraordinary provision for."[8]

At the White House, Hayes noncommittally called the nomination of Garfield "the best that was possible," but he was not so charitable about the selection of Garfield's running mate. "The sop thrown to Conkling in the nomination of Arthur," he growled, "only serves to emphasize the completeness of his defeat. He was so crushed that it was from sheer sympathy that this one was thrown to him."[9] Sympathy, however, was something seldom extended to the spiteful and combative Conkling; the gesture obviously was extended more out of fear about what wrath the vituperative party leader might impose on the Garfield campaign if completely ignored.

In the fall electioneering that followed, all the nominees stayed off the campaign trail and limited themselves to writing letters of acceptance that essentially endorsed their parties' platforms. Arthur, apparently to counter his record as New York customhouse collector, made a point of noting that he favored continued civil service reform. But one of his principal points was a slap at his own removal as collector: "The tenure of office should be stable."[10] Garfield, in a new campaign phenomenon, greeted hosts of daily callers from the front porch of his farmhouse in Mentor, Ohio.

Instead of campaigning, Arthur, now the state Republican Party chairman, immersed himself in the campaign's details, personally scheduling and overseeing the travels of Grant and Conkling in New York and the Midwest. Arthur assessed "voluntary contributions" from federal and state workers in great amounts in much the same way he had done as the customhouse collector. Garfield and Arthur carried New York State, and in the largest turnout of qualified voters in the nation's history, 76.4 percent, they were elected over Hancock and English.

After the inauguration, Arthur, with his long experience as an effective "spoilsman" in New York, hoped and expected to have a major say in the distribution of patronage, especially to the Empire State. But Garfield made clear from the first: "I will not tolerate nor act upon any understanding that anything has been pledged to any party, state or individual."[11] When Conkling, rebuffed over several Garfield decisions, turned to his old political subordinate Arthur, he found the new vice president ill-positioned to be of much help.

In mid-March, Conkling was summoned to the White House, where Garfield told him he was willing to make several New York appointments involving Conkling men, but not to the lucrative customhouse post once held by Arthur. Two days later the names of five Conkling men were sent to the Senate, but none for a cabinet post. Worse for Conkling, Garfield made an appointment that the *New York Herald* deemed a direct slap at Conkling, putting in the New York customhouse "a sharp politician . . . who [would] know how to work it for all it is worth against Conkling."[12]

Demonstrating where his loyalty rested, Arthur went to the White House at one point to urge Garfield to pull the offending job offer, but to no avail. Instead the president, determined to establish his primacy, withdrew the nominations of the five Conkling men. Conkling and Tom Platt, New York's other U.S. senator, were outraged and submitted their resignations to Arthur in the presiding officer's chair, sending the chamber into an uproar.

Conkling and Platt returned to Albany to push for their speedy reelection as a further demonstration of their political strength at home and that their fight with Garfield was not over. Vice President Arthur also returned to Albany to aid his old political colleagues. The *New-York Tribune* warned: "If General Arthur does not desire four years of public contempt he would do well to desist from the business in which he is now engaged before his inexcusable indiscretion becomes a National scandal. . . . The moral of his performances is that we must not expect to change a man's nature by electing him to the Vice-Presidency."[13]

The fight over the reelection bids of Conkling and Platt droned on for more than seven weeks, with no resolution. All this time, Arthur put his vice presidency on the back burner as he stayed at Conkling's side in Albany, returning to Washington only on weekends. On July 1, Platt suddenly dropped his bid for Senate reelection, after a Republican foe on a stepladder peered through an open transom of a hotel room and caught him in bed with a woman who was not his wife. The story swept through Albany and beyond, but Conkling and Arthur held firm.[14]

That same morning at Washington's Baltimore and Potomac Railroad Station, President Garfield strolled in with Secretary of State James Blaine on his arm. The president was en route to the commencement exercises at his alma mater, Williams College, in central Massachusetts, and then on to a vacation with his family. Already aboard the train were four other cabinet members and their wives, awaiting Garfield and Blaine. Suddenly a short and scrubby-looking man with a dark brown beard appeared behind them, drew a revolver and shot Garfield in the back. As the president fell, the attacker fled, but a District of Columbia policeman who had heard the shots ran down the man in the station's reception room and arrested him. "All right," the man said quietly. "I did it and will go to jail for it. I am a Stalwart, and Arthur will be president."[15]

The assailant was identified as Charles Guiteau, a mentally unbalanced government job seeker with grandiose ideas about obtaining a diplomatic post. The forty-eight-year-old assailant knew neither Garfield nor Arthur but had sent Garfield letters expressing interest in working in Vienna or Paris, and after the election was given to hanging around the State Department, where Blaine once encountered him and told him to stop making a pest of himself. When caught, police found on him a letter dated that day in which he had written that he bore "no ill will toward the President . . . [but] his death was a political necessity."[16] Garfield in fact was still alive, but severely wounded.

In another letter to Arthur, Guiteau informed him of what he had done, assuming Garfield was dead, and offered recommendations for a new cabinet. There was some immediate speculation, soon ended, that Arthur might have been involved in a plot. In any event, his qualifications to assume the presidency immediately came under editorial fire. The *New York Times* declared, "Active politicians, uncompromising partisans, have held before now the office of the Vice President of the United States, but no holder of that office has ever made it so plainly subordinate to his self-interest as a politician and his narrowness as a partisan."[17] Twice after hearing the news, Arthur went to the White House inquiring about Garfield's condition but was not told.

Through all this, Conkling clung to his effort in Albany to be reelected to the Senate. When the Conkling forces finally went down to defeat in late July, some of his old Stalwarts called on him at his Fifth Avenue Hotel suite to commiserate, but Chester Arthur was not among them now. By this time Garfield's condition had seriously deteriorated, and the vice president secluded himself in his home in New York, where no word was passed to him about the prospect of having to assume presidential responsibilities. At August's end, Blaine proposed to the cabinet that Arthur be called to Washington to take over the presidential duties, inasmuch as the Constitution said only that the "Powers and Duties" of the presidency were to "devolve" to the vice president "until the disability [of the president] be removed." But Arthur declined even to rush to Washington. The end for Garfield finally came on September 19, and a state supreme court judge was produced to swear Arthur in as the twenty-first president.

His ascendancy was marked by considerable apprehension, in light of his checkered career as a close ally of Conkling, even to the point of breaking with Garfield in their notorious clash over federal patronage to New York. Governor Charles Foster of Ohio put the matter as optimistically as possible in predicting, "The people and the politicians will find that Vice President Arthur and President Arthur are different men."[18]

Arthur's vice presidency had lasted only six months, and the shock of his elevation, as well the springing of a flood of hopeful goodwill from the country, seemed to sober him to his new responsibility. He was advised by friends to keep Garfield's cabinet for a time if only for the appearance of continuity, but many expected, and many others feared, that he would bring Conkling into his inner circle. The new president asked all cabinet members to stay on at least until the next session of Congress in December, and all did. In mid-October, however, Blaine asked to be allowed to resign, as friends urged him to prepare to make another presidential bid in 1884.

Conkling, still nursing his political wounds and hatred of Blaine, made clear his desire to replace his old enemy as secretary of state. But Arthur was well aware by now that such a move would be seen widely as turning his new administration over to his old political chieftain. Conkling himself called on the new president, offering to serve in his cabinet and presenting him with federal patronage demands for New York, the foremost of which was removal of Garfield's choice as collector of the New York customhouse.

Conkling, rebuffed, left in renewed anger. Other Conkling machine Stalwarts were invited to sumptuous White House receptions and dinners, but there was no rush to give them positions as had been widely expected. One old machine friend, John O'Brien, observed, "He isn't Chet Arthur any more, he's the president."[19]

Arthur did, however, retain some sense of obligation toward Conkling. In February 1882, he sent his old political boss's name to the Senate to fill a vacancy on the Supreme Court, but Conkling rejected it and retired from public life. During this time, Garfield's assassin was tried for murder and convicted. An appeal to Arthur to intervene on the grounds of insanity was rejected, and Guiteau was hanged.

In the congressional elections of 1882, continued allegations of government corruption contributed to Republican loss of the House and a narrower majority in the Senate. To the amusement of many, Arthur, the old Conkling political spoils man, in his first annual address to Congress embraced Garfield's call for civil service reform, including competitive tests for government jobs based on the British system. In January 1883, Congress passed and Arthur signed an act establishing the bipartisan Civil Service Commission, following the lead laid down by Garfield.

The nation's fourth accidental president generally trod carefully in legislative affairs but did use his veto power on a few occasions. To great surprise as an old spoils man, Arthur vetoed a classic "pork-barrel" rivers and harbors appropriations bill through which legislators had approved millions of dollars for their districts for years.[20] Congress overrode the veto, but Arthur won wide editorial praise for his action.

After a respectful grieving period following Garfield's death, Arthur had the White House redecorated and opened it to a great many sumptuous dinners, with his sister Mary serving as hostess for her widowed brother. He eventually took to the presidency with relish, and his personal demeanor did much to counter the negativity and doubts that had greeted his assumption of the first office. In 1882, however, he suffered an attack of what later was described as Bright's disease, a serious kidney ailment that often proved fatal. In March 1883 he confided to his son, Alan, that he was so ill he could hardly perform his presidential duties, and in May the *Hartford Evening Post* reported, "He has repeatedly given his friends to know that under no conceivable circumstances would he again be President."[21]

Nevertheless, Arthur continued to receive favorable comments for his stewardship, which had been greeted with such misgivings upon Garfield's death. None other than Mark Twain was quoted in the *Chicago Daily News* in August as observing: "I am but one in the 55,000,000; still, in the opinion of this one fifty-five millionth of the country's population, it would be hard indeed to better President Arthur's administration. But don't decide till you hear from the rest."[22] Newspaper surveys of leading Republicans and editors, though, found Arthur trailing Blaine, even in New York samplings. Contrary to certain newspaper reports, Arthur let it be known he would welcome the chance to lead the party again in 1884 but said nothing about the state of his health, which was gradually deteriorating.

At the Republican National Convention in June, Blaine entered as the clear frontrunner. Arthur, who did not attend, ran a respectable second on the first ballot but slipped gradually, and Blaine was nominated on the fourth roll call. When Tom Platt, who seconded Blaine's nomination, asked Conkling to endorse his candidate, lawyer Conkling characteristically and acidly replied, "No thank you. I don't engage in criminal practice."[23]

That fall, Blaine narrowly lost the presidency to the Democratic governor Grover Cleveland of New York. Arthur, his health further declining, returned quietly to his law office in New York, where on November 17, 1886, he finally succumbed to Bright's disease. Chosen vice president in an irresponsible manner and often at odds with the president he served while in that position, Chester Arthur comported himself honorably as Garfield's successor in achieving some of the fallen president's prime objectives. Associated with political corruption in his earlier years, he redeemed his reputation with his signature on the most significant civil service reform of his time.

CHAPTER 21

THOMAS A. HENDRICKS
OF INDIANA

I n the annals of American vice presidents, no occupant of the office had a more tortuous route to achieving it than the Democrat Thomas A. Hendricks of Indiana. In the course of that route, he earned a controversial reputation as an opportunist with views on race that cast a shadow on a political career marked by as many defeats as victories.

Rejected as a vice presidential running mate of Samuel J. Tilden of New York in 1876, Hendricks was first used eight years later as a foil in an effort to block the presidential nomination of Governor Grover Cleveland of New York. When that failed, he became Cleveland's successful running mate in a balancing move on the 1884 Democratic ticket, marking the party's first victory since the Civil War. Only nine months later, sudden death claimed him, leaving his record marred by a clinging racial bias.

Ironically, as a young lawyer Hendricks brought suit against a white neighborhood tough who assailed and sought to get a black boy thrown into jail simply for talking to him. Hendricks got the assailant jailed instead by convincing a jury that attacking one of inferior social position was a greater offense.[1] That case, however, did not foretell a racial animosity that would later surface in his political career.

Born in a farmhouse near Zanesville, Ohio, on September 7, 1819, Hendricks was six months old when his father, John, moved the family to Indiana and became a successful farmer and operator of a general store in Shelbyville. After graduating from Hanover College, young Hendricks studied law, began a practice in Indiana, and in 1848 entered politics, winning a seat in the Indiana House of Representatives. He was a delegate to the state constitutional convention, where he revealed his anti-black bias, leading an effort to enact "Black Laws" upholding racial segregation and limiting immigration of free blacks into Indiana. In one speech, he declared, "The races are different—physically, intellectually and morally. . . . They cannot meet and mingle, in a state of social and political equality without a violation of the laws of nature and a gross outrage of all our better feelings, and without producing a degradation of our own race."[2]

In 1850 Hendricks was elected to Congress, served two terms, and as a disciple of Senator Stephen A. Douglas of Illinois was a strong supporter of popular sovereignty and the extension of slavery into the West. He backed Douglas's controversial Kansas-Nebraska Act, which repealed the Missouri Compromise, costing Hendricks reelection. In 1860 he ran for the governorship of Indiana but lost.

With the outbreak of the Civil War, Hendricks became a War Democrat in the state party deeply split over the war. He found himself in sharp conflict with the leading Indiana Peace Democrat, Jesse Bright, the U.S. Senate president pro tem, who in early 1862 was expelled for writing a letter to the Confederate president Jefferson Davis, suggesting that the rebel army buy rifles from an Indiana firm. Hendricks was elected by the state legislature to take the seat in the next term. Meanwhile, he rallied fellow War Democrats to defeat anti-war resolutions in the state legislature.

Upon taking his seat in the Senate in 1863, where there now were only ten Democrats to thirty-three Republicans, Hendricks became the party leader and as a War Democrat had frequent access to President Lincoln while maintaining a partisan posture. Shortly before Lincoln's death, Hendricks called on the president at the White House, where Lincoln told him, "We have differed in politics, Senator Hendricks, but you have uniformly treated my administration with fairness. Presently there will be no differences between us." Whereupon Lincoln took Hendricks by his arm and led him to a window overlooking the Potomac and beyond, into Virginia, saying, "Within a few months there will be such universal good feeling over there that it will bring us all together."[3] It was hardly one of Lincoln's most prophetic visions.

In a speech on the Senate floor on April 7, 1864, one week before the assassination, Hendricks opposed abolition on these grounds: "It is not a favorable time for us to lay our hand upon the work of the fathers." With the nation at war and with the Southern states excluded, he argued, the move should await bringing them back into the fold.[4] He insisted he was never in favor of the subjugation of the South, but for "the prosecution of the war upon such a policy as will secure a return of the Southern people, that there may be prosperity and greatness and enterprise of the North at the same time."[5]

Indeed, after Lincoln's death Hendricks was conspicuously sympathetic to southern whites and hostile to freedmen's rights. He opposed the post-war constitutional amendments that were at the heart of Reconstruction— the Thirteenth abolishing slavery, the Fourteenth providing due process protection, and the Fifteenth barring denial of suffrage on racial grounds. He reminded Radical Republicans that Lincoln had declined to sign, and instead had pocket-vetoed, the Wade-Davis Bill, which would have barred reentry of southern states unless 50 percent of their citizens signed an iron-clad oath that they had never supported the Confederacy.

Hendricks also fought against the repeal of the fugitive slave laws prior to the constitutional abolition of slavery and generally resisted all forms of social integration. "I say we are so different," he observed emphatically, "that we ought not to compose one political community."[6] And later: "I say that our fathers were right in saying that this was a white man's government, to be controlled by white men. I say that I do not deem the negro to be my equal."[7]

When the Indiana legislature went Republican in 1868, Hendricks was not offered a second U.S. Senate term. Critics argued that he had not originated nor was he identified with any prominent policy or legislation and that he was noted principally as an obstructionist, especially on issues involving race and Reconstruction. Despite his skimpy record of achievement in the Senate, however, Hendricks was popular there for his candor and leadership of the minority views he represented.

Despite those controversial positions, Hendricks was offered as a presidential candidate that year at the Democratic National Convention, in New York, and in a tempestuous and drawn-out fight over three days, he actually led the balloting briefly on the twenty-second ballot, before the delegates turned to Governor Horatio Seymour of New York. Hendricks subsequently returned to Indiana and ran for its governorship once more but was again defeated. He was mentioned again as a presidential prospect in 1872 but instead ran for the governorship of Indiana yet again, and this time he won. Coming from an important swing state, Hendricks seemed poised for another presidential bid in 1876, but investor advocates of "hard money" achieved the nomination of their like-minded Tilden.

As a consolation, Hendricks, as an advocate of "soft money" to ease farmers' ability to pay their debts, was made the Democratic vice presidential nominee to balance Tilden's currency stand. In his acceptance speech, he struck a conciliatory note, observing, "Gold and silver are the real standards of value," but adding, "Our national currency will not be a perfect medium of exchange until it shall be convertible at the pleasure of the holder."[8] The Democratic ticket of Tilden and Hendricks won the popular vote by 251,000 ballots but fell one vote short of an electoral college majority. Then a special commission awarded all disputed votes in four states to the Republican ticket of Rutherford B. Hayes and William A. Wheeler, and the election was theirs.

Four years later, Indiana Democrats considered pushing Hendricks for president one more time, but while on vacation in Hot Springs, Arkansas, he suffered a stroke. He later also developed a lameness in one foot, but nevertheless in 1884, with an ailing Tilden declining a second try himself, Hendricks made known he was willing once again. Tilden, hearing that Hendricks had talked of a reprise of the Tilden-Hendricks ticket, chided him, "I do not wonder, considering my weakness!"[9] But by now Hendricks was seen as a perennial candidate for some office or another, and he attended the Democratic convention in Chicago in early July prepared to nominate the former Indiana senator Joseph E. McDonald.

In the first session, the temporary chairman, Governor Richard B. Hubbard of Texas, drew cheers and applause for Tilden and Hendricks for their honorable acceptance of the election commission's denial of their 1876 quest. Nevertheless, the nomination seemed well in hand for Governor Grover Cleveland of New York, with the convention's largest delegation behind him. But rival Tammany Hall Democrats, led by New York City mayor John Kelly, launched a stop-Cleveland scheme, whereby the front-runner might be derailed by the backing of a dark horse, settling on a willing Thomas Hendricks. Early the next morning, when the popular Hoosier, "robbed" of the vice presidency in 1876, entered the hall, Kelly men jumped up and tried to launch a loud floor demonstration and stampede for him. But only the Tammany men joined the cry of "Hendricks! Hendricks!"[10] An alert Cleveland man had caught wind of the scheme, roused Cleveland delegates from their beds to block it, and the brief insurrection was snuffed out.[11]

Cleveland prevailed as a hard-money advocate who could not only win New York but also bring liberal Republicans to his camp, and Hendricks, once again as a ticket-balancing soft-money man from a swing state, landed the vice presidential nomination a second time.[12] In the fall campaign, Cleveland essentially stayed on the sidelines, making only two explicitly political appearances while his Republican opponent, James G. Blaine, the "plumbed knight" of Maine, traveled widely. But Hendricks, determined not to have the national office elude him as it had as Tilden's running mate in 1876, campaigned hard, particularly after July 21, when the Buffalo *Evening Telegraph* broke the sensational news that Cleveland had fathered a son born of a local widow ten years earlier.

The story was spread widely by other newspapers, often without noting that Cleveland was a bachelor at the time. The Democratic candidate, however, admitted he was the father of the boy who bore his name and that he had assumed responsibility, providing for the child's needs and helping the woman, Maria Halpin, who had fallen into heavy drinking, in relocating and starting a business. The boy was settled in an orphanage and later adopted. The episode gave rise to the oft-repeated Republican campaign chant: "Ma! Ma! Where's my Pa? Gone to the White House, ha, ha, ha!" Cleveland's demeanor after the boy's birth, however, on balance probably won as much voter support as his paternity cost him.[13]

The Tilden-Hendricks ticket received an unexpected boost when, during a dinner in Blaine's honor at the plush Delmonico's in Manhattan, the pastor of the Murray Hill Presbyterian Church, Dr. Samuel D. Burchard, rose and grandly promised Blaine: "We are Republicans, and we don't propose to leave our party and identify ourselves with the party whose antecedents have been Rum, Romanism and Rebellion." The Democrats had assigned a stenographer to take down remarks at the dinner, and soon the slur, interpreted as aimed at the Irish Catholics and the South, was spread across the country.[14] It was estimated later that Burchard's remarks cost Blaine critical Irish and Catholic votes, particularly in New York. Cleveland and Hendricks won by the narrowest margin up to that time, with 48.5 percent of the vote compared with 48.26 percent for Blaine and his running mate, John A. Logan.

Blaine later wrote to a friend, Francis Fessenden, "I should have carried New York by 10,000 if the weather had been clear on election day and Dr. Burchard had been doing missionary work in Asia Minor or Chochin China."[15] As for the paternity issue involving the Democratic nominee, the party faithful were soon riffing, "Hurrah for Maria! Hurrah for the kid! I voted for Cleveland, and damned glad I did."[16]

As vice president, Hendricks had little influence in the Cleveland administration and, as a champion of agrarian interests, differed with the new president's business and industrial orientation. Also, as a seeker of federal patronage for Indiana Democrats, he lacked the zeal for reform that became a hallmark of Cleveland's presidency and was unsympathetic to Cleveland's embrace of civil service improvements under the Pendleton Act.

Hendricks's own pressures on the administration for more patronage jobs to Indiana Democrats earned him the derogatory label "Vice President of the Spoilsmen." He did, however, abide by the civil service reforms, while noting that only 15,000 federal employees were subject to them, leaving 125,000 others to be dealt with through old-fashioned patronage.[17]

In the spring of 1885, Hendricks set off on a vacation to Atlantic City and then on to Yale and Harvard for receptions and speeches at their law schools. Once home in Indianapolis, he and his wife enjoyed a round of social events with friends, and he appeared to be in good health. But on November 24 at a reception he suddenly looked pale and tired, and a doctor was called. Hendricks told him, "I am free at last." He went to bed and never woke up, dying peacefully at age sixty-six.

For the fifth time, the vice presidency became vacant as a result of the death of its occupant. Thus, in ten of the first eighteen presidencies, there was no sitting vice president, raising a serious question of prospective presidential succession. But the vice presidency by now had come to be so lightly regarded that few seemed to care. Upon Hendricks's death, the order of presidential succession set in 1792 placed the Senate president pro tem and then the Speaker of the House next in line. But both offices were also vacant at this time, and there was also the possibility, with the Republicans in the majority in the Senate, that the next successor would be of the opposite party to the Democrat Cleveland.

Therefore, in 1886, Congress passed a law removing congressional leaders from the line and replaced them with the president's cabinet members behind the vice president, making more likely that a new president would be of the same party. The secretary of state, as the senior cabinet official, would be first, followed by the others according to the date their department was established. That procedure remained until 1947, when congressional leaders were returned to the order, with the House Speaker first and then the Senate president pro tem, on the grounds that any president should first have been elected by the people.

The new line of presidential succession could not of course be attributed solely to Hendricks's sudden death. But the congressional leaders were alerted once more to a long-neglected problem, although the new line of succession did not deal with the issue of a vice presidential vacancy itself. That would take more vacancies and eighty years before ratification of the Twenty-Fifth Amendment, providing for the presidential nomination of a new vice president with the assent of Congress. In the end, Hendricks's service in the second office could be said to be memorable chiefly for an action taken by others upon his leaving it.

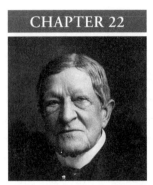

CHAPTER 22

LEVI P. MORTON
OF NEW YORK

L evi Parsons Morton was one of the nation's most successful bankers and
businessmen when he began dabbling in the world of politics, then
eventually became vice president of the United States in the election of
1888. From the humblest beginnings he built a fortune, became a lieutenant
of the New York political boss Roscoe Conkling, and passed up a chance
to be vice president under President James A. Garfield before accepting the
office under President Benjamin Harrison. After undistinguished service in
that office, he became the governor of New York but never really mastered
the skills of politics, unlike the skills of finance, which had made him a giant in that world.

Morton came from a long line of Puritan New England stock. In 1814
his father, the Reverend Daniel Oliver Morton, had moved from the family
home in Middleboro, Massachusetts, to Shoreham, Vermont, near Lake
Champlain. In 1816 Daniel graduated from Middlebury College, took
over a small Congregational church, and married his wife, Lucretia, who
on May 16, 1824, gave him a son, Levi. The father was a strong advocate
of temperance in alcohol and also a condemner of slavery. In his church he
set aside a "negro pew" for the few slaves in the community to share in the
Sabbath worship. Despite young Levi's thorough grounding in the religious
life, he chose a career in business rather than in the church, leading one

of his grandfathers to write, "I hear that Levi is prospering in this world's goods. I fear lest it be at cost to his soul."[1]

Because Levi's father could not afford to send him to college, at age fourteen the boy took a job in a general store in Enfield, New Hampshire, for a salary of fifty dollars a year plus room and board in the home of his employer. He moved on to a somewhat more lucrative job in Concord, and when the prospering owner decided to open a branch in Hanover, home of Dartmouth College, he sent Levi to manage it. At the age of twenty-one Levi took over the branch when the owner was about to close it.[2] There he also met and married his future wife, Lucy Young Kimball. She didn't care for his first name, so she took to calling him by his initials, and he came to be known among his family and closest friends as LP.[3]

With his business prospering, Morton became active in the civic and then the political communities. As an ardent Whig, he served as the toastmaster at a celebratory dinner after the election of President Zachary Taylor in 1848. He joined a series of large business and banking firms and in 1851 took a partner, Junius Spencer Morgan, father of J. Pierpont Morgan, a rising young banker. They merged into a broader firm called J. M. Beebe, Morgan and Company. Finally, he moved to New York and, with another partner, set up his own wholesale dry goods firm called Morton, Grinnell and Company.[4]

In advance of the Civil War, Morton focused on buying southern cotton for the textile mills in New England and sending northern manufactured products to the South, an arrangement demolished when war broke out in 1861. As the war progressed, his business recovered, and he segued into banking, forming Morton, Bliss and Company, which was linked to a London house known as Morton, Rose.

During the war, British shipping firms built warships for the Confederacy in violation of international neutrality laws. Afterward, Senator Charles Sumner, chairman of the Senate Foreign Relations Committee, demanded that Britain pay huge compensation, including the U.S. annexation of Canada, for damages inflicted on American ships by British-built Confederate vessels. They came to be known as the Alabama Claims, after one such ship that had sunk or damaged Union shipping. Into this controversy stepped Morton and his British partner, Sir John Rose, to engage in international arbitration. The British finally agreed to pay fifteen million dollars, to be disbursed through Morton, Rose, and beyond that the Americans consented to ignore the British dealings with the Southern rebellion.[5]

In the same year, Morton's wife, Lucy, died, and two years later he married Anna Livingston Reade Street, a New York socialite who brought him entrée into the city's social and political circles. He already had become a friend of President Grant and one of Grant's main political backers, Senator Roscoe Conkling, boss of the New York Republican Stalwarts.

In 1876 Morton became the financial chairman of the Republican National Committee, and two years later he won a seat in Congress from a fashionable Manhattan district. A tall and erect man of quiet elegance, he immediately took his place as an important cog in the Conkling machine and as a desirable host of social and political gatherings at his spacious home. Among his friends in Congress was Representative James A. Garfield of Ohio.

In 1880, Morton attended the Republican National Convention as part of Conkling's effort to win a third presidential term for Grant and to block his bitter rival, James G. Blaine. Morton cast his vote for Grant through all thirty-six ballots, even as a resulting deadlock led the Blaine forces to throw their votes to Garfield, a late dark-horse entry. Garfield, realizing he needed a New Yorker as his running mate, turned to Morton, who after seeking Conkling's advice declined the nomination. Garfield then offered it to another New Yorker and Conkling man, Chester Arthur, who became vice president and then president upon Garfield's assassination.

Morton instead agreed to serve as Garfield's campaign finance chairman, apparently assuming he would be appointed secretary of treasury in a Garfield administration. But Garfield was reluctant to choose a prominent banker, although Morton had agreed to give up his professional endeavors to serve. Garfield later wrote in his diary that Morton was "under misapprehension" that he had been promised the treasury post, insisting, "It would be a congestion of financial power at the money centre and would create jealousy in the West."[6]

Morton, reelected to the House, meanwhile had cast his eye on the U.S. Senate seat, and Conkling calculated that placing him in the cabinet would clear the field for his own friend Tom Platt, also seeking the seat. Morton, feeling he was entitled to the Senate post after having given up the vice presidential nomination, demanded that Conkling ask Platt to withdraw, but Conkling declined.

Garfield and Morton remained on good terms through all this, and shortly before Garfield's inauguration he offered Morton the cabinet position of secretary of the navy, which Morton accepted. Conkling was not pleased; he informed Garfield that New York would rather have no cabinet seat if it could not be the Treasury. In the middle of the night, Conkling and Vice President Elect Arthur urgently went to Morton's lodgings, roused him, and got the loyal Conkling lieutenant to withdraw his acceptance of the navy post. In his diary the next day, Garfield wrote, "Morton broke down on my hands under the pressure of his N.Y. friends, who called him out of bed at 4 this morning to prevent his taking the Navy Dep't. . . . The N.Y. delegation are in a great row because I do not give the Treasury to that state."[7]

Many other Morton friends urged him not to pass up the chance to serve in the Garfield cabinet in some capacity. He wrote later about contacting Garfield to tell him of his willingness: "I would, if he so desired, accept the position of Secretary of the Navy, but as I had been a hard-working business man, I should prefer, if agreeable to him, the post of Minister to England or France. . . . He then offered me the position of Minister to France, which I accepted."[8]

Morton had not yet sailed for Paris when Garfield was shot at the train station in Washington, D.C., on July 2, 1881. Eighteen days later, when Morton departed, the president was still clinging to life. His death on September 19 brought home Morton's realization of his fateful decision in declining Garfield's offer to be his vice presidential nominee. Morton remained in his diplomatic post, performing largely ceremonial duties, including presiding at France's presentation of her gift of the Statue of Liberty, destined to grace the entrance to New York Harbor.

Platt backed Morton for the Senate in 1885 and again in 1887 to no avail, as the New York Republicans were badly split. In 1888, James Blaine, in declining health, chose not to seek the presidential nomination again, and Platt put New York behind the Indiana senator Benjamin Harrison, the grandson of President William Henry Harrison, the hero of the Battle of Tippecanoe. Blaine, vacationing in Italy, wrote Morton, "The tendency I think is toward a Western candidate for President. If this is so, you will have a splendid opening for V.P. if you desire it and set your New York friends to work."[9]

Morton did so and was nominated. He admittedly was not much of a public speaker and left that aspect of the campaign to the articulate Harrison, concentrating instead on organization, fund-raising, and his broad contacts in the business and banking world. The Republican ticket lost the popular vote by ninety thousand ballots but won in the electoral college over the Democrats Grover Cleveland, the president seeking reelection, and his running mate, Allan G. Thurman of Ohio. In demeanor, Harrison and Morton offered the country a cameo of solid Republicanism of conservative and religious values.

As president of the Senate, Morton chaired a body heavily populated with successful businessmen and bankers like himself, of which he was among the most prominent. But his business acumen was of little help to Harrison on critical political matters. Senator Henry Cabot Lodge of Massachusetts at one point sought to bring to the floor a so-called force bill that would have obliged the southern states to permit black men to vote in protection of their civil rights. The rigorously even-handed Morton declined to interfere with a Democratic filibuster, and the force bill finally was moved aside without action.[10]

By 1892, Morton's independence as president of the Senate had cooled Harrison toward him, and he was dropped from the Republican ticket, replaced by an old New York friend and publisher, Whitelaw Reid. Blaine resigned as Harrison's secretary of state to run again for president himself, and old party bosses like Platt and Matthew Quay of Pennsylvania signed on with Blaine. Platt meanwhile, foreseeing a likely Harrison defeat at the hand of Cleveland seeking to regain the presidency, persuaded Morton to run for the governorship of New York in 1894. Cashing in on his great popularity in his home state, Morton won easily, providing a steady and reliable hand in business and banking experience to the state.

In 1896, Platt offered Morton as New York's favorite son for the party's presidential nomination at age seventy-two. Platt hoped to derail the bid of Governor William McKinley of Ohio, fearing he might consider free-silver currency in his platform, threatening the entrenched gold standard worshipped in the eastern financial centers. But Platt as a strategist was no match for McKinley's campaign manager, Mark Hanna, who returned the Republicans to the White House.

Upon the defeat, Morton rejoined the banking world, where he built the Morton Trust Company, and in 1909 he accepted a bid from J. P. Morgan to merge into what became the giant Morgan Guaranty Trust Company. After a successful career in politics that had brought him to Congress, the vice presidency, and the governorship of his state, Levi Morton retired from the banking world in his eighties and died on his ninety-sixth birthday, likely more revered and almost certainly more remembered for his private activities than for his government service.

CHAPTER 23

ADLAI E. STEVENSON

OF ILLINOIS

I n the history of politics in Illinois, one of the most illustrious names is that of Adlai E. Stevenson. But it is the fate of the twenty-third vice president of the United States that the reference usually is not to him but to his namesake grandson, who twice ran for the presidency and twice lost. And while the grandson remains heralded in Democratic legend as the epitome of morality and integrity in politics, the grandfather's niche is found in his strong and consistent partisanship and office peddling.

The first Adlai Ewing Stevenson actually came from Kentucky, where he was born on the family farm of John Turner Stevenson and his wife, Eliza, on October 23, 1835. The family originally came from Presbyterian stock in Scotland and northern Ireland before immigrating to Pennsylvania, North Carolina, and finally the small town of Blue Water, Kentucky. There young Adlai attended a one-room schoolhouse lorded over by a tyrannical schoolmaster long remembered thereafter.[1] The family raised tobacco until 1852, when a severe frost destroyed the season's crop. The father, an owner of slaves, freed them, packed up sixteen-year-old Adlai and the rest of the family, moved to Bloomington, Illinois, where some other relatives lived, and bought part ownership of a sawmill.[2] They left behind not only relatives but also slavery, which was barred in Illinois, and country life for the then-booming town.

Young Adlai worked in the sawmill, taught at a local school, and attended

Illinois Wesleyan. Then, with his parents' help he returned to Kentucky and enrolled at Centre College, in Danville, where political debates first whetted his interest. There he also met the daughter of headmaster Reverend Lewis Warner Green, Letitia, whom he would later marry. But first his father's death obliged him to return to Bloomington to run the sawmill. When the Reverend Green died, Letitia moved near Bloomington, where she and Stevenson finally were wed in 1866. They had three daughters and one son, Lewis, who would later be the father of the second and more famous Adlai Stevenson.[3]

In the course of starting up a practice in law, the first Adlai inevitably became enmeshed in politics, at a time when the Democratic and Whig Parties were being challenged by a number of new splinter groups over issues ranging from slavery and immigration to trade and tariffs, the most prominent of those groups being the Know-Nothings. He was admitted to the bar in 1858, the year of the famous Lincoln-Douglas debates for a U.S. Senate seat. Hearing some of them and inspired, he ran for town council in Metamora but lost, although he was later elected a district attorney in 1864.

With the Civil War raging, largely unexamined and unexplained until later was the able-bodied Stevenson's absence of military service or uniform. In the summer of 1863, an assistant provost marshal came to Metamora to register all unmarried men between twenty and forty for the federal draft, and Stevenson's name appeared on the list. Long thereafter, political foes alleged that Stevenson had bought his way out of military service. There was no record, however, that he had hired a substitute as was allowed, that he had paid what was called "blood money" of three hundred dollars to escape the draft, as his younger brother William had done, or that he was excused for medical reasons. Some speculated later that he may have qualified for exemption as a widow's son who had taken on the responsibility of providing for the rest of the family, although he was not living with his mother at the time.

Later also, Stevenson was accused of joining the Knights of the Golden Circle, a group said to support the Confederacy and to actively oppose the draft. As he became more prominent in Democratic politics, other allegations were aired, including one that he had sold pistols to draft dodgers.[4] Unquestionably he was politically ambitious and perhaps felt—as a later vice president, Dick Cheney, asserted about his lack of service in the Vietnam War—that he had "other priorities."

In 1869, Adlai and Letitia Stevenson moved from Metamora back to Bloomington, where he joined a cousin, James S. Ewing, in forming the law firm of Stevenson and Ewing, later one of the state's best known. His genial nature and reputation as a witty storyteller made for friendships that crossed party lines and encouraged him to reach higher in politics.

In 1874, on a wave of resentment toward the Republican Party resulting from the economic panic of the previous year, Stevenson ran as a Democrat for the U.S. House of Representatives in the normally Republican Thirteenth Illinois Congressional District. His Republican opponent, a colonel of the Union's Bloomington regiment in the Civil War, was no pushover. He used a pitch aimed at local Democrats and the new reformers that much later would be called "class warfare" politics. Stevenson in turn railed against the "Republican moneyed interests of this country and their conspiring bondholders," who exploited "the overtaxed and impoverished people."[5] Stevenson, however, always tempered his assaults with storytelling, as in his tale of a convicted murderer sentenced to hang while a local politician appeared on the same gallows platform. The murderer, when asked what his last wish was, demanded that he be hanged before the politician was allowed to speak.

Some Republicans against Stevenson brought up the allegations of disloyalty during the Civil War. When one heckler yelled out during a speech, "You were a Confederate sympathizer and a Knight of the Golden Circle," Stevenson shot back, "My friend, you are a liar. I want you to understand me. Anyone else who makes that statement is a willful and a deliberate liar."[6] His allegiance to the Union was clear in many ways, but the fact that he had not worn the uniform and had not been in combat hounded him thereafter.

On Election Day, he was confronted at the polls by temperance crusaders demanding that he sign a pledge opposing the sale of liquor in Bloomington. Although he was a teetotaler, he refused, saying it was an individual choice. He won the House seat in a three-man race.

Only two years later, when the Republican governor Rutherford B. Hayes of Ohio won the presidency in the controversial campaign against the Democrat Samuel J. Tilden, more Republicans turned out, and Stevenson narrowly lost the House seat. He won it back in 1878 but lost it again in 1880 and in 1882. After that roller coaster ride, his political future looked grim. Of his congressional service, Stevenson told his friends, "I will pillow my head consoled by the thought that no act of mine has made the poor man's burden heavier."[7]

Back in Bloomington, he worked for the election of the Democratic presidential nominee Grover Cleveland and in 1885 became his first assistant postmaster general, charged with overseeing fifty-five thousand fourth-class post offices across the country. Somewhat surprisingly but boldly, he expressed public disappointment with his own president's slow pace in replacing Republican and independent federal officeholders with Democrats. When the *New York World* editorially scolded Cleveland, reminding him of "the obligations which an Administration elected by a great historical party owes to that party" after so many years of Republican control of the White House, Stevenson agreed.

Soon he was doing his best to make up for the lost time. Local postmasters, often farmers whose post offices became the gathering places for community and political gossip, were appointed at Stevenson's pleasure and became a convenient recruitment tool for political allies and foot soldiers. The task sharpened his talent for the useful patronage giving that became a hallmark of his public service, even as civil service reforms broadened.

He welcomed and often rewarded job seekers who became his political helpmates, having no hesitation about ousting Republicans and replacing them with Democrats, to the point of being known as "Adlai the Axeman." The Republican *New York Herald* dubbed him "a man who uses the guillotine freely and is decapitating thousands."[8] Detractors had a field day, while approving Democrats shortened his job title to "General," ironically giving some the impression that he had engaged in the high military service whose absence had brought the critics' charges of disloyalty.

In 1892, the New Yorker Cleveland sought to regain the presidency. He was easily nominated on the first ballot, and the Democrats looked for a mate from a midwestern state with a large electoral vote. Stevenson came from a large and by now well-known Illinois family, and his reputation as a congenial and accommodating "spoilsman" at the U.S. Post Office Department might also attract hopefuls for federal jobs.[9] From the convention floor, an Illinois delegate offered Stevenson as "a man that is known by every woman, child and voter that ever licked a stamp, in every village and hamlet in the land."[10] He, like Cleveland, was nominated on the first ballot. The Republicans meanwhile renominated President Benjamin Harrison and took the New York publisher Whitelaw Reid as his running mate.

In keeping with the still-prevailing custom, Cleveland eschewed virtually all personal campaigning, leaving the chore to Stevenson. The fame of "Uncle Adlai" as an arresting storyteller kept him in demand, and he was particularly effective in his native South. There he railed against the Republican force bill calling for federal monitoring of southern elections to protect the voting rights of former slaves, warning it would "disturb harmonious relations between blacks and whites and create the old race prejudice so bitter under carpetbagger regimes."[11]

On the currency issue, Stevenson tempered his pro-silver stance in deference to Cleveland's support of gold, typically phrasing his endorsement for "a sound honest money and a safe circulating medium." Critics accordingly labeled him a great straddler,[12] but the Cleveland-Stevenson ticket won handily.

With Cleveland a gold-standard man and Stevenson at best favoring a mixture of silver and gold in backing the nation's currency, the new vice president kept his silence on the issue. Early in the new term Cleveland considered calling a special session of Congress to seek repeal of the Sherman Silver Purchase Act of 1890, which in his view had already gone too far in threatening the dominance of gold reserves. One hard-money backer wrote Cleveland, apparently worried about the possibility of Stevenson suddenly succeeding him: "I wish you had Congress in session now. You may not be alive in September. It would make a vast difference to the United States if you were not."[13]

Late that spring, as the Stevensons were starting on a goodwill tour of the West, a bizarre episode occurred that if publicly known might have aroused similar concerns about what could happen if Cleveland were to die or become disabled and Stevenson the silverite become president, with a stock market panic already building. On May 5, the president, a longtime cigar smoker, noted a small growth on the roof of his mouth but thought nothing of it. But by mid-June it had enlarged to a painful and worrisome size. His wife, Frances, called the family physician, a prominent New York surgeon, who identified the growth as a malignant tumor that had to be removed. The surgeon recalled later that Cleveland would not agree to the operation unless it could be done in secret and would leave no telltale scar. Cleveland explained that public knowledge could shatter confidence on Republican Wall Street over a possible return to silver currency if the pro-silver vice president were to assume the Oval Office.

Neither Stevenson nor any cabinet member was told, although under the presidential succession act then in force, executive power would have been placed in his hands if the president was physically unable to carry out his duties.[14] It was decided the operation could not be performed in the White House nor at the Cleveland summer retreat at Buzzards Bay, Massachusetts, where snooping reporters were likely to find out. The president himself came up with the solution. A close wealthy friend owned a luxury yacht, the *Oneida,* on which Cleveland often had gone fishing in Long Island Sound and off the coast of Cape Cod. No suspicions would be aroused if he was aboard for several days. A small team of surgical experts was assembled along with a prominent New York orthodontist assigned to construct an artificial jaw that, when installed, would in time enable Cleveland to speak normally.[15]

Shortly after the unknowing Stevensons had embarked on their western trip, Cleveland took a private Pullman train to Jersey City, having a few cigars and whiskeys en route. Then he boarded a ferry to Manhattan and spent the night on the *Oneida* for what was advertised as a fishing cruise in the waters of Long Island Sound. In the morning the president's huge frame was strapped to an oversized wicker chair in the yacht's saloon as he underwent the surgery under anesthesia. In all, five teeth, a part of his palate, and his whole upper jaw were removed in the nearly ninety-minute operation. The jaw was replaced with a vulcanized rubber device, and to masquerade the truth, aides spread the word that Cleveland was having difficulty with his dentures.[16] Important to him, his large moustache remained intact through it all. Two days later on the night of Independence Day, he was up and about on the *Oneida,* anchored off the coast of Sag Harbor, at the eastern end of Long Island, with the world none the wiser.[17]

The next night the president arrived late at Gray Gables, his summer retreat, where a United Press reporter collared the chief surgeon on the porch of the house and asked him about an account that a cancer had been found and removed. The surgeon dodged, but by the next morning, the wire story had been picked up by newspapers around the country. Stevenson was in

Chicago attending Fourth of July festivities at the World's Fair, and when he heard the reports he left for Cape Cod to find out for himself what was going on. But Cleveland swiftly had a telegram sent to the vice president, assuring him all was well and asking him to go the West Coast for a series of meetings with party officials, guaranteeing he was kept in the dark. Soon Cleveland was back on his feet, his artificial jaw in place and working like a charm. When a second suspicious-looking growth was found, it was back aboard the *Oneida* for more surgery that proved to be minor.

Meanwhile, the state of the economy had grown worse, with more banks and manufacturing plants closing. Cleveland by now had called for that special session of Congress to consider repeal of the Silver Purchase Act, hoping it would stabilize the economy. Stevenson, as president of the Senate, found his muted neutrality sorely tested while a filibuster against a repeal droned on. Claiming he had no power to stop it, he was accused by repeal advocates of "lacking the courage to refuse dilatory motions." In any event, with no tie vote materializing, which would have enabled Stevenson to weigh in, the silver act was repealed after a compromise on the gradual reduction of silver purchases, which only enraged many silverites.[18] With the Democrats so divided on the currency question, Cleveland came to see Stevenson and his silver allies as so detrimental to the economy that at one point he jokingly observed, "The logical thing for me to do . . . was to resign and hand the Executive Branch to Mr. Stevenson."[19]

Stevenson throughout his vice presidency remained popular on the social circuit for his humorous storytelling, but he never broke into Cleveland's inner circle. Yet by now, his name was being mentioned as a possible Democratic presidential nominee once Cleveland finished his second term. But when the 1896 national party convention met, again in Chicago, Stevenson was accorded only alternate delegate status and waited in Bloomington for a call that never came. Although he had a long record as a silverite, his accommodating posture toward Cleveland on the currency issue reinforced the view that after all he was a straddler. The *New York Times* observed editorially, "The Vice President says nothing but immaterial pleasantries. He could be readily adjusted to a sound money plank or a declaration for free silver. He would feel quite as much at home with one position or the other."[20]

On the other hand, the man who carried the message for silver at the convention, the thirty-five-year-old Nebraska congressman William Jennings Bryan, was anything but tongue-tied on the issue. His historic and defiant oration against the gold standard electrified the convention and brought him the nomination on the fifth ballot. Stevenson was left with a few scattered votes on each roll call.

When Bryan spoke in Bloomington in the fall, Stevenson introduced him, and upon Bryan's loss to McKinley of Ohio, he returned to his home town. Four years later, when the center of Bloomington was destroyed by fire, Stevenson joined in a campaign to rebuild it. In 1900, he was surprised to learn he had been nominated for another vice presidential term as Bryan's running mate in his second bid for the presidency, as an old silverite.

In the campaign, Stevenson largely left debating the currency question to Bryan, "the Boy Orator of the Platte," and focused on foreign policy. He took on making the case against American imperialism in his view of its manifestation not only in the Spanish-American War but also in the U.S. occupation of Puerto Rico and the Philippines. He called for abandonment of the latter occupation, arguing, "Sixty thousand [American] soldiers are now in the Philippine Islands. How much more will be the sacrifice of treasure and life before the conquest is completed? And when completed, what next?"[21]

In November the Bryan-Stevenson ticket was badly beaten by McKinley and his new running mate, Governor Theodore Roosevelt of New York, failing to carry even Stevenson's home state of Illinois. Eight years later at age seventy-three, Stevenson ran for the governorship of Illinois and beat four other Democrats in the state primary, campaigning across the Land of Lincoln by horse and buggy and the new auto car. In the fall, he opposed the Republican incumbent, Charles Deneen, saying after all his years as a prime Democratic spoilsman that he stood as a nonpartisan. "If elected," he promised, "I will represent the whole people and I will never run again."[22] He came close enough to call for a recount, within twenty-two thousand votes of more than a million cast, but he was turned down by the Republican state legislature. Four years later, he put himself before the Illinois voters again, this time for a U.S. Senate seat, but failed to win the Democratic nomination.

On Christmas Day, 1913, Stevenson's wife, Letitia, died at age seventy-one at home in Bloomington. Six months later, on June 14, 1914, the twenty-third vice president died at seventy-nine in a Chicago hospital after a nervous breakdown and complications. Among those who mourned his death after a long career at the highest levels of politics was his fourteen-year-old grandson, destined later to write an even more cherished page in the history of the Democratic Party. He succeeded where his grandfather had failed in becoming the governor of Illinois but twice later fell short of the higher goal of the presidency, seldom displaying the extreme partisanship of his less-acclaimed forebear.

CHAPTER 24

GARRET A. HOBART

OF NEW JERSEY

T
he twenty-fourth vice president of the United States was a man who considered himself a corporate lawyer and businessman first and foremost. He boasted, "I make politics my recreation,"[1] and he had never held an elective office higher than that of state senator in New Jersey. But Garret Augustus Hobart proved to be such an astute operative in both worlds and was so regarded by President William McKinley, under whom he served, that he was utilized almost as the country's assistant president.

Not since Martin Van Buren had served in the second office under Andrew Jackson had any presidential running mate been brought so importantly into a national administration as "Gus" Hobart was in McKinley's acceptance of him in 1896. With the single exception of Van Buren, none of the other vice presidents up to Hobart's time had taken office with any truly significant role in the policies of the administration to which he was elected. After Van Buren's service to Jackson as a key political and policy adviser to him during his climb to national power, Van Buren had continued in his own climb, culminating in his election to the presidency in 1836. In Jackson's first term, Van Buren was the president's secretary of state, and Jackson was expected to choose Van Buren for the second term.

Hobart by contrast hardly knew the president with whom he was called upon to serve. He had risen in prominence in the world of finance rather than national politics. His family roots traced back to Puritan New England, where his ancestors were ministers who had first settled in Charlestown, Massachusetts, in the 1630s. Their descendants moved to New Hampshire and eventually to New Jersey in the 1840s. A grandfather helped found Queens College, later renamed Rutgers. His father, Addison Hobart, was a schoolteacher, and his mother was Sophia Vanderveer, of New Amsterdam Dutch stock.[2] After their marriage in 1841 they settled in Long Branch, near the Atlantic shore, where the future vice president was born on June 3, 1844, the second of three boys.[3]

Gus Hobart's father built his own schoolhouse, attended by his sons, and young Gus progressed so rapidly that he was placed in a class with his older brother. Of military age when the Civil War began, Gus did not serve, focusing instead on preparations for a career in law. He graduated near the top of his class at Rutgers in 1863 and came under the tutelage of a friend of his father's named Socrates Tuttle, a prominent lawyer in the town of Paterson. Although up to this time the Hobarts had been Democrats, Tuttle's involvements in Passaic County Republican politics eventually converted young Hobart.[4] In 1869, he married his tutor's daughter Jenny and had two children with her.[5]

Admitted to the bar in 1866, Hobart served in succession as the county grand jury clerk and, after Tuttle became mayor of Paterson in 1871, as his father-in-law's city counsel. His local political climb was swift after that; he was elected to the New Jersey Assembly in 1872, elected as Speaker in 1874 at age thirty, elected to the state Senate two years later, and five years after that as the Senate president.[6] Meanwhile, he had plunged into Republican affairs, attending every national convention starting in 1876, and at the same time conducted a hugely successful legal practice representing industrial enterprises, all of which made him the consummate Gilded Age political-and-business operative. Seldom appearing in a courtroom, he served on a host of corporate boards as an adviser on matters of law and finance. As a court-appointed receiver, he paid particular attention to rescuing railroads in bankruptcy or other trouble, while also investing in some of them.[7]

In 1895, Hobart was so highly regarded in the railroad field that he was appointed to the critical three-man Joint Traffic Association, arbitrating disputes concerning rates of thirty-two railroads with tracks running between New York and Chicago. His legal and business work also dealt with supplying water to such growing cities as New York, Newark, and Jersey City. Hobart's involvement in such lucrative public utilities eventually raised major ethical questions about his dual role, including allegations of corruption.[8]

Also in 1895, when he was credited with the election of his friend John Griggs as the governor of New Jersey and with making it a Republican state, he began to emerge as a likely easterner to bring strength to a national ticket headed by the Ohioan McKinley.[9] In April 1896, the Republican Party of New Jersey endorsed him for the vice presidency, a move he did not openly encourage, although indicated his availability.[10]

But even at this point Hobart was best known as a shrewd representative of water and railroad interests in his state and the neighboring New York and Pennsylvania, and it was in his pursuit of these interests that he had become a powerful Republican figure in New Jersey. He had turned down chances to run for the governorship, preferring to concentrate on enriching himself monetarily as well as increasing his political influence, which he would continue even in his vice presidency. It was Hobart who convinced McKinley to back the gold standard in the party platform after considering a mixed silver and gold currency.[11]

Mark Hanna, the Ohio industrialist and political kingmaker usually credited with McKinley's political rise and success, was impressed with Hobart's business credentials and knowledge of politics in the East. Within a large pool of former cabinet and other officeholders available to be McKinley's running mate, Hobart not only agreed with him on gold over silver but also fit comfortably into the profile of a desired and inoffensive Republican ticket partner. McKinley actually had wanted his old friend House Speaker Thomas R. Reed to run with him, but Reed wanted the presidential nomination or nothing. McKinley quickly found Hobart to be both congenial and politically astute and was willing to have Hobart at his side at the Republican convention.[12]

On leaving for St. Louis, Hobart told his wife, "It is a nice thing friends want my nomination but really I do not want it, and do not know what to do about it. If I have enough votes to make my candidacy respectable, it will be all I want."[13] As the convention approached, he wrote to her, "I am heart-sick over my own prospects. It looks to me I will be nominated for Vice-President whether I want it or not, and as I get nearer to the point where I may, I am dismayed at the thought. . . . If I want a nomination, everything is going my way. But when I realize all that it means in work, worry, and loss of home and bliss, I am overcome, so overcome I am simply miserable."[14]

But neither was he indifferent. When Senator Matthew Quayle, the boss of the Pennsylvania Republican Party, asked Hobart to release him from a pledge to vote for him, he told Quayle, "Certainly, but I tell you, Quayle, I will be nominated without the act of your [Pennsylvania] delegation," which in the end voted for him anyway.[15]

Hobart was correct, and after McKinley's presidential nomination he won the second place on the ticket on the first ballot. Together with McKinley and Hanna, he concocted the strategy for the fall election campaign. McKinley had planned to base it on his well-established espousal of high protective tariffs in legislation bearing his name. But Hobart, as an eastern financier, encouraged him, and Hanna, to focus more on a spirited defense of the gold standard in behalf of banking and financial interests, about which he was so well informed.

It was, he argued, the way to defeat his Democratic foe, William Jennings Bryan, who had rocketed to his party's presidential nomination by ranting against mankind's political crucifixion "upon a cross of gold." Hobart told Hanna, "The silver heresy is the only issue upon which we have a chance of winning. We can stir the country with the menace of a change in the money standard that will reduce the purchasing power of the dollar to half a dollar."[16] In a speech in Paterson, he took the lead in challenging Bryan's silver policy, saying, "Such a debasement of our currency would inevitably produce incalculable loss, appalling disaster and national dishonor."[17]

In Hobart's letter of acceptance, he won wide praise for saying clearly what McKinley could not bring himself to utter: "An honest dollar, worth one hundred cents anywhere, cannot be carved out of fifty-three cents of silver plus a legislative fiat."[18] The *New York Sun* was prompted to observe, "This is a debate that should have come from the lips of Major McKinley months ago."[19]

In the tradition of the day, McKinley in Canton, Ohio, and Hobart in Long Branch, New Jersey, conducted front-porch campaigns, greeting those who called at their homes, defending the gold standard, and doing little speech making, although Hobart did attend some local rallies in his home state. Meanwhile, Bryan traveled tirelessly around the country, hawking the support of free silver and reprising his famous assault on gold, which resonated strongly with farmers and in rural America generally. He covered some eighteen thousand miles whistle-stopping by train and making more than six hundred speeches in a gargantuan one-man effort to match the much larger campaign treasury amassed by Hanna with Hobart's assistance.[20] They tapped millions from railroad and other corporate interests, which financed heavy mailings and surrogate speakers while McKinley stayed home, talking gold and high tariffs from his rocking chair.

John Hay, soon to become McKinley's secretary of state, observed during the fall that Bryan was "begging for the presidency as a tramp might beg for a pie."[21] McKinley, while actually sympathetic to a policy of bimetallism, was persuaded by Hobart to pivot sharply to upholding the gold standard to reinforce his backing in the business and banking community. The strategy worked; on Election Night the McKinley-Hobart ticket soundly defeated Bryan and running mate Arthur Sewall of Maine, a banker opposed to the gold standard. Bryan's popular total was larger than any previous winner, but he was stymied in the industrial Northeast, where big business reigned over populism.[22]

Before the inauguration, Hobart wound up much of his business affairs but not all. He resigned from official positions in companies that did heavy business with federal agencies, but he declined to divest himself from every corporate board on which he served. "It would be highly ridiculous for me," he proclaimed, "to resign from the different companies in which I am officer and a stockholder whose interests are not in the least affected, or likely to be, by my position as Vice President. I have no intention of resigning all the offices that I hold."[23]

Notably, one he refused to relinquish was his post as a rate arbiter on the Joint Traffic Commission, which clearly was involved in business before the Interstate Commerce Commission and railroad legislation before Congress. Indeed, the Supreme Court would soon declare unconstitutional a midwestern forerunner of the Joint Traffic Commission, and a month after Hobart's inauguration he took part in ruling on a rate increase involving the Erie Railroad, to which he had ties.

Upon his election, the *Chicago Daily News* prophesied, "Garret A. Hobart will not be seen or heard until, after four years, he emerges from the impenetrable vacuum of the Vice Presidency."[24] But in his inaugural remarks, Hobart served notice that, unlike his predecessor Adlai Stevenson, as president of the Senate he would not be reluctant to assume a greater role in expediting Senate business in the face of what some might see as dilatory practices. He had no intention of being a mere ornament in the Senate or in the new administration for that matter.

Two weeks after taking office, Hobart took it upon himself to drop in at the Treasury Department for a chat with the new secretary, Lyman George. When an aide, not recognizing him, told him the secretary was too busy to see him, Hobart simply left his calling card, asking the aide to give it to George "when he is disengaged," obliging the embarrassed aide to apologize later.[25] On another occasion, however, the new vice president insisted on deference. When the British ambassador, Sir Julian Pauncefote, declined to call on Hobart before the vice president first made a courtesy visit to him, Hobart refused and held fast, until the British Foreign Office ordered the ambassador to back down. The diplomatic controversy made news, and telegrams to Hobart congratulated him for holding his ground.[26]

Hobart's firmness paid dividends for a successor vice president two administrations later, when Theodore Roosevelt's standby, Charles Fairbanks, and his wife were invited to a senator's dinner in honor of the French ambassador and his wife. The hostess asked Mrs. Fairbanks whether she would mind giving precedence to them. The Second Lady replied, "But that matter was settled once and for always by Vice President Hobart and Mrs. Hobart, was it not?" The chastised hostess raced back to the dining room and changed the seating place cards accordingly.[27]

McKinley and Hobart quickly became close friends and governing partners. Although the vice president was not invited to cabinet meetings, the president and his cabinet members frequently consulted with him on matters dealing with their departments. Arthur Wallace Dunn, a Washington correspondent who covered the White House from the presidency of Benjamin Harrison to that of Warren Harding, later observed, "For the first time in my recollection, and the last for that matter, the Vice President was recognized as somebody, as a part of the administration, and as a part of the body over which he presided."[28]

In June 1897, however, his continued role as a railroad rate arbiter triggered allegations from the chairman of the Interstate Commerce

Commission that he had violated anti-trust laws. "Mr. Hobart must have known the way the pool [of railroad interests] would be viewed by the public," William C. Morrison declared, "but he contented himself with taking the stand of Eastern capitalists that a pool is a legitimate railroad aid." The Supreme Court later ruled the arbitration arrangement unconstitutional, and Hobart resigned from the post in November, escaping further legal action.[29]

With the president's wife, Ida, suffering from epilepsy, Hobart's wife, Jennie, became a constant presence in the White House, helping with social obligations there, to the president's great relief and sense of appreciation. She wrote later in her memoir, "Many a time he sent for me at the eleventh hour to come to some White House dinner. My presence, he said, gave him confidence. A request from the President is in reality a command. It meant I must cancel any previous engagement and come, however inconvenient."[30] When a woman reporter inquired about her "duties at the White House," she replied, "I have no duties there." The reporter persisted: "But since Mrs. McKinley is an invalid, all Washington understands that you are virtually First Lady." Mrs. Hobart told her, "Anything I do at the White House is only at the request of President and Mrs. McKinley. I have neither desire nor intention to assume any prerogatives of the Mistress of the White House, but I am happy to help when requested."[31]

But the relationship was more than that. The foursome became particularly close, both in Washington and on vacations they shared at Lake Champlain. The wealthy Hobarts leased a mansion on Lafayette Square directly across Pennsylvania Avenue from the White House, where they held many dinners for senators and foreign dignitaries at what came to be called "the Cream White House." One such guest was Prince Albert of Belgium. And both McKinley and Hanna frequently crossed Pennsylvania Avenue for breakfast with the vice president or after hours to play cards and talk.

Jennie Hobart later remembered the president spending "long evenings, over boxes of perfectos, in consultation with the Vice-President on perplexing problems of state." McKinley also counseled with Hobart on business and investment matters, to the point of turning over his own presidential salary to Hobart to invest for him. In the winter of 1898 the *New York Times* reported, "Mr. Hobart is already a tower of strength to the administration. . . . [The Hobarts] are themselves in great demand at all the most exclusive entertainments in Washington, and are quite unspoiled by the unusual attentions they are receiving."[32]

As presiding officer of the Senate as well, Hobart proved to be conscientious and attentive in the chair, having earlier served in the same capacity as president of the New Jersey Senate. The *Washington Post* observed, "The Senate has been more businesslike than at any time during many years past," and on the only occasion Hobart was called up to break a tie vote, he opposed a bill proposing self-government for the Philippines in the wake of the Spanish-American War.[33]

After the sinking of the American warship *Maine* in Havana Harbor in February 1898, Hobart took McKinley aside and advised him that the Senate was in near revolt over the president's resistance to declaring war on Spain. McKinley finally asked for and obtained a declaration in April. In casting his one tie vote, Hobart made possible the American retention of the Philippines after the brief and successful war, though he himself was leery of the United States embarking on any imperial course. As for the notion of self-government for the Filipinos, McKinley declared as pockets of resistance continued, "It is not a good time for the liberator to submit important questions concerning liberty and government to the liberated while they are engaged in shooting down their rescuers."[34]

In domestic matters, McKinley depended more and more on Hobart's counsel in the administration. In 1898, he brought John Griggs, the man Hobart had helped elect to the governorship of New Jersey, into the cabinet as attorney general. The vice president also became a political emissary to the Republican bosses in New Jersey and New York. But the year also brought hardship to the Hobarts. Late in the year, he was found to have a serious heart ailment, and by April 1899 speculation began on whether he would be up to a strenuous reelection campaign in 1900. Hanna insisted to reporters that in light of his appreciated service, "nothing but death or an earthquake can stop the renomination of Vice President Hobart."[35]

McKinley's reliance on him was seen again when the president, averse to unpleasant personal encounters, asked him to call on Secretary of War Russell Alger to resign in the wake of heavy criticism of mismanaging the war with Spain. Alger was a close Hobart friend, but the vice president got Alger to step down amid press speculation that Hobart had personally added a financial sweetener to achieve the desired end.[36] The *New York Sun* reported that Alger's resignation had come as a result of Hobart's "crystal insight" and "velvet tact." The vice president, severely ailing, had his wife compose a wire to McKinley: "My 'crystal insight' is still clear but the nap is slightly worn off my velvet tact vide the New York Sun."[37]

Hobart's health continued to lag, and in August allegations surfaced that he was involved in a plot to gain control of New York City's water franchise that would require payment of five million dollars a year, nearly twice that being currently paid, to a fake firm without the ability to deliver the water. The *New York Times* charged that the scandal led "to the political threshold of the administration itself" and that "every rascal in the job, be he near the President, be he in the Senate Chamber, or be he a third-rate Tammany hack, must have his Constitutional chance to show he is not guilty."[38] A state investigating committee issued a host of subpoenas but none to Hobart, and eventually the investigation died out without further implicating him.

In early November, in seclusion in Paterson with his health further ebbing, Hobart announced his retirement from all his business connections, adding that he would not be returning to Washington. On November 21, Hobart died with fifteen months remaining in his vice presidential term, having attained perhaps greater utility, if not recognition, in the post than any of its previous holders since Van Buren. At the same time, Hobart's continued engagement in private business affairs was a caution to future occupants of the second office. An obvious requisite of any successful vice president was commitment to the agenda of the president above all else, and Hobart seemed often to have had a dual focus that cast a shadow over an otherwise constructive tenure in the office.

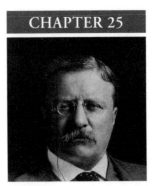

CHAPTER 25

THEODORE ROOSEVELT
OF NEW YORK

The death of Vice President "Gus" Hobart fifteen months before the end of his term required President William McKinley to start looking for another running mate in his expected pursuit of a second term in 1900. An unusual political circumstance in the state of New York and in its internal intrigues brought one of the most dynamic occupants to the vice presidency up to this time, but he was a man who neither yet wanted nor sought the office—the governor of New York, Theodore Roosevelt. He served in it only seven months, but that period was a prelude to one of the nation's most vibrant presidencies.

The uncommon condition that set Roosevelt's course to becoming president-in-waiting, and shortly afterward to the presidency itself, was the concern of Senator Thomas Platt, New York's Republican leader, that Roosevelt's independence and willpower would erode Platt's influence in the political domain over which he ruled. Roosevelt had attained the governorship only after an agreement with Platt to consult with him on major appointments and in general to pay proper homage to the man known in the Empire State as "the easy boss" of the party machine. While Roosevelt adhered to that arrangement, his forceful and exuberant nature led Platt to determine that his own life would be better off with a new governor in Albany. And he concluded that his purpose would be conveniently served by having Roosevelt in effect kicked upstairs to the second office in the land.

In a letter to his closest political friend, Henry Cabot Lodge of Massachusetts, during his first years as governor, Roosevelt wrote, "I have found out one reason why Senator Platt wants me nominated for the Vice-Presidency. He is, I am convinced, genuinely friendly, and indeed I think I may say, really fond of me, and is personally satisfied with the way I have conducted politics; but the big money men with whom he is in close touch and whose campaign contributions have certainly been no inconsiderable factor in his strength, have been pressing him very strongly to get me put in the Vice-Presidency so as to get me out of the state."[1]

Roosevelt, enjoying immensely the executive power he was wielding as governor of the country's most important state, did not consider that proposed office a step up for him. He was well aware of its reputation as a political dead end and its usual minimal utility by the president. While it was true that McKinley had brought Hobart into his inner circle as few of his predecessors ever had done with their vice presidents, Roosevelt had no reason to surmise with his own reputation for power wielding that he would be given similar deference were he to become McKinley's second vice president.

There was a certain irony in the situation wherein a distinctly political hack like Platt would be instrumental in the fortunes of a man of aristocratic birth like Theodore Roosevelt. Theodore was the grandson of Cornelius Van Schaack Roosevelt, one of New York's first real-estate scions and millionaires and the namesake son of a prominent philanthropist. In a rare self-deprecating assessment of himself upon his father's death at only age forty-six, Roosevelt said, "I often feel badly that such a wonderful man as Father should have had a son of so little worth as I am."[2]

Young Theodore Roosevelt, although still a student at Harvard at the time and nothing yet on his résumé to contradict that appraisal, had grounds to expect a successful career ahead, if not particularly in politics. Born into family wealth to the home of Theodore Senior and Martha Bulloch Roosevelt on Manhattan's fashionable east side on October 27, 1858, he suffered from the start from debilitating asthma. But under the prodding and guidance of his father, he eventually overcame the affliction through rigorous exercise and sheer determination. He later recalled that Theodore Senior had pointedly told him at the age of twelve, "You have the mind but you have not the body, and without the help of the body the mind cannot get as far as it should. You must *make* your body."[3] The boy responded conscientiously, throwing himself into more than just body-building calisthenics and boxing. He also embraced the outdoor life, including hiking and hunting, which became a core of his physical being thereafter, along with a fascination with all aspects of wildlife.

While at Harvard, Teddy, known in the family then as "Teedie," met Alice Lee, a vivacious seventeen-year-old, of Chestnut Hill, outside Boston, and immediately set his cap for her. After a two-year courtship and a final bachelor's adventure out west with younger brother, Elliot, he and Alice were married in late October 1880, and after a brief and isolated stay at the Roosevelt summer home in Oyster Bay, Long Island, they moved to midtown Manhattan. The groom entered Columbia Law School and began writing a history of the War of 1812, demonstrating his determination to lead a multifaceted life that continued throughout his days.

Young Roosevelt also explored political engagement for the first time, amid family reservations. Roosevelt himself was wary of entering politics as a sole occupation. "I did not then, and I do not now believe," he wrote later, "that any man should ever attempt to make politics his only career. It is a dreadful misfortune for a man to grow to feel that his whole livelihood and whole happiness depend on his staying in office."[4]

Considering his own "bringing-up and convictions," he wrote that the Republican Party was his only recourse, and it was "treated as a private corporation." Nevertheless, when he first asked around among colleagues how to proceed, he said, he was told, "Politics were 'low'; . . . the organizations were not controlled by 'gentlemen'; . . . I would find them run by saloon-keepers, horse-car conductors." Describing his response, he wrote, "I answered that if this were so it merely meant that the people I knew did not belong to the governing class . . . and that I intended to be one of the governing class; that if they proved to be too hard-bit for me I supposed I would have to quit, but that I certainly would not quit until I had made the effort and found out whether I really was too weak to hold my own in the rough and tumble."[5]

After a break for a belated honeymoon trip to Europe, during which he left his wife behind for a few days as he climbed the Matterhorn, Roosevelt left law school, entered the political wars as a candidate in 1882, and was nominated and elected to the New York State Assembly three times in what was known as a "silk stocking" district. But in February 1844, family matters rushed to the fore, first in joy with the birth of his first daughter, which was quickly and grimly followed with the death of his mother of typhoid fever and then of his wife, Alice, of Bright's disease. This vital and vibrant man wrote in his diary the night of his wife's death: "The light has gone out of my life."[6] And later in a private memorial: "When my heart's dearest died, the light went from my life forever."[7]

Already somewhat of an insomniac, Roosevelt turned to work to fill the daily hours of grief, returning to Albany to immerse himself as best he could in his legislative duties. He commuted regularly between Albany, where he navigated a series of bills through the Assembly, and his Manhattan district, and in April 1884 he attended the state Republican Party convention in Utica.

But these political matters could not drive off the personal sorrow that gripped him. He never publicly mentioned his wife again and, seeking refuge, he left his infant daughter, who also was named Alice but was called Baby Lee, in the care of his maiden sister and headed for the Badlands of the Dakota Territory. There he bought a shack on a site for a small cattle ranch and toured the territory on horseback, later finding a more suitable locale for his planned spread. After a brief and apparently uncomfortable visit in New York with the baby and his family, he retreated again to his ranch and life as a cowboy. He drove his own cattle, hunted, and supervised the construction of Elkhorn Ranch, on the Little Missouri River, all the while building his strength in keeping with his father's instruction to fashion a body that was the match of his mind.

Gradually his zest for politics returned and along with it romance. Two years after the death of his first wife, he became secretly engaged to Edith Crowe, a friend of his sister Corinne. In 1886, he was nominated for mayor of New York but ran a poor third, and shortly after the election he and Edith embarked by Cunard liner for England, where they were married in the presence of the bride's mother and sister, living in London. After a fifteen-week honeymoon tour of England, France, and Italy, the couple returned to New York, where Roosevelt learned his ranch had been hit hard by a bitter winter. Yet he credited his cowboy experience later with hardening him for the many difficult days that would lie ahead of him.

When the Republican Benjamin Harrison sought the presidency against

Grover Cleveland in 1888, Roosevelt undertook a speaking tour for Harrison in key midwestern states. Afterward, his friend Lodge interceded directly with the victorious Harrison for Roosevelt, who hoped to be appointed an assistant secretary of state. But the new secretary, James Blaine, balked, and Roosevelt, at age thirty, was instead named a Civil Service commissioner at the annual salary of thirty-five hundred dollars.[8] Reform under the Pendleton Act of 1883 was close to his heart, and he plunged into the task with customary zest. He embarked on a housecleaning tour of post offices that confirmed Roosevelt meant business, and he was reappointed in 1892.

In 1895, Roosevelt became the police commissioner of New York City and the head of the Police Board. Almost at once he fired the chief of police of the notoriously corrupt force and one of its most brutal inspectors, taking dead aim at saloon keepers who routinely violated the city's prohibition of intoxicating liquor sales on the Sabbath. Personally undertaking nighttime raids across the city, Roosevelt laid down the law to his precinct police officers to close down any establishments serving alcohol between midnight Saturday and midnight Sunday. "No matter if you think the law is a bad one; you must see that your men carry out your orders to the letter," he told them. "If it proves impossible to enforce it, it will only be after the experiment of breaking many a captain of the police."[9]

By the end of June 1895, 97 percent of the city's saloons were closed down on Sunday, in the face of loud complaints from the Democratic organization against a law that Roosevelt said "was intended to be the most potent weapon in keeping the saloons subservient allies to Tammany Hall." The controversy put Roosevelt's name on every lip in New York, whether wet or dry.

When prominent New York reporter Jacob Riis observed that the police commissioner had his eye on the presidency, Riis put the question directly to Roosevelt, who responded angrily, "Don't you dare ask me that! Don't you put such ideas into my head. No friend of mine would ever say a thing like that." Then Roosevelt put his arm over Riis's shoulder and told him he must never "remind a man at work on a political job that he may be President. It almost always kills him politically. He loses his nerve; he can't do his work; he gives up the very traits that are making him a possibility." After a pause, he continued, "I must be wanting to be President. Every young man does. But I won't let myself think of it; I must not, because if I do, I will begin to work for it, I'll be careful, calculating, cautious in word and act, and so—I'll beat myself."[10]

If Roosevelt did not yet let himself think about the presidency, he clearly did muse at this time about getting back on the federal track. In 1896 he arranged an interview with Mark Hanna, chief political adviser to Governor William McKinley of Ohio, the Republican presidential nominee. He offered to campaign vigorously for McKinley in the fall, a most welcome offer to Hanna, whose plan was to have McKinley conduct a front-porch campaign from his home in Canton. With the Democratic presidential nominee, William Jennings Bryan, already lighting up the West with his emotional speech decrying the gold standard, in which he referred to the crucifixion of mankind on a cross of gold, Hanna put Roosevelt on Bryan's trail. He whistle-stopped across Illinois, Michigan, Minnesota, and the prairies, refuting the Bryan message with his own gruff and pointed pitch in support of gold—an aristocratic easterner with the Wild West swagger of a rugged cattle rancher.[11]

When McKinley was easily elected over Bryan, Roosevelt had reason to expect that his hope to be named an assistant secretary of the navy would soon follow. But apparent concerns of McKinley that Roosevelt might be a loose cannon and political hesitation by the New York Republican boss Tom Platt held up the appointment for a time, until Roosevelt met with Platt. The party boss said thereafter that Roosevelt "would probably do less damage to the [party] organization" in that federal position in Washington than mucking about in New York.[12]

Roosevelt was a good fit for the navy post, having written a well-received book on the War of 1812 right out of Harvard and maintaining a keen interest in naval affairs thereafter. He advocated an expansion of the American fleet in Pacific and Caribbean waters to deal with real or potential naval threats from Spain. Revolution in Cuba against its Spanish ruler had broken out in early 1895, with strong sympathies in the United States for the insurgents. The fighting in Cuba eventually had deleterious economic consequences for American commerce with that country, which Spain regarded as indisputably part of its empire. The situation coincided with growing American sentiments for expansionism, which Roosevelt saw as a need for a stronger navy.

As the Cuban insurrection dragged on through 1897, McKinley sent a message to Madrid in mid-September saying the fighting on the island had brought "upon the United States a degree of injury and suffering which can not longer be ignored." He called on Spain to "put a stop to this destructive war" with an honorable settlement.[13] Madrid decided to give Cuba autonomy, followed by amnesty to political prisoners and the release of any Americans in Cuban jails. But Spain as a sovereign power would continue controlling military and foreign policy in Cuba. This response was a far cry from the American objective, which was independence for the island. Madrid warned that any foreign interference "would lead to an intervention which any nation possessing any self-respect would have to repel by force."[14]

Spain's autonomy plan went into effect on January 1, 1898, but protest riots led many in the U.S. Congress to agitate for recognition of Cuban independence. The McKinley administration sent the American navy on winter maneuvers in the Caribbean, and the battleship *Maine* was at Key West awaiting orders. In what appeared to be a conciliatory diplomatic gesture, the ship was sent into Havana Harbor, but on the night of February 16, the ship suddenly was destroyed in a huge explosion. Not waiting for the findings of a court of inquiry, Roosevelt fired off his belief that the ship "was sunk by an act of dirty treachery on the part of the Spaniards."[15] The Hearst and Pulitzer newspapers jumped to the same conclusion, and their circulations soared.

Roosevelt by now had alerted Navy Secretary John Davis Long that in the event of armed conflict he intended to resign his desk job and join the fight. He told the head of the New York National Guard he wanted to be commissioned to lead a regiment, citing three years' service in the state militia and acting "as sheriff in the cow country" in the Dakota Badlands.[16]

In a private letter to a friend, Roosevelt declared of the prospect, "I like life very much. I have always led a joyous life. I like thought and I like action, and it will be very bitter to leave my wife and children; and while I think I could face death with dignity, I have no desire before my time has come to go out into the everlasting darkness. So I shall not go into a war with any undue exhilaration of spirit or in a frame of mind in any way approaching recklessness or levity."[17]

When the war came, Roosevelt was given the rank of lieutenant colonel in a cavalry regiment under the command of Colonel Leonard Wood, a greatly admired friend. Quickly trained in San Antonio and shipped via Tampa to Cuba, the volunteers were a mix of western cowboys and Indians and eastern playboy horsemen, soon dubbed the "Rough Riders."[18] They subsequently took part in the famous charge up San Juan Hill with Roosevelt on horseback in the lead, and press reports of his daring and heroism soon made him a national hero.

When the short and victorious war ended in August, the Republican Party in New York, seeking a candidate for governor in the fall of 1898, cast a sharp eye on the returning Roosevelt. But the state party boss, Tom Platt, was not at all certain he wanted this reform-minded dynamo in the seat of power in Albany and a prospective challenger to his party leadership. Platt finally agreed to back Roosevelt on the promise that he would be consulted on key appointment and policy decisions.

In the fall campaign against the Democratic judge Augustus Van Wyck, Roosevelt whistle-stopped across upstate New York with uniformed Rough Riders prominently in view, regaling large crowds. He won the election on sheer personal magnetism, and it was not long until Platt began to think of getting him out of Albany by running him for vice president in 1900. Roosevelt's closest political friend, Lodge, liked the idea. "I do not pretend to say that the office in itself is suited to you and to your habits," he wrote to Roosevelt, "but for the future it is, in my judgment, invaluable. It takes you out of the cut-throat politics of New York, where I am sure they would have destroyed your prospects, if you had remained two years longer, and it gives you a position in the eyes of the country second only to that of the president."[19]

When Vice President Garret Hobart died in November 1899, Roosevelt's name was increasingly heard as McKinley's next running mate. But he told Lodge of the prospect, "I am a comparatively young man yet and I like to work. I do not like to be a figurehead. It would not entertain me to preside over the Senate."[20]

In early February 1900, Roosevelt informed reporters, "Under no circumstances could I or would I accept the nomination for the vice-presidency." At one point he told Platt, "The more I have thought it over the more I have felt that I would a great deal rather be anything, say a professor of history, than vice president." Platt, to such observations, reflected,

"Roosevelt might as well stand under Niagara Falls and try to spit the water back as to stop his nomination."[21]

Soon, however, Roosevelt was saying, "I believe that I would be looked upon as rather a coward if I didn't go," in reference to the nominating convention, and by late spring he wrote to Lodge, "I did not say that I would not under any circumstances accept the vice presidency." While still denying interest, he went to the convention and called on several state delegations wearing an old army cap, which skeptics came to call "an acceptance hat."[22]

Hanna by now had become dead-set against having the free-spirited and freewheeling Roosevelt on the ticket. As a stampede for him began to mount, Hanna was in despair, asking other convention delegates of the prospect of Roosevelt becoming vice president, "Don't any of you realize there's only one life between that madman and the presidency?"[23]

To the satisfaction of New York boss Platt, the ticket of McKinley and Roosevelt was nominated unanimously, shunting the unmanageable Rough Rider off the New York stage and more than ever into the national spotlight. Roosevelt readily and enthusiastically took up the role of active campaigner, telling Hanna, "I am as strong as a bull moose and you can use me to the limit," which the campaign manager did.[24]

Roosevelt made 573 speeches in 567 towns in 24 states crisscrossing the country for more that 21,000 miles. He repeatedly identified the Democratic presidential nominee, Bryan, as his opponent, taking him on in defense of American expansionism and the war with Spain. He campaigned defending gold in the Northeast and imperialism across the Midwest and the Rocky Mountains, where his rugged outdoorsman role played particularly well. At first he resisted the barnstorming, arguing, "It does not seem to me that a canvass from the rear end of a railway train, as a kind of rival to Bryan, is dignified, and therefore a wise thing for me."[25] But Hanna insisted, and the trip proved to be an excellent vehicle for the former cowboy, lashing out repeatedly against Bryan and silver as he flashed his fierce, toothy glare at mesmerized audiences. On Election Day, the Republican ticket coasted to victory. Hanna, still depressed about Roosevelt now a heartbeat from the presidency, wrote to McKinley, "Your duty to the country is to live for four years from next March."[26]

After their inaugurations, Roosevelt's reservations about having to preside over the Senate proved to be unwarranted. The usual winter special session lasted only four days and adjourned until the following December. But McKinley seldom consulted Roosevelt on policy and appointments, instead generally looking upon him with a certain wariness toward his combustible nature.

At the end of summer, he and McKinley each undertook a tour, the president visiting the Pan-American Exposition, at Buffalo, on September 6, and Roosevelt visiting Lake Champlain, in Vermont. After a leisurely lunch, Roosevelt was summoned to the telephone. It was Buffalo calling, to tell him that President McKinley had just been shot in the chest and stomach by a young anarchist, later identified as Leon Czolcosz, and was undergoing surgery. Roosevelt left at once for Buffalo, not knowing whether McKinley would survive, and on arrival he maintained a bedside vigil.

The chest wound was not serious but the other was. The next morning, however, the president seemed to be doing better, and after the weekend Roosevelt was told he need not stay, and for public consumption it would be better that he not. Thereupon, expecting McKinley's recovery, Roosevelt departed to a cabin in the Adirondacks for a short stay with his awaiting family. Six days after the shooting, with McKinley seemingly on the mend, the Roosevelts began a hiking party. But early the next afternoon a telegraph messenger found the hikers and brought Roosevelt the news: McKinley had died. Theodore Roosevelt was president of the United States, even before the formal taking of the oath of office.

Some years earlier, he had written that a vice president "should so far as possible represent the same views and principles which have secured the nomination and election of the president, and he should be a man standing well in the councils of the party, trusted by his fellow party leaders and able in the event of any accident to his chief to take up the work of the latter just where it was left."[27]

But Roosevelt, reformer at heart and with aggressive foreign policy notions, was not McKinley. He had no intention of being a mere caretaker of his predecessor's agenda, and his personal flare for leadership produced considerable reforms in politics, including trust-busting and federal regulation of the railroads. On his first day as president, he told reporters at the White House, "I want you to understand at the start—I feel just as much a constituently elected President . . . as McKinley was. I was voted for as Vice-President, it is true, but the Constitution provides that in the case of the death or inability of the President, the Vice-President shall serve as President. And, therefore, due to the act of a madman, I am President and shall act in every word and deed precisely as if I and not McKinley had been the candidate for whom the electors cast the vote for President. That should be understood."[28]

Once again, a man who had accepted running for the vice presidency without enthusiasm had found that decision to be the most critical of his political career. He embarked on one of the most colorful presidencies in the nation's annals. In December 1901, with Roosevelt in only his second month as president, the Senate approved the second Hay-Pauncefote Treaty, in which the British agreed to allow the United States on its own to build and fortify a canal linking the Atlantic and Pacific Oceans. Then, in November 1903, Roosevelt encouraged an insurrection that produced the independence of the Republic of Panama and paved the way for the start of construction of the Panama Canal across the Central American isthmus, perhaps Roosevelt's greatest foreign policy initiative.[29]

In a coal strike in May 1902, which might have paralyzed the nation, Roosevelt threatened to nationalize the railroads and run them with federal troops, forcing arbitration. And in foreign relations, he won a Nobel Peace Prize in 1910 for mediation efforts in the Russo-Japanese War. After a second White House term with a vice president of his own, Roosevelt retired from public life but only for a time, soon to resume his political career, as we shall see in a succeeding chapter.

CHAPTER 26

CHARLES W. FAIRBANKS
OF INDIANA

Into the twentieth century, an axiom of presidential ticket making held that it was wisest to provide geographical balance to the party's slate, choosing a running mate for the presidential nominee from a section of the country other than his own. In 1904, the Republican Party adhered to this counsel by selecting as President Theodore Roosevelt's partner Senator Charles Warren Fairbanks, a native of Ohio resettled in Indiana.

Fairbanks was not the choice of Roosevelt, who had shown only mild interest in the identity of a running mate. Mentioning the matter to his eldest son, Ted, however, he said of Congressman Robert B. Hitt of Illinois, a prominent member of the House Foreign Affairs Committee, "He would be an excellent candidate, and if I should be elected, he would be of all men the pleasantest to work with."[1] The observation at least hinted of some possibility of making use of his vice president.

But many Old Guard Republican leaders preferred Fairbanks as a trustworthy conservative more in the McKinley mode, and Fairbanks, like Hitt, also came from the Midwest and would provide geographical balance to the ticket. At the nominating convention in Chicago, however, Hitt asked that his name be withdrawn, so Fairbanks was nominated by voice vote. It fell to him, as with Roosevelt in 1900, to carry the brunt of the fall campaign while Roosevelt mainly stayed in Washington running the country. But more than anything Fairbanks said or did on the campaign trail, Roosevelt's huge popularity and force of personality were what carried the day over the lackluster Democratic presidential nominee, Judge Alton B. Parker of New York, and his running mate, Henry Gassaway Davis, a wealthy eighty-two-year-old West Virginian. The choice of Davis obviously was not made with his longevity in mind.

Although Roosevelt himself had endured the customary underutilization during his own brief vice presidency, he was not inspired any more than most previous chief executives to put the second officer to work in any significant role in his administration. He had functioned without a vice president through his abbreviated first term, and at any rate Fairbanks was too orthodox a conservative to fit in with Roosevelt's increasingly reformist and progressive style and ideas.

Notably, in 1896 Roosevelt had written in regard to choosing a vice president, "It would be an unhealthy thing to have the Vice-President and President represented by principles so far apart that the succession of one to the place of the other means change as radical as any party overturn" by election. But when it came to making the choice for his prospective administration, Roosevelt disregarded his own advice and went along with the party leaders' desire.[2]

Charles Fairbanks was a the ninth-generation descendant of Jonathan Fayerancke, an English Puritan who had settled in Dedham, Massachusetts, in 1636. Fairbanks was born on a farm in Union County, Ohio, on May 11, 1852, the son of Loriston Monroe Fairbanks, a farmer, and Mary Adelaide Smith Fairbanks, also of Union County. He was an industrious and studious boy obliged to help work the farm. A somewhat daring youth who loved to hunt and ride, he once broke an arm while successfully breaking a colt resisting his mount. Soon after, still wearing a sling, he caught and stopped a runaway team of horses.

By age fifteen he had earned enough money to enter nearby Ohio Wesleyan University, where he was elected one of three editors of the college newspaper. Upon Fairbanks's graduation, an uncle, a general manager of the Western Associated Press, got him a job as a reporter, first in Pittsburgh and then in Cleveland, where he went to law school for one term and was admitted to the Ohio bar. At age twenty-two, he moved to Indianapolis, where he married Cornelia Cole, a former fellow student at Ohio Wesleyan. Hired as a lawyer with the Chesapeake and Ohio Railroad, his law practice soon thrived, focusing on corporate and transportation affairs in cases before the federal courts in Indiana, Ohio, and Illinois.[3]

Fairbanks's opposition to strikers in a railroad labor dispute in Indianapolis in 1877 drew the attention of Republican leaders in Indiana. Through the next decade and beyond he worked for various party candidates, and after another Hoosier Republican, President Benjamin Harrison, lost the White House in 1892, Fairbanks undertook rebuilding the party in disarray. In 1896 he became chairman of the party's national convention in St. Louis and delivered the keynote address, the Indiana delegation, and the state for William McKinley in his victory over the Democrat William Jennings Bryan.[4]

Fairbanks's railroad connections enhanced his standing in the party as he parceled out largesse in the form of railway passes to political associates. He became a majority owner of the state's largest newspaper, the *Indianapolis News,* and its chief rival, the *Indianapolis Journal,* increasing his political clout in behalf of the Republican Party in the state. He held no elective office but became an important voice in presidential politics, because Indiana often was the source of nominees for the national ticket, mostly for the vice presidency.

In 1896 also, the Republicans took control of the Indiana state legislature, and grateful party members elected Fairbanks to the U.S. Senate. There he became a loyal and helpful McKinley ally as chairman of committees limiting immigration and imposing literacy tests for entry. He originally questioned going to war against Spain in 1898 but supported McKinley when war was declared. In a dispute with Canada over the border with Alaska, the president appointed Fairbanks to the Joint High Commission considering the issue. He endeared himself to Alaskans by declaring that he opposed the "yielding of an inch of United States territory," and later the city of Fairbanks was named for him. One of his most advanced positions was his backing the demand of black soldiers fighting in Cuba to be led by black officers.[5]

After the war, with McKinley seeking reelection in a rematch against Bryan in 1900, his chief political adviser, Mark Hanna, hoped to block the vice presidential nomination of Theodore Roosevelt with the candidacy of Senator Fairbanks. But Fairbanks declined being a sacrificial lamb, hoping to make his own bid for the presidency after McKinley was reelected and finished his second term. Fate decisively intervened with the president's assassination in 1901 and the ascendancy of Roosevelt to the White House.

Fairbanks's hopes for a future presidency now seemed dimmer than ever. Hanna himself was being pushed by Old Guard Republicans for the 1904 presidential nomination against the despised Roosevelt. But in February of the election year, Hanna died, leaving Fairbanks as the closest Republican left with any connection to the departed McKinley. Roosevelt, however, had by this time cemented his hold on the party, and his nomination for a presidential term in his own right was assured. To assuage and accommodate the Old Guard, party leaders decided that it would be prudent to bestow the vice presidential nomination on the loyal old Charlie Fairbanks.

But Indiana's senior senator insisted he had no interest in the vice presidency and wanted to remain in the Senate. As the pressure mounted from Republicans in Indiana and nearby states, however, Fairbanks agreed to be offered to the convention. Of his eventual selection, Roosevelt was said to remark, "Who in the name of heaven else is there?"[6]

After Roosevelt had been duly nominated for another term, he quietly acquiesced despite his earlier declarations of preferring an ideological soul mate in the job. Senator Chauncey M. Depew of New York seconded the Fairbanks nomination, rather incongruously reminding the delegates of some of the great men in the nation's history who had held the office, whose company Fairbanks seemed hardly destined to join.

"It seems to me," Depew said, "that we have not given enough importance to the office of the Vice-President of the United States. It was not so among the fathers. Then of the two highest potential Presidential possibilities, one took the Presidency, the other the Vice-Presidency. But in the last forty years, ridicule and caricature have placed the office almost in contempt. Let us remember that Thomas Jefferson, let us remember that old John Adams, let us remember that John C. Calhoun and George Clinton and Martin Van Buren were vice presidents of the United States. Eighty millions of people want for vice president a presidential figure of full size."[7] With this rather amusing bit of hyperbole, Indiana's favorite son was unanimously nominated as Roosevelt's running mate.

In the ensuing campaign, Fairbanks took to the campaign trail but with neither the fire nor the charisma of the hero of San Juan Hill. He tried to make up for those shortcomings with thoroughness and diligence. But

Fairbanks's cold and stilted manner earned him the nickname "the Icicle" and prompted Peter Finley Dunne's Mr. Dooley to pen: "Th' republican convintion labored, too, like a cash register. It listened to three canned speeches, adopted a predigested platform, nominated a cold storage vice president, gave three especially cheers and wint home. The convintion's mind all made f'r it met."[8]

Fairbanks boasted about his own abstemiousness, talking about his preference for wholesome buttermilk. But when a reporter covering a lawn party that Fairbanks hosted in honor of Roosevelt learned that Manhattans had been served, he was widely ridiculed as "Cocktail Charlie" to the taunting of prohibitionists.[9]

But the presence of Fairbank on the ticket was irrelevant. Roosevelt's own force of personality swept the pair to victory on Election Night. Late that night, the victorious Roosevelt dictated a surprise announcement to reporters in the White House that had to be an encouragement to the ambitious Fairbanks: "On the fourth of March next I shall have served three and a half years, and this three and a half years constitutes my first term. The wise custom which limits the President to two terms regards the substance and not the form. Under no circumstances will I be a candidate for or accept another nomination."[10] The declaration gave Fairbanks considerable basis for seeing himself as the next president. Once in the vice presidency, though, he found himself treated much the same as nearly all of his predecessors, the revered and the forgotten as well.

In 1896, when Roosevelt was the New York City police commissioner, he had written an article in the *American Monthly Review of Reviews* arguing for much wider involvement by the vice president in his administration, including attending cabinet meetings with the president and being allowed to vote in the Senate rather than simply presiding and breaking ties.[11] In the presidency, however, he showed no such interest in having Fairbanks looking over his shoulder, although the vice president did lend what help he could provide toward passing legislation sought by Roosevelt—and blocking bills the White House did not want.

At the same time, Fairbanks, as a former senator, was not favorably disposed toward some of Roosevelt's efforts to expand executive powers at the expense of the legislative process. In the president's campaign against some of the most powerful corporate trusts, he preferred to rely on powers within his executive mandate rather than having to cope with the long and circuitous legislative route and political opponents on Capitol Hill. In intraparty rows on issues, Fairbanks often sided with the senators rather than with his own president.

Roosevelt in turn had little regard for Fairbanks's abilities, a view widely shared in the press. When Roosevelt told Finley Peter Dunne he was considering going underwater in a submarine, the author of the "Mr. Dooley" sketches replied, "You really shouldn't do it—unless you take Fairbanks with you."[12] Roosevelt indeed did join one of the early dives of the USS *Plunger,* one of the first American submarines, but there was no record that he took Fairbanks with him then or on other such adventures.

By December 1907, Roosevelt seemed to be having qualms about his impetuous announcement that he wouldn't run again. He wrote a friend, "I hate for personal reasons to get out of the fight here," and "I have the uncomfortable feeling that I may possibly be shirking a duty."[13] But he had given his word, and so he turned to his secretary of war and close friend, William Howard Taft of Ohio, to run. Taft preferred being named to the Supreme Court but agreed, with Roosevelt's strong support. Roosevelt by now had little but contempt for the persevering Fairbanks, ignoring him and being more concerned about the challenge to Taft from the New York governor Charles Evans Hughes.

Before the 1908 Republican National Convention in Chicago, however, reports of support not only for Hughes but also for Fairbanks baffled Roosevelt. He told a Hughes supporter, "Do you know who we have the most trouble in beating? Not Hughes—but Fairbanks! Think of it— Charlie Fairbanks! I was never more surprised in my life. I never dreamt of such a thing. He's got a hold in Kentucky, Indiana, and some states that is hard to break. How and why is beyond me. It is easier to win delegates away from Hughes right in New York than to win them away from Fairbanks in those states."[14]

By the time the convention opened, however, the only real challenge to Taft was from Roosevelt supporters in the hall. They responded to a mention of the president by the permanent chairman Lodge with nearly an hour-long demonstration peppered by shouts of "Four More Years!" and "We Want Teddy!"[15] Later in the day, Taft was easily nominated and, in November, beat the Democrat William Jennings Bryan, running and losing for a third time.

After completion of his vice presidential term, Fairbanks returned to Indiana and resumed involvement in Republican Party politics there. After a serious split in the ranks, he lent himself to efforts to restore unity in Indiana and as a result briefly prolonged his career in national politics, as we shall see in a succeeding chapter.

CHAPTER 27

JAMES S. SHERMAN

OF NEW YORK

Most presidents-elect up to this time had been quite content to adhere to the tradition that their running mates elected with them essentially go their own way, which was to the Senate to preside in leisure, free of any serious involvement in the administration. But that was not to be the case in 1909, when William Howard Taft of Ohio had as his vice president elect James Schoolcraft Sherman, a journeyman House of Representative leader from New York, whom he had handpicked to be his successor as president.

Taft, who was naturally regarded as a progressive of the Roosevelt school, anticipated he was going to have his hands full dealing with the Old Guard reactionary Speaker of the House, "Uncle Joe" Cannon. So he called in Sherman, known as "Sunny Jim" for his smiles, his easy-going disposition, and his talent for persuasion, and told him, "I am going to rely on you, Jim, to take care of Cannon for me. Whatever I have to do there [in the House] will be done through you." But Sherman, who as vice president was elected on his own, replied, "Not through me. You will have to act on your own account. I am to be Vice President, and acting as a messenger boy is not part of the duties of the Vice President."[1]

This was hardly an auspicious beginning of an official relationship or a personal one for that matter. Sherman may have felt he had nothing to lose, because a president has no constitutional power to fire the vice president. In any event this initial brush-up did not bar the two men and their families from sharing the box of honor at the inaugural ball. Thereafter, in fact, Taft and Sherman worked closely together on legislative matters while the vice president remained outside the Taft administration inner circle. The moderate Sherman had been tapped as Taft's running mate to accommodate the Old Guard in a split Republican Party after nearly eight years of Roosevelt's progressivism. His personal style helped soften conservative concerns that Taft would stick to the same progressive course.

As a supporter of high tariffs, Sherman was believed to be persuasive in nudging Taft in that direction, to the chagrin of a principal administration critic in the party, progressive leader Senator Robert La Follette of Wisconsin. Taft later credited Sherman's "charm of speech and manner, and his spirit of conciliation and compromise" for good relations on Capitol Hill. But he took note as well of "a stubborn adherence" to his principles, observing, "It would be unjust to Mr. Sherman to suggest that his sunny disposition and his anxiety to make everybody within the reach of his influence happy, was any indication of a lack of strength of character, of firmness of purpose, and of clearness of decision as to what he thought was right in politics."[2]

Sherman's independence emerged fairly early in his life. Born on October 24, 1855, in Utica, New York, where his father, Richard Sherman, published a Democratic newspaper and ran a food canning plant, he followed a path that led him into the Republican Party. After graduating from nearby Hamilton College in 1878 and its law school a year later, he was admitted to the state bar in 1880 and set up a law practice with a brother-in-law. In 1881 he married Carrie Hancock, who gave him three sons. In Utica, Sherman joined several fraternal clubs and at age twenty-nine was elected as mayor as a Republican. Two years later, he was elected to Congress and, with the exception of one short break, served in public office at the national level for the rest of his life. His only loss came in 1890, when his support for the unpopular high McKinley Tariff cost him his House seat, but he won it back in the next election.

With his congenial disposition and party fealty, Sherman became the center of a band of younger House Republicans from New York, showing no conspicuous interest in any leadership post and deferential to the advancement of his colleagues. He also emerged as an effective parliamentarian and through the years was called upon by whichever House Speaker was in the chair to sit in for him when the House met as the Committee of the Whole. The designation permitted freer debate and the amendment of bills; in fact, Henry Cabot Lodge said that Sherman "gradually came to be recognized as the best chairman of the Committee of the Whole whom that great body had known in many years."[3]

In 1900, with the retirement of Speaker Thomas B. Reed, Sherman ran for the office but lost to David B. Henderson of Iowa. Sherman then became Henderson's chief lieutenant, a role he continued with Henderson's famed successor, "Uncle Joe" Cannon. As chairman of the Committee of the Whole in 1896, Sherman presided over the House debate on tariff legislation that rejected the lower rates advanced by the Democratic president Cleveland and raised them in keeping with the Republican president McKinley's objectives.

When the assassination of McKinley in 1901 ushered in a more progressive and reformist administration under Theodore Roosevelt, Sherman stood staunchly with the Republican Old Guard. He had by now inherited his father's food canning business and opposed legislation calling for more precise labels reporting the weights and measures of various canned items. A crusader for greater accuracy proposed that "Sunny Jim" Sherman be renamed "Short-weight Jim."[4]

While Sherman was denied an official leadership position in the House, within Republican Party ranks his popularity and fund-raising abilities in the business community brought him the chairmanship of the Republican State Conventions in New York in 1895, 1900, and 1908 and the chairmanship of the GOP Congressional Campaign Committee in 1906. At the 1908 state convention, with President Roosevelt having announced he would not run again and having proposed William Howard Taft as his successor, the New Yorkers backed their governor, Charles Evans Hughes, for president and Sherman for vice president.

Upon Taft's nomination, he hoped for a more progressive running mate. But Speaker Cannon and other House Republican leaders pushed for their genial friend "Sunny Jim," arguing that a western presidential nominee needed a New Yorker on the ticket. According to Congressman Chauncey Depew in a later memoir, Taft's political managers had already shopped around the second spot to several other Republicans from key states and then had to let them down easily. The device, Depew reported, was to call each of them, ask whether they would accept the vice presidential nomination, and before they could say yes, to take any hesitation as a no and hang up. That way, Depew wrote, the recipients of the call could say later they had been asked but had turned it down.[5]

Others were romanced with the possibility of being Taft's running mate, but all did indeed reject it. Speaker Cannon rose and made a fiery appeal for Sherman that sealed the deal, somewhat placating the disappointment of the Old Guard still wary of Taft as a progressive ally of the retiring Roosevelt. William Allen White wrote at the time that sticking Taft with Sherman marked "the revolt of the conservative Republican Party against . . . liberal leadership."[6] In the general election, Sherman dutifully campaigned for Taft, who won easily over the perennial loser Bryan, though it was doubted that with Sherman's low national profile he affected the outcome.

Although Sherman as the new vice president had at the outset rejected Taft's efforts to have him "handle" Speaker Cannon, he later stepped in to help the president in other ways. When the 1910 congressional elections rolled around, Sherman carried out presidential assignments designed to strengthen the administration's influence. But when Taft sent him into Wisconsin to try to prevent the Senate renomination of La Follette, he had no success.

Taft also dispatched Sherman to his home state of New York to try to referee a party split that put the vice president into a struggle with former president Roosevelt over the election for governor. The Republican incumbent, Hughes, had just been appointed by Taft to the U.S. Supreme Court but was not to take the seat until mid-October, to enable him to complete some of his most-sought objectives in the state. One was legislation providing direct primary elections for public office rather than legislative selection, and Hughes had called a special session in June to consider it. Hughes had asked Roosevelt to endorse the progressive idea, and he had agreed. Taft also favored it, and Roosevelt saw the opportunity to demonstrate some unity on the reform and hence shore up the party in New York.

But Roosevelt didn't take into account the opposition of the Old Guard to the legislation, which would reduce its powers. And some wondered whether Roosevelt might be gearing up to get control of the party again in New York preparatory to another presidential run. Sherman as a status-quo regular warned, "We must stand up and hold matters together or the party is busted."[7]

In the end, the Direct-Elections Bill was defeated, and the regulars gloated at giving Roosevelt a political black eye. One leader of the anti-Roosevelt effort crowed, "Teddy is licked to a frazzle. We no longer worship the gods, we laugh at them."[8] But the progressives, in hoping to nominate one of their own for governor, persuaded the old Rough Rider to run for temporary chairman against Sherman, chosen by the Old Guard for the post. When Sherman called Taft and informed him of Roosevelt's seeking the temporary chairmanship, the president said he had no objection. Sherman sounded an alarm to Taft: "Why, don't you know that he will make a speech against you and the administration, and will carry the convention . . . and take the machinery out of the hands of your friends?" Taft told Sherman, "You must understand distinctly that you cannot involve me in a fight with Mr. Roosevelt over such a question."[9]

By this time relations between Taft and the former president who had chosen him as his successor were shredding, and the regulars pressed on, endorsing Sherman. When Taft read of the vote in the afternoon newspaper, he reportedly observed, "They have defeated Theodore," and laughed.[10] But that was not the end of the story.

Roosevelt, upset over Taft's seeming preference for Sherman over himself in this local wrangle, pressed Taft through an intermediary to issue a denial. The president, who remained so deferential to Roosevelt that he still referred to him as "the president" while owning the title himself, cravenly provided it. He wrote that he had done all he could to prevent the Sherman-Roosevelt contest. But the former president observed, "I am sorry that the Old Guard have put themselves in such shape that I shall have to go in and try to smash them," twenty years after he had first struggled for control of the state organization.[11]

At the state convention, however, Roosevelt was elected as temporary chairman after all, and his candidate for governor, Henry L. Stimson, was duly nominated but lost the election in a year the Republicans dropped twenty-five other governorships, eight U.S. Senate seats, and control of the House of Representatives.

Taft's breach with Sherman only got deeper when Taft appointed Stimson as his secretary of war, apparently as a gesture toward Roosevelt. As Old

Guard concerns rose, talk began of running Sherman against Taft in 1912, and the vice president focused on strengthening his support in New York. But Taft told associates he believed Sherman was more interested in using the state as leverage to retain the vice presidency for a second term. By this time, in 1911, Taft and Roosevelt had come to agree that Sherman was bad business. Once, when the vice president at a church affair began to quote from the Bible, Roosevelt was said to have whispered to Taft, "When Jim Sherman quotes scripture, the devil must shake all hell with his laughter."[12]

Taft for his part began to think about dumping Sherman in 1912 for Governor Herbert S. Hadley of Missouri, in the hope of picking up some border and southern states. But Hadley was now committed to the possibility that Roosevelt might change his mind and run for president again. When an exhausted Robert La Follette had a physical breakdown in February of the election year, removing him from presidential contention, Roosevelt, despite his vow not to seek the presidency, did indeed jump into the race for the Republican nomination.

The former president demonstrated his continuing popular appeal in several state primaries, but Taft managed to hold on to enough state organizations to claim the nomination. Sherman, rallying for Taft, helped carry the New York delegation for him. An outraged Roosevelt bolted the party convention and formed his own, known as the Progressive or "Bull Moose" Party, making it a three-way race, which in effect handed the presidency to the Democratic nominee, Governor Woodrow Wilson of New Jersey.

In the meantime, the disheveled Republicans renominated Sherman as Taft's running mate, making him the first sitting vice president so chosen to run again since John C. Calhoun, eighty years earlier. Sherman never made it across the finish line. He accepted the renomination, but Bright's disease, a major kidney illness, prevented him from campaigning in the fall, and a few days before the election he died at age fifty-seven. Taft had to decide whether to name a replacement, but party leaders decided doing so would not be appropriate, so Taft ran alone and finished a poor third behind the winner, Wilson, as well as Roosevelt. For the purpose of recording the electoral count, the Republican National Committee chose Nicholas Murray Butler, the president of Columbia University, to complete the party's ticket.

As for Roosevelt, he returned to private life in 1913, championed American entry into World War I on the Allied side, and sharply criticized the

American neutrality that continued until U.S. entry in 1917. Thereupon he sought to lead a volunteer unit, a latter-day version of the Rough Riders, to fight in France but was denied a commission. At only age sixty, he died in his sleep on January 6, 1919, only two months after the end of the war, having experienced one of the most vigorous and colorful lives of any American political figure in war and peace. Originally disdainful of the vice presidency as a political dead end that he preferred to avoid, he nevertheless gained greater national power and international influence from it than any previous "accidental" president.

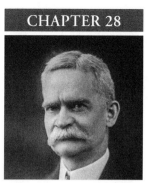

CHAPTER 28

THOMAS R. MARSHALL

OF INDIANA

Perhaps no previous vice president was more poorly treated up to this time than Thomas Riley Marshall of Indiana. He came perilously close to the presidency as a result of the serious physical incapacity of President Woodrow Wilson in October 1919, yet was kept in the dark about it. To his credit, when he learned of Wilson's perilous condition, Marshall intentionally eschewed any word or deed that might have cast him as an opportunistic usurper of the highest office.

His benign response to the tempting situation did not stem from a lack of political ambition. In the 1912 presidential election, Marshall, as governor of Indiana, had entertained thoughts of winning the Republican nomination in what might well have been a deadlocked convention. Instead he settled for the vice presidency, and although the shortcomings of the office were well understood by him, he had neither the hubris nor the unscrupulous nature even to attempt to exploit the situation that presented itself in the second of the two terms he served.

Born in Columbia City, Indiana, on March 14, 1854, Marshall was the only child of a country doctor and his wife. Young Tom attended schools in Warsaw and Fort Wayne and then Wabash College, joining the Phi Gamma Delta fraternity and achieving admission to Phi Beta Kappa. The most notable episode at Wabash was a two hundred thousand dollar libel suit against him and other staff members of the college paper for an article writing that a woman had been "kicked out" for flirting under a table with boys at her boardinghouse. After jury selection the case was dismissed at the request of the woman and her husband. The college paper later retracted the story and issued an apology. Marshall spent much of his free time at the county courthouse, viewing and listening to trials, afterward talking trial tactics with the lawyers and whetting his ambition to follow their career course.[1]

Marshall returned to Columbia City in 1873 and joined a small local law firm there, becoming an attorney of the Whitley County Court at age twenty-one. A confirmed bachelor for the next twenty years, he lived with his mother there until her death in 1894. Less than a year later, he married Lois Kimsey, a clerk in the office of her father, the county clerk in neighboring Angola. Marshall at this time was a heavy drinker, conspicuously seen hungover in court, until his wife talked him into being a teetotaler for the rest of his life, even to the point of being an occasional lecturer on temperance.[2]

Marshall was a short man who seldom weighed more than 125 pounds and walked with a slight limp.[3] He was an avid reader with a quick mind and retentive memory but limited objectives. "I had then as I now have the happy faculty of superficiality," he wrote whimsically later. "It enabled me quickly to learn any subject to which I put my mind, and just as quickly to forget it when I no longer needed it."[4] He was regarded by friends to be intellectually lazy but had the fortune of having a law partner who handled the heavy lifting, and they made a winning and prosperous partnership.

Marshall's beginnings in politics were predictable and inauspicious. His grandfather had been elected as a county clerk in the days when Andrew Jackson was organizing what became the Democratic Party. Both Marshall's grandfather and father remained Democrats through the Civil War, giving up their Methodist church membership when their minister threatened to banish them unless they stopped voting Democratic. Marshall's biographer cited the grandfather saying he was willing to take his chance on hell but never on the Republican Party.[5]

Young Tom Marshall worked in the party starting in his early twenties, became secretary of his county convention in 1876, but lost his first election for prosecuting attorney in 1880. Discouraged, he did not run for public office again for twenty-eight years, though continued to serve on the state party central committee and to speak for other Democratic candidates. In 1906, he was pressured to run for Congress but refused, happy with his small-town life and good income. In 1908, a local newspaperman launched the idea that Marshall be nominated for the governorship, apparently without Marshall's knowledge. A pamphlet was printed and circulated, first in his congressional district and later around Indiana in general. Without campaigning he was nominated, and that fall he stumped tirelessly, delivering 169 speeches, or as his wife put it, the same speech 169 times.[6]

His campaign for governor was marked by seeming indifference to the outcome. He frequently told listeners he had a solid law practice back home and didn't care whether he became governor or not. When the party organized a train tour of Democratic candidates across Indiana, and Marshall learned it was being financed by the state brewery industry, he refused to travel on it. He rode on day coaches, paying his own way, so if elected he would be unencumbered by political debts.[7] On Election Night, Marshall was elected, but the Democrats lost all but two other state offices and control of the state Senate, giving him a mixed legislature in his first two gubernatorial years.

In 1912, with his governorship soon to end by the state's term limits, he decided to seek the Democratic presidential nomination as Indiana's favorite son. With Governor Woodrow Wilson of New Jersey short of a majority, the Indiana party chairman Tom Taggart bartered the state's delegates in a deal that put Wilson over the top on the forty-sixth ballot and made Marshall his running mate. Wilson did not learn of the deal until the next morning and simply acceded, though confiding to an ally that he judged Marshall "a very small caliber man."[8] After all this, Marshall at first rejected the office on the grounds that the salary of twelve thousand dollars a year was too little, and he could live better as a lawyer back in Columbia City. But his tearful wife changed his mind.

In the fall campaign against the Republican nominee, President Taft, and former president Roosevelt in his newly formed Progressive or Bull Moose Party, Wilson carried a heavy share of the load, but Marshall pitched in. He set an unprecedented and remarkable condition; once again he paid for all expenses for himself and his wife, who accompanied him throughout the campaign.[9] The Republican Party was so devastatingly split that the result was predictable and lopsided: Wilson and Marshall, 41.9 percent of the popular vote and 435 in the electoral college; Roosevelt and Hiram Johnson of California, 27.4 percent and 88 electoral votes; Taft and James Sherman of New York, 23.2 percent and 8 electoral votes.

Marshall came into the vice presidency with no legislative experience and the confidence to match, but he took to his lot with good cheer and wit. After his first day presiding over the U.S. Senate, he remarked that his place in the chamber didn't differ much from a monkey cage, quipping, "Except that the visitors do not offer me any peanuts."[10] He wrote later, "I soon ascertained that I was of no importance to the administration beyond the duty of being loyal to it and ready, at any time, to act as a sort of pinch hitter . . . to acknowledge the insignificance of the office, to take it in a good-natured way; to be friendly . . . to deal justly with those over whom I was merely nominally presiding."[11]

On certain issues such as women's suffrage and prohibition, however, he expressed his personal opposition, saying of the former only, "I never talk about it; Mrs. Marshall is opposed to it. That settles me on the question." On the latter, he told the Virginia Bar Association, "I do not use liquor, never serve it at my table, and I wish to God that no one else did. But I object to the way prohibition has been imposed, though again I insist, now that it is here, it must be enforced."[12]

In March 1914, around the second anniversary of the elections of Wilson and Marshall, Wilson's wife, Ellen, suffered a fall, after which she was diagnosed with Bright's disease. She died five months later, sending the president into a period of deep grief and depression. About a year later, when Marshall was on a trip to the Far West, he learned that Wilson was about to marry a second wife, Edith Galt. He sent her a folksy congratulatory letter, along with a native wool blanket woven by an American Indian woman for a Navajo chief, saying he hoped it was "worthy to be trodden underfoot by the great White Chief." In reporting on the warm note from Marshall, biographer Daniel J. Bennett noted, "It would, however, do little to thaw the icy demeanor of Edith Wilson, or change her thinly disguised disdain for Marshall and his wife,"[13] as future events would confirm.

After the sinking of the British liner *Lusitania* in May 1915, with the loss of many Americans, Marshall argued that Americans who boarded such ships were in effect setting foot onto British soil and should expect to bear the consequences, and criticism mounted. The *New York Times* editorially observed that Marshall "should have sense enough not to embarrass the President by utterances at odds with his settled policy, and should not spatter flippant epigrams on an international tragedy. . . . If Indiana cannot raise men of presidential calibre, she should at least try to train mediocre men in some of the negative virtues. She should train them to keep silence when they have nothing to say."[14] But if Marshall's occasional observations shocked and rankled many, they also won him some public respect as a man who spoke his mind.

Despite Marshall's frequent squabblings with senators, usually Republicans, over some of his parliamentary rulings, he mixed firmness with humor and eventually was regarded as one of the better Senate presidents up to that time. Eventually, the same *Times* editorial board declared him "an American patriot, and the words he speaks have a sense and sanity that are urgently needed. . . . Some of the things he says may be regarded as platitudinous, but they can only be so regarded by men who do not know Thomas Riley Marshall. . . . Nobody has yet appeared as well qualified as the Vice President to state in plausible terms the longing of a great many American citizens to get back to where they used to be."[15]

For all of Marshall's substantive observations, however, his best-remembered utterance came as a whispered aside from the Senate president's chair as one Senator Joe Bristow of Kansas droned on one day about what the country needed: "What this country needs," Marshall offered, "is a really good five-cent cigar."[16] But the origins of the quote were later disputed. In any event, Marshall's sense of humor was a hit in the Senate, and he often served it up for the more sober and intellectual Wilson. Shortly after their first nomination, he gave the president a book on Indiana humor inscribed: "From your only Vice, Thomas R. Marshall."

But Marshall's standing in the White House was sometimes shaky. In the course of one general discussion with Wilson over party and political matters, his close adviser Colonel Edward House suddenly raised the question of whether Marshall should be dumped from the ticket in 1916 in favor of Newton Baker, the former mayor of Cleveland and Wilson's secretary of war.

House reported later what Wilson said in a commentary on how the vice presidency was then perceived: "He felt that Baker was too good a man to be sacrificed. I disagreed with him. I did not think that any man was too good to be considered for Vice President of the United States. I thought if the right man took it, a man who has his confidence as Baker has, a new office could be created out of it. He might become Vice President in fact as well as in name, and be a co-worker and co-helper of the President. He [Wilson] was interested in this argument but was unconvinced that Baker should be, as he termed it, sacrificed."[17]

House recollected that his suggestion to Wilson reflected the thoughts of other party leaders, and he puzzled at the indifference of the intellectual Wilson to the notion. Wilson's biographer John Milton Cooper Jr., of the University of Wisconsin, observed, "The idea of a vice president who might serve as a co-president should have appealed to Wilson. Having spent so much of life studying political systems and institutions, he was better equipped than anyone else to grasp the merits of this idea. Having an able and trusted vice president such as Baker at his side during his second term could have made a big difference in management and policy, particularly when it became a wartime presidency."[18]

Apparently Wilson made no comment on a second term for Marshall at the time. As early as October 1915, however, with Marshall's candor and witticisms drawing increasing comment and some criticism, Wilson had been reported as commenting, "It would be unlucky to run the same team twice." Wilson denied having said it, but rumors continued, and one close Wilson friend, the former ambassador to Turkey Henry Morgenthau, also began to boost Newton Baker. But Baker squelched the talk, saying he was not a candidate. Many years later he said he had been informed that Wilson really did want him as his 1916 running mate, but when the president himself said nothing to him about it, he figured it wasn't so.[19]

Meanwhile, a group of professional politicians moved to squelch any anti-Marshall talk. When Governor H. R. Fielder of New Jersey asked Wilson for his view on the matter, the president quickly sent back a note saying it was not his place to state a preference but also that Marshall had been "loyal and generous to the extreme," adding, "He has given me every reason to admire and trust him."[20] And when the Democratic senator Henry Ashurst of Arizona pointedly asked Wilson whether he wanted Marshall as his running mate again, the answer was: "I have a very high regard for Vice President Marshall and I wish you would tell him so." Well, did he support him for renomination? "Why, yes," Wilson replied, and Marshall was routinely nominated by acclamation.[21]

In the fall campaign, Marshall continued speech making, focusing on the far western states, while Wilson only reluctantly got involved in the late stages. But only a few weeks before the 1916 election, Wilson and his closest political advisers now realized the election would be very close and that Hughes might edge him out.

The prospect led Colonel House to suggest a bizarre scheme whereby Wilson, before the results were in, would get his secretary of state, Robert Lansing, and Vice President Marshall to resign and then appoint Hughes to replace Lansing. Wilson himself presumably would then resign before the completion of his term in March. "The course I have in mind," House wrote in his diary, published much later, "is dependent upon the consent and cooperation of the Vice President."[22] Under the presidential succession then in place, with the vice president resigned and then the president as well, Hughes would become president and thus avoid the awkward and perilous four-month interregnum that then existed between the election and the inauguration of the new president.

House approached Lansing and Wilson with the idea. Lansing was willing, but Wilson was noncommittal. Two days before the election, however, Wilson wrote a letter in shorthand, then typed it, and sealed it with wax in an envelope and had it hand-delivered to Lansing. In it, he advocated the idea, citing the wartime conditions and writing, "No such critical circumstances in regard to our foreign policy have ever before existed," adding that he had "no right to risk the peace of the nation by remaining in office after I had lost my authority."[23] As for Marshall's possible acquiescence in the plan, constitutionally he had been separately elected, and Wilson had no legal power simply to fire him, but it would have been hard for Marshall not to go along had Wilson pressed him.

Later some disputed whether Wilson had actually asked Marshall to step aside, although the vice president in a September 1916 campaign speech in Terre Haute did say, "If I believed the European war would last during the remainder of the present administration, and there was a likelihood of a calamity befalling President Wilson that would shift the burden of responsibilities to my shoulders, I would resign my office."[24]

The observation drew a fierce condemnation from one of Marshall's home-state newspapers, the *Fort Wayne Sentinel,* saying outsiders who didn't know him would "wonder what sort of a wild and woolly fool he is . . . lacking in backbone, nerve and manhood." The editorial concluded, "If he feels that way about his office he should never have accepted a renomination and . . . it is not yet too late for him to retire."[25]

Much later, after Marshall's ultimate retirement, he reportedly told a close friend, J. C. Sanders, that Wilson had indeed asked him to resign but that he had refused because he had been elected to serve a full four-year term, and he intended to serve it out.[26]

In any event, Wilson took no action on Colonel House's idea, and the outcome of the election eradicated the cause for concern. In a night-long nail-biter, with Wilson going to bed believing he had lost the election, the Wilson-Marshall ticket narrowly prevailed over Hughes and Fairbanks when California went to the Democrats by fewer than four thousand votes, giving the Democrats 277 in the electoral college compared with 254 for the Republicans.

When Wilson took the country into the war in 1917, Marshall threw himself into making speeches to raise funds for Liberty Loan Bonds. But until then, he had adhered to the president's neutrality proclamation while being outspoken about the drift to war. In 1915, he had said the United States had no right to tell any European country what kind of government it should have and that American businessmen should not make loans to England and France if true neutrality was to be observed.

When Wilson submitted war preparedness bills to Congress, Marshall guardedly told him the country would support "reasonable" steps and that the country "endorsed his efforts to maintain peace with honor."[27] After the United States became a combatant with the declaration of war on April 6, 1917, however, he apologized for his earlier mild position. He now questioned how "a God-fearing man in the twentieth century of civilization could have dreamed that any nation, any people or any man could be neutral when right was fighting wrong."[28]

In advance of the 1918 congressional elections, Marshall somewhat naively proposed to Wilson that he, Marshall, make a speech "announcing that the only question before the American people was winning the war and standing behind the president." He said he asked Wilson, "Should I not propose that both Democrats and Republicans nominate men pledged to these two objects and let the people make a choice? . . . I also suggested proposing to the Republican party to close up all political headquarters and to expend money saved thereby in Red Cross and other war activities."

Wilson rejected the notion, Marshall said, telling him he "expected to issue a call shortly before the election for a Democratic Congress, and had no doubt that the people would give it to him because they had refused him nothing so far."[29] So with misgivings Marshall followed the partisan course and instead inflamed rival party resentment of the sort that would later poison Wilson's efforts to win Senate ratification of the peace treaty with Germany.

In those congressional elections, Marshall regretted their being held in wartime, but he threw himself behind Wilson's push for election of a Democratic Congress. At Wilson's specific request, Marshall, in a late campaign speech in Wisconsin, launched a sharply partisan attack uncommon to him on a Republican congressional nominee who actually supported Wilson on the war, asking him, "Do you doubt that Republican success will be hailed at home and abroad as repudiation? Do you want the election returns celebrated in London and Paris, where Wilson is honored, or in Berlin and Vienna where he is hated?"[30] But Marshall's uncharacteristically demagogic words backfired. On Election Night, the Democrats lost control of the Senate and the votes that might otherwise have sustained Wilson later in his fight for the Peace Treaty of Versailles.

A week after that election, the armistice ending the shooting was signed, and on December 4, 1918, for the first time in the nation's history, an American president left the country for Europe, to negotiate the treaty between the Allied Powers and the defeated German Empire. Marshall, asked by a reporter what he thought of a notion that the duties of the president should be transferred to him in Wilson's absence, said, "I have not the slightest desire nor intention of interfering with the President, unless I am forced to, and that will be of infinite regret to me." He said he supported Wilson's trip, then reassured, "Most certainly do not want his job while he is away." He added, "That does not mean I am dodging responsibility. . . . I will meet it squarely and accept whatever responsibility was placed upon me."[31]

Before departing, Wilson designated Marshall to preside over his cabinet meetings while he was away, but the president actually called the first cabinet meeting in his absence by cable from sea. In taking over, Marshall pointedly told the attendees he was acting at Wilson's request and also at their request, that he was there "informally and personally" and was "not undertaking to exercise any official duty or function."[32] He also made a point of observing that he did not accept the notion that a vice president needed to be kept better informed of his president's policies in order to be able to carry them out in the event that anything happened to him. "A vice president might make a poor president," he said, "but he would make a much poorer one if he attempted to subordinate his own mind and views to carry out the ideas of a dead man."[33]

After sitting at the head of the table for only a few cabinet meetings, Marshall stopped attending. Upon completion of the negotiations for the peace treaty, Wilson returned to Washington and plunged into the struggle over Senate ratification against Republican senators led by Chairman Henry Cabot Lodge of the Senate Foreign Relations Committee, none of them invited to the negotiations. When the treaty failed, Wilson embarked on a tour of the country to sell it to the American people, against the advice of his White House physician, Dr. Cary T. Grayson. For twenty-two days, Wilson traveled more than eight thousand miles by train, making about forty speeches and en route increasingly complaining to his wife about severe headaches.

On the night of September 26, 1919, after a speech in Pueblo, Colorado, Edith Wilson called Grayson to examine the restless president. The doctor concluded at this point only that he was "suffering from nervous exhaustion" but that "his condition [was] not alarming."[34] Under the doctor's orders Wilson returned to the White House, and six days later, he suffered a massive stroke that partly paralyzed his left side. Edith Wilson found him lying unconscious on his bathroom floor and summoned Grayson, who issued a terse statement saying little more than "the President is a very sick man" and that "absolute rest is essential for some time."[35] Grayson, together with Wilson's secretary, Joseph P. Tumulty, and Mrs. Wilson, decided that the president have no visitors and that only the most pressing business be brought to him.

Through all this, Vice President Marshall was not informed of the seriousness of Wilson's plight. At the time of the attack, he was in Hoboken, New Jersey, along with Secretary of State Robert Lansing, greeting the arriving king and queen of Belgium and their son. Wilson's condition clearly raised the question whether under the Constitution he should be declared unable to carry out his presidential duties and, at least temporarily, that they be bestowed on the vice president. In Edith Wilson's later memoir, she wrote that her husband's neurologist said it was imperative that she shield Wilson from anything that might upset him, explaining, "Every time you take him a new anxiety or problem to excite him, you are turning a knife in an open wound. His nerves are crying out for rest, any excitement is torture to him."[36]

She wrote that she thereupon asked the doctor, "Then had he better not resign, let Mr. Marshall succeed to the presidency and he himself get that complete rest so vital to his life?" The doctor replied, she wrote, "No. Not if you feel equal to what I have suggested. For Mr. Wilson to resign would have a bad effect on the country, and a serious effect on our patient. He has staked his life and made his promise to the world to do all in his power to get the Treaty ratified and make the League of Nations complete. If he resigns, the greatest incentive to recover is gone; and as his mind is clear as crystal he can still do more with even a maimed body than anyone else." Marshall's wife, Lois, reported years later that Grayson said he had urged Wilson to resign but that he had refused.[37]

Lansing, by the nature of his responsibilities in foreign policy, was brought into the small inner circle who knew Wilson's true condition and was the first to raise the question of presidential disability and succession. Lansing handed Tumulty a copy of the Constitution, from which he read the pertinent language. Tumulty, shaken, was said to have replied, "Mr. Lansing, the Constitution is not a dead letter with the White House. I have read the Constitution and do not find myself in need of any tutoring at your hands of the provision that you have just read. You may rest assured that while Woodrow Wilson is lying in the White House on the broad of his back I will not be a party to ousting him." At that, Grayson entered the room. Tumulty turned to him and added, "And I am sure that Dr. Grayson would never certify to his disability."[38] Grayson agreed. Tumulty wrote later, "It is unnecessary to say that no further attempt was made by Mr. Lansing to institute ouster proceedings against his chief."[39]

Lansing, as the ranking member of the cabinet, nevertheless called a meeting of the other members to discuss Wilson's condition with Grayson, but after hearing the doctor they seemed satisfied that no action was necessary. When Wilson later learned that Lansing had done so without Wilson's knowledge and authorization, he demanded and got the resignation of the secretary of state.[40]

With the rumors of Wilson's health intensifying in Washington, Tumulty decided that Vice President Marshall should be alerted in an unofficial manner of the president's condition. Tumulty informed Secretary of Agriculture David Houston, who was to have lunch with Marshall the next day, to so advise him. Houston wrote later that Marshall "was evidently much disturbed and expressed regret that he was being kept in the dark about the president's condition. . . . [He said] that it would be a tragedy for him to assume the duties of the President, at best . . . that he knew many men who knew more about the affairs of government than he did; and that it would be especially trying for him if he had to assume the duties without warning."[41]

Two weeks after the previous stroke, Wilson developed a serious prostate blockage that doctors said would require surgery, which could be fatal, but Mrs. Wilson rejected it. After a few hours the blockage resolved itself, but the crisis convinced Tumulty, Grayson, and Lansing that Marshall had to be told all. But would such notification constitute the triggering of the presidential disability language in the Constitution? It was decided, probably by Tumulty, that the best way would be to enlist a trusted and dependable White House reporter, J. Fred Essary, of the *Baltimore Sun*, to so advise the vice president. Essary reported later that when he did so, Marshall was stunned and speechless, staring at his folded hands on his desk.

Marshall decided to go to the White House to discuss the situation directly with Wilson, but the president's wife refused to admit him to the sickroom. Marshall vowed that nothing would persuade him to take any action short of a resolution of Congress or a written direction from Mrs. Wilson. He firmly told his secretary, Mark Thistlethwaite, "I am not going to seize the place and then have Wilson, recovered, come around and say, 'Get off, you usurper!'"[42] And he told his wife, "I could throw this country into civil war, but I won't."[43]

Meanwhile, official papers requiring Wilson's attention or signature were shuttled to Edith Wilson for her own decision on whether they should be seen or signed by the president. Some signed documents bore a shaky handwriting that led to speculation and doubt as to whether it was Wilson's hand that signed them. A Republican senator, Albert Fall, gushed, "We have a petticoat government! Mrs. Wilson is president!"[44]

All this while, Marshall was presiding over the Senate debate on the peace treaty and ratification of Wilson's dream of a league of nations, with the United States as a member. Senators of both parties approached him to assume the presidency or at least its duties; aware that Marshall supported Wilson on the treaty but believing he might accept some modifications that Wilson had rejected, they hoped he might be the vehicle for a breakthrough. But Marshall stood firm.

Years later, he wrote, "Those were not pleasant months for me. The standing joke of the country is that the only business of the vice-president is to ring the White House bell every morning and ask what is the state of health of the president. If there were a soul so lost to humanity to have desired his death, I was not that soul. I hoped that he might acquire his wonted health. I was afraid to ask about it, for fear some censorious soul would accuse me to a longing for his place. I never have wanted his shoes. Peace, friendship and good will have ever been more to me than place or pomp or power."[45]

Beyond that, Marshall knew that the daunting Edith Wilson held a low opinion of this witty and unaffected man, and he had no intention of getting on cross purposes with her. He told columnist Arthur Krock of the *New York Times*, "No politician ever exposes himself to the hatred of a woman, particularly if she's the wife of the President of the United States."[46] Mrs. Wilson's own judgment of her husband's ability to function as president during this time, dealing with matters of state, was severely questioned later. The chief usher in the White House, Irwin "Ike" Hoover, who saw Wilson immediately after Mrs. Wilson found him collapsed and in the days thereafter, wrote later that there "never was deception so universally practiced in the White House as it was in those statements given out from time to time."[47]

Eventually, Wilson's health stabilized sufficiently for Marshall to undertake some speech engagements outside Washington. On November 23, 1919, he was addressing a convention in Atlanta when he was called to the telephone. Told that the vice president was in the middle of his speech, the caller replied, "Well, I guess he'll come now. President Wilson has just died in Washington." When the message was conveyed, Marshall passed it on to the audience, saying, with head bowed, "I cannot continue my speech. I must leave at once to take up my duties as Chief Executive of this great nation. I cannot bear the great burdens of our beloved chieftain unless I receive the assistance of everybody in this country." As he and wife Lois left the stage and the auditorium organist started playing "Nearer My God to Thee," Marshall phoned the White House and was told the call was a hoax; Wilson still lived.[48]

In 1920, Marshall threw his hat into the ring, but beyond Indiana there was little support for him. When the rival Republicans nominated Governor Warren G. Harding of Ohio for president and Governor Calvin Coolidge of Massachusetts for vice president, Marshall sent Coolidge a telegram: "Please accept my sincere sympathy."[49] Wilson, to the surprise of many, finished out his term in 1921, and Marshall with him. Soon after, President Harding appointed Marshall to the Lincoln Memorial Commission. On June 1, 1825, Marshall died of a heart attack at the Willard Hotel in Washington, where, not well-off enough to buy a home in the area, he had spent some of his eight years as vice president.

Along with being a small man in stature, Thomas Marshall of Indiana was perhaps also, as Woodrow Wilson once said, "a small caliber man" in terms of intellect and erudition. But in the restraint and grace he displayed in those dark days when Wilson seemed at death's door and the presidency might well have passed to him, he demonstrated qualities that earned him distinction in the vice presidency that few other occupants, past or present, have ever achieved.

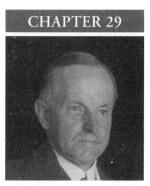

CHAPTER 29

CALVIN COOLIDGE
OF MASSACHUSETTS

Over the fireplace in the home of Calvin Coolidge in Northampton, Massachusetts, hung a placard that read, "A wise old owl lived in an oak; the more he saw the less he spoke. The less he spoke the more he heard; why can't we be like that old bird?"[1] Some years later, when he had become the leader of his country, a prominent society lady sitting next to Coolidge at a Washington dinner party said to him, "Oh, Mr. President, you are so silent. I made a bet today that I could get more than two words out of you." He replied, "You lose."[2]

The man known as "Silent Cal" also attributed his political climb from his position in the state legislature, then as mayor of Northampton, lieutenant governor and governor of Massachusetts, and finally as vice president and president of the United States to his reticence. "I have never been hurt by what I have not said," he declared.[3]

Indeed, his elevation from local and state politics to the national stage as the nation's twenty-ninth vice president did not come out of self-promotion by Coolidge. The genesis was the Republican governors' irate reaction at their party's 1920 national convention in Chicago to the smoke-filled cabal, where U.S. senators chose one of their own, the affable and moderate Senator Warren G. Harding of Ohio, for the presidential nomination.

When the "Senatorial Soviet," as one critic later called it, sought also to anoint another colleague, Senator Irvine L. Lenroot of Wisconsin, as the vice presidential nominee, a rebellion broke out. As Senator Medill Mc-Cormick of Illinois was placing Lenroot's name in nomination, a delegate from Oregon, the former state supreme court justice Wallace McCamant, interrupted with a cry of "Coolidge! Coolidge!" that rang through the hall.

Earlier, with Coolidge's acquiescence, the Massachusetts delegation had entered his name for president, even though, characteristically, as he wrote later in his autobiography, he "did not wish to use the office of governor in an attempt to prosecute a campaign for nomination for some other office."[4] He therefore did not permit his name to be entered in any state primaries, and the former newspaperman Harding was nominated.[5] Prior to the nominations for vice president, Coolidge had informed the Massachusetts delegation that he did not want his name offered for that position either. The political boss of the state's western portion, W. Murray Crane, had passed the word: "Don't put the governor up. He's been beaten once, and he doesn't want a second defeat."[6]

The Oregon delegation meanwhile had come to Chicago instructed to vote for Senator Henry Cabot Lodge of Massachusetts, but Lodge too had asked that his name not be put forward. Consequently, McCamant demanded the floor, saying, "But there is another son of Massachusetts who has been much in the public eye during the past year," referring to Coolidge's celebrated firmness in putting down a Boston police strike in 1919.[7] When McCamant offered him as Harding's running mate, the convention exploded in approval, and Coolidge was overwhelmingly nominated over Lenroot, the choice of the senatorial cabal.

Calvin Coolidge's typically terse remarks in snuffing out that police strike—"There is no right to strike against the public safety by anybody, anywhere, anytime"—had brought him instant national acclaim.[8] At a time when the country had grown weary of conflict, including the labor unrest following the Great War, Coolidge's words insisting on the maintenance of law and order at home resonated widely, as did his personal placid demeanor.

The choice, however, was not quite the spontaneous action suggested by the popular narrative. Crane and Frank W. Stearns, a Boston businessman who had attended Amherst College with Coolidge, had circulated a seventy-thousand-copy printing of Coolidge's inspirational speeches called

Have Faith in Massachusetts to all prospective convention delegates.[9] So Coolidge's name was on their minds well before the Oregonian's call to his colors on the convention floor.

Although Coolidge gained his first fame and political fortune as governor of Massachusetts, his roots and general outlook on life came more from neighboring Vermont, where he was born in Plymouth Notch on the Fourth of July, 1872, to the proprietor of the local post office and general store and his wife. They named him John after his father, but he always was called Calvin. A sister, Abby, was born three years later. Their father also ran the family farm and later opened a blacksmith shop. Their mother was a gentle woman of fair complexion who died from injuries suffered in a carriage accident caused by a runaway horse when Calvin was only twelve years old.[10] His sister died a few years later. His grandfather left him forty acres of Vermont farmland, with the intent that he work it for the rest of his life.

When Calvin was only two months old, his father was elected to the Vermont legislature. Calvin's own frugality in mercenary matters and his temperate behavior were an inheritance from his Vermont beginnings. Of his neighbors, he wrote later, "Their speech was clean and their lives were above reproach. They had no mortgages on their farms. If any debts were contracted they were promptly paid. Credit was good and there was money in the savings bank."[11] The town of Plymouth Notch was grounded in democratic principles, and young Calvin followed its early political meetings and discussions with great interest. His father at times also served as a local constable, sheriff, justice of the peace, and tax collector and often took him to court hearings.

Young Coolidge left the farm and a local one-room schoolhouse at age thirteen to attend Black River Academy, in nearby Ludlow, where he first encountered the Constitution and also studied history, Latin, and Greek. From there he attended and graduated from Amherst College, in Massachusetts, where he distinguished himself as a public speaker. Each summer he returned home to help work the farm. He was lean, physically and facially unimpressive, with a tranquility that belied a scholarly intensity. Taken in by a law firm in Northampton, a few miles from Amherst, he passed the bar, then undertook the practice of law there. He was elected to the Northampton City Council in 1898, as city solicitor in 1899, and became an interim clerk of the county court. He married Grace Goodhue at her home in Burlington, Vermont, in 1905 and later wrote of their marriage, "We thought we were made for each other. For almost a quarter of a century she has borne with my infirmities, and I have rejoiced in her graces."[12]

In 1906 Coolidge was elected to the first of two one-year terms in the Massachusetts legislature, going door to door and asking for votes in the old-fashioned way, with his customary brevity.[13] In 1910 he was elected as mayor of Northampton, thereafter becoming a member of the Massachusetts Senate and then its president. In 1912, he negotiated settlements in a strike at the Lawrence Duck Mill, which produced a wage increase for the workers and was a forerunner to the most notable such intervention of his career.

He commuted by train to Boston and, when elected as lieutenant governor in 1916, rented a cheap hotel room there and served on the governor's council, oversaw the state's penal institutions and the governor's granting of pardons, and was acting governor in the absence of the Republican governor Samuel W. McCall. In 1918 Coolidge was elected to succeed McCall only a few nights before the armistice was signed ending the Great War in Europe. One of his first acts as governor was to sign an appropriation of ten thousand dollars for a reception for the Yankee Division, and he subsequently pushed through a hundred-dollar bonus for the troops. In a rare burst of personal extravagance, the new governor added to his one-room lodging at the dingy Adams House in Boston, expanding his space to include another room and connecting bath, and shelled out two and a half dollars in monthly rent for it, a dollar more than he had been paying. Meanwhile, Mrs. Coolidge remained in Northampton caring for the well-being of their sons.

As governor, Coolidge took particular interest in the affairs and needs of the state's military veterans, establishing a state employment commission to help their transition to civilian life. He visited state prisons to inspect living conditions and appointed commissions to consider pensions for state workers and maternity benefits for female employees. He reorganized the state government, reducing its more than one hundred agencies to twenty, giving himself greater control in the process.[14]

Early in his tenure at the State House, on Beacon Hill, as labor unrest broke out in Boston and around the country, the city's police were up in arms over low wages endured during the war and deplorable living conditions in their station house. As a legislator, Coolidge had been sympathetic to their lot but not to any resort to strike against a public-service entity, a position also held by the city's police commissioner, Edwin Curtis. To avert trouble, Curtis got the city government to raise policemen's pay two hundred dollars a year, and Coolidge suggested to the Democratic mayor, Andrew James Peters, that something be done about improving sleeping conditions at the station house.[15] Otherwise, the governor tried to stay out of the dispute and the gathering storm.

The Boston police, however, were prohibited from joining any outside union, and the breaking point came when many formed the Boston Social Club, which sought affiliation with the American Federation of Labor. When the AFL complied, Commissioner Curtis acted quickly, suspending nineteen members of the force who had led the organizing. They were tried and discharged. Coolidge, for all his sympathy for the police officers' wage and condition demands, saw the dispute in terms of their duty to protect the public safety and sided with Curtis. He asked, however, "Can you blame the police for feeling as they do when they get less than a street car conductor?"[16]

Even without their organizers, the police officers voted to strike, and nearly all of them walked out, leaving their badges behind. Coolidge said he had no authority to interfere, despite the mayor's urging him to call out the National Guard.[17] On the night of September 9, 1919, mobs filled the streets around Scollay Square, and riots and looting broke out elsewhere in the city. Mayor Peters finally called out the Boston State Guard, in effect taking over from Curtis, and President Woodrow Wilson declared, "A strike of the policemen of a great city, leaving that city at the mercy of an army of thugs, is a crime against civilization."[18] Only then did Coolidge himself act, calling out the state's National Guard and restoring Curtis, he said, "for the purpose of assisting me in the performance of my duty," to bring order to the streets of Boston.[19]

The Boston strike quickly collapsed. If Coolidge was tardy in responding the crisis, the outbreak of violence gave him the opening to reinforce his basic position that the first duty of a police officer was maintaining the peace, not deserting his post to advance his own well-being. The AFL president Samuel Gompers, disputing the governor's argument, insisted that whatever disorder had occurred was due to "the assumption of an autocratic and unwarranted position by the commissioner of police" against the right of policemen to strike.[20] Gompers further noted that in Washington, Wilson had not ordered dismissal of District of Columbia police who had affiliated with the AFL and asked why Coolidge could not show the same forbearance.

The governor replied, "The right of the police of Boston to affiliate has always been questioned, never granted, [and] is now prohibited. The suggestion of President Wilson to Washington does not apply to Boston. The police [in the District] remained on duty. Here the Policemen's Union left their duty, an act which President Wilson described as a crime against civilization. Your assertion that the commissioner [in Boston] was wrong cannot justify the wrong of leaving the city unguarded. That furnished the opportunity [to riot]; the criminal element furnished the action." Then came the concluding sentence that won Coolidge national acclaim in a time of growing labor unrest and public fears: "There is no right to strike against the public safety by anybody, anywhere, anytime."[21]

Although Coolidge had tread very cautiously in the matter, even seemingly to the point of timidity through the first stages of the crisis, his firm response to Gompers cast him as a hero in defense of the public. Coolidge himself was said to have declared, "I have just committed political suicide."[22] But he was overwhelmingly reelected in 1919 and now was a national figure beyond the borders of his native New England, being mentioned for a place on the Republican national ticket in 1920. And in the revolt at the convention in Chicago against the efforts of U.S. senators to make it an all-senatorial slate of Harding and Lenroot, Coolidge was stampeded through for the vice presidential nomination.

In his acceptance speech, he struck a particular note of morality, calling for American blacks "to be relieved from all imposition, to be defended from lynching, and to be freely granted equal opportunity," a liberal position not often associated with his dominant conservatism.[23] In the campaign that followed against the Democratic ticket of the Ohio governor

James M. Cox and a young assistant navy secretary from New York named Franklin D. Roosevelt, Harding promised Coolidge a major role. He told reporters in Coolidge's presence, "I think the Vice President should be more than a mere substitute in waiting. In reestablishing coordination between the Executive Office and the Senate, the vice president can and ought to play a big part, and I have been telling Governor Coolidge how much I wish him to be a helpful part of a Republican administration."[24]

In the campaign, Harding's strategists resorted to another front-porch candidacy from his home in Marion, with only selected trips to a few major cities, and Coolidge stuck to New England until October. Then the Republican National Committee directed him to make an eight-day swing through the South. After objecting, "I ought not to be away so long from Massachusetts and . . . my abilities do not lie in that direction," he dutifully went.

Meanwhile his Democratic counterpart, FDR, stumped energetically and enthusiastically by train, ridiculing the Republican stay-home approach, saying, "We will drag the enemy off the front porch."[25] The competing vice presidential speech making was a prelude to the future in Coolidge's mild expositions of the status quo and FDR's advocacy of further social reform.[26] But the focus of the public that fall was not on any running-mate sideshow.

In July, Cox and Roosevelt had visited the ailing Wilson, and Cox had pledged to him that American participation in the League of Nations would be a paramount objective of the Democratic campaign, but the public was weary of Wilson and his failed fight for the Versailles Treaty. In the end, that weariness, coupled with the postwar recession and the Republican promise of a return to normalcy, produced a landslide GOP victory.

After the election, Harding suggested greater responsibilities for his vice president, noting they both had served as lieutenant governors with active roles in governance. Three days after their inauguration, Harding sent Coolidge a written invitation to join his cabinet meetings. "It has seemed to me that the second official of the Republic could add materially to the fullness of his service in this way," Harding wrote. "I am quite aware that there is no constitutional or statutory provision for such participation but cabinet councils are wholly of an advisory nature in any event, and I am sure your presence and your suggestions will be welcome to the members of the Cabinet and I know they will be gratefully received by me."[27]

Coolidge gladly took Harding up on his offer but commented only when asked, though he also took advantage of his association with the cabinet members to inform himself of their activities, requesting additional information from them as he desired. He later observed, "[From] my position as President of the Senate and in my attendance upon the sessions of the Cabinet, I thus came into possession of a very wide knowledge of the details of the government."[28]

The Coolidges, upon moving to Washington, settled into a four-room apartment in the Willard Hotel, on Pennsylvania Avenue two blocks from the White House, taking over the lodgings of the vice president's predecessor, Thomas Marshall. While Coolidge's parsimoniousness was legendary, he made a good case for the country to provide an official residence for its vice presidents, who, absent heavy administrative duties, were often obliged to assume social obligations. "It was necessary for me to live within my income," he wrote later, "which was little more than my salary and was charged with the cost of sending my boys to school. . . . My experience convinced me that an official residence with suitable maintenance should be provided for the Vice-President."[29] But Congress brushed aside any efforts to provide one.

One story goes that one night soon after the Coolidges moved in at the Willard, a fire broke out, sending the residents and guests to the lobby in various degrees of undress. When the fire was under control, Coolidge headed up the stairs, only to be stopped by the fire marshal, who asked him, "Who are you?" Coolidge replied, "I'm the vice president." The marshal told him to go ahead, then suspiciously asked, "What are you vice president of?" Coolidge: "I'm the vice president of the United States." The marshal further impeded him: "Come right down. I thought you were the vice president of the hotel."[30]

Coolidge unlike many, if not most, other vice presidents professed to enjoy presiding over the Senate and to respect the institution and the performance of its members. He wrote later, "If the Senate is anything it is a great deliberative body and if it is to retain a safeguard of liberty it must remain a deliberative body. I was entertained and instructed by the debates." At the same time, he observed, "The Senate had but one fixed rule, subject to exceptions of course, which was to the effect that the Senate would do anything it wanted to do. When I had learned that, I did not waste much time on the other rules, because they were so seldom applied." As vice president, he was never called upon to break a tie vote, which seemed to satisfy him well enough.[31]

As for the vice presidency itself, Coolidge easily accommodated himself to its limitations as a man who recognized his own. His close political friend and counselor Frank Stearns reported that Coolidge had once told him, "My conception of my position is that I am vice president. I am a member of the administration. So long as I am in that position it is my duty to uphold the policies and actions of the administration one hundred percent up to the point where I cannot conscientiously agree with them. When I cannot conscientiously agree with them it is my duty to keep silent."[32]

Silence was a condition that came easily, even constitutionally, to him, and he adhered to it throughout his vice presidency. When the economy turned sour early in the Harding presidency, producing steep Democratic congressional gains in 1922, Coolidge essentially held his tongue. If he did not have the power to bring change, he seemed to prefer being uninvolved.

For all Coolidge's loyalty to Harding and his efforts to maintain cordial relations with the cabinet and within the Republican Party, some resentments smoldered among Old Guard senators, who would have preferred Lenroot or another of their club as Harding's vice president. A Boston newspaper speculated that Massachusetts Republicans preferred to have Coolidge run for the U.S. Senate seat in 1924.

But late on the night of August 2, 1923, after two and a half years in the vice presidency, fate interceded. Coolidge, visiting the family farmhouse in Plymouth Notch, was sleeping in an upstairs bedroom when his father awakened him with word of Harding's sudden death. By kerosene lamp, John Coolidge, as a notary public, administered the oath of presidential office to his son.[33] Years later, when a portrait artist, Charles Hopkinson, trying to encourage some animation in the sober Coolidge's face, asked him what his first thought was upon learning that Harding had died and he had become president, Silent Cal, without an change of expression, replied, "I thought I could swing it."[34]

For the next nineteen months, Coolidge would fill the rest of Harding's unexpired term as five previous accidental presidents had done, leaving the vice presidency vacant. And so the secretary of state, Charles Evans Hughes, would for the time being stand, in the tired phrase, a heartbeat away from the presidency. Coolidge made clear that in inheriting the presidency he accepted the concept that he was to be a "caretaker," declaring, "It is a sound rule that when the President dies in office it is the duty of his successor for the remainder of that term to maintain the counsellors and policies of the deceased President."[35] But if there was such a rule, it often had been honored in the breach in past transfers of power and would be so again in the future.

The first step by the new president was indeed to ask members of the Harding cabinet to stay in place. But the old poker-playing cronies of Harding knew their time was up under Coolidge, not a man susceptible to the patronizing of such individuals. He did, however, inherit with the presidency a pair of major scandals in the Harding administration in which he was not involved and about which he had little awareness at the time.

The first concerned Colonel Charles R. Forbes, director of the Veterans Bureau and a drinking and poker-playing companion of Harding, who had been put in charge of construction and supervision of new veterans' hospitals and of a host of warehouses jammed with surplus supplies and equipment from the Great War. Forbes and some associates proceeded to pocket huge amounts of money from building contracts and surplus sales, which financed lavish parties and travel, all under the nose of the casual, fun-loving, and unsuspecting Harding. Forbes finally resigned in February 1923 and left the country about six months before Coolidge assumed the presidency, but the scandal's odor lingered.

Three weeks after Forbes resigned, his closest associate, Charles F. Cramer, committed suicide, and less than three months after that, Jess Smith, an unscrupulous sidekick of Attorney General Harry Daugherty, Harding's chief political adviser and fixer, followed suit. Daugherty himself had been charged with corrupt practices and was threatened with impeachment, but his close tie with Harding saved him for a time.

Once Coolidge had moved into the Oval Office, more damaging to the reputation of the Republican Party was the stench of the infamous Teapot Dome scandal of the year before. Unbeknownst to Harding, key members of his administration had engaged in massive looting of the nation's oil reserves at a site about fifty miles north of Casper, Wyoming. Secretary of the Interior Albert B. Fall, a former U.S. senator from New Mexico, had conspired with Secretary of the Navy Edwin Denby to persuade Harding to sign an executive order in June 1922, transferring the Naval Petroleum Reserve to the Interior Department. Thereupon, lucrative exploitation rights were sold to private interests at great profit to the conspirators. A Senate investigating committee did not undertake a fumigation of the whole mess until late October 1923, two months after Harding's death, but he did become aware of his cabinet members' betrayal in his last months.

Coolidge himself had been acquainted with Forbes, Fall, Denby, Daugherty, and Smith in the course of attending Harding cabinet meetings and had recognized their unsavory natures. But in keeping his place, Coolidge said nothing, except for preaching the virtues of clean government, to which he was personally dedicated. Yet he would have to carry the public remembrance of the scandals into his later quest for a presidential term of his own.

The new president's first serious test was dealing with an approaching strike of anthracite coal miners in Pennsylvania. Two weeks after Harding's death, he called two inconclusive meetings with the union leader John L. Lewis and mine operators and then summoned Governor Gifford Pinchot to the White House and appointed him a special coal strike mediator, to no avail. The strike of 150,000 strikers began on September 1, and the president announced he was told by legal advisers that he had no power to seize the mines. But a two-year agreement was reached a week later giving the miners a 10 percent wage increase, and the mines reopened.

Meanwhile, William M. Butler, the president's prospective campaign manager for 1924, got busy lining up the delegates needed for the presidential nomination. Expected challenges from Pinchot and Detroit auto magnate Henry Ford fizzled, and thus the stage was set for the party's convention, at which the only substantive business would be the selection of Coolidge's running mate. A story was afoot that Coolidge wanted Senator William E. Borah of Utah on the ticket and that when the president proposed it to him, Borah asked, "Well, at which end?"[36]

But the second office remained so low in esteem that when the convention opened in Cleveland in June, it seemed the job once again would have to be shopped around. After other rejections, the party finally decided on a running mate for Coolidge whose brilliance, outgoing nature, and fiery and commanding independence would offer a promise of lifting the much-maligned vice presidency out of the shadows.

CHAPTER 30

CHARLES G. DAWES
OF ILLINOIS

O ne of the most accomplished of all American vice presidents joined
the second presidential term of the accidental president Calvin
Coolidge in 1925. But his outspokenness and gruffness in contrast
with the mild-mannered Silent Cal produced one of the most unusual odd
couples to share the two highest offices in the land up to that time. Charles G.
Dawes came to the vice presidency after a heralded career that included his
becoming the first director of the Bureau of the Budget, then comptroller
of the currency, and supply czar for the American Expeditionary Forces in
Europe during World War I. Thereafter he was credited with putting Europe's economy back on its feet and overseeing reparations sought from the
defeated Germany, which won him a share of the 1925 Nobel Peace Prize.

Dawes was of aristocratic stock from colonial days, whose family traced
its roots back to the Massachusetts Bay Colony in 1635, when William
Dawes arrived from England. Another William Dawes rode with Paul Re-
vere from Charlestown to Lexington on April 18, 1775.[1] And another relative was a senior partner in a mercantile firm named Dawes and Coolidge,
coincidentally bringing together forebears of men who, nearly three hundred years later, would become in reverse order the Republican president
and vice president of the United States.

Charles Gates Dawes was born in Marietta, Ohio, on August 27, 1865.
His father, Rufus R. Dawes, ultimately a brigadier general in the Union

army, volunteered in April 1861 upon President Lincoln's call and recruited a hundred others to serve under him at Antietam and in subsequent Civil War battles. In 1864 during a furlough he married Mary Beman of Marietta, daughter of a railroad builder and banker. Dawes became an official of the Marietta Iron Works and soon branched out into oil and gas exploration in southeastern Ohio, adding to his growing wealth. The panic of 1873 broke him, obliging him to start anew in the wholesale lumber business, where he eventually prospered again and served a single term in Congress.[2]

Upon his graduation from Marietta College and the Cincinnati Law School, young Charles moved to Lincoln, Nebraska, where he became a prominent anti-monopoly attorney for the Lincoln Board Trade and other clients. There he met and became close friends of William Jennings Bryan and John J. Pershing, later the commander of American forces in the Great War. Dawes and Bryan were members of an informal discussion group called the Lincoln Round Table, in which they debated key issues of the day, including the currency controversy that Bryan later glamorized with his famous "cross of gold" speech at the 1896 Democratic National Convention. Pershing was not a member of the group but joined them in a similar group, dubbed Debates at the Square Table, at a local restaurant.[3]

Dawes won statewide attention as a witness before a Senate committee on railroad affairs and another before the Nebraska Board of Transportation. In the latter, when the state auditor chided him about his criticisms of a host of discriminatory rates, Dawes responded by accusing the man of "riding in special cars at the expense of the railroads." When the auditor shot back, "I guess you would ride, too, if you had the chance," Dawes replied, "Not if I were drawing a salary and was paid by the people to stay home and protect their interest and do my duty."[4]

By 1893, as Dawes's law practice grew, he became a bank director and formed the Dawes Block Company, owning and managing major office buildings in downtown Lincoln. His friend Pershing, also a lawyer, meanwhile was teaching military science and tactics and commanding enrolled cadets at the University of Nebraska as a second lieutenant. When he approached Dawes about joining him as a partner, Dawes advised him, "Better lawyers than either you or I can ever hope to be are starving in Nebraska. I'd try the Army for a while yet. Your pay may be small, but it comes very regularly."[5] So Pershing remained on that fateful course.

Dawes survived the panic of 1893 and afterward acquired a power company in Wisconsin and another in Evanston, Illinois. In 1895 he moved to Chicago, where he made his home for the rest of his life. The previous year, he had met Governor William McKinley of Ohio, and McKinley's campaign manager, Mark Hanna, enlisted him to oversee the Ohioan's presidential bid in Illinois. Dawes's first major political undertaking came at the Republican state convention of 1896, where at the age of thirty he delivered the Illinois delegation to the Ohio governor, who was later nominated by a landside over Speaker Tom Reed of Maine at the national convention in St. Louis.

Sitting in the press gallery not far from where Dawes watched the proceedings was Bryan, his old colleague and debater at the Lincoln Round Table, now a reporter for the *Omaha World Herald.* Two weeks later in Chicago, Bryan unexpectedly set the Democratic convention afire with his memorable harangue against the gold standard. Dawes, in attendance, sent a telegram to McKinley: "Went to the Democratic Convention. Sat on the platform. Heard my old friend, William J. Bryan, make his speech on the platform's silver plank. His oratory was magnificent, his logic pitifully weak. I could not but have a feeling of pride for the brilliant young man whose life, for so many years, lay parallel to mine, and with whom the future may yet bring me into conflict, as in the past."[6]

Six days later Dawes joined Hanna and other Republican leaders at McKinley's home in Canton, where the presidential nominee declared he would not compete with the silver-tongued and silver-driven Bryan on the stump but would campaign from his front porch. "I am going to stay here and do what campaigning there is to be done," McKinley told Dawes. "If I took a whole train, Bryan would take a sleeper; if I took a sleeper, Bryan would take a chair car; if I took a chair car, he would ride a freight train. I can't outdo him, and I am not going to try."[7]

In Chicago, Dawes handled the dispensing of campaign funds out of the McKinley national headquarters campaign while Hanna traveled the country raising them, and hordes of McKinley supporters went to Canton as Bryan stumped feverishly across the land. On Election Night, McKinley beat Bryan by more than half a million popular votes and by nearly one hundred in the electoral college.

Dawes immediately became the subject of speculation about a cabinet post in the McKinley administration but pointedly asked supporters not to address the new president on the matter. After the election, according to Dawes's diary, McKinley said he often thought he owed his nomination to Dawes in light of Dawes's vital campaign work in Illinois. Dawes continued, "He . . . was anxious to know whether his failure to give me a Cabinet appointment would, in any way, alter our intimate and constant friendship."[8] Then McKinley offered Dawes the post of comptroller of the currency, an independent position reporting to Congress, which he cheerfully accepted and carried out without political interference. Dawes often lunched and dined with the president and was a constant confidant as McKinley wrestled with the aftermath of the sinking of the *Maine* in Havana Harbor, which led to the brief war with Spain.

But Dawes now had his eye on a U.S. Senate seat from Illinois in 1902 and told McKinley of his intention to step down as comptroller. McKinley himself, in the face of some urging that he seek a third term, issued a statement squelching the notion, which prompted Vice President Theodore Roosevelt to invite Dawes to spend the night with him at his Oyster Bay home to discuss the 1904 presidential nomination—for TR, of course. Dawes promised Roosevelt his support in Illinois. But then came the shooting of McKinley in Buffalo, from which at first the president showed signs of survival. Three days afterward, Dawes met Roosevelt for lunch again to discuss the 1904 campaign, apparently with an expectation of McKinley's recovery and with his pledge not to seek a third term in mind.

But with the death of his friend the president, Dawes's support for the Senate seat soon faded. He returned to his highly successful business and banking pursuits, writing "with joy of a man entering from a political atmosphere to one where promises are redeemed and faith is kept."[9] In succeeding years, Dawes fought for stronger enforcement of anti-trust laws, tried to cope with closing banks in the mid-1900s, and later personally engaged himself in charitable works. Upon the sudden death of his only son, Rufus, at twenty-two, Dawes built and endowed a hotel home for unemployed men in Chicago, later ran bread wagons for the destitute during the city's frigid winters, and only occasionally lent a hand to friends in Republican politics.

When the United States finally entered the war in Europe in April 1917, Dawes, at age fifty-one, called on his good friend Pershing, now a major general and the commander of the American Expeditionary Forces, to obtain a commission as a major in the Corps of Army Engineers, having once worked as a railroad surveyor. In taking the position, Dawes turned down an offer from Herbert Hoover, just named the U.S. food administrator in charge of controlling domestic grain prices.

After training with the Seventeenth Engineers Regiment and promotion to the rank of lieutenant colonel, Dawes and his unit were the first to reach France, landing at Le Havre on a cattle boat. Pershing made him head of the army's General Purchasing Board over all supplies in Europe, and he eventually was put in charge of the Military Board of Allied Supply, often going to the front to assure himself that the most pressing needs were being met. To the war's end, both he and Pershing favored fighting on to total victory, with Dawes writing in his diary on October 3, 1918: "This war must be fought to finish, not negotiated to one."[10] Five weeks later, however, the armistice was declared.

While wrapping up his work on the Military Board, Dawes was called on by Hoover to take charge of a military commission to dispense relief to the German civilian population. But Pershing declined to release him. Finally, after receiving the Distinguished Service Medal, the highest civilian wartime honor, Dawes went home to Chicago. There a boomlet for his presidential candidacy in 1920 awaited him, with his old friend but Democratic political rival William Jennings Bryan in the forefront. He declined the candidacy, and after ten ballots at the Republican convention, the ticket of Harding and Coolidge was nominated and subsequently elected over the Democratic governor James M. Cox of Ohio and Franklin D. Roosevelt of New York.

Three months later, Dawes was summoned before the House Committee on War Expenditures as the American Expeditionary Forces' chief purchasing agent and to his immense irritation was called on the carpet. "Is it not true that excessive prices were paid for some articles?" one inquisitional congressman asked. Dawes shot back, "When Congress declared war, did it expect us to beat Germany at twenty percent discount? Sure, we paid high prices. Men were standing at the front to be shot at. We had to get them food and ammunition. We didn't stop to dicker. Why, man alive! We had a war to win! It was a man's job!" The interrogator continued: "Is it not true that excessive prices were paid for mules?" Dawes erupted with his favorite epithet: "Hell and Maria! I would have paid horse prices for sheep, if the sheep could have pulled artillery to the front!"[11]

For much of the seven hours he sat before the committee, Dawes gave the committee what for, peppering his testimony with the odd declamation from his old Nebraska days. In reporting the flamboyant episode, newspapers wrote it as "Hell'n Maria!" which was thereafter often associated with the otherwise proper Dawes.

About a month before the inauguration, Harding offered Dawes the post of secretary of the treasury. He turned it down, telling the president-elect that as a member of the cabinet he would have no authority over the others to do what he considered necessary to put the economy in order. According to Dawes's biographer, he told Harding, "But, as your assistant secretary or assistant President or whatever you might call it, I could, if I could sit by your side and issue executive orders. Just because the United States Government is the biggest business in the world, there is no reason why it should be the worst run. But only one man can make it run right, and that is the President of the United States."[12]

Here again was another high-level proposal similar to that of Colonel House's to Woodrow Wilson to create an executive position as first assistant to the president. Dawes made no mention of enhancing the role of the vice president, and in any event Harding still insisted that Dawes was the right man to bring the national budget into balance and should undertake it as head of the treasury. Again Dawes declined but told Harding the only job that would tempt him was director of the budget. Some months later, that offer was made and accepted. Before the conversation ended, Harding told Dawes he regretted running for president, was happier in the Senate, and after four years in the White House he intended to step down. "I'd like to see you nominated and elected president in 1924," Harding told him. "I will do what I can to help you."

In 1923, when Senator Charles Curtis of Kansas, according to his own later memoir, urged Harding to seek a second term rather than leave the presidential nomination to Coolidge, Harding replied, "Charlie, you are not worried about that little fellow in Massachusetts, are you?" Harding put his hand on Curtis's shoulder and added, "Charlie Dawes is the man who is going to succeed me!" A month later, however, Harding was dead, and Vice President Coolidge was president.[13]

In his first year as head of the Budget Bureau, Dawes saved 1.75 billion dollars and reduced the federal debt by 1 billion, even as taxes were lowered, and the surplus continued in succeeding years. In 1923, with Germany in shreds after its defeat in the Great War, Harding appointed Dawes to head the Committee of Experts of the Allied Reparations Committee. Its task was to put Germany's economy on its feet so that the battered country could pay the reparations imposed by the Treaty of Versailles. Through the injection of two hundred million dollars in American and other Allied loans, the plan stabilized the German currency, established the Reichsbank, restructured the nation's railroads, and raised reparations funds by issuing rail and industrial bonds, with a one-year moratorium on payments. But critics later argued that it also opened the door to Hitler's takeover of power. Nevertheless, Dawes was awarded a share of the Nobel Peace Prize for his work,[14] and he returned to Chicago to much public acclaim.

With the acclaim came a groundswell of speculation that he would be chosen as Coolidge's running mate as the Republican nominee for vice president in 1924.[15] The frontrunner was the Illinois governor Lowden, and although nominated on the second ballot, he declined. Next, the party national chairman William Butler sought out Hoover, but his setting of farm prices during the war was judged likely to lose many farm states for the ticket. Coolidge next sounded out Senator William E. Borah of Idaho, who as previously noted asked, "At which end?"[16] Finally the convention turned to Dawes, and he was nominated on the third ballot.

The president, however, made a point afterward to read and edit Dawes's acceptance message, an indication that he had no intention, if elected, of giving Dawes much deference in his administration. In the campaign, Coolidge's participation was severely curtailed in July by the sudden death of his sixteen-year-old son, Calvin Jr., as a result of a seemingly inconsequential stubbing of his toe while playing tennis, causing blood poisoning. Coolidge was distraught, and his normal disinclination to campaign was compounded by the family tragedy. He eschewed the front-porch tactic and made few speeches, all of them low key, obliging Dawes to take up the slack against the Democratic nominee, John W. Davis of West Virginia.

Dawes focused on the principal threat to Coolidge, the Progressive entry, Robert W. LaFollette of Wisconsin, attacking him as a proponent of "red radicalism" and shouting "Hell'n Maria!" to the crowds' delight. Davis, frustrated by LaFollette's appeal to Democratic liberals and Coolidge's reticent appeal to conservatives, was stymied. The scandals of the Harding years seemed not to rub off on the staid and proper Coolidge. Davis lamented later, "I did my best . . . to make Coolidge say something. I was running out of anything to talk about. What I wanted was for Coolidge to say something. I didn't care what it was, just so I had someone to debate with. He never opened his mouth."[17]

So Coolidge left the heavy lifting to Dawes, who in four months traveled fifteen hundred miles and delivered more than a hundred speeches. Repeatedly he asked the crowd to reject LaFollette's call for congressional override of labor-backed judicial decisions, demanding, "Where do you stand? With President Coolidge on the Constitution and the flag, or on the sinking sands of socialism?"[18] The three-way race split the opposition to Coolidge and Dawes, and they won by a landslide.

Coolidge, however, gave little indication of gratitude to Dawes for stepping in on the campaign trail as he had done. Unlike Harding, who had invited Coolidge to sit in at cabinet meetings, Coolidge made no such offer to Dawes. A few weeks after their election, having not heard from the president on the matter, Dawes, possibly to save face, wrote to him saying he did not want to attend, saying doing so "would set a precedent that would sometimes prove a very injurious thing to the country." He offered, "Suppose in the future some President with the precedent fixed must face the determination of inviting a loquacious publicity-seeker into his private councils or affront him in the public eye by denying him what had come to be considered his right—how embarrassing it would be."[19]

In this, Dawes seemed to protest a bit much, considering all his experience as a presidential adviser in several fields. Coolidge's own position seemed puzzling, given that as vice president he had seen how helpful sitting in on cabinet meetings had been to him when he moved into the presidency. Soon after, in advance of their inauguration, Dawes wrote again suggesting to Coolidge, "In view of my unfamiliarity with Senate procedures, I think it best to get to Washington in time to be posted a little." But Coolidge ignored "posting" him, a slight that later might have saved Dawes much embarrassment and Coolidge much disappointment in having a cabinet appointment rejected by the Senate over which Dawes presided.[20]

In taking the vice presidential oath in March, Dawes ignored the notion that the occupant of the second office should be seen and not heard. He surprisingly seized the spotlight to harangue members of the Senate for wasting their time engaging in filibusters and other excesses. Of the Senate Rule 22, requiring a two-thirds vote to close down debate, Dawes loudly lectured that it "at times enables senators to consume in oratory those last precious minutes of a session needed for momentous decisions [and] places in the hands of one or a minority of senators a greater power than the veto power exercised under the Constitution by the President of the United States, which is limited in effectiveness by an affirmative two-thirds vote."[21]

Dawes's lecture to the senators was hardly a message to assure a smooth beginning to his role as presiding officer of their proud body. Worse, it took the play in news coverage from Coolidge, whose face was said to stiffen, but he made no open rebuke of the haughty Dawes. Nevertheless, a coolness clearly set in between the two men, diminishing the contribution Dawes might have made to the administration. Later, Dawes also took his case against the Senate filibuster to the stump, proclaiming that unless the issue went "to the people the fundamental institutions of the country [would] suffer."[22] But the matter remained for the Senate to decide, and so the filibuster survived.

Subsequently, Dawes committed an even more memorable faux pas during a lengthy debate on the Senate floor over the confirmation of Charles Warren, a controversial member of the Sugar Trust whom Coolidge wanted as his attorney general. Dawes, told by the majority and minority leaders there would be no vote that day because six senators had indicated they wanted to speak, asked a senator to preside and headed back his Willard Hotel apartment for a nap. Unexpectedly, five of those senators decided not to take the floor. Majority Leader Charles Curtis called for the vote on the nomination, and fearing the possibility of a tie requiring the vice president to break, Curtis sent word to Dawes to return to the Senate at once. He dressed quickly, raced down to the Willard lobby, and hailed a cab to the Capitol. But before he arrived, the vote did produce a tie. One Democrat who had voted for Warren switched his vote, thereby defeating Coolidge's choice. Had Dawes been present, he could have broken the tie in Warren's favor.

Coolidge, obviously chagrined, resubmitted Warren's name, but this time it failed by seven votes.[23] This was the first time in nearly sixty years that the Senate had denied a president a cabinet nomination. Later, some speculated that Dawes might have snoozed intentionally, because at the 1924 Republican convention in Cleveland, Warren had cast the sole vote in the Michigan delegation against Dawes.[24]

As a result, Dawes became the brunt of humiliating ridicule. Someone placed a sign over the entrance to the Willard lobby reading "Dawes Slept Here." Soon after, he was showing a friend around the Capitol and took him to the Supreme Court, where a particularly boring case was being heard, causing some of the justices to seem about to nod off. Chief Justice William Howard Taft, spotting Dawes in the chamber, sent him a note that said, "Come up here. This is a good place to sleep!"[25] Also, at the 1926 Gridiron dinner, at which high government officials were spoofed by members of the Washington press corps, Dawes was given a large clock, supposedly from Coolidge, with the admonition to stay awake because more ties were anticipated.[26] All this inevitably jeopardized any presidential ambitions Dawes harbored.

In the Senate, the strong-willed Dawes found ways to get around the tradition that the presiding officer was not to enter into or affect the outcome of legislative debate. From 1924 to 1928, he negotiated a deal whereby a major bill authorizing the sales of surplus food abroad and another extending the charters of the Federal Reserve Bank were passed.

In 1927, when Coolidge shocked the nation by tersely announcing, "I do not choose to run," for another term the following year, Dawes was mentioned as a possible Republican nominee, but he too announced he was not interested and would back his old friend Governor Lowden of Ohio. On leaving the Senate, Dawes did nothing to hide or retract his contempt for the filibuster. In his book, *Notes as Vice President,* Dawes cited a senator telling him at the time that the membership finally thought highly of him as the presiding officer, adding, "But the Senate got very tired of you at the beginning of your service." Dawes shot back, "I should have to think that the Senate was as tired of me at the beginning of my service as I am of the Senate at the end."[27] And in his farewell speech to the chamber, he said of his assault on the Senate rule: "I take nothing back."[28]

Writing of the second office on June 27, 1928, Dawes surprisingly provided a view contrary to the prevalent dismissive one: "The superficial attitude of indifference which many public men assume toward the office of Vice President of the United States is easily explained. It is the office for which one cannot hope to be a candidate with sufficient prospects for success to justify the effort involved in a long campaign. One's political availability for nomination to the position cannot be determined until the nominating convention has in effect decided upon the head of the ticket. . . . The office is largely what the man in it makes it—which applies to all public offices. The fact that the Vice President in the Senate Chamber cannot enter into debate is considered a disadvantage, yet for that reason he is removed from the temptation to indulge in the pitiable quest for that double objective so characteristic of many Senate speeches—the placating of public opinion and of an opposing local constituency at the same time. For his prestige as a presiding officer, it is to his advantage that he neither votes nor speaks in the Senate Chamber. Outside the Senate Chamber, his position as Vice President gives him a hearing by the general public as wide as that accorded any Senator, other things being equal." Yet he concluded, "The occupancy of a public office, unless decorated with public respect, is a curse to anyone."[29]

All this was a generous assessment of the importance and actual influence of the vice president from a man who certainly enjoyed more of both in his positions as an appointed private citizen, in both war and peace.

In April 1929, the new president, Herbert Hoover, appointed Dawes as the American ambassador to Great Britain, and in 1932 he was named head of the new Reconstruction Finance Corporation, established to help banks and corporations recover from the Great Depression. But in June of that year he abruptly resigned to attend to the near collapse of his own Central Republic Bank of Chicago. Dawes reorganized the bank as the City National Bank and Trust Company of Chicago and paid off its loans. His stock as a financial wizard remained so high that there was some talk in 1932 of dumping Hoover's chosen running mate, Charles Curtis of Kansas, to bring some "Hell'n Maria" fire to the Republican ticket. But Dawes was too engaged in rescuing his bank to consider the possibility. On April 23, 1951, he died at age eighty-five, still not broken to the saddle of political limitations imposed on any subordinate office.

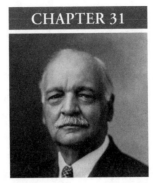

CHARLES CURTIS
OF KANSAS

A s the first American vice president of Native American lineage, Charles Curtis of Kansas rode a colorful course to national prominence, starting as a horserace jockey, speaking the Kaw language of Kansas Indians, and living with his maternal grandparents on the Council Grove reservation, sixty miles from Topeka. Despite this rather bizarre path to his political career, Curtis, known in his youth as a daring "half-breed Indian," developed into a skilled practical politician. That reputation, however, never earned him any role in policy in the star-crossed administration of Herbert Hoover, in which he served.

Curtis was born in 1860 in North Topeka, in a mixed white and Indian community of what was then the Kansas-Nebraska Territory, a year before Kansas was admitted to the Union under the Wyandotte Constitution. He was the son of Orren A. "Jack" Curtis, a white man, and Ellen Pappan, who was one-quarter Kaw Indian, and a great-great grandson of a Kansas-Kaw chief called White Plume, who aided the Lewis and Clark expedition into the Northwest in 1804. Curtis's grandmother, Julie Gonville, of mixed French and Indian heritage, and her husband, Louis Pappan, a French trader, lived on a federal land grant near Topeka in 1825 under a Kansas-Kaw treaty for "half-breeds."

Young Charlie spoke French as well as Kaw before learning English. His mother died when he was three, and in 1863, his father was called into the Fifteenth Kansas Cavalry of the Union Army, commissioned a captain.[1] Subsequently, he remarried, divorced, and married again, was dishonorably discharged from the Union army after hanging three "bushwhacker" prisoners, then pardoned.[2] The father was a poor influence on his son, so young Charlie continued to live with his grandparents on the reservation. His grandfather Louis Pappan ran a small ferry across the Kansas River, charging a dollar a wagon, until Charlie's father bought him out and operated it for a time.[3]

Charles Curtis's biographer, Don C. Seitz, wrote, "As a child little Charlie always thought of himself as an Indian. When he was a year old he was given a smart pony named Kate and was taught to ride her bareback, clinging to her mane to keep from falling off. By the time he was three he could ride alone at some speed, and his mother had already taught him to swim by dropping him in the Kansas River and letting him splash around by himself."[4] Years later Charlie wrote, "Until I was eight I lived there [on the reservation], happy and contented, playing, riding horses and learning very little." He also amused himself by chasing jackrabbits, prairie chickens, and quail and downing them with bow and arrow.[5]

In 1869, upon an attack by hostile Cheyenne Indians, Charlie was sent on foot to Topeka for help, a cross-country feat that won him local fame and later accusations of gross exaggeration and dramatization. It was later found that word of the approaching attack had been leaked.[6] In any event, his paternal grandparents, William and Permelia Curtis, decided the boy needed to grow up in more "civilized" circumstances, so he went to live with them in North Topeka.

By now, at the age of nine, Charlie was an excellent bareback pony rider, taking part in his first horserace on a track built by his grandfather Curtis. Known eventually as "the Indian Boy," he continued to ride for the next seven years, winning steadily. He became a favorite of local gamblers and betting prostitutes, who showered him with clothes and other presents.[7] The owner of a particularly good Kansas horse named Tilden hired Curtis to race him regularly, and they toured the Southwest without losing. Curtis later recalled riding for another owner in Texas who summoned him for final orders before a particular race. The owner, seated with a rifle across his knees, told him, "Son, the last dollar I have in the world is on this race. If you don't win, don't stop when you cross the finish line. Keep right on going." Curtis made sure he won.[8]

Grandfather Curtis proved to be a great benefactor to young Charlie, assuming parental responsibility for his errant son. His death in 1873 was a severe to blow to the boy. Still intrigued by the tribal life, Charlie left Topeka and joined his other grandparents, Louis and Julie Pappan, traveling with the Kaw tribe to the Indian Territory in Oklahoma. But his welcoming grandmother told him if he stayed he would wind up like most of the other men there, with inadequate education and a dismal future. He took her advice, returning to Topeka to resume life with his other grandmother, Permelia Curtis, now a widow.

She put him on the straight and narrow, requiring him to give up horseracing and go to a decent high school. He did not, however, abandon his association with horses. He rented a livery hack and ran a profitable service, meeting incoming trains, and for a time sold news he gathered along the way to the *Topeka Times*.[9] Thereafter he studied law, and in 1881, at age twenty-one, he was admitted to the Kansas bar. By this time, Charlie had inherited federal land from his mother under Indian treaties around Topeka,[10] opened a real estate business, and started his own law firm. Three years later he married Anna Baird, and she bore him three children in a marriage of nearly forty years.[11] They also took in his half-sister Dolly.

Meanwhile he had followed his grandmother into the Republican Party, becoming a foot soldier in Topeka for the presidential nominee James A. Garfield in 1880. Four years later, still remembered as the popular jockey, he ran for county attorney in Shawnee and won. In the election he was supported by the local liquor interests, both his father and grandfather having run saloons in North Topeka. But upon his election he cracked down on prohibition enforcement, as the law he had sworn to enforce required. He held a retainer from the liquor interests, however, who mistakenly figured they had bought him. He noted that while he himself was not a teetotaler, it was his obligation to enforce the law, and he intended to do so.

In 1889, Curtis ran for the U.S. Congress but lost by a single vote. Later, the editor William Allen White of the *Emporia Gazette* took him under his wing, and Curtis, with his dominant personality and his background, won the seat essentially by default in 1892, a year of otherwise Populist success in the state. The House Republican leader Tom Reed also took to Curtis, giving him a leadership position in the House.[12]

White well captured Curtis's political appeal thus: "His enemies made the mistake of stressing his Indian blood in ignominy. When he appeared in a little town the people went out to see the Indian. What they saw was a gallant young Frenchman, suave, facile, smiling, with winning ways and a handshake that was a love affair itself." But, White went on, they also saw that internally his governing spirit had been New England, inherited from his stolid Grandmother Curtis.[13]

In Congress, Curtis focused on the House Indian Affairs Committee, drafting and passing a bill in 1898 that abolished many Indian treaty and mineral rights and placed them under the Interior Department, where his committee role could best look out for the interests of the Kaw tribe. In 1902 he also wrote legislation that gave him and his children title to certain Kaw lands in Oklahoma.[14] In 1898 he wrote the Curtis Act, allowing residents of Indian Territory to incorporate towns and elect their own officials.[15]

In 1907, he was elected by the Kansas state legislature to fill a vacancy in the U.S. Senate. He later lost the seat in a Republican Party split over a high tariff policy that he supported, but in the first direct election for the Senate in Kansas in 1914, Curtis won it back and became the Senate Republican whip. In 1919, while hardly a progressive, he led the floor fight for the Nineteenth Amendment, providing women's suffrage.[16]

At the Republican National Convention in Chicago in 1920, Curtis, as head of the Kansas delegation, was among the senators who in the infamous "smoke-filled room" pushed through the presidential nomination of Warren G. Harding. Curtis's role gave him entrée to the Harding inner circle of poker-playing cronies at the White House after the election. In 1923, when Harding was facing a stiff fight for a second term, Curtis reportedly inquired whether he intended to keep the dour Coolidge as his running mate. Harding interrupted by telling him if there was to be switch, "Charlie Dawes is the man!" But fate intervened with Harding's assassination.

Curtis meanwhile continued to move up the party ladder in the Senate, becoming the majority leader in 1925. There he served more as a traffic cop on legislation and generally supported the Coolidge administration, though occasionally breaking with it to back state interests, as in farm relief. When in 1928 Coolidge vetoed such a bill, however, Curtis voted to sustain in a show of solidarity.

In 1928, Curtis challenged Herbert Hoover for the Republican nomination, denying he was really seeking only the vice presidency. He argued that to nominate the Great War relief czar, a man with no political experience, would place "a hopeless burden" on the Republican ticket.[17] But farm protests against Hoover and his opposition to some major Harding-Coolidge administration bills were not enough to bar his first-ballot nomination in Kansas City.

Hoover first considered as his running mate the Progressive senator George W. Norris of Nebraska but settled on Curtis, known as "Egg Charlie" for his heavy support of the poultry industry. As a solid farm-state leader, Curtis signed on despite differences with Hoover on farm legislation. The reporter Thomas L. Stokes wrote of Curtis's acceptance of the role: "He had eaten his bitter words, but he was suffering from indigestion, you could see."[18] For the first time, both Republican nominees came from west of the Mississippi.

On the Democratic side was New York's governor Alfred E. Smith, seeking to become the first Roman Catholic president, and Senator Joseph T. Robinson of Arkansas, a Protestant and a teetotaler, balancing off Smith's prominent beer drinking. Smith's Catholicism, as well as his gruff if friendly street smarts developed on the sidewalks of New York, made him seem foreign to many Americans outside the teeming cities of the East and did him in. Hoover and Curtis were easy winners, giving little hint of a Democratic sea tide to come four years later.

Curtis moved comfortably into the presiding officer's chair but sometimes asserted authority that seemingly went beyond its constitutional limit. He seemed to many in the Senate to play now to his Indian origins, filling his Senate office with native artifacts and often posing in Indian headdress. He appeared to chafe at the lesser influence than he had enjoyed as the Senate majority leader and began to insist on deference to his vice presidential stature. One aspect was a search he began for an official vice presidential residence, where he could entertain as he thought the position warranted, beyond the Mayflower Hotel suite he rented.

Curtis fixed on a mansion in downtown Washington owned by the wealthy widow of Senator John B. Henderson of Missouri, a brownstone castle only a few blocks north of the White House on Sixteenth Street, which she wished to have named the Avenue of the Presidents. She even sold some parcels of land along it as an enticement for foreign embassies to locate there. She had offered a house there to Vice President Coolidge, but he declined. Curtis, hoping to pick up on the offer, sent his sister Dolly to examine the house, and she came back excited about the prospect. But in the end Mrs. Henderson's relatives balked, and nothing came of an official vice presidential residence until the 1970s, when Vice President Nelson A. Rockefeller donated his mansion on upper Massachusetts Avenue for that purpose.

Curtis later found himself embroiled in a diplomatic spat when Dolly got into a feud with Alice Roosevelt Longworth, the daughter of President Theodore Roosevelt and the wife of House Speaker Nicholas Longworth, over a matter of protocol. When Curtis's wife died, his sister invited the vice president to live with her at her Washington home, where she would serve as his official hostess at diplomatic and congressional dinners. Alice, it seems, raised an objection with her husband that at such dinners Dolly should be seated after the dean of the diplomatic corps and his wife but before other diplomatic and congressional wives. The Longworths used Dolly's show of pretense to boycott Prohibition-era "dry" dinners the Speaker didn't care to attend anyway. In the end, Secretary of State Henry L. Stimson placed Curtis's sister after the dean of the diplomatic corps and his wife but before other diplomatic wives.[19]

William Allen White in the *Emporia Gazette* wrote, "If Washington does not do right by our Dolly, there will be a terrible ruckus in Kansas. We will be satisfied with nothing less than she be borne into the dinner on the shoulders of Mrs. Nick Longworth, seated at the center of the table as an ornament with a candelabra in each hand and fed her soup with a long-handled spoon by the wife of the Secretary of State."[20]

Curtis himself suffered major ridicule during the Washington march of bonus-seeking veterans in 1932. The vice president had presented himself as a major figure of sympathy for the Great War veterans marching for early payment of the bonuses that Congress had promised them. Although Curtis had never served in the military, he often cited his father's Civil War service in asking for veterans support. But when the marchers came and encamped around Washington and the Capitol, he called on Hoover to call out troops to disperse them.

In July, the architect of the Capitol had its lawn sprinklers turned on, so the marchers, rather than encamping, decided to march single file around the Capitol. Curtis declared he had not authorized the march and ordered them off the property. But the District of Columbia police chief told him only the president could call out the army or move them. So Curtis then took it upon himself to call out the marines, which made him even more the brunt of ridicule.[21]

It was in this context that voices were heard calling for dumping Curtis from the next Republican national ticket. Curtis himself talked about going home to Kansas and running for the Senate again. But with the Kansas delegation still behind Curtis, Dawes reiterating he was not available, and no other Republican willing to hitch his wagon to Hoover and the Depression, Curtis was renominated.

As a little native color, about all he added to the Hoover cause in the subsequent election was his Indian heritage. On the campaign train, an Indian maiden reciting "Hiawatha" performed from time to time on the rear platform. Curtis campaigned heavily, particularly in the West, but was often heckled by veterans for his role in the dispersal of the Bonus Army in 1932. When a veterans' group presented a petition to the Senate censuring Hoover, Curtis demanded that the language be deleted but was told to strike it out himself, and the leader of the group in leaving refused to shake the vice president's hand.[22] It was a fitting coda to what is widely considered a failed vice presidency in a failed administration. In November, Hoover and Curtis, unable to extricate themselves from the political carnage of the Great Depression, were snowed under by the New York Democratic governor Franklin Delano Roosevelt and his running mate, House Speaker John Nance Garner of Texas.

Curtis, rather than going back to Kansas, stayed in Washington. In 1935, he became chairman of the Republican Senatorial Campaign Committee, hoping he could restore his reputation in the party by returning it to majority status in the Senate. But before the 1936 election he died of a heart attack at age seventy-six at the home of sister Dolly. He never regained his earlier political success or his popularity as the Indian jockey and has been more remembered as the inspiration for Alexander Throttlebottom, the hapless vice president who applied for a public library card but couldn't get the required two references in the Broadway stage hit *Of Thee I Sing,* by George and Ira Gershwin.

CHAPTER 32

JOHN NANCE GARNER
OF TEXAS

W hen John Nance Garner became Speaker of the House of Representatives in 1931, he attained the highest public office to
which he had ever aspired. With considerable reluctance, he
then traded it in for another that he later famously described as "not worth
a bucket of warm spit," or at least that was the sanitized version of what he
actually said.

His assessment no doubt grew out of his experience. Serving as president-in-waiting for arguably the most powerful American chief executive
in history was often a most frustrating responsibility. Garner was vice president to Franklin Delano Roosevelt for the first eight of FDR's thirteen-plus
years, long enough to inspire Garner to seek to take the office from him and
to end his own more than forty-year political career in the failed effort. Yet
for most of their association, "Cactus Jack" was regarded by many as the
most constructive vice president up to his time, helping his president carry
out the policies he did not always favor.

Garner was born on November 22, 1868, three years after the end of
the Civil War, in the town of Blossom Prairie, Red River County, Texas. He
was the namesake son of a Confederate cavalry officer whose family came
from colonial roots in Virginia by way of Tennessee. His grandmother was
a direct descendant of Sir Robert Walpole, prime minister of England.[1] His
Scots-Welsh father was a hard-working farmer who raised the boy in a Texas

log cabin. Young Garner had only four years of primary education, walking three miles twice a day to an unpainted schoolhouse. With Texas entering statehood, politics became a constant subject of discussion at home, and his father often took him to local debates, giving him political aspirations of his own. At age eighteen, John set off for Vanderbilt University, in Nashville, but for reasons of inadequate preparation, health, and finances soon returned home and found a job in a local law firm. At twenty-one he was admitted to the Texas bar and set up practice in the county seat of Clarksville.[2]

With little thought and no hesitation, young Garner ran and lost a bid for his first public office as a city attorney. Feeling run down, he went to a doctor and was told he had tuberculosis. To relieve his respiratory afflictions, in December 1892 he moved to Uvalde, in the dry Rio Grande Valley west of San Antonio. There he joined a local law firm and began to ride the judicial circuit for hundreds of miles over nine counties through what was known as cattle-and-cactus country. He often bedded down on the ground at night. At one point he took ownership of the Uvalde *Leader* in lieu of a legal fee, gathering, writing, and printing local items.[3]

In 1893, he was elected a county judge, the same year he met Mariette "Ettie" Rheiner, who became his wife and life-long secretary. Garner served as ex-officio county school superintendent, charged with overseeing a local poor fund. When he learned that some Mexicans had used the dole to buy tequila and whiskey, he began giving harmless placebos to those suspected of doing so. A few days later, Garner's political foes spread the word that a welfare recipient had died of the "pills" Garner had given him. They blamed the man's alleged death on Garner, and the bad publicity cost him his judgeship. But shortly afterward, the "dead" man, who had been kept out of sight until after the election, reappeared on the local streets. Garner said later of his defeat by trickery, "It was the best thing that ever happened to me." Had he not lost that seat, he said, he probably wouldn't have run for and been elected to the Texas Legislature in 1898.[4]

There he won a reputation as a deft and fair mediator between railroad and shipping interests. In a debate over the state flower, he proposed the cactus blossom but lost out to the bluebonnet. Henceforth, the nickname "Cactus Jack" stuck to him. Another legislative nonstarter was his plan to carve Texas into five states to give it more U.S. senators, but when a colleague asked, "Who would get the Alamo?" the notion died.[5]

In 1896 Garner was a delegate to the Democratic state convention in Corpus Christi to choose a nominee for a vacant congressional seat. Armed with ten proxy votes, Garner threw in with Rudolph Kleberg, part owner of the famous King Ranch, in return for being named chairman of the convention's redistricting committee in the booming state. Kleberg was nominated for the House seat and then elected. As the committee chairman, Garner carved a new legislative district out of his home county and surrounding area and won election to Congress from it in 1902 and reelection for the next thirty years.[6]

Upon his initial election, Garner immediately issued a declaration of independence, telling his constituents he wanted to hear their views, then clarifying his position: "But when a piece of legislation is in its final form and comes up for a vote, you won't be there. You will be down here attending to your business. I propose to make up my mind on any measure and cast my own vote according to what I think is in the public interest."[7]

He was, however, essentially a loyal party man on most matters and slowly rose to leadership posts. When President Woodrow Wilson finally called on Congress to declare war on Germany in 1917, Garner voted for the resolution and summoned his only son, Tully, recently graduated from college. "Son," he asked, "how do you feel about going to war?" The boy replied, "I aim to go, Dad." Garner answered, "I'm glad to hear it, for you've got to go. I couldn't have cast that vote to send other fathers' boys to war if I hadn't known I was sending my own."[8]

By the 1920s, Garner was the ranking Democrat on the House Ways and Means Committee. He became a regular attendee at Speaker Joe Cannon's poker-and-whiskey club, called the Boar's Nest, the predecessor of one of Garner's own clubs when he attained his great ambition. But he did not have an easy path to his prime goal, the speakership. After the landslide election of Herbert Hoover, the enlarged Republican majority in the House easily retained Nicholas Longworth in the chair. The defeat, however, left Garner as the undisputed Democratic leader in the House, and soon Longworth and Garner teamed up in what came to be known as "the Board of Education." It was a bipartisan watering-hole hideaway on the floor above the Capitol rotunda, where the daily dispensing of wisdom and whiskey prevailed, along with the "education" of wayward legislators.

Once asked why it was so called, Garner said, "You get a couple of drinks in a young congressman and then you know what he knows and what he can do. We pay the tuition by supplying the liquor."[9] While prohibition was still the law of the land, attendees at the Board would ignore it as they engaged in Garner's favorite toast: "Now we'll strike a blow for liberty!" Afterward, Republican Longworth would give Democrat Garner a ride to his hotel in the Speaker's car and often pick him up for work the next morning as well.[10]

In 1930–31, politics and mortality contrived to bring Garner his life's wish. After the year's congressional elections, the control of the House was in doubt, to the point that Longworth sent Garner a telegram: "Whose car is it?" Garner replied, "Think it's mine. Will be pleasure to let you ride."[11] Garner was wrong at that moment but not for long. By the time of the opening of the next House session, fourteen members, including Longworth, had died. After special elections to replace them, Garner was elected as Speaker by three votes.

Garner became a harsh taskmaster of the House Democrats. He told them, "You are at the controls. You must remember that you are in command and are no longer the minority party."[12] With the Great Depression now enveloping the country, he appealed for a balanced budget, uncharacteristically taking to the House floor with an impassioned plea for necessary programs and the taxes to pay for them. He warned, "I believe that if this Congress should decline to levy a tax bill there would not be a bank in the United States in existence in sixty days that could meet its depositors." Challenging the whole chamber, he went on, "I want every man and every woman in this House who . . . is willing to try to balance the budget to rise in their seats." At first there was silence, then one by one nearly every member stood. Garner continued, "Now, if they don't mind, those who do not want to balance the budget can rise in their seats." None did.[13]

The first interest in Garner as a national candidate came from William Randolph Hearst, the newspaper tycoon, who raised the possibility in a radio talk in early January of the election year. They had known each other when Hearst was in the House of Representatives, and when Garner was asked at his daily press conference, "What have you got to say about your presidential candidacy?" he shot back, "I haven't a word to say. I am trying to attend to my business here. Now I'll talk about anything else you want to."[14]

Garner's adamant resistance did not, however, still a rising interest in

Texas, but Garner held fast. After visiting Hoover on one occasion, he offered, "I always thought of the White House as a prison, but I never noticed until today how much the shiny latch on the Executive office door looks like the handle on a casket."[15]

Garner's real interest was cementing his hold on the House speakership. He told his biographer, "I have no desire to be President. I am perfectly satisfied right here in the Speaker's office. I worked twenty-six years to get to be Speaker. If we win this election I will have a comfortable majority to work with in the House. If we are on the political upswing as it looks, I will have a longer tenure as Speaker than any other man ever had." He said he had no intention of doing anything that might deadlock the Democratic National Convention against the nomination of the presidential front-runner, Governor Franklin D. Roosevelt of New York.[16]

But with Hearst leading the way in California and Treasury Secretary William McAdoo also in Garner's corner, the Democratic primary in the Golden State in May 1932 surprisingly gave Garner the state's forty-four delegates over New Yorkers' FDR and rival Al Smith. Together with the Texas delegation, Garner went into the convention with ninety delegates and a scattering of second-place support.

McAdoo, speaking for the California delegation, had promised, "California will stay with Garner until hell freezes over."[17] But Roosevelt's floor manager, James A. Farley, told Garner the convention would deadlock unless Roosevelt went over the top on the next roll call. Garner said later, "So I said to Sam, 'All right, release my delegates and see what you can do. Hell, I'll do anything to see the Democrats win one more national election.'"[18] The floodgates opened, FDR was nominated on that ballot, and Garner was nominated as Roosevelt's running mate by acclamation.

In the fall campaign, Garner was happy to be pitted against Hoover, painting him as a tool of Wall Street, and he went off for two weeks of hunting and fishing. At Farley's urging, he made a few speeches but was convinced the election was in the bag. Meeting Roosevelt in Hyde Park, Garner told him, "All you have to do is stay alive until election day. The people are not going to vote for you. They are going to vote against the depression."[19] And he added, "Hoover is making speeches, and that's enough for us."[20] Later, after delivering a speech to businessmen in New York, Garner said, "I got on a train and came back to Texas. I had no more to say about the campaign. I had not campaigned for the nomination for vice-president. I didn't want the office. I wanted to stay on as speaker of the House."[21]

On Election Day, the Roosevelt-Garner ticket won forty-two of the forty-eight states, and Garner was also elected to the House for the sixteenth time but resigned his House seat to take the vice presidency. Accepting the limits of the office, he declared, "I am nothing but a spare tire and have nothing to say. I believe it is my duty as vice president not to do any talking about government policies. I owe that to the boss. He is spokesman for the administration." And he told his old friends in the press corps, "I will always be glad to see you, but don't ask me to talk. That is not my job anymore. The man who is moving into the White House will do the talking."[22] Later, however, he acknowledged, "I couldn't get it into my head that I shouldn't express my own views instead of agreeing with the president about everything. I had the feeling that it was my duty to express honest views, whether they agreed with the president [or not]."[23]

Less than three weeks before FDR and Garner were to be sworn in as president and vice president, Garner came fatefully close to the presidency itself. On February 15, 1933, President-elect Roosevelt was riding in a motorcade in Miami with Mayor Anton Cermak of Chicago when an unemployed and disgruntled bricklayer named Giuseppe Zangara fired five times at the car, killing Cermak and wounding four others, but Roosevelt escaped unscathed. Had the president-elect been slain, the vice president elect would have been sworn in as president on March 4.

After nearly a lifetime in one of the highest leadership positions in Congress, Garner was not likely to go gently into semiretirement as a benign Senate presiding officer. He carried out its routine duties with good humor, as when the despised Senator Huey Long of Louisiana, the infamous Kingfish, paused in a filibuster and demanded that Garner require the presence of all senators. Garner replied, "In the first place the senator from Louisiana should not ask that. In the second place, it would be cruel and unusual punishment!"[24]

In the first term, relations between FDR and Garner were generally cordial but with each man holding firmly to his own views. Early on, when Roosevelt declared a bank holiday to cope with any rush on the banks to withdraw deposits, Garner argued for a federal guarantee on deposits, but Roosevelt balked. At a dinner at the National Press Club, its president,

Bascom Timmons of the *Tulsa World,* later Garner's biographer, sat between them and heard FDR say, "It won't work, John. You had it in Texas and it was a failure and so it was in Oklahoma and other states. The weak banks will pull down the strong. It's not a new idea, and it has never worked." Garner replied, "You'll have to have it, Cap'n, or get more clerks in the Postal Savings banks. The people who have taken their money out of the banks are not going to put it back without some guarantee. A national guarantee can be made to work. Depositors are not going to run on banks which have a government insurance."[25] In the end, Roosevelt relented and took credit for the move.

When Roosevelt began considering diplomatic recognition of the Soviet Union in 1933, the two men went off on a fishing trip together to West Virginia. Garner, a veteran of the House Foreign Affairs Committee, took the occasion to tell the president, "You ought not to recognize Russia." FDR shot back, "You tend to your office and I'll tend to mine."[26]

All this time, Garner never took the trouble of shielding his regret at having left the House speakership for the vice presidency. He told one interviewer, "When I was elected vice president it was the worst thing that ever happened to me. As Speaker of the House I could have done more good than anywhere else." He often referred to the speakership as the second most important office in the federal government. His only public complaint about his most widely published derision of the vice presidency—that it wasn't "worth a bucket of warm spit"—was that it was reported incorrectly. What he had really said, he insisted, was that it wasn't "worth a bucket of warm piss," complaining, "Those pantywaist writers wouldn't print it the way I said it."[27] He also said, "Becoming vice president was the only demotion I ever had."

But Roosevelt came to regard Garner as a man of down-to-earth wisdom to be consulted on all manner of affairs, calling him "Mr. Common Sense."[28] On the other hand, the president complained to Farley when Garner was too free in discussing administration strategies with his old legislative cronies. In 1935, when a veterans' bonus bill was under consideration, Garner privately suggested to FDR that for tactical reasons he veto it "in temperate language so as not to incur the ill-feeling of veterans," and then have Congress override the veto. FDR agreed, then fumed on learning that Garner had told some senators of the plan, leaving the president open to a charge of bad faith. "I can't believe Jack let it out," he told Farley. Roosevelt then got the veto sustained to save face.[29] Garner's alleged leaks from cabinet meetings led other members to watch what they said and to hang back afterward to get Roosevelt's private ear. Garner called the practice "staying for prayer meeting."[30]

In 1936, the Roosevelt-Garner ticket was renominated by acclamation and reelected in a landslide with minimal campaigning, carrying forty-six of the forty-eight states over the Kansas governor Alfred M. Landon and the Chicago newspaper publisher Frank Knox. The result led to the rephrasing of the old saying of Maine, as a national bellwether, to read, "As Maine goes, so goes Vermont." But the political success could not quell Garner's growing concern about the first-term avalanche of reform legislation warranted by the Great Depression, in his mind of questionable wisdom now. He told his biographer, "The watchword for Democrats should be amend, amend, amend during the next four years. We are not putting out a fire. There is no reason why we can't balance the budget now. You can repeal unwise and unworkable laws but you can't repeal the public debt."[31]

Beyond that, Garner was unhappy about the advent of a wave of sit-down strikes and unemployment and later FDR's ill-conceived inspiration to pack the Supreme Court after its rejection of key New Deal initiatives. Finally he was most disturbed, as the specter of war clouds rumbled increasingly from Europe with the rise of Adolf Hitler, of an unprecedented third-term bid by an American president.

The country at this time was hit by a wave of strikes in the auto industry, led by the Congress of Industrial Organizations (CIO) president John L. Lewis and his Union of Automobile Workers, hitting many General Motors and Chrysler plants. Garner told his biographer that when Roosevelt said he "couldn't get those strikers out without bloodshed," the vice president replied, "Then John L. Lewis is a bigger man than you are if you can't find some way to cope with this."[32] Later, Garner said of the confrontation, "I think that is the only angry discussion we ever had. I disagreed with him many times and expressed my viewpoint as forcefully as I could, but there were no brawls."[33]

In FDR's second inaugural address, he signaled an expansion of his New Deal agenda, memorably referring to "one-third of a nation ill-housed, ill-clad, ill-nourished." But he had already encountered resistance from the

Supreme Court, which by the end of its 1936 term had reviewed nine New Deal laws and ruled seven of them unconstitutional. The latter included the National Industrial Recovery Act creating the National Recovery Administration, and the Social Security and Wagner labor acts also appeared to be in jeopardy.

Fifteen days after Roosevelt's address, he jolted Congress by sending it a radical court reorganization bill. The first Garner knew of it was when Roosevelt read it to him. Hoover, on hearing the plan, labeled it "court packing," and the label stuck, kicking off the biggest row of the FDR years. The bill, obviously inspired by the Supreme Court's resistance to New Deal reform schemes at the heart of the Roosevelt economic recovery plan, called for the presidential appointment of six additional justices, one for every sitting justice over the age of seventy. The rationale was that the existing nine could not keep up with the court's workload. The Democratic senator Carter Glass of Virginia likened FDR's gambit to putting in "a lot of judicial marionettes to speak the ventriloquisms of the White House."[34]

In the midst of the resulting uproar, Garner suddenly headed back to Uvalde for a previously planned vacation, believing earlier that Congress would have adjourned by that time. But the Senate debate on the court-packing bill droned on, and Roosevelt fumed again. He asked Farley, "Why in hell did Jack have to leave at this time for? . . . This is a fine time to jump ship. What's eating him?"[35] Farley cooled Roosevelt off for a time, and then a few weeks later the president wrote Garner a conciliatory letter persuading him to return. "I miss you because of you yourself, and also because of the great help [you could bring] to the working out peacefully of a mass of problems," the letter said.[36]

Garner returned to Washington after attending a senator's funeral in Arkansas. On the train back, he held a session of the "Board of Education" with the senators aboard and took a good nose count on how the Senate would vote on the court reform. On arrival he went to the White House and was asked by Roosevelt how he found it. "Do you want it with the bark on or off, Cap'n?" Garner asked. "The rough way," FDR said. "All right, you are beat," Garner told him. "You haven't got the votes."[37] Farley wrote later, "I don't think the President ever forgave Garner. I believe this marked the beginning of coolness on his part. In the past he had accepted criticism from Garner good-naturedly, evidently aware Jack would finally support him even against his own judgment. Thereafter things were never the same between them, so I judged from my seat at the Cabinet table."[38]

But by this time the Supreme Court problem had evaporated. Before a watered-down version of the bill could be brought to a final vote, the court had changed course. It suddenly reversed a 1936 decision that had declared a minimum-wage law in Washington unconstitutional and shortly afterward upheld the Wagner labor act. In June, one of the court's conservative justices retired, giving Roosevelt his first opportunity to appoint a more liberal judge.[39] With a rash of subsequent retirements, Roosevelt was able to appoint five liberal justices within thirty months, all to his satisfaction.

Meanwhile on March 4, 1937, Roosevelt told a dinner party that he planned to retire in January 1941, at the end of his second term, in keeping with the Washington tradition. With another recession hitting in 1937–38, Roosevelt was obliged to launch another spending program that fell short of the need to achieve his goal of full employment in his second term. In his Democratic Party, the growing breach between northern liberals and southern conservatives undercut the progress of the New Deal reform, and right-wing agitation against communism and other perceived un-American threats was mounting.

The political outcome of the party's division was another divisive FDR decision in the 1938 congressional election campaign: to seek the defeat of foes of liberal Democrats, a strategy quickly denounced as an intramural "purge." Garner, as an unvarnished loyal Democrat, was against it. He told Roosevelt, "I don't think you ought to try to punish these men, Cap'n. On many details of party principles men disagree. Some branch off in one direction and some in another. Men who oppose you on one thing are for you on another and there is always a legislative program for which you have to find votes. . . . You may have reason to be provoked at them, but you can't defeat the Southern senators and if you defeat the Democrats in the North you will get Republicans instead."[40]

With war clouds darkening and rumbling with Hitler's march into Austria in March 1938, Garner said, this was no time for party disunity. But Roosevelt went ahead anyway. Garner blamed the so-called liberal Brains Trust around FDR for seeking to weed out conservative Democrats. In July, the president delivered a radio fireside chat defending his decision to campaign against dissident Democrats and then took aim at them in a swing by train across the West and South. All were reelected, but other Democrats lost eighty-one seats in the House, eight in the Senate, and eleven governorships in a conspicuous slap at the president.

Meanwhile, at the Texas Democratic convention, Garner was unanimously endorsed for president in 1940, to which he gave no encouragement. On returning to Washington, the vice president flatly confronted Roosevelt on whether he intended to seek a third term. He told Washington correspondent Ray Tucker he had advised FDR that he had to decide whether he was "gonna get on or get off," also telling him, "For God's sake, Mister President, have the baby or let it go!"[41]

In July 1939, Farley proposed to Garner that he join him and Secretary of State Cordell Hull in opposing a third term. When FDR proposed the development of "a revolving fund fed from the earnings of government investments . . . to finance new projects when there is a need for extra stimulus of employment," Garner said the idea "in some particulars is the worst that has come up here. It gives the president discretion to spend billions where he wants to, how he wants to and when he wants to" without annual congressional appropriations.[42] The legislation, somewhat reduced, passed the Senate, but the House refused even to consider it. In a cabinet meeting, Garner also opposed the shipment of oil, scrap metal, and other war materiel to Japan, declaring, "I never thought a white man ought to sell knives to Indians."[43]

The last two years of the second term drove Roosevelt and Garner further apart, as the vice president objected to more spending, to what he saw as use of relief funds for political purposes, and to FDR's leftward swing. With the 1940 presidential election more than a year away, *Time* magazine wrote of Garner, "His enemies say that, having long bided his time, this 70-year-old sagebrush poker-player at last holds the makings of a royal flush and can scarcely contain himself when he looks at a pot he might win." But Garner told the magazine, "I am not giving a living soul permission to speak for me or to put forth my name as a candidate—but I'm not telling anybody not to."[44]

Roosevelt for his part continued to tell all interrogators, in public and in private, that he would not accept a third term. When a reporter for the *New York Times* asked again, the president singled him out by name, saying, "Bob Post should put on a dunce cap and stand in the corner."[45] At the same time, he made clear he was dead against any third term for anybody, but with Hitler's invasion of Poland and the declarations of war by France and Britain, a Roosevelt draft spread swiftly.

Finally, in December, Garner issued a forty-five-word statement: "I will accept the nomination for President. I will make no effort to control any delegates. The people should decide. A candidate should be selected at the primaries and conventions as provided by law, and I sincerely trust that all Democrats will participate in them."[46] Roosevelt had no comment.

At the Democratic National Convention in Chicago, neither Roosevelt nor Garner was present, choosing to remain in Washington. In an obviously orchestrated kabuki dance, the convention chairman, Alben W. Barkley of Kentucky, pulled from his pocket a letter from Roosevelt saying he had no "desire or purpose to continue" as president and declaring his delegates were "free to vote for any candidate."[47] The statement created an uproar and an immediate floor demonstration for FDR, organized by the Chicago mayor and party boss, Edward J. Kelly. Immediately as well, the hall erupted on cue with calls of "We want Roosevelt!" and "America wants Roosevelt!" amplified to an ear-splitting pitch by a single voice in the basement, quickly labeled by the press "the Voice from the Sewers."[48] A huge photograph of FDR was raised in the hall, and he was overwhelmingly nominated for an unprecedented third term.

First Lady Eleanor Roosevelt, at her husband's request, flew to Chicago and personally presented Secretary of Agriculture Henry A. Wallace, the Iowa farmer-agronomist, as her husband's choice as his running mate. The selection was unenthusiastically received in the hall, as will be seen in the next chapter, but accepted by the convention.

In September, Garner returned to the Senate to finish his duties as presiding officer and attended cabinets meetings at the White House despite his overt role of rebellion. As for his sentiments toward Roosevelt, he predicted after the election, "Roosevelt will be a candidate for a fourth term if he lives. He will never leave the White House except in death or defeat."[49]

In retirement, Cactus Jack and Ettie Garner talked of world travels, but the plans went for naught when she was stricken with Parkinson's disease. They celebrated their golden wedding anniversary with family and friends at home in Uvalde in 1945, and a wheelchair-bound Ettie died three years later at age seventy-eight. John Nance Garner continued at home for nearly twenty-two more years, until fifteen days before his ninety-ninth birthday on November 7, 1967, when a coronary occlusion brought his death, with his son, Tully, and friends at his bedside. To this day, visitors can explore the Garner Museum in Uvalde, laden with scrapbooks, photos, letters, and telegrams from the famous who have toured it or corresponded with arguably the most revered Texan never elected president.

CHAPTER 33

HENRY A. WALLACE
OF IOWA

With John Nance Garner, Roosevelt's vice president in his first two terms, out of favor after his rebellion against FDR's third term and his New Deal agenda, the president decided he was not going to leave the selection of his next running mate to the Democratic National Convention in 1940. Upon his renomination in Chicago, Roosevelt wanted a man unquestionably loyal not only to him but also to his liberal agenda. And with war now broken out in Europe, he was also obliged to consider the important role foreign policy would play in the next four years.

The president therefore had been casting his eye on his secretary of state, Cordell Hull, but Hull said he felt he "could render far more valuable service in the troubled days ahead by staying at the State Department." On three separate occasions Hull said this to FDR, until the president finally told him, "If you don't take it, I'll have to get Henry Wallace to run."[1]

The man Roosevelt mentioned to Hull seemed a most unlikely individual to be considered for the second political office in the nation. As FDR's secretary of agriculture, Henry Agard Wallace was not widely regarded as a working politician; rather, he was known as a classic man of the soil who had grown up on a farm in Iowa and had made his name as a pioneer in developing new strains of corn, the state's prime crop. His roots were distinctly in the rural life. His Scots-Irish forebears had emigrated from Ireland as early as 1734 to western Pennsylvania, outside Pittsburgh, and thence to Iowa. His father, Henry Cantwell Wallace, called Harry, a farmer and publisher of farm journals, himself rose to be secretary of agriculture under Presidents Warren Harding and Calvin Coolidge.[2]

Born into the staunch young Republican farm family of Harry Wallace in rural Adair County, Iowa, on October 7, 1888, young Henry, as he was called then, was engulfed in farm life from an early age. He made a successful career in agriculture quite apart from politics. His namesake grandfather, known as Uncle Henry, wrote for and then published farm journals.[3] His father became editor of the *Iowa Homestead,* the state's largest and leading farm journal, a professor of agriculture at Iowa State, and later publisher of his own highly profitable family paper, *Wallaces' Farmer.* When the family moved to the outskirts of Des Moines, young Henry tended his own garden and in time became fascinated with studying and growing corn.

In those days, corn farmers emphasized the appearance of their crop; competitive corn shows were held in which ears were judged by the orderliness of their kernels and their "perfection." In 1903 Young Henry wrote an article in the family journal asking, "What's looks to a hog?" arguing it was flavor that mattered.[4] He demonstrated the point with his own carefully treated cobs. In 1904, the young farmer took a special course at Iowa State on growing quality corn, then went back to the family paper, and for more than twenty years devoted himself to the breeding of quality corn.

In 1913, at age twenty-four, the shy and somewhat eccentric Henry Wallace went to a picnic in Des Moines where he met a pretty and demure young woman half a year older, named Ilo Browne. He courted her relentlessly, and even though he seemed a bit strange to her friends, they were married in May 1914.[5] Together they bought a farm with his sparse savings and the sale of some property she had inherited, then began a business in corn production and dairying.

When the United States entered the Great War, both Wallaces, now the parents of a young son, were opposed to it and the profiteering that went with it but were not pacifists. When Congress passed the military draft in May 1917, calling all men between the ages of twenty-one and thirty, Henry, at twenty-eight, signed up. Heavily engaged in the farm and helping his father edit the family paper, he sought an exemption on the grounds of his family status and occupation and was classified 3-J—exempt as engaged in necessary agricultural work. He did not, as some critics suggested much later, file as a conscientious objector.[6]

By the time the war ended in November 1918, farmers were enjoying prosperous days, but after the armistice farm prices for corn and other crops began to fall. After the election of 1920, the Republican presidential nominee Warren Harding named the elder Wallace secretary of agriculture, and his son stepped in as editor of *Wallaces' Farmer.*[7] The senior Wallace died in 1924, and his son took over as publisher of the influential family farm journal.

In 1926, Henry and eight other Iowans formed a company to develop, raise, and sell a special hybrid corn called Pioneer Hi-Bred. After a few difficult start-up years at the onset of the Great Depression, Wallace joined forces with a young Coon Rapids salesman named Roswell Garst, kicking off what ultimately would be a multimillion-dollar high-yield hybrid corn empire in a revolution of American farming.[8]

In the fall of 1929, *Wallaces' Farmer* bought its rival, the *Iowa Homestead,* and Wallace became editor of the joint publication. But the merger failed to withstand the eroding farm economy, and in 1932 the Wallace family had to drop ownership. Henry continued as editor, while also engaging in a personal religious quest that soon won him a reputation as a mystic. The furthest he would go in admitting it was to say he was "probably a practical mystic . . . that if you envision something that hasn't been, that can be, and bring it into being, that is a tremendously worthwhile thing to do." He said he shared the view of a friend "who believed that God was in everything and therefore, if you went to God, you could find the answers," adding, "Maybe that belief is mysticism. I don't know." In Des Moines, he often attended meetings of the local Theosophical Society.[9]

En route to a European vacation in 1929, Wallace visited an art museum in New York run by a Russian expatriate painter, peace activist, and self-styled guru named Nicholas Konstantinovich Roerich. They struck up a strange correspondence that later produced what came to be known as "the guru letters," a considerable embarrassment to Wallace for the somewhat bizarre otherworldly discussions they revealed. Roerich turned out to be a con artist who milked wealthy Americans for support of his enterprises. In 1935 Wallace finally severed all connections with Roerich and his wife, who fled to India without paying the taxes owed. The fiasco haunted Wallace long after and fed the impression that he was indeed a mystic who bore watching and might even be dangerous.

As neither mysticism nor Herbert Hoover in the White House had been able to lift Iowa and the rest of the Farm Belt and the country out of its economic despair, Wallace began to look to the Democratic Party in the early 1930s, although without much enthusiasm for its ambitious New York governor, Franklin D. Roosevelt. But in the spring of 1932, Wallace received a totally unexpected visitor in Henry T. Morgenthau Jr., a friend and neighbor of Roosevelt and also a publisher of a farm journal. Morgenthau talked up FDR as a friend of agriculture. A few days after the Democratic National Convention in Chicago nominated Roosevelt for the presidency, Wallace was invited to have lunch at FDR's home in Hyde Park. Roosevelt engaged his guest for nearly two hours with questions about agricultural matters, without ever once raising politics or any possible appointment. Several weeks later Wallace was asked to help draft a major speech on farm policy that would commit Roosevelt to domestic crop allotments aimed at increasing prices for farmers without overproduction. FDR delivered the speech in Topeka, and Wallace thereafter threw himself into writing in support of the president's policy, lobbying farm leaders and speaking at numerous political meetings.

The focus on the farm vote paid big dividends. For only the second time since Iowa statehood, the state went Democratic, and Roosevelt was easily elected over Hoover. Wallace was offered the post of secretary of agriculture, the same office his revered father had occupied under Harding.[10]

The first Department of Agriculture appointment Wallace made was of a Republican named Milton Eisenhower, brother of the army major Dwight D. Eisenhower, without regard to his party, to be Wallace's personnel policy director. Wallace called an immediate conference of the nation's farm leaders who agreed that "farm production must be adjusted to consumption" and domestic allotment instituted to reduce production and restore buying power.[11]

The emergency Agricultural Adjustment Act, to cope with spreading farm foreclosures and plunging crop prices, was written in a week, and the House passed it without amendment in another week. In the Senate, however, the bill stalled and was saved only by an outbreak of violence in the small town of Le Mars, Iowa. A mob of six hundred farmers seized a judge considering a farm foreclosure, put a noose around his neck, and threatened hang him, but cool heads prevailed. The governor of Iowa declared martial law and sent troops to disband "the Corn Belt rebellion," so the Senate finally passed the bill, and Roosevelt signed it.

The frenetic energy that burst from the new farm secretary's department became the talk of Washington, sparking a raft of hiring as he tackled the task of dealing with huge crop surpluses, coupled with planned crop reductions to achieve livable commodity prices for farmers. Young and idealistic lawyers with names like Abe Fortas, Adlai Stevenson, and Alger Hiss flocked to the department as a cutting edge of the Roosevelt agenda. Wallace, as the genius behind hybrid seed boosting corn production across Iowa, was ironically charged now in his new post with the task of cutting that production, in the interest of higher prices for the farmers who planted his prized product.

As part of the program, Wallace caused a particular furor by raising cotton and pork prices for farmers by cutting production, having them plow under ten million acres of cotton and slaughter six million young pigs. To critics, Wallace blandly observed, "Perhaps they think that farmers should run a sort of old-folks home for hogs."[12] Farm prices in some cases doubled under his plan.

In 1936, the innovative New Deal agenda whose crest Wallace was riding was abruptly interrupted when the conservative-led Supreme Court ruled the Agricultural Adjustment Act unconstitutional by a 6–3 vote. The majority opinion said farming was "a purely local activity" that was not subject to federal regulation. Wallace was both incredulous and irate, writing, "Were agriculture truly a local matter in 1936, as the Supreme Court says it is, half of the people in the United States would quickly starve."[13] The decision was not a surprise, however. The previous May, the court had unanimously struck down the business version of the AAA, the National Industrial Recovery Act, signaling the legal fight against the New Deal ahead. Wallace reflected much later that when that happened, he had thought, "We're not going to be caught flat-footed as these boys are," if the Supreme Court were to invalidate the entire AAA.[14]

Wallace quickly set his mind to salvage the critical farm relief program. The result was the Soil Conservation and Domestic Allotment Act, designed to cut production and raise farm prices. Congress speedily passed it and Roosevelt signed it, greatly impressed with Wallace's resilience and ingenuity. The law was challenged but upheld. Wallace, more determined than ever that his boss be reelected that November, took his wife to the courthouse in Des Moines, where they both registered as Democrats for the first time.

But when FDR pushed his scheme to pack the Supreme Court, Wallace quietly lamented it, observing thereafter, "It was the last time the New Deal really breathed defiance. From then on, while many of us didn't realize it, it was a downhill slide, very much a downhill slide."[15]

Long before Roosevelt finally made clear he would seek a third term, he had made up his mind that chief aide Harry Hopkins would be his running mate. Serious illness, however, struck Hopkins in February of the election year, and by May he took himself out of contention. When Garner and Farley announced they would challenge FDR, all Wallace would say was that he would support any New Dealer nominated.

Finally, on April 9, 1940, world events forced Roosevelt's hand with the German invasion of Denmark and Norway, making it all but inevitable that he would seek a third term to forge national unity. FDR retained his silence on the matter, but when a group of Iowans approached him in May about supporting Wallace for president on the first ballot at the Democratic National Convention, he told them to desist. Wallace quickly assured him he had had no hand in it and would follow his boss's wishes.

He was aware by now, however, of the chance that Roosevelt might pick him as his running mate. At a dinner in New York, when he told the FDR aide Sam Rosenman he believed the president should run again, Rosenman replied, "In that case, you'll have to be the vice president."[16] But Wallace went into the convention without having any word from FDR about his intentions.

In a meeting with Farley in Hyde Park before the Democratic convention, Roosevelt had hinted he would run again and that he might choose the agriculture secretary to run with him. Farley later wrote that he told FDR, "Boss, I'm going to be very direct with you. Henry Wallace won't add a bit of strength to the ticket. . . . I think it would be a terrible thing to have him President. . . . I think you must know that people look on him as a wild-eyed fellow." Roosevelt replied only, "The man running with me must be in good health because there is no telling how long I can hold out.

You know, Jim, a man with paralysis can have a breakup at any time. While my heart and lungs are good and the other organs are functioning along okay . . . nothing in this life is certain."[17]

Two days after the fall of France to the Nazis, the Republicans convened in Philadelphia and surprisingly nominated a political neophyte, Wendell L. Willkie of Indiana, a folksy, rumpled, and appealing public utilities executive. He was given as his running mate Senator Charles McNary of Oregon, the Senate minority leader and coauthor of farmer-friendly agricultural bills in the Harding and Coolidge adminstrations, obviously calculated to help the GOP ticket in the Farm Belt.

At the subsequent Democratic convention in Chicago, at which Roosevelt was renominated, FDR by now had settled on Wallace, and he made it clear he would have no alternative. Nevertheless, Hopkins advised the president of rising opposition to Wallace. According to Grace Tully, Roosevelt's secretary, when Hopkins told him that "the convention might not go for Wallace, the Boss really got his Dutch up. 'Well, damn it to hell,' he barked at Hopkins, 'they will all go for Wallace or I won't run, and you can jolly well tell them so.'"[18]

To calm the waters, Eleanor Roosevelt flew to Chicago and took a seat on the convention rostrum next to Wallace's wife, Ilo, and awaited her turn to speak. When Wallace's name was placed in nomination to be FDR's running mate, boos and catcalls were heard from the galleries; one delegate grabbed an open microphone and complained, "Give us a Democrat! We don't want a Republican!"[19]

Back in Washington, Roosevelt sat at a card table in the Oval Office playing solitaire and listening to the convention on the radio. Sam Rosenman later described the scene: "As the fight got more and more acrimonious, the President asked Missy [LeHand, another secretary] to give him a note pad and a pencil. Putting aside his cards he started to write. The rest of us sat around wondering what he was writing. . . . Finally he laid his pencil down, turned to me [Rosenman] and said: 'Sam, take this inside and go work on it; smooth it out and get it ready for delivery. I may have to deliver it quickly, so please hurry it up.'"[20]

What FDR finally wrote was a message to the convention that in light of the "discord" that had surfaced, he was "declining the honor of the nomination for the presidency."[21] The statement was sent to Harry Hopkins, who pocketed it awaiting the right time to release it. FDR phoned him and told him he had decided on Wallace but gave him no instructions about what he had written. When Hopkins informed him the convention had expected that the choice would be left to the delegates and there would be sharp objection, the president curtly snapped back, "It's Wallace."[22] Hopkins dutifully called Wallace with the news. As word leaked out, the mood at the convention became increasingly restless, even surly.

When it was Mrs. Roosevelt's turn to speak, she rose and made a firm appeal for support for her husband. She did not mention Wallace, but her intent was clear. "We people in the United States have got to realize that we face now a grave and serious situation," she said. ". . . We cannot tell from day to day what will come. This is no ordinary time, no time for thinking about anything except what we can best do for the country as a whole, and that responsibility is on each and every one of us as individuals. . . . This is a time when it is the United States we fight for."[23]

The First Lady brought the conventioneers to their feet in cheers. Wallace was nominated on the first ballot, and half an hour after midnight, Roosevelt addressed the convention by long-distance hookup, thanking the assemblage for accepting his choice of Wallace, adding that his practical idealism would be of great service to the president individually.[24] He never had Hopkins deliver the letter written in anger in the Oval Office, which could have changed history.

Roosevelt's strong-arm selection of Wallace was the most blatantly personal and unilateral choice of a presidential running mate up to this time. With the third-term issue offering the Republican Party a potent weapon to raise against FDR, Wallace in the fall campaign pitched in with speeches through the Farm Belt as Roosevelt whistle-stopped by train across the industrial states, claiming economic recovery and assuring anxious mothers, "Your boys are not going to be sent into any foreign wars."[25]

The race was closer than the Democrats had expected in the popular vote, but Roosevelt and Wallace won decisively in the electoral college. The American voters were determined not to change horses in the middle of the stream of a cataclysmic world war.

As vice president, Wallace spent his first months speaking in support of FDR's lend-lease deal with Britain and presiding over the debate on it in the Senate before it was passed by Congress and signed by the president in mid-March 1941. In July, Roosevelt made good on his earlier magazine musing about making the vice president "useful" by appointing Wallace as chairman of the new Economic Defense Board, to be "a policy and advisory agency." It was to deal with all manner of international economic matters relating to American involvement as a noncombatant in the European war and what might come after its end. It was the first such stipulated executive role for a vice president, and Wallace eagerly grasped it. After Roosevelt and Winston Churchill joined in the Atlantic Charter, FDR also put Wallace at the head of the Supply Priorities and Allocations Board (SPAB) to oversee the speedy dispatch of armaments to the British. These moves made him the most engaged vice president in history.

In October 1941, Wallace became one of the few Americans privy to the nation's greatest military secret. Vannevar Bush, head of the Office of Scientific Research and Development, met with the president and vice president and informed them of the conclusions of separate American and British scientific experts that it was possible to build an atomic bomb of indescribable destructive force and that the Nazis were also pursuing it. The only immediate decision was FDR's instruction that if such a weapon were to be built, only he would decide whether to do so and when to use it.[26] In late November, Roosevelt ordered that the research go forward, and he appointed the Top Policy Committee, which included Wallace, to oversee it.

On December 7, 1941, when Wallace was in New York engaging in public preachings of the need to step up war preparations while thinking beyond to peacetime, the news broke of the Japanese attack on Pearl Harbor. He flew back to Washington and went directly to the White House for night-long talks with Roosevelt and Undersecretary of State Sumner Welles. When FDR called on Congress to declare war on Japan for the "date which will live in infamy," Wallace emerged as a major spokesman for the administration, particularly in rallying public support behind the war effort.

About five weeks later, however, shortly after the influential James Reston of the *New York Times* had written that Wallace was "not only Vice President but 'Assistant President,'" Roosevelt suddenly summoned Wallace and Donald M. Nelson, executive director of the SPAB under Wallace, to the Oval Office. He told them he was creating still another superagency, the War Production Board under a single chairman, and he would be . . .

Nelson, not Wallace! After a shocked Nelson left, Wallace neither asked nor was told why he had not been selected, inquiring only whether FDR wanted him to remain on the board as a member, and he was told yes.[27] Wallace also retained his chairmanship of the Board of Economic Warfare (BEW), responsible for the financing and purchasing of wartime raw materials from foreign sources and for postwar planning.

Though not a bureaucrat at heart, Wallace found himself entangled in a series of bureaucratic fights, the worst of which were with FDR's secretary of commerce, Jesse Jones, and Secretary of State Cordell Hull over BEW affairs. Wallace particularly castigated Jones on the grounds that he had failed to stockpile certain vital materials. When Jones fired back, calling Wallace's allegations "hysterical" and "filled with malice and misstatements," Roosevelt asked James Byrnes, director of the Office of War Mobilization, to referee the fight.

Wallace finally wrote Roosevelt a firm letter calling on the president to appoint a commission to investigate the situation and either fire him or give him the power he needed to do his job as BEW chief. FDR, fed up with the feud, abolished the BEW and put its functions under a new agency with a new director. Jones crowed at the outcome and later wrote, "Mr. Wallace was out of a war job. He was once more just the Vice President with little to do but wait for the president to die, which fortunately did not occur while Henry was Vice President."[28] The liberal columnist I. F. Stone, taking Wallace's side, wrote that Roosevelt "now, smugly even-handed, equally rebukes the loyal and the disloyal, the lieutenant who risked his political future for the war effort and the lieutenant who sabotaged it. Justice itself could not be more blind."[29]

The whole row naturally raised questions about Wallace's political future. He lost his prime wartime staff job but had been elected to the vice presidency and could not be fired from it. But as the end of FDR's third term loomed ahead and as the war's end was not in sight, the question of whether Roosevelt would seek a fourth term was now under wide discussion. By the end of August 1943, Wallace himself assumed that Roosevelt would indeed run again and believed he was still in the president's good graces. But when he got advice from friends to start lining up support from party leaders and potential 1944 convention delegates, he declined as not his style.

A Gallup Poll in March gave Wallace the highest favorable rating of potential FDR running mates in 1944. But within the Roosevelt inner circle and among the party's political bosses, there were conversations about removing Wallace from the line of presidential succession in the approaching election. They all knew of the toll that the war had taken on the health of the already invalided FDR and were aware that in nominating the next candidate for vice president they might well be choosing the next president. Ed Flynn, the New York Democratic boss, told Roosevelt that Wallace was now perceived as "the candidate of the radicals" and that the challenge was to find the Democrat "who would hurt him least."[30]

Roosevelt, however, in a preconvention meeting with Wallace, assured him he was his choice to be his running mate again and, at Wallace's pointed request, would be willing to say that if he, FDR, were a delegate to the convention he would vote for Wallace. The next day, FDR finally announced his intention to seek a fourth term but made no mention of his running mate. Meanwhile, the national party chairman, Bob Hannegan, also approached Wallace, urging him to step aside, but was told, "I will not withdraw as long as the president prefers me."[31]

Roosevelt also told him, Wallace wrote later, that the president's political advisers thought Wallace would hurt the ticket, to which the vice president replied, "If you think so, I will withdraw at once." FDR said it was "mighty sweet" of him to offer, but he would not consider accepting it. The meeting ended with the two men shaking hands and the president saying only, "While I cannot put it just that way in public, I hope it will be the same old team." But as Wallace was heading for the Oval Office door, Roosevelt strangely added, again according to Wallace, "Even though they do beat you out at Chicago, we will have a job for you in world economic affairs."[32]

That night, six days before the opening of the Democratic National Convention, Flynn, Hannegan, national party treasurer Ed Pauley, Postmaster General Frank Walker, and Mayor Ed Kelly of Chicago had dinner with Roosevelt at the White House. Further details of this political coup against the sitting vice president will be found in the next chapter, but it suffices to say here that not only Wallace's personal fate but also the course of American presidential politics and history was at stake in the outcome.

Roosevelt sent another letter to the convention on July 14, not made public until its opening. After acknowledging the likely rumors floating around, he wrote, "I am wholly willing to give you my own personal thought in regard to the selection of a candidate for vice president. . . . The easiest way of putting it is this: I have been associated with Henry Wallace during his past four years as vice president, for eight years earlier while he was secretary of agriculture, and well before that. I like him and I respect him and he is my personal friend. For these reasons I personally would vote for his renomination if I were a delegate to the convention." But then the president tellingly added, "At the same time, I do not wish to appear in any way as dictating to the Convention. Obviously the Convention must do the deciding. And it should—and I am sure it will—give great consideration to the pros and cons of its choice."[33]

Four years earlier, he had not hesitated to dictate his choice of Wallace in no uncertain terms. Now he was openly inviting the convention to ignore his transparently worded "endorsement." Wallace himself later observed that Roosevelt could not have been "a well man" in full command of his faculties at the time or he would have told the vice president "clean and straight" that he didn't want him on the ticket, especially since Wallace had offered to withdraw.[34] But he chose to take at face value the statement's part about the president's personal preference for him.

Wallace, now in Chicago to second Roosevelt's renomination, vowed, "I am in this fight to the finish."[35] In his seconding speech for FDR's renomination, he triggered a demonstration for himself from the labor-packed galleries, saying the only question to be answered at the convention was whether the party believed "wholeheartedly in the liberal policies for which Roosevelt has always stood."[36] By implication he was urging his own continuation as FDR's most liberal ally, and his speech electrified the crowd. Maybe his foes in the party were wrong, and he could be nominated after all.

The roll call of the states for presidential nomination gave FDR an easy, though not unanimous, first-ballot victory. Roosevelt, now at a naval base in San Diego, accepted the nomination in a talk piped into the convention hall, saying that although he wanted to retire he felt could not do so with the nation still at war. He said he would not campaign "in the usual sense" and would press on to win the war and secure the peace. A long and well-planned demonstration for him ensued on the floor, but as it was dying down, the Chicago Stadium suddenly erupted in calls of "We Want Wallace! We Want Wallace!"[37]

Hannegan, fearing a stampede, demanded and finally succeeded in getting the convention chairman to gavel through an adjournment until the next morning. Through the night, the anti-Wallace political bosses worked key state delegations, and the next day Chicago police, on orders from Mayor Kelly, clamped down on admission to the hall. Nevertheless, on the first ballot for vice president Wallace led, but significantly short of a majority. On the second ballot the party bosses loyal to FDR started squeezing, and their choice, Senator Harry S. Truman of Missouri, was put over the top with a late rush of delegates from Flynn's New York.

The defeated Wallace had made a remarkably strong run, to the point that Grace Tully, as she said later, heard FDR say he was astonished the Iowan had drawn such powerful support on the first two ballots and would have insisted on him had he thought he could be nominated. But unlike 1940, when FDR had the luxury of focusing on politics and fought for Wallace, in 1944 he was consumed by the war, aging and in decline, and vulnerable to the entreaties of his political lieutenants.

Roosevelt's deception of Wallace ended the vice president's chances for a second term. He was now down but not out. On the night of the nominations, Roosevelt sent him a telegram that read, "You made a grand fight and I am very proud of you." Then it added, "Tell Ilo not to plan to leave Washington next January."[38] What he meant would not immediately become clear, and Wallace publicly dismissed Roosevelt's duplicity with perplexity. He observed later that it was a lot of trouble to go to: "All he needed to do was call me in and say, 'I don't want you to run.'"[39]

In late August, Roosevelt invited Wallace to the White House and followed up on his vague telegram reference. He told his guest he wanted him to remain in his expected fourth administration and could have any cabinet post except the State Department, because he could not ask his old friend Cordell Hull to step aside. FDR had told Wallace earlier that he intended to get rid of Jesse H. Jones, his arrogant commerce secretary, whom FDR derisively called "Jesus H. Jones." So Wallace, long a bitter foe of Jones, suggested, "Well, if you are going to get rid of Jesse, why not let me have secretary of commerce, with RFC [the Reconstruction Finance Corporation] . . . thrown in? There would be poetic justice in that." The deal was struck.[40] That fall, Wallace campaigned diligently for Roosevelt's reelection, focusing on the Farm Belt, as he no doubt would have done had he been campaigning for his own reelection. He traveled with little or no staff, in a demonstration of his pride and independence.

Only a couple of days after the end of Wallace's term as vice president did Roosevelt fire Jones and clear the way for the Iowan's appointment as secretary of commerce. He was not destined, however, to have a satisfying tenure in it. Upon the death of Roosevelt in April, the elevation of Truman to the Oval Office, and the end of the European war in May 1945, Wallace's views on conciliation with the Russians toward a postwar peace put him in conflict with the Truman administration's hard-nosed foreign policy. After a Wallace speech led Truman to forbid him to speak out further on the subject, the president finally demanded his resignation, and Wallace returned to private life.

Increasingly focused on seeking a less confrontational posture with the Soviet Union during the developing Cold War, Wallace ran for president in 1948 on the Progressive Party ticket but won only 2.4 percent of the vote in the upset Truman victory over the Republican Thomas E. Dewey. In retirement, Wallace continued his controversial foreign policy views toward the Soviet Union, as well as his longtime genetic experimentation on corn and other crops, and was an early critic of the American involvement in Vietnam.

Afflicted with Lou Gehrig's disease in later life, Wallace died on November 18, 1965, in Danbury, Connecticut. For four years he arguably had been the most involved and helpful vice president in the administration in which he served since Martin Van Buren. But his strong independent streak and developing anti-war positions eventually cast him as an outsider focused on a worldview that many Americans came to see as visionary, but others condemned as naive or even disloyal.

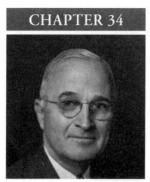

CHAPTER 34

HARRY S. TRUMAN
OF MISSOURI

The thirty-fourth vice president was a former midwestern haberdasher, county judge, and U.S. senator who, less than three months after assuming the office, found himself in the presidency at one of the most critical junctures in the nation's history.

Born a common farm boy to John and Martha Ellen Young Truman on May 8, 1884, on a six-hundred-acre farm of his grandfather's near the small town of Lamar, Missouri, young Harry Truman had no middle name, just the middle initial *S*. It was the result of a compromise in honoring his two grandfathers, Anderson Shipp Truman and Solomon Young.[1] As a young boy Harry suffered from poor eyesight. Fitted with thick-lensed eyeglasses, he avoided sports and opted instead for heavy reading.

In 1890, the family moved to Independence to afford young Harry a proper education, and in 1900 he got his first real taste of politics when his father took him to the Democratic National Convention in Kansas City, where William Jennings Bryan was nominated for the presidency a second time. In 1903 when the family went bankrupt after speculating in grain futures, the Trumans moved to Kansas City, where his father got a job as a night watchman at a grain elevator. Harry yearned for a career in the army, but his weak eyesight cost him a West Point appointment, so he took up a job as a clerk in a local bank until 1905, when the Trumans moved to another farm, outside Harrisonville. Upon his father's death in

1914, Harry took over working the large spread, spending much of his free time practicing on the family piano and delving into American history.[2]

The work was hard and the return minimal. In the meantime, Harry had met and started dating a young local woman, Elizabeth (Bess) Wallace, and after a year proposed marriage in 1911, but she turned him down. He persisted over the next six years, to no avail. He involved himself in some mining ventures that disappointed him,[3] and when the United States entered the war in Europe in 1917, he enlisted. At age thirty-three he was two years over the draft-age limit and, in any event, qualified for exemption as a farmer critical to the war effort. But he left the farm in the hands of his mother and sister, got into the army by memorizing the eye chart used to check his vision, and was given command of a National Guard company in Kansas City, with the rank of first lieutenant. In France, he led Battery "D" of the 129th Field Artillery into the Meuse-Argonne sector in the final days of fierce fighting before the armistice ending the war.[4]

Through all this, Harry regularly wrote to Bess, describing the war and thereafter the sights in Paris from the view of this unsophisticated farm boy. Upon his return home, they were finally married in Independence on June 28, 1919, and moved in with her mother in what proved to be a permanent arrangement.[5]

A month prior to the wedding, Harry and a local wartime buddy, Eddie Jacobson, a former clerk at a Kansas City clothing store who had run a canteen with Harry in the army, leased a store in downtown Kansas City. They opened a men's haberdashery—shirts, ties, and all the other accessories of the modern smart gentleman's attire. The business started off with a burst of success, and Harry was a personal advertisement for the store, always nattily dressed.

One day in 1921, another old army buddy named Jim Pendergast dropped by with his father, Mike Pendergast, head of the city's Tenth Ward Democratic Club. Harry was surprised to be asked whether he might want to run for the eastern Jackson County judgeship. It was more an administrative than a judicial position, overseeing road contracts and the like, and he immediately accepted.[6] Around this same time, with a postwar drop in farm prices and general recession, the Truman and Jacobson enterprise went bankrupt, and Harry spent the next fifteen years paying off debts accumulated from the store.[7]

Fortuitously he was elected as county judge in February 1922 for a two-year term, paying $3,465 a year. Harry wrote later of the period, "Went into business all enthusiastic. Lost all I had and all I could borrow.... Mike Pendergast picked me up and put me into politics and I've been lucky."[8] He made clear it was Mike who was his original savior, not Mike's brother Tom, who came to be the boss of the notorious Pendergast Democratic machine in Kansas City but was unknown to Truman until later.

After only two years as a county judge, however, a split in the Democratic ranks cost Truman his judgeship, which was lost to a Republican. The defeat in 1924, his only one in twenty-six more years in public life, was lightened by the birth of his only child, Mary Margaret, destined to play a central if uncommon role in her father's political career. While waiting to run again in 1926, Truman sold memberships to the Kansas City Automobile Club and kept in touch with Jim and Mike Pendergast. He also finally met Tom Pendergast, who persuaded him to run for chief judge on his old court, and he won two four-year terms.

During this time, the Pendergast machine thrived financially under boss Tom through local and state patronage and government contracts for roads and other public construction works. Part of Truman's mandate was awarding and overseeing such contracts, and he guardedly avoided suspicions of real or imagined favoritism on the part of the machine. He proposed and pushed through a bond issue for a new network of county roads built by low-bid contractors, later lauded by the Independence *Examiner*. As for Tom Pendergast, Truman wrote of one conversation with him regarding three complaining contractors: "These boys tell me you won't give them contracts," Pendergast began. Truman replied, "They can get them if they are low bidders, but they won't get paid for them unless they come up to specifications." Pendergast told the complainers, "Didn't I tell you boys? He's the contrariest cuss in Missouri."[9]

Truman's success as the presiding judge of Jackson County and his ability to get along with the Pendergast machine on his terms led him to approach Tom Pendergast in 1934 about running for the U.S. House of Representatives. The party boss had already promised the nomination to someone else and countered with an offer to be the Democratic nominee for the U.S. Senate, an offer already turned down by three other Democrats.[10]

While the offer gave Truman considerable organizational support in the

Democratic primary against two Missouri congressmen, he had to combat allegations of being a mere tool of the machine. He survived and won the seat on the basis of his reputation as an honest and hard-working county judge. In the Senate, he avoided the spotlight and plunged into committee work. In his first term as a member of the Senate Interstate Commerce Committee, he coauthored, along with Chairman Burton K. Wheeler of Montana, a new transportation act regulating rail, truck, and other shipping interests.

Truman's hopes for a second term, however, were imperiled by the prosecution of his benefactor Tom Pendergast for tax fraud in 1939. Truman came to Pendergast's defense, telling the *St. Louis Post-Dispatch* that "political animus" was involved, adding, "I am not one to desert a ship when it starts to go down."[11] Pendergast was convicted, but the anti-Pendergast vote split, and Truman was reelected.[12]

American preparedness was now expanding in the face of the war in Europe. Truman, as a member of the Senate Military Affairs Committee, a colonel in the reserves, and aware of the shortage of army officers in early 1941, sought a commission from U.S. Army Chief of Staff George C. Marshall. Marshall told him that at fifty-six he was too old ("We don't need old stiffs like you—this will be a young man's war") and that he could do more in the Senate to advance national defense.[13] So Truman called on Roosevelt at the White House and proposed the creation of a special Senate committee to oversee the implementation of defense contracts. The result was the Truman Committee, which catapulted its founder into national prominence as war came closer and eventually enveloped America. Truman traveled the country tirelessly as a watchdog of what, after Pearl Harbor, became the nation's war production effort, while continuing to give strong support to FDR's New Deal agenda.

Truman's performance and the machinations of some good political friends were soon to put him on the path to the vice presidency. When Roosevelt decided in July 1944 that he would run for a fourth term, he was persuaded by his chief political strategists that Wallace should not be retained as his running mate. Apparently to let Wallace down easily, the president insisted on going through a masquerade that ultimately brought Truman into the picture. FDR disingenuously told Wallace he preferred him but was leaving the choice to the convention delegates.

As related in the previous chapter, the anti-Wallace strategists dined with Roosevelt at the White House in what FDR's poker-playing friend and raconteur George Allen dubbed "the conspiracy of the pure at heart." They did not consider Wallace one of them, but rather an altruistic do-gooder with an otherworldly air foreign to their club. As Allen wrote, "They were determined that Roosevelt's successor would not be the boomerang-throwing mystic from the place where the tall corn grows."[14]

The list of Wallace's possible replacements started quite naturally with James F. Byrnes, oft referred to as the "assistant president" and FDR's original preference. But Ed Flynn, the New York party boss, had already reported that Byrnes wouldn't do, "because he had been raised a Catholic and had left the Church when he married, and the Catholics wouldn't stand for that; organized labor, too, would not be for him; and since he came from South Carolina, the question of the Negro vote would be raised."[15]

Flynn wrote later that he and the president "went over every man in the Senate to see who would be available, and Truman was the only one who fitted." Flynn continued promoting Truman, saying his record as head of the Senate investigating committee on the defense program was "excellent," his labor votes were good, he came from a border state, and had never made any "racial" remarks. Of Truman, Flynn wrote, "He just dropped into the slot. It was agreed that Truman was the man who would hurt him [FDR] least."[16]

During the strategists' dinner, the president suddenly injected the name of the liberal Supreme Court justice William O. Douglas, who at age forty-nine seemed to intrigue him. Observing that because of his youth he had "a kind of Boy Scout quality," Roosevelt added that he played an "interesting game of poker" and had finished at the top of his class at the Columbia Law School. None of the political bosses at the table seemed interested; Douglas, like Wallace, was not a professional politician as they were.[17]

Finally, Roosevelt turned to Hannegan and said, "All right, Bob. Start talking." The party chairman seized the opportunity to boost his fellow Missourian Harry Truman as a loyal, popular, and effective New Deal senator who, in coming from a border state, could help the ticket in the South. Roosevelt raised the question of Truman's age, which he thought was nearly sixty. FDR's son-in-law John Boettiger was sent to fetch a Congressional Directory, which showed that Truman had just reached sixty, but Pauley intercepted it and held it before Roosevelt could ask again. The president finally cut off the meeting by saying both Truman and Douglas looked like strong candidates and, according to some recollections, turned to Hannegan and said, "Bob, I think you and everyone else here want Truman."[18]

As the visitors got up and started out of the room, the president took Postmaster General Frank Walker aside. "Frank," he asked, "will you go over tomorrow and tell Jimmy [Byrnes] that it's Truman and that I'm sorry it has to be this way?"[19] On the stairs down to the first floor, Walker, knowing Roosevelt's penchant for changing his mind, whispered nervously to Hannegan of FDR's comment about Truman: "Go back and get it in writing." Claiming he had forgotten his coat, Hannegan ducked back in and asked Roosevelt for a note. The president scribbled on an envelope and handed it to him. He dashed back down the stairs and told Walker, "I've got it."[20] In his rush, Hannegan did not look at what FDR had written until later. Rather than mentioning Truman only, he had also listed Douglas as acceptable to him as his running mate.[21]

Meanwhile, Byrnes was still under the impression that he was the president's choice. Hannegan and Walker informed him after this meeting that the odds now favored Truman or Douglas. Byrnes, disconcerted, phoned FDR, who told him, as Byrnes wrote later, "You are the best qualified man in the whole outfit and you must not get out of the race. If you stay in, you are sure to win."[22] On the basis of that conversation, Byrnes called his old Missouri friend and told him, "Harry, the old man is backing me. I'm going to be the vice presidential nominee. Will you make the nominating speech?"[23] Truman told him he'd be happy to. According to Byrnes, on the Saturday before the convention opened, Ed Kelly called him from Chicago. He said the argument that blacks would be against him had been discredited, adding, "The President has given us the green light to support you and he wants you in Chicago." Byrnes caught the next available plane and was told by Kelly and Hannegan of FDR's instructions to them: "Well, you know Jimmy has always been my choice from the very beginning. Go ahead and name him."[24]

Before long the report was out that FDR wanted Byrnes. Roosevelt was again sending out different signals to different suitors. Hannegan turned to Kelly and reminded him that FDR had also said, "Clear it with Sidney

[Hillman]," the president of the Amalgamated Clothing Workers of America and an organizer of a new CIO political action committee committed heavily to Roosevelt's reelection. It proved to be a pivotal caveat; Hillman wanted no part of Byrnes.

On the same Sunday morning before the opening of the convention, Truman met a stone wall when urging Byrnes's nomination over eggs with Hillman, later telling oral historian Merle Miller, "I told him I was going to nominate Jimmy, and he said, 'Harry, that's a mistake. Labor will never support Byrnes. He's against labor. His whole record proves it.' And I said, 'Who the hell do you want then?' He said, 'We're supporting Wallace but we have a second choice, and I'm looking right at him.'" Truman also met with Philip Murray, head of the CIO, and heard the same comments. He told Miller, "But I said, 'You needn't be for me. I am not going to be a candidate.'"[25]

Meanwhile, Ed Flynn continued to pursue his case for Truman at Roosevelt's bidding. With the president en route by train from Hyde Park to San Diego for an appearance at the naval base there, Bob Hannegan caught up with Roosevelt in the Chicago rail yards of the Rock Island Railroad, where the train was briefly sidetracked. Joined by Mayor Kelly, Hannegan got FDR to write a note addressed to him in longhand: "Dear Bob, you have written me about Harry Truman and Bill Douglas. I should, of course, be very glad to run with either of them and believe that either one of them would bring real strength to the ticket. Always Sincerely, FDR."[26] Roosevelt's implication that he was being sincere as always was a nice if unintentional touch.

Hannegan would have preferred that Roosevelt mention only Truman, but the president chose otherwise. The note was postdated July 19, two days after the opening of the convention, and Hannegan pocketed it, not eager to reveal that it also included Douglas's name. An account of the episode by Roosevelt's secretary, Grace Tully, held that originally the president had written Douglas's name first, to the distress of Hannegan, who feared readers would conclude that Douglas, not Truman, was his prime choice. She wrote that at the earlier White House meeting Hannegan had come out and handed her the letter and told her, "Grace, the president wants you to retype this letter and to switch the names so it will read Harry Truman or Bill Douglas," and that she did so.[27] Later investigation by the Wallace biographers John C. Culver and John Hyde found, however, that both the handwritten and the typed letter bore Truman's name first. So much for the what-could-have-beens of a Douglas presidency and all that could have followed.[28]

At the ensuing convention, when FDR's renomination was confirmed and shouts of "We Want Wallace!" rained down from the galleries, Hannegan finally decided to release to reporters the FDR letter naming both Truman and Douglas. Then, playing his trump card, he arranged a private hotel room meeting with Truman and a few of the other bosses. In a prearranged scenario, the president placed a call to the room. Hannegan picked up the phone and held it away from his ear so that all present could hear. FDR's easily recognized voice blared into the room: "Bob, have you got that fellow lined up yet?" Hannegan replied, "No, Mr. President, he is the contrariest Missouri mule I've ever dealt with." Roosevelt commanded, "Well, you tell him that if he wants to break up the Democratic Party in the middle of a war, that's his responsibility," and hung up. Hannegan turned to Truman: "Now what do you say?" Truman: "Oh, shit. Well, if that's the situation I'll have to say yes, but why the hell didn't he tell me in the first place?"[29]

Truman was nominated in an outcome that the press widely described as a triumph of bossism and Truman as a good but undistinguished man. The *New Republic* wrote, "He will make a passable Vice President, but Truman as President of the United States in times like these?"[30] As for the nominee himself, the first time he saw Roosevelt thereafter he was shocked at the president's faltering physical appearance, realizing that if elected he might soon find himself president.

The defeated Henry Wallace pledged support of the Roosevelt-Truman ticket and campaigned vigorously for it in the fall. Truman meanwhile crisscrossed the country in what clearly was a subordinate role, even though Roosevelt had a limited part in the campaigning for reasons of his health and the war. Those closest to the president observed his weariness and aging but kept it to themselves. Little was said about the question of succession that hung over the campaign.

The Republican *Chicago Tribune,* which in 1948 would claim journalistic infamy with its page-one photo and headline proclaiming, "DEWEY DEFEATS TRUMAN," labeled him "Truman the bankrupt. Truman the pliant tool of Boss Pendergast in looting Kansas City's county government, Truman the yes-man and apologist in the Senate for political gangsters."[31] None of this labeling, however, seriously threatened the Democratic ticket. On Election Day, the result was the closest of the Roosevelt presidency, by a margin of three million votes in winning thirty-six of the forty-eight states over Dewey and John Bricker of Ohio.

Truman eased into the role of president-in-waiting. As a former senator, he was familiar with the ways of the body in which he now became presiding officer, and as such he held an open-door policy toward his old colleagues. One of his first tasks was to encourage the Senate confirmation of Henry Wallace as secretary of commerce in his unusual retention in the administration.

Only two days after the inauguration, FDR, under the deepest secrecy, slipped away aboard the cruiser *Quincy* for Malta, in the Mediterranean, and then on by plane to the Black Sea and the Yalta Conference with Winston Churchill and Joseph Stalin. Truman was left at home with no special instructions on his duties other than to contact the White House if any urgent matter occurred.

Six days after having been sworn in, Truman was faced with a sensitive political decision. His old Missouri benefactor, the Kansas City boss Tom Pendergast, died at age seventy-two, nearly five years after he had finished serving a prison term for conviction of tax evasion. Truman had had no contact with him since that time but decided that as an old friend and recipient of Pendergast's support, he had a personal obligation to attend his funeral in Kansas City. His much-photographed presence drew considerable news-media coverage and criticism, but he declined to turn his back on his old friend.[32]

A couple of weeks later in Washington, Truman showed up at a National Press Club canteen for servicemen and entertained them at the piano. Movie actress Lauren Bacall accommodatingly and alluringly posed on the piano as he played, providing photographers with a field day that brought more criticism down on him. The pictures brought some delight to many fans but not to the vice president's wife, Bess, who told him not to play the piano in public thereafter.[33]

On March 1, after Roosevelt had returned from Yalta, Truman sat behind him on the raised platform of the House chamber. The president reported in optimistic but halting terms the results of that historic meeting, which later was to bring Republican allegations of the "surrender" of Eastern Europe to the Russians. "I saw the president immediately after his speech had been concluded," Truman wrote later. "Plainly he was a very weary man."[34]

The new vice president saw Roosevelt only twice more, on March 8 and March 19, before FDR departed ten days later for his vacation cabin, "the Little White House," in Warm Springs, Georgia, for a hard-earned and much-needed rest. Two weeks later, on the afternoon of April 12, Truman was in the Senate president's chair as routine business droned on. The Senate recessed just before five o'clock. Truman walked over to his office, just off the chamber, and told his aide Harry Vaughn that he would be at House Speaker Sam Rayburn's office if Vaughn had to reach him. Eluding the Secret Service guard recently assigned to him, Truman walked briskly across the Capitol through the rotunda, over to the House side, and down another flight to Rayburn's "Board of Education."

On arrival, Rayburn told Truman, "Steve Early [the White House press secretary] wants you to call him right away." The vice president mixed himself a drink and dialed the White House. A tense Early asked him to come "as quickly and quietly" as he could. According to aide Lew Deschler, who was also present in Rayburn's office, Truman turned pale and declared, "Jesus Christ and General Jackson," a favorite expletive. Then he walked out, ran across the ground floor of the Capitol to his Senate office, grabbed his hat, and left, ordering Vaughn to tell nobody.

His driver took him down Pennsylvania Avenue and entered the northwest gate, where two ushers awaiting him took him to the elevator up to the residential quarters on the second floor. Mrs. Roosevelt was waiting in her study along with Early and her daughter and son-in-law. Greeting Truman, she put her hand on his shoulder and said simply, "Harry, the president is dead." He stood there a moment, before asking her, "Is there anything I can do for you?" She replied, "Is there anything *we* can do for *you*? For you are the one in trouble now."[35]

Only eighty-two days after Truman's swearing-in as vice president, Roosevelt's death of a cerebral hemorrhage had made him president. His first order as chief executive was to authorize Eleanor Roosevelt to use a government plane to fly to Warm Springs. Then he summoned the Roosevelt cabinet and phoned the news to his shaken wife. He took the oath of presidential office, administered by Supreme Court Chief Justice Harlan Fisk Stone, then asked all the cabinet members to remain in their posts.

As they left the room, the senior member, Secretary of War Henry L. Stimson, stayed behind. He told Truman there was a matter of the most utmost importance he needed to discuss with him concerning a new weapon of unbelievable power, but gave him no further details. The next morning, the first of his presidency, Truman went to the Oval Office and met with several cabinet and war officials, including Stimson. But again in the rush and confusion of the new situation, the war secretary told him nothing more of what he had briefly mentioned the night before.

Truman surprised Congress by going to Capitol Hill for lunch with a group of his old legislative friends, mostly from the Senate, and told them earnestly he needed their help. When he came out of the lunch a large group of reporters who had covered him in the Senate were waiting. "Boys, if you ever pray, pray for me now," he said. "I don't know if you fellows ever had a load of hay fall on you, but when they told me yesterday what had happened, I felt like the moon, the stars, and all the planets had fallen on me."[36]

Amazingly, not until twelve days after FDR's death did Stimson remind Truman that he had a most important secret to impart to the president. In a brief letter, the war secretary wrote, "I mentioned it to you shortly after you took office but have not urged it on you since on account of the pressure you have been under. It, however, has a bearing on our present foreign relations and has such an important effect on all our thinking in this field that I think you ought to know about it without further delay."[37]

On April 25, the day the United Nations Conference was opening in San Francisco, Stimson arrived alone at the White House. Later he was joined only by General Leslie G. Graves, head of the Manhattan Project, which developed the atomic bomb. Stimson handed Truman several typewritten pages, the first sentence of which read, "Within four months we shall in all probability have completed the most terrible weapon ever known in human history, one bomb of which could destroy a whole city."[38]

This was arguably the most significant development in terms of world history ever to be placed before any American president, or for that matter any other world leader. There was immediate agreement among the other Allied leaders informed that use of such a weapon would bring a swift end to World War II. Remaining, however, was the concern over what the existence of such a weapon would mean to world survival, especially if the United States were to go ahead and put it to use. In the first months of Truman's presidency, therefore, he was confronted with what turned out to be the most critical decision of the nearly eight years of his fateful presidency.

When his presidency came to an end, in January 1953, Harry S. Truman retired to his home in Independence, later to be judged one of the nation's most respected, even loved, White House occupants and perhaps the best of the nine "accidental presidents." More than any other circumstance, his ascendancy to the Oval Office without knowledge of the atomic bomb offered a paramount reason for keeping vice presidents fully informed of the most critical secrets of the administration in which they are serving.

Roosevelt himself should have told Truman about the bomb's development before his death, particularly as a man who much earlier had proposed the idea of making the vice president a sort of assistant president. At the time, however, FDR already had Byrnes in that role, and upon assuming his fourth term in the presidency, he had rushed off to Yalta with his mind already fully occupied.

Seven weeks after Roosevelt's return, he was dead and Truman was president, only then informed about the greatest military weapon ever developed, now in his hands. He had been chosen for the vice presidency out of purely political considerations by FDR's closest political operatives, without much thought of what sort of national leader he might be if destiny were to so dictate. One might expect that now the lesson would have been learned that the selection requires greater care and wisdom for the benefit of party and nation. Yet vice presidential choices continued to be made often by political calculation and even in some cases by whim, as the occupants largely remained lightly regarded in terms of substantive governance.

CHAPTER 35

ALBEN W. BARKLEY
OF KENTUCKY

A t his party convention in 1948, when President Harry Truman proposed a nominee for his old job of vice president, he first sounded
out Supreme Court Justice William O. Douglas, four years earlier
a finalist in President Franklin Roosevelt's musings on a replacement for the
incumbent Henry Wallace on the Democratic ticket. Douglas was said now
to have brushed off the idea, rather inelegantly, by saying he had no interest
in being "Number Two to a Number Two man."[1] So Truman turned to an
old friend in Senate Majority Leader Alben W. Barkley, one of the chamber's
most loved and respected leaders, who four years earlier had been dismissed
for the job of vice president as too old at age sixty-seven. Now, at seventy-
one, Barkley apparently wasn't too old for Truman, who in hearty health
didn't seem to include possible presidential succession in his reckoning, even
after he himself had reached the presidency by way of it.

Barkley, with his jovial nature, his gift as country storyteller, and his
talent for campaign oratory, made a particular contribution to the lore of
the second office. He became known and loved throughout America as
"the Veep," a nickname his ten-year-old grandson Stephen preferred to
"Mr. Vice President." Telling reporters where it came from, Barkley said,
"I must admit I get a warm feeling when I hear it."[2]

"The Veep" had a storybook beginning, literally born in a log cabin on
the farm of his grandfather Alben Graham Barkley in a tiny town called

Wheel in Graves County, Kentucky, on November 24, 1877. He bragged that he had traced his ancestry back to Roger de Berchelai, a Norman follower of William the Conqueror. A family member, John Berkelley, had come to America and settled in Virginia around 1618, the father of ten children and, four years after arriving, the victim of a fatal Indian attack. Barkley traced his direct lineage to a Scots-Irish Presbyterian named Henry Barkley, born in 1740 in Rowan County, North Carolina, and his son Robert, who fought in the American Revolution. Named Willie Alben Barkley by his father, John Barkley, and his mother, Electra, Alben hated the name "Willie" so went by his middle name, declaring later that he couldn't have stomached "going through a Kentucky childhood with the name of 'Willie' and later trying to get into politics!"[3]

Alben's earliest relatives in politics were two cousins, a Kentucky congressman named James A. McKenzie and Vice President Adlai E. Stevenson, grandfather of the Democratic presidential nominee in 1952 and 1956. As a boy, Alben worked as a hand on the wheat and tobacco farms of neighbors and later worked his way through the small Marvin College as its janitor, while also keeping up with his chores on the family farm. He studied Latin and Greek and honed his skills for later campaign stumping as a member of the Periclean Debating Society, inspired by another Kentuckian, Henry Clay, a one-time National Republican who, in 1844, became the Whig nominee for president.

Young Barkley, however, was an avid Democrat, becoming a proponent of free silver and its brilliant oratorical champion William Jennings Bryan, a man he later met and befriended. He took a job as a traveling salesman of cooking crockery and, after graduation from Marvin, enrolled for a year at Emory College in Oxford, Georgia. Thereafter he taught briefly at Marvin, moved to Paducah, and began reading for a law degree. He became a clerk for the Kentucky congressman Charles K. Wheeler, learning shorthand in the process, and was admitted to the bar in 1901. Two years later, at twenty-five, he married a Paducah girl, Dorothy Brower, and they had a son and two daughters.

In 1905, Barkley ran for and won his first public office, as McCracken County prosecuting attorney. A rumor grew over later years that he had campaigned on a mule. He subsequently wrote in his autobiography, "This story is a base canard, and here and now I want to spike it for all. It was not a mule—it was a horse . . . a one-eyed horse."[4] One of his first duties in office, he wrote later, was to send an old friend to jail, "an embezzling county official" who had been elected on the same ticket with him. "Before the sheriff took him away, I made a point of seeing the man I had convicted. I shook his hand and wished him well. He later rehabilitated himself and remained my good friend; he told me my gesture of friendliness had meant a good deal to him when he was down. I have always remembered that incident and have tried not to judge people too harshly."[5]

From prosecuting attorney, Barkley next was elected as a county administrative judge of the sort that gave Harry Truman his political start in Missouri. In 1912, Barkley ran for the U.S. House of Representatives in a four-man race. All four traveled together by horse and buggy or occasionally an automobile, to keep down expenses. Barkley won, going to Congress on the same day that the Democrat Woodrow Wilson was inaugurated as the president. Soon after Barkley sought an interview with Wilson on a patronage matter and became a disciple of his.

As a newcomer to Washington, Barkley served notice that he did not intend to hang back. Early on he also went to Wilson seeking his support for a constitutional amendment that would end each session of Congress after an election in early January rather than March 4, thus barring defeated legislators from serving so long into the new year. Wilson told Barkley he was sympathetic, but he had too much else on his plate.[6] It was an idea that later came to pass, with Barkley's cosponsorship.

The Kentuckian had differences with Wilson in politics, though not on substance. During the Great War, Barkley advised the president he thought it was a mistake not to go "barnstorming," as Wilson put it, for reelection in the 1916 campaign, an election Wilson nearly lost. In 1918, Barkley advised him not to campaign against his critics in Congress but to ask merely for a Congress sympathetic with his war efforts and the peace objectives. The Democrats lost working majorities in both houses that year. Barkley said later this may have been a factor in the Senate failure to ratify the Versailles Treaty and with it the Covenant of the League of Nations.[7] In 1919, Barkley also appealed to Wilson to push for giving women the right to vote. In October, he voted for prohibition and upon passage observed the law but later voted for its repeal.

In 1923 Barkley ran for governor, traveling across Kentucky and building a reputation for tireless campaign stumping, offering a seemingly endless store of country tales delivered with gusto and a bellowing voice from the frame of a lumberjack. He lost the race, but his efforts were a prelude to his election three years later to the U.S. Senate over the incumbent Republican. By the 1930s, he had risen to an assistant to Senate Majority Leader Joseph T. Robinson of Arkansas.

In 1932, Barkley was called on for the first time to deliver the keynote address at the Democratic National Convention. He triggered a forty-five-minute floor demonstration when he called for repeal of prohibition and as usual talked at great length. Humorist Will Rogers in his newspaper column wrote, "Now comes Senator Barkley with the 'keynote.' What do you mean, 'note'? This was in three volumes. Barkley leaves from here to go to the Olympic Games to run in the marathon. He will win it, too, for that race lasts only three or four hours."[8]

In the campaign that fall, accompanying Franklin D. Roosevelt in Corbin, Kentucky, Barkley told the train-side crowd that he recognized the faces looking up at him from his previous campaign visit to the town four years earlier. "The reason I know you are the same people," he said, "is that after four years of Hoover, you are all wearing the same clothes that you had on four years ago!" FDR roared his approval.[9]

Roosevelt's election ushering in the era of the New Deal found no stronger supporter than Barkley. He wrote later, "We were a sick nation when Franklin D. Roosevelt came into office. I shall never forget the thrill with which the nation responded to his inspiring inaugural declaration that 'the only thing we have to fear is fear itself.' After twelve years of numbing *laissez faire* it was a dynamic experience to serve in the Congress which, in the memorable 'first hundred days' of the Roosevelt administration, began to bring the nation back to health."[10]

In 1936, Barkley again delivered the keynote speech at the Democratic convention. He spoke out on his concern about the Supreme Court's growing resistance to and disagreement with key legislative initiatives by the administration to lift the country out of the Great Depression, questioning the court's narrow grounds for opposition. While he respected the court as an institution, he said, he insisted that the Democratic Party sought only to treat the Constitution as "a living, moving, vital instrument of government not to be preserved in a museum."[11]

Accordingly, after reelection, when Roosevelt suddenly proposed in 1937 that the membership of the Supreme Court be enlarged by the addition of up to six justices, Barkley was generally in sympathy. He was prepared to support FDR, knowing the size of the court had been altered in the past. But FDR dropped the bombshell on Congress, and on his own leaders, without warning or a concerted plan to get his proposal enacted. Both Majority Leader Robinson and Barkley, as his assistant, were caught flat-footed when a rebellion in the Senate's Democratic ranks erupted. The day before the issue was to come up for debate, Robinson called a meeting in his office and concluded after a nose count that the votes for passage were unlikely.

The next morning, Barkley got a phone call telling him Robinson had died of a heart attack in his apartment, alone, with his wife visiting family in Arkansas. The floor fight on the measure was postponed. In the midst of all this chaos, Roosevelt chose to write to Barkley as the acting majority leader of the Senate. But it so happened that Barkley's leadership was not going unchallenged. A Mississippi conservative also was seeking the post, and FDR's "My Dear Alben" salutation was seized upon as evidence that the president was taking Barkley's side in a major Senate matter. In a secret ballot of Democratic senators, Barkley won by a single vote. Afterward, according to Barkley, the president told him, "Although I took no hand in the contest, I'm glad you were elected."[12]

Barkley's leadership of the Senate was in sharp contrast to that of the tough and decisive Robinson. The new leader was more inclined to persuade and compromise with fellow senators while entertaining them with his yarns. He was not as effective in the face of Democratic divisions. As a result, in his first year as leader, some critics nicknamed him "Bumbling Barkley."[13]

But with the advent of World War II, the party became more cohesive in the Senate behind his determined and clear leadership in support of national defense and wartime needs. He facilitated aid to the European Allies through changes in neutrality laws, particularly the enactment of the Lend-Lease Act of 1941, which threw a lifeline to the struggling British.

Later, in 1942, Barkley himself was under consideration for a Supreme Court vacancy, in which he had not expressed an interest. When Roosevelt chose another man in January 1943, he wrote Barkley a note: "Dear Alben:

I do not know whether you will be disappointed or not in this Supreme Court matter. Personally, I would not be." Roosevelt went on to describe Barkley as "a sort of balance wheel [in the Senate] that has kept things moving all these years," explaining further, "I had to come to the conclusion that there are nine Justices but only one Majority Leader in the Senate—and I can't part with him in that capacity."[14]

In 1944, Barkley entertained thoughts of being Roosevelt's running mate, having been extremely engaged in promoting the New Deal agenda as the Senate majority leader. There was, however, one notable exception to Barkley's support. He had just worked exhaustively in getting a $2.3 billion tax bill through the Senate to continue financing the war against Germany and Japan. FDR, having sought a whopping $10.5 billion for that purpose, threatened to veto the bill as woefully inadequate. Barkley told FDR if he sent over a veto he, Barkley, would "be compelled to say something about it in the Senate." Roosevelt replied, "Of course, you have that right."[15]

Barkley's solid support of FDR had been unquestioned up to now, but when the president went ahead with his threatened veto, the majority leader became particularly incensed at the incendiary language Roosevelt used in rejecting the bill. He called it "a tax-relief bill providing relief not for the needy but for the greedy," saying he had asked Congress for "a loaf of bread" and was handed instead "a small piece of crust" of "many extraneous and inedible matters." Barkley wrote, "To me, $2.3 billion is no crust."[16]

The next day Barkley took the Senate floor, angrily charging that the president's message was "a calculated and deliberate assault upon the legislative integrity of every member of Congress," adding, "I do not propose to take this unjustifiable assault lying down." He charged that in reading the tax bill, Roosevelt "had gone forth with a searchlight and magnifying glass to find inconsequential faults."[17] He called a Democratic caucus and resigned his leadership, saying that if Congress had "any self-respect yet left it [would] override the veto."[18] His declaration was greeted on the Senate floor and in the galleries with wild applause, enhancing his esteem in the Senate.

On leaving the Senate Democratic caucus, Barkley was besieged by awaiting reporters seeking his comment. "Boys," he told them in classic

Barkley style, "I'm afraid I'm like the Swede who proposed to his girl while driving. She said yes, and then they drove along for five miles in silence. Finally she asked him, 'Why don't you say something?' The Swede replied, "Ay tank Ay say too much already!'"[19]

Surprised at the resignation, Roosevelt wrote Barkley another "Dear Alben" letter, urging him to reconsider and urging his fellow senators not to accept the resignation or to "immediately and unanimously" reelect him. Barkley was indeed reelected, and the House and Senate overwhelmingly overrode and killed the FDR veto. In his conciliatory letter, Roosevelt concluded, "Your differing with me does not affect my confidence in our leadership nor in any degree lessen my respect and affection for you personally."[20] But Barkley wrote later, "I am in no position to state with certainty that the episode revolving around Mr. Roosevelt and me over this tax bill affected my future political career. Nevertheless it is legitimate to reflect on what might have happened if this episode had not transpired."[21]

Roosevelt's selection of Truman over Barkley did not seem to sour the Senate leader's relations with his old Senate colleague when Truman became president. They became an effective team in pushing further New Deal legislation, now labeled the Fair Deal under Truman. But when tough economic times returned and the Republicans took over control of the House and Senate for the first time since the Great Depression, Barkley was reduced to the Senate minority leadership. In the approach to the 1948 presidential election, it seemed a foregone conclusion that Truman would lose a bid for reelection to the Republican Tom Dewey, nominated a second time after his defeat by FDR in 1944. Therefore, it seemed also that the Democratic vice presidential nomination would be worth even less.

Prior to the convention, Truman's aide Clark Clifford passed the word to insiders that the president had telephoned Supreme Court Justice William O. Douglas, bypassed by FDR in 1944 for Truman as his running mate, and sounded him out about taking the nomination this time around. Douglas wanted time to consider, but he finally said he wasn't interested. An insulted Truman, mixing his metaphors, told a friend, "I stuck my neck all the way out for Douglas and he cut the limb out from under me."[22]

At the Democratic National Convention in Philadelphia, Barkley again was chosen to deliver the keynote address, this time to a glum and dispirited party anticipating the worst outcome. He rose to the occasion, firing up the delegates with a classic Barkley assault on the Republicans. Chiding the Republicans for attacking the New Deal, he asked, "What is this cankering, corroding, fungus growth which every Republican orator . . . denounced with unaccustomed rancor, then in their adopted platform hugged to their political bosom as if it were a child of their own loins? It was recovery. The new Roosevelt administration breathed into the nostrils of every worthy American enterprise a breath of new life, new hope and new determination."[23]

The demonstration that followed Barkley's stirring battle cry lasted so long that many said later he had talked himself into the vice presidential nomination. Farley said, "The convention made up the President's mind for him" on his running mate.[24] In any event, in light of the convention's reaction, Truman phoned Barkley the next day, congratulating him on the speech and offering him the nomination. "Why didn't you tell me you wanted to be Vice President?" he asked. "I didn't know you wanted the nomination." Later, Barkley wrote of his reply, which sounded a bit haughty: "Mr. President, you do not know it yet." Truman responded, "Well, if I had known you wanted it, I certainly would have been agreeable"—hardly a ringing endorsement. Barkley replied that if it was the will of the convention he would accept but added that the nomination would have to come quickly. He explained rather petulantly, "I am not interested in any biscuits that have been passed around hot to other people and come to me cold."[25] According to his wishes, he was nominated unanimously.

In a fighting speech given at two in the morning, arousing the slumping delegates, Truman assured them, "Senator Barkley and I will win this election and make these Republicans like it—don't you forget it!" He assaulted "the worst Eightieth Congress" ever and announced he would be calling it back into a special session to act on an array of liberal bills, saying about the legislators, "They can do this job in fifteen days if they want to do it. They will still have time to go out and run for office" afterward.[26]

In the most dramatic whistle-stop presidential campaign up to this time, Truman rode the rails across the nation attacking the Republican "do-nothing Congress." Barkley saw him off from Union Station with "Mow 'em down!" to which Truman replied, "I'll mow 'em down, Alben, and I'll give 'em hell!" which became his campaign battle cry.[27] At the same time, Barkley tirelessly introduced the prop-stop campaign, flying in a chartered DC-3 nicknamed *The Bluegrass* across thirty-six states in six weeks in support of the winning ticket in November.

As vice president, Barkley undertook presiding over the Senate he had for so long and so recently ruled as the Democratic leader. He had less influence in its deliberations than he had had as its majority leader, but his experience in the Senate made him a valuable aide to Truman, through his long personal friendships and associations. He attended Democratic committee meetings, sat in on Truman cabinet sessions, and was the first vice president to be made a member of the National Security Council under the 1947 act creating it.

During Barkley's vice presidency, however, the Democratic majority had shrunk to only two seats, and his parliamentary rulings from the chair were sometimes challenged successfully. In 1949, when he ruled against a point of order by the segregationist Democratic senator Richard B. Russell in a civil rights debate, he was overridden by the Senate. But other senators lauded him for taking a principled stand to end the southern filibuster.[28]

In the summer of 1949, Barkley, a widower, suddenly electrified and entertained social Washington with a whirlwind courtship, after which he married a widow, Jane Rucker Hadley of St. Louis, thirty-four years his junior. They had met at a dinner party given by her friends Clark Clifford, the Truman counsel, and his wife, Marny. They became favored guests on the capital social circuit.

In 1950, Barkley was making a speech in Illinois when he was notified of the attempted assassination of Truman by Puerto Rican nationalists while he stayed temporarily at Blair House, across Pennsylvania Avenue from the White House. As a consequence, Truman ordered Secret Service protection for the vice president, and five agents were assigned. Barkley balked and got the squad reduced to two, playing games with them, once eluding their shadow by hopping on a Washington bus just to take a ride.[29]

During the Korean War, Truman left the congressional campaigning of 1950 to Barkley, and although the Democrats suffered some losses, they retained control of both the House and Senate. In 1952, before Truman said whether he would seek another term, which was possible under an exemption in the Twenty-Second Amendment, Barkley actively pondered a presidential candidacy of his own. Truman expressed his affection for "Old Barkley" but noted that at seventy-four his age was a factor against him.

At the time, however, Truman apparently had two other men in mind for the Democratic presidential nomination. One was General Dwight D. Eisenhower, commander of the Great Crusade in Europe, which had vanquished Nazi Germany. The other was a rising political star, Governor Adlai E. Stevenson II of Illinois, grandson of a previous vice president under Grover Cleveland and, as it happened, a distant cousin of Barkley. Eisenhower, courted by both major parties, finally decided to run for the presidency as a Republican. Stevenson, while having announced he would run for reelection as governor, was called to the White House by Truman to consider seeking it in the event that Truman decided not to run for another term. Afterward, Stevenson called Barkley, told the vice president of his visit to Truman, and sought his advice. Barkley quickly informed him that he was thinking of running for the presidency himself.

In late March of the presidential election year, Truman announced he would not run. The other leading Democrat was Senator Estes Kefauver of Tennessee. Barkley didn't believe Kefauver could win and finally decided to announce that while he would not actively seek the nomination, he would accept it. About a week before the opening of the convention, Barkley got a call in Paducah to attend a "must" conference in Washington. The party chairman Frank McKinney opened the session, according to Barkley, by telling him, directly in the president's presence, that Truman had decided to back him for the nomination. McKinney said the president would not make a public statement to that effect but would urge his Missouri delegation to support Barkley. At this point, Barkley wrote later, he asked, "What about Governor Stevenson?" He was told that it was certain he would not run.

In the end, Barkley met at the convention with sixteen top labor leaders, asking their support. They all turned him down, saying they still liked and admired him, but he was now too old for the job. That afternoon, he called Truman and told him he was withdrawing from the race.[30]

In the ensuing campaign Barkley backed the nomination of his distant cousin Stevenson and his running mate, Senator John J. Sparkman of Alabama, in their futile effort to beat the national hero Eisenhower and his ticket mate, Senator Richard M. Nixon of California. After the inauguration of the Republicans, the Barkleys attended a reception at the home of the former secretary of state Dean Acheson. The gathering of the defeated Democrats occasioned Barkley to recall the story of the French husband whose wife had died and her paramour cried broken-heartedly at her funeral, at which the husband consoled, "Don't take it so hard, my friend. I shall marry again."[31]

Two years after retiring to Kentucky at age seventy-six, Barkley won back his old Senate seat from the incumbent Republican. His victory contributed to a one-seat Democratic majority that made Senator Lyndon Johnson of Texas the majority leader. On April 30, 1956, Barkley delivered another keynote address with his customary gusto, this time to a mock convention at Washington and Lee University. He ended by saying that after all his years in the Senate, he had become a freshman again and was "glad to sit on the back row," adding, "for I would rather be a servant in the House of the Lord than to sit in the seats of the mighty." Thereupon, as the student audience heartily applauded, Alben W. Barkley collapsed on the spot and died of a massive heart attack at age seventy-nine.[32]

As "the Veep," he may have been the most publicly beloved of all the men to serve in the office, but few would argue he was very influential. Barkley's advanced age and inexperience in foreign policy left questions concerning the wisdom of Truman's selection in terms of potential presidential succession, barely three years after he himself had experienced having "the moon, the stars, and all the planets" dropped on him.

CHAPTER 36

RICHARD M. NIXON
OF CALIFORNIA

S eldom was the selection of a vice presidential nominee less relevant to the outcome of an election than was that of the Republican Richard Milhous Nixon in 1952. The huge popularity of the party's presidential nominee, General Dwight D. Eisenhower, leader of the Great Crusade against Nazi Germany during 1941–45, assured a landslide victory for the Eisenhower-Nixon team.

In that 1952 election, as a junior senator from California, Nixon rode Eisenhower's coattails into national prominence. What little drama there was in the campaign came from a controversy surrounding Nixon's financial support. He deftly extricated himself and the GOP ticket from it with a television performance for which long afterward he has been remembered.

This controversy, the only perceived threat to Eisenhower's election, involved the disclosure of a "secret Nixon fund" raised by wealthy Californians to cover the travels of Eisenhower's running mate, seized upon by the Democrats to cast the vice presidential nominee as a bought candidate. Nixon confronted the allegations by going on national television with a plea of middle-class frugality, capped by his defense of keeping his daughter Julie's dog, Checkers, the gift of a political contributor. Nixon urged viewers to call or write the Republication National Committee to say whether he should withdraw from the ticket, and predictably the vote was overwhelmingly in his favor, effectively taking the decision on his fate from Eisenhower's hand.

The maneuver was in keeping with Nixon's skill in political self-preservation up to that time and long thereafter, in the vice presidency and in his public career that followed. Only the crimes of the Watergate break-in of the Democratic National Committee in 1972, whose cover-up was engineered by Nixon and exposed in a tenacious Senate committee investigation, dramatically drove him into political exile.

Richard Nixon was born in the small Southern California town of Yorba Linda, in suburban Los Angeles, on the morning of January 9, 1913, the second son of Frank and Hannah Milhous Nixon. The father was a onetime trolley driver and fruit ranch hand, and the mother a devout Quaker and graduate of nearby Whittier College. They lived in a small clapboard bungalow built by Frank the year before Nixon's birth, and a year later a third son, Francis Donald, was born, joining Richard and Harold, then five years old.

The Milhous clan was of German-Irish Quaker stock who settled in the William Penn colony in eastern Pennsylvania in 1729, migrated to Indiana in 1854, and moved to Southern California in the late 1880s. The Nixon side, of English, Scottish, and Irish roots, first settled in northern Delaware in 1731 and fought in the Revolutionary War. Frank Nixon was born in Ohio in 1878 and became a motorman in Los Angeles in 1907.[1] After a failed effort to raise lemon trees, Frank abandoned the orchard in 1919, as well as subsequent hopes to find oil on the land. The father took the setbacks hard. He was a stern disciplinarian with his sons, but Richard earned a reputation as an intelligent, studious, and solitary young man.[2] With his mother's encouragement, he took piano lessons, maintained excellent grades in school, and helped at the grocery the family ran for a time. He had his first involvement in politics at Whittier High School, where he won an oratorical contest as part of a debating team. Later when he attended the local Whittier College, he was on the football team but played little as a third-stringer. He was, however, elected student president in his senior year, graduated second in his class, and went on to Duke Law School on a scholarship. He passed the California bar in 1937 and joined a Whittier law firm. In the meantime he had met Thelma Ryan, called Patricia or Pat, a graduate of the University of Southern California, a fellow amateur among the Whittier Community Players, and a new teacher at Whittier Union High School. In 1940 they married.[3]

By the time war came with the attack on Pearl Harbor, Nixon had already been recruited through a Duke faculty member to join the Office of Price Administration in Washington. But in mid-August 1942 he quit that position, enlisted in the navy, and handled transportation duties in the South Pacific, in Bougainville and on Green Island in New Guinea. He returned to San Diego in 1944 and then finished out his enlistment at a naval facility in Maryland. In September 1945 some Whittier Republican businessmen summoned him from Maryland to California to consider running for Congress against the five-term incumbent Democrat, Jerry Voorhis. Nixon showed up wearing his naval uniform and was chosen to take on the liberal Voorhis in 1946. In a debate, Nixon attacked Voorhis as the tool of a labor political action committee that Nixon described as communist-infiltrated—establishing a pattern of negative campaigning that would mark much of his career.

There actually were two such labor groups, the one supporting Voorhis not a union offshoot and not targeted by critics for communist ties. Nixon's campaign manager, Murray Chotiner, intentionally tied Voorhis to the suspected communist front, and in the debate Nixon confronted Voorhis with a mimeographed copy of that labor group's endorsement of the Democratic candidate. On Election Night, Nixon won 57 percent of the vote, part of a nationwide Republican sweep of Congress.[4]

Sworn in as a member of the House of Representatives in January 1947, Nixon was placed on the House Un-American Activities Committee (HUAC). Amid the growing public fears of communism, which were raised by the right wing of the GOP, the committee was made to order for Nixon, fresh from his exploitation of the "Red Scare" in the campaign against Voorhis. He gained central stage in the case of the State Department official Alger Hiss, who was brought before the committee and accused of past communist affiliations by a *Time* magazine editor and former member of the Communist Party, Whittaker Chambers. Before a subcommittee chaired by Nixon, Hiss first denied having ever met Chambers but then acknowledged he had met him by another name. Chambers accompanied HUAC investigators to a pumpkin patch on his farm on Maryland's Eastern Shore, where he extracted from a hollowed-out pumpkin some undeveloped films of State Department documents and other material—the soon-famous Pumpkin Papers. The sensational story kept Nixon in the headlines into early 1950, when Hiss was indicted and finally convicted of perjury. With the statute of limitations having run out on any possible espionage charges, Hiss served forty-four months of a five-year jail sentence.[5]

After only four years in the House, Nixon decided to run for the Senate seat against the three-term Democratic congresswoman and glamorous actress Helen Gahagan Douglas, wife of the Broadway and Hollywood star Melvyn Douglas. She was an aggressive critic of HUAC and of Nixon's methods, and her staunchly liberal views made her an obvious target for Nixon's aggressive tactics. Her attacks on HUAC's Red-baiting and on a loyalty oath that California required from its state university faculty cemented her nickname as "the pink lady," which the Nixon campaign adopted. The Nixon headquarters then widely circulated what came to be known as "the Pink Sheet," a flyer printed on pink paper detailing the most prominent votes she shared with the left-wing New Yorker Vito Marcantonio, while boasting that Nixon had "voted exactly opposite to the Douglas-Marcantonio Axis!"[6] Douglas took to referring to Nixon as "Tricky Dick," the label destined to stick to him the rest of his political career. Nixon insisted, "If there is a smear involved, let it be remembered that the record itself is doing the smearing."[7] But many years later in a memoir, Nixon's longtime press adviser Herb Klein acknowledged, "The pink sheet was a smearing distortion."[8] Nonetheless, on Election Night, Nixon routed the actress-politician by nearly seven hundred thousand votes.

Shortly after Nixon's victory, his finance chairman for that campaign began soliciting prominent California supporters for a bank account to help pay for expenses in an active incumbency, just as had been done for Nixon when he was in the House. Known simply as "the fund," its donors were mainly Southern California oil and manufacturing men who had been in on the ground floor of Nixon's political career.[9] He used the money for travel, mail, and other practical expenses, including Christmas cards to donors.

Many of Nixon's California enthusiasts reasoned that his next political step might well be the governorship, with the incumbent, Earl Warren, considered unlikely to seek a fourth term and instead to pursue a presidential bid in 1952. Nixon was committed to Warren, the state's favorite son, but had his eye on another prospective presidential candidate, General Dwight D. Eisenhower. Nixon attended a secret meeting of Eisenhower supporters at which the former Minnesota governor Harold Stassen was urged to run for president as a stalking horse against the other leading prospect, Senator Robert A. Taft, to ease the path for Eisenhower if he could be persuaded to run as a Republican.[10] Earl Warren's own presidential hopes would ride on a Taft-Eisenhower deadlock at the Republican convention. Nixon repeated his endorsement of Warren while also urging Eisenhower to get into the race, saying, "He owes it to his party to state his views before the nominations are made."[11]

Tom Dewey, keeping Nixon secretly onboard, dangled the vice presidential nomination with Eisenhower under his nose. In late May at the Texas party convention, the Taft forces elected their slate to the Chicago convention, obliging the Ike supporters to send a competing delegation. The Eisenhower strategists raised an issue of "fair play" that would appeal to delegations with favorite-son candidates, like California, joining in.

When Warren and the state delegation boarded the train from Sacramento to Chicago on July 3, Nixon was not aboard. He joined it in Denver and set out on what later was dubbed "the great train robbery" of separating the California delegation from its unwitting governor. For his own "guidance," Nixon undertook a secret poll of California delegates' preference for an alternative if Warren were to bow out. Warren was furious at the gambit and demanded that the poll results, indicating stronger support for Eisenhower than for Taft, not be published, and Nixon was so "ordered," but inevitably they were leaked.

With Nixon functioning as what Dewey later called a "fifth column" within the California delegation, Nixon declared the nomination "still wide open," adding with feigned detachment that if either Taft or Eisenhower was nominated, the delegation would press for the state's more conservative senior senator, William F. Knowland, for the vice presidency.[12]

Having completed his undercover work aboard the train, Nixon slipped off at Cicero, outside Chicago, and was taken by car into the city. When the train pulled into Union Station, the waiting buses, which earlier had been decked out with banners reading "Warren for President," now read "Eisenhower for President," with the switch suspected as Murray Chotiner's handiwork, adding to Warren's agitation and anger at Nixon.[13] The

California delegation caucused on the proposed "fair play amendment," which would prevent previously seated Taft delegates from voting on more than a hundred contested delegates. Nixon seized the microphone, arguing that the Taft delegates be excluded on the grounds that they had been illegally chosen. The fair play amendment easily carried. Many Californians thought they were helping Warren's cause, and the Texas delegates for Eisenhower were seated.

Later, the Dewey associate Herb Brownell asked Eisenhower whether he had a preference for his running mate. "I thought the convention had to do that," he replied, apparently unaware he had any say in the matter.[14] After briefly mentioning some other names, they agreed on Nixon. The next day, for all the maneuvering over the California delegation, it held firm for Warren on the first ballot, which ended with Eisenhower leading with 595 delegates compared with 500 for Taft. Then Minnesota, previously behind Stassen, switched to the general, and he was nominated. Henry Cabot Lodge walked over to the California delegation and informed Nixon that the vice presidential nomination was his, and he immediately accepted.

As the fall campaign began, running mate Nixon quickly embraced the traditional role as attack dog, referring to the Democratic presidential nominee, Stevenson, as "sidesaddle Adlai," who "like all sidesaddle riders, his feet hang well out to the left."[15] Soon, however, he was to take center stage with the disclosure of and intense news-media focus on that little fund from California helpmates. When a panelist on *Meet the Press* in mid-September asked Nixon about it, he referred the questioner to the Californian handling the fund.

By this time, word of the slush fund had been trumpeted by the then-liberal *New York Post* under the headline "SECRET NIXON FUND!" Based on a report that some of the money went to hire the Nixons a maid, the subhead read, "Secret Rich Men's Trust Fund Keeps Nixon in Style Far beyond His Salary."[16] Back in California the Nixon campaign train was now wending its way through the Central Valley and just pulling out of the small town of Marysville when a voice called out to the candidate, "Tell 'em about the $16,000!"—the amount reported in some of the newspaper accounts.[17] Nixon, hearing it, ordered the train halted and made a full-throated defense of the fund on the grounds that his use of it actually saved taxpayers' money.

Meanwhile, the Democratic National Chairman, Stephen Mitchell, called on Eisenhower to demand Nixon's resignation from the ticket. The general, fighting on a battlefield unfamiliar to him, expressed to reporters on his train his confidence that Nixon was an honest man, but added, "Of what avail is it to carry on this crusade against this business of what has been going on in Washington if we ourselves aren't clean as a hound's tooth?"[18]

Under pressure from both Dewey and Eisenhower to tell his side of the story, Nixon agreed, and the result was the famous "Checkers speech," which ultimately prevented the expulsion of young Julie's spaniel and kept her father on the 1952 Republican ticket. With wife Pat sitting just to his side, Nixon proceeded to lay out his personal financial history, mixing facts and figures with a heavy dose of sentimentality that included his disclosure: "Pat doesn't have a mink coat but she does have a respectable Republican cloth coat, and I always tell her that she'd look good in anything."[19] Nixon called on viewers to write to the Republican National Committee— notably, not to Eisenhower—and say whether they thought he should stay on the ticket or resign.[20] Soon after, a telegram finally arrived from Eisenhower urging him to meet the presidential candidate's entourage in Wheeling, West Virginia, for a dramatic, heavily photographed reunion. Ike read a wire from the party national chairman, Arthur Summerfield, reporting overwhelming support for keeping Nixon on the ticket. The Eisenhower-Nixon team would remain intact.

With his place on the Republican ticket assured, Nixon resumed his campaign with a vengeance. He labeled Stevenson "Mr. Truman's stooge" and "a graduate of Dean Acheson's spineless school of diplomacy which cost the free world six million former allies in the past seven years of Trumanism." He reminded voters of his own role in the Hiss case whenever possible, characterizing Stevenson's defense of the former State Department official as "going down the line for the arch traitor of our generation." Nixon topped even himself by blasting Stevenson as having "a Ph.D. degree from Acheson's College of Cowardly Communist Containment."[21] Stevenson responded by accusing Nixon of practicing "McCarthyism in a white collar."[22] On the positive side, all the Republicans needed was their indisputable slogan: "I Like Ike." By Election Night, the results were predictable: an Eisenhower-Nixon landslide.

Once in office, Eisenhower made Nixon chairman of a committee overseeing government contracts, invited him to sit with the cabinet, and asked him to intervene with his friend Joe McCarthy to try to moderate his behavior. In part to get Nixon away from Red-hunting and in part to educate him in foreign policy, Eisenhower sent him on a seventy-day tour of Asia, during which he visited nineteen countries for substantive talks with national leaders.

In the second year, however, with important congressional elections approaching, Eisenhower put Nixon back on the campaign trail as the administration's designated hitter. McCarthy made clear, with polls indicating a spurt in his popularity, that he had no intention of keeping his promise to Nixon to cool down his politically advantageous hunt for communist subversion. In time, however, when McCarthy tried to subpoena a key White House aide and Eisenhower asserted executive privilege against it, the Senate voted to "condemn" its surly member, sending him into political oblivion. Two years later, he died of alcoholism. Not until the second half of October 1954 did Eisenhower stir himself to hit the campaign trail for the midterm congressional elections, and for all of Nixon's energies, the Republicans lost seventeen House seats, two in the Senate, and control of both chambers.

In 1955, Eisenhower sent Nixon on a second foreign trip, to Central America and the Caribbean, and when Eisenhower himself went to Geneva for a summit on arms control, he asked Nixon to preside over a cabinet meeting and another with the legislative leaders. Meanwhile, Ike mused about possible successors if he didn't seek reelection, and Nixon was among four men on the list, although behind the secretary of the navy and former Texas banker Robert B. Anderson. But Eisenhower was in apparent good health and on the top of his game.

On the afternoon of September 24, 1955, Eisenhower's press secretary, Jim Hagerty, called Nixon from Denver, where the president had been vacationing, telling him, "The President has had a coronary."[23] Hagerty passed on Ike's orders that Nixon was to continue to run cabinet and National Security Council meetings in his absence, to demonstrate the government was functioning without letup. In the cabinet room, Nixon purposely took his regular chair, not the president's, and gave the Oval Office a wide berth, operating out of his office as president of the Senate on Capitol Hill.

As for the conduct of foreign policy, Eisenhower pointedly informed Nixon that Secretary of State Dulles was to remain in charge.[24]

The Eisenhower men did not want to encourage any talk other than that their leader would make a full recovery and run again. When he rebounded and finally agreed to seek a second term, it became known he was considering a new running mate for 1956, with the focus again on Bob Anderson of Texas. The Eisenhower speechwriter Emmet Hughes wrote that the president had told him of Nixon, "I've watched Dick a long time and he just hasn't grown. So I just haven't honestly been able to believe that he is presidential timber."[25]

In December, Eisenhower had a three-hour conversation with Hagerty about possible successors, throwing out such names as Tom Dewey, Earl Warren, and the president's brother Milton. Ike finally asked his press secretary, "What about Nixon?" Hagerty told him he thought he was fine as his running mate but not as a president. So on the day after Christmas, the president called Nixon in and dropped a political bomb on him. In deciding whether to seek a second term and taking note of his recent heart attack, he said he had hoped that after four years the Republican Party would be strong enough to elect someone else. But it hadn't happened and that Nixon's own popularity had not climbed "as high as he had hoped it would." Therefore, he said, it might be better for Nixon to get off the ticket for 1956 and accept a Cabinet post that would boost his standing in the country.[26] Nixon was dumbstruck.

Eisenhower told him he could have any job except secretary of state or attorney general, which were secure for Dulles and Brownell. What about secretary of defense? Nixon said he would agree only if Ike thought his administration would be better served if Nixon got off the ticket. But obviously he was of no mind to cut his own political throat. After New Year's, Eisenhower brought up the subject several other times, and when Nixon responded the same way each time, Ike would patronizingly say only, "I think we've got to do what's best for you."[27]

The matter dragged on until the end of February, when Eisenhower finally announced he would run again, with his doctors' blessing. He ducked on whether Nixon would be his running mate. At his next weekly news conference, he dodged again, saying, "I told him he would have to chart his own course and tell me what he would like to do."[28] The awkward situation dragged on for another two months. Finally in late April, Nixon bit the bullet and told Ike he believed the best course for both of them was for him to be his running mate again, and Eisenhower, perhaps trapped by his own indecision, acceded.

In early June, Nixon's position of being "a heartbeat away from the presidency" raised some more temporary concern when Eisenhower suffered a sudden attack of ileitis, an intestinal affliction that required a two-hour surgical procedure. But the patient recovered rapidly, and Nixon replicated his role as a benign standby, which had won him praise during Ike's coronary experience.

Still, Nixon was not in the clear. Harold Stassen, now an Eisenhower aide on arms control, suddenly launched a stop-Nixon effort. But the president cut it off, and Eisenhower and Nixon were easily renominated. Ike gave Nixon his marching orders to defend the administration against the renominated Stevenson's attacks but with the caution that it wasn't necessary to attack him personally.

When for the most part Nixon complied, the traveling press corps began writing about a "New Nixon." When Stevenson derided him as "a man of many masks" who "has put away his switchblade and now assumes the aspect of an Eagle Scout," Nixon simply turned the other cheek,[29] speaking of the economic prosperity and the booming stock market of the first Eisenhower years, the peace achieved in Korea, and the lull in the Cold War.

In the last week of the campaign, when the British, French, and Israelis attacked Egypt and the Soviet Union suppressed a people's uprising in Hungary, support for Eisenhower as a military hero surged. The most Stevenson was able to make out of the situation was to raise the specter of a Nixon presidency if Eisenhower were reelected. "Distasteful as this matter is," he said in allusion to Eisenhower's health and age, "I must say that every piece of scientific evidence we have, every lesson of history and experience, indicates that a Republican victory tomorrow would mean that Richard M. Nixon would probably be president of this country within the next four years."[30] But voters again were focused on and enamored of Eisenhower, not Nixon, and the Republican ticket won a second landslide victory, though the Democrats retained control of Congress by a slightly larger margin.

The second Eisenhower-Nixon term began quietly, though jolted by the sudden emergence of a space race with the Soviet Union. The firing of the first man-made satellite, called Sputnik, challenged the assumed American technological superiority. Nine months into the term, however, presidential succession intruded again. Nixon was summoned to the White House and informed that Eisenhower had suffered a stroke and was "confused and disoriented." Aide Sherman Adams told him, "You may be president in twenty-four hours." But the next morning Nixon and Adams called on Eisenhower at his bedside and found him stable and alert. Nixon held his first press conference at the White House, saying, "I would like to scotch once and for all any reports that the President is in a condition that would make it necessary for him to consider resigning."[31]

The matter of succession now had Ike's attention. He wrote a draft letter of resignation and gave copies to Nixon, Dulles, and Rogers, saying that if he were disabled and aware of it, he would simply direct Nixon to take over. If he were too disabled, Nixon would make the determination and "serve as Acting President until the disability had ended." The president wrote he hoped Nixon would consult with Adams, Dulles, and his doctors but that Nixon would be "the individual explicitly and exclusively responsible," then added, "I will be the one to determine if and when it is proper for me to resume the full exercise of the powers and duties of the office."[32]

In all it was a remarkable assignment of power to Nixon. Eisenhower intended that the letter be secret, but when he told the press of its existence there was such a clamor that Hagerty finally released pertinent segments. The letter raised more questions about legality and implementation than it answered. Fortunately the president recovered without the plan having to be followed.

Meanwhile, Nixon agreed to undertake an eighteen-day tour of South America. In late April 1958, his traveling party was well received in the first stops, until Caracas, Venezuela. Riding in a closed limousine, the Nixons were pelted with rocks and other objects, forcing the motorcade to stop. The mob rocked Nixon's limo, forcing them to take refuge in the American Embassy. There, apologetic Venezuelan government officials called on a cool and controlled American vice president, who made the most politically of the imbroglio.

The trip alerted the administration to the need for a more vigorous diplomacy in South America and was a major boost for Nixon. The Gallup

Poll in June showed him leading Stevenson as a potential foe in 1960 and running close to Senator John F. Kennedy. On the eve of the 1958 congressional elections, Dewey for one advised Nixon to stay out of them: "Your conduct in South America finally has taken the blinders from eyes of many Democrats. . . . You are a national asset that should not be wasted." But when Eisenhower told him, "I would give a year of my salary if we could win either the House or the Senate,"[33] Nixon had no choice. He campaigned in twenty-five states, covering twenty-five thousand miles, yet the Republicans lost forty-eight seats in the House and twelve in the Senate.

In 1959, Eisenhower's brother Milton dreamed up an idea that the president embraced as a means to lighten his workload—the creation of two assistant presidents, one in charge of foreign policy and the other of domestic affairs. But Nixon and Dulles both saw it as a means of putting another layer between the president and the cabinet, and Nixon particularly viewed such a development as a diminution of his influence. The idea was dropped.

In July, Nixon went to Moscow to open an exhibition on American life as part of a cultural exchange program and to meet with the Soviet premier, Nikita Khrushchev. Part of the Nixon visit was to be shown on Russian television. At an exhibition including a model American home, the two men heatedly argued the comparative merits of their countries' technological and economic advances, in what came to be known as "the kitchen debate." Nixon was captured on camera pointing his finger aggressively at Khrushchev.[34] The Nixons spent five more days touring the Soviet Union and returned to a hearty Washington reception and wave of public approval.

It was now the fall of 1959, approaching the last year of Eisenhower's final term under the Twenty-Second Amendment's two-term limit, and Eisenhower was still silent on his choice for a successor. The only credible potential challenger to Nixon was Governor Nelson Rockefeller of New York, elected by a landslide the previous November. But he turned down entreaties of New Hampshire Republicans to challenge Nixon in their first-in-the-nation presidential primary, which Nixon won easily. With Rockefeller in the wings, Nixon flew to New York for a late-night dinner at which he made a direct pitch to Rocky to run with him. The governor repeated that he had no interest in being vice president, later arguing that he was not built "to be standby equipment." After more than six hours of negotiation over various convention platform planks, they signed what came to be known as the "Compact of Fifth Avenue." Conservative Republicans, distressed that Nixon had made a secret pilgrimage to the liberal New York governor, called it "surrender." But Nixon insisted he had won out by getting the governor to drop certain language critical of Eisenhower's defense policy. Most important politically, the trip erased the last potential barrier to Nixon's nomination.[35]

The convention chose Nixon by acclamation, and, after meeting with a host of party leaders, he announced that Senator Henry Cabot Lodge of Massachusetts would be his running mate. Lodge was Eisenhower's favorite for the nomination, but the president in all was not of much material help to Nixon. In an August news conference, when asked to give an example of a Nixon idea that he had adopted, Eisenhower replied, "If you give me a week I might think of one. I don't remember."[36] Interestingly at the next presidential press conference, nobody asked.

The highlight of the fall campaign against the Democratic team of Kennedy and Johnson was a series of four nationally televised debates between the presidential nominees. Eisenhower had advised Nixon not to debate Kennedy, but his vice president was extremely confident of his debating skills, especially after his encounter with Khrushchev, so he ignored the counsel.[37] The first debate was on foreign policy, and on the basis of his globe-trotting experience, Nixon was generally seen to have an advantage going in. But Kennedy's strong self-confidence and grasp of the issues, coupled with a visibly weary and deferential performance by Nixon, turned the tables. Nixon had unwisely pledged to visit all fifty states, and the ordeal had left him ragged before the television cameras compared with the alert, fresh, and handsome Kennedy. Television viewers polled afterward rated Kennedy the winner, even though many radio listeners thought Nixon had the better answers.

The remaining three televised debates were anti-climactic, now that Kennedy had demonstrated that his youth, at forty-three, and his lack of comparable experience were not handicaps. In a nail-biting Election Night, Nixon went down to defeat by three-tenths of 1 percent of the vote—49.9 for Kennedy, 49.6 for Nixon—but by 303–219 in the electoral college. As the most visible of all vice presidents up to that time, Nixon licked his wounds and two years later ran for governor of California but lost again, leading him to tell reporters memorably in Los Angeles, "You won't have Nixon to kick around anymore, because, gentlemen, this is my last press conference."[38]

It was, of course, not his last. Six years later he ran for the presidency again and was elected in 1968 and reelected in 1972, until brought down by the break-in of the Democratic National Committee headquarters at the Watergate office complex in 1972 and the subsequent White House cover-up. These events led to his resignation on August 8, 1974, after which Nixon went into virtual exile in California. Thereafter, however, he wrote several books on public policy and a long memoir that kept his ideas before the country, even as he remained out of party and public affairs until his death on April 22, 1994.

Richard Nixon probably did more than any previous vice president to elevate the office in the eyes of average Americans. But what followed ultimately obscured that distinction. His role of goodwill ambassador around the world won him much notoriety and acclaim. In political seasons, however, the role of the president's and the party's hatchet man and the Watergate scandal colored much of the American public's view of him. His pursuit of politics at all costs eventually brought him to the Oval Office, but in the end it also drove him from it.

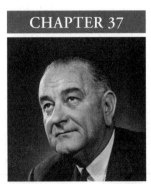

CHAPTER 37

LYNDON B. JOHNSON

OF TEXAS

D espite the gestures of some presidents to give their understudies a more significant role in their administrations, the reputation of the vice presidency remained low in the minds of power wielders in Washington in the mid-twentieth century. So when Senate Majority Leader Lyndon Johnson was approached in 1960 by the Democratic presidential nominee, John F. Kennedy, to be his running mate, Johnson's acceptance was both surprising and puzzling. As a tough, overbearing, and crafty politician, he was widely regarded at the time as second only to the president himself in terms of influence in national public affairs.

Why Kennedy wanted Johnson, however, was easy to comprehend. As an overwhelmingly popular Texan and southerner, LBJ could help deliver votes in his state and region that otherwise might seem out of reach for a Yankee liberal from Massachusetts. Beyond that, having him under JFK's tent as vice president would remove a potential rival power center on Capitol Hill. From Johnson's point of view, he might have calculated that with a Democrat in the Oval Office, his own clout as party leader in the Senate would be seriously diminished, so he might as well be inside that tent.

Johnson may have expected that he would wield even more influence on legislative matters on Capitol Hill as the president's man there. But matters were not to work out that way. Instead, destiny intervened with the assassination of Kennedy in November 1963 and catapulted Johnson to the presidency itself. There, his extraordinary political talents eventually came into play in building a remarkable legislative record, only to be marred by a calamitous war in Vietnam.

Lyndon Johnson's roots in rural Texas Hill Country, in the central part of the state, hinted at a career in politics, though never at reaching the heights that were to come. A great-great-uncle, John Wheeler Bunton, a tall transplanted Tennessean, was a signer of the Republic of Texas Declaration of Independence and a hero of the war with Mexico, which prompted that declaration.[1] A grandfather, Joseph Wilson Baines, was a teacher, lawyer, newspaperman, Texas secretary of state, and member of the state legislature.

Lyndon's father, Sam Ealy Johnson Jr., was a farmer and young Texas state legislator, and his mother, Rebekah Baines Johnson, an elocution teacher. The two shared an interest in politics and often spent their dates listening to political orators, including William Jennings Bryan. They were married in 1907, and their second son was born on a farm near the small town of Stonewall on August 27, 1908. Lyndon's mother, as a college graduate, did not appreciate her husband's gruff country ways and speech, and she found adjustment to farm life difficult and depressing. She compensated by concentrating on young Lyndon, her favorite among his brother, Sam Houston, and three sisters, Rebekah, Josepha, and Lucia, focusing on his education at home and as he advanced through grade and high school levels.[2]

From some of his earliest days, the boy talked politics with his father, who when Lyndon was about ten would take him to Austin during legislative sessions and as he campaigned.[3] Sam and Lyndon liked to talk and, as the boy got older, to argue, but the men who engaged them saw one difference: Lyndon always insisted on winning.[4] And he seemed to learn by talking and listening, not by reading much. In his family he was known to skimp on doing homework but got by as a quick study. When his father was away, leaving Lyndon with chores around the house, he would push them off on his siblings.[5]

During Lyndon's grade-school years, his father fell on bad economic times in his real estate and other financial ventures, requiring severe belt-tightening, which nonetheless did not free him from deep debt. Living now in Johnson City, a poverty-stricken backwater where the Depression came as early as 1924, Lyndon took the circumstances particularly hard. Upon

Lyndon's graduation from the local high school, his parents insisted that Lyndon go to college, despite their financial straits, but the boy refused. The only job available was road work, and he abhorred physical labor. When four of his local friends went to San Marcos to register for college, he went along on his father's orders but returned to Johnson City without signing up.

Subsequently, again ignoring the wishes of his father, Lyndon ran away and joined four older boys in buying an old Model-T Ford and driving to California in quest of preferable work. Eventually they split up, and he wrote later, "Up and down the coast I tramped. Washing dishes, waiting on tables, doing farm work when it was available, and always growing thinner."[6] By his eighteenth year, in late 1925, he was back in Texas, working for the State Highway Department. He fell in with some older and wilder companions, developed a conspicuous if awkward swagger, and came home one night bloodied in a one-sided fight.

He finally agreed, in 1927, to go to Southwest Texas State Teachers College, and he talked his way into a campus job and its meager sustenance, inflating his résumé by falsely claiming he came from the founders of Johnson City. He inflated his IQ and his grades as well and made the college debating team but, because of his boasting, exaggerating, and dominating conversation, was not very popular. He earned the nickname Bull Johnson, which the campus *College Star* explained this way: "Bull: Greek philosophy in which Lyndon Johnson has an M.B. degree."[7]

In 1928, extravagant purchases such as expensive clothes and a car left him unable to pay his tuition, so he took a teaching job at $125 a month at a Mexican school in the small south Texas town of Cotulla. On arrival he was made principal, at last in charge of something, with five housewife-teachers under his authority. In June 1929, he returned to college in San Marcos, where he broke into campus politics and developed the persuasive powers that would come to be his trademark. After graduation, he got a job teaching public speaking at Sam Houston High School, in Houston, and coaching the school debating team, which reached the state finals.[8]

In Lyndon's second year there, he received a phone call from Richard Kleberg, a scion of the King Ranch dynasty in Texas and a newly elected Texas congressman looking for a secretary to head his office in Washington. Five days later, with a leave of absence from Houston High, Johnson was on his way to a career in national politics that would not end until he reached its pinnacle.[9] Kleberg enjoyed being in Congress but had other interests, including golf, polo, hunting, and an eclectic range of endeavors that gave his secretary, later called administrative assistant, a heavy workload and wide latitude in handling it. Kleberg authorized Johnson to answer and sign letters in the congressman's name and make phone calls identifying himself as Kleberg.[10] Johnson also ran the congressman's successful 1932 reelection campaign.

In 1934, he met Claudia "Lady Bird" Taylor, a recent University of Texas graduate and daughter of well-off parents. He proposed marriage on the first day they met and then conducted a whirlwind courtship that included a visit to the impressive King Ranch before heading off to Washington, alone. They were married in San Antonio two and a half months later and set up housekeeping there in a one-bedroom apartment. Johnson used his Texas connections to become the state director of the new National Youth Administration, where he first met FDR.[11] Lyndon and Lady Bird later moved to Austin, where he focused on finding construction jobs for young workers, enabling them to stay in school, and kept his eyes open for political opportunities.

In 1937, when a Democratic congressman from central Texas died, Johnson's father-in-law bankrolled him to run for the seat. In a six-man field, 28 percent of the vote was enough to win, and Johnson was elected as a solid backer of Roosevelt's agenda. When Roosevelt next visited Texas, Johnson met him and won appointment to an important House subcommittee.[12] Now under the guiding wing of the senior Texas congressman Sam Rayburn, Johnson became a champion of rural electrification, power, and public housing projects in his district. Then in 1941, when Texas's senior senator, Morris Sheppard, died of a stroke, Johnson decided to run in the special election. Linking himself again to Roosevelt, on Election Night he appeared to be on the way to victory over Governor Lee "Pappy" Daniels. But Daniels scraped up enough late-reported rural votes of questionable legitimacy to edge Johnson out by 1,311 out of more than 350,000 votes cast.[13]

Barely a month later, when Japan attacked the American fleet at Pearl Harbor and brought the United States into the war, Johnson was drawn into it as well. During his failed campaign for the Senate, he had promised voters, "If the day ever comes when my vote must be cast to send your boy to the trenches, that day Lyndon Johnson will leave his Senate seat and go with him."[14] In fact, several months earlier he had been commissioned as a lieutenant commander in the U.S. Naval Reserve, and the day after Pearl Harbor he wrote to Roosevelt asking him to assign him "immediately to active duty with the Fleet."[15] He thereafter stood up in the House of Representatives and won unanimous consent for an indefinite leave of absence.

FDR got Johnson assigned to Navy Undersecretary James Forrestal, and Johnson, along with his congressional aide John Connally, later a governor of Texas, was sent to the U.S.–New Zealand Command in San Francisco. Meanwhile, Lady Bird ran his congressional office in his absence. Aware that this stateside duty would not help his political career, Johnson flew back to Washington to lobby for overseas duty. Through Forrestal, Roosevelt sent him to the Pacific with a message to General Douglas MacArthur to provide what Johnson later called "a very low-ranking set of eyes and ears" for the president.[16]

Johnson flew to MacArthur's headquarters in Melbourne, Australia. From an airfield on Port Moresby, he decided to hitch a ride on a B-26 bomber making a run over a Japanese target. Two bombers were available for him and two army colonels. They boarded the first one; the other was shot down, and all aboard were drowned. Johnson's bomber also came under attack by Japanese fighters but managed to return safely. For unexplained reasons, MacArthur awarded Johnson a Silver Star, although he did not engage in any military action, and no one else aboard got one.[17]

Eight days after the mission, Roosevelt ordered that members of Congress on active duty return to inactive duty and to their political offices. Of the eight involved, four resigned their seats and stayed on duty in uniform. The other four, including Johnson, returned to Washington. When he ran for reelection in 1944 and in 1946, his opponents called him on breaking his pledge to serve "in the trenches" with other Americans, and one of them charged that FDR's order was "an excuse to return to an air-cooled foxhole in Washington."[18] But Johnson trumpeted his "combat" service in these and future campaigns.

Still determined to move across the Capitol to the Senate, he ran again in 1948. In keeping with the postwar climate, he also did not hesitate to stamp himself as an unvarnished anti-communist and, in the South, as anti-union, without surrendering his populist strain. He campaigned fervently across his broad state by helicopter against Governor Coke Stevenson in the election, which required a runoff between the two top finishers. Johnson trailed Stevenson by about 70,000 votes going into the runoff, and when it was completed, Stevenson was ahead by only 349 votes with 40 uncounted. But some Johnson precincts came in late under suspicious circumstances, and LBJ was declared the winner by 87 votes, thereafter dubbed "Landslide Lyndon."[19]

Johnson rode into the Senate at a propitious time, along with the Harry Truman upset of Thomas Dewey and the Democratic control of both houses of Congress. He allied himself with the conservative veteran Richard Russell of Georgia. Two years later, when the two top Democrats in the Senate were defeated, Johnson, with Russell's backing, ran for and won the second post as majority whip. In 1954, with the Democratic leadership again vacant, Russell helped his protégé capture it. After barely six years in the Senate, Lyndon Johnson was ruling the roost as majority leader.

With Dwight Eisenhower easily reelected in 1956 with a Republican Senate, Johnson was reduced to minority leader for two years. But when the Democrats regained control in 1958, he returned as majority leader for the next six, cementing his reputation as arguably the strongest and most effective occupant of that office in its history. With his own membership divided between southern conservatives led by Russell and the influx of northern liberals like Humphrey, Johnson's masterful talent for compromise—a deft mixture of arm-twisting and sweet cajolery—dominated. It was soon known on Capitol Hill as the "Johnson Treatment," featuring LBJ as a commanding figure cornering his prey with chest-piercing finger and jutting jaw or gangling arm wrapped over the shoulder of his victim.

The man seemed a force of nature but not immune to nature's capriciousness. In 1956, he was suddenly stricken with a heart attack but returned after a few weeks to his old hard-driving self, as if to make up for the lost time. In 1957, as the country experienced the start of its historic pivot in civil rights from deep segregation of the races, especially in the South, to integration in schools, housing, and other public accommodations, Johnson became its champion. With bipartisan support, the Senate and House passed the first major civil rights act since Reconstruction days.

In 1958, economic woes for the Eisenhower administration contributed to a Democratic landslide in the midterm congressional elections. The party's two-seat majority in the Senate swelled to thirty, emboldening liberals to increase their demands on Johnson, both in their voice in the Senate and for a progressive agenda. His strength in the party remained centered in the chamber that he ruled with an iron hand but was not reflected to any such degree outside it.

Nevertheless, Johnson now entertained presidential ambitions for the 1960 campaign. He assumed his Senate mastery could assure him a major place in the competition for the party nomination that summer. Rayburn insisted he declare openly, but Johnson declined, saying he had his Senate leadership responsibilities to handle.

In the early primaries, Kennedy and Humphrey battled in Wisconsin and West Virginia, with the young Yankee senator emerging as the frontrunner and Humphrey bowing out. Kennedy then painstakingly courted party leaders at the city and state levels around the country, building delegate commitments.

Johnson meanwhile held his fire, in what was a severe underestimation of his pulling power outside his congressional orbit. He did not announce his presidential candidacy until July 5, only days before the opening of the national party convention in Los Angeles.

The showdown came when LBJ and JFK met in a joint appearance before the Texas and Massachusetts delegations. Johnson chided his younger competitor for missing many Senate quorum calls while out campaigning. Kennedy wryly conceded Johnson's superior attendance record and endorsed him—for another term as Senate majority leader. With Johnson having failed to reach out beyond the Senate to build a campaign organization, the outcome was predictable: a first-ballot victory for JFK, winning nearly twice as many delegates as Johnson.

Unlike in 1956, when the presidential nominee Stevenson threw the choice of running mate to the convention and Kennedy lost, this time Kennedy was going to do the choosing himself. As a northern liberal he was well aware of his weakness in the South. Kennedy's chief aides drew up a list with Johnson's name at the top, considering Kennedy's need to carry Texas's electoral votes. Furthermore, the new nominee had agreed with his brother Robert that if Johnson indicated he wanted to be asked or thought he was entitled to the right of first refusal, then he would have to be asked.[20]

Other accounts argue that the offer was made in the expectation that Johnson would turn it down, preferring to retain his huge power base in the Senate, where he was up for reelection that fall and certain to be returned by Texas voters. John Kennedy went to Johnson's hotel suite personally to make the offer. Robert Kennedy told Schlesinger later, "He [JFK] never dreamt that there was a chance in the world that he would accept it."[21]

Robert Kennedy said he was in his brother's suite when JFK returned, saying, "You just won't believe it. . . . He wants it. . . . Now what do we do?" In light of all the opposition to Johnson voiced by labor leaders, they finally decided that "Bobby" would go back and try to get LBJ to withdraw. Bobby then made the effort, offering to make Johnson chairman of the Democratic National Committee, a crumb that Kennedy could not have seriously believed Johnson would swallow. As Robert Kennedy told Arthur Schlesinger later, Johnson "just shook and tears came into his eyes, and he said, 'I want to be Vice President, and if the president will have me, I'll join with him in making a fight for it.'" To which Bobby said he replied, "Well, then that's fine. He wants you to be Vice President if you want to be Vice President."[22]

A slightly different version came from Phil Graham, the *Washington Post* publisher and friend of both Kennedy and LBJ. According to Graham, Johnson told him that after Robert's visit, LBJ phoned JFK and was told, "Bobby's been out of touch and doesn't know what's been happening." John Kennedy then reassured Johnson that he wanted him, and both men made public statements that LBJ had accepted the offer.[23]

The key question remained: why did Johnson agree to accept the vice presidential offer when arguably he already was the second-most powerful politician in Washington as Senate majority leader? Speaker Sam Rayburn, who had first counseled Johnson to reject it, later changed his mind. A close Johnson friend reported that LBJ explained to him that "power is where power goes, thinking he could run Congress from the vice presidency."[24] But in so saying, LBJ demonstrated a mistaken confidence that the power was embodied in himself rather than in the office he held, and hence he could take it with him.

According to historian Doris Kearns Goodwin, who worked closely with LBJ after his retirement, "Johnson recognized that his power in the Senate had depended in part upon having a passive Republican President

[Eisenhower] in the White House. . . . The world he had mastered so well would no longer be his. Even if Kennedy lost, Richard Nixon would be no Eisenhower; he would not accord the Majority Leader the respect or the power Johnson had enjoyed in the 1950s. Better, then, to help young John Kennedy."[25]

Once the furor over Kennedy's surprise selection of Johnson passed, the two men plunged into the general election campaign. Johnson stumped heavily across the South and wound up the campaign in Texas; in spite of his presence on the ticket it needed selling right up to the end. In the Adolphus Hotel in Dallas a few days before the election, Republican women coming from a Nixon rally subjected Lyndon and Lady Bird Johnson to a rowdy and hostile reception. With television cameras capturing the scene, Johnson took his sweet time working his way through the crowds in the hotel lobby.[26] On Election Night, Kennedy and Johnson beat Nixon and Lodge by three-tenths of 1 percent in the popular vote, with the Democratic ticket carrying Texas, making it believable if not certain that having the southerner Johnson on the ticket accounted for part of the victory.

In organizational meetings for the new administration, Johnson was invited to the Kennedy house in Palm Beach for critical political meetings of the Kennedy circle. When the new secretary of defense, Robert McNamara, recommended Johnson's old aide, John Connally, for secretary of the navy, Johnson was not consulted until Kennedy informed him of the appointment.[27] Johnson urged that Senator J. William Fulbright of Arkansas be appointed secretary of state, but Robert Kennedy balked, citing the peril of racial complications in his coming from a segregated state. Kennedy then nominated Dean Rusk, who phoned Johnson in Texas and offered to discuss foreign relations with him, but Johnson huffily waved him off.[28]

Right after New Year's, Johnson was briefly sworn in for another Senate term in advance of the inauguration and sat in on the Senate Democratic Caucus, which he had chaired for eight years. At Kennedy's suggestion, the easy-going senator Mike Mansfield of Montana agreed to take over as majority leader. At this first meeting with JFK, Mansfield in turn suggested that Johnson, as incoming president of the Senate, be invited not only to attend but also to preside at future caucuses. The notion, which few doubted was Johnson's own idea, disturbed many senators and outraged a few. In a vote on the odd arrangement, forty-five acquiesced and seventeen voted against. The uneven support amounted to a humiliating rebuff. Johnson attended the next caucus but immediately turned over the gavel to Mansfield and never attended again.[29] He did, however, appropriate the large and ornate Senate office from which he had reigned as majority leader, called by other senators the Taj Mahal.

Shortly after the inauguration, having been reminded of his proper place in the legislative branch, LBJ set out to assure for himself a substantial role in the executive. He had an aide draw up an executive order for Kennedy's signature stating he would have "general supervision" over certain federal agencies, including the National Aeronautics and Space Administration. The presumption on Johnson's part was quickly shortstopped by the Kennedy staff and never signed by the president, if indeed he ever saw it.[30] LBJ was, however, the first vice president to be given an office in the Executive Office Building adjacent to the White House.

Beyond these initial gestures seemingly toward self-aggrandizement, Johnson settled into the vice presidency with full awareness of his position, declaring to his staff that he intended to give Kennedy his total allegiance and expected his aides to do the same. That did not mean, however, that he never fell into brooding over his lack of influence or limited utilization, particularly in his specialty of steering legislation past congressional pitfalls and marshes. But having once had his wrist slapped by his old colleagues in the Senate, he uncharacteristically retreated.

Kennedy did make his vice president chairman of the Presidential Committee on Equal Opportunity, which gave him a voice in civil rights matters, and chairman of the National Aeronautics and Space Council. He also was a member of the National Security Council and attended cabinet meetings but was notably quiet. Even on occasions when Kennedy would invite him to comment, he often would plead insufficient knowledge of inside information on which to offer a constructive observation. He was not in charge, and that seemed to make all the difference in his demeanor.

During the first crisis of the Kennedy administration, the disastrous attempt to land Cuban military exiles at the Bay of Pigs with the objective of ousting the communist leader Fidel Castro, Johnson was at his Texas ranch entertaining the West German chancellor Konrad Adenauer and apparently out of the loop. When a friend asked JFK why he hadn't included Johnson, he explained, "You want to talk to the people who are most involved, and your mind does not turn to Lyndon because he isn't following the flow of [diplomatic] cables."[31]

Kennedy did, however, follow Eisenhower's practice of dispatching his vice president on foreign missions, despite Johnson's very limited experience abroad. Early in their first year, JFK sent him on an important fact-finding visit to Southeast Asia. And in August 1961, Kennedy rushed LBJ to Berlin as a show of solidarity when the Russians suddenly slapped together a makeshift wall separating the Eastern zone, under their control, from the Western, under supervision of the Americans, British, and French. As an American convoy of armored trucks carrying U.S. troops rolled into West Berlin via the corridor through East Germany, LBJ was there to greet them, and afterward he addressed the parliament and another crowd outside the city hall. His visit proved to be a morale booster for the German people and for Johnson himself.[32] Other foreign trips followed, on which he segued from diplomat to politician and plunged into crowds shaking hands, to the delight of the locals.

But, as Johnson's special assistant Booth Mooney wrote later, "State Department stiff-collars, at home and abroad, were dismayed by such goings on. They wished the President would keep his Vice President in the United States. They passed among themselves with appreciative chuckles the statement of an assistant secretary in State that 'like some wines, Lyndon does not travel well.' Certainly there was no doubt that he upset the routine of every American embassy he visited. Which could not have mattered less to him."[33]

The most revealing window into Johnson's influence in foreign-policy crises came during the October 1962 Cuban missile crisis. The vice president was a member of the Executive Committee of the National Security Council, or Ex Comm, created to deal specifically with the discovery that the Soviet leader Nikita Khrushchev had secretly slipped ballistic missiles onto the island. In Robert Kennedy's account of the crisis, *Thirteen Days,* Johnson is mentioned only as "attending intermittently, at various meetings."[34]

But at one point when a message came from the Kremlin indicating the Russians would remove their missiles if the United States would take theirs out of Turkey, Johnson at first seemed to seize on it. Then, noting that the Soviets had shot down an American U-2 photo-reconnaissance plane, killing the pilot, and there had been no U.S. response, he warned that the failure to respond militarily would convey weakness on Kennedy's part. Robert Kennedy said in an oral history later, "After the meetings were finished, [LBJ] would circulate and whine and complain about our being weak."[35]

Whether or not Johnson's thoughts on a deal involving the American missiles in Turkey had any influence on the final swap, it was a crisis breaker, though unannounced at the time and not publicly acknowledged until years later, long after American missiles had been quietly removed from Turkey. According to Robert Kennedy in his chronicle, when the crisis finally ended, the president said to him, in obvious reference to the Lincoln assassination soon after the Civil War had ended, "This is the night I should go to the theater." Bobby shot back, "If you go, I want to go with you."[36] Bobby did not spell it out, but one could speculate that he didn't want to be around for the resulting Lyndon Johnson presidency if Jack Kennedy was going to meet Lincoln's fate.

With the missile crisis finally behind the administration, thoughts turned in 1963 to matters of civil rights, including the violence at the University of Mississippi over the admission of the first black student, James Meredith. Johnson was not involved, and when Kennedy began planning a broad civil rights bill and LBJ was asked his thoughts, he essentially limited his comments to the timing and tactics he would employ in seeking to pass it. With the approaching presidential election year, a restless and disappointed Johnson complained to friends about slights by Kennedy aides and the possibility of being dumped from the 1964 ticket. The previous May, Kennedy had been asked about rumors that Johnson might be dropped from the ticket. He replied, "Well, I don't know what they'll do with me, but I'm sure the Vice President will be on the ticket if he chooses to run. We were fortunate to have him before—would again—and I don't know where such a rumor could start."[37]

All this came amid administration concerns about a Democratic civil war in Texas between John Connally, the governor at the time and LBJ's old lieutenant, and the state's more liberal forces, led by the outspoken U.S. senator Ralph Yarborough. With the next presidential election in mind, the administration decided that President Kennedy should undertake a political trip to the Lone Star State to try to patch things up in the Texas Democratic family. It was to be a triumphal visit to San Antonio, Houston, Fort Worth, and Dallas.

Early on Johnson had advised against a trip that would put the president in the middle of a seething party feud. Connally insisted on handling the Texas end of the planning and in advance met with Kennedy with no notice to Johnson. When the Kennedy party set off for Texas, Yarborough hitched a ride on *Air Force One* and en route likely got the president's ear on his beefs with Connally and with Johnson. In an effort to bring the feuding sides together, Johnson was to ride with Yarborough in the motorcades, but Yarborough had refused. An incredible fandango ensued, with LBJ prompting White House aides to drive the balking senator like a Texas steer into the desired corral. After several failed attempts, Yarborough was finally herded into Johnson's car for the Dallas motorcade.

Shortly after 12:30 P.M. Central Standard Time, past the Dallas intersection of Houston and Elm Streets, a shot rang out. Two cars behind the presidential limo, agent Youngblood turned and lunged toward the vice president of the United States, ordering him, "Get down!" President Kennedy and Governor Connally were both hit, the president fatally. In the vice presidential car, Yarborough called out, "Oh, my God! They've shot the president!" Youngblood told Johnson simply, "An emergency exists. When we get to where we're going, you and me are going to move right off and not tie in with the other people." Johnson muttered, "OK, partner."[38]

The lead cars in the motorcade immediately peeled off and headed for Parkland Memorial Hospital, where Kennedy and Connally were swiftly wheeled into separate trauma rooms as doctors rushed in and administered to them. Efforts to revive the president were unavailing, and at about 1:00 P.M. Jacqueline Kennedy, at her husband's side, was told that he had expired. At that moment, by virtue of JFK's assassination, Lyndon Baines Johnson became president of the United States. Governor Connally, who had lapsed into a semicoma, survived his wounds and went on to be reelected in 1964.

The most shocking presidential drama since the assassination of Abraham Lincoln, nearly a century earlier, played out on and was conveyed to the American people through the immediacy of television. So was the scene of the official transfer of presidential power when Johnson was sworn in from the cabin of *Air Force One,* parked at Love Field, in Dallas. He took the oath of office from an old Texas friend, the federal district judge Sarah Hughes, with his wife, Lady Bird, and a blood-spattered Jacqueline Kennedy as witnesses.

Johnson as the new president joined in the national mourning but also moved rapidly to strike a theme of continuity by embracing major aspects of the Kennedy agenda, most notably in the realm of civil rights. In a stirring address to Congress, he rallied the nation with "let us continue" Kennedy's goal of racial and social equality, pledging in the words of the old Negro spiritual, that "we shall overcome" the divisions in the country.

Left vacant again until the following year's presidential election was the vice presidency. Johnson, yet another accidental president, was easily elected to a full term in his own right in November 1964, over the weak Republican nominee, Senator Barry Goldwater of Arizona. Johnson instituted his version of social and economic advancement in what he called the Great Society, with the most ambitious domestic agenda since Franklin D. Roosevelt's New Deal had lifted America from the Great Depression.

But Johnson's continuation and then escalation of the U.S. participation in the war in Vietnam proved to be the undoing of his highest aspirations. He attempted simultaneously to raise the quality of life for the neediest Americans through costly social programs at home and to wage an ever more draining and futile war abroad, undertaken to stop the spread of communism around the globe. This policy of "guns and butter" ultimately forced him to abandon the quest for another presidential term in 1968, ostensibly to focus on ending the war in Vietnam. Instead it went on for another seven years.

Before peace finally was achieved, Johnson died at age sixty-four on January 23, 1973, at his Texas ranch. As the presidential standby for nearly three years, he was never utilized to the fullness of his governmental experience, energies, and imagination, demonstrating only later the qualities that the highest office requires when the power of the presidency moved unexpectedly to him.

The personal closeness and shared liberal outlook between Lyndon

Johnson and his choice for vice president might have been expected to bring the second office to its highest peak. But, as we shall see in the next chapter, LBJ's domineering ways and the ultimate humiliations he was to inflict on his standby would only reinforce the public perception, and the reality, of the limited influence of another vice presidency.

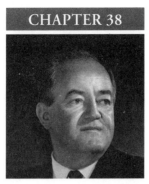

CHAPTER 38

HUBERT H. HUMPHREY
OF MINNESOTA

Aprime requisite for the American vice presidency is loyalty, and
Hubert Humphrey had it in overabundance toward his president,
Lyndon Johnson. That loyalty to the man, and to most of his legislative objectives, undeniably brought the vice presidency to Humphrey in
1964. But his unwillingness thereafter to separate himself from LBJ over
the Vietnam War, which was bringing Johnson down, eventually brought
Humphrey down with him as he reached for the White House on his own.

Humphrey started out in the small-town footsteps of his namesake father as a pharmacist. Born in the small Dakota town of Wallace on May 27,
1911, in a room over the family drugstore, "Pinky" Humphrey, as he was
called, later moved on with his family to Doland, still in South Dakota but
near the Minnesota border, where Hubert Horatio Humphrey Sr., known
as HH, opened another drugstore. His son, a mischievous but otherwise
well-mannered boy, worked at the soda fountain and became a pharmacist
himself. But a lot of talking was always in him, as a champion member of
the school's debating team. He took after his father in his two main interests beyond family—politics and the spoken word.[1]

When the Great Depression hit the prairie states, wheat and other grain
prices plummeted, and in 1926 the two banks in Doland failed. His father
was forced to start selling goods other than pharmaceuticals and also began
vaccinating farm animals to make ends meet. In 1931, HH moved the

business to the larger town of Huron, South Dakota, where a dust storm hit the next year. In 1936, President Franklin D. Roosevelt came there on an inspection tour, and HH, now the local Democratic Party chairman, took Hubert Jr. to meet him.

Hubert Jr. was sent to a pharmacy college in Denver, completed a two-year course in six months, and returned to the store. The next year he married a local girl, Muriel Buck, and moved to Minneapolis to complete his schooling. But Hubert had more in mind than peddling pills, as he told his father.

Majoring in political science, he was elected to Phi Beta Kappa and upon graduation got a small teaching fellowship at Louisiana State University, in quest of a doctoral degree and a college teaching career.[2] He taught political science at Minnesota through the summer of 1941, then took a job instructing Minnesota teachers in FDR's Works Projects Administration (WPA). He later moved into other New Deal agency posts, including state director for war production training and assistant state director of the War Manpower Commission.[3] Meanwhile, as crime mounted in Minneapolis, young Humphrey ran for the mayoralty in 1943 at the age of thirty-one, finishing second in a nine-man field but losing a runoff against the incumbent, Mayor Marvin Kline. Courted thereafter by Republicans to join their ranks, he declined, wedded as he was to the party of his father and FDR.

Humphrey soon concluded, however, that the Democratic Party in Minnesota as then constituted was a losing proposition. He brought about a merger with the Farmer-Labor Party, then the third political force in the state, creating the Democratic Farmer Labor Party (DFL), soon to be the dominant force in Minnesota politics.[4] Many in the new party wanted to nominate Humphrey for governor, but with the war still on he decided to enlist.

Well before Pearl Harbor he had been classified as 3-A and exempted from the draft as a father. (His daughter, Nancy, was born in 1939.) Later, as teacher of air force officers at Macalester College, he was reclassified as 2-A as an "essential civilian." He asked that his exemption be removed, was reclassified as 1-A, and got as far as an army induction center, where he was turned down for a double hernia, lung calcification, and color blindness.[5] All this history would later be revisited when political foes repeatedly accused him of draft dodging, which he refuted with draft board documents and affidavits.

Humphrey then plunged into the politics of FDR's bid for a fourth term, leaving his teaching job at Macalester and serving as the president's Minnesota coordinator. In 1945, he filed again for the mayoralty of Minneapolis and was elected at age thirty-four over the incumbent.[6] His reformist agenda not only reduced crime but also combatted racial discrimination and anti-Semitism in the city. In 1947, during a time when communist elements had begun to infiltrate the DFL, Humphrey went to Washington for the founding meeting of Americans for Democratic Action (ADA), formed to strengthen anti-communist political and labor involvement in the Democratic Party, and was elected vice chairman.[7]

In the summer of 1948, Humphrey was propelled into the national spotlight when he led the fight for a strong civil rights plank in the party platform at the Democratic National Convention in Philadelphia. He argued strenuously with Senator Scott Lucas of Illinois for a stronger and more explicit plank in defiance of the party's southern wing. Lucas at one point demanded to know: "Who does this pipsqueak think he is?"[8] When the committee voted to send its own plank to the convention floor, Humphrey joined in writing a single additional paragraph calling on Congress to guarantee the rights of "full and equal political participation . . . equal opportunity of employment . . . , security of person, and equal treatment in the service and defense of our nation."[9]

Lucas and others warned that this plank would split the party and cost the Democrats the 1948 election. But Humphrey went ahead. "There are those who say . . . we are rushing this issue of civil rights," he said. "I say we are a hundred and seventy-two years too late. There are those who say this issue is an infringement on states' rights. The time has arrived for the Democratic Party to get out of the shadow of states' rights and walk forthrightly into the bright sunshine of human rights."[10] The Humphrey plank triggered a walkout of southern delegates, but the convention passed it, and Harry Truman was easily nominated over Senator Richard Russell of Georgia, supported by southern delegates who remained behind.[11]

Humphrey's success at the convention, followed by his outspoken opposition to the Taft-Hartley Act (also known as the Labor Management

Relations Act), which was despised by organized labor, and his firm defense of the Marshall Plan to rebuild Europe after World War II, swept him into the U.S. Senate that November, as Truman upset Dewey for the presidency. It could be said that Humphrey talked his way into the Senate, making nearly seven hundred speeches as a full-throated disciple of the New Deal agenda. As the Democrats won control of both houses of Congress, he was the first Democrat elected to the Senate from his state in nearly half a century. As icing on the cake, Humphrey became the ADA chairman and a prime spokesman for the party's liberal wing.

None of this endeared him to the southern Democrats, who for so long had dominated the Senate. He locked horns with them over Taft-Hartley, seen in Dixie as protection against union incursions into the region. Humphrey also plunged into the fight over civil rights but was rebuffed by a phalanx of filibustering southern Democrats and allied Republicans.

The Minnesota freshman cosponsored a host of social welfare bills, including a health insurance plan for the elderly that sixteen years later became Medicare. Along the way, he rounded off some of his brash edges and with his natural ebullience won the name the "happy warrior." He became close to another member of the Senate class of 1948, Lyndon Johnson, who had ties to the old southern lions.

In 1952, President Truman's political operatives asked Humphrey to run as a favorite son in the Minnesota primary, a move that kept out Senator Estes Kefauver, a declared challenger to Truman. When Truman decided not to seek a second full term, Humphrey helped deliver the Minnesota delegation to Adlai Stevenson, and in 1953 with Johnson's help, Humphrey was given a seat on the prestigious Foreign Relations Committee.

In 1958, he had an eight and a half hour meeting with the Soviet leader Nikita Khrushchev at the Kremlin, with the discussion ranging from agriculture and trade to the division of Berlin, which Khrushchev menacingly called "a bone in my throat."[12] The meeting's extraordinary length became instant news around the world, triggering more talk of national office for the ambitious Minnesotan.

Humphrey finally took the plunge in 1960, taking on Kennedy for the Democratic presidential nomination in early primaries in Wisconsin and West Virginia. He had neither the Boston Irish charm nor the money of his rival's father, Joseph Kennedy, a former ambassador to Britain. The tacit issue in the race was Kennedy's Catholicism; no one of his faith had ever been elected to the presidency, and the first one who ran, Al Smith of New York, had been soundly beaten. But Humphrey was called "Wisconsin's third senator" because of mutual interests and his work in behalf of his Badger State neighbors, and he had high hopes of winning there.

The race took a difficult turn for Humphrey in West Virginia. Kennedy threw heavy resources into the state and, in a high-risk strategy, played on prospective anti-Catholic sentiment to make religious tolerance an open issue. In his first appearance in Fairmont, Kennedy asked, "Is anyone going to tell me I lost the primary before I was born?" Citing his award of a Purple Heart in the Pacific, he declared, "No one can tell me that I am not as prepared as any man to meet my obligations to the Constitution of the United States."[13]

Then, in a state where Franklin D. Roosevelt had achieved saintly dimensions, the Kennedy camp brought in the late president's namesake son, who strongly suggested that Humphrey had been a draft dodger in the late war. "I don't know where he was in World War II," he would say, handing out papers professing to substantiate the charge. Humphrey wrote later that the only thing he remained "unforgiving" of in the Kennedy campaign in West Virginia was FDR Jr.'s continued slander after evidence of the untruths had been provided to the Kennedy campaign.[14]

In a primary campaign in which candidates were "slated" with popular local candidates in the various counties and money passed hands regularly, the Kennedy wealth easily outspent the Humphrey shoestring effort. At a dinner in New York, Kennedy felt comfortable making a joke about it: "I got a wire from my father: Dear Jack, don't buy one more vote than necessary. I'll be damned if I'll pay for a landslide."[15] But a landslide it was in West Virginia, Kennedy winning the primary with 60.8 percent of the vote. Returning to the Senate, Humphrey at LBJ's urging was named majority whip.

When John F. Kennedy was assassinated in Dallas in November 1963, Humphrey was immediately drawn into the inner circle of the new president, Lyndon Johnson. In LBJ's speech to a joint session of Congress, he said, "No memorial or eulogy could more eloquently honor President Kennedy than the earliest passage of the civil rights bill for which he fought so long." As the bill's floor leader, Humphrey received LBJ's marching orders to achieve that goal, which he did the next June, after seventy-five days of debate and filibuster.[16] Humphrey experienced the presidential transition from his ringside seat, watching some old Kennedy hands stay and others move on when LBJ placed his own people into positions of influence and prestige while striving to advance the agenda of his fallen leader and at the same time asserting his desire and will to shape his own presidency.

Soon the 1964 presidential election was upon Johnson, and with it the issue with which he had intimate acquaintance—the selection of a running mate. In May, LBJ told Humphrey he'd prefer to have him as his running mate, provided no obstacles came up, a signal that his performance as Senate majority whip would be critical to the outcome.[17] In the meantime, Johnson enjoyed stirring the pot by dropping names of governors and other officials as prospects, sometimes letting Humphrey in on the game, sometimes not.

Through all this, Humphrey's name and that of his Minnesota colleague in the Senate, Eugene J. McCarthy, were most frequently mentioned, along with Secretary of Defense Robert McNamara and Attorney General Robert Kennedy. McNamara reported later that Johnson had offered him the vice presidential nomination before the convention. When he declined, he said, LBJ proposed to make him his "number one executive vice president in charge of the cabinet," which sounded like creating an assistant presidency, which McNamara also declined.[18]

So while Johnson may have "preferred" to pick Humphrey, he apparently was not yet settled on him. The one thing he did know was that he didn't want Robert Kennedy waiting in the wings for his departure. Johnson thereupon conferred with his old adviser, Clark Clifford, about the best way to let Robert Kennedy down. Clifford dreamed up the ludicrous rationale read aloud by Johnson at a hastily called meeting with reporters: "It would be inadvisable for me to recommend to the Convention any member of the Cabinet and or any of those who meet regularly with the Cabinet. . . . In this manner, the race has been considerably narrowed."[19]

It certainly had, at least by one, without Robert Kennedy even being mentioned. Kennedy responded by sending telegrams to fellow cabinet members, saying, "Sorry I took so many of you nice fellows over the side with me."[20] Left in the boat of prospective vice presidential nominees were Gene McCarthy and Hubert Humphrey. McCarthy, fed up with being a foil in Johnson's little game, sent a telegram to LBJ saying he should go ahead and pick Humphrey. So after Humphrey had worked out a compromise over a Mississippi delegate fight at the convention, Johnson summoned him to the White House and told him he would be his running mate, cautioning him to say nothing of it to anybody, not even to his wife, Muriel. Soon after, Humphrey was called to the White House again, this time accompanied by Senator Tom Dodd of Connecticut. James Rowe, a Democratic insider and Humphrey confidant, told Humphrey that LBJ's inclusion of Dodd was "just a cover" and that he wanted "to continue the speculation."[21]

On arrival, Johnson's aide Jack Valenti led Dodd in to see LBJ while Humphrey cooled his heels in the parked limo. He finally dozed off until a knock on the window stirred him, and he was ushered into the Presence—obviously more drama building. Johnson asked Humphrey again of the vice presidency: "Why would you want to have the job? You know it is a thankless one." He told Humphrey that the relationship between a president and his vice president "is like a marriage with no chance of divorce." Johnson finally relieved Humphrey by saying, "If you didn't know you were going to be vice president a month ago, you're too damn dumb to have the office."[22]

In the fall campaign, Humphrey and his party traveled by a chartered plane dubbed the *Happy Warrior,* and his own staff prepared speech drafts that not surprisingly were to be cleared by the Johnson White House.[23] It was obvious from the start that Goldwater and his ultrapartisan running mate, Congressman William Miller of upstate New York, would be no match for Johnson and Humphrey. The Democratic ticket easily won a landslide 61.1 percent of the popular vote and a whopping 482 electoral votes to 52.

As vice president, Humphrey became a member of the Johnson cabinet and his National Security Council, and LBJ also gave him the chairmanship of a host of executive agencies dealing with civil rights, efforts against poverty, the Peace Corps, and the space program. Humphrey served as a liaison with the nation's mayors and navigated the legislative agenda through Congress. Included in Humphrey's achievements over the next years were passage of the voting rights act and pursuit of bills on Medicare, the Model Cities Program, and the domestic Marshall Plan.

A serious cause of friction between Humphrey and Johnson, however, was the Vietnam War. In February 1965, as Viet Cong and North Vietnamese attacks on the South intensified and Johnson ordered the bombing of North Vietnam in retaliation, Humphrey expressed doubts about this strategy at á National Security Council meeting. He sent Johnson a memo arguing that the action "in fact adopted Goldwater's position" and risked the intervention of Communist China and the Soviet Union, as well as draining resources from the Great Society agenda at home. Johnson, fearing leaks, was not pleased with the communiqué. Humphrey said later that LBJ told him, "We don't need all those memos, Hubert."[24]

What concerned Johnson more was that, in front of others, Humphrey was offering views that differed from LBJ's own, which he had warned the vice president never to do. Soon Humphrey was being frozen out of meetings, yet was still expected to sell the president's war goals and policies to Congress and the public. His carrying of LBJ's water on Vietnam particularly vexed fellow liberals, and by year's end a Gallup Poll found that 56 percent of those surveyed didn't want Humphrey as a future president. He summed up his acceptance of his subservient role by telling one interviewer, "I didn't become vice president with Lyndon Johnson to cause him trouble."[25]

On Christmas Day, 1965, however, Johnson ordered a pause in the bombing of North Vietnam, saying, "We're going to try it Hubert's way."[26] But the pause didn't last and the bombing was resumed, followed by Johnson's decision to send Humphrey on another mission to sell the war, a two-week swing through India and nine Far East countries of the Pacific Rim, including South Vietnam. Johnson sent Jack Valenti along to report back on the vice president's performance. Throughout, Humphrey defended the Johnson policy, tying himself more inextricably to it while talking himself back into LBJ's good graces.

When asked about Robert Kennedy's suggestion that the insurgent Viet Cong's political arm, the National Liberation Front, be brought into the South Vietnamese government as a way to bring peace, Humphrey's reply was instant: "Putting the Viet Cong in the Vietnamese government would be like putting a fox in the chicken coop. . . . We are not going to permit the VC to shoot their way into power."[27] The statement not only cemented Humphrey's commitment to Johnson's policy but also roiled the political waters back home among former liberal supporters.

In March 1966, Humphrey played a key role in the Senate's rejection of an attempt to repeal the Gulf of Tonkin Resolution. Johnson thereupon raised the American troop level in Vietnam to 380,000 by the end of the year, which amounted to a confession that the war was not going as well as the administration had suggested to the American people. Meanwhile, the Gallup Poll showed disenchantment with the Democratic administration, generating some speculation that Robert Kennedy would replace Humphrey as LBJ's running mate in 1968. When Hubert told an audience in St. Louis that he was sure Johnson would keep him, Johnson chastised him for saying so. Humphrey was obliged to comment a few days later, "The realities of politics require that a president have many options. . . . I don't predict whom he will want in 1968."[28]

Johnson apparently was having doubts about his own future, telling Valenti in September, "I won't be around then," but adding, "They would say I was playing politics if I resigned and gave the job to Humphrey. My own party has turned against me, and the Republicans are chiming in. We probably need a fresh face. Humphrey would start with a clean slate. . . . As of now, I have lost Congress."[29] A year later, he dictated a draft letter of resignation to his press secretary, George Christian, but nothing more came of it.

On Election Night in 1966, despite Humphrey's campaigning through twenty-six states, the Democrats lost forty-seven House seats, three in the Senate, and eleven governorships. The mercurial Johnson put Humphrey in the deep freeze again, amid increasing reports of gratuitous presidential rebuffs of his vice president. After a second Humphrey trip to Southeast Asia, he came back with more doubts about the prospects and of success. He urged Johnson to switch from an offensive military strategy to one of containment and negotiation. Still, he remained LBJ's public mouthpiece on the war and was sent to Congress to cajole more money for his Great Society agenda in what was now being labeled a policy of "guns and butter."

Many advocates of the "butter" part still admired the domestic agenda but were dead against the "guns" portion. A couple of University of North Carolina alumni, Allard Lowenstein and Curtis Gans, approached Robert Kennedy to head a Democratic dump-Johnson effort. Kennedy declined. They also courted Gene McCarthy, who first told them, "I think Bobby should do it."[30] But he later agreed, announcing his candidacy on the last day of November 1967.

Fueled by the anti-war protest and a sizable army of college dropouts and graduates, McCarthy entered the New Hampshire primary. Johnson loftily declined to campaign, sending surrogates instead. Then, on the last day of January 1968, the lunar New Year celebration of Tet in Vietnam, the supposedly decimated Viet Cong forces suddenly swarmed over major South Vietnamese cities, shattering assurances of Humphrey and others that the war was going well. Despite U.S. claims that the enemy had suffered major casualties, the Tet Offensive had a demoralizing effect on American public opinion at home.

In New Hampshire on Election Night, the absent president "won" but with only 49.4 percent of the vote in the Democratic primary compared with a surprising 42.2 percent for the little-known senator from Minnesota. The result was widely reported as a huge upset and a ringing denunciation of Johnson's war in Vietnam. Kennedy had been following McCarthy's run and now was reconsidering. He had been saying he wasn't challenging Johnson because he didn't want any of his own efforts to be seen as a personal vendetta or to be accused of splitting the Democratic Party. But the vote in New Hampshire, he said, had shown there already was "deep division" in it. Kennedy thereupon entered the presidential race.[31]

In the next Democratic primary, in Wisconsin, it was too late for Kennedy to get on the ballot, and McCarthy was on the verge of defeating the president outright. Two nights before Wisconsin Democrats voted, Johnson went on nationwide television and, after telling the country he had decided to restrict the bombing of North Vietnam in the hope of encouraging peace talks, declared, "I shall not seek, and I will not accept, the nomination of my party for another term as your president."[32] In the wink of an eye, Hubert Humphrey's longtime dream of the presidency suddenly had been resurrected, at least as the likely heir to the support of much of the Democratic establishment.

Johnson summoned Humphrey to the White House and told him he did not intend to take sides in the race. Considering the low state of LBJ's popularity, it wasn't the worst news Humphrey could have heard. He made a key strategic decision. It was too late to develop a campaign from scratch through the primary-election process, so he would stay out of the primaries and rely on his longtime connection with party leaders and the labor movement. The assassination of Dr. Martin Luther King Jr. in Memphis in April brought the campaign to a sudden halt, and it was not until later in the month that Humphrey finally declared his candidacy and continued to pile up delegates without entering a single primary.

The climax came in California. Kennedy, rebounding in Oregon from the only defeat a Kennedy had ever suffered anywhere, got back on track by defeating McCarthy there. But his Election Night celebration in the Ambassador Hotel ballroom in Los Angeles was suddenly shattered by more assassin's bullets, as Robert Kennedy was departing through a kitchen passageway. He died about twenty-six hours later in a nearby hospital after surgery.[33] From it all Hubert Humphrey now emerged as the Democratic hope to salvage the White House from the grasp of the anointed Republican nominee, Richard Nixon.

The honor, however, had come at a heavy price for Humphrey. In July, Johnson resumed the heavy bombing of North Vietnam as Humphrey continued to stand uncomfortably behind him, and angry protesters at his rallies chanted, "Dump the Hump!" A pro-Humphrey committee wrote a Vietnam platform plank designed to be acceptable to LBJ. But when Humphrey showed it to him, Johnson warned, "Hubert, if you do this I'll just have to be opposed to it, and say so."[34] He said it could jeopardize developments in the Paris peace negotiations. Humphrey submitted a rewrite of the plank, and Johnson rejected that one as well.

At the convention in Chicago, for which Mayor Richard J. Daley ordered out the full city police force, the plank supporting Johnson on Vietnam beat the anti-war plank by a ratio of three to two, setting off more protests in the streets in what a postconvention investigation later said had turned into a "police riot." Many angry and disruptive protesters created mayhem, shouting, "Hey, hey, LBJ! How many kids have you killed today?"[35] But on the one roll call for the presidential nomination, Humphrey won easily. Having failed at a last-minute effort to persuade Ted Kennedy to be his running mate, he settled on Senator Edmund Muskie of Maine.

The convention did not mark an end to Humphrey's torment. Kicking off his fall campaign against Nixon and running mate Governor Spiro Agnew of Maryland, Humphrey was a man walking on eggs in any discussion of Vietnam, for fear of incurring the further wrath of Johnson. When he said in Philadelphia he thought some American forces could start coming home later in 1968 or early 1969, Johnson interjected, "No man can predict when that day will come."[36]

Nixon meanwhile, ready to exploit the slightest daylight showing between Humphrey and LBJ, offered, "It would be very unfortunate if any implication was left in the minds of the American people that we were able to bring home our forces now because suddenly the war was at an end." He went on, "I for one don't want to pull the rug out from our negotiations in Paris."[37]

By now, Humphrey's campaign manager for the fall campaign, the Kennedy veteran Larry O'Brien, told Humphrey regarding Vietnam, "You have to prove you are your own man. You're not going to be elected president unless people are convinced you stand on your own two feet—and this is the issue you can prove it on!" An irate Humphrey replied, "Damn it, I'm on my own two feet," and set to work with his advisers on a tougher speech on the war.[38]

The next night, fifteen minutes before airtime, Humphrey phoned Johnson and told him what he was going to say: "As President I would be willing to stop the bombing of North Vietnam as an acceptable risk for peace," adding, "If the government of North Vietnam were to show bad faith, I would reserve the right to resume the bombing."[39] He wrote later that Johnson just listened and then said, "I gather you're not asking my advice." Humphrey told him that what he would say would "in no way jeopardize" what the president was trying to do. Johnson replied, "Well, you're going to give the speech anyway. Thanks for calling, Hubert," and he hung up.[40]

The speech delivered in Salt Lake City liberated the vice president, answered the hecklers, and was an immediate spur to desperately needed fund-raising. Joseph Califano, a key Johnson White House aide, wrote later, "Humphrey's speech turned the campaign into a horse race but Johnson never forgave him for it."[41] Nixon demonstrated his concern by suggesting in his fashion that Humphrey ought to clarify his statement "and say he is not undercutting the United States position in Paris."[42]

In the next days on the stump, the crowds grew larger, the hecklers desisted, and the Nixon lead in the polls began to narrow. The ADA executive board endorsed Humphrey and, tardily, so did McCarthy.

Meanwhile, Lyndon Johnson increased his efforts to achieve a breakthrough in the peace negotiations in Paris. On television he reported that the Hanoi regime had agreed to have the Saigon government participate, and the National Liberation Front would be permitted a role. Humphrey was jubilant. But suddenly the Saigon regime was boycotting the Paris talks after all, rejecting any participation by the NLF. Humphrey obviously was crushed.

Johnson was furious. He turned over to Humphrey pertinent classified information garnered in wiretaps at the South Vietnamese Embassy in Washington, including a phone call from Anna Chennault, the Chinese-born widow of the World War II flying ace General Claire Chennault, who was a friend of the South Vietnamese leaders and a strong Nixon supporter and confidante. She was heard, according to Clark Clifford's memoir, conveying "a simple and authoritative message from the Nixon camp" that Thieu would get a better deal in any peace negotiations if he were to wait until Nixon was elected and in office.[43] The reason Johnson didn't make use of the information himself, Clifford wrote, was that he did not want to further disrupt any negotiations, because "he was really ambivalent about whether he really wanted Humphrey to be elected" and was more concerned about "what his place in history would be."[44]

As for Humphrey, he wrote later in his memoir, "I wonder if I should have blown the whistle on Anna Chennault and Nixon. He must have known about her call to Thieu. I *wish* I could have been sure. Damn Thieu. Dragging his feet this past weekend hurt us. I wonder if that call did it. If Nixon knew. Maybe I should have blasted them anyway."[45] Joe Califano wrote later that Humphrey's refusal to use the information "became the occasion for a lasting rift" between him and LBJ.[46]

In any event, no firm evidence became public about the Anna Chennault caper, and in an extremely close election, Nixon won with 43.4 percent of the popular vote to 42.7 percent for Humphrey and 13.5 percent for the former Alabama governor George C. Wallace, running as an American Independent. Nixon got 302 electoral votes, 32 more than he needed, compared with 191 for Humphrey and 45 for Wallace, all from the South. In his memoir Johnson argued that the failure of the Saigon regime to go to the Paris peace talks "cost Hubert Humphrey the presidency."[47]

Beyond that, the defeat of Hubert Humphrey meant the end of Johnson's Great Society, embodying some of the most innovative ideas for implementing liberal social goals since the New Deal. Despite Johnson's personal pettiness and often ill consideration of his vice president, Humphrey served LBJ well, if often uncomfortably and torn by his own doubts about Johnson's policies on the war.

A committed public servant who reveled in "the politics of joy" even when it was joyless, Humphrey returned to the Senate in 1971, winning the Minnesota seat being vacated by Eugene McCarthy. He sought the presidency in 1972, winning some state primaries, but lost the Democratic nomination to George McGovern, with the Vietnam War still a centerpiece of the campaign. He was reelected to the Senate in 1976 and served into the next year, when he was hospitalized with terminal bladder cancer. He bid a tear-inducing good-bye to his decades of colleagues with dramatic speeches to the Senate and the House. He died on January 13, 1978, at the age of sixty-six, beloved in his own party and respected outside it, despite allowing his sense of loyalty to Lyndon Johnson to cloud his political judgment on the war in the most critical moments of his political life.

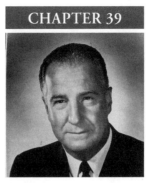

CHAPTER 39

SPIRO T. AGNEW
OF MARYLAND

Until Spiro Agnew's time in office, probably no American vice president had brought more attention to it, was more controversial during his incumbency, or left it in greater disgrace. As the governor of Maryland, "Ted" Agnew was relatively unknown nationally when he was unexpectedly chosen by the presidential nominee Richard Nixon as his running mate in the tumultuous year of 1968, but Agnew rose like a rocket in that campaign and thereafter. His climb was fueled by his aggressive yet entertaining rhetoric against a variety of political targets. But after nearly five years of Agnew's controversial prominence, his career imploded in a personal scandal that ended in resignation to avoid impeachment and imprisonment.

Agnew's childhood and early adult years gave no hint of the controversies that eventually would envelop him. He was born of a Greek immigrant father and a western Virginia mother in a second-floor rear apartment over a florist shop in Baltimore on November 9, 1918, two days before the armistice ending World War I. He was an average child, not particularly athletic, and an average student, winning acceptance in his Forest Park High School crowd as a piano player. The school being highly rated, young Agnew was admitted to Johns Hopkins University, majoring in chemistry, but didn't do well and dropped out. Later, while taking law school night classes at the University of Baltimore, he worked as an assistant insurance underwriter, where he met his future wife, Judy. Three months before the

Japanese attack on Pearl Harbor, he was drafted into the army, six months later he was commissioned as a second lieutenant, and three days after that, he and Judy were married. He was shipped overseas in March 1944 and that winter took part in the Battle of the Bulge in France, his unit then pushing into Germany by war's end. He returned with a Bronze Star and the Combat Infantryman's Badge.[1]

After a brief time as an assistant personnel manager for a small super-market chain, Agnew was called up for the Korean War as a reserve officer, although he now had three children. He was about to be shipped overseas again when the army recognized it had made a mistake and discharged him, sending him back to his job at the supermarket. Because of his legal train-ing he was "promoted" to interrogating petty shoplifters. He soon quit and opened a small law firm with a friend in suburban Towson, the Baltimore County seat. As a Republican he won a seat on the county board of zoning appeals and soon became chairman. He set his sights on the county execu-tive position in 1962, offering himself as a civil libertarian and a champion of civil rights, and won as a result of a Democratic split, becoming the first Republican to hold the office in the twentieth century.[2]

Agnew got the county council to create a new human relations com-mission, but during a local dispute over alleged racial discrimination, he scolded demonstrators for their "impatience and resentment" when the dispute was not being resolved to their liking. He finally stepped in and completed a compromise that the commission had been on the verge of reaching, taking credit.

At any rate, Agnew was beginning to cement his reputation as a strong but moderating liberal voice for civil rights in the state, embracing such things as open-housing legislation without offending Republican dogma. He told one Democratic audience, "Most of the voices raised so far in the civil rights controversy are either militantly integrationist or militantly segregationist. There is a great need to hear voices from calm moderates of both races," the implication being, like his own.[3]

Agnew had barely gotten into harness as the county executive in June 1963 when he decided to take a hand in presidential politics. He decided that in 1964 neither the ultraconservative senator Barry Goldwater of Ari-zona nor the ultraliberal governor Nelson Rockefeller of New York would be able to unite the Republican Party and defeat President John F. Kennedy, expected to seek reelection. So he went to Washington and, in vain, urged the surprised moderate senator Thomas Kuchel of California to seek the 1964 nomination.

In 1964, when Rockefeller's candidacy crashed and Governor William Scranton of Pennsylvania was induced to try to save the party from Goldwater, Agnew became his Maryland chairman and was with a loser again, but the brief association boosted his reputation as a progressive. In 1965, when he first met Rockefeller, Agnew was impressed with his commanding personality and organizational skill and began to see him as the party's 1968 standard-bearer after all. Agnew also wrote Richard Nixon, not yet personally known to him, to sound him out on his political plans. Nixon was now practicing law in New York after his failed bid for governor in California but didn't answer for months, leading Agnew to tell a political associate, "That damn Nixon, he won't even answer your letters. No wonder he can't get elected."[4]

It was clear that Ted Agnew was getting restless in his job as a county executive, and as he approached the end of his four-year term he decided to run for governor. The Republican nomination in the strongly Democratic state of Maryland was not in great demand, and Agnew, as the highest-ranking Republican statewide officeholder, had no serious primary opposition in 1966. In the midst of all the racial turmoil at that time, the Democratic voters handed Agnew a huge gift by nominating a blatantly segregationist perennial also-ran named George Mahoney, a wealthy paving contractor. Taking dead aim at the talk of open housing, Mahoney adopted as his campaign slogan "Your Home Is Your Castle—Protect It!" and won the nomination on the strength of a white backlash vote.[5]

In the general election, Agnew challenged Mahoney to a debate, but Mahoney refused, whereupon Agnew made much of a Mahoney rally at which Ku Klux Klan stickers were seen. Despite some allegations of a shady Agnew deal connected with the proposed construction of a bridge to be built parallel to the existing one across the Chesapeake Bay, which were raised again later in his career, Agnew won the general election over the outspoken segregationist, further enhancing his own reputation as a civil rights stalwart.

Taking office in January 1967, Agnew inherited a Democratic-controlled legislature in Annapolis. He supported and passed a limited open-housing plan that would apply only to new houses and new apartment units, still defending the right of the individual owner of an existing home to sell to a buyer of his choice—apparently his version of Mahoney's "Your Home Is Castle" slogan. It was the first open-housing legislation passed in Maryland history, further embellishing his pro–civil rights record.[6]

Early on, Agnew also called on the General Assembly to authorize three new bridge sites across the Chesapeake, and one was eventually chosen after he had disposed of his share of the land involved, supposedly settling the matter. In time, however, his aloofness and jibes at uncooperative Democratic legislators wore thin. When a young state delegate, Paul Sarbanes, later a U.S. senator, balked at Agnew's education cuts in "the East Coast version of the Ronald Reagan budget" in California, Agnew dismissed his criticism as "a Sarbanality." It was a demonstration of his way with words that soon would become his trademark.[7]

Meanwhile, Agnew's interest in presidential politics and his efforts to bring more progressive leadership to the Republican Party had not waned. In April 1967 he brushed aside Rockefeller's declaration that he was strongly backing Governor George Romney of Michigan for the 1968 party nomination and began to court him anyway. In May, Rockefeller agreed to see Agnew in his Manhattan office but would not budge in his disinterest in running. In July, however, Romney made his infamous remark of having received a "brainwashing" from the American generals in Vietnam and his candidacy began to go south. Soon after, in response to a *Time* magazine cover touting a Rockefeller-Reagan "dream ticket," Rockefeller declared flatly, "I am not a candidate, I'm not going to be a candidate, and I don't want to be President."[8]

Romney's campaign meanwhile collapsed so thoroughly that he was forced to withdraw from the race two weeks before the opening 1968 primary in New Hampshire, won overwhelmingly by Nixon. Soon after, though, Rockefeller gave a go-ahead to the presidential draft Agnew had been pushing. Rockefeller scheduled a televised news conference ostensibly to declare his candidacy, and Agnew invited the Annapolis press into his office to share the great moment with him. As all eyes were glued to the television set, the blow came. "I have decided," Rockefeller said, "to reiterate unequivocally that I am not a candidate campaigning directly or indirectly for the Presidency of the United States."

Agnew sat there, frozen and humiliated, as Rockefeller explained that "a considerable majority of the party's leaders" had made clear they wanted Nixon as their nominee. Nixon agents swiftly fielded the disappointed Agnew on the short hop, recruiting him to their cause.[9]

Two developments in Maryland now crystallized Agnew's political thinking and sharpened his view on law enforcement in dealing with racial protest in a way that coincided with Nixon's own. First, students at Bowie State College, a predominantly black school in the state university system, complained about decrepit dormitories, triggering a boycott and demanding that Agnew come to the campus. He refused and ordered Bowie State closed. Then, just as news broke of the assassination of Dr. Martin Luther King Jr. in Memphis, all hell broke loose in Baltimore among its black population. Fires and vandalism spread, killing six and injuring seven hundred, with thousands more arrested. Local black moderate leaders took to the streets to cool the rioting, but to little avail.

On the night before King's assassination, Stokely Carmichael, a young evangelist of Black Power, had shown up in a tough black Baltimore neighborhood allegedly preaching, "The only way to deal with a white man is across the barrel of a gun." When Agnew heard this, he was furious.[10] He summoned a hundred moderate Baltimore black leaders, who sat stunned as he read them the riot act, with uniformed, armed state troopers at his side. He charged that these well-respected moderates "ran" in the face of intruding Black Power rabble-rousers. They angrily walked out, declaring that when "the chief executive [of Maryland] should be calling for unity, he deliberately sought to divide us."[11]

The story of Agnew's confrontation was big news in Maryland and was picked up by the wire services and brought to Nixon's attention. That summer at the Republican convention in Miami Beach, at two private sessions with party leaders on the party's prospective choice for vice president, no one even mentioned Agnew until Nixon did. A Nixon pollster confided later that a survey investigating which Republican would most help the ticket found that Nixon would run strongest alone, so he chose the little-known Agnew, whose latest views on domestic violence closely resembled his own. "The name of Spiro Agnew is not a household name," the new running mate wistfully acknowledged to reporters. "I certainly hope that it will become one within the next couple of months." Few who heard him express that wish could have foreseen how soon it would come to pass.[12]

The day after Nixon disclosed his choice, he held a press party at nearby Key Biscayne. An amiable Nixon at poolside proudly explained, "There is a mysticism about men. There is a quiet confidence. You look a man in the eye and you know he's got it: brains. This guy has got it. If he doesn't, Nixon has made a bum choice."[13] He had chosen a potential president by his gut feeling.

In the ensuing campaign, Agnew was assigned to secondary markets and told to aim his criticisms at the Democratic presidential nominee, Hubert Humphrey, which he did with relish. But as a novice in the national arena, he invited criticism. When he accused Humphrey of being "soft on communism" and "squishy soft" on crime, he drew comparisons to the Red-hunting Joe McCarthy and to Nixon himself in his early campaign against Helen Gahagan Douglas and was described as Eisenhower's hatchet-man in attacks on Adlai Stevenson.[14] The Nixon aide John Sears was dispatched to keep an eye on Agnew.

The vice presidential nominee seemed to stumble from one gaffe to another. When a reporter asked him in Chicago whether he was concerned there weren't many blacks in his crowds, Agnew replied, "When I am moving in a crowd I don't say, 'Well, there's a Negro, there's an Italian, and there a Greek and there's a Polack,'" using the derisive word for a Pole. Later when leaving Las Vegas on his campaign plane, he observed a portly, native-born Japanese American reporter from the *Baltimore Sun* snoozing in a seat and asked, "What's the matter with the fat Jap?"[15] Agnew professed not to realize he was being offensive, but as time went on his rhetoric hardened to the point that his promise to be a household name was well on the way to reality.

Nevertheless, with Humphrey having his hands full justifying Johnson's escalation of the Vietnam War, Nixon and Agnew made the most of law-and-order issues in the face of rising street protest against the war, street crime, and racial conflict. On Election Night, Nixon and Agnew edged Humphrey and Edmund Muskie of Maine by seven-tenths of 1 percent of the popular vote, 43.4 percent to 42.7 percent, with the third-party nominee, George Wallace, winning a surprising 13.5 percent. In the electoral college, the Republican ticket won 301 votes compared with 191 for the Democratic and 46 for Wallace.

Agnew embarked on the vice presidency with high hopes, but from the start he was frozen out by the tight-knit Nixon staff. He conscientiously undertook presiding over the Senate, but as the first Senate president in nearly a quarter-century not to have been a member, he stumbled concerning a traditional prohibition against trying to lobby a senator on the floor. When he asked the conservative GOP senator Len Jordan of Utah whether the administration had his vote on a particular measure, the indignant Jordan replied, "You did have, until now." Soon after, the senator announced that henceforth the "Jordan Rule" would apply: If Agnew tried to lobby him again, he would vote the other way. Agnew apologized and backed off.[16]

Initially Agnew was loaded with responsibilities, a few of them real, most of them showcases. He was a member of the cabinet and the National Security Council and chairman of a host of councils dealing with urban affairs, economic policy, intergovernmental relations, and the space agency. As a former governor, he was responsible for dealing with governors, county executives, and mayors, becoming a shortstop fielding their gripes. Agnew had particular trouble with his old hero, Rockefeller of New York, who insisted on dealing directly with John Ehrlichman, Nixon's chief aide on domestic matters.[17]

Ehrlichman and Bob Haldeman, known derisively in the White House as "the Germans," themselves functioned as shortstops, keeping Agnew out of the presidential loop they constituted with Nixon and, on foreign policy, with Henry Kissinger. Agnew wrote later that Haldeman once told him, "The President does not like you to take an opposition view at a cabinet meeting, or say anything that can be construed to be mildly not in accord with his thinking."[18]

Agnew soon turned to the political side of his job, selling the administration to the public, looking to the 1970 midterm elections. That suited him; he found speech making more personally rewarding and less arduous than being entangled in bureaucratic tasks. It also gave him an opportunity to repair his somewhat tarnished image, with what came to be known as Agnewisms, preaching the anti-liberal, anti-protest gospel of "the silent majority" to the masses.

In Dallas six days before the huge November 15, 1969, Vietnam

Moratorium Day protest on campuses around the country, he asked, "Should the establishments of this country . . . cringe and wring their hands before a small group of misfits seeking to discredit a free system because they can't effectively compete and find success elsewhere? I find it hard to believe that the way to run the world has been revealed to a minority of pushy youngsters and middle-aged malcontents. . . . Only the president has the power to negotiate peace. Congress cannot dictate it, the Vietnam Moratorium Committee cannot coerce it, and all the students in America cannot create it."[19]

Agnew continued his tirade in New Orleans, declaring, "A spirit of national masochism prevails, encouraged by an effete corps of impudent snobs who characterize themselves as intellectuals." He said, "If the Moratorium had any use whatever, it served as an emotional purgative for those who felt the need to cleanse themselves of their lack of ability to offer a constructive solution to the problem."[20] In collaboration with the Nixon speechwriters Pat Buchanan and William Safire, the vice president was reintroducing himself to America. Noting the furor he was creating, he said, "It appears that by slaughtering a sacred cow I triggered a holy war. I have no regrets. I do not intend to repudiate my beliefs, recant my words, or run and hide."[21]

Also in that November, shortly after Nixon had made a televised speech in defense of his Vietnam policy, Agnew took on network news analysts who had observed that there was little new in the policy. Agnew assaulted their "instant analysis and querulous criticism," declaring that Nixon had the right to communicate with the American people without having his words and thought "characterized through the prejudices of hostile critics before they can even be digested." He questioned the concentration of power "in the hands of a tiny and closed fraternity of privileged men, elected by no one, and enjoying a monopoly sanctioned and licensed by the government" and suggested it was "a form of censorship."[22] His remarks were taken as a declaration of war on the television industry, raising concerns about loss of federal broadcast licenses. The next time Nixon made a televised speech, the network analysts limited themselves to perfunctory recaps of what he had said.

Next, Agnew targeted the print press, particularly the *New York Times* and the *Washington Post,* and it was clear by now that Ted Agnew was having a whale of a time making himself "a household name." He sprayed his audience with alliterations, speaking of "partisans of passion," "supercilious sophisticates," and, later, "nattering nabobs of negativism" and "hopeless, hysterical hypochondriacs of history." To suggestions that Agnew was going too far, Nixon asked only that his administration leaders remember that "when the action is hot, keep the rhetoric cool."[23] Agnew, however, was emboldened by now to try to assert more influence in the White House, particularly as pushback against Ehrlichman. "We couldn't program Agnew to leave a burning building," Ehrlichman wrote later.[24]

In August 1970, the Nixon speechwriters were told to target Democratic liberals and again worked closely with Agnew on a catchy description of those in their aim. They came up with "radical liberals," sometimes shortened to "radiclibs," a catchall that even caught in its web a New York Rockefeller Republican, Senator Charles Goodell, who would lose in November. Agnew was now riding high in the Gallup Poll, running third nationally behind only Nixon and the Christian evangelist Billy Graham.

At one late fall planning meeting, however, he artlessly told Nixon, "Mr. President, as I travel around I get a great many questions about our 1972 ticket." Nixon merely dodged, telling him, "Of course, this far ahead the President can't say anything. Just say we're only thinking about November of 1970. You can say, 'The President has shown great confidence in me so far, and I hope it will continue.'"[25] For all the mayhem that Agnew had wrought on his targets, the Republicans picked up only two Senate seats, losing nine in the House and eleven governorships.

At the postelection Republican Governors Conference in Sun Valley, Idaho, Agnew was dispatched to inform the attendees that Nixon was appointing as his new secretary of treasury a former governor, John B. Connally of Texas—a Democrat. To the Republicans present, including the eleven who had lost in November and were looking for new jobs, the news was not welcome. Agnew also lectured them not to place blame or offer excuses for the losses suffered, "even when it masquerades as constructive criticism."[26]

One of the surviving governors, Tom McCall of Oregon, called the vice president's remarks "a rotten, bigoted little speech" and "the most divisive speech ever given by such a high official."[27] At a private meeting with the governors, Agnew confronted McCall, who replied sarcastically, "I'm not sure I said 'rotten.'" He denied that he had ever called for Agnew to be dumped from the ticket in 1972 but simply had raised the question of whether Nixon would want to run with someone who had campaigned "with a knife in his shawl."[28]

In 1971, when Nixon was in sensitive consultations on opening relations with what was then called Communist China, the subject of Taiwan came up at a meeting of the National Security Council. When UN Ambassador George H. W. Bush reported that the United States didn't have enough votes to save Taiwan's UN seat, Agnew spoke up: "Mr. President, I think it's very simple. The Security Council has every right to do whatever they want, and we have every right to kick their asses out." The next day, according to the Nixon aide William Timmons, Haldeman informed Agnew, "Your presence won't be required at NSC meetings henceforth."[29]

Shortly afterward, as part of a proposed thaw with mainland China, an American table-tennis team played a vastly superior Chinese team using second-string players as a gesture of friendship, and the Americans still lost. But an end to a trade embargo between the two countries followed, and Nixon was praised for his "ping-pong diplomacy." Agnew in a late-night bull session with some reporters said he thought the United States had taken a propaganda beating, that relations with Taiwan would suffer badly, and the United States would appear too eager to reach an accommodation with China. According to the White House tapes, when Nixon heard about this, he told Henry Kissinger, "I suppose you saw what our Peck's Bad Boy did yesterday . . . where he popped off as he does, on this subject, not knowing his ass from his face."[30] Word was passed to Agnew to leave comments on foreign policy to the president.

What Agnew didn't know at the time was that Nixon and Kissinger were deep in secret dealings on a groundbreaking visit of Nixon's to mainland China. Nixon was startled when Agnew suggested that inasmuch as he was going to South Korea for the inauguration of the president, he might just pop over to China! A stammering Nixon turned Agnew off without revealing his own plans.[31] Soon after, when traveling in Africa, Agnew indelicately told one leader there that he disagreed with Nixon on China, whereupon the president complained to Ehrlichman, "Twice Agnew has proposed that *he* go to China! Now he tells the world it's a bad idea for me to go! What am I going to do about him?"[32]

On April 7, 1971, in a taped Oval Office talk with Haldeman, Nixon mused on how he might get Agnew to resign before the 1972 election and then nominating John Connally to replace him as vice president. "We've got to do something, but I don't know what the Christ to do," Nixon said. "What's he [Agnew] going to resign for? . . . Decides to own a television network and so forth? That would be great. Get somebody to buy CBS and have Agnew run it."[33]

After further discussion, Nixon suddenly came up with a brainstorm. "Hey, Bob. Let me ask you about the [Supreme] Court. . . . I'm very much afraid if you put Agnew on, it would raise holy hell in the country, of course."[34] Here was an American president so eager to get his vice president out of the line of presidential succession that he was perfectly willing to shunt him to the highest judicial bench. The notion was dropped for the moment, to be revived soon after.

As for Connally, he saw the vice presidency as a dry hole and continued to resist Nixon's entreaties. In mid-July, the president took him to the mountaintop, describing how the job would be different for him: "You in the job would be basically the president's stand-in. . . . Basically everybody would know it. . . . If there was something important to do, you would do it."[35] But Attorney General John Mitchell still favored Agnew, arguing that Connally as a Democrat could not win Senate confirmation. "Before long," Ehrlichman wrote later, "Mitchell had talked with Nixon, and soon most of the Connally-for-Agnew stars had gone out of the president's eyes."[36]

In September, Ehrlichman again mentioned Agnew, and Nixon offered, "Agnew once told me he wanted to be on the court," referring to the U.S. Supreme Court. Haldeman: "God, that would really rip things up. Talk about your blockbusters. They'll say, 'What's the shoe Nixon's gonna drop next?'" Nixon (defensively): "He'd be a damned good judge." And moments later: "Agnew's a red-hot lawyer. I say why not put him on the court?"[37] In the end, Nixon dropped the idea, but according to Haldeman's diaries, "He still thinks he should indicate his support [for Agnew] whether or not he intends to drop him later, and he thinks also it's a good way to get the P out of the black VP question [nominating an African American] which is sure to arise."[38] Pat Buchanan said later, "By then Nixon realized, 'Look, if you tear this ticket up, you're gonna antagonize and alienate the whole conservative movement, for whom Agnew was a tremendous hero

. . . and why would you do that when it looked like you were playing with a pat hand?"[39]

Through all this, Agnew was out on the campaign trail hammering the Democrats in general and Ed Muskie in particular as the perceived frontrunner. On the night of June 17 a group of burglars hired by the Committee to Reelect the President broke into the Democratic National Committee headquarters at the Watergate office complex in Washington. They were caught by police, triggering the investigation that ultimately drove Nixon from the presidency.

For once, the freezing out of Agnew from the Nixon inner circle was serendipitous for him, keeping him free of an involvement in the break-in itself and the cover-up. The yet-to-be fully investigated episode did not inhibit the landslide reelection of Nixon and Agnew in November, when the Democratic presidential nominee, Senator George S. McGovern, and his running mate, R. Sargent Shriver, carried only the state of Massachusetts and the District of Columbia.

A week after the reelection, Nixon was already fretting about Agnew's expected bid to take over the presidency in 1976. "I'm not sure he's the one to succeed me in 1976—but we may be stuck with him," he told Ehrlichman. "By any criteria he falls short. Energy? He doesn't work hard; he likes to play golf. Leadership? Consistency? He's all over the place." Haldeman suggested, "Maybe the Vice President needs your 'benign neglect.'" Nixon agreed, "Yes, that should be our strategy."[40]

Before long, there would be nothing regarding Agnew for Nixon to joke about. Five days before the second Nixon-Agnew inauguration, a Baltimore County contractor showed his lawyer a subpoena calling him before a grand jury investigating construction kickbacks to Baltimore County officials. When the lawyer told him he would have to tell what he knew or lose immunity against prosecution, the contractor blurted out that he could not do that, explaining, "Because I have been paying off the vice president."[41]

Thus began a long and dramatic episode that ended nearly nine months later with Agnew's resignation in disgrace after pleading nolo contendere to multiple charges of taking bribes as the Baltimore County executive, the governor of Maryland, and even as the vice president. The contractor told of making payoffs to Agnew for county and state contracts that Agnew had steered to him back in Maryland and were still generating income for his firm. These were made in the basement of the White House, including one of about ten thousand dollars in cash.[42]

As the case developed, Nixon and his chief confidants began to think of Agnew's troubles in relation to Nixon's own Watergate dilemma, and the beleaguered president began to entertain thoughts of giving up. On April 17, 1973, a White House tape caught him telling Kissinger, "I've even considered the possibility of, frankly, just throwing myself on the sword, and letting Agnew take it. What the hell."[43] And eight days later: "You know, people say, 'Impeach the president.' Well, then, they get Agnew."[44] When someone raised the question of Nixon's physical safety, he called Agnew his "insurance policy," adding, "No assassin in his right mind would kill me. They know that if they did they would end up with Agnew!"[45]

In mid-May, the first stories on the Baltimore investigation of the contractor broke in the *Wall Street Journal* and the *Washington Post* without implicating Agnew. On July 16, Alexander Butterfield of the White House staff jolted the Senate Watergate investigating committee with the existence of the recording system in the Oval Office. The noose was getting tighter on Nixon and also on Agnew. White House chief of staff Alexander Haig was informed that prosecutors had enough evidence to charge the vice president with "forty felony counts for violations of federal statutes on bribery, tax evasion and corruption."[46]

Questions were raised, however, whether under the Constitution a president or vice president could be indicted and removed by any measure other than impeachment—trial by the House and conviction by the Senate. The White House lawyers reasoned that if Agnew as vice president could avoid indictment, so could Nixon as president. By this time, however, the insurance policy theory had worn thin, and Nixon wanted Agnew out. He sent Haig and the political adviser Bryce Harlow to tell Agnew he wanted him to resign. Agnew later characterized them as having "brought the traditional suicide pistol to my office and laid it on my desk."[47] He refused without a chance to make his case directly to Nixon, to no avail.

In the end, Attorney General Elliot Richardson agreed to remove a prospective felon from the line of presidential succession and to enter into plea bargaining with Agnew's lawyers before the federal judge in the case. He recommended that Agnew not be imprisoned but did not stipulate it as a condition of the plea bargain. The judge sentenced Agnew to three years of unsupervised probation and a fine of ten thousand dollars. After resigning, Agnew read a summary statement of guilt, in which he admitted taking payments that he did not report on his income tax returns but insisted they had not influenced his official actions.[48] Then he walked out of the courtroom a free but disgraced and bitter private citizen.

Nixon wrote later of the resignation in terms of his own fight for political survival: "While some thought his stepping aside would take some of the pressure off the effort to get the president, all it did was open the way to put pressure on the president to resign as well."[49] Agnew had to borrow the $10,000 to pay his fine from his friend Frank Sinatra, who also loaned him $200,000 to pay bills, which included one from the Internal Revenue Service for $150,000 in unpaid back taxes, which, he wrote later, he repaid by 1978.[50]

Upon his resignation Agnew launched a business career in part based on connections made during his overseas travel as vice president, particularly in the Middle East and South America. He was reported to be involved in a land deal in Kentucky, a coal mine in Oklahoma, and a mysterious relationship with a South Korean businessman known for lavishly entertaining American congressmen. In 1976 he formed a nonprofit educational foundation and was later accused by the Anti-Defamation League of B'nai B'rith of planning to use it "for the purpose of organizing a movement to reflect his anti-Israeli, pro-Arab views."[51]

Agnew also wrote a novel about a vice president who intends to run for president and clashes with the incumbent on foreign policy in ways suggesting his own experiences with Nixon. He never saw Nixon again but seventeen years later attended his funeral in Yorba Linda, California, where he was well received by old Nixon administration colleagues. A year later outside the Senate chamber over which he had presided, he attended a ceremony at which a bust of him was dedicated, observing, "I am not blind or deaf to the fact that some people feel that this is a ceremony that should not take place."[52]

The man who declared upon his surprise nomination for the vice presidency in 1968 that he was not a "household name" but vowed to become one had at least succeeded in that. Years later he told of walking down a street in Copenhagen and being stopped by an American stranger who declared, "You're Spiro Agnew! Lay some rhetoric on me, man!"[53] He became more famous, or notorious, for his manner of speaking than for any con-tribution he ever made as vice president, under a president who largely avoided and ignored him. Spiro Agnew died of leukemia on September 17, 1996, at age seventy-seven and was buried in Towson, Maryland, with little public notice.

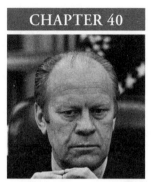

CHAPTER 40

GERALD R. FORD JR.

OF MICHIGAN

O n December 6, 1973, for the first time in American history, a man not elected to the vice presidency took the office. On the heels of the sudden resignation of the incumbent Spiro T. Agnew, who was facing indictment on charges of bribery, corruption, and income-tax evasion, President Richard M. Nixon chose House Minority Leader Gerald R. Ford to replace him. Nixon was the first in history to invoke the Twenty-Fifth Amendment to the Constitution, ratified only six years earlier to provide, for the first time, for filling a vacancy. Only twenty months later, Ford found himself the president of the United States as a result of Nixon's own forced resignation in the White House cover-up of the 1972 break-in of the Democratic National Committee headquarters at the Watergate office complex, in downtown Washington.

Ford was an amiable man who had served a quarter of a century in the House of Representatives, with no greater ambition than someday to become its Speaker. He was the unwitting political beneficiary of the only back-to-back resignations of a duly elected presidential–vice presidential team in the nation's history. Soon after, out of compassion or to try to put the whole episode behind him, Ford pardoned Nixon. At least in part because of that decision, Ford lost the presidency himself in the next election.

Ford was chosen by Nixon for the vice presidency in large part because he was well liked by members of both parties in Congress and seemed certain to be confirmed. Nixon's preference was for John Connally, the former Democratic governor of Texas, for whom the president had hoped to shove Agnew aside in order to make Connally his running mate in 1972. But Agnew had declined to step aside and was kept on the Republican ticket in the face of his great popularity within the Grand Old Party. Nixon knew now that as a converted Republican, Connally could not have been confirmed by the Democratic-controlled Congress, and so he turned to Ford, who could be. Ford's confirmation came twenty-seven days after his nomination, with the office vacant until then.

The brief vice presidency of Jerry Ford was as an extremely trying one. At the time he took over from Agnew, the man who had anointed him was in a desperate fight for his own political survival as more details of the Watergate scandal unraveled, imperiling the second Nixon term. Ford was ideally positioned to serve as Nixon's liaison with Congress, but almost from the outset he was obliged to rally to his benefactor's defense. He had to do so without knowing the truth or falsity of the suspicions that Nixon had somehow been involved in the fiasco or at least involved in an effort to cover up his own awareness of it. But Ford had always been a loyal Republican and in fact a friend of Nixon in their mutual service in the House, and they shared humble beginnings as small-town boys who served in the navy after the attack on Pearl Harbor, before going into politics.

The man who became Nixon's second vice president was born Leslie Lynch King Jr. in Omaha, Nebraska, on July 14, 1913, the namesake of a father who was physically abusive and threatening to the boy's mother, Dorothy Gardner King, leading to a divorce when her son was still an infant. She took him to Grand Rapids, Michigan, where they lived with her parents. There she met and married a paint salesman, Gerald Rudolf Ford, who, although he never legally adopted the boy, renamed him after himself and provided mother and son a secure and loving home. "He was the father I grew up with, the father I loved and learned from and respected," his stepson said later.[1]

Tall and husky, Jerry Ford Jr., became an Eagle Boy Scout, a good student with a friendly disposition, and a star athlete, playing on his high school football team. He got a part-time job slinging hamburgers at a local diner, where one day in 1929, when Jerry was sixteen, a stranger came in and introduced himself as Jerry's birth father. Leslie King Sr. took him to lunch at a nearby restaurant, telling him how well off he now was and how he had just come from Detroit, where he had bought a new Lincoln luxury car. King, inquiring whether he could help financially, handed the boy twenty dollars and asked him if he wanted to go with King to live in Wyoming, where he said he owned acres of ranch land. Young Ford, full of resentment, replied, "No, I like it here."[2]

Ford went on to be named all-state center on his high school team and won a scholarship to the University of Michigan, where he starred as a freshman but was a benchwarmer on the varsity behind an all-American center for two years before making the All-Big Ten team as a senior. He was picked for the East-West Shrine charity game and received offers from the Green Bay Packers and the Detroit Lions to play professionally but elected to take a job as an assistant football and boxing coach at Yale, intending to go to law school there.

At first Ford was turned down for law school admittance, so he took a summer job as an intern forest ranger at Yellowstone National Park. Upon returning to Yale he was admitted to the law school. Through a friend in Michigan, he met a beautiful and sophisticated young woman named Phyllis Brown, who became his first love. When she became a professional model, she recruited him to join in a *Look* magazine picture spread of a ski weekend in Vermont and to appear with her on a cover of *Cosmopolitan*.[3] After working as a volunteer in the 1940 presidential campaign office of Wendell Willkie and graduating from Yale, he decided to return to Grand Rapids to practice law, but Phyllis remained in New York.

Ford formed a new law practice with an old Michigan fraternity brother, Phil Buchen, but on the day after Pearl Harbor he enlisted in the navy. He was made an athletic training officer, first at the Naval Academy in Annapolis and then at a preflight school in Chapel Hill, North Carolina. In early 1943 he was assigned to the USS *Monterey*, a small aircraft carrier whose planes saw action against Japanese targets in the Gilbert Islands and later in support of amphibious invasions elsewhere in the Pacific. As a gunnery officer, he endured kamikaze attacks, and in thirteen months he and other crew members earned eleven battle stars. He also survived a huge typhoon that nearly washed him overboard and at war's end was discharged as a lieutenant commander.[4]

Back in Grand Rapids, Ford began dating a soon-to-be divorcée named

Betty Warren, who was a local department-store fashion designer, and preparing for a primary run for Congress against the incumbent backed by the long-time local Republican boss. Influenced by his exposure to the internationally minded Willkie, he campaigned in 1948 in western Michigan, supporting the United Nations and the Marshall Plan for recovery of Europe, and won the election at age thirty-four. A month later he and Betty were married.

As a freshman in the House, Ford became good friends with a fellow Republican, Richard Nixon. He ingratiated himself with Nixon by writing to commend him for his performance in the Alger Hiss case. When his reputation mounted as a loyal, steady, and industrious Republican, he turned down an opportunity to be the party nominee for the Senate in 1952 after the death of his political ideal, Arthur Vandenberg, preferring to remain where he was.[5] He joined Nixon and others in forming the Chowder and Marching Society, a social club of House Republican World War II veterans. In 1959, he helped replace the likeable but aging Joe Martin of Massachusetts with the feisty Charlie Halleck of Indiana as the House minority leader. In 1960, some Michigan Republicans boosted him to be Nixon's running mate, but Nixon had already made up his mind on Henry Cabot Lodge, even as he solicited recommendations from Ford and other rising Republicans.[6]

In the 1960 campaign, Ford joined a Republican "truth squad" that trailed Democratic presidential nominee John Kennedy to rebut his claims at news conferences. In 1963 Ford was elected to the number-three post in the leadership as chairman of the House Republican Conference. After the death of JFK, President Lyndon Johnson appointed Ford to the blue-ribbon Warren Commission, which investigated the assassination, concluding that the assailant, Lee Harvey Oswald, had acted alone and that there was "no evidence of a conspiracy."[7]

After the shellacking the Republicans took in 1964 with Barry Goldwater as their presidential nominee, losing thirty-eight House seats, a group of Young Turks moved against Halleck with the easy-going Jerry Ford as their candidate. Ford became the House minority leader, only one step short in his ambition for the speakership. But once in office in 1965, Ford could do little to stop the avalanche of legislation that Johnson was to enact, with large Democratic majorities in both houses and the legacy of JFK behind him. Ford, however, was outspoken in his belief that Johnson was not committing enough power, short of nuclear weapons, to win in Vietnam and told him so, warning that if the war dragged on he would lose the public's support.[8]

Johnson was not happy with Halleck's replacement by Ford, jibing that the Michigander had "played too much football without a helmet" and he was so dumb that he couldn't "walk and chew gum at the same time."[9] In 1968, Ford as House minority leader gaveled open the Republican National Convention that nominated Nixon on the first ballot and was invited to a midnight conference of party leaders to consider the choice of a running mate. Sitting next to Ford, the presidential nominee turned to him and said, "I know that in the past, Jerry, you have thought about being vice president. Would you want it this year?" Ford told him thanks but no thanks.[10] Once again as in 1960, Nixon was serenading the leaders, letting them think they had a say in the matter when he had already decided. The next morning Ford got a phone call from a Nixon aide telling him the candidate's choice was Spiro T. Agnew of Maryland. "I shook my head in disbelief," Ford wrote later.[11]

Nixon won the election narrowly over the Democrat Hubert Humphrey, but the Republicans gained only five seats in the House, leaving Ford twenty-six short of what he would have needed to be promoted to Speaker. But as minority leader he looked forward to working with a Republican president, and he wrote, "I believed we would have a good chance to win to the House [in 1972] with his reelection."[12]

With both houses of Congress remaining in Democratic hands, Nixon embarked on his presidency determined to assert as much executive power as he could in dealing with the legislature. He put one of his chief aides, John Ehrlichman, in charge of dealing with Congress on domestic affairs, which put him on a collision course with Ford in the House. Ehrlichman referred to the leaders there as "that Congressional herd of mediocrities" and said of his first meeting with Ford, "I was not impressed. It was clear in our first conversation in 1969 that he wasn't thrilled to be harnessed to the Nixon Administration. I came away from his office with the impression that Jerry Ford might have become a pretty good Grand Rapids insurance agent; he played a good game of golf, but he wasn't excessively bright."[13]

In 1969 amid speculation that he was acting at the behest of the White House, Ford initiated a campaign to impeach Supreme Court Justice

William O. Douglas in a period during which two Nixon nominees for the court, Clement F. Haynsworth and W. Harrold Carswell, were rejected. Douglas's lifestyle—multiple marriages and divorces, some to women forty years his junior, financial irregularities, and his liberal philosophy—was raised against him, leading to Senate committee hearings at which Ford testified. He denied he had ever been asked by Nixon or his White House to bring the impeachment charges, and the matter was dropped, but it left a shadow over Ford's reputation.[14]

The stormy political year of 1972 was highlighted by the foiled June break-in of the Democratic National Committee headquarters by burglars in the hire of the Nixon reelection committee. The Democratic chairman of the House Banking and Currency Committee, the seventy-nine-year-old Wright Patman of Texas, undertook an investigation of the money trail of payments to the burglars, whereupon Nixon's right-hand man, Bob Haldeman, wrote in his diary that Nixon "wants to be sure we put the screws on Congress to turn off the Patman hearings."[15] At a taped meeting with Haldeman and the White House counsel John Dean, Nixon specifically mentioned some Republican committee members whom Ford should approach, including one ambitious member: "After all, if we ever win the House, Jerry will be the speaker and he could tell him if he did not get off— he will not be chairman, ever."[16] On the committee vote to hold hearings, all sixteen Republicans voted against, along with four opposing Democrats, and the hearings were abandoned, by a vote of twenty to fifteen.

On Election Day, despite the unfolding Watergate scandal, Nixon and Agnew easily won reelection, and it appeared the matter would blow over. Ford continued in the House as a loyal Nixon ally through two political explosions that in a short time would rocket him first into the vice presidency and then the presidency. First, the forced resignation of Agnew in October 1973, described in chapter 39, and then Nixon's own culpability in the Watergate cover-up, which forced him to resign as well the next August, made Gerald Ford the fortieth vice president and then the thirty-eighth president without having been elected to either office.

With Agnew on the way out, Nixon drew an assurance about the popular Ford from the Democratic House Speaker Carl Albert: "He would be the easiest man that I know of to confirm in the House of Representatives. There wouldn't be any question in my mind but that he would be confirmed, and it would not be a long, drawn-out matter either." Later, Albert claimed, "We gave Nixon no choice but Ford. Congress made Jerry Ford President."[17] So Nixon, having abandoned hopes of replacing Agnew with John Connally, turned to good old Jerry Ford, everybody's friend on Capitol Hill, the safe bet to be confirmed by Congress under the new Twenty-Fifth Amendment.

On October 12, Nixon called Ford in, told him he was his choice, and asked him what his political plans were. Ford told Nixon he had promised his wife, Betty, that he would retire from politics after finishing his vice presidential term and had no plans to run for president after that. "Well, that's good," Nixon replied, according to Ford, "because John Connally is my choice for 1976. He'd be excellent."[18] Ford knew where he stood from the start.

Congressional hearings were held from November 7 through 26 on Ford's confirmation. According to Alexander Haig, Nixon's chief of staff at the time, both Democrats and Republicans in Congress let Nixon know that support of Ford would be contingent on release of the White House tapes. Haig wrote later he feared that a continued vacancy in the vice presidency as the Watergate inquiry grew closer to Nixon might yet put Carl Albert in the Oval Office.[19]

On October 20 in an act of open defiance, Nixon ordered Attorney General Elliot Richardson to fire special prosecutor Archibald Cox. Richardson flatly refused and resigned, as did his deputy William Ruckelshaus for the same reason, in what came to be known as the "Saturday Night Massacre." The deed was then done by the third in command at the Justice Department, Solicitor General Robert Bork. The Supreme Court ordered that the tapes be turned over to the Senate investigating committee, and the Ford confirmation finally went forward.

In late November the Senate overwhelmingly endorsed Ford, and a week later the House completed his confirmation. He was sworn in with Nixon present, even as new Watergate pressures continued to imperil Nixon's own security as president. The new vice president identified himself as "a Ford, not a Lincoln," a modest comparison with which most in the chamber, knowing him well, could agree. William Greider of the *Washington Post,* one of the nation's most perceptive and fair reporters, wrote of him, "The more they thought about Jerry Ford, the more they thought of him."[20]

Nixon told Ford he wanted him to attend cabinet and National Security

Committee meetings and be his chief liaison with his old colleagues in Congress. But under the threatening circumstances to Nixon, Ford was put to work shoring up the Republican Party around the country for the next eight months. As the year dragged on, there were disclosures, including the embarrassing eighteen-and-a-half-minute gap in one of the tapes being transcribed by Nixon's personal secretary, Rose Mary Woods. Ford's travels became virtually a nonstop defense of the man who had put him a heartbeat from the presidency. He found himself repeatedly insisting he believed in Nixon's innocence of covering up his administration's and his own involvement in the whole sordid affair and its aftermath. But Ford's defense of Nixon was a limited one, in that he kept saying Nixon was "innocent of any impeachable offense."[21]

As the *Washington Post* reporter covering Ford's vice presidency, I interviewed him in early July 1974 aboard *Air Force Two* about the noose tightening around Nixon's neck and the difficulty of defending the man he might well soon succeed. He did not want even to talk about the prospect, as if doing so would be an act of disloyalty. Nonetheless, he acknowledged that he was probably hurting himself politically with his continuing profession of Nixon's innocence but said anything less would be taken as abandonment of him.

On the final weekend of this salvage mission, as Ford was campaigning and speaking in Mississippi and Louisiana, key Republicans, including the Senate minority whip Robert Griffin of Michigan, learned of the "smoking gun" tape of June 23, 1972. On it, only six days after the Watergate break-in, Nixon spoke of efforts to cover up the White House involvement. Word was flashed to Ford, and on returning to Washington he issued a brief statement saying it would serve no useful purpose for him to say anything at all regarding the possible impeachment of Nixon.[22] As Ford's longtime aide Bob Hartmann wrote later, "No longer was [Ford's task] to save the president who appointed him but to save the presidency he might inherit."[23]

On August 1, Haig came to Ford's office and asked him whether he was ready to assume the presidency "in a short period of time." Ford said he was, and according to him a discussion ensued of the Twenty-Fifth Amendment and also of the presidential powers of pardon. Ford wrote of what Haig told him: "According to some on Nixon's White House staff, Nixon could agree to leave in return for an agreement that the new president—Gerald Ford—would pardon him. Haig emphasized that these weren't his suggestions." Ford went on to note, "Because of his references to pardon authority, I did ask Haig about the extent of a President's pardon power," and Haig cited a White House lawyer as saying, "A President does have authority to grant a pardon even before criminal action has been taken against an individual."[24] Intentionally or not, Haig seemed to have planted the notion in Ford's head.

On the night of August 8 on nationwide television, Nixon announced that he would resign the next day, rationalizing his reason for doing so: "I hope I will have hastened the start of the process of healing which is so desperately needed in America."[25] It was hardly a confession of wrong-doing, attributing his decision to loss of sufficient support in Congress to go on. The next morning, after Nixon had made emotional farewell remarks to his staff and others in the East Room of the White House and flown into California exile, Ford took the presidential oath in the same room and declared to a relieved nation, "Our long national nightmare is over." Aware that he had just become the first president not elected by the people after having been the first vice president not elected by them, he said, "If you have not chosen me by secret ballot, neither have I gained office by secret promises. I have not campaigned either for the presidency or the vice presidency. I have not subscribed to any partisan platform, I am indebted to no man and to only one woman, my dear wife Betty, as I begin the most difficult job in the world."[26]

To fill the vacancy caused by his ascendance to the presidency, Ford chose the former governor Nelson A. Rockefeller of New York, soon confirmed. On Sunday morning, September 8, Ford announced the unconditional pardon for all of Nixon's alleged Watergate sins, saying neither Nixon and his family nor the country at large could stand the drawn-out ordeal that a criminal prosecution would have entailed. "My conscience tells me it is my duty," he told a shocked nation, "not only to proclaim domestic tranquility but to use every means that I have to insure it."[27]

The first protest came from Ford's newly appointed press secretary, Jerald terHorst, previously the Washington bureau chief of the *Detroit News,* who instantly became a hero to many in the press corps for submitting his resignation on the spot to his old Michigan friend. Around the country, the conclusion was drawn: that a deal had been struck whereby Ford had agreed to pardon Nixon before becoming president himself. Ford flatly denied the allegation and testified before the House Judiciary Committee investigating the matter.

In any event, Ford served in the Oval Office through the remainder of the second term to which Nixon had been elected. In 1976, despite saying earlier that he would not seek a term of his own, Ford did so. He turned back a strong challenge for the Republican nomination from the former governor Ronald Reagan of California in that year's primary elections and at the party national convention in Kansas City. But the long shadow of the Nixon pardon hung over his general-election campaign against the former Democratic governor Jimmy Carter of Georgia, and he lost narrowly that November.

In gaining the Oval Office, Jerry Ford far exceeded his earlier quest to become House Speaker. But in his eight months as vice president he was unwittingly reduced to the role of a bit player in what is generally considered to be the worst American political scandal up to that time. Years later, his pardon of Nixon was judged by many as wise as well as compassionate, yet would remain the most controversial if memorable act of his presidential tenure.

In retirement, the still robust Jerry Ford lived an active physical life, playing golf and skiing at homes in Rancho Mirage, California, and Vail, Colorado, and lecturing for nearly thirty more years. He died at age ninety-three on the day after Christmas 2006 and was buried at the Ford Presidential Museum, in his hometown of Grand Rapids, Michigan.

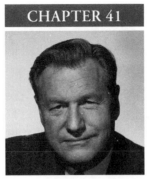

CHAPTER 41

NELSON A. ROCKEFELLER

OF NEW YORK

I n the country where it's said that every mother's son can become president, Nelson Aldrich Rockefeller was one of the relatively few who could legitimately say, as he did later in life, "When you think of what I had, what else was there to aspire to?"[1] One of the five grandsons of John D. Rockefeller, touted as the richest man in the world, Nelson fell one rung short as the forty-first vice president. After failing to be elected to the presidency and famously saying he wasn't built to be "standby equipment," he finally accepted appointment to the second office in 1974 by President Gerald R. Ford, himself elevated to the highest office upon Richard M. Nixon's resignation in the Watergate scandal.

Rockefeller's early notoriety came to him as an heir to the millions of the founder of the Standard Oil Company, but his roots also sprang from political soil as the maternal grandson of U.S. Senator Nelson W. Aldrich of Rhode Island. As Senate majority leader, Aldrich was regarded the prime defender of the nation's great trusts and combines and was dubbed "the arch-representative of protected, privileged business" by muckraker Lincoln Steffens.[2] He used his influential position in the Senate to become a multimillionaire himself through the sale of his trolley lines in Providence to the New Haven Railroad. Young Nelson's advancement rose initially through the Rockefeller name and empire, and he turned to elective politics only after a series of appointive positions in government, including those in the administrations of the Democratic president Franklin D. Roosevelt. They convinced him that the power he sought had to be attained through his own political enterprise. While Nelson Rockefeller never achieved the one goal he thought worthy of his aspirations, he brought a high degree of progressivism and public service to what came to be known as Rockefeller Republicanism.

He was born in Bar Harbor, Maine, on July 8, 1908, to Abby Aldrich and John D. Rockefeller Jr. during their summer vacation there. Nelson was a lusty nine and one-quarter pounds, a hint of the stocky and rugged man he would become. As fall approached the family moved back to the Rockefeller mansion on West Fifty-Fourth Street in Manhattan, where Nelson and his siblings had Central Park as their playground.

Nelson was not a particularly studious boy, more inclined to mischief and a gregariousness that made him popular but a bit of a trial for his parents, who naturally had high ambitions for him. He finished high school in the lower third of his class and could not qualify for admission to Princeton to follow his older brother, John. Instead he went to Dartmouth, whose president, Ernest M. Hopkins, was a family friend. There he buckled down and in 1930 made Phi Beta Kappa, graduating cum laude.[3] By this time he had met and courted Mary Todhunter Clark, granddaughter of George B. Roberts of Philadelphia, president of the Pennsylvania Railroad. The marriage, immediately after Nelson's graduation, pleased both socially conscious families. The couple embarked on a nine-month cruise around the world, a wedding gift from the groom's grandfather, John D. Sr., along with twenty thousand dollars in pocket money.[4]

Young Nelson had written to his parents that he didn't want "just to work [his] way up in a business that another man has built" and gain control only many years later, but that's what happened.[5] While his father was building the new Rockefeller Center in midtown Manhattan, Nelson obtained a real-estate broker's license and set about finding business tenants for what would be the world's largest office complex. He lured tenants by offering bargain rents, to the point that he was sued by competitors, unsuccessfully. His enterprise led his father to naming Nelson president of Rockefeller Center in 1938.

Three years earlier, Nelson had made an investment in a Standard Oil subsidiary, the Creole Petroleum Company in Venezuela, then became a member of its board, and began to build his own fortune, along with forming a deep interest in Latin America and its art.[6] During an intense inspection trip of Creole Petroleum's facilities and the surrounding countries, Rockefeller developed a strong concern over the plight and living conditions of its workers. He went among them political-campaign style in his open and glad-handing way, which later would be a trademark of his political success at home. News of his grandfather's death in 1937 brought him flying home, after which he lectured the top Standard Oil officials about their social responsibilities to their workers.

Rockefeller also became involved in promoting modern art, a passion of his mother. He survived an early fiasco when the celebrated left-wing Mexican artist Diego Rivera painted a huge mural for Rockefeller Center depicting a Moscow May Day scene and a likeness of the communist icon Vladimir Lenin. Amid a public protest, it had to be destroyed.[7] After an apprenticeship on a junior advisory committee, in 1939 Rockefeller became president of the family's Museum of Modern Art, known as MoMA, and navigated his way through other disputes in the tempestuous art world. "I learned my politics at the Museum of Modern Art," he joked later.[8]

On return from another trip to South America in early 1940, Rockefeller met President Franklin D. Roosevelt and raised his concerns about Nazi infiltrations there. He presented elaborate plans to FDR for coordinating U.S. economic policies throughout Latin America. The president was greatly interested but had already named a dynamic New York lawyer, James Forrestal, as his eyes and ears in South America. But Forrestal was more focused on intelligence and military aspects, so a new federal position, coordinator of Inter-American Affairs, was concocted for Rockefeller.[9]

After Pearl Harbor, all four of Rockefeller's brothers were in the armed services, and in August 1942 Nelson went to Roosevelt and told him, "You're my commander-in-chief. Any time you want me in the Army, I'm ready to go."[10] The president told him he wanted him right where he was and would tell him if that changed. In 1944, Secretary of State Cordell Hull resigned in ill health and was replaced by his undersecretary, Edward Stettinius. He shook up his top subordinates, and at Roosevelt's urging Rockefeller was made assistant secretary of state for Latin American affairs.

But Rockefeller's efforts to achieve greater regional unity among the

South American states were seen by some within the State Department as undercutting its prime focus on creating the United Nations Organization. When Roosevelt died in April 1945, Harry Truman assumed the presidency and named his old Senate colleague and friend James F. Byrnes secretary of state. In August, Rockefeller was dismissed, only thirty-seven years old, and still determined to make his mark in international affairs, particularly in Latin America.

He returned to his family's enterprises and, in concert with his brothers, achieved generational transition of control. As a private citizen, Nelson undertook a sort of independent Marshall Plan for Latin America, creating the American International Association, focused on strengthening the region's health, education, and agricultural infrastructure as a broad philanthropic, nonprofit undertaking. He also established the International Basic Economy Corporation, which provided shipping and heavy farm equipment at low prices to fishermen and farmers, sinking millions of his own money into the enterprise and losing it.[11]

In 1952, with the Republican Dwight D. Eisenhower elected to the White House after a twenty-year GOP absence, Rockefeller proposed to him a sweeping government reorganization and recommended three names to head it, not listing his own. The new president bought the idea and put his brother Milton in charge with Nelson as an associate. One product of the review was the new Department of Health, Education and Welfare, created in June 1953, with Rockefeller as undersecretary. Once under the Eisenhower administration tent, Nelson got the president to name him special assistant for foreign affairs in 1954. One of his chief contributions was the "Open Skies" proposal for aerial inspections over the United States and the Soviet Union to reduce the prospect of a surprise military attack, an idea of a young Rockefeller consultant from Harvard named Henry Kissinger. Eisenhower presented it at the 1955 summit conference in Geneva to wide national and international acclaim.[12]

At year's end, with only one year left in Eisenhower's first term, Rockefeller returned to New York and formed America at Mid-Century, a special-studies project to examine future national problems. He gathered the best minds he could find, which was a distinctly Nelson Rockefeller practice.

It had become abundantly clear to Rockefeller by now that to be truly effective he had to hold the public office where the power resided. The state

Republican chairman Judson Morhouse clearly wanted Rockefeller to seek the governorship in 1958, but it was a hard sell. Many Republicans in the state doubted whether the Democratic incumbent, W. Averell Harriman, could be defeated and whether Rockefeller as a member of one of the America's richest families could ever be elected, especially with the GOP reputation as the party of the rich. According to Rockefeller's account of Tom Dewey, "He slapped me on my knee and laughed out loud and said, 'Nelson, you're a great guy but you couldn't get elected dogcatcher in New York.'"[13]

Nevertheless, with Malcolm Wilson, a twenty-year state assembly veteran taking him on a personal tour of nearly all of the Republican-strong upstate counties, Rockefeller was nominated on the first ballot at the state convention.[14] Overcoming a stilted speaking style with his ebullient, back-slapping manner, he campaigned across the state, greeting everyone on big-city and small-town streets with a robust "Hiya, fella!" expressing his appreciation for their reception with an effusive "Thanks a thousand!" as if to avoid any reference to his own fortune of millions. He was easily elected.[15]

As governor, Rockefeller went to work, swiftly asking for and receiving a major gasoline tax and income and other tax increases to fund his ambitious spending plans. Continuing his formula of tapping into the best available minds on any subject, he formed as many as fifty task forces in his first two years in Albany. They addressed needs in such areas as fiscal policy, labor, education, job retraining, rent control, economic expansion, and hospital and schoolroom construction.[16]

Rockefeller's auspicious start encouraged press inquiries about a possible presidential candidacy in 1960. But Richard Nixon as the vice president under the hugely popular President Eisenhower had by now built a commanding lead in the polls. In the fall of 1959, when Rockefeller undertook a series of speaking engagements across the country, what he heard was not at all encouraging to his chances for the Republican nomination. On the day after Christmas he surprised the political community by making a "definite and final" announcement that he would not be a candidate for president in 1960, adding, "Quite obviously I shall not at any time entertain any thought of accepting nomination to the vice presidency." Besides, it was clear he was having a great time as governor. He said he intended to keep working to strengthen the party and expected to support its 1960 nominee, without mentioning Nixon.

At the same time, Rockefeller remained unhappy about what he saw as Eisenhower's accommodating posture toward the Cold War threat from the Soviet Union, but he held his tongue because of a summit meeting with Nikita Khrushchev scheduled for the spring. When an American U-2 spy plane was shot down over Soviet territory and the Russians flaunted their capture of pilot Francis Gary Powers, however, the summit collapsed, and Rockefeller reconsidered. He called on the Republican Party to speak out more aggressively, saying, "It would be false and frivolous, and ultimately damaging to both nation and party, to dismiss criticism of specific American conduct as a peril to our national unity."[17]

Two weeks later, he issued a "call for plain talk," saying, "I am . . . deeply concerned that those now assuming control of the Republican Party have failed to make clear where this party is heading and where it proposes to lead the nation." Rockefeller said, "We cannot . . . proceed—nor should anyone presume to ask us to proceed—to march to meet the future with a banner aloft whose only emblem is a question mark."[18] But all he got for his warning for a lack of clear objectives was an irate Eisenhower and broad criticism within the party for doing the work of the opposing Democrats. Having decided not to contest Nixon in the Republican primaries, Rockefeller was now shooting at him from outside the tent and further alienating party stalwarts.

The battle soon shifted to the writing of the party platform in advance of the 1960 convention in Chicago. Rockefeller's men raised other questions over the civil rights and national security planks, so while in New York, Nixon decided to intervene personally. Rockefeller agreed to meet Nixon but insisted that he come to his Fifth Avenue apartment. After dinner and a three-hour discussion, the fourteen-point "Compact of Fifth Avenue" was hammered out. Half the points dealt with national defense. Rockefeller crowed over the outcome but still did not endorse Nixon, claiming the New York delegation was going to the convention uncommitted. The platform committee's conservatives, led by Barry Goldwater, revolted, calling the deal the "Munich of the Republican Party."[19]

Eisenhower was particularly irate at the deal, which also called for a reorganization of the federal government, an idea he had planned to offer to

Congress on leaving office. On Nixon's arrival at the convention, it fell to him personally to thrash out the differences, strengthening the civil rights plank to satisfy Rockefeller and fashioning the national defense plank to mollify the Eisenhower camp. In the end, Rockefeller had demonstrated his clout over the platform but at the price of appearing self-aggrandizing and unwittingly showcasing Nixon's own negotiating and peace-making aptitude.

Despite all this turmoil, Nixon was easily nominated on the first ballot but lost the election to John F. Kennedy in the closest presidential election yet. Hoping to resurrect his political fortunes, Nixon ran for the governorship of California in 1962 but lost again, providing Rockefeller another crack at the Republican presidential nomination in 1964. This time he took the traditional course by entering select primaries and put all his considerable energies and financial resources into the pursuit of it.

In the meantime in 1961, Rockefeller had taken the political risk of separating from his wife of thirty years, after a fire swept the Executive Mansion in Albany in May, revealing that they were occupying separate suites. She moved to her apartment in New York, never to return.[20] But the revelation did not interfere with his reelection in 1962, and in 1963 he married the just-divorced Margaretta "Happy" Fitler Murphy, a socialite and former member of his gubernatorial staff and eighteen years his junior, an event that proved to be a great detriment to his 1964 presidential bid.

In the staid Republican Party of the day, and indeed throughout the country, Rockefeller's decision to end a marriage of more than three decades and to marry a much younger recent divorcée had the political community buzzing. Republicans in New Hampshire, voting in the 1964 kickoff primary of the season, jolted the two frontrunners, Rockefeller and Barry Goldwater, by giving the prize instead to a stealthy write-in campaign for Henry Cabot Lodge, with Goldwater second and Rockefeller a disappointing third. To recover, Rockefeller sounded a cry against a takeover of the party by the "radical right" and moved his campaign to the more liberal Oregon in May, where he bested Lodge, with Goldwater running third.

Meanwhile, the Goldwater operation was working the state conventions diligently. He and Rockefeller came into the final important primary in California in June, going all out in the state that likely would determine the nominee. Rockefeller decided there to attack his party's right wing as

the core of the Goldwater support, charging that it sought to write off minority voters with a white, southern strategy. He subsequently said he was
not attacking "responsible conservatism in our party," but the ideological
battle lines were joined.[21]

Back in New York on the eve of the primary, Happy Rockefeller was
awaiting the birth of their first child. Against the pleas of his political
advisers, the anxious father-to-be hastily flew back East to be with her, arriving in time to welcome Nelson Junior to the family. As the candidate's
strategists feared, his decision rekindled the whole saga of his divorce and
remarriage. He won liberal Northern California but lost the heavily conservative south and thus the state. An eleventh-hour effort to advance the
moderate governor William Scranton of Pennsylvania as a stop-Goldwater
candidate fizzled, and at the Republican National Convention in San Francisco, Rockefeller was roundly booed by the raucous Goldwater crowd.

Once nominated, Arizona's favorite conservative went down to a landslide defeat at the hands of President Lyndon B. Johnson in November.
Rockefeller went back to the governorship of New York, licking his wounds
and contemplating whether he could pick up the pieces of his shattered
party in the next presidential election.

After winning a third term in Albany in 1966, Rockefeller professed he
was finished with being a divisive figure in the national party. Concerning
1968 he declared, "I am not a candidate for president. I am determined not
to be used as an instrument to split the unity of progressive Republicans
behind a candidate who can win in 1968."[22]

Instead, he decided to back Governor George Romney of Michigan, also
just reelected, and pledged a reported two hundred thousand dollars for
Romney's campaign. But from the start Romney, although leading in the
early polls, had trouble adjusting to the national stage. He couldn't articulate well his position on the Vietnam War, and in a Detroit television interview in August 1967, he made a soon-infamous characterization about a
recently completed fact-finding tour: "I just had the greatest brainwashing
anybody can get when you go over to Vietnam. Not only by the generals,
but also by the diplomatic corps."[23] When reporters learned what he had
said, they pounced on it as evidence of his gullibility and unpreparedness
for the presidency, and the Romney stock began to fall.

In mid-October, Rockefeller, Romney, and also Governors Ronald

Reagan of California and Spiro Agnew of Maryland were passengers on a National Governors Conference cruise on the SS *Independence* from New York to the Virgin Islands and back, labeled by the political press corps the "Ship of Fools." On deck one afternoon Rockefeller was asked about a *Time* magazine cover depicting Reagan and himself as the Republican "dream ticket" for 1968. Rockefeller said he appreciated the notion but repeated he was not a candidate, adding for the first time, "And I don't want to be president."[24] Romney took heart, but as the cruise ship plied the Atlantic waves, his own political ship continued to take on water. Before the first Republican primary voting in New Hampshire, Romney dropped out, handing Nixon an easy first victory.

Rockefeller was now reassessing. His first notion was to avoid the next primaries and go back to liberal Oregon, where he had won the 1964 GOP primary, and take on Nixon there. Instead, he announced, as he had in 1960, that inquiries within the party indicated there was no desire for another challenge to Nixon and that he would not run after all, while leaving himself available for a call he did not expect to come.

Subsequent developments, however, persuaded Rockefeller to reconsider yet again. Rockefeller could not abide the notion of a Nixon presidency, which appeared more likely after Lyndon Johnson's sudden withdrawal from contention for reelection, followed by the jolting assassinations of Martin Luther King Jr. and then Robert Kennedy. He mounted another personal and late television advertising effort to dissuade the Republican National Convention from anointing Nixon and instead switch to him, but it got him nowhere. For all his obvious personal dislike of Nixon, Rockefeller campaigned for the nominee's successful election in 1968, after which he went back to New York and in 1970 won a fourth term as governor.

In September 1971, he encountered his greatest challenge in office with a takeover of the state prison in Attica by twelve hundred inmates, who held thirty-nine correctional officers and guards hostage. The prison was ultimately recaptured in an armed and lethal assault, in which thirty-nine inmates and hostages were killed, in the worst mark against Rockefeller's long tenure in Albany.

In 1972 Rockefeller campaigned for Nixon for reelection, with little thought of being further engaged in Washington politics. In November

1973, when Rockefeller's former cheerleader, Vice President Ted Agnew, was forced to resign, Nixon bypassed Rockefeller and filled the vacancy with Gerald Ford. The next month, Rockefeller resigned as governor after fourteen years to enable his loyal lieutenant governor, Malcolm Wilson, to take over and run as the incumbent in the next election. Rockefeller thereupon established the new Commission on Critical Choices for America and seemed resigned to private life.

But when Nixon's Watergate woes drove him from the presidency in 1974, making Ford president and leaving another vice presidential vacancy, the man who had once insisted that he was "not built to be stand-by equipment" agreed to fill it. Unspoken by him was the possibility of moving closer to his unfulfilled presidential ambition.

Through several weeks in November and December 1974, House and Senate committees, in considering Rockefeller's nomination, asked him about many loans and gifts he had given to officials in his state with no evidence of how or when the loans were repaid. But there was little penetrating inquiry into possible quid pro quos in such arrangements. A Senate committee report acknowledged there had been no probing of the huge wealth of the Rockefeller family or "how this wealth in combination serves to enhance the economic influence" of the mighty brood.[25] It seemed that Nelson Rockefeller's willingness to serve as vice president was seen as a generous public service in itself. The confirmation got through both houses of Congress as required by the Twenty-Fifth Amendment, but only after four months in which the nominee declined to take part in the administration, a delay that impeded his or his highly touted staff's immersion in its policy setting and implementation.

Rockefeller's constitutional role as the presiding officer of the Senate soon conveyed to him that he would be dealing with tougher adversaries than those who customarily faced him in the state legislature in Albany. In a sensitive fight over a motion to liberalize the Senate's anti-filibuster rule, he tried to ignore a call for recognition by the conservative senator James Allen of Alabama and proceeded with a roll call, only to be rebuked by Goldwater. When he insisted there was Senate precedent for him to decline to recognize a parliamentary inquiry, the blunt Arizonan told him, "That is what it says, but I never thought I would see the day when the chair would take advantage of it."[26] Rockefeller finally apologized to Allen and the Senate, but the political harm was done as far as the conservatives were concerned.[27] They took Rockefeller's action on the cloture rule as confirmation that, despite his efforts to appear more moderate than he had been as a governor, he remained a leader of the party's diminishing liberal wing.[28]

In offering the vice presidency, Ford had promised to put Rockefeller in charge of domestic policy. But almost at once Rockefeller ran into resistance from Ford's new White House chief of staff, Donald Rumsfeld, who coveted that portfolio himself as head of the Domestic Council. Rockefeller appealed to Ford and finally won out, but Rumsfeld, in keeping with a Ford no-new-spending rule, managed to achieve deep cuts in its budget, thwarting much of Rockefeller's grandiose plans. Also, in taking on a specific line assignment and trying to run it as he would have as a governor, Rockefeller tied himself down to a bureaucratic responsibility that inhibited his ability to function as a general adviser to Ford.[29]

Rockefeller pressed on, however, with ideas for a hundred-billion-dollar energy independence authority with a mind to relieve the nation's dependence on foreign oil. Its design was a major achievement for him in the Ford administration, but he made the mistake of being its very visible chief advocate, drawing fire from conservatives who eventually shot it down in Congress. When Rumsfeld managed to saddle Rockefeller with the oversight of an administration investigation of the Central Intelligence Agency, it was another burdensome diversion, which in time was derided by critics as a whitewash compared with a more aggressive congressional inquiry.[30] On top of all that, Rockefeller remained committed to family and interests in New York, commuting there weekends, often leaving himself out of touch.

Meanwhile, in early 1975, conservative Republicans began to consolidate behind Reagan as the obvious candidate to dethrone Ford, the accidental president, with standby Rockefeller as added baggage. In May the former secretary of defense Melvin Laird, a key Ford political lieutenant, floated the idea of throwing the vice presidential nomination open to the 1976 national convention. Goldwater chimed in that Rockefeller "might make a fine secretary of state" in the next Ford administration. In early June a group of conservative Senate Republicans called for an open convention to choose both the presidential and vice presidential nominees, since neither of the incumbents had been elected by the people.[31]

In an unwise gesture to keep peace with the party's right wing in the South, Ford selected his secretary of the army, Howard (Bo) Callaway, a former Georgia conservative congressman, to be his campaign manager. After Ford had formally announced his candidacy, Callaway held a free-wheeling press conference at the campaign headquarters in which he pointedly made clear this was an effort to elect Ford only, not Rockefeller. A few weeks earlier Ford had said his personal preference was to run with Rockefeller, but it was up to the party convention. "I am confident both of us can convince delegates individually and as a team we should both be nominated," he said.[32]

But in an abundance of candor, Callaway observed, "A lot of Reagan people are not supporters of Rockefeller, and I want it clear to them that we want their support [for Ford] whether they support Rockefeller or not."[33] Despite denials from the White House that Ford wanted his vice president off the ticket and was using Callaway as his hit man, Callaway only fed that impression by volunteering to reporters that Rocky was his "Number One problem." Rockefeller, furious, called Callaway and Ford, but the damage was done.[34]

Rockefeller himself hit the campaign trail in the South to, as he put it, "prove to them I don't have horns," and Ford seemed determined to stick with him, saying, "He has done a superb job. He has been a good teammate. I don't dump good teammates." But through most of 1975, the complaints about Rockefeller by Republican conservatives continued, and according to Ford in late October his vice president told him, "Mr. President, I'll do anything you want me to do. I'll be on the ticket or off the ticket. You just say the word." Ford replied, "There are serious problems, and to be brutally frank, some of these difficulties might be eliminated if you were to indicate that you didn't want to be on the ticket in 1976. I'm not *asking* you to do that, I'm just stating the facts."[35] A close Ford aide, James Cannon, later quoted Ford on the episode: "It was the biggest political mistake of my life. And it was one of the few cowardly things I did in my life."[36]

And so, a year before the election, Rocky got off the ticket; he had had enough. Hitting back at Callaway, he told a press conference that his presence on the ticket was "just not worth it," adding, "I came down here to help [Ford] in connection with solving problems, not dealing with party squabbles. Therefore I eliminated myself."[37] So were his presidential ambitions over at last? "Listen, I wouldn't have accepted the vice presidency if I hadn't been willing to take the presidency should, God forbid, something happen to the President," he said. "So I am not going to kid you that I came down here with no thought of the presidency in mind."[38]

With that, Nelson Rockefeller committed himself to Ford's election and to campaign for him in 1976. After the election, Rockefeller finished out the less than three months left in his term as vice president and retired from politics. He spent the last two years of his life focused on his interest in the arts and died in New York on January 26, 1979. Nelson Rockefeller was a man particularly well qualified by energy, imagination, and experience to be the president of the United States and to serve well and with distinction as vice president. But he never had the opportunity regarding the first and was frustrated by underutilization and then abandoned in the second role. And with his departure, the New York brand of ambitious liberalism known as Rockefeller Republicanism also vanished.

CHAPTER 42

WALTER F. MONDALE
OF MINNESOTA

In 1976, an American vice president was truly chosen both for his qualifications to be president and as a governing partner when the Democratic presidential nominee, the former governor Jimmy Carter of Georgia, selected Senator Walter F. "Fritz" Mondale of Minnesota to be his running mate. Even before Carter was assured of the nomination, he had set in motion a selection process focused on his vice presidential nominee's experience, that nominee's compatibility with Carter, and his potential to serve as chief subordinate in a fully integrated administration in Washington.

Carter's deliberate quest for a genuine partner in governance resulted from his own determination to have such a vice president and from Mondale's requirement in acceptance that he be so utilized. But the care taken in choosing Mondale also came in the wake of the botched 1972 running-mate selection by the previous Democratic presidential nominee, Senator George McGovern. On that occasion, McGovern had not clinched his nomination against his competitor, Senator Hubert Humphrey, until the party convention itself, leaving little time beforehand for a more thorough consideration of a running mate. Not until the next morning did McGovern address the matter, and in what proved to be inadequate vetting he selected Senator Thomas Eagleton of Missouri.

Some years earlier, Eagleton had twice undergone electric shock treatments for mental illness, but he never so informed a McGovern aide when asked if there was anything detrimental in his background. The news at the time was considered so potentially damaging to the Democratic chances that McGovern finally convinced Eagleton to step aside, triggering a drawn-out and embarrassing quest for a replacement. After several turndowns, McGovern chose R. Sargent Shriver, head of the Peace Corps in the administration of his brother-in-law John F. Kennedy. As previously noted, that fall the McGovern-Shriver ticket was buried in the landslide reelection of the Republicans Richard Nixon and Spiro Agnew.

Four years later, the whole calamitous McGovern experience gave Carter more reason to undertake the intensive process by which he and his staff personally chose his own running mate. It was particularly appropriate in light of Carter's intention to make his vice president significantly more than a mere standby figure in his administration. In mid-April 1976, Carter had his staff compile a list of as many as four hundred prominent Democrats, from which he culled about two dozen vice presidential prospects. He also had before him a detailed memorandum from his key Georgia political strategist, Hamilton Jordan. Before Carter interviewed anyone, Jordan advised him, "It is important that you have clear in your mind the role that you would want the Vice President to play in the campaign and in a Carter administration. . . . Historically, the vice presidency has not been a good job because the President has not allowed it to be." Jordan also advised Carter to pick someone whose abilities he really respected and intended to use, even bringing him directly into the White House.[1]

Jordan designed an elaborate rating system to evaluate the contenders in terms of ability, integrity, and acceptance within the party, from which five senators emerged, one of whom was Mondale, along with a number of governors and other members of Congress. Carter concluded early that his wisest choice would probably be a senator who knew his way around Washington and would counter the complaint against Carter as a total outsider. In the days leading up to the convention, Carter had his senior adviser and close friend Charles Kirbo oversee the inquiries into the personal and professional backgrounds of the most prominent Democrats. Then Carter himself interviewed seven of them, summoning Mondale to his home in Plains, Georgia, for lengthy conversations.

Carter and Mondale had briefly met only twice before, but in advance of their Plains meeting, Mondale and his Senate chief of staff, Richard

Moe, began looking into Carter's own record and background. Moe drew up a working paper on how Mondale might best function as a working vice president for a president who lacked any experience in Washington, and that preparation made a distinct impression on Carter. "Every question that came up on an issue," the close Carter aide Greg Schneiders recalled, "Mondale not only could spell out clearly and succinctly his own position, but knew exactly what Carter's position was, and where the two differed."[2]

When the question of an earlier Mondale withdrawal from presidential consideration came up, Mondale told Carter he had been willing to campaign long and hard if he believed he had a chance of winning but had been realistic in concluding otherwise. Meeting reporters afterward, Carter said he had no doubt that Mondale, if selected, would be an aggressive campaigner, to which Mondale broke in: "What I said at the time was that I did not want to spend most of my life in Holiday Inns. But I've checked and found they've all been redecorated. They're marvelous places to stay and I've thought it over and that's where I'd like to be."[3] In the end, personal compatibility proved to be an essential element in the decision. The morning after Carter's own nomination, he phoned Mondale and got his quick acceptance.

Walter Frederick "Fritz" Mondale, born on January 5, 1928, in Ceylon, Minnesota, was the son of the Reverend Theodore Mondale—changed from Mundal in the old country. The family had emigrated from Norway in 1856 and settled in southern Minnesota in 1864, where Theodore Mondale was born in 1876. In 1902, he married a local girl, Jessie Larson, and in 1911 he became a minister in the Methodist church.

After some profitable years in which he was able to buy two farms as investments, a sharp drop in farm prices after World War I plunged him into foreclosure on both of them, and a fatal illness of encephalitis at the same time took his wife from him, leaving him with two young sons, Lester and Clifford. Before her death, Jessie, concerned about the fate of their sons, urged him to start courting an unwed friend, Claribel Cowan, and in 1925 the widower Theodore married her. An internal church row found him and his young family shipped to Ceylon, where Fritz was born and raised in a family of strong progressive inclinations in the Great Depression years.[4]

Hardship followed the family as it moved around Minnesota, finally settling in the town of Elmore. The parents conveyed to Lester and Clifford and then to Fritz, Pete, and Mort, the sons born of their own marriage, their strong religious and political convictions about charity and good works, as had also been the case with Jimmy Carter's upbringing in rural Georgia. Drinking and smoking were firmly prohibited in the Mondale household. Fritz grew up as a somewhat mischievous and athletic boy and became a star football player in Elmore, nicknamed "Crazylegs" for his shifty running style. Family trips in a makeshift trailer, including one to Washington, whetted his interest in politics.

In the fall of 1946, he enrolled in Macalester College, in St. Paul, and later that year his political science instructor took him to a rally at a union hall in Minneapolis. There he first laid eyes on Hubert Humphrey, who had helped lead the merger of the state's radical Farmer-Labor Party with its moribund Democratic Party and had become mayor of Minneapolis. Mondale was transfixed by the thirty-five-year-old Humphrey's rousing call to the party colors. He got to shake Humphrey's hand and was put to work handing out flyers for Humphrey's reelection campaign.

A fight for control of the Minnesota Democratic Farmer Labor Party was underway among Farmer-Labor radicals, including local communists and Democratic regulars led by Humphrey. Humphrey ran for the U.S. Senate in 1948, and Mondale became a foot soldier in the effort, heading the Humphrey campaign in a key congressional district that was carried in a landslide.[5]

At Macalester, Mondale affiliated with Students for Democratic Action, the campus offshoot of Americans for Democratic Action, later dropping out of college and moving to Washington as the SDA national secretary. In 1951, Mondale finished his degree at the University of Minnesota, then enlisted in the army during the Korean War and was stationed at Fort Knox, Kentucky. Upon his discharge a year later, he entered the university's law school, marrying Joan Adams in 1955, graduating in 1956, and practicing law in Minneapolis until 1960. In 1958 he ran the successful campaign of Orval Freeman for the governorship and was rewarded with an appointment as the state attorney general, at thirty-two the youngest in the country.

Under Mondale's leadership, his staff won convictions in a massive case of fraud and corruption involving executives of the Sister Elizabeth Kenny Foundation, a huge Minneapolis-based charitable institution for the benefit of children crippled by polio and other debilitating diseases. Some of the officials, including the former mayor Marvin Kline, were found guilty. In 1963, Mondale led the state attorneys general in the famous U.S. Supreme Court case in behalf of Clarence Earl Gideon, an indigent prisoner convicted after denial of free counsel. And in 1964, at the behest of Humphrey, Mondale shaped a compromise at the Democratic National Convention in the fight over seating the Mississippi delegation. Finally, in 1965, another gubernatorial appointment put Mondale in the U.S. Senate, replacing Humphrey after his 1964 election to the vice presidency.

In 1968, Mondale and Senator Fred Harris of Oklahoma managed Humphrey's successful campaign for the Democratic presidential nomination after LBJ dropped out. In 1969, Mondale finally broke with Johnson on the war in a speech at Macalester College, and in 1971 he voted to halt American military involvement in Cambodia. Two years later he co-sponsored the War Powers Resolution, stipulating that the president inform Congress of any U.S. military action taken and report periodically on its progress, subject to congressional termination. The resolution was subsequently and routinely ignored by the executive branch.

In 1973, during the Watergate scandal, which eventually drove Nixon from office, Mondale undertook to explore a presidential bid of his own for the 1976 presidential nomination. "After more than a year of constant travel, constant fund-raising and constant speaking," he wrote later, "I had pulled about even with 'None of the Above' in national opinion surveys, and I dropped that bid—to widespread applause." It was then that he made the comment that he didn't want to spend his life in Holiday Inns. But what he also said in late November 1974 was: "Basically I found I did not have the overwhelming desire to be President which is essential for the kind of campaign that is required," adding, "I don't think anyone should be President who is not willing to go through fire."[6]

By the time the 1976 party convention rolled around, however, Mondale had second thoughts, at least about running for the vice presidency. When he became one of Jimmy Carter's finalists for the job, he was both willing and prepared. "When Fritz came down to Plains," Carter wrote later, "he had really done his homework about me and the campaign. More important, he had excellent ideas about how to make the vice presidency a fulltime and productive job. He was from a small town as I was, a preacher's son, and shared a lot of my concerns about our nation [and] we were personally compatible."[7]

Carter himself received high marks in the news media for the care and deliberation he demonstrated in making the choice of an esteemed legislator to help him navigate the shoals of political Washington, in the event they got there together the next January. When the fall campaign heated up in earnest, Mondale plunged in. But by far his greatest contribution was in the nationally televised debate with the Republican vice presidential nominee, Senator Bob Dole of Kansas, the sharp and acerbic World War II combat hero.

In any presidential campaign, the prime role for running mates is that of the medical Hippocratic oath—first, do no harm. But Dole had a reputation as a political attack dog, and he also harbored a deep hostility toward the Democratic Party. He was also bitter over the severe wounds he had suffered as a World War II officer in Italy. At first in the debate, Dole displayed his playfully jibing side, observing, "I think tonight may be sort of a fun evening. I've known my counterpart for some time. We've been friends and we'll be friends when this debate is over. And we'll be friends when this election is over—and he'll still be in the Senate."[8]

But Dole's personal rancor came boiling out in his biting answer to a question from the debate panel. The veteran Associated Press reporter Walter Mears asked why in 1974 he had said that Ford's pardon of Nixon for the Watergate crimes had been "prematurely granted and mistaken." Dole snapped back that Watergate wasn't a very good campaign issue, "any more than the Vietnam war would be, or World War I or World War II or the Korean War—all Democrat wars in this century." Then he added, "I figured up the other day if we added up all the killed and wounded in Democratic wars in this century, it would be about 1.6 million Americans, enough to fill the city of Detroit." An incredulous but calm Mondale pounced: "I think Senator Dole has richly deserved his reputation as a hatchet man tonight. Does he really mean that there was a partisan difference over our involvement in the fight against Nazi Germany?"[9]

The Carter campaign strategists concluded that Mondale had done so well and Dole so poorly that they quickly produced a television ad showing both men with a voice-over that said, "What kind of men are they? When you know that four of the last six vice presidents have wound up as presidents, who would you like to see a heartbeat away from the presidency?" Actually, it was four out of seven at that time, but the point was the same.[10] In the extremely close election, which Carter and Mondale won by only 2.2 percent, many fingers pointed primarily to Ford's pardon of Nixon for his loss. But Dole's reference to "Democrat wars" got its share of mentions as well.

Even before the winners were sworn into office, Carter was true to his word about making Mondale a real partner. Carter summoned him to Plains again for further discussions. Mondale had Richard Moe draft a memo laying out the key elements in their thinking. Mondale had talked at length with Humphrey about his friend's own experiences as vice president under Johnson. "I knew that if I didn't see everything Carter saw, even the classified material," Mondale wrote in his memoir, "I could not be an effective adviser."[11]

On Mondale's arrival in Atlanta, Hamilton Jordan met him, and Mondale asked him how Carter had reacted to the memo, a copy of which he had sent to Jordan. "Oh, the memo," Carter's right-hand man said. "Just double-space it and he'll agree to everything." And so it was. Mondale remembered that Carter told him, "I want you to be in the chain of command— a vice president with the power to act in the president's place," and gave Mondale his own office in the White House, a break in precedent.[12] A major difference between Humphrey's experience with LBJ and Mondale's with Carter was Carter himself, who was above delivering the sort of deep personal humiliations that Johnson had routinely dealt to subordinates.

In anticipation of assuming the presidential powers of war and peace, Carter included Mondale in all preinauguration briefings. "It was obvious to me that in a nuclear exchange, the President might well be incapacitated, and the Vice President, as the new Commander in Chief, had to be fully qualified to assume his duties," Carter wrote later.[13] Mondale also was the first vice president to be sent the highly classified Presidential Daily Brief (PDB), including the latest foreign-policy intelligence.

During the transition, he was assigned to prepare an action agenda for the first months of the Carter administration, and about three weeks before its inauguration, each member of Carter's new cabinet was given a twenty-nine-page memo of Carter's weekly schedule through the approaching March, prepared by Mondale.[14] Unlike most past cases, Mondale's staff was totally integrated with Carter's, an indication of the shared agenda they had, rather than Mondale being given specific side assignments like those that had often been shunted to past vice presidents.

Mondale himself was placed entirely in the loop for receiving all policy papers going to the president, and he usually saw Carter on a daily basis. A regularly scheduled lunch meeting between the two was a staple of their weekly calendars. Mondale also functioned as a sort of long-range traffic cop for issues to be taken up by the president in an orderly fashion, including foreign travel for each of them.

At the outset, Mondale insisted that he not be given the direction of any agency, such as the Domestic Council, which had bogged down Rockefeller, or any major area of responsibility beyond the agenda setting. When Carter proposed that he serve as his White House chief of staff or take on dealing with Africa as his special task, Mondale begged off, successfully making the case that he could better serve as a generalist and senior adviser without portfolio.[15] Nor did he want to be caught in bureaucratic wrangling with cabinet heads working the same side of the issues street. With Carter new to Washington and many Georgians with little experience there given key White House positions, Mondale's direct general counsel was much needed, as seen almost at once.

One matter not included in the early cabinet meeting, and hence not subject to comment by the cabinet, was a sudden decision by Carter less than a month in office to veto federal funding for some eighteen water projects, mostly in the western states. They were pet projects of senior members of the House and Senate and often tagged as pork-barrel handouts. Carter added insult to injury by failing to consult with or notify the affected legislators in advance, to Mondale's chagrin. But Carter was determined to tackle inflation and balance the federal budget by the conclusion of his term.

Mondale finally alerted Carter to the political as well as the budgetary aspects of the issue, advising that he veto the most egregious pork-barrel items and yield on the others in the interest of party peace. But newcomer Carter dug in his heels. "Eventually we rounded up enough votes to sustain a veto," Mondale wrote later, "but House Speaker Tip O'Neill called the president and proposed a compromise—to suspend the projects rather than cancel them. Carter agreed, but that only infuriated several members of

Congress who, at some risk to their congressional friendships, had promised to support us. In the end, a year later, Carter finally did sign a bill cancelling several of the projects on his list. So we won a little on the merits, but we lost a lot on the politics."[16]

Mondale's influence had its first major test in helping shape a major affirmative action case before the Supreme Court. A young white student from Minnesota named Allan Bakke alleged he had been denied admission to the University of California medical school in deference to less-qualified black students. Carter's attorney general and old Georgia friend, Griffin Bell, had his staff produce a draft in support of Bakke that would run contrary to Carter's own general support of affirmative action. Mondale weighed in with Carter, asking him, "Why do we need this fight now? The administration is already battling with its liberal allies. Why provoke them more and turn away from our campaign promise to promote affirmative action?"[17] Mondale's intercession eventually helped bring the brief into line with Carter's commitment to this critical civil rights principle.[18]

Mondale concluded early in his new job, "Many of the lawmakers I called the old whales, the powerful veteran committee chairmen [of his own party], had little interest in seeing us succeed. They were profoundly skeptical of this Democratic outsider, and they were scheming right from the start to find ways of testing and diminishing him. They were almost as happy with a Republican president as a Democratic president because the big point was getting their own way."[19]

Carter had hoped to kick off his administration with an economic stimulus bill composed of a jobs program, public works spending, and an individual tax rebate of fifty dollars as symbolic evidence that the Democrats felt the public's pain. But as the economy began to show an uptick, Carter scrapped the rebate to the severe distress of many congressional leaders. The actions disturbed Mondale as well while he sought to run interference for the Georgian newcomer.

Mondale used his weekly private lunches with Carter to alert him to the political elements of some of his plans that may have eluded him. "I had hoped I might help Carter navigate these shoals, or at least avoid collisions with our friends," he wrote later. "I spent a lot of time up on the Hill with senators and members of the House picking up information that I would bring to the president." He said of their private lunches: "[They] proved to be one of our most valuable ideas—just the two of us, no staff, no fixed agenda, totally honest. I often used those lunches for politics because Carter didn't like to bring politics into our meetings with cabinet officials and agency staff. This was my chance to tell him what I was hearing and how I interpreted it."[20]

Mondale, however, found himself in the administration of a man who led with more head and less heart than Mondale did. Carter's agenda was the captive of his justifiable concern over the restraints imposed by federal debt and inflation, at the cost of diminished social programs that Mondale favored. Speaking as a traditional liberal, Mondale said of his personal challenge dealing with Carter: "I tried to keep our constituency together by forcing [the liberals] to confront the inflation issue, and I fought within the administration to prevent unnecessary budget cuts. It was a tough job for an old progressive like me."[21]

Reviewing their administration in a memo to Carter after their first seven months, Mondale wrote, "I think it is important that I devote more time to strengthening our relationship with those constituencies [of the old Democratic coalition] and persuading them that our interests and theirs are inextricably tied together."[22] The matter came to a head in mid-1978 at a party conference in Memphis at which Mondale's good friend Ted Kennedy called on the Democrats to "sail against the wind" of economic restraints in support of their old social agenda. Mondale defended Carter's anti-inflation worries, in a prelude to the inevitable clash to come in Kennedy's decision to challenge Carter's bid for reelection in the 1980 Democratic presidential primaries.

Before then, however, Carter orchestrated the one foreign-policy achievement that would crown his otherwise troubled presidency—the 1978 personal peace negotiations refereed by him between Egypt's Anwar Sadat and Israel's Menachem Begin at Camp David, Maryland, which ended in their historic peace treaty. Mondale played an unobtrusive role as an ice-breaker in separate private talks with Sadat and Begin in advance of their meeting at Camp David and as an encourager to each of them once there. Carter wrote of the vice president later in his memoir: "Mondale handled everything possible for me in Washington, and took a helicopter up to Camp David whenever he could get away at night or on weekends."[23]

Carter included Mondale in most major meetings and often used his vice president as an intermediary with each of the visiting principals. Carter meanwhile tenaciously urged them not to waste the opportunity he had afforded them, and he eventually succeeded.[24] The next year, Mondale also played a key role with the State Department specialist Richard Holbrooke in getting Carter to agree to take a leading part in a multination rescue of Southeast Asian boat people—refugees fleeing the war-torn region by sea.[25]

Overshadowing both these foreign-affairs achievements, however, were two episodes that most seriously damaged the Carter presidency. The first came in the late summer of 1978, when Carter made the domestic decision that caused the worst breach in his relationship with Mondale. With Middle East oil prices soaring and a severe energy crisis plaguing the country, the president planned a major speech on it, then abruptly canceled it and summoned a host of outside kibitzers to Camp David to counsel him on what do to. For twelve days, the energy experts and various political leaders trooped to the Maryland hideaway for seminars that seemed only to underscore Carter's indecision. The president's pollster, Patrick Caddell, weighed in with data suggesting that the American people had lost confidence in their president, and Carter decided he had to make a speech addressing that conclusion.

Mondale wrote later of Caddell's notion: "He argued that the public was having a sort of psychological breakdown after several bad years in American politics. He thought Americans simply couldn't grapple with the gravity of a challenge as severe as an international energy crisis. Caddell proposed that Carter speak to the public about this failure of will and urge them to buckle up and deal with it." But, Mondale wrote, "I thought that was a dead end." Referring to psychological texts Caddell had brought with him, Mondale told him, "Pat, I've read all those books and they don't have a damn thing to do with the price of energy or the next election."[26]

Of the internal staff debate that ensued with the president, Mondale wrote later, "By late afternoon I was pretty upset, and probably for the only time, I broke with Carter. . . . I said I don't believe this problem is in people's heads. . . . These are real problems. People can't get gas. Their paychecks are getting smaller. They're worrying about their heating bills." Further, Mondale told Carter, "You can't blame the American people for the problems they face. We were elected to be a government as good as the people, yet now we're proposing to say that we need a people as good as the government. You can't sell that." Mondale wrote later, "I probably got a little angry as I finished my case, something I can't remember ever happening with Carter and me, and I probably made an ass of myself. But I was afraid that this would be the end of our administration."[27]

Carter took Mondale for a walk to cool him down, but in the end the president delivered a crisis-in-confidence address that immediately was dubbed his "malaise speech," although he never used that word. It left an impression of incompetence and confusion that hung over Carter and his administration long afterward.

Mondale was also distressed by a Carter decision at Camp David to shake up his cabinet, calling for the resignations of all members and accepting five, apparently in an effort to show toughness and strength. Mondale wrote later, "I think our administration never recovered from that week. Congress was caught by surprise. Wall Street was rattled. The general public seemed flummoxed. The Republicans said Americans weren't depressed about America, they were frustrated with us."[28]

Even more damaging in public opinion was the storming by Iranian student radicals of the American Embassy in Tehran on November 4, 1979, and the taking of 101 American diplomats and other personnel as hostages. The attack came shortly after Carter had reluctantly agreed to admit the ailing and exiled shah of Iran to the United States for medical treatment, a decision in which Mondale had concurred. For the next 444 days, the hostages were held under the most humiliating circumstances, an episode made infinitely worse for Carter when a helicopter rescue mission ordered by him was badly botched in the Arabian desert, leaving eight dead among the American forces.

On top of all this woe came Ted Kennedy's decision to challenge Carter for the 1980 presidential nomination. The development was particularly trying for Mondale because he and Kennedy were good friends, and they shared most of their party's liberal positions and aspirations. In Carter's diary on June 29, 1979, he wrote, "I had lunch with Fritz. He thought my comment concerning 'whipping Kennedy's ass' was ill-advised. His is kind of a lonely voice. Some of my staff members say it was the best thing for morale around the White House since the Willie Nelson concert."[29]

Mondale was particularly chagrined at Carter's decision early in the election year to stay off the campaign trail and conduct what was called a

"Rose Garden strategy" of focusing on the national and international crises, leaving to Mondale the role of chief campaign surrogate. Carter did, however, agree to join Kennedy and a third candidate, Governor Jerry Brown of California, in a debate sponsored by the *Des Moines Register*, scheduled for the first week of the election year.

On Christmas Day of 1979, however, the Soviet Union invaded Afghanistan in support of an internal coup there, leading Carter to impose an embargo on grain sales, in spite of a previous pledge in Iowa, the nation's corn capital, never to do so. Kennedy immediately attacked the embargo, saying it would hurt Iowa farmers without punishing the Russians, who could get the grain they needed elsewhere. Three days later, with the Iran hostage crisis also still unresolved, Carter pulled out of the debate, saying he was hoping soon "to bring the Iranian matter to a head" and hence there was no way he could leave Washington.[30] The newspaper offered to shift the site there, but Carter declined.

In Des Moines, Mondale seized on Kennedy's criticism of the embargo, accusing him of trying to capitalize on "the politics of the moment." Although Mondale himself had advised Carter not to order the embargo, he said supporting it was "the patriotic route to take." When a reporter asked the vice president if he was accusing Kennedy of being "unpatriotic," Mondale said only, "I've said what I've said." Kennedy, learning of the remark, shot back, "I don't think I or the members of my family need a lecture from Mr. Mondale or anyone else about patriotism."[31]

Years later, in his memoir, Mondale wrote, "This was hard for me. Kennedy's position was my position; I didn't think the grain embargo would hurt the Soviets much, but I knew it would hurt American farmers and turn the farm states against us." He wrote he "regretted immediately" saying, "Kennedy should support the president at a time like this," adding, "I was tired and I shouldn't have said it. Ted took offense, and I took it back right away, and by the next morning he had accepted that. But it was bruising."[32]

Worse from the viewpoint of the Carter campaign, Kennedy's challenge dragged on through June and left the Democratic Party badly split. With the Republican nominee, Ronald Reagan, overcoming doubts about the competence of a former movie star to be president, he and his running mate, the former UN ambassador George Bush, won a clear-cut victory on Election Night in both the popular vote and the electoral college.

Despite failing to win a second term, Mondale could claim some significant victories in his four years as vice president. He was instrumental in the creation of the Department of Education; he also was a key figure in the enactment of the Panama Canal treaties transferring the canal to Panamanian control, in the rescue of the Vietnamese boat people, and particularly in his assistance to Carter in bringing a successful conclusion to the Israeli-Egyptian peace talks at Camp David. He was credited also with moderating some of Carter's deeper budget cuts affecting the poor and the middle class while retaining enough political capital to achieve his party's presidential nomination four years later.

In 1984, Mondale made a political comeback by winning the Democratic nomination over Senator Gary Hart of Colorado, who ran as an insurgent against the party establishment candidate. Mondale won strong labor backing and turned the tables on the charismatic Hart, the 1972 campaign manager of George McGovern, by questioning his substance. The Mondale campaign dusted off a television advertising slogan of the day, asking of Hart in his own ad, "Where's the beef?" It halted Hart's early surge, but Mondale did not clinch the nomination until the final day of the last 1984 primaries.

In his convention acceptance speech, aware that he was trailing Reagan in the polls, Mondale rolled the dice, boldly declaring, "Let's tell the truth. Mr. Reagan will raise taxes and so will I. He won't tell you. I just did." It caused Reagan's deputy campaign manager, Lee Atwater, to remark that Mondale deserved "an A-plus for boldness" but predicted that Mondale would "get an F-minus in the end."[33] He was right. Mondale explained much later, "I thought one way of dealing with Reagan was to show more confidence, solid experience in dealing with the budget. It didn't get me anywhere."[34]

In a long-shot effort to pull out the general election, Mondale nominated the New York congresswoman Geraldine Ferraro as the first female in American history to be on a major national ticket. The ticket won an impressive vote among women, but in vain. Mondale himself could not match the Reagan appeal, and a hope in his camp that a rambling performance by the aging president in their first debate would benefit the challenger was dashed in the second. Reagan won the audience by jokingly observing, "I will not make age an issue of this campaign. I am not going to exploit, for political purposes, my opponent's youth and inexperience."[35] Mondale acknowledged later that he knew he was beaten after that.

Reagan's reassurance of his competence in that second debate brought an even greater landslide victory in November for him and Vice President Bush, who captured all but 13 of the 538 electoral votes, losing only Mondale's home state of Minnesota and the District of Columbia. Mondale went back to law practice in Minneapolis.

Mondale's defeat did not end his public service, though. In 1992, upon the presidential election of his fellow Democrat Bill Clinton, Mondale was offered the ambassadorship to Moscow, which he accepted but later thought better of it as a poor fit for him and ultimately declined it. Clinton came back and offered him Japan, which he accepted and served happily and effectively for four years, returning in late 1996 to Minnesota, where he engaged in DFL Party affairs with no intention to ever run for public office again.

But in 2002, the Democratic senator Paul Wellstone, campaigning for a third term less than two weeks before the election, perished in a small plane crash that also claimed his wife and a daughter. Wellstone's campaign manager pleaded with Mondale to run in Wellstone's place as the only Democrat who could hold the seat and assure Democratic control of the Senate. Reluctantly, he agreed. But a large and emotional memorial service for Wellstone, attended by leading figures of both political parties, turned into a political rally in the hands of unthinking partisan Democratic speakers. The tone was deeply resented by attending Republicans and many other grieving Minnesotans. On Election Night, Mondale, then age seventy-four and hindered by the poisoned circumstances, lost by three percentage points to the Republican mayor of St. Paul, Norm Coleman, and returned again to the practice of law in Minneapolis.

Mondale, because of his intimate service with Carter in the White House, was arguably the most well-prepared man for the presidency who ran for but never attained it. Still, his service in the vice presidency, shaped largely by his own hand in collaboration with his president, became the model for future presidents in making constructive use of the office, if they chose to follow it.

CHAPTER 43

GEORGE H. W. BUSH

OF TEXAS

The cliché endures that the vice presidency is the prime stepping-stone to the presidency. But after John Adams and Thomas Jefferson, the first two vice presidents, were elected to the presidency in their own right, only two others have since made it—Martin Van Buren in 1836 and, more than a century and a half later, George Herbert Walker Bush in 1988. The nine others who rose to the presidency achieved it as a result of eight presidential deaths and one resignation.

In most of the early years after Adams and Jefferson, the elected vice presidents lacked the distinction required for the presidency or served in such subordinate and near-invisible roles in their administrations that they did not warrant consideration for the highest office. Van Buren was an exception as the chief political strategist and adviser to President Andrew Jackson, and his presidential candidacy was seen as a means to continue the Jackson policies. Likewise, 152 years later, Bush's presidential candidacy was cast by many Republicans as the closest thing to a third term of President Ronald Reagan, whose agenda Bush loyally embraced for eight years. Although he succeeded in being elected, he proved to be no Reagan, either in charisma or in policy, and in the end was denied reelection in 1992.

Coloring within the lines was a trademark of the senior George Bush. His ancestors on the English and Scottish sides of his family could boast of distant ties to royalty, and his grandparents and parents raised him with a proper respect for courtesy, piety, and self-reliance. His paternal grandfather, Samuel Prescott Bush, after graduation from Stevens Tech, took various railroad jobs in the Midwest before settling in Columbus, Ohio. There he became the president of a company manufacturing railway car equipment and the first president of the National Association of Manufacturers.[1]

Samuel Bush's son, Prescott, George's father, attended Yale, served briefly as a field artillery captain in France in World War I, on return moved to St. Louis, and went into business. There he met and married Dorothy Walker, daughter of the wealthy investment banker George Herbert Walker. Soon after, he went to work for the U.S. Rubber Company in Tennessee and then in Milton, Massachusetts, where young George, the second of five children, was born on June 12, 1924, and named for his maternal grandfather.[2] A by-product of the name eventually was another tag hung on him that later led to derision, especially from political foes. Grandfather Walker had come to be called "Pop" by his sons, so as young George was growing up they called him "Little Pop" or "Poppy," and it stuck to him with a gentle vengeance outside the family long afterward.[3]

The family moved to Greenwich, Connecticut, and Prescott Bush soon joined the New York banking and investment firm of W. Averell Harriman, of which his father-in-law was president. At Yale, he had become a member of the secret elite Skull and Bones Society, where a fellow Bonesman was Roland Harriman, brother of W. Averell. When the firm merged with another Wall Street powerhouse, Brown Brothers, Prescott became one of twelve partners and, not surprisingly, a Republican, though not yet interested in political office.[4]

Young George attended the exclusive Greenwich Country Day School and then Phillips Academy, at Andover, Massachusetts. There he was not rated a distinguished student but excelled in sports as captain of the soccer and baseball teams. He was six months from graduation and planned to follow in his father's footsteps at Yale when the Japanese bombed Pearl Harbor. He told his father that college would to have wait, because he intended to enlist in the navy on this eighteenth birthday in June 1942.

During Christmas break, George met Barbara Pierce at a local country club dance, and they started dating. On his birthday he was sworn in as an ordinary seaman in Boston. Soon after, he was shipped off to navy preflight training in North Carolina as an aviation cadet. He became a combat pilot, and on a bombing run in the Bonin Islands, in the Pacific, his plane was hit. He continued to the target, dropped his bombs, and leveled off, telling his two crew members to bail out. Neither survived, but he jumped into the sea, where an hour and a half later an American submarine picked him up.[5] He rejoined his squadron and ultimately flew fifty-eight combat missions. Home on leave, he married Barbara on January 6, 1945, and on July 6 of the following year, his first child was born, named George Walker Bush but called Junior in the family.

After the war was over, George Senior entered Yale in the fall of 1945, joining his elder brother, Prescott Junior, called Pressy. There, in addition to being captain of the baseball team, he turned out to be a diligent student, making Phi Beta Kappa and graduating in two and a half years. The Yale connection, as it was intended to do, paid off for George. Through a fellow Bonesman, he got into the Texas oil business at a portable drilling rig equipment company in Odessa, where he earned $375 a month as a clerk. After transfers to several towns in California where he sold rigs, he and his young family moved back to Texas, to Midland, a booming oil town just east of Odessa.

He became a partner in an independent oil production company, and the couple added a daughter, Robin, and three more sons—John Ellis Bush (Jeb), Neil Mallon Bush, and Marvin Pierce Bush. They lost Robin to leukemia at age three, after which another daughter, Dorothy (Doro) was born.[6]

Meanwhile, back East, Prescott Bush Sr. got into politics. In 1950 he ran for the U.S. Senate from Connecticut and lost narrowly but in 1952 won the other, recently vacated, Senate seat. He became a strong supporter and occasional golf partner of President Dwight D. Eisenhower and one of the first Republicans to denounce the Red-baiting tactics of Wisconsin's senator Joseph R. McCarthy. After two six-year terms, Bush retired in declining health.[7]

In 1953, son George Bush's firm, boosted with a fortuitous investment of about half a million dollars from an uncle, Herbert Walker, and others, merged with another independent oil operation, Zapata Petroleum. In 1959 it split between inland and offshore sectors, with Bush becoming president of Zapata Offshore and moving his family to Houston. Like his father's success earlier, George Bush's success in business provided him enough money to go into politics.

When the still young Republican Party in Texas began to encounter inroads from the far-right, fiercely anti-communist John Birch Society, Bush was recruited to be the party's chairman. As a somewhat naive champion of party unity, he at first tried conciliation with the Birchers, and when he ran for the U.S. Senate in 1964, his opponent, the liberal Democratic incumbent Ralph Yarborough, tagged him as "the darling of the John Birch Society."[8] Although a longtime supporter of the United Negro Fund, Bush opposed the Civil Rights Act of 1964 and also the first nuclear arms treaty with the Soviet Union and backed Barry Goldwater for president in a conspicuous effort to associate with the dominant conservatism in Texas. Those attempts often conflicted with the GOP moderation of eastern Republicans, including his own father.

In the end, Bush lost to Yarborough for the Senate seat but ran ahead of all the other Texas Republican candidates as well as Goldwater that year. He later expressed regrets that in courting the right wing he had failed to repudiate the "irresponsibility" of some of Goldwater's supporters.[9] In 1966, Bush took on a more modest challenge, winning the House seat from Houston. As a congressman, George Bush was more in tune with his father's moderate views than with Texas conservatism. In spite of his 1964 vote against civil rights, he opposed racial segregation and supported an LBJ surtax to support the war in Vietnam and Great Society programs. And in 1968 he backed open housing in the Civil Rights Act of that year, citing the service of black troops in Vietnam.[10]

In 1970, Bush ran for the U.S. Senate and lost again, but reentered public service as the American ambassador to the United Nations, appointed by President Richard Nixon. After the 1972 landslide reelection of Nixon over the Democratic senator George McGovern, Nixon tapped Bush to relieve Senator Bob Dole of Kansas as chairman of the Republican National Committee. Bush was not thrilled with the appointment but accepted it as loyal Republican soldier. Nixon told him he was not involved in the Watergate mess, and Bush said that was good enough for him. He traveled around the country attesting to the president's innocence.[11]

Then came a bump in the road in the summer of 1973 with the

disclosure that Vice President Agnew was facing likely indictment on allegations of corruption as the Baltimore County executive and the governor of Maryland. In October, Agnew resigned to escape a jail term, and Nixon was faced with selecting a replacement under the new Twenty-Fifth Amendment. Texas Republicans pushed Bush for the job, but Nixon chose the popular House minority leader, Gerald Ford, as sure to be confirmed by Congress as required.

Meanwhile, the investigation of the Watergate crimes and cover-up continued, and amid more disclosures via the tapes recorded in the White House, Bush finally concluded that he had been misled. On the most incriminating "smoking gun" tape, Nixon was heard telling Haldeman, his chief of staff at the time, to get the CIA to block the FBI's investigation. So finally, on August 6, 1974, Nixon called a cabinet meeting at which he proceeded to discuss—inflation!

According to Alexander Haig, Nixon's new chief of staff, Bush, invited by Nixon to attend, "suddenly seemed to be asking for the floor. When Nixon failed to recognize him, he spoke anyway. Watergate was the vital question, he said. It was sapping public confidence. Until it was settled, the economy and the country as a whole would suffer. Nixon should resign. . . . Nixon brushed Bush aside, saying it might be a good idea to call a domestic summit conference on the economy. Bill Saxbe, the attorney general, spoke up. 'Mr. President, I don't think we ought to have a summit conference,' he said. 'We ought to be sure you have the ability to govern.'"[12] On August 9, 1974, Nixon resigned, turning the presidency over to Ford.

With the vice presidency vacant, a poll of Republican leaders expressed their support for Bush, but the new president instead chose Governor Nelson Rockefeller of New York. Apparently as an alternative prize, Bush was offered his choice of ambassadorships to London or Paris but asked instead for the China portfolio as chief of the U.S. Liaison Office, the United States not then having established a formal embassy there. Ford agreed, and Bush was shipped off to Beijing for thirteen months, before being recalled to become director of the Central Intelligence Agency. The CIA then was under severe congressional scrutiny and had been called "a rogue elephant." Bush's friends warned he was heading into a political dead end, but once again he decided he could not reject a presidential call and took the post.

In 1979, with Carter looking increasingly likely to become a one-term president, Bush announced his candidacy for the Oval Office. The former California governor Ronald Reagan, who had given Ford stiff opposition for the 1976 Republican nomination, also decided to run again. In a large field in the 1980 Iowa caucuses, Bush surprised with a victory over Reagan, who was caught napping with minimal personal campaigning in the state. Suddenly Bush was in the national news claiming he now had the "Big Mo"—for momentum.

But the Reagan campaign woke up in New Hampshire, ambushing a petulant Bush in a televised debate involving the full field in what he had expected would be a one-on-one face-off with Reagan. Bush charged, correctly, that he had been sandbagged, and in the ensuing primary Reagan routed him, 50 percent to 23. Not only did Bush's "Big Mo" fade thereafter; his irritated reaction to the surprise debate appearance of the other candidates, orchestrated by Reagan's campaign manager, left a bad taste with Reagan that further cooled a chilly relationship between the two.[13]

As the contest for the nomination went on, Bush characterized Reagan's plan for balancing the budget and simultaneously cutting taxes and raising defense spending as "voodoo economics," widening the breach. When Bush denied ever using the term, a reporter produced a tape recording of him saying it. When he was repeatedly asked by reporters whether he would accept the vice presidential nomination, his pat answer was, "Take Sherman and cube it." He meant he shared in spades what the Union general William Tecumseh Sherman had said in memorably dismissing any presidential candidacy: "If nominated I will not run; if elected I will not serve."[14]

In any event, the men around Reagan were thinking in another direction. As early as May in advance of the Republican convention, Reagan was prodded by some aides to ask former president Ford whether he would be interested in being Reagan's running mate. Ford said he was not, but at the convention Reagan was persuaded to try again. Among the arguments used on Reagan was that he would have Bush as the alternative if he didn't get Ford to run.

Ford, probably unwittingly, opened the talk to public scrutiny when Walter Cronkite of CBS asked him in a television interview whether they were talking about "something like a co-presidency." Ford never used that term, but it got Reagan and his chief strategists to thinking of what might be lost in such an arrangement, and they finally thought better of the idea.

Dick Cheney, Ford's former White House chief of staff, recalled later that in exploratory talks with Bill Casey, Reagan's campaign manager, "it was stunning how much they were willing to give up. We came away thinking, 'This is nuts.'"[15]

After the election Reagan said about the Cronkite interview: "[It] was part of what was making me realize that this thing was out of hand. . . . I began to wonder if all of us in our belief in the dream ticket, if we had thought beyond the election. Everything was based on the election; it was not based on thinking about how it would work."[16]

Finally, Reagan and Ford, after conferring one more time, concluded that the scheme posed too many questions of implementation and areas of responsibility. As Ford left Reagan's hotel suite, Reagan mopped his brow and said, "Now where the hell's George Bush?"[17] He called Bush at his hotel suite and asked him to be his running mate. Bush broke out his trademark crooked grin and gave his wife the thumbs-up sign. Bush thus eagerly put the Sherman-like statement behind him and became Reagan's loyal partner on the Republican ticket that trounced Jimmy Carter and Walter Mondale in November.

After their inauguration, the always amiable Reagan followed Carter's example of giving his vice president his own office within the White House, providing him with the Presidential Daily Brief and a weekly private lunch. He also chose as his chief of staff Bush's close friend and adviser James A. Baker III, who kept a sharp eye for decent treatment of the new vice president.

Reagan put Bush in charge of a task force on regulatory reform and made him chairman of a crisis management team, a task previously assigned to the president's national security adviser. But at once, he wrote, his new secretary of state, Al Haig, "was on the phone going through the roof, saying he didn't want the vice president to have *anything* to do with international affairs; it was *his* jurisdiction, he said, and he told me he was thinking of resigning." To mollify him, Reagan drafted a short statement that made clear the obvious: "that the secretary of state was my primary advisor on foreign affairs."[18] Bush, however, was importantly involved in manning the White House situation room during certain foreign-policy crises.

Haig's fixation on jurisdictional turf was soon to be displayed in public.

Only ten weeks into the new administration, on the afternoon of March 30, 1981, an assassination attempt on Reagan outside the Washington Hilton hotel put Bush literally a heartbeat from the presidency. The president was rushed to nearby George Washington University Hospital, where surgeons removed a bullet from within an inch of his heart.

Bush was on a short speaking trip to Texas, and his plane was just taxiing down an airport runway when he was notified, so the party headed back to Washington. While the president's condition was still in doubt, the immediate question arose over who was in charge. Haig, apparently confused about the order of presidential succession and crisis procedure, raced from the White House situation room to the press room and declared that "constitutionally, the line to succession ran from the president to the vice president to the secretary of state." Haig was wrong; the Speaker of the House and the Senate president pro tem came after the vice president in accordance with a 1947 change in the law. He then added that it was up to the president "to decide he wants to transfer the helm," and "as of now, I am in control here in the White House, pending the return of the vice president, and in close touch with him." In terms of the immediate crisis there was nothing wrong with that, but in saying "I am in control," Haig left an impression with some that he thought he was next in line to take over the country.[19]

In any event, Reagan survived surgery and quickly recovered, leaving Bush in standby mode. In 1984, the president announced early that he would keep Bush on the ticket for reelection. When the 1984 Democratic presidential nominee, Walter Mondale, chose the first woman on a major national ticket, the New York congresswoman Geraldine Ferraro, Bush had a dicey challenge on his hands. Through much of his career, he had been chided and then ridiculed about his upper-crust background, prep school dress, all-around gentlemanly ways, and urge to please. This rap became what was called by foes the "wimp factor," yet to attempt to counter it with toughness in his one scheduled television debate with Ferraro that fall could be regarded as unseemly by voters.

Ferraro, herself a tough politician who rose in her profession with the street smarts of her district in Queens, proved to be no pushover. During an exchange about the terrorist attacks on American facilities in Lebanon, she criticized Reagan's lack of response, and Bush, coming to Reagan's defense, condescendingly offered to "let me help you" understand the situation. Ferraro shot back, "Let me just say, first of all, that I almost resent, Vice President Bush, your patronizing attitude that you have to teach me about foreign policy. I've been a member of Congress for six years. I was there when the embassy was held in Iran."[20]

Bush survived the debate, but the next morning, at a rally of longshoremen in blue-collar Elizabeth, New Jersey, he was caught on an open microphone morphing into Macho Man by telling someone in the crowd, "We tried to kick a little ass" in the debate. Then, seeing the mike, he blurted, "Whoops! Oh, God, he heard me! Turn that thing off!"[21] And so the "wimp factor" clung but had no bearing on the outcome of the election, which Reagan and Bush won easily.

With Reagan ineligible to run again in 1988, Bush was poised to try for the presidency a second time, with his greatest strength his strict loyalty to the retiring president. For all that, he earned the derogatory label of "lapdog" from the conservative columnist George Will, who himself had once coached Reagan for a presidential debate and then commended him for his performance. But Bush took care not to seem eager to take advantage of any opportunity presented by a Reagan illness or mishap. In July 1985, when Reagan was hospitalized again for intestinal cancer and signed a temporary transfer-of-power to Bush for the period he would be under anesthesia, Bush stayed at the vice presidential residence up on Massachusetts Avenue rather than going to the White House, following Nixon's example during Eisenhower's illnesses.

Bush's prospects seemed to slip when the Republicans lost control of the Senate in the 1986 off-year congressional elections. And when the Reagan administration got into hot water over the selling of arms to Iran and siphoning off profits to aid the Contra insurgents in Nicaragua in direct contravention to congressional prohibition, the trail led suspiciously close to Bush. His claim of superior foreign-policy experience as a former CIA director and head of White House crisis management made it difficult to contend he was unaware of what had been going on.

When a CIA-funded plane carrying arms to the Contras was shot down and an American crew member was captured, the first alert went to Bush's national security adviser, Donald Gregg. According to a later investigation into the Iran-Contra affair, Gregg was an overseer of the operation.[22] Bush claimed to have been "out of the loop," saying that when the subject came up at a critical White House meeting, he was "off at the Army-Navy football game."[23] But in this and other Reagan adventures in the Caribbean, including the brief invasion of Grenada, Bush was at a minimum a silent partner.

In the first 1988 preconvention caucuses in Michigan, Bush barely won and then finished a dismal third in Iowa behind Bob Dole and the right-wing evangelist Pat Robertson. There, he got into a spat with the television anchor Dan Rather, who pressed him so hard on what he did and didn't know about the Iran-Contra deal that Bush showed some fire, and in the process countered the "wimp factor" held against him. He bounced back with a strong showing in debate against Dole, and in the New Hampshire primary his campaign ran a tough television ad saying he would not raise taxes and accusing Dole of "straddling" the issue. Dole snapped back, saying Bush should "stop lying" about his record, and came off as a hot-headed sore loser.

Thereafter Bush swept most of the Super Tuesday primaries en route to the 1988 Republican nomination and the campaign in the fall against the Democratic nominee, Governor Michael Dukakis of Massachusetts, and his running mate, Senator Lloyd Bentsen of Texas. In a bravado gesture to the conservative Republican anti-tax crowd in his acceptance speech at the convention, Bush proclaimed, enunciating each word, "Read my lips! No new taxes!"[24] It was a crowd-pleasing gambit he would come to regret later.

In a major surprise, Bush chose a lightly regarded Republican senator from Indiana, J. Danforth Quayle, grandson of the conservative Indiana and Arizona newspaper entrepreneur Eugene Pulliam. Asked later why he chose Quayle, Bush said vaguely because Quayle "represents the next generation and the future."[25] The selection triggered much criticism over the youth and inexperience of the boyish, forty-one-year-old Dan Quayle, who went on to commit gaffes in the campaign, described in the following chapter, but none of this had a detrimental effect on the outcome. The team of Bush and Quayle was elected in November by 53.4 percent of the popular vote compared with 45.6 percent for Dukakis and Bentsen, and in the electoral college by 426 to 111.

For the next four years, Bush occupied the Oval Office in his own right, but he was unable to hold on to presidential tenure despite a major foreign-policy achievement. In 1990 he ordered an invasion of Iraq with U.S. and allied forces, which reversed a military conquest of Kuwait by the Iraqi dictator Saddam Hussein. The swift military action sent Bush's popularity soaring at home, but it could not be sustained in the face of a clinging economic recession. He failed to blunt a strong Democratic assault in 1992 and was replaced by the Democratic presidential nominee Bill Clinton.

Bush's candidacy and election in 1988 did not hold up in either passion or policy in his failed 1992 reelection bid. The senior Bush retired with his wife, Barbara, to Texas. In the face of subsequent natural disasters around the globe, he joined with former president Clinton in massive fund-raising relief efforts that brought each of them esteem in their later years.

In terms of Bush's role in the evolution of the vice presidency as a force in governance, however, neither in his own performance in the office nor particularly in his selection of a running mate did he stand out. Bush's choice of Quayle was widely seen as both startling and irresponsible after he himself had come a heartbeat from the presidency in the near assassination of Reagan. He escaped any penalty for it in winning his first term and lost his quest for reelection more for his failure to improve the economy, in the face of an appealing Democratic challenger and campaigner named Bill Clinton.

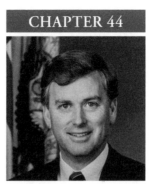

CHAPTER 44

J. DANFORTH QUAYLE
OF INDIANA

N
o American vice president came to office under a heavier cloud than Dan Quayle, despite his record of respectable if not outstanding service in the United States Senate and before that in the House of Representatives, from Indiana. The senior George Bush's choice of the youthful Quayle was widely regarded as a blatantly political one, based on providing some sex appeal and charisma to the bland Bush image rather than any experience or intellectual heft Quayle would bring to the Republican ticket.

The extreme secrecy with which Bush kept his choice to himself, even from his closest staff associates, compounded the surprise of Quayle's entry onto the national political stage. It generated a frenzied vetting of his background by a particularly curious and diligent news media. Reporters were especially fixed on discovering not only why Quayle had been selected but also what there was about him and his personal and political background that qualified him to assume the presidency if circumstances so required.

In advance of the opening of the 1988 Republican National Convention in New Orleans in August, the Bush pollster Bob Teeter had drawn up a list of about twenty prospective running mates, soon whittled down to about a dozen, including several of whom were regarded as mere decoys. Senator Bob Dole of Kansas and Congressman Jack Kemp were considered the favorites. Beyond Quayle's youth and possible appeal to a younger generation, another reason he was on the list could have been that Bush wanted his own Bush as vice president. That is, perhaps he wanted a totally loyal and uncomplaining Republican who would happily serve in the shadow of the president as Bush had done as Reagan's standby for eight years.

Dan Quayle seemed a pleasant enough fellow from a well-off Indiana family of deep conservative Republican roots. His maternal grandfather, Eugene Pulliam, was a successful publisher of small to moderate-sized newspapers there and in Arizona. But he was not a believer in inherited wealth or in giving his children or their children a free ride through life; they were all expected to work. He did, however, give Dan's father, James Quayle, a job as the advertising manager and sports editor of his paper in Lebanon, Indiana, where "Danny," as he was called, was born on February 4, 1947, to Jim and Corinne Pulliam Quayle. The boy was named after James A. Danforth, a marine friend of his father who had been killed in Germany in World War II. Soon after, the family moved to Huntington, Indiana, where Jim Quayle became the publisher of another Pulliam paper,[1] and then on to Arizona to still another.

During young Dan's junior year at Scottsdale High School, where he played on the golf team, the family moved back to Huntington, where he quickly made the high school varsity team and his father became publisher of the local *Herald-Press.* Dan was deeply into all sports and school antics, and in the summers he worked as a reporter and advertising salesman at his father's paper and in the press room melting down printing plates and cleaning out ink fountains. Both Grandfather Pulliam and Jim Quayle insisted that Dan carry his share of the workload.

At DePauw University, in Greenville, Indiana, Quayle joined Delta Kappa Epsilon fraternity and focused on varsity golf. A gag circulated on campus that "Dan Quayle managed to get from the Deke house to the golf course for four years without ever having to go through a classroom." It was a major exaggeration, Ted Katula, the school's athletic director said later, but he confirmed that Quayle was an outstanding player who, he said, would have been a top amateur golfer had he decided to stay with the game. "He had a very friendly nature about him," Katula said, "but he was serious about his golf game. He was in his own world when he got on a golf course." At the same time, Quayle, for all the family money, worked part of the way through DePauw, waiting tables and doing chores in the kitchen of a sorority house.[2]

The United States was now getting entangled in Vietnam, and there were anti-war demonstrations on the DePauw campus, but Quayle never got involved in them.[3] Although Quayle graduated as a political science major, there was considerable dispute about whether he had ever taken or passed the comprehensive examination in the course required for his degree. Of more concern to him at the time, however, as it was with many other college seniors, was whether he would be caught in the military draft before graduation. Six days before that event, Dan joined the Indiana National Guard with some help from family friends. He managed to be assigned to a public information unit, where he had to report once a month to a camp about fifty miles south of Indianapolis. There he helped turn out a small newspaper on Guard activities, which took about half a day.[4]

While in the Guard, Quayle decided to go to law school, but his mediocre college grades were not good enough to get him into the Indiana University program. However, an old family friend and teacher at its night school extension with Purdue got him admitted there, where he met and married another law student, Marilyn Tucker.[5]

Quayle's interest in public office was whetted by briefly working for the state attorney general and governor, and he and Marilyn practiced law together before he resumed work at the family newspaper in Huntington. Later, ironically for one who became a whipping boy for the press, Quayle attributed his core conservative hostility toward government to his background in the newspaper business. "People in the newspaper business hate the government. They distrust the government," he told his biographer. "It is the last unregulated business. It is almost immune from regulation," said this eventual champion of deregulation. "It is deeply ingrained in them that the government should keep hands off, that government cannot do any good, that it only brings trouble. That distrust is deeply ingrained in me."[6]

In 1976, Quayle was recruited by the local county Republican chairman to challenge an eight-term Democratic congressman, and at age twenty-nine he won the first of two terms in the U.S. House. As a down-the-line conservative, Quayle was seen by critics as he had been in college, as more focused on athletics than on his legislative duties. A colleague recalled, "People called him a 'wet head' because he was always coming out of the [House] gym. His attendance record was lousy. . . . They didn't know where he was a lot of the time. He'd be in the gym or he'd sneak off to play golf and they'd have to call around to find him [for House votes]."[7] Most memorably, in 1978 he introduced a bill to cut off food stamps for participants in a coal strike when a University of Maryland professor estimated that the federal government was spending more than $430,000 a day supporting the strikers. The bill got nowhere.

Easily reelected, in 1979 Quayle cast himself as a staunch Cold War warrior, urging the shelving of Jimmy Carter's second arms limitation treaty until all Soviet Union troops were removed from Cuba. He continued to find time to play golf, including joining a weekend trip to a Florida resort with other House Republicans at which a soon-to-be-famous lobbyist named Paula Parkinson shared their group cottage. The episode came to light the next year when he ran for the Senate against the incumbent Democrat Birch Bayh, who was seeking an unprecedented fourth term from Indiana.

Marilyn Quayle's reaction to the rumor that her husband had slept with Parkinson was that if he had a choice between golf and sex, golf would win out every time. Quayle won the Senate seat as one of the beneficiaries of a fierce campaign effort by the National Conservative Political Action Committee, which drove a host of veteran Democratic senators, including Bayh, from office, abetted by the popularity of Ronald Reagan at the head of the Republican ticket.

Quayle attributed his Senate election, however, to his own efforts to escape from what he saw as a boring and "awful job" in the House, where "you can't get anything done."[8] In the Senate, though, he at first was no more involved with legislation than he had been in the House. When the new president Reagan failed to act quickly enough on a campaign pledge to abolish the Department of Education, Quayle introduced such legislation, which also languished.

Meanwhile, the thirty-three-year-old freshman senator now lamented his switch from the House. He told his Indiana biographer, "I miss my peer group. There aren't many senators under thirty-five with children under six. There are no basketball games. People don't get together in groups on the floor and tell stories. There are no groups or cliques here. In the House you have little clubs." He was said to be "sneaking over to the House in the late afternoon to play basketball."[9]

In May 1982, when the president of his alma mater DePauw invited

Quayle to deliver that spring's commencement address, which carried with it an honorary degree, an irate faculty voted against the invitation. But to save the president and the school further embarrassment, enough faculty members changed their votes on a second ballot, and the invitation went forward. The campus radio station, however, reported on what was supposed to be an off-the-record faculty meeting, resulting in two students being fired and a third being suspended and then resigning from the station, charging censorship. When Quayle learned of the actions, he urged the station manager to reinstate them, declaring his firm support of First Amendment rights of a free press, but the suspensions stood. Quayle gave the address and received the honorary degree.[10]

As a strong Reagan man in the Senate, he supported the president's 1981 tax cuts and then his subsequent tax increase of nearly ninety-nine billion dollars, despite continuing his unremitting opposition to higher taxes. But with the rate of unemployment among young blacks as high as 40 percent, he lobbied to save youth job training from Reagan's ax. A subcommittee he chaired drafted, with the Democratic senator Ted Kennedy, the Quayle-Kennedy Job Training Partnership Act, providing $3.9 billion to be dispensed at the local and state levels.

The bipartisan legislation added some heft to Quayle's reputation, and he was easily reelected to the Senate in 1986. Little was heard from him into the presidential year of 1988, but from time to time he dropped by the office of Vice President George Bush, by now a presidential candidate. Through increased speaking on the Senate floor, attendance at Senate Republican lunches also attended by Bush, and more of those drop-ins to Bush's vice presidential office, just off the Senate floor, Quayle made himself known to the vice president.

Next, Quayle took some positions in the Senate that aligned him with Bush on matters in dispute within the Reagan administration, particularly the Intermediate-Range Nuclear Forces Treaty with the Soviet Union. That summer he urged Bush to press Reagan to veto a three hundred billion dollar defense budget bill he considered cut too deeply by the Democrats, while agreeing with Bush that discretion on arms control be reserved to the president. Reagan used his veto, highlighting the Republicans' pro-defense posture entering the 1988 campaign. Quayle said later, "That was the turning, that was the major point" in his relationship with Bush.[11]

As the 1988 convention opened and Bush was nominated on the first ballot, the only suspense left was the identity of his running mate. Any idea of Dan Quayle as a nominee for vice president of the United States would have been regarded as sheer fantasy. Bush did not reveal his choice even to Reagan until the president was boarding his plane from the convention city, New Orleans. Bush was determined, on the advice of the media adviser Roger Ailes, to use his selection to demonstrate that after eight years under Ronald Reagan's shadow he was taking charge of his own course. Also, he wanted to show he was not the bland figure so often painted by critics but capable of springing a surprise, throwing a "long ball" as Ailes put it, at a convention having little drama.

After Reagan had departed, Bush called Quayle and then boarded an old paddle-wheel riverboat down the Mississippi to the New Orleans pier, where Quayle was told to meet his arrival. Watching the scene on television from their hotel room were the two seasoned political professionals already assigned to run the vice presidential campaign—Stuart Spencer of California, on old Reagan and Ford hand, and Joe Canzeri of New York, a veteran of Nelson Rockefeller campaigns. They didn't know Quayle, and he didn't know them.

Dan and Marilyn Quayle were at dockside, and when Bush disembarked and introduced his running mate, the ebullient young Hoosier raced forward and enthusiastically embraced his political benefactor. As Quayle grabbed the thunderstruck Bush in a bear hug, Spencer, watching the TV screen, told his sidekick, "Well, we gotta correct that."[12] Quayle himself later described his effervescent entry into the national limelight thus: "I was talking like a junior senator in campaign overdrive. I was picked, in part, for my youth, but this was a little too youthful—not vice-presidential nor, given the nature of that office, potentially presidential . . . but I was energized and proud, and I was wearing my emotions on my shirtsleeves."[13]

Thus began the "handling" of Dan Quayle that was to guide, and torment, the new Republican vice presidential nominee between then and the election in November. Canzeri was immediately dispatched to pick up Quayle at his hotel to prepare him for what was to come. The next morning at a news conference, Quayle was subjected to a withering bombardment about everything from the Paula Parkinson golf weekend to his National Guard service and failure to serve in Vietnam, and he did not handle himself well. He brushed off the query about Parkinson and called the question about not serving in Vietnam "a cheap shot." And he added naively, "I did not know in 1969 [when he entered the Guard] that I would be in this room today."[14]

Quayle was paraded that night into each of the television network booths at the convention hall. When Tom Brokaw of NBC asked whether he had received special help in getting into the National Guard, he acknowledged that "phone calls were made." When Dan Rather at CBS asked him what his worst fear was, he blurted out, "Paula Parkinson." The rumor soon spread that Quayle would be dropped from the ticket. But according to Rich Bond, who had run Bush's upset caucus victory in Iowa in 1980, the immediate orders concerning the rumor were: "Squash it. Squash that one like a bug."[15] Memories of the fiasco that had followed George McGovern's dumping of Tom Eagleton in 1972 assured that quick decision.

In another news conference in his home town of Huntington, Quayle offered more evasive or confused answers while local supporters jeered the inquisitorial press. He was brought back to Washington for what Bond called "Dan Quayle goes to candidate school," run by his professional campaign handlers.[16] Spencer and Canzeri said, "We knew we were going to have to script him," but as stories mounted about how Quayle was being "handled," he grew more irritated. In September before the City Club of Chicago he threw away the script prepared for him on national defense and winged it. He was disorganized, guilty of misquotes, and performed poorly.[17]

The nadir of Quayle's troubles came in his debate with the Democratic vice presidential nominee, Senator Lloyd Bentsen. When asked what was the first thing he would do were he suddenly to become president, Quayle haltingly said, "First I'd say a prayer for myself and for the country I'm about to lead, and then I would assemble [the president's] people and talk." Tom Brokaw pressed him on what he actually would do, and he answered by talking about his experience. "I have far more experience than many others who sought the office of vice president in this country," he said. "I have as much experience in the Congress as Jack Kennedy did when he sought the presidency." Bentsen pounced. "Senator," he said, "I served with

Jack Kennedy. I knew Jack Kennedy. Jack Kennedy was a friend of mine. Senator, you are no Jack Kennedy." Quayle lamely replied, "That really was uncalled for, Senator."[18]

The Quayle camp was stunned, in part because Quayle had made that comparison on earlier occasions, and his advisers, including his wife, had counseled him to abandon it. Long after the debate, he insisted, "The comparison of myself and Kennedy on this point was relevant, because by 1960 he had served six years in the House and eight in the Senate, almost what I had, and he was running for the presidency itself."[19] Canzeri later blamed the misstep on Quayle's short attention span, cruelly observing, "He was like a kid. Ask him to turn off a light, and by the time he gets to the switch, he's forgotten what he went for."[20] Quayle blamed it all on his handlers, writing later, "My biggest mistake was allowing myself to be put in a position where I couldn't take responsibility for anything—my schedule, my press availability, my own words and movements."[21]

As destructive as the exchange with Bentsen was to Quayle's credibility, on Election Night the Bush-Quayle ticket won over the Democratic ticket of Michael Dukakis and Bentsen. Quayle now had a second chance to make a good impression on the American voters. On the eve of the inauguration of the new administration, he quoted Winston Churchill on what he had just been through: "There is nothing more exhilarating in life than to be shot at without result."[22]

In taking office, Quayle concentrated on two executive responsibilities given to him, chairing the National Space Council and the Council on Competitiveness, where he could carry the conservative flag against troublesome environmental regulations. He also undertook ceremonial duties abroad, with some political risk. Meeting in El Salvador with the retiring president, José Napoleón Duarte, he clumsily said the United States would "work toward the elimination of human rights." On return, when the Republican National Committee censured the Louisiana legislator and former Ku Klux Klansman David Duke, Quayle commended the RNC for its "censorship" of him.[23]

On an early Quayle trip to the Far East, a host of American reporters signed up for what came to be called the "gaffe watch." They were rewarded on a refueling stop when he treated the locals to a geography lesson, Quayle style: "Hawaii has always been a very pivotal role in the Pacific. It is in the Pacific. It is a part of the United States that is an island that is right here." At a stop in Pago Pago, American Samoa, where the famous resort is pronounced "Pango Pango," he botched it as "Pogo Pogo," as in the jumping stick or the old cartoon character. And he addressed a group of local schoolchildren as "happy campers," leading the Samoan delegate to Congress to complain that he seemed to be "implying that the people of Samoa are simple, illiterate natives camped out in the jungle."[24]

Back home, in discussing the United Negro Fund, whose slogan at the time was "A mind is a terrible thing to waste," it came out of Quayle as "What a waste it is to lose one's mind, or not to have a mind, is very wasteful. How true that is."[25] Quayle himself admitted that saying he had simply "mangled" the motto wasn't enough. "I fractured, scrambled and pureed" it.[26]

When an earthquake hit Northern California as millions of Americans watched a World Series game in San Francisco, Quayle inspected the damage and called it "a heart-rendering sight" at which "the loss of life will be irreplaceable."[27] Who could make up such malapropisms? But in an interview with the *Dallas Morning News* in November, Bush said Quayle would "absolutely" be his running mate again in 1992 if he wanted to be. When United Press International asked Quayle whether he might seek the presidency himself in 1996, he acknowledged, "Anytime you get into politics, being president crosses one's mind."[28]

Soon after, Bush was en route to Malta for a summit meeting with the Soviet leader Mikhail Gorbachev when a coup attempt was made against President Corazón Aquino in the Philippines. On the advice of deputy national security adviser Robert Gates, Quayle called a meeting of the National Security Council and conveyed to Bush through White House communications its recommendation that American air cover be provided to keep rebel planes on the ground. Bush so ordered, this limited action worked, and the coup was foiled. Afterward, Quayle took credit as the man in charge with Bush airborne, noting, "I was the one asking the questions, seeking the options and pushing for a consensus."[29] Chairman of the Joint Chiefs of Staff Colin Powell, also involved, later disputed his view. Powell wrote that it was his own intervention with Bush's secretary of defense, Dick Cheney, that avoided a tougher response, but he allowed that the vice president "did perform well in the Philippine situation," though his aides "put a spin on the story that exaggerated Quayle's role."[30]

In early 1990 Bush sent the vice president to Latin America on an important damage-control mission after the administration's invasion of Panama to overthrow dictator Manuel Noriega in violation of the charter of the Organization of American States. Two countries on Quayle's itinerary, Mexico and Venezuela, balked at receiving him. But Quayle completed the other stops satisfactorily and without incident, except for another episode that kept the gaffe watch at work.

In Chile, Quayle took his wife to the port city of Valparaiso for lunch and some tourist shopping. There he bought a carved wooden figurine of a smiling native, whose top slid up to reveal its lower frontal anatomy popping up. Marilyn Quayle saw her husband about to buy it, so he desisted, but later he sent a Secret Service agent back to get it for him. In the news media, the stories about the "anatomically correct doll" overshadowed all the constructive work Quayle had done on the trip. In a speech to the National Press Club on return, an irate Marilyn called the doll episode "an ugly chapter in journalism and an ugly chapter in my own personal life."[31]

One area in which Quayle was an unqualified success was in fundraising for the party going into the 1990 midterm elections. By some estimates he raised more than fifteen million dollars for Republican candidates by segueing from the nice kid from Indiana into a slashing partisan. Noting he had beaten incumbents in his House and Senate races in Hoosierland, he bragged, "Believe me, you don't beat incumbents by saying we're all going to do a good job and I'm a nice guy. You beat incumbents by going for the jugular and by hammering the issues over and over again."[32]

An important disagreement between Bush and Quayle came in the wake of a mushrooming deficit and the president's resulting June 1990 decision to break his 1988 convention pledge of "no new taxes." His agreement to a compromise with the Democratic congressional leaders shocked and angered fellow Republicans, especially conservatives, including Quayle. He wrote later that he had told Bush, "You shouldn't do it. You got a bad deal and you should walk away." But in the end he played the good soldier, "lobbying for a plan my heart wasn't in," rationalizing that doing so "actually gained me a more sympathetic ear than I might have gotten otherwise."[33] In any event, in the midterm congressional elections the Republicans lost one Senate and eight House seats.

In May 1991, when Bush was hospitalized with an irregular heartbeat after jogging and a surgical procedure was considered to deal with it, more questioning ensued of Quayle's remaining in the direct line of presidential succession. The concern proved unnecessary when Bush quickly returned to his Oval Office desk. Still, *Time* ran photos on its cover of five Republicans "who could be president," omitting Quayle, and *Newsweek* showed him swinging a golf club and asked, "The Quayle handicap. . . . Is he a lightweight—or smarter than you think?" Nevertheless, Bush reiterated his intention of keeping him on the ticket. His running mate, he said, was getting "a bum rap in the press, pounding on him when he's doing a first-rate job."[34] On subsequent trips to Japan and to central and eastern Europe, Quayle was free of gaffes, but he got little press credit for it, not qualifying as news.

The vice president did gain high marks and favorable publicity, along with sharp criticism from critics within labor and environmental circles, for his chairmanship of Bush's Council on Competitiveness. Under Quayle, the council sought to alter federal rules regarding everything from airplane noise to opening wetlands for commercial development. He said his mission from Bush was "to make sure that 'regulatory creep' . . . does not get back into his administration" and that he was "the last stop before the president" to curb excessively restrictive inhibitions to business.[35] House Democrats later blocked the council's appropriations, with the Virginia congressman James P. Moran calling it "a back door to the White House" for campaign contributors seeking a private hearing on regulatory issues.[36]

In 1992, as Bush began his quest for reelection with Quayle at his side, he had to deal with two new threats: a primary challenge from the former Nixon speechwriter Pat Buchanan and the third-party candidate, the Texas business tycoon Ross Perot. In New Hampshire, which in 1988 had put Bush back on track after a humiliating third-place finish in the Iowa caucuses, he had not yet returned to express his appreciation, and Buchanan was poised to make the most of it.

As Bush was off to Tokyo, saying his objective was to create more markets for American products and hence more jobs, Buchanan had a large map of New Hampshire plastered on a factory wall in Manchester and sent a giant searchlight into the heavens for Bush's plane. He told crowds that Bush should "put a Denver boot on Air Force One"—anchoring it in place—and maybe then Bush would find time to return to New

Hampshire. When the Bush campaign finally sent Quayle to the state with the message that he still cared, Buchanan chided the president for sending "little Danny, the pit puppy" to do political battle with him.[37]

Quayle arrived in Nashua only hours after word had come from Tokyo that Bush had become ill and collapsed while attending a state dinner, rekindling the question of presidential succession. As soon as *Air Force Two* landed, the vice president was asked again about his qualifications to take over if necessary. "I'm ready," he curtly answered and walked off.[38]

After returning from his foreign trip, when Bush finally got to New Hampshire a month before the primary, he was armed with cue cards, one of which instructed him to let the locals know he cared. It read: "Message: I care." So he read it to them![39] Bush did not have to take a back seat to the gaffe champ, his vice president.

Quayle, the solid family man, peddled family values hard in the remaining state contests. In California, Quayle blamed riots in Los Angeles on a "breakdown of family structure, personal responsibility and social order," including women irresponsibly bearing children out of wedlock. He pointed to one of the most popular television shows of the day, *Murphy Brown,* in which the main character becomes an unwed mother. "It doesn't help matters," he said, "when prime time TV has Murphy Brown—a character who supposedly epitomizes today's intelligent, highly paid, professional woman—mocking the importance of fathers, bearing a child alone, and calling it just another 'lifestyle choice.'"[40] He set off a firestorm, bringing the battle over abortion rights squarely into the campaign, pleasing conservatives but with uncertain effect on the election. Bush kept his head down, but Quayle, unrestrained by imposed "handlers" this time around, played the notoriety for all it was worth.

Rumblings of dumping him from the ticket were heard once more, these from the Republican senator James Jeffords of Vermont and some others. But Quayle's chief of staff at the time, William Kristol, said later, "The people involved never had the nerve to really move beyond talk to conspiring."[41] Also, talk of removing Quayle would only resurrect questions about Bush's selection of him in the first place. So nothing happened.

In the fall campaign, Quayle played the usual running mate's role of covering second-tier markets. In his one debate with the Democratic nominee Al Gore, he focused more on the man at the top of the ticket, Bill Clinton, criticizing his personal history and contending that Clinton did "not have the strength of character to be president."[42] Quayle acquitted himself well enough and could not reasonably have been blamed for the ensuing Republican defeat, clearly the result of Bush's own failure to inspire confidence in the economic recovery he tried to sell or in himself.

In April 1999, as a private citizen, Quayle declared his candidacy for the Republican presidential nominee for 2000, and in August, he entered the Iowa straw poll in advance of the state's 2000 precinct caucuses. He finished a dismal eighth and dropped out of the race. He resumed residence in Arizona and became chairman of the Competitiveness Center of the Hudson Institute. What had begun as a surprisingly easy climb up the political ladder eventually faded in an epidemic of unfortunate mishaps, many self-inflicted. His four years in the vice presidency did nothing to enhance the esteem of the office or his own, despite diligent service and good intentions. In the end, his tenure cast as much judgment on the man who put him in the line of presidential succession as on the good-natured Dan Quayle himself.

CHAPTER 45

ALBERT A. GORE JR.

OF TENNESSEE

Conventional wisdom was thrown to the winds in 1992 when the Democratic presidential nominee Bill Clinton of Arkansas chose another son of the South, Al Gore of Tennessee, as his running mate. Ignoring a tradition that a national ticket strategically should have geographical balance, Clinton selected a contemporary of his own region, putting a young face on the Democratic ticket.

Although Gore's family roots were unquestionably deep in southern soil, he actually was born in Washington, D.C., on March 31, 1948, and for much of his youth he resided there as the offspring of a brilliant United States senator whose name he bore. During sessions of the Senate, Albert Arnold Gore Sr. and wife Pauline kept an apartment in the stylish Fairfax Hotel, near Embassy Row, and young Albert Junior lived there, attending the exclusive private St. Albans School, within walking or busing distance. It was in many ways a restricting life for the boy, who nevertheless maintained high grades and was seen by students as well-behaved and cautious, though highly competitive in sports. He was captain of a not-very-good football team and in the words of one female classmate "just dabbled in being one of us."[1] While there he met his future wife, Mary Elizabeth Aitcheson, called Tipper, who attended another private school.

When the Senate was not in session, the Gores lived on the family farm in Carthage, Tennessee, where the boy enjoyed the country life and was subject to many of the chores of the rural South. He was the Gores' long-awaited first son, born nearly ten years after their daughter, Nancy, and his arrival rekindled Albert Senior's wish for a boy on which to lay his highest hopes. Young Al's path to his father's political prominence did not, however, follow a straight line. In fact it took several detours—through Harvard as an undergraduate, to the Vietnam War as an enlisted man, and to daily journalism and law school in Nashville—before he finally arrived in Congress at the age of twenty-eight and in the Senate six years later.

His father was in many ways a typical southern farmer, who made a modest living raising Black Angus cattle and tobacco. But as a senator in 1956, he would not sign the Southern Manifesto, which rejected the federally enforced desegregation of the public schools. He denounced it as a "spurious, inane, insulting" document and "the most unvarnished piece of demagoguery" he had ever read. A year later he voted for the Civil Rights Act, barring discrimination in voting based on race or color, further antagonizing much of the white voting population in the region.[2]

His son's major detour to Vietnam was the product of a personal dilemma young Albert faced as he approached his Harvard graduation in the spring of 1969. Like many of his fellow seniors who strongly opposed American involvement in the war, he would soon be subject to the military draft and the decision whether to wait for it to swallow him up or choose the other options: to seek a graduate student or conscientious objector deferment, flee to Canada, or enlist on his own. As the son of a famous senator who was also a vocal critic of the war and faced a stiff challenge to his reelection the next year, Albert Junior was obliged to weigh his decision in terms of not only his own future but also that of his father. He chose the only course that would be seen as upholding his own honor and the likely political viability of his father, and upon graduation he enlisted in the army as a private for a two-year hitch.

Richard Neustadt, the celebrated government professor, counseled Gore: "If you want to be part of the country twenty-five years from now, if you want any future in politics, you've got to serve."[3] But that was well before Gore had made any firm decision to follow his father's footsteps; at the time he was not expressing any inclination to do so.

In the army he was classified as a journalist—he had worked as a *New York Times* copy boy one summer—and was sent to Fort Rucker, Alabama, where he worked on the base newspaper. The next spring he and Tipper were married at the National Cathedral in Washington, and that summer and fall he appeared in uniform in some television commercials for his father's reelection, but in vain. As a critic of the war in Vietnam, Albert Senior lost his Senate seat, and shortly afterward his son was shipped to Vietnam. There he saw no combat, spending the next five months as a military reporter writing stories about fellow soldiers for their local newspapers back home.

On return home, Gore got a job as a reporter at the Nashville *Tennessean* and took night classes at Vanderbilt University in religion and law while contemplating a possible future in journalism. With encouragement from the editor John Seigenthaler, he took to investigative work, all the while resisting the urging of family members, especially his mother, to try his hand in his father's domain.

But in 1976 Albert Senior's old House district became open, and at age twenty-eight, to his parents' great satisfaction, Albert Junior ran and won it. In the House, he made himself an expert on the exotica of arms control, to the discomfort of Democratic liberals, who felt he was getting in over his head. When Tennessee's senior Republican senator Howard Baker resigned in 1984, Gore ran and was elected to his father's old stamping ground.

Only two years after entering the Senate, again prodded by his father's ambition for his son and by his own, Al Gore startled most of the rest of the political community by deciding to reach for the Democratic presidential nomination in 1988. He hoped at first to ride his expertise in arms control and support of a strong military to establish himself as the southern candidate. He further burnished his rightward swing by emphasizing his support of Ronald Reagan's invasion of Grenada in 1981 and of aid to the Contra rebels in Nicaragua. Another rival, Congressman Richard Gephardt of Missouri, accused him of "pandering to the right wing of the party."[4] In keeping with his southern strategy, Gore also ducked New Hampshire, the first primary state. His sharpened edge by now had antagonized all the other candidates, who wondered why the thirty-nine-year-old Tennessean was even in the race.

Why he was positioning himself as the southern candidate became clear on Super Tuesday, when he won five southern state primaries. But he faltered in Illinois, Michigan, and Wisconsin and headed for New York, where his campaign totally collapsed. Gore's defeat seemed to end Albert Gore

Senior's lifelong dream that his son would one day become president of the United States. It ushered in a period of depression for the son that was only deepened about six months later when his own son, six-year-old Albert, was nearly killed running into the path of a moving car.

Gore finally shook off the near tragedy and wrote a book on his growing concerns about the perils to the environment, *Earth in the Balance,* which became a best-seller. He also returned to the Senate, where he prepared for another reelection campaign in 1992 and was one of ten Democrats to support President Bush's use of military force to reverse the Iraqi strong-man Saddam Hussein's invasion of neighboring Kuwait. He had reason to believe any dreams for national office were over.

In 1992 he was out promoting the book on which he had diligently worked over the past two years, when Governor Bill Clinton of Arkansas won the Democratic presidential nomination and addressed the selection of a running mate. After George Bush's startling selection of Dan Quayle to run with him on the Republican ticket, Clinton was determined that his own choice be seen as clearly qualified to assume the presidency if required. Gore's experience in foreign policy and the environment shored up Clinton's weaknesses, and in a two-hour meeting between the two southerners who did not know each other well, a developing compatibility emerged that sealed the deal.

Immediately upon adjournment of the Democratic convention in New York, a caravan of buses carrying the candidates, staffs, and several bus-loads of reporters flowed across much of the eastern United States in what was soon dubbed "Bill and Al's Excellent Adventure." Each had his own bus, but before long they were riding together, getting more acquainted, swapping campaign stories, and generally comporting themselves like two young buddies on a summer's lark. Wherever the bus caravan stopped, throngs of locals flocked to see and hear the candidates.

They shared the speaking chore like a duet, breaking the tradition that the principals seldom campaign together. They worked up a routine that came off in time as more vaudeville or road show than political exercise. Gore would warm up the crowd with a rollicking jibing of the opposition ticket: "Bush and Quayle have run out of ideas. They're run out of energy. They're run out of gas, and with your help come November, they're going to be run out of office!" He would conclude the pitch shouting, "It's time for Bush and Quayle to go!" Then he would ask the crowd: "What time is it?" and the response would come with a roar: "It's time for them to go!" Through all this, the supposedly wooden robot Al Gore would grin contagiously while Clinton would throw his head back and roar as if he were seeing and hearing it all for the first time.[5] Often the two candidates would sit together on the lead bus, talking away for long periods as the reporters cooled their heels outside. Once, the pair sat gabbing so long that the press corps en masse started to rock the bus until they sheepishly emerged.

In the late fall, a single vice presidential debate was held. For Quayle, it was an opportunity to redeem himself after four years of his humiliating "You're no Jack Kennedy" spanking by the 1984 Democratic running mate Lloyd Bentsen. Early in the debate Gore injected that bad memory for Quayle by offering him a deal: "If you don't try to compare George Bush to Harry Truman, I won't compare you to Jack Kennedy." But then, Gore made the same allegation of unpreparedness by recalling how Truman was suddenly called to the presidency with the death of FDR with World War II still going on in the Pacific.[6]

Thereafter in the debate, Quayle gave a much better accounting of himself and easily exceeded low expectations by largely focusing on Clinton rather than Gore. Postdebate polling still rated Gore the winner, but he was afforded little credit, considering the perceived view of Quayle. In November, Clinton-Gore won easily as voter participation—55.2 percent—rose for the first time in thirty-two years.

After the election, Clinton and Gore met in Little Rock and worked out an agreement on how the new vice president would function, patterned after the Mondale model in the Carter administration. In a break with the Mondale model, Gore also would have specified fields of interest, areas in which he had already developed expertise, such as arms control and disarmament, the environment, high tech, including the Internet, and other new means of communications.[7]

Yet the new vice president's hope and intention of being Clinton's prime right-hand man was complicated by others within the president's own circle vying for the role. First among them obviously was wife Hillary. She particularly seemed to some administration aides to resent Gore's role and his face time with her husband. Gore for his part kept a sharp personal eye for Oval Office meetings about which he may not have been apprised.[8] As

Clinton got himself into various scrapes, foreign and domestic, Gore remained solidly in support. According to Clinton's national security adviser, Anthony Lake, "If you're vice president, it's possible to pick and choose, to be there on some issues and take a walk on others that could have a tough edge to them." But Gore, he said, "never took a walk," at least not at this juncture.[9]

Domestically, Gore took on a direct Clinton assignment to review the performance of the federal establishment, a review known in shorthand as "reinventing government." After an intense six-month study, Gore made 384 recommendations for overhauling and streamlining government regulations and rule making, claiming they would save taxpayers $108 billion and eliminate 252,000 federal jobs in the next five years.

Perhaps more influential in his political stature was Gore's leading role in late 1993 in winning congressional approval of the new North American Free Trade Agreement (NAFTA) with Mexico and Canada, ending most tariffs and other taxes among three countries. The pact was put forward as a major weapon for creating new markets for American goods among the neighboring states and more jobs at home. The failed third-party candidate of 1992, Perot, took up the fight. He colorfully proclaimed that passage would trigger a "giant sucking sound" of lost jobs in the American economy caused by many domestic companies moving to Mexico to take advantage of sharply lower labor costs.

Gore was recruited to challenge Perot to a televised debate on NAFTA and Clinton agreed. Gore realized the debate posed a considerable risk for him, and he prepared for the encounter with a mock rehearsal similar to those he had undergone in debating Dan Quayle the previous year. Against Perot, he took a needling approach, peppering him with questions about some of his famously off-the-wall claims and thereafter was credited with giving NAFTA a strong boost in Congress, which passed both houses with bipartisan support.

But other problems in the administration continued to intrude on its public approval, casting doubts on the political value of the vice presidency for the man so obviously with his eye still on the Oval Office. Investigation of the Clintons' involvement in a questionable land purchase in Arkansas, dubbed "Whitewater," and the demise of Hillary Clinton's secrecy-prone quest for universal health care reform contributed to midterm congressional elections in 1994 that gave the Republicans control of the House for the first time in forty-one years, along with the Senate. A conservative "revolution" led by the bombastic Newt Gingrich of Georgia made him House Speaker, bent on bringing down Bill Clinton, with uncertain ramifications for Al Gore.

In early 1995, the president clearly was in a funk, obliging him to respond to a question about his diminishing clout by insisting, "The president is relevant here."[10] At Gore's urging, Clinton enlisted an old pollster-strategist, Dick Morris, to design an expensive television advertising campaign that deftly moved him more to the center of the political spectrum in what was called "triangulation," positioning him somewhere between the poles of liberalism and conservatism.

Gore and Morris both pressed Clinton to take Gingrich head on with his own balanced budget proposal. Clinton finally called the Speaker's bluff, warning he would close down the government rather than yield to Gingrich's demand for various social service cuts. Charging, "The Republican Congress has failed to pass most of its spending bills," Clinton sent home eight hundred thousand federal workers, closing many public facilities, including national parks, a move that backfired on Gingrich.[11] The president carried the day and shortly was back on track, and Gore with him.

The costly television advertising campaign that accompanied the comeback strategy, unusually early in an election cycle, obliged Gore to engage in heavy fund-raising through the Democratic National Committee (DNC). It soon brought negative news media attention to the vice president, putting an unwelcome spotlight on him in advance of the Clinton-Gore reelection campaign of 1996. Many big-cash donors not only attended fund-raising dinners around the country but also had access to the White House and even some overnight stays in the Lincoln Bedroom. Gore held nearly two dozen coffees in the Executive Mansion, some attended by Clinton, and made numerous phone calls to potential donors. All this effort raised a reported $8.74 million. Such calls were not unusual, except that an 1882 law, the Pendleton Act, prohibited asking for or raising campaign contributions from federal offices and buildings, and Gore made many of them from his office in the West Wing.

The furor over Gore's solicitation of campaign funds intensified after the convention when reporters began looking into the "bundling" of large amounts for the DNC from the Asian American community, by John Huang, an executive of an Indonesian banking firm. The most eyebrow-raising event was a fund-raiser at a Buddhist temple in suburban Los Angeles at which Gore spoke and more than a hundred thousand dollars was raised. The temple had a federal tax exemption, prohibiting its use in seeking political contributions at such events. Gore insisted he understood it was not to be a fund-raiser and made no overt pitch for campaign money.[12]

Subsequent evidence made clear that the temple event was what it appeared to be, and a year later Gore acknowledged it was a "political event" at which it was "inappropriate" for him to engage in fund-raising. Seven times he cited a lawyer's conclusion, in lawyerly language, that "no controlling legal authority" prevented him from making soliciting calls from his White House office.[13]

None of this, however, was enough to bar the easy 1996 reelection of Clinton and Gore over the uninspiring Republican team of Bob Dole of Kansas and Jack Kemp of New York. But further congressional inquiries into fund-raising involving Gore continued well into 1997.

At an international summit on the perils of global warming and other climate change, held in Kyoto, Japan, at year's end, the administration's proposal on limiting greenhouse pollution disappointed advocates. Gore at first decided not to attend this major meeting on the issue with which he was so identified. He finally made a brief trip, promising the other conference attendants only that the United States would provide "increased negotiating flexibility" in discussions. He returned with only modest agreement on emissions goals achieved in the first serious effort at reducing global warming, but enough to keep alive what for him was a crusade.

Greeting him on his return was a shocking revival of the womanizing allegations against Clinton that had long haunted his political career. This time it was the revelation that a young White House intern named Monica Lewinsky was said to have had sexual relations with Clinton within the Oval Office itself. Clinton denied the story emphatically but with more word games that only enhanced suspicions of his truthfulness raised in previous sagas. Gore met them with a categorical acceptance and pledge of support, saying, "The president has denied the charges, and I believe him."[14] Gore purposely traveled with the beleaguered president, making no mention of the scandal. When Clinton admitted to a grand jury that he had had "inappropriate intimate contact" and deeply regretted it, Gore said only it was "time to take what he said to heart and move on to the people's business."[15]

As the investigation of Clinton's sexual misconduct proceeded on a track that was eventually to lead to impeachment by the House of Representatives, Gore gamely focused on legislative objectives close to his interests. But as Clinton's personal misdeeds drew more menacing to his presidency with each new disclosure, Gore's own role in the inner circle inevitably diminished. In one meeting Clinton held with cabinet members and Democratic congressional leaders, Gore was said to have urged them all to stand behind the president, while warning him, "Mr. President, I think most of America has forgiven you, but you've got to get your act together."[16]

In the 1998 midterm congressional elections, for which Gore loyally campaigned, the Democrats surprisingly held the line, yielding no Senate seats while picking up five in the House. Gore got some more welcome news in the fall when Attorney General Janet Reno announced she would not recommend appointment of an independent counsel to look any further into Gore's fund-raising activities.

But on December 19, 1998, the House voted two articles of impeachment against Clinton, one for lying under oath to a grand jury and one for obstructing justice, sending the matter to the Senate for trial. Immediately afterward, eighty House Democrats were bused to the White House, where they gathered on the South Lawn. As a red-eyed Clinton stood by, Gore said of the occasion, "This is the saddest day I have seen in our nation's capital." He added that while Clinton had admitted that what he had done was wrong, so was "invoking the solemn power of impeachment [against him] in the cause of partisan politics." Gore said, "What happened as a result does a great disservice to a man I believe will be regarded in the history books as one of our greatest presidents."[17]

The statement was startling in its fulsome endorsement of the Clinton record if not of the man himself. Clinton was subsequently acquitted of the impeachment charges against him, saved only by votes of Democratic senators, many repulsed by the whole sordid mess.

But Gore's endorsement notwithstanding, he, like most previous vice presidents who had sought the presidency, ultimately strove to establish his own identity. In launching his 2000 presidential campaign in Carthage, Gore decided to low-ball his participation in the Clinton administration and did not to ask Clinton to play a major role in his campaign. Also, in light of Gore's embarrassing and arguably illegal excesses in fund-raising, he had to guard against more bad stories as he strove to finance his own effort.

The major challenge to Gore came from the former senator Bill Bradley of New Jersey, famed as a Princeton and New York Knicks basketball star. In a debate in Iowa on farm policy, Gore researchers found a local farmer whose land had been flooded and placed him in the debate audience. He asked Bradley about an obscure vote of his against a disaster relief amendment. Bradley, taken aback, fumbled the question with a weak and evasive answer and never recovered.[18] Gore, with strong labor and agricultural support, not only won the Iowa caucuses but also went on to beat Bradley in the New Hampshire primary and subsequent state contests, driving Bradley from the race.

Selecting his running mate, Gore broke new ground by choosing Senator Joseph Lieberman of Connecticut, a dedicated moderate and champion of the state of Israel, as the first member of the Jewish faith to serve on a national ticket. The Republican nominee, Governor George W. Bush of Texas, meanwhile asked the former congressman and defense secretary Richard Cheney to find the best running mate for him, and Cheney wound up being chosen himself, as described in the next chapter.

In emulation of the Clinton-Gore bus tours, Gore and Lieberman kicked off their campaign on a Mississippi riverboat but failed to replicate the magic of the earlier romp; their chemistry was just not there. Gore set a populist tone for the campaign by declaring, "The difference in this election is, they're for the powerful, we're for the people."[19] In saying so, Gore appeared to be casting his lot more with the old FDR and Truman Democrats than with the New Democrats of Clinton, a matter that in time came to be a bone of contention with the cantankerous Lieberman.

In what was developing into an extremely close race between Gore and Bush, the vice president joined the first of three debates with high expectations against the Ivy Leaguer–turned–Texan son of a former president, known for often wrestling with the English language and getting pinned. In the first meeting Gore came off as a bullying know-it-all, to his detriment in postdebate analyses. Some of Bush's answers brought smirks, audible sighs of impatience, and incredulity and raised eyebrows from the superior-posturing Gore.

The campaign ended with polls indicating a very close race but with no indication of the astonishing and unprecedented outcome. Although Gore had won the national popular vote by more than half a million ballots, neither candidate had a majority in the electoral college. After weeks of recounting and appraising a relative handful of votes in the single state of Florida, Bush was awarded its twenty-five electoral votes and the presidency in a split decision of the United States Supreme Court. In a battle of lawyers and political wits between the Gore and Bush campaigns, the highest federal court, of Republican majority composition at the time, voted to intervene in a state election against the court's own longstanding precedent to leave such matters to the lower courts.

And so Albert A. Gore Jr. was obliged to decide whether this shattering blow to his lifelong aspiration would end his political career or whether he would try a third bid. He was only fifty-two years old and had plenty of time to seek the presidency again in 2004, or 2008, or even beyond. Instead, Gore turned away from politics altogether and created for himself a distinguished career as a groundbreaking thinker and innovator in the field of global environment. In 2007, he won a Nobel Peace Prize for his work and wrote an award-winning book alerting the world to the perils of climate change, *An Inconvenient Truth.* He became, among other things, the founder and chairman of the Alliance for Climate Protection and Current TV but seemed destined to be remembered in the history books as the victim of perhaps the single-most significant political decision ever handed down by the highest judicial body in the land.

RICHARD B. CHENEY
OF WYOMING

Many leading American public figures in the early years shunned the vice presidency as a political dead end. But as time passed, many others looked to it as the best stepping-stone to presidential nomination. In 2000, Richard Cheney had no such expectation as a man whose history of multiple heart attacks seemingly disqualified him. Instead, he agreed to assist a presidential nominee in finding a running mate, vetting a number of prospects on their qualifications, and in the end finding—himself. He then disavowed any intention to reach higher, content to focus on defending and enhancing the power of the office to which he vowed not to aspire.

Yet it fell to Cheney, in the first hours of the September 11, 2011, terrorist attacks on American soil, to assert ultimate presidential powers in directing the nation's first responses to the crisis. It was Cheney who, shortly after the first two hijacked aircraft struck the Twin Towers of the World Trade Center, in New York, learned of another seized plane heading toward Washington and issued the order to shoot it down. He said later he had acted after conveying the situation to President George W. Bush. But there was, and has remained, conflicting testimony and evidence of any such notification. There was also the question of whether, beyond the imperative of immediate action, any authority ever existed for a vice president to issue such an order. Nevertheless Dick Cheney unhesitatingly filled the breach in behalf of the president and thereafter functioned more in the nature of an assistant president than any of his forty-five predecessors.

Indeed, one perceptive analyst of the Bush-Cheney relationship has argued convincingly that although Cheney was "the most powerful vice president in U.S. history," his real legacy is "his role as co-president." Shirley Anne Warshaw, a professor of political science at Gettysburg College, has written that he took advantage of Bush's inexperience in dealing with Congress and foreign policy to carve out for himself, with Bush's full acquiescence, a clear "division of labor" in the running of his administration. At the start, with Bush more interested in and occupied with a faith-based agenda popularized as "compassionate conservatism," Warshaw wrote, Cheney was able to take control of the key policies in the fields of energy, national security, and, eventually, the extension of presidential power that were at the heart of the George W. Bush White House years. And when the 9/11 terrorist attacks intruded, the response and the subsequent pivot to the invasion of Iraq naturally fell to Cheney's assigned area of responsibility, with Bush again relying on him with his superior experience and aggressive assertion of that extended power.[1]

Still, critics charged that in his actions Cheney flirted with long-term damage to both the presidency and the vice presidency, claiming he usurped the first and made the second the instrument of great constitutional mischief. As a result, future presidents may become warier about how they delegate to their presidents-in-waiting, keeping them on a shorter leash than Bush allowed Cheney.

The man who generated such musings came from solid American stock, reaching back to ancestors who arrived from England in the 1630s, when the first of his Puritan ancestors sailed to the New England coast. There they and their descendants took part in the building of a new nation, and eventually his great-grandfather Samuel Fletcher Cheney was engaged in its preservation. In the mid-1800s, Samuel moved his family west to Defiance, Ohio, and when Confederate forces fired on Fort Sumter he joined the Union army, serving for the duration of the Civil War. He survived thirty-four battles in that time and also marched with General William Tecumseh Sherman from Atlanta to the sea and later with him past the White House, where they received and returned the salute of President Andrew Johnson.

Richard Herbert Cheney, the father of the future vice president, was working for the Soil Conservation Service in Syracuse, Nebraska, when in 1940 he met and married Marjorie Dickey, daughter of the owner of the café where bachelor Cheney took his meals. On January 30, 1941, the young Cheneys had a son, also named Richard, born in Lincoln. After Pearl Harbor the elder Richard worked for the Department of Agriculture and in 1944 joined the navy. On his return he went back to Lincoln and the Soil Conservation Service and later was transferred with his family, now including another son, Bobby, and a daughter, Sue, to Casper, Wyoming. Both parents, beneficiaries of the New Deal in the 1930s and 1940s, were loyal FDR Democrats.[2]

Young Dick became an avid fisherman and a football player at the local high school, where he met Lynne Vincent, a top student who also excelled as a baton-twirling majorette, and began his courtship of her. In 1958, Dick Cheney, selected for Wyoming Boys State, attended an academic summer camp at Northwestern University. A local independent oilman offered Cheney a full scholarship to the oilman's alma mater, Yale, for which he was a regional recruiter.[3]

It was quite a culture change for the boy from the plains and mountain states to be thrown in with many graduates of elite prep schools. Later, he wrote about his study habits: "I found some kindred souls, young men like me, who were not adjusting very well and shared my opinion that beer was one of the essentials of life."[4] After his freshman year, he lost the scholarship but was allowed to return with a student loan, but he "continued to accumulate bad grades and disciplinary notices." In the spring of 1962, he was kicked out of Yale.[5]

Returning to Wyoming, he joined the International Brotherhood of Electrical Workers as a ground man, laying power transmission lines there and in Utah and Colorado. After work, he would join fellow crew members in local bars, later writing about that time, "I managed to get arrested twice within a year for driving under the influence."[6] Aware he was on the wrong course and told by his girlfriend, Lynne, that he would have to change his ways or lose her,[7] Cheney then stayed out of the bars. He moved to Laramie and enrolled at the University of Wyoming, and in 1964 they were married in Casper. Under a grant, half of which was paid by the state Republican Party, he worked as an intern at the State of Wyoming Legislature in Cheyenne, leading to a Ford Foundation fellowship and work in the Madison office of the Republican governor Warren Knowles of Wisconsin, where he and Lynne continued graduate work at the University of Wisconsin. He traveled with the campaigning Knowles, further whetting his appetite for practicing politics.

Earlier, upon attaining draft age at eighteen, Cheney had registered and twice thereafter was classified 1-A, but over the next eight years he applied for and received four student deferments and a fifth in 1966, when Lynne was pregnant.[8] He later wrote that had he been called up in the draft he "would have been happy to serve,"[9] but years later in 1980, at the time of his Senate confirmation hearings to be secretary of defense, he acknowledged, "I had other priorities in the 1960s than military service."[10]

In 1968, Cheney received an American Political Science Association fellowship in Washington and was interviewed for a job by the freshman Republican congressman Donald Rumsfeld of Illinois. He apparently didn't impress Rumsfeld and signed up to work for Wisconsin congressman Bill Steiger.[11] Subsequently he was hired to handle congressional relations for the Office of Economic Opportunity, the anti-poverty agency. He came under, of all people, Don Rumsfeld, drafted by President Richard Nixon to downsize the agency. When Rumsfeld was made Nixon's director of the Cost of Living Council, Cheney went with him.[12]

Upon Nixon's resignation in August 1974, the new president, Gerald Ford, chose Rumsfeld to head his transition team, bringing Cheney along. When Ford made Rumsfeld his White House chief of staff, Cheney became Rumsfeld's deputy at age thirty-three, without ever having met Ford. In a subsequent shakeup in November 1975, Ford sent Rumsfeld to the Pentagon as secretary of defense and put Cheney in the top White House staff job at age thirty-four.

Through all this time, Dick Cheney had been regarded as essentially a mild-mannered, hard-working bureaucrat of little-revealed ideological cast. The Secret Service code name for Cheney was "Backseat," and it seemed appropriate. When Ford suggested that his chief of staff be given cabinet status, he demurred, observing later, "The top staff guy is still a staff guy."[13]

In advance of Ford's bid for a full term in 1976, Cheney and Rumsfeld, aware of conservative dissatisfaction with the liberal vice president Nelson Rockefeller as next in the line of presidential succession, urged Ford to drop him as his running mate. They wrote Ford a detailed memo and attached their signed letters of resignation. "This wasn't a matter of saying unless you accept our recommendations, we will quit," Cheney wrote later. "Rather, we were telling Ford that if his idea of changes included moving us, we'd make it easy for him."[14] In any event, Ford finally got Rockefeller to step aside while publicly saying otherwise, but the Republican ticket lost anyway to Democrats Jimmy Carter and Walter Mondale.

Four years later at the national convention in Detroit, as a lowly freshman congressman from Wyoming, Cheney joined former Ford administration officials in weighing the prospect of having Ford as the retired president become Ronald Reagan's running mate—the fanciful "copresidency." Both Ford and Reagan eventually rejected the idea.

Cheney climbed rapidly in the Republican congressional leadership, in 1986 serving on the House committee investigating the Iran-Contra affair, wherein the Reagan administration illegally traded arms in return for financial aid to the anti-communist rebels in Nicaragua. On this committee, the Cheney staff aide David Addington argued that as commander in chief the president had unchallengeable executive powers. Cheney joined him in declaring that the Constitution "does not permit Congress to pass a law usurping Presidential power" and that any such laws "should be struck down."[15] He also wrote a long paper attacking "congressional overreaching in foreign policy," and he called for repeal of the War Powers Resolution, saying he could not accept "such a limited view of the president's inherent constitutional powers."[16]

In 1989, Reagan's successor in the Oval Office, the senior George Bush, called on Cheney to come to the rescue again when the Texas senator John Tower's nomination to be secretary of defense was rejected by the Senate. Reluctantly, after having survived two heart attacks, Cheney agreed to take over the Pentagon and was confirmed. After a third heart attack, he had successful bypass surgery and ran the Pentagon with his recommended appointee, General Colin Powell, as his chairman of the Joint Chiefs of Staff. They were an effective team through the ouster of the Panamanian dictator Manuel Noriega at the end of 1989 and the dramatic months of the reversal of Saddam Hussein's Iraqi invasion of Kuwait in 1991. Cheney demonstrated his penchant for control of the news media by sharply limiting coverage of the buildup to the American military response, requiring monitoring of reporters' interviews and then a total blackout on the ground in the decisive stages that drove the Iraqi forces out of Kuwait.

In the summer of 1992, Bush sounded out Cheney about returning to the White House as his chief of staff, but Cheney preferred to remain at the Pentagon. When Bush failed in reelection in 1992, Cheney went back to Wyoming and private life. In early 1994, he considered a presidential campaign of his own for 1996, set up a political action committee, and started testing the waters. But he was getting nowhere and decided that at age fifty-three there was still time to have a lucrative career in the private sector. "I said I would like to be president but I said I wasn't going to run," he observed in a later interview for this book. "If I didn't win, my health history would be blamed and that would disqualify me for future jobs. . . . I really put politics behind me."[17]

In late 1995 Cheney joined the giant Halliburton oil services company and took over as chief executive officer at the start of 1996. In 1999, he discussed the possibilities of managing the presidential campaign of Texas governor George W. Bush but decided to stay at Halliburton. He told Joe Allbaugh, the governor's chief of staff, "I've never met a happy vice president," quoting Gerald Ford as saying his brief time was "the worst period in his public life" and that it was his job "to shoot down" costly programs sought by Ford's vice president, Nelson Rockefeller.[18]

As early as March 2000, Bush had Allbaugh ask Cheney whether he would be interested in being Bush's running mate. The answer was no. Among the reasons that Cheney said later he told Allbaugh: "Wyoming is a sure state. If he needs me to carry Wyoming, he's not going to get elected anyway." In a subsequent meeting with Bush and Karl Rove, Bush's political adviser, Cheney said he told the prospective candidate that as head of a large oil company, his four previous heart attacks, and having been "kicked out of Yale and with two DUI's," he would be an easy target. Rove agreed, Cheney said.[19] After Bush's nomination, however, the Texas governor Bush asked Cheney to head the search for another running mate, and as a loyal Republican and proven staff man Cheney agreed to take on the task.

Cheney set up a small search team that included his elder daughter, Liz, her husband, Phil Perry, and Addington.[20] Cheney acknowledged later that in the process there usually were two lists of prospective nominees, one for "public consumption" to placate certain figures or party factions, and the "real" one of actual prospects.[21]

Each vice presidential prospect who was asked to supply detailed background information was told he was on "a very short list."[22] One of those approached, the former governor Lamar Alexander of Tennessee, said when he agreed to be vetted that Cheney said, "We'll get together. The only thing was, I never heard from him again."[23] In fact, Cheney wrote subsequently that Bush had told him "more than once, 'Dick, *you're* the solution to my problem.'"[24] Cheney finally said he would consider being Bush's running mate, but he had a few preliminary conditions: "I needed to . . . go through all the reasons he *shouldn't* pick me. . . . I didn't want him to be surprised, and I needed to make sure he vetted the vetter."[25] But Cheney himself said he did not fill out the questionnaire required of the others.

From all this it was not unreasonable to conclude that Dick Cheney, in his fortuitous position, was able to make himself in the end, as one biographer later put it, "the least worst option."[26] Dan Bartlett, later the communications director in the George W. Bush administration, observed, "Cheney was pushing on an open door," while being able to leave the impression that he was not angling for the nomination for himself.[27]

In the legal battle of campaign lawyers and strategists leading up to the eventual election of Bush and Cheney, they left the combat to others in Florida. As the legal maneuvering to secure the presidency dragged on, the prospective vice president elect returned to Washington and assumed the task of preparing for the transition of power. In the transition process, most of the key White House staff jobs went to Bush loyalists from Texas. But Cheney saw to it that not only were some of his own loyalists placed on his vice presidential policy staff but also some were made assistants to the president, integrated with the White House staff.

Early in his vice presidency, he asked Addington as his general counsel to review the procedures under the Twenty-Fifth Amendment, whereby he would be required, in the event of an incapacitated president, to "immediately assume the powers or duties of the office as Acting President."[28] But what if the vice president himself became incapacitated, a pertinent question in light of Cheney's history of multiple heart attacks? Cheney wrote a letter of resignation, signed it, and added a written instruction to Addington to present the letter to Bush "if the need arises."[29]

Nine days after taking office, Cheney announced he would head a White House task force on energy policy that ostensibly would focus on the debate over global warming and other environmental issues. But in reality it would go far beyond that to a matter close to Cheney's concerns—the protection and extension of presidential power. His first challenge was to counter Bush's statements in the 2000 campaign indicating he accepted the scientific findings that man-made carbon emissions contributed to the "greenhouse effect" and climate change. Cheney suggested that the president dodge the issue by saying that "given the incomplete state of scientific knowledge of the causes of, and solutions to, global climate change," he favored a further examination of various "innovative options."[30]

The task force, with formal membership limited to executive branch staff but with the advice and testimony of unidentified outside participants in complete secrecy, soon raised the hackles of suspicious environmental groups. While the ongoing participation of all the major energy-producing companies was invited, more than a dozen "green" advocates were heard on a single day and were never invited back.[31] Because the industry figures were not "members" of the task force, the White House insisted their identities did not have to be disclosed. Cheney persuaded Bush to go to court to protect his constitutional right to seek and obtain advice without public disclosure, as part of what advocates called the power of the "unitary executive."

The executive shielded its disclosure by using the same all-purpose justification that would be invoked by Justice Department lawyers in other, later arguments for the executive's right to use all means to obtain intelligence to preserve national security without legislative or judicial interference. Cheney later noted, "On the scale of risks, I am more concerned about depriving the president of his ability to act than I am about Congress's alleged inability to respond."[32]

In mid-April, two House committees turned for help to the General Accounting Office, the investigative arm of Congress. Its director, David Walker, wrote directly to Cheney for the names of all participants and records of all task force meetings. Addington, as the vice president's legal counsel, replied that the GAO as a legislative body "could not intrude into the heart of Executive deliberations." Cheney, ignoring Walker, wrote directly to the House and Senate, stating that complying "would unconstitutionally interfere with the functioning of the Executive Branch." When a federal judge ordered Cheney to appear and explain, he declined, and the matter eventually went to the Supreme Court, which sent it back to a lower court, where it died; Cheney's "unitary executive" defense survived for the time being.[33] "It was a major victory both for us and for the power of the executive branch," he wrote later.[34]

In these first months of the administration, Bush handed Cheney another special portfolio, monitoring national security, and the gathering of intelligence against terrorist threats to American interests at home and abroad. Less than a month before the 2000 election, a small boat in Aden Harbor, in Yemen, had nearly sunk the navy destroyer USS *Cole.* Cheney declared, "Any would-be terrorist out there needs to know that if you're going to attack, you'll be hit very hard and very quick. It's not time for diplomacy and debate. It's time for action."[35]

Accordingly, on May 8, 2001, Bush announced the creation of the new Office of National Preparedness, in which Cheney would plan for the "consequence management" of any domestic attack, particularly with weapons of mass destruction.[36] The vice president had barely begun when, three months later, Bush and Cheney read the Presidential Daily Brief warning, "Bin Laden Determined to Strike in U.S."

On the morning of September 11, Cheney was at his desk in the White House when without warning the first of the Twin Towers of the World Trade Center was hit by a hijacked jet plane. He immediately placed a call to Bush, who was visiting an elementary school in Sarasota, Florida. Unable to reach the president at once, within minutes Cheney was hustled out of his office by Secret Service agents to a secure underground bunker, the Presidential Emergency Operations Center. He finally reached Bush aboard *Air Force One* and advised him not to return to Washington at once. Meanwhile, as fragments of information came to Cheney and a second plane hit the second tower, a military aide informed him that still another unauthorized commercial jet was swiftly approaching Washington. Twice the aide asked the vice president whether combat air patrol pilots had the authority to shoot down a suspected hijacked plane, and each time without hesitation Cheney said yes.[37]

The vice president had no specific authorization to give the order but acted as the emergency warranted. The exact details of whether Cheney ever sought and got Bush's approval were never satisfactorily resolved.[38] About a half hour after giving the order, however, Cheney reached Rumsfeld at the Pentagon and told him, "Pursuant to the president's instructions I gave instructions for [the hijacked planes] to be taken out." When Rumsfeld asked, "Who did you give that direction to?" Cheney replied that he gave it to the pilots, reached through air force communications.[39]

Thus began arguably the most dramatic episode in U.S. history of the nation being pulled into war and Cheney's unexpected role in it. In ordering the first American defensive and retaliatory blow, he spent the next momentous hours as the prime conduit to the president, until Bush, after being diverted to Barksdale Air Force Base, in Louisiana, and then to Strategic Air Command headquarters, near Omaha, returned to the nation's capital that night. Two days later, with key members of the National Security Council relocated to Camp David, Bush and Cheney began initial talks about going after the al Qaeda perpetrators. Cheney wrote later in his memoir, "Although we had discussed Iraq earlier in the day, I also took time now to say that Afghanistan, where the 9/11 terrorists had trained and plotted, should be first," before dealing with "the threat Iraq posed" to the West with its suspected development of weapons of mass destruction.[40]

Cheney's performance in those first minutes and hours after the 9/11 terrorist attacks presaged the dominant role he would play in the remaining years of the George W. Bush administration. Ironically, he had been prepared for it in a way by his part in the Reagan administration's 1980s secret "continuity of government" drill called Project 908. Teams of essential federal officials were spirited out of Washington to undisclosed locations around the country, and Cheney, as a member of the congressional leadership, led one of the teams in a classified exercise of keeping the government going in the face of an enemy attack.[41] This time it had been no drill, and Cheney slipped easily into the hierarchy of command, not by calculation, but by circumstance. Thereafter his determination to maintain the power of the executive branch in the conduct of the war arguably made him the most influential vice president in American history.

In an appearance on NBC News's *Meet the Press* five days later, Cheney acknowledged the importance of working "the dark side, if you will," to find the terrorists, probing into "the shadows in the intelligence world . . . without any discussion, using sources and methods that are available to our intelligence agencies."[42] Thus the vice president broached the subject of surveillance that would eventually engulf him as the highest advocate of what came to be known as "robust interrogation" methods against suspected terrorists.

At Cheney's instruction through Addington, a thirty-four-year-old deputy in Justice's Office of Legal Counsel, John C. Yoo, was assigned to write the legal cover for use of torture to break the will of captured terrorists.[43] Yoo, an American-born son of South Korean immigrants, argued that an American president, as commander in chief of the armed forces under Article II, Section 2, had "plenary" or absolute powers, particularly in wartime. Yoo wrote that no law "can place any limits on the President's determinations as to any terrorist threat, the amount of military force to be used in response, or the method, timing, and nature of the response."[44]

Furthermore, the legal framework was classified, protected from congressional or public scrutiny. The practical effect was to leave the direction of what the administration called "the war on terror" in the hands of the president and of this uncommonly powerful vice president. Without seeking required congressional authorization for warrantless domestic spying, Cheney brought to Bush a simple presidential "signing statement" drafted by Addington, creating the new Terrorist Surveillance Program, and he signed it three weeks after the 9/11 attacks.

Captured and detained prisoners were sent to a prison facility at the U.S. naval base at Guantánamo Bay, Cuba, posing more questions as to their status under international law. Cheney had Addington draw up a draft stipulating that captured terrorists had no right to any American court procedure and could be held indefinitely. If they were to be tried at all it would be by military commissions run by the Pentagon.

When the concerned secretary of state Colin Powell initiated a panel to consider the matter, Cheney ignored it, and when Attorney General John Ashcroft went to the White House to object, Cheney and Addington told him they had already run the military commissions by their man in the Office of Legal Counsel. Cheney declared that no terrorist deserved to be "treated as a prisoner of war" protected by the Geneva Conventions, which among other things prohibit the use of torture to extract information.[45] In making the decision public, Bush used Addington's artful guideline: that they would be dealt with "humanely and, to the extent appropriate and consistent with military necessity, in a manner consistent with the principles of the Geneva Conventions."[46] Cheney subsequently insisted in an interview, "We don't torture. That's not what we're involved in. We live up to our obligations in international treaties."[47]

Meanwhile, Cheney urged Bush to press the United Nations on Iraq's repeated violations of UN resolutions against the acquisition of weapons of mass destruction (WMDs) and to plan for possible military action. In October 2002, Congress authorized the use of military force against Iraq, and in November the UN Security Council voted unanimously to give Saddam Hussein "a final opportunity to comply with its disarmament obligations" by providing immediate and unrestricted access to UN weapons inspectors.[48]

In late January 2003, with sixteen words in his State of the Union address to Congress, Bush unwittingly triggered accusations that, to justify military intervention, he was using false information about an Iraqi quest for uranium required to manufacture WMDs. "The British government," he said, "has learned that Saddam Hussein recently sought significant quantities of uranium from Africa," which turned out not to be the case.[49]

Cheney got further involved after seeing in his classified daily intelligence briefing a Defense Intelligence Agency report that the government of Niger had signed an agreement to sell five hundred tons of the rare material a year to Baghdad. He asked the CIA for clarification. Unknown to Cheney at the time, Valerie Plame Wilson, an agent of the CIA's Counterproliferation Center, had volunteered that her husband, Joseph Wilson, familiar with Niger as a former U.S. ambassador to Gabon, might be willing to go and investigate. He did so and found no evidence of any such sale.

Meanwhile, the administration's prime premise for the urgency in invading Iraq was coming under increasing doubt. Cheney paid several visits to the CIA, ostensibly to press for more proof. The president finally sent a reluctant Colin Powell to the UN armed with what Powell insisted was an air-tight indictment against the Iraqi regime. He spent nearly three hours before television cameras offering "facts and conclusions based on solid intelligence" that, in his contention, established the existence of weapons of mass destruction and the means to make and hide them. But Powell offered only diagrams and sketches of such alleged equipment rather than actual photos from an administration famed for its high-altitude, high-definition technology. Later, Powell's own tardy skepticism led him to say that the presentation was "the lowest point in [his] life" and a "blot" on his distinguished military and diplomatic career. When the Security Council appeared unwilling to approve a further use-of-force resolution, Bush decided to act without one.[50]

On the night of March 19, 2003, on intelligence that Saddam Hussein might be at a certain site in Iraq, Bush got Cheney alone and asked him whether he should go after the Iraqi strongman. Cheney advised him to do so, and so began the U.S. invasion. The air attack failed to hit its prey, but Operation Iraqi Freedom was underway.

That summer, Cheney found himself embroiled in a dispute over the false report of Iraq's quest for uranium in Niger and Joseph Wilson's trip there rebutting the claim. All hell broke lose when columnist Robert Novak identified Wilson's wife, Valerie, as "an agency operative on weapons of mass destruction," attributing the information to "two senior administration officials." She was thereby deprived of the anonymity of her classified status, leaving the CIA with much egg on its face. Democratic legislators jumped all over the story, and on July 30 the agency quietly asked that the FBI investigate the leak.

The eventual upshot was a special prosecutor's 2005 indictment of Cheney's chief of staff, I. Lewis "Scooter" Libby, on one count of obstructing justice, two of perjury, and two of making false statements, followed by his 2007 conviction on four of those charges. He was not charged with leaking classified intelligence, apparently because two years earlier Bush had signed an executive order extending to the vice president, for the first time in U.S. history, the power to classify and declassify documents. According to the author Charlie Savage, this made Cheney "the full equal to the president" in terms of releasing such information.[51] Hence, if Cheney told Libby to inform reporters that Wilson's wife was a CIA operative, as alleged in grand jury testimony, his action in Addington's view amounted to a declassification.[52]

The columnist Novak, who died in 2009, never named his sources, but Deputy Secretary of State Richard Armitage, a close lieutenant to Secretary Colin Powell, acknowledged to the Justice Department that he had told Novak of Valerie Plame Wilson's CIA job. Bush commuted Libby's sentence of jail time but, to the outspoken disappointment of Cheney, declined to pardon his chief of staff. The vice president wrote later, "In the long term, where doing the right thing counts, George W. Bush was, in my view, making a grave error. 'Mr. President,' I said, 'you are leaving a good man wounded on the field of battle.'"[53] Later, Cheney said in an interview that the matter was "probably the most tense aspect of our relationship," but that he "appreciated the fact that [Libby] did not have to do any prison time."[54]

Another casualty of the whole affair was the relationship between Cheney and Colin Powell. After a cabinet meeting on October 7, 2003, reporters asked Bush who had leaked Valerie Plame Wilson's employment at the CIA, and he said he didn't know but wanted the truth. Cheney wrote later, "Thinking back, I realize that one of the few people in the world who could have told him the truth, Colin Powell, was sitting right next to him."[55] But one other person who might have been able to tell Bush the truth was Cheney himself. In front of the grand jury, Libby said he did not recall Cheney's telling him to inform reporters about Wilson's wife but that it was possible.[56] In a later interview for this book, Cheney said, "The leaker was not in my office," adding that the leaker was Armitage.[57]

The most heated controversy surrounding Cheney as the 2004 presidential campaign approached was his unsubstantiated contention of a possible link between the 9/11 terrorist attacks and the Saddam Hussein regime. It finally raised some speculation about Cheney being dropped from the Republican reelection ticket. Cheney reported later that on three occasions he suggested to Bush that he might consider replacing him, but Bush said each time he wanted to stick with his vice president.[58]

In the campaign, Cheney kept a relatively low profile. The election was close, with Bush and Cheney winning with 51 percent of the popular vote and 286 electoral votes compared with 48 percent and 251 votes in the electoral college for Kerry and Senator John Edwards of North Carolina, his running mate. There was insufficient sentiment for changing horses during wartime.

In the second term, when Hurricane Katrina hit the Gulf Coast and obliterated much of New Orleans, Bush asked Cheney to head up a cabinet-level relief task force, but he declined, insisting, "It would put me in a role that was primarily symbolic . . . a figurehead without the ability really to do anything about the performance of the federal agencies."⁵⁹ Bush didn't hesitate to call Cheney out for his refusal. According to an aide at the meeting, Bush said, "I asked Dick if he'd be interested in spearheading this. Let's just say I didn't get the most positive response." Then, turning to Cheney, Bush asked, "Will you at least go do a fact-finding trip for us?" Cheney replied, "That'll probably be the extent of it, Mr. President, unless you order otherwise."⁶⁰

In the war in Iraq, the capture of Saddam Hussein provided a balm to impatience at home for a time, but Cheney only left himself open to charges of false optimism by declaring in May 2005 that the war was "in the last throes."⁶¹ By late 2006, as the war in Iraq dragged on, Bush finally decided, against Cheney's strenuous objections, to remove Rumsfeld at the Pentagon and replace him with Robert Gates, a man of strong resolve but of more pliable and diplomatic manner. Concerned about a drift in determination to see the fight through, Cheney lobbied hard and successfully for a major troop increase, which Bush finally embraced, sending a surge of twenty thousand more troops into Iraq. Also, significantly for Cheney, the American detention center at Guantánamo remained open, and by 2007 the course of American policy in Iraq was essentially set for the rest of the Bush presidency. Although in 2005 Congress approved limits on the interrogation of detainees complying with the Geneva Conventions, Bush subsequently signed an executive order basically endorsing Cheney's advocacy of harsh methods, drawing a line only against unspecified "cruel, inhuman or degrading treatment or punishment."⁶²

In the 2008 presidential campaign, both Bush and Cheney took a back seat, and upon the defeat of the Republican ticket of Senator John Mc-Cain of Arizona and Governor Sarah Palin of Alaska, Cheney returned to Wyoming, where he regularly expressed criticism of Democratic efforts to end the military conflicts in Iraq and Afghanistan. In the summer of 2010, he again underwent a successful implant of an electronic device to assure the proper functioning of his heart.

Of all other American vice presidents up to Cheney's time, none had made more of the office, both in affecting policy and in defending and expanding the power of the executive branch of the government. Cheney and his chief aides authored more muscular rules for dealing with enemy combatants than ever set before under a concept of unlimited presidential power, especially in time of war. Yet his zeal in cementing the vice presidency's stature and influence in high executive policy also drew much bitter and angry opposition, escalating, for good or ill, the public profile of the office to a record high and the powers delegated to or seized by him as well.

CHAPTER 47

JOSEPH R. BIDEN JR.
OF DELAWARE

B y the time two vice presidents—Al Gore and Dick Cheney—had enjoyed significant roles in the administrations in which they served, the office had finally begun to lose its reputation as a political dead end. Still, some politicians who already held influential positions were not sure they wanted to serve in a job whose prime constitutional role was to wait in the wings as a standby for the president.

One such man was Senator Joe Biden of Delaware, chairman of the powerful Senate Foreign Relations Committee and before that chairman of its Judiciary Committee. In both positions, Biden had been intricately engaged in the nation's most critical involvements in international and legal affairs. In 2008, at age sixty-five when the Democratic presidential nominee Barack Obama approached him about being his running mate, Biden's prospects for succeeding to the presidency after four or eight years of an Obama administration seemed slim.

Biden had already run twice for the presidency himself without success, in 1987 for the 1988 Democratic nomination and then in early 2008. Both times he had returned to the Senate, where he had comfortably and contentedly served for thirty-six years. So when speculation first started about his possible selection as vice president, he denied interest, as well as in being secretary of state in the next Democratic administration. "They are the only two things that would be of interest to anyone," he said in April. "I've made it clear I don't want either one of them. . . . I'm satisfied where I am right now." When Obama asked him whether he would agree to be vetted for the vice presidency, he reported, "I said I'd have to think about it."[1]

By the time Obama had clinched the nomination after a long primary battle with Senator Hillary Clinton of New York, he met with Biden at a Minneapolis hotel and pointedly asked him, in light of his long and prominent experience in the Senate, "Will this job be too small for you?" Biden, setting his terms, replied, "No, not as long as I would really be a confidant." Then he added, "The good news is, I'm sixty-five and you're not going to have to worry about my positioning myself to be president. The bad news is I want to be part of the deal."[2] With Obama's assurance that Biden would have the same basic arrangement as Carter and Walter Mondale had in terms of frequent and ready access to the president, including the weekly private meetings first initiated between them, Biden finally agreed. Also understood was that Biden would not be saddled with any administrative or departmental responsibilities that would impinge on his role as a general senior adviser across the board, in recognition of Biden's broad experience.[3]

Biden's route to the vice presidency was a long one from humble beginnings in blue-collar Scranton, Pennsylvania. It was marked by unusually early political success but also deep personal tragedy, overcome by determination and resolute family support. Born on November 20, 1942, almost a year after America's entry into World War II, he was the first child of Joe Biden Senior and the former Jean Finnegan. He was a lithe and athletic boy from English and French stock on his father's side but clearly a dominant Irish Catholic influence on his mother's. His paternal grandfather, Joseph H. Biden, emigrated from Liverpool to Baltimore in 1825. His maternal grandfather, Ambrose Finnegan, whose immigrant parents were apple pickers in upstate New York, was an acclaimed quarterback at Santa Clara in California before moving to Scranton, where he worked for coal and gas companies in the heart of the anthracite coal country of the Allegheny Mountains.[4]

Joe Senior and a cousin prospered during the war working for an uncle who manufactured a watertight sealant for merchant marine ships, so much so that they both owned the fastest new cars and piloted a small plane on hunting trips to the Adirondacks and polo matches on Long Island. Joe Senior subsequently was transferred to a Boston suburb with his family, where a daughter, Valerie, was born, Joe Junior's best friend and later his first campaign manager.

After the war, however, the good times ended, and Joe Senior entered into a couple of unsuccessful enterprises with his cousin, including a crop-dusting business over Long Island. He moved the family back to Scranton and the small home of Grandfather Ambrose in the Green Ridge neighborhood of Irish, Italian, and Polish families, where two more boys, Jimmy and Frank, were born. Joe Junior got his first taste of politics at Ambrose Finnegan's, where on Sundays, after mass and afternoon dinner, neighborhood men would gather around the kitchen table talking sports and politics.

In Green Ridge, he enjoyed a scrappy Tom Sawyer childhood of playing baseball and cops and robbers, committing various pranks, and absorbing a Catholic school education. He was a good student despite suffering a severe case of stuttering, for which he was roundly ridiculed by others in his classes. But sympathetic nuns helped him through patient coaching, and eventually he conquered it to the point that he later came to be known for his oratory—and the length of it.[5]

When Joe Senior took a job selling automobiles in Wilmington, Delaware, and moved the family there, Joe Junior was enrolled in Archmere Academy, a Catholic prep school, where he was a class leader and in football a speedy receiver. He moved on to the University of Delaware, where a promising football career was cut short by a spring-break trip to Nassau. There he met Neilia Hunter, a beautiful college student from upstate New York. Soon on weekends he was borrowing a convertible from Joe Senior's car lot and commuting 320 miles round trip to see her, leaving no time for football. On graduating from Delaware, he was admitted to the Syracuse University Law School, near Neilia's family home.[6]

Writing later in his memoir, he explained an incident during his first year there: "I botched a paper in a technical writing course so badly that one of my classmates accused me of lifting passages from a *Fordham Law Review* article." He was called before a faculty board to explain, and the board concluded that he hadn't intentionally cheated but required him to repeat the course. He did so, but more than twenty years later the incident would still add fuel to growing impressions that he was a serial plagiarist. After his second year he and Neilia were married, and with diligent tutoring from his new wife he graduated in 1968, and they moved to Wilmington, with the intention of Joe starting a small law practice.[7]

After briefly working for a large and prestigious firm that defended major corporations, Biden decided it wasn't for a young lawyer from a working-class background. He signed on as a public defender and then found a firm more to his political liking. While he was in Syracuse, during and after the April 1968 assassination of Dr. Martin Luther King in Memphis, Wilmington had been the victim of severe riots in the heavily black-populated Valley section of the city, which spread downtown. Delaware's Democratic governor Charles L. Terry Jr. called out all thirty-eight hundred National Guard troops to patrol the most troubled neighborhoods nightly and kept the troops there until the following January—the longest such military presence in any American city since the Civil War.[8] Disappointed with the occupation and with the state Democratic Party, Biden registered in Delaware as an independent and in 1968 voted for the Republican Russell Peterson, who ousted Terry. "But I couldn't bring myself to register as a Republican because of Richard Nixon," he explained later.[9]

In Wilmington he got involved in a citizens' fight against intrusive highway plans and was approached to run for the state General Assembly. He declined but joined a local Democratic forum of young progressives concerned that the state party was dragging its feet on school integration, open housing, and other civil rights issues.

At age twenty-seven Biden was encouraged by a retiring member of the New Castle County Council to seek his seat. He ran, on essentially family energies and manpower, and won by two thousand votes in a nominally Republican district. Even before he had served a day on the council, he decided to run for the United States Senate in 1972 and won that too, weeks before he would reach the required age of thirty, upsetting the veteran Republican senator Caleb Boggs.

On the occasion of his thirtieth birthday, shortly before Inauguration Day, the Biden family held a twin celebration. Then Joe, Neilia, and their young family of two boys, Beau and Hunter, and an infant girl, Naomi, moved into a new home in suburban Wilmington and prepared both for Christmas and Joe's impending swearing-in. While hunting for a home away from home in Washington, Biden got a phone call informing him that his wife and baby daughter had been killed and the boys injured in a car accident.

Biden's sons eventually recovered, but in his own shattered state he at first thought of giving up the Senate before being sworn in. His closest family members and some notable would-be Senate colleagues, however, urged him to take the oath, if only as some personal catharsis to see him through the tragedy. He finally did so, at the hospital where son Beau was still recovering. On that occasion he declared, "If, after six months or so, there's a conflict between being a good father and being a good senator," he would resign. He explained to Delawareans, "We can always get another senator, but they [his sons] can't get another father."[10]

To that end, Biden began a routine that continued with few exceptions during his sons' convalescence and on throughout his Senate career: commuting to care for the boys. His family life subsequently stabilized with a long courtship and marriage in 1977 to his second wife, Jill Tracy Jacobs Biden, a community college teacher who continued in her own profession while embraced by the boys as their second mother. Biden's youth, tragic personal story, and open manner soon drew many speaking engagements around the country. As a member of the Senate Judiciary Committee, he was in the middle of all major civil rights debates. After easily winning a second term in 1978, his name was floated at the 1980 Democratic National Convention as a possible 1984 presidential candidate. But he demurred, saying, "It's difficult to be the kind of father I want to be and go flat out [campaigning] for two years."[11]

Reelected to the Senate in 1984, Biden became chairman of the Judiciary Committee and ran for the 1988 Democratic presidential nomination and simultaneously led a fight against the confirmation of the ultra-conservative federal judge Robert Bork to the Supreme Court. Suddenly accused of plagiarism in borrowing from a speech about blue-collar roots by a British Labor politician without attributing the remarks to him, followed by resurrection of the charges at Syracuse Law School of improperly citing a reference source in that *Fordham Law Review* article, Biden ended his bid for the 1988 nomination, observing, "There will be other presidential campaigns but there may not be other opportunities for me to influence President Reagan's choice for the Supreme Court."[12] In the end, Biden prevailed as the full Senate declined to confirm Bork by the largest rejection of a Supreme Court nominee ever delivered.

Back in the Senate, Biden threw himself into his work on the Foreign Relations Committee as well as the Judiciary Committee. On a speaking tour, he suffered an intercranial aneurysm at the base of his brain that required emergency surgery and later a second aneurysm and surgery that kept him out of the Senate for seven months. On his return he plunged into work again, winning the approval of a major anti-drug bill and the creation of a national drug czar after six years of crafting. He was easily reelected that fall.

In June 1991, Biden found himself in the center of another contentious political fight to fill another Supreme Court vacancy, upon the retirement of the eighty-two-year-old Justice Thurgood Marshall, the first African American on the highest bench. Not surprisingly, President George H. W. Bush nominated another African American, but his choice of the ultra-conservative federal judge Clarence Thomas was a bombshell, particularly because Bush declared him to be the person "best qualified at this time" to replace the legendary Marshall, legal hero of the civil rights movement.[13]

The nomination of Thomas, a federal judge for only a year and widely regarded to be the most rigidly conservative black jurist in the land and no intellectual heavyweight, guaranteed another bitter battle with Democrats, including Biden. Once again Biden was faced with an appointment that, if confirmed, could radically change the ideological composition of the court.

In the course of the hearings, a former subordinate of Thomas named Anita Hill alleged that as head of the Equal Employment Opportunity Commission he had made improper sexual advances to her. Thomas made a full and categorical denial of all allegations, then turned indignant, claiming the charges had "done a grave and irreparable injustice" to him and his family.[14] He labeled the hearings "a high-tech lynching for uppity blacks who in any way design to think for themselves" and who would be "lynched, destroyed, caricatured by a committee of the U.S. Senate, rather than hung from a tree."[15] In spite of Hill's personal testimony and that of other black women who said they had heard of various sorts of sexual harassment from Thomas, he was confirmed by a vote of 52 to 48, the most votes ever cast against a successful nominee.

In 1996, Biden won his fifth six-year Senate term and in 2001 became chairman of the Senate Foreign Relations Committee. Upon the terrorist attacks on New York and the Pentagon on September 11, he pledged his support to President George W. Bush's determination to locate and kill or capture the perpetrators finding haven in Afghanistan. But in 2002, when the administration pivoted its attention to Iraq under the flawed belief that strongman Saddam Hussein had weapons of mass destruction poised to hit Western democracies, Biden held committee hearings exploring Bush's intentions and where they might lead. Pointedly, he asked, "When Saddam Hussein is gone, what would be our responsibilities [thereafter]?" He also questioned "whether resources can be shifted to a major military enterprise in Iraq without compromising the war on terror in other parts of the world."[16]

As Vice President Cheney continued to beat the drums for war, Biden joined the Republican senators Richard Lugar of Indiana and Chuck Hagel of Nebraska in a Senate resolution that would give Bush authority to use force to disarm Saddam Hussein only if other means failed. But according to the Senate majority leader at the time, Trent Lott of Mississippi, President Bush ordered him: "Derail the Biden resolution, and make sure its language never sees the light of day again."[17] Lacking sufficient Democratic support, Biden dropped the resolution and finally, in October, voted for Bush's use-of-force resolution with the caveat that it be acted on only as a last resort.[18] It was an action that would haunt Biden long afterward. In the end, because Bush had told him personally he had not made up his mind to invade Iraq, Biden said later, "I thought it would give him a stronger hand to get Saddam Hussein to act responsibly, and it was a very bad bet I made."[19]

And so on March 18, 2003, the invasion began with Rumsfeld's "shock and awe" assault on Iraq, which dispersed the dictator's army and drove him into hiding and eventual capture in mid-December. But an insurgency continued, causing Democrats at home to conclude that a regime change in their own country was imperative to end the war and causing Biden to weigh what his own role in achieving it should be. In mid-August, however, he declared that his seeking the presidency again in 2004 was "too much of a long shot."[20]

Instead, he threw his support behind Senator John Kerry of Massachusetts, like-minded on the quagmire the Iraq War had become. But Kerry fell victim to unwarranted smears against his combat service in Vietnam and renewed jingoism stirred up by Bush supporters, and he lost narrowly. Biden began to consider running for president again in 2008, especially when Kerry decided not to try a second time.

In January 2007, Biden declared his intention to seek the Democratic nomination again, vowing not to make the mistakes that had forced him from the presidential arena two decades earlier. He seemed well aware of and adjusted to the odds against him, running against the popular former first lady Hillary Clinton and an engaging newcomer, Senator Barack Obama, seeking to become the first African American president.

In the campaign, it was clear from the start that the Democratic candidates' positions on the war in Iraq would be critical. Biden joined in sponsoring a nonbinding resolution in the Senate against Bush's surge of twenty thousand troops into the country, but it fell four votes short and was dropped. A bigger political problem for Biden was the lack of campaign money and the appeal of Senator Clinton to women and of Senator Obama to the black community. Though Biden continued to be a leading voice against the war in Iraq, calling for repeal of the 2002 authorization to Bush for use of force, he could get no traction, particularly with a proposal to partition the country.

Biden continued his penchant for delivering long and detailed speeches on the stump, but he demonstrated his awareness of the problem with good humor at a nationally televised debate in Orangeburg, South Carolina, when asked by the moderator if he could manage this time around to curb his verbosity. He replied, "Yes," and flashed a broad smile. More seriously, his thoughtful responses in the string of debates during 2007 and early 2008 drew praise and statements of agreement from the other contenders, including Obama. The Biden campaign capitalized on the phenomenon by running a television ad that said simply what his challengers were saying: "Joe's right." But Biden found himself lost in the pack, seldom called on early or often to comment in the debates. In one of them, when finally invited by the moderator, he feigned surprise and said, "Oh, no, no, no, no! Don't do it, no! Don't make me speak!"[21]

In the first 2008 voting in the Iowa precinct caucuses, he finished fifth with an abysmally embarrassing 1 percent and dropped out, recognizing that too much time had passed and he was no match for Obama and

Clinton. He returned to the Senate again, telling a Wilmington reporter that he was not interested in being secretary of state or vice president if the next administration was a Democratic one. "I can have much more influence, I promise you, as chairman of the Foreign Relations Committee than I can as vice president," he said.[22]

Once Biden was out of the race, Obama approached him in late January for help in the remaining primaries, but Biden told him he intended to remain neutral until the voters had picked the party nominee. He promised both Obama and Clinton that he would work tirelessly for whichever of them won. "If you win," he told Obama, "I'll do anything you ask me to do," to which Obama replied, according to Biden later, "Be careful, because I may ask you a lot." Biden said Obama told him, "The only question I have is not whether I want you in this administration. It's which job you'd like best."[23]

Once Obama decided that if he were to choose Hillary Clinton as his running mate, husband Bill might be "too big a complication," he chose Biden, according to Obama's campaign manager, David Plouffe. "We knew Biden could be somewhat long-winded and had a history of coloring outside the lines a bit," Plouffe said later, "but honestly, that was very appealing to Obama, because he wanted someone to give him the unvarnished truth. What do you need in a vice president? He knows and understands Congress, has great foreign policy and domestic experience. He had the whole package from a VP standpoint."[24] What finally persuaded Biden to accept the nomination was Obama's promise, if elected, to involve him as a governing partner in the new administration.

In the fall campaign Biden dutifully took on the task of engaging the Republican opposition. After describing the GOP presidential nominee, John McCain, as "genuinely a friend" of his and a courageous war hero, Biden insisted, "You can't change America and end the war in Iraq when you declare 'no one has supported President Bush in Iraq more than I have,' . . . when you know your first four years as president will look exactly like the last eight years of George Bush's presidency."[25] And in a rap at Cheney while he was at it, Biden told the Democratic National Convention in Denver, "No longer will the eight most dreaded words in the English language be: 'The vice president's office is on the phone!'"[26]

Biden's potentially most dangerous event was his debate with McCain's surprise running mate, Governor Sarah Palin of Alaska, a charismatic and aggressive newcomer on the national stage. But he remained cordial toward her while demonstrating a clearly firmer grasp of the issues raised and focusing on McCain as a willing heir to the policies of George W. Bush, now sinking in the popularity polls. A postdebate poll by United Press International found Biden the clear winner, though Palin was credited with exceeding the low expectations set for her. When at a fund-raiser in Seattle Biden blurted that Obama probably would be tested in an early international crisis, Obama was reported later to have chewed out his running mate for the gaffe,[27] but after the campaign Obama said of Biden's performance in the primaries, "He could be a very disciplined candidate, so that was not a major concern to me."[28] On Election Day, the ticket of Obama and Biden prevailed with 52.9 percent of the popular vote and 345 in the electoral college compared with 45.7 percent of the popular ballots and 173 electoral votes for McCain and Palin.

In the transition period, Biden said he intended to "restore the balance" in the vice presidency, seeming to suggest he would return it to its subordinate while still significant role in the executive branch, rather than the dominant role it appeared to have played under Cheney in the previous administration. Biden followed Cheney's practice of staffing the vice president's office with ranking specialists in foreign and diplomatic policy and economic affairs paralleling those on the president's staff. But these specialists were to be integrated into the White House operation rather than forming the separate power center that had evolved under Cheney.

Once sworn in, Biden embarked on a trip for Obama to Iraq, Afghanistan, and Pakistan to make a personal assessment of the policy in place, and at home he undertook oversight of the implementation of the new president's economic stimulus package, known as the American Recovery and Reinvestment Act. He became the prime contact point for governors, mayors, and other local officials in tracking progress and problems around the country. Although Biden had signed on to be a general adviser, he agreed to chair the new Middle Class Task Force as close to his interests, dealing with child care, elderly care, college student assistance, and savings for retirement.

In the first weeks of his administration, Obama also sent Biden to the annual European conference on security in Munich, where he reported the new president's determination "to set a new tone not only in Washington but in America's relations around the world," to "work in a partnership wherever we can, and alone only when he must," striving "to act preventively, not preemptively . . . starting with diplomacy."[29] Biden pledged to "press the reset button" with Russia to halt "a dangerous drift" in relations with that old enemy, while giving assurance to former members of the Soviet Union of U.S. recognition of their sovereignty.[30] That summer he went to Ukraine and Georgia for the same purpose.

As Obama considered requests from the American generals for more ground troops beyond the twenty-one thousand he had already agreed to send to Afghanistan, Biden reminded him of the original mission of rooting out al Qaeda terrorists. A compromise was struck for which Biden was said to have persuaded the president to proceed on a limited basis. Such advice was in keeping with his own role as a team player compared with Cheney in the previous administration, which he called "a divided government" between "Cheney and his own sort of separate national security agency and . . . the [official] National Security Agency."[31]

In late August, the NATO and U.S. commander in Afghanistan, General Stanley McChrystal, pushed Obama on the request for more ground troops, pointedly warning that unless more were sent in the next year, defeat of the insurgents might not be achievable. In response, over the next three months the president plunged into ten closed-door meetings with chief military, diplomatic, and political advisers at Camp David, with Biden at his side tenaciously arguing against what he saw as a drift from the counterterrorism mission that had justified the initial troop deployments. As a kibitzing Cheney accused Obama of "dithering" and inviting defeat, Biden dug in as the devil's advocate against the demands of the generals.

The result was a compromise in which McChrystal would get a surge of additional troops, but with a deadline of July 2011 to start their withdrawal. Biden argued that the strategy was what was important, not the number of troops added. In an Oval Office meeting in November, Obama polled the military chiefs, and they all signed on, committing to the timetable.[32] Later, when Obama was asked what he thought of critics' view that Biden had "lost" that debate, he said, "I don't think anyone who was party to the very, very exhaustive discussions we had would say that. Joe was enormously helpful in guiding those discussions. The decision that ultimately emerged was a synthesis of some of the advice he gave me, along with the advice of the generals."[33] As the troop surge progressed amid continued criticism from Democratic liberals, Biden repeatedly insisted unequivocally that the timetable for starting to pull American combat troops from Afghanistan would hold and subsequently would be completed by 2014.

In January 2014, former Obama secretary of defense Robert Gates, a Republican carryover from the George W. Bush administration, in a memoir accused Biden of "poisoning the well" against the military leaders supporting the surge. "All too early in the administration," Gates wrote, "suspicion and distrust of senior military officers by senior White House officials—including the vice president—became a problem for me as I tried to manage the relationship between the commander in chief and his military leaders. . . . I think he [Biden] has been wrong on nearly every major foreign policy and national security issue over the past four decades." A White House spokesperson swiftly defended the vice president, asserting, "From his leadership in the Balkans in the Senate, to his effort to end the war in Ira, Joe Biden has been one of the leading statesmen of his time and has helped advance America's leadership in the world. President Obama relies on his good counsel every day."

In the fall of 2010, Biden turned to the customary political role of vice presidents in working to maintain Democratic control of Congress in the midterm elections. But Republicans nevertheless won a majority in the House of Representatives with a surge of their own, from an emerging conservative Tea Party movement. The result was a stiffly obstructionist opposition party that flowered a bitter partisanship in Washington for the rest of Obama's first term.

Winding down his oversight of the American Recovery Act, in early 2011 Biden was assigned as the administration's "legislative fireman" in debt-ceiling and deficit-reduction battles that dragged on through the next two years. With his decades-long experience on Capitol Hill, he led budget negotiations with new House Speaker John Boehner and Senate Minority Leader Mitch McConnell, paving the way for Obama's direct intervention but ultimately falling short of a ballyhooed "grand bargain" with Boehner to swap tax cuts for new revenue. The result was an agreement on a "sequestration" of deep mandatory cuts in domestic and military spending if no other agreement could be reached by the end of 2012.[34] It was not, providing only an unsatisfactory coda in the continued debate over deficit reduction.

As the 2012 presidential campaign approached, Biden turned to the political wars, among some fanciful press speculations that he might be dropped from the Democratic ticket in favor of Secretary of State Hillary Clinton, despite her disavowal of interest and Obama's reinforced support of his vice president. Biden precipitated one minor flap in May when on *Meet the Press* he volunteered that he had come to accept same-sex marriage, at a time when Obama was silent on the controversial matter. Cast by some as an embarrassment to the president, it actually served to smoke him out on an issue of increasing strength and significance to party liberals, who were growing restive about the cautious and pragmatic leader of their party. Of that occasion Biden said later, "There's never been a time when I've said anything substantively . . . that I don't think or know he's already there. I knew where he was, but a lot of people said, 'Well, maybe I should have let him say "I'm coming with gay marriage,"' but for me it was a matter of basic civil rights." The next morning, Biden recalled, Obama "came in laughing and said, 'Well, you told me. . . . I knew you'd say what you think.'"[35]

In the fall campaign, after Obama had stumbled badly with a flat performance in his first debate against the Republican presidential nominee, Mitt Romney, Biden was credited with recovering for the Democratic ticket with an aggressive debate confrontation with the GOP running mate, Paul Ryan. Biden said later that after it looked like he and the president "needed a bump," he took on Romney for his disparagement of "47 percent of Americans" as people who are bribed by federal benefits and Ryan for dividing the populace into "takers and makers."

"I can speak with authenticity about the middle class," Biden said, "and it was a very good setup between me and Romney, because it almost offended me with his disregard for the folks I grew up with." The 47 percent remark, Biden said, "went to the heart of it, because I *am* that 47 percent, my family is that 47 percent, the things I value most are those people. . . . Even if they told me not to, I couldn't have been quiet [on] the 47 percent. That was the fundamental divide."[36] In claiming the mantle of champion of the middle class, Biden boosted the Democratic spirit. Obama then recovered in two subsequent debates with Romney, resulting in reelection of the Obama-Biden team.

As their first term came to an end, jolted just before Christmas with the horrible mass murder of twenty first-grade children and six adults in a Newtown, Connecticut, schoolroom, Obama chose Biden to lead a national response for stronger gun controls demanded by an outraged and grieving American public. Despite a broad and energetic campaign, the effort fell short in the opening months of the second term, but Biden vowed to continue pursuing his goals.

In all this, Biden could claim, however, that he had delivered on his pledge to "restore the balance" in a more limited but still influential role in the office compared with that of his immediate predecessor, Dick Cheney. Biden, seventy years old at the time but physically fit, did or said nothing to discourage speculation that he might make a third try for the presidency in 2016. His service alone in his first vice presidential term seemed worthy of such speculation. But with a continued expectation that Hillary Clinton might make a second bid for the Oval Office, it seemed more likely that Joe Biden would conclude his lengthy political career one step short of that long-held ambition.

Biden, in noting that Cheney had freed himself of the same speculation in taking himself out of consideration as a future presidential candidate, mused at the time that such talk continued about himself. "I haven't taken it out of the possibility, it's not where I am," he said, "but the good news for me from my perspective is that everything that would make me a viable candidate also is the very thing that would make me a good vice president. As long as I'm seen, and as long as I do a good job here, which I hope I did the first four years, of taking on important projects, executing them well, being a part of a team that makes this a successful administration, that's the stuff that will make me viable, and so I don't have to make that decision now, and I haven't, for real. . . . That's a familial decision that you don't get to make alone. I also don't want to get into a position where everything I did was viewed through the prism of I'm running for the nomination, because I think that diminishes the degree to which I can be helpful to the president."[37]

In any event, Joe Biden's wide-ranging vice presidency had already provided in its own right a model for future occupants of the office and for the open collegiality and compatibility between Obama and Biden, which became a positive element in the administration's governance of the nation.

THE EVOLVING
ASSISTANT PRESIDENCY

When the founding fathers conceived the office of the vice presidency, for all the cavalier manner of its conception as a by-product of the electoral college, they anticipated it might produce the second most-qualified citizen to lead the country. The Constitution having stipulated that the vice presidency would go to the runner-up in the presidential balloting, the choices in the first two elections honored that expectation. John Adams and Thomas Jefferson were high among the revolutionary era figures in the esteem of their contemporaries, and on balance their subsequent presidencies were judged favorably by history.

But there was little evidence that the founders had given serious thought to the prospect that the vice president thus elected might actually become president. The Twelfth Amendment, ratified in 1804, provided for separate elections of the two officers in order to avoid the selection of candidates of rival political factions, as Federalist Adams and Anti-Federalist Jefferson were in their joint election of 1796. A presidential vacancy then would have meant a sharp change in factional control of the nation.

The next five vice presidents—Aaron Burr, George Clinton, Elbridge Gerry, Daniel Tompkins, and John C. Calhoun—for one reason or another were found wanting as presidential material or otherwise tarnished their service by personal shortcomings or misbehavior. None was the particular choice of the president under whom he served, or was chosen by him at all, or was a significant partner in his administration. Nor was the second office much of a stepping-stone to the presidency for years after Adams and Jefferson. After Clinton and Calhoun, the only two vice presidents to serve under two different presidents, none other was renominated for a second term by a party caucus or convention for seventy-six years, until 1890, when James S. Sherman was elected to serve under William H. Taft. And none was reelected until Thomas A. Marshall in 1916, to continue serving under Woodrow Wilson.

It was not until selection of the eighth vice president, Martin Van Buren, in 1832 that a president, Andrew Jackson, decisively chose the man he wanted and then made him a key political and policy adviser. Van Buren earlier was Jackson's presidential campaign manager and then his secretary of state in the first term. When Calhoun resigned as Jackson's first vice president, Van Buren become his vice president for his second term. In 1836, Richard Johnson, the ninth vice president, was selected by the U.S. Senate to serve under President Van Buren after failing to win a majority in the electoral college. Little in Johnson's background suggested he was of presidential caliber, and he eventually spent much of his time as the vice president back in Kentucky, running a hotel and saloon.

In 1864, in one of the most significant early cases of a president hand-picking his running mate, Abraham Lincoln shunted aside his first-term vice president, Hannibal Hamlin, a strong critic of slavery, in favor of Andrew Johnson, a War Democrat, to run with him for his second term. Lincoln determined that he needed a Union fusion ticket to win reelection and gain time to end the Civil War. It was a fateful decision in terms of how the South was treated in the Reconstruction policies that followed.

In subsequent years, presidential nominees usually left the selection of their running mates to political party advisers who ran their campaigns. Senator Marcus Hanna, the Ohio kingmaker who masterminded William McKinley's election in 1896, chose a successful businessman, Augustus Hobart, to be the twenty-fourth vice president. Hobart served as McKinley's personal financial adviser as well as his virtual assistant president. But in 1900, after Hobart's death, Hanna strenuously objected to pressure from the New York Republican boss Thomas Platt that led to the nomination of Governor Theodore Roosevelt as McKinley's second-term running mate and as the twenty-fifth vice president. After the election, Hanna memorably told the president, "Now it is up to you to live."[1]

In 1932, basic calculations and arrangements handled by Franklin D. Roosevelt's political advisers lured House Speaker John Nance Garner to be his running mate and the thirty-second vice president during two FDR terms. But in 1940, for the third term, Roosevelt insisted on Secretary of Agriculture Henry Wallace as his standby, threatening not to run himself if the Democratic convention did not accept his choice. And in the aging Roosevelt's fourth campaign in 1944, key political advisers sold him on the fateful selection of Harry Truman as the thirty-fourth vice president.

In 1952, the political neophyte Dwight D. Eisenhower was unaware that choosing a running mate was in his hands as the Republican presidential nominee. He left the selection to New York political advisers Thomas E. Dewey and Herbert Brownell, who orchestrated the nomination of Richard Nixon to be the thirty-sixth vice president. Thereafter, however, presidential nominees increasingly chose their running mates themselves, though usually with seasoned political advisers at their elbows.

In 1960 amid much internal opposition, John F. Kennedy chose Lyndon B. Johnson to strengthen his chances in the South. In 1964, LBJ tapped Hubert Humphrey after much false histrionics. In 1968, Richard Nixon went through a charade of consulting party leaders but then surprised them by picking Spiro Agnew as his running mate. The choice eventually raised questions about leaving the selection in the hands of a single person.

In 1980, Ronald Reagan reluctantly turned to George H. W. Bush after flirting with the possibility of choosing former president Gerald Ford. In 1988, Bush kept his decision from his closest advisers before disclosing Dan Quayle as his running mate, to the shock and consternation of his political brain trust. And in 2000, when Republican presidential nominee George W. Bush left it to Richard Cheney to find him a running mate, Cheney in a sense chose himself, becoming the forty-sixth and arguably the most powerful and controversial of all vice presidents.

Of the nine vice presidents who eventually ascended to the presidency, eight by death of the incumbent and one by the incumbent's resignation, only two—Theodore Roosevelt and Harry Truman—were later generally judged to have been superior chief executives. A third, Lyndon Johnson, received high grades for domestic legislative achievements, but they were overshadowed by the historic American military withdrawal from Vietnam.

Furthermore, until the past half century most elected vice presidents neither carried out significant responsibilities nor were even given the opportunity to carry them out. Accordingly, the office was not seen as a pathway to the presidency; on the contrary, as an otherwise ambitious Daniel Webster, who rejected the Whig Party nomination in 1848, observed, "I do not propose to be buried until I am dead."[2]

Eventually, however, the concept of a de facto assistant president emerged out of occasional suggestions for a more formal designation. In 1956, the former Republican president Herbert Hoover proposed to a Senate subcommittee that an "administrative vice president" be created by Congress to relieve the president of his growing managerial burdens. But the idea was rejected on the grounds that the legislative branch ought not dilute the president's own responsibilities.

The rather off-handed attitude toward the vice presidency began to change after 1972, when the Democratic presidential nominee, George McGovern, only belatedly addressed choosing his running mate. When it was learned that his selection, Senator Thomas Eagleton of Missouri, had previously undergone shock therapy for mental illness, Eagleton was dropped from the ticket. McGovern, reflecting on the fiasco, proposed that more time be allotted after the presidential roll call for the nominee to weigh his choices and that he submit several names to the convention from which to choose his running mate. More important, he argued that responsibility for the selection should not rest in the hands of a single individual.[3]

Four years later, the Democratic presidential nominee, Jimmy Carter, was determined that there be no repetition of the preceding election's troubles. He personally interviewed finalists vetted by aides before choosing Senator Walter Mondale of Minnesota, pointedly identifying him as qualified to assume the presidency if required and preparing him accordingly in office. That model has been generally followed thereafter in both major parties, though not all. In 1984, Mondale, as the Democratic presidential nominee, oversaw the vetting process, but his choice of the little-known congresswoman Geraldine Ferraro as his running mate was obviously politically motivated, based on a bid for women's votes. Her presidential qualifications escaped the thoughts of most veteran political observers.

Mondale himself later defended the choice in an interview for this book, saying, "I didn't see how a campaign against Ronald Reagan could win with just an all-male ticket. I had to shake up the cards some way. If I left a legacy," he said, "it's that I was part of opening the political party, the legal process, to women, and choosing Ferraro was a big step forward."[4]

Mondale also said he regretted going through the process of personally vetting his prospective running mates, all of whom he already knew, unlike Carter in 1976. As for Ford, he said that after his flirtation with Reagan to be his running mate in 1980, he thought the vice presidential vetting process was "more show than substance."[5]

In 1988, three months before the senior George Bush, as Reagan's vice president seeking to succeed him, shockingly chose Dan Quayle as his running mate, the *Report of the Twentieth Century Fund Task Force on the Vice Presidency* overoptimistically declared, "The public, ever more aware of the need for successor presidents who can fill the office ably and faithfully, has taught politicians that they cannot increase their chances to win the election except by applying governance criteria to the selection of vice-presidential candidates."[6] It also said that a presidential nominee "who pays insufficient attention to governance criteria in choosing the vice-presidential nominee, will suffer for it in the election. . . . Ultimately, the price of a rash or overly 'political' nomination for vice president is paid in the coin of the realm: votes on election day."[7] That was hardly the case in the election of the Bush-Quayle ticket.

In 2008, the political community was jolted again when the Republican presidential nominee, Senator John McCain, chose the nationally obscure governor Sarah Palin of Alaska as his running mate. McCain had met her only once, briefly, before she was hurriedly interviewed and presented to the public. Palin proved to be a charismatic candidate but transparently ill-informed on many major issues, again raising questions about the judgment of the man who chose her and that of his key political advisers. The decision continued to fall essentially to the presidential nominee, whether by diligent scrutiny of prospects or personal whim.

Through all this, one prominent presidential scholar argued whether there ought to be a vice president at all. In a minority view, the late historian Arthur M. Schlesinger Jr., as a member of the 1988 Twentieth Century Fund Task Force, contended, perhaps with Hubert Humphrey in mind, that the office was "as often a maiming as a making experience, a process of emasculation rather than of education," and should be abolished.[8]

But the most recent vice president interviewed for this book, Joe Biden, emphatically defended the office as indispensable today. "The way the world has changed, the breadth and scope of the responsibility an American president has," he said, "virtually requires a vice president to handle serious assignments, just because the president's plate is so very full."[9]

Assuming the vice presidency is here to stay, the key question remains: should the choice of a potential "accidental" president be left in the hands of one individual? Several alternatives have been suggested, including conducting vice presidential primaries during the presidential primary period and leaving the choice to the national party convention. But such primaries would necessarily preclude participation of a party's top prospects seeking the presidency itself, thus characterizing the remaining contenders as second-raters. Also, letting the party convention decide would invite internal division and risk saddling the presidential nominee with an unwanted or disruptive running mate. In 1956, the Democratic presidential nominee, Adlai Stevenson, threw the selection to the convention, which chose Senator Estes Kefauver of Tennessee, in a losing cause. No presidential nominee of either major party has repeated that practice since then.

In 1974, when Spiro Agnew was forced to resign the vice presidency and Nixon was obliged to nominate his replacement, he chose Gerald Ford essentially because he was advised by congressional leaders in both parties that Ford would be most easily confirmed. Less than nine months later, however, when Ford in turn had to fill the vice presidential vacancy as a result of his own ascendancy, he selected Nelson Rockefeller as a man who distinctly had presidential qualifications. Later, Ford told me, "Some presidents pick a running mate who will not compete with them in public relations, in world recognition, and so forth, and I think that's unfortunate. A president ought to pick his running mate because he adds strength to the president. Some presidents pick vice presidents who are not at any point going to compete with them. . . . I never understood why presidents as candidates occasionally select somebody who is really not going to be as popular or as highly regarded as themselves."[10]

In 1976, for the first time the two major parties agreed to add a vice presidential debate to the schedule of the televised presidential debates that had begun in 1960 with the Kennedy-Nixon confrontations. Dole faced the Democratic standby nominee, Mondale, in a debate marked by a damaging display of anger and resentment by Dole. The incident later was cited as a factor in the defeat of the Ford-Dole ticket, although others mentioned Ford's pardon of Nixon as a more likely explanation.

Since 1984, when Vice President Bush faced Congresswoman Ferraro, the vice presidential debate has been a regular feature of the fall election, elevating public awareness of the office if not voters' decisions on Election Day. In 2012, after President Obama was perceived to have slipped in his first debate with the Republican nominee, Mitt Romney, Vice President Joe Biden aggressively debated the Republican running mate, Paul Ryan, and was credited with putting the Democratic ticket back on track to its reelection on Election Day.

Equally important in raising the visibility of vice presidents in the public eye has been the increasing willingness of presidents to give them conspicuous roles, beyond the ceremonial, in the business of their administrations. Ever since the Eisenhower-authorized globe-trotting of Richard Nixon in the 1950s and the sharply increased utilization of the standbys in the Mondale model of governance in the 1970s, the office has been elevated well beyond the ridicule and near anonymity it endured for so long in years prior to World War II.

Cheney, probably the most empowered vice president in history, said in an interview for this book, however, that "the president is the president," and it all depends on what he seeks in his standby. "The only way it will work is if the president wants you to play a role," he said. Citing the unhappy experience of Lyndon Johnson in the second office, he said with a touch of sarcasm, "Lyndon Johnson would have been a great vice president, but they buried him."[11]

It is clearly imperative now that a presidential nominee retain and exercise the prerogative to choose his running mate and to make constructive use of the experience, talents, wisdom, and energies of his choice if both are elected. Recent governing partnerships have underscored the need and advantages of personal compatibility and policy harmony for effective administration of the public's business. Biden insisted, "The thing that makes it work here is that the president and I are simpatico, ideologically and politically." He reported that on a daily basis he spent about four hours with Obama, giving him "unvarnished advice" and a commitment that if ever he disagreed with the president on a major issue, he would resign.[12]

This arrangement can only be as productive as the president desires and permits, requiring the vice president's acceptance of the subordinate role in the governing equation, best illustrated in recent years by the Carter-Mondale, Clinton-Gore, and Obama-Biden relationships. The requisite compatibility also existed between the junior Bush and Cheney, though this vice president's role appeared to grow so outsized as to raise questions of excessive vice presidential influence, particularly in the conduct of foreign policy. Cheney said compatibility "has to be professional; it doesn't have to be personal." But Biden said Cheney in his eight years in the office "kicked the vice presidency up a couple of notches. He took on a different, expanded role. . . . And I don't mean it [was] just because of W; it's also because the world gets increasingly complicated."[13]

After attaining the presidency, Ford, whose personal compatibility was tested in his vice presidency during Nixon's Watergate downfall, said that while the vice president need not be a subservient yes-man, "he has to be a team player." He continued, "He can't go off on a separate tangent on every major issue. When he can't be a spokesman affirmatively for the president, he ought to be quiet. But it doesn't enhance the vice president, either," he added, "to always be echoing what the president says."[14] Ford noted that as Nixon's vice president he proclaimed the man's innocence in the Watergate cover-up until he learned otherwise, and then his only recourse was to say nothing.

Discounting the eight vice presidents who rose to the presidency by death of the president and the one by resignation, only five other vice presidents were later elected to the highest office in their own right—Adams, Jefferson, Van Buren, Nixon, and Bush—and of these only Jefferson and Nixon were reelected. So the vice presidency as a stepping-stone to the Oval Office has been a rare phenomenon since the earliest days when Adams and Jefferson first achieved it as presidential runners-up. In five of the last nine elections, however, a vice president has been his party's presidential nominee, and two—Nixon and the senior Bush—were winners.

What of the vice presidency itself? First of all, with the expansion of the responsibilities of the most recent occupants, should they continue to preside over the Senate, as specified in the Constitution? The arrangement giving them one foot in the executive branch and the other in the legislative seems to be, if not a conflict, then certainly unpropitious. In practice, the vice president long ago gave up regularly taking the chair for Senate sessions, usually occupying it only in anticipation of a tie vote. Yet that specified task can be crucial on a matter of legislative importance to the president. The existing arrangement works no substantial inconvenience on a vice president. Mondale later remembered that the office was no particular burden "and not worthy of efforts to change the Constitution" where it stipulates such service.[15]

But Cheney, after leaving office, said of the job, "I considered it an asset." He said he was welcomed to the Republican Senate Caucus with open arms as an ex officio member of the club. It enabled him to keep up on inside political and legislative information to convey to the president and to push for administration policies.[16]

Aside from presiding over the Senate, what role can a vice president best perform? Absent being placed in charge of a cabinet department, some occupants have assumed major responsibilities in areas of their expertise that may overlap with the duties of a cabinet member. Gore, beyond an assigned job to explore government organization, became an influential advocate of energy independence and of various environmental concerns in the Clinton administration. Cheney ran a task force on energy and later was the key Bush administration figure in national security matters, including the wars in Afghanistan and Iraq and the treatment of enemy detainees. But he often seemed to crowd Bush's defense secretary and ranking Justice Department figures in determinations on matters of legality in the reach of presidential powers and in establishing a separate vice presidential office that sometimes appeared to act on its own.

Mondale later questioned whether Cheney's tenure posed a threat of an excessively powerful vice president given unusually free rein. "What happens," he asked, "when, as Cheney did, a vice president uses his office to go into the dark side, and runs a kind of secret, separate government, unaccountable, even less accountable than the president? To manipulate, in this case, a weaker president?"

Alleging "abuse of vice presidential power," Mondale cited the role of Cheney's chief of staff, I. Lewis Libby, in the outing of CIA employee Valerie Plame Wilson, as part of efforts to intimidate her and her husband, Joseph Wilson, over "what was going on in Iraq," and the Bush administration's incorrect insistence that weapons of mass destruction existed there.

"Cheney was up to his eyeballs in that," Mondale said, "because that's what they did there. They managed news. We have to be worried about that happening again, because it happened once."[17]

With presidential acquiescence, Mondale and Biden have functioned as across-the-board general advisers to the president, at his side or looking over his shoulder as principal kibitzers. All six vice presidents starting with Mondale have served to one degree or another as generalists unencumbered by cabinet-like managerial responsibilities. Years after his tenure, Mondale said, "I often said I don't want to do anything that somebody else is doing. This should not be a make-work office." Making the vice president a cabinet member or agency chief, he said, would be a waste of time and would put him "in the middle of chains of command, and a pleader for an agency rather than giving overall advice to the president." Such a notion, Mondale said, "goes back to the days when they were trying to find something for the vice president to do, and that's no longer a problem."[18]

Biden recalled his response when Obama asked him what he wanted as a portfolio: "I said I don't want a portfolio." He noted that Al Gore as vice president had a consequential one in dealing with government reorganization and the environment. "But when you take on a portfolio no matter how consequential, it takes you out of the action in terms of having an impact on the decision process of the president. . . . Why would you want to have the job unless you could attempt to impact on outcome on all the important decisions?"

Biden actually turned out functioning as a hybrid when at the start of his first term Obama assigned him to oversee the disbursement of his administration's economic stimulus and its implementation, through local and state chief executives and federal cabinet members. His role, Biden said, was judged necessary by Obama because the broad task required crossing jurisdictions, federal departments, and agencies. It worked, Biden said, "because everybody knew that when I showed up I was speaking for the president."[19]

Under this approach to the vice presidency, some recent occupants have been free to function as assistant presidents in the fashion envisioned by FDR nearly a century ago when he ran, unsuccessfully, for the office. It's also been suggested that a modern-era president should have two vice presidents, one to handle ceremonial chores and the other administrative duties.

But Mondale said, "The stature of the vice president would be greatly diminished," adding, "vice presidents don't have any problem handling both functions."[20] They are also called on increasingly to carry the brunt of political combat and party building, putting on a partisan cloak that often subjects them to being called "hatchet men." Mondale argued that policy and politics can't be separated, saying, "I don't see how a nonpolitical vice president can be of any use to a president."[21] Biden said a vice president risks repudiation if he goes after an opponent on personal grounds but can and must engage in debate on political philosophy.[22]

In any event, the responsibilities of vice presidents, both in policy and politics, have become so numerous that all now have substantial staffs of their own. Their staff's effectiveness, both Mondale and Biden have said, depended on their being thoroughly integrated with the staff of their presidents. Cheney, in contrast, maintained one that in many ways appeared to be independent of the Bush staff, even as he also placed personnel in key Bush administration positions. In the Carter administration, Mondale's chief of staff, Richard Moe, was a regular attendee in the president's daily staff meetings, as have Biden's chiefs of staff in Obama's presidency.

For all its dependence on staffing, however, the presidency continues to be in the hands of one individual. And transcending all other questions about the vice presidency is whether the selection of its occupant should remain with that single person, chosen by the people but left alone to choose his potential successor. This chronicle of the vice presidents, their early inactivity in governance eventually emerging as a de facto assistant presidency, argues emphatically for keeping the selection where it always has been. No primary election, or vote by convention, or assemblage of political wise men can prudently substitute for the presidential nominee's considered judgment about which prospective running mate can best assist him in governing the nation.

Of course, leading up to that responsibility, the presidential nominee will also weigh the political ramifications of the choice in terms of achieving the presidency. But the two factors need not be mutually exclusive. The wise and responsible party standard-bearer will select a vice presidential nominee who not only is qualified to assume the presidency but also can help him or her win it, or at least not impede that quest because of political or personal factors.

At the same time, Americans at the ballot box should take time to evaluate the presidential nominees in terms of their judgment in choosing a running mate. There may be no better yardstick of a prospective president's responsibility than this decision, tentatively placing someone "a heartbeat away" from the leadership of the country. Failure to act wisely and soberly should raise serious public doubts concerning the presidential nominee's own worthiness to assume the nation's highest office. The sign that Harry Truman placed on the Oval Office desk—"The Buck Stops Here"—should apply as well on this critical decision to all those who seek the presidency for themselves.

ACKNOWLEDGMENTS

This book is a chronicle of all forty-seven American vice presidents, from John Adams to Joseph R. Biden, and the evolution of their office over nearly 225 years, from early oblivion to current significance. It draws first on many of the essential vice presidential biographies of the eighteenth, nineteenth, and twentieth centuries and the start of the twenty-first, listed among the titles in the bibliography. A starting point was the work of the United States Senate Historical Office staff on the men who have simultaneously served by constitutional dictate as presidents of the Senate. I am particularly grateful to Donald A. Ritchie, the U.S. Senate historian, for setting me off on a challenging course, and to the Library of Congress staff for facilitating my access to the more than three hundred books consulted in this project.

Building on these invaluable sources, I have relied on my own reporting in Washington and around the country from 1954 to the present. It has included interviewing and traveling with every occupant of the second office from Richard Nixon to Joe Biden and covering every president who chose them. My efforts have been made possible by a National Endowment for the Humanities fellowship grant for 2012–13, gratefully acquired through recommendations from former vice president Mondale and the former Republican vice presidential nominee Bob Dole, and were smoothly squired through the application process by Jim Turner of the NEH staff.

Most of the vice presidents, especially the early ones after Adams and Jefferson, remain little known to their countrymen. In the process of reviewing them, I have attempted to make the case for more responsible selection of the men and, now, women sought as presidential running mates. The book is a plea, too, for greater voter responsibility in holding presidential nominees and presidents to account in placing one individual a single act of fate or circumstance away from the highest office.

Personal experience has played a role in this pursuit. As a newspaper reporter, the matter of presidential succession has been brought home to me in witnessing at close range the assassination of one presidential candidate, Robert F. Kennedy, in Los Angeles in 1968, a failed attempt against President Gerald R. Ford in Sacramento in 1975, and two months later a realistic hoax involving a fake pistol against the presidential candidate Ronald Reagan at the Miami International Airport. All these incidents, as well as joining a death watch over another presidential hopeful, the Alabama governor George C. Wallace, at a hospital in suburban Washington in 1972, underscored for me the imperative of the wise and thoughtful selection of presidential running mates, particularly in a land of growing gun violence and, in at least one case, of corruption in high government places.

I thank particularly three of the surviving vice presidents—Walter Mondale, Richard Cheney, and Joe Biden—for granting interviews for this book and all the others who have talked to me over time, including the late Hubert Humphrey and Gerald Ford and Dan Quayle, about the office they held and their notions on their satisfactions enjoyed and frustrations endured along the way. I am also grateful to many vice presidential aides, most notably Richard Moe, chief of staff to Mondale at the time of his selection. He helped prepare the Minnesota senator in the summer of 1976 for the key discussions with Democratic presidential nominee Jimmy Carter that led to the Carter-Mondale ticket that fall and their partnership, which became the model for subsequent White House leadership teams.

I am grateful as well for the assistance and counsel of the staffs at Smithsonian Books, led by Carolyn Gleason, as well as Christina Wiginton, and for the meticulous editing of Robin Whitaker, all in the quest of enhancing public awareness of the second office and what has become the de facto assistant presidency. Finally, my wife and fellow author, Marion Elizabeth Rodgers, and my always supportive children have my thanks for their encouragement during the three years of researching and writing this chronicle.

Jules Witcover
Washington, D.C.

NOTES

INTRODUCTION

1. McCullough, *John Adams,* 402.
2. Madison, *The Constitutional Convention,* 92.
3. Witcover, *Crapshoot,* 13.
4. Ibid.
5. Ibid., 14–15.
6. Ibid., 15.
7. Ibid.
8. Lyon, *The Constitution and the Men Who Made It,* 230.
9. Witcover, *Crapshoot,* 15–16.
10. Ibid., 16.
11. Ibid., 16–17.
12. Lyon, *The Constitution and the Men Who Made It,* 231.
13. Ibid., 248.
14. Ibid., 231–32.

1. JOHN ADAMS

1. Horsman, "The Elections of 1789 and 1792," 5.
2. Kaminski, *George Clinton,* 170.
3. Ibid.
4. Ibid., 17.
5. Ibid., 172.
6. Hatfield, *Vice Presidents of the United States,* 6.
7. McCullough, *John Adams,* 392.
8. Hatfield, *Vice Presidents of the United States,* 6.
9. McCullough, *John Adams,* 402.
10. Ibid., 447.
11. Ibid., 392.
12. Ibid., 399.
13. Ibid.
14. Ibid., 402.
15. Ibid., 404.
16. Ibid., 405.
17. Ibid.
18. Ibid, 406–7.
19. Ibid., 407.
20. Ibid., 410.
21. Ibid., 417.
22. Ibid., 421.
23. Ibid., 417–18.
24. Ibid., 429.
25. Ibid.
26. Ibid., 425–26.
27. Ibid., 434.
28. Ibid., 422.
29. Kerber, "The Federalist Party," 1:10.
30. Chernow, *Alexander Hamilton,* 422.
31. McCullough, *John Adams,* 447.
32. Ibid., 448.

33. Ibid., 449, 452.
34. Ellis, *First Family,* 166.
35. McCullough, *John Adams,* 458.
36. Ibid., 452.
37. Ibid.
38. Ibid., 459.
39. Ibid., 462.
40. Schlesinger, *History of U.S. Political Parties,* 1:xxxv.
41. McCullough, *John Adams,* 462.
42. Ibid., 464.
43. Ibid., 465.
44. Witcover, *Party of the People,* 47.
45. McCullough, *John Adams,* 465.
46. Ibid., 465–66.

2. THOMAS JEFFERSON

1. Wibberley, *Man of Liberty,* 4, 15–29.
2. Ibid., 64.
3. Ellis, *American Sphinx,* 42–44.
4. Ibid., 47–49.
5. Ibid., 65–66.
6. Ibid., 66.
7. McCullough, *John Adams,* 448.
8. Ibid., 473.
9. Ibid., 474.
10. Kurtz, *The Presidency of John Adams,* 229.
11. McCullough, *John Adams,* 483.
12. Ibid., 489.
13. Binkley, *American Political Parties,* 79.
14. Bowers, *Jefferson and Hamilton,* 373.
15. McCullough, *John Adams,* 503.
16. Pancake, *Thomas Jefferson and Alexander Hamilton,* 247; McCullough, *John Adams,* 505.
17. Pancake, *Thomas Jefferson and Alexander Hamilton,* 250.
18. McCullough, *John Adams,* 521.
19. Ibid., 536.
20. Ibid., 536–37.
21. Ibid., 577–79.

22. Cunningham, "The Election of 1800," 32.
23. Ibid., 34–35; McCullough, *John Adams,* 545.
24. Ellis, *First Family,* 204–5.
25. Cunningham, *The Jefferson Republicans,* 240.
26. Ibid., 186.
27. Ellis, *First Family,* 204–5; McCullough, *John Adams,* 545.
28. Cunningham, *The Jeffersonian Republicans,* 240.
29. Ibid., 241; Schachner, *Thomas Jefferson,* 652.
30. Schachner, *Thomas Jefferson,* 653.
31. Ibid.
32. Ibid.
33. Bowers, *Jefferson in Power,* 245–46.
34. Cunningham, *The Jeffersonian Republicans,* 242.
35. Schachner, *Thomas Jefferson,* 657.
36. Ferling, *Adams vs. Jefferson,* 191.
37. Ibid., 193.

3. AARON BURR

1. Isenberg, *Fallen Founder,* 224.
2. Lomask, *Aaron Burr,* 299–300.
3. Ibid., 299–301.
4. Isenberg, *Fallen Founder,* 230.
5. Lomask, *Aaron Burr,* 302.
6. Ibid., 309–11.
7. Ibid., 313.
8. Cunningham, *The Jeffersonian Republicans in Power,* 205; Isenberg, *Fallen Founder,* 246.
9. Ibid., 206.
10. Isenberg, *Fallen Founder,* 231–33.
11. Ibid., 247–50.
12. Cunningham, *The Jeffersonian Republicans in Power,* 206.
13. Isenberg, *Fallen Founder,* 247.
14. Blum et al., *The National Experience,* 180.
15. Ibid., 164.

16. Ibid., 181.
17. Cunningham, *The Jeffersonian Republicans in Power*, 211–12.
18. Bowers, *Jefferson in Power*, 236.
19. Ibid., 213–14.
20. Ibid., 253.
21. Isenberg, *Fallen Founder*, 253.
22. Chernow, *Alexander Hamilton*, 673.
23. Isenberg, *Fallen Founder*, 255.
24. Ibid., 257.
25. Ibid., 258.
26. Ibid., 259.
27. Ibid., 260–61.
28. Chernow, *Alexander Hamilton*, 262, 693.
29. Lomask, *Aaron Burr*, 352–53.
30. Isenberg, *Fallen Founder*, 265–66; Chernow, *Alexander Hamilton*, 701–4.
31. Isenberg, *Fallen Founder*, 267–68.
32. Chernow, *Alexander Hamilton*, 717; Lomask, *Aaron Burr*, 357.
33. Lomask, *Aaron Burr*, 361; Chernow, *Alexander Hamilton*, 718.
34. Isenberg, *Fallen Founder*, 273–34.

4. GEORGE CLINTON

1. Kaminski, *George Clinton*, 275.
2. Ibid., 21.
3. Ibid., 24–25.
4. Ibid., 26.
5. Ibid., 280.
6. Spaulding, *His Excellency George Clinton*, 289.
7. Ibid., 290–91; Kaminski, *George Clinton*, 283.
8. Spaulding, *His Excellency George Clinton*, 292; Kaminski, *George Clinton*, 280–81.
9. Spaulding, *His Excellency George Clinton*, 287; Cunningham, *The Jeffersonians in Power*, 280–81.
10. Kaminski, *George Clinton*, 289–90.
11. Ibid.
12. Ibid., 293.

5. ELBRIDGE GERRY

1. Billias, *Elbridge Gerry*, 3–5.
2. Ibid., 9.
3. Ibid., 47.
4. Ibid., 48, 49.
5. Ibid., 52.
6. Ibid., 87.
7. Ibid., 195, 199.
8. Blum et al., *The National Experience*, 167–68.
9. Billias, *Elbridge Gerry*, 316–17.
10. Wills, *James Madison*, 116.
11. Risjord, "Election of 1812," in *Running for President*, 70.
12. Billias, *Elbridge Gerry*, 308–10.
13. Ibid., 309; Austin, *The Life of Elbridge Gerry*, 375.

6. DANIEL D. TOMPKINS

1. Irwin, *Daniel D. Tompkins*, 198.
2. Hatfield, *Vice Presidents of the United States*, 74.
3. Irwin, *Daniel D. Tompkins*, 202.
4. Ibid., 208; Cmiel, *Democratic Eloquence*, 80.
5. Irwin, *Daniel D. Tompkins*, 210–11.
6. Ibid., 211.
7. Ibid., 223.
8. Ibid., 230.
9. Ibid., 251–52.
10. Ibid., 249.
11. Ibid., 262.
12. Ibid., 280.
13. Ibid., 283.
14. Hatfield, *Vice Presidents of the United States*, 78.
15. Irwin, *Daniel D. Tompkins*, 288.
16. Ibid., 299.
17. Ibid., 309.

7. JOHN C. CALHOUN

1. Bartlett, *John C. Calhoun*, 114.
2. Ibid., 28.

3. Wiltse, *John C. Calhoun: Nationalist, 1782–1828,* 41–42.

4. Bartlett, *John C. Calhoun,* 59.

5. Capers, *John C. Calhoun, Opportunist,* 34.

6. Cole, *Martin Van Buren and the American Political System,* 28.

7. Bartlett, *John C. Calhoun,* 99–100, 103.

8. Ibid., 100.

9. Wiltse, *John C. Calhoun: Nationalist, 1782–1828,* 156.

10. Bartlett, *John C. Calhoun,* 101.

11. Wiltse, *John C. Calhoun: Nationalist, 1782–1828,* 160.

12. Ibid., 314; Hatfield, *Vice Presidents of the United States,* 87.

13. Ibid., 89.

14. Ibid., 92.

15. Wiltse, *John C. Calhoun: Nationalist, 1782–1828,* 329–30.

16. Bartlett, *John C. Calhoun,* 135.

17. Binkley, *American Political Parties,* 117.

18. Wiltse, *John C. Calhoun: Nationalist, 1782–1828,* 348.

19. Remini, "Election of 1828," 417.

20. Wiltse, *John C. Calhoun: Nationalist, 1782–1828,* 389–90.

21. Remini, "Election of 1828," 496.

22. Bartlett, *John C. Calhoun,* 167.

23. Ibid., 168

24. Ibid., 185–86.

25. Cole, *Martin Van Buren and the American Political System,* 217.

26. Schlesinger, *The Age of Jackson,* 55.

27. Cole, *Martin Van Buren and the American Political System,* 127.

28. Remini, "Election of 1828," 498.

29. Witcover, *Party of the People,* 144.

30. Ibid.

31. Ibid., 144–45.

32. Ibid.

8. MARTIN VAN BUREN

1. Cole, *Martin Van Buren and the American Political System,* 16.

2. Ibid., 18–19.

3. Hatfield, *Vice Presidents of the United States,* 106.

4. Cole, *Martin Van Buren and the American Political System,* 123.

5. Van Buren, *The Autobiography of Martin Van Buren,* 149.

6. Ibid., 141.

7. Ibid., 209–10.

8. Ibid., 217.

9. Ibid., 219.

10. Ibid., 228.

11. Ibid., 230.

12. Ibid., 232.

13. Ibid., 233.

14. Blum et al., *The National Experience,* 248.

15. Ibid., 240.

16. Cole, *Martin Van Buren and the American Political System,* 239.

17. Ibid., 239–40.

18. Ibid., 251–52.

19. Hatfield, *Vice Presidents of the United States,* 114.

20. Blum et al., *The National Experience,* 249.

9. RICHARD MENTOR JOHNSON

1. Hatfield, *Vice Presidents of the United States,* 121.

2. Ibid., 123.

3. Feller, "The Election of 1836," 134.

4. Cole, *Martin Van Buren and the American Political System,* 261.

5. Hatfield, *Vice Presidents of the United States,* 125.

6. Silbey, "The Election of 1836," 584–86.

7. Hatfield, *Vice Presidents of the United States,* 127.

8. Feller, "The Election of 1836," 134.

9. Wilentz, "The Election of 1840," 152.

10. Cole, *Martin Van Buren and the American Political System*, 263.

11. Hatfield, *Vice Presidents of the United States*, 127.

12. Silbey, "The Election of 1836," 588.

13. Hatfield, *Vice Presidents of the United States*, 128.

14. Cole, *Martin Van Buren and the American Political System*, 357.

15. Hatfield, *Vice Presidents of the United States*, 130.

16. Ibid.

17. Ibid.

18. Wilentz, "The Election of 1840," 150.

10. JOHN TYLER

1. Crapol, *John Tyler*, 8; Chitwood, *John Tyler*, 202.

2. Hatfield, *Vice Presidents of the United States*, 142.

3. Ibid., 9.

4. Ibid., 10.

5. Witcover, *Crapshoot*, 36.

6. Monroe, *The Republican Vision of John Tyler*, 81.

7. Hatfield, *Vice Presidents of the United States*, 142.

8. Seager, *And Tyler Too*, 56–58.

9. Remini, *Andrew Jackson and the Course of American Democracy*, 36.

10. Chitwood, *John Tyler*, 115.

11. Monroe, *The Republican Vision of John Tyler*, 73.

12. Hatfield, *Vice Presidents of the United States*, 128.

13. Chitwood, *John Tyler*, 154.

14. Ibid., 166–69.

15. Ibid., 173.

16. Ibid., 175.

17. Seager, *And Tyler Too*, 135.

18. Chitwood, *John Tyler*, 188.

19. Hatfield, *Vice Presidents of the United States*, 145.

20. Pastan, *The Smithsonian Book of Presidential Trivia*, 180.

11. GEORGE M. DALLAS

1. Seigenthaler, *James K. Polk*, 73.

2. Ibid., 78.

3. Ibid., 76.

4. Ibid., 80–81.

5. Belohlavek, *George Mifflin Dallas*, 88.

6. Ibid., 88–89.

7. Ibid., 90.

8. Ibid., 92–93.

9. Ibid., 96.

10. Seigenthaler, *James K. Polk*, 92–93.

11. Belohlavek, *George Mifflin Dallas*, 100.

12. Ibid.

13. Ibid., 102.

14. Seigenthaler, *James K. Polk*, 115–16.

15. Belohlavek, *George Mifflin Dallas*, 112.

16. Hatfield, *Vice Presidents of the United States*, 158.

17. Belohlavek, *George Mifflin Dallas*, 114.

18. Ibid., 115.

19. Ibid., 124.

20. Seigenthaler, *James K. Polk*, 152.

21. Belohlavek, *George Mifflin Dallas*, 134.

22. Hatfield, *Vice Presidents of the United States*, 151.

12. MILLARD FILLMORE

1. Rayback, *Millard Fillmore*, 2–3.

2. Ibid., 14.

3. Ibid., 150–51.

4. Quoted by Troy, "The Election of 1848," 187.

5. Ibid.

6. Ibid., 189.

7. Ibid., 191.

8. Rayback, *Millard Fillmore*, 185–86.
9. Ibid., 192.
10. Blum et al., *The National Experience*, 299–300.
11. Hatfield, *Vice Presidents of the United States*, 174.
12. Ibid., 175.

13. WILLIAM R. KING

1. Hatfield, *Vice Presidents of the United States*, 183.
2. Remini, *Henry Clay*, 424.
3. Hatfield, *Vice Presidents of the United States*, 183.
4. Remini, *Henry Clay*, 573.
5. Ibid., 574.
6. Ibid.
7. Ibid.
8. Hatfield, *Vice Presidents of the United States*, 185.
9. Ibid.
10. Ibid.
11. Ibid., 186.
12. Ibid., 181.

14. JOHN C. BRECKINRIDGE

1. Hatfield, *Vice Presidents of the United States*, 194.
2. Heck, *Proud Kentuckian*, 42.
3. Ibid., 61.
4. Ibid., 63.
5. Ibid., 74.
6. Hatfield, *Vice Presidents of the United States*, 197.
7. Blum et al., *The National Experience*, 349.
8. Heck, *Proud Kentuckian*, 85.
9. Ibid., 89.
10. Ibid., 98.
11. Hatfield, *Vice Presidents of the United States*, 198.
12. Heck, *Proud Kentuckian*, 102; William C. Davis, *Breckinridge*, 276.
13. Heck, *Proud Kentuckian*, 106.

14. Hatfield, *Vice Presidents of the United States*, 198.
15. Ibid., 199.
16. Ibid.

15. HANNIBAL HAMLIN

1. H. Draper Hunt, *Hannibal Hamlin of Maine*, 4–6.
2. Ibid., 17.
3. Ibid., 23.
4. Ibid., 25.
5. Ibid., 29.
6. Ibid., 48.
7. Ibid., 62.
8. Ibid., 48.
9. Ibid., 81.
10. Ibid., 83–84.
11. Ibid., 88–89.
12. Ibid., 91.
13. Ibid., 102.
14. Ibid., 117.
15. Ibid., 118.
16. Ibid., 119; Hamlin, *The Life and Times of Hannibal Hamlin*, 354–55.
17. Hunt, *Hannibal Hamlin of Maine*, 122.
18. Ibid., 126.
19. Hamlin, *The Life and Times of Hannibal Hamlin*, 367; Hunt, *Hannibal Hamlin of Maine*, 139.
20. Hunt, *Hannibal Hamlin of Maine*, 147.
21. Hamlin, *The Life and Times of Hannibal Hamlin*, 406–7.
22. Blum et al., *The National Experience*, 353.
23. Hunt, *Hannibal Hamlin of Maine*, 154.
24. Ibid., 155.
25. Ibid., 156.
26. Ibid., 156–57.
27. Ibid., 156–58.
28. Ibid., 159–60.
29. Ibid., 162.

30. Ibid., 166.

31. Ibid., 172.

32. Ibid., 173.

33. Ibid., 177.

34. Ibid., 179–80.

35. Ibid., 182.

36. Trefousse, *Andrew Johnson,* 177.

37. Hunt, *Hannibal Hamlin of Maine,* 188–89.

38. Ibid., 189–90.

39. Ibid., 191.

40. Ibid., 193.

41. Ibid., 194.

42. Ibid.

43. Ibid., 198–99.

44. Ibid. 199–200.

16. ANDREW JOHNSON

1. H. Draper Hunt, *Hannibal Hamlin of Maine,* 180.

2. Trefousse, *Andrew Johnson,* 32–33.

3. Ibid., 43–45.

4. Ibid., 57.

5. Ibid., 43, 63.

6. Lately Thomas, *The First President Johnson,* 140; Trefousse, *Andrew Johnson,* 119–21.

7. Thomas, *The First President Johnson,* 146.

8. Ibid.

9. Ibid.

10. Ibid., 152.

11. Ibid., 160; Trefousse, *Andrew Johnson,* 130.

12. Thomas, *The First President Johnson,* 163–64.

13. Ibid., 168.

14. Trefousse, *Andrew Johnson,* 140.

15. Thomas, *The First President Johnson,* 206–7.

16. Ibid., 229.

17. Ibid., 234, 242–43.

18. Ibid., 268–69; Trefousse, *Andrew Johnson,* 180.

19. Thomas, *The First President Johnson,* 274.

20. Trefousse, *Andrew Johnson,* 180.

21. Thomas, *The First President Johnson,* 272–73.

22. Trefousse, *Andrew Johnson,* 180.

23. Ibid.

24. Ibid., 182.

25. Thomas, *The First President Johnson,* 279; Trefousse, *Andrew Johnson,* 183.

26. Thomas, *The First President Johnson,* 279; Trefousse, *Andrew Johnson,* 183.

27. Thomas, *The First President Johnson,* 279.

28. Ibid., 279.

29. Ibid., 294.

30. Ibid., 291.

31. Hunt, *Hannibal Hamlin of Maine,* 195.

32. Ibid., 196–97.

33. Trefousse, *Andrew Johnson,* 189–90.

34. Ibid.

35. Ibid., 191; Thomas, *The First President Johnson,* 303.

36. Trefousse, *Andrew Johnson,* 190.

37. Ibid., 194.

38. Thomas, *The First President Johnson,* 317–18.

39. Trefousse, *Andrew Johnson,* 211–12.

40. Ibid., 217.

17. SCHUYLER COLFAX

1. Willard H. Smith, *Schuyler Colfax,* 2–4.

2. Ibid., 10.

3. Ibid., 13.

4. Hatfield, *Vice Presidents of the United States,* 224.

5. Ibid., 226.

6. Smith, *Schuyler Colfax,* 218–19.

7. Ibid., 221.

8. Ibid., 223.

9. Ibid., 225.

10. Ibid., 227.

11. Ibid., 233–34.
12. Trefousse, *Impeachment of a President*, 38–39.
13. Ibid., 306.
14. Ibid., 310.
15. Ibid., 317.
16. Hatfield, *Vice Presidents of the United States*, 227.
17. Ibid., 329; Gray, ed., *Gentlemen from Indiana*, 75–77.
18. Smith, *Schuyler Colfax*, 330.
19. Ibid., 331.
20. Ibid., 332.
21. Ibid., 347–48.

18. HENRY WILSON

1. McKay, *Henry Wilson, Practical Radical*, 8.
2. Abbott, *Cobbler in Congress*, 8.
3. Ibid., 80–81.
4. Ibid., 81–82.
5. Ibid., 82.
6. McKay, *Henry Wilson, Practical Radical*, 111.
7. Abbott, *Cobbler in Congress*, 109.
8. Ibid., 156.
9. Ibid., 161–62.
10. Ibid., 178.
11. Ibid., 189.
12. Ibid., 203.
13. McFeeley, "The Election of 1872," 305.
14. Hatfield, *Vice Presidents of the United States*, 238.
15. Ibid.

19. WILLIAM A. WHEELER

1. Howells, *Sketch of the Life and Character of Rutherford B. Hayes*, 12.
2. Ibid., 5–8.
3. Ibid., 11.
4. Ibid., 13–14.
5. Ibid., 16.
6. Ibid., 23.

7. Polakoff, *The Politics of Inertia*, 104–35, 180–82.
8. Howells, *Sketch of the Life and Character of Rutherford B. Hayes*, 16–17.
9. Ibid., 20.
10. Hatfield, *Vice Presidents of the United States*, 243.
11. Nevins, foreword to John F. Kennedy's *Profiles in Courage*, xiv.
12. Polakoff, *The Politics of Inertia*, 123.
13. T. Harry Williams, ed., *Hayes*, 69, 129.
14. Hatfield, *Vice Presidents of the United States*, 247.
15. Ibid.

20. CHESTER A. ARTHUR

1. Ackerman, *Dark Horse*, 61.
2. Thomas C. Reeves, *Gentleman Boss*, 18–19, 42.
3. Ibid., 60; Ackerman, *Dark Horse*, 18, 62.
4. Reeves, *Gentleman Boss*, 63, 76–77.
5. Karabell, *Chester Alan Arthur*, 33.
6. Reeves, *Gentleman Boss*, 147.
7. Ibid., 180; Ackerman, *Dark Horse*, 128.
8. Reeves, *Gentleman Boss*, 183.
9. Ibid., 184.
10. Ibid. 189.
11. Ibid, 206.
12. Ibid., 224.
13. Ibid., 234–35.
14. Ibid., 236.
15. Ibid., 236–37.
16. Ibid., 237.
17. Ibid., 241.
18. Ibid., 245.
19. Ibid., 260.
20. Ibid., 280–81.
21. Ibid., 318.
22. Ibid., 369.
23. Ibid., 387–88.

21. THOMAS A. HENDRICKS

1. Hensel, "A Biographical Sketch of Thomas A. Hendricks," 197.
2. Gray, ed., *Gentlemen from Indiana,* 126.
3. Holcombe and Skinner, *Life and Public Services of Thomas A. Hendricks,* 267.
4. Ibid., 264.
5. Ibid., 265–66.
6. Hatfield, *Vice Presidents of the United States,* 263.
7. Gray, ed., *Gentlemen from Indiana,* 133.
8. Hensel, "A Biographical Sketch of Thomas A. Hendricks," 244–45.
9. Nevins, *Grover Cleveland,* 147.
10. McElroy, *Grover Cleveland,* 1:83; Graff, *Grover Cleveland,* 53.
11. Hirsch, "Election of 1884," 1571.
12. Ibid., 1572.
13. Ibid., 1574–75; Graff, *Grover Cleveland,* 60–64.
14. Hirsch, "Election of 1884," 1578.
15. Ibid., 1581.
16. Graff, *Grover Cleveland,* 66.
17. Holcombe and Skinner, *Life and Public Services of Thomas A. Hendricks,* 375.

22. LEVI P. MORTON

1. McElroy, *Levi Parsons Morton,* x.
2. Ibid., 31.
3. Ibid., 20.
4. Ibid., 33–43.
5. Ibid., 56–58.
6. Hatfield, *Vice Presidents of the United States,* 271.
7. Ibid.
8. McElroy, *Levi Parsons Morton,* 129–30.
9. Ibid., 171.
10. Hatfield, *Vice Presidents of the United States,* 273.

23. ADLAI E. STEVENSON

1. Jean H. Baker, *The Stevensons,* 83–85.
2. Ibid., 83–86.
3. Hatfield, *Vice Presidents of the United States,* 279.
4. Baker, *The Stevensons,* 97–100.
5. Ibid., 121.
6. Ibid.
7. Ibid., 127.
8. Ibid.
9. Morgan, "The Election of 1892," 1720.
10. Baker, *The Stevensons,* 147.
11. Ibid., 150.
12. Ibid., 149.
13. Hatfield, *Vice Presidents of the United States,* 281.
14. Algeo, *The President Is a Sick Man,* 53–55.
15. Ibid., 63–79.
16. Ibid., 91–92.
17. Ibid., 91–97.
18. Baker, *The Stevensons,* 165–66.
19. Hatfield, *Vice Presidents of the United States,* 282.
20. Baker, *The Stevensons,* 168.
21. Ibid., 176–77.
22. Ibid., 178.

24. GARRET A. HOBART

1. Magie, *The Life of Garret Augustus Hobart,* 30, 41.
2. Ibid., 2.
3. Ibid., 1.
4. Ibid., 13, 20–24.
5. Ibid., 25.
6. Ibid., 25, 28–30.
7. Ibid., 31–34.
8. Ibid., 34–37.
9. Ibid., 49, 50.
10. Ibid., 58–70.
11. Ibid., 64–68.

12. Hatfield, *Vice Presidents of the United States,* 290–91.

13. Magie, *The Life of Garret Augustus Hobart,* 75.

14. Ibid., 74.

15. Ibid., 78.

16. Connolly, "Vice President Garret A. Hobart and Nineteenth-Century Republican Business Politics," 1, 20.

17. Ibid., 27.

18. Magie, *The Life of Garret Augustus Hobart,* 103.

19. Ibid., 104–5.

20. Blum et al., *The National Experience,* 530–31.

21. Schlesinger and Frent, eds., *Running for President,* 2:xiv.

22. Blum et al., *The National Experience,* 531–32.

23. Connolly, "Vice President Garret A. Hobart and Nineteenth-Century Republican Business Politics," 27–28.

24. Ibid., 33–34.

25. Ibid., 29.

26. Ibid., 30.

27. Hobart, *Memories,* 3–4, 44.

28. Hatfield, *Vice Presidents of the United States,* 291.

29. Connolly, "Vice President Garret A. Hobart and Nineteenth-Century Republican Business Politics," 31–32.

30. Hobart, *Memories,* 14.

31. Ibid.

32. Connolly, "Vice President Garret A. Hobart and Nineteenth-Century Republican Business Politics," 29.

33. Magie, *The Life of Garret Augustus Hobart,* 154.

34. Gould, *The Presidency of William McKinley,* 151.

35. Connolly, "Vice President Garret A. Hobart and Nineteenth-Century Republican Business Politics," 33.

36. Ibid., 34.

37. Gould, *The Presidency of William McKinley,* 176; Hobart, *Memories,* 68–69.

38. Connolly, "Vice President Garret A. Hobart and Nineteenth-Century Republican Business Politics," 37.

25. THEODORE ROOSEVELT

1. Auchincloss, *Theodore Roosevelt,* 37.

2. Ibid., 10.

3. Ibid., 12.

4. Roosevelt, *The Autobiography of Theodore Roosevelt,* 37.

5. Ibid., 38.

6. Edmund Morris, *The Rise of Theodore Roosevelt,* 241.

7. Nathan Miller, *Theodore Roosevelt,* 158.

8. Morris, *The Rise of Theodore Roosevelt,* 392–93.

9. Ibid., 497–98.

10. Ibid., 510–11.

11. Ibid., 552–53.

12. Auchincloss, *Theodore Roosevelt,* 26.

13. Gould, *The Presidency of William McKinley,* 69.

14. Ibid., 75.

15. Morris, *The Rise of Theodore Roosevelt,* 600.

16. Auchincloss, *Theodore Roosevelt,* 27.

17. Morris, *The Rise of Theodore Roosevelt,* 609.

18. Ibid., 620–28.

19. Hatfield, *Vice Presidents of the United States,* 301.

20. Miller, *Theodore Roosevelt,* 334.

21. Ibid., 338.

22. Gould, *The Presidency of William McKinley,* 216–17.

23. Witcover, *Crapshoot,* 55.

24. Morris, *The Rise of Theodore Roosevelt,* 729.

25. LaFeber, "The Election of 1900," 1897.

26. Miller, *Theodore Roosevelt,* 342.

27. Hatfield, *Vice Presidents of the United States,* 305.

28. Irving G. Williams, *The Rise of the Vice Presidency*, 84–85.

29. Miller, *Theodore Roosevelt*, 398–409.

26. CHARLES W. FAIRBANKS

1. Gould, *The Presidency of Theodore Roosevelt*, 135.

2. Irving G. Williams, *The Rise of the Vice Presidency*, 84.

3. William Henry Smith, *The Life and Speeches of Charles Warren Fairbanks*, 21–24.

4. Hatfield, *Vice Presidents of the United States*, 314.

5. Ibid.

6. Nathan Miller, *Theodore Roosevelt*, 438.

7. Smith, *The Life and Speeches of Charles Warren Fairbanks*, 211.

8. J. M. Cooper Jr., "The Election of 1900," 29.

9. Gray, *Indiana's Favorite Sons, 1840–1940*, 185.

10. Edmund Morris, *Theodore Rex*, 364; Gould, *The Presidency of Theodore Roosevelt*, 139.

11. Williams, *The Rise of the Vice Presidency*, 88.

12. Ibid., 89.

13. Gould, *The Presidency of Theodore Roosevelt*, 271.

14. Williams, *The Rise of the Vice Presidency*, 89–90.

15. Morris, *Theodore Rex*, 526.

27. JAMES S. SHERMAN

1. Williams, *The Rise of the Vice Presidency*, 93; Anderson, *William Howard Taft*, 132.

2. Hatfeld, *Vice Presidents of the United States*, 329.

3. Ibid., 326.

4. Ibid., 327.

5. Depew, *My Eighty Years of Memories*, 176–77.

6. Williams, *The Rise of the Vice Presidency*, 92.

7. Gould, *The Presidency of Theodore Roosevelt*, 113.

8. Ibid.

9. Pringle, *The Life and Times of William Howard Taft*, 564.

10. Manners, *TR and Will*, 175–76; Pringle, *The Life and Times of William Howard Taft*, 565.

11. Brands, *TR,* 675.

12. Gould, *The Presidency of Theodore Roosevelt*, 97.

28. THOMAS R. MARSHALL

1. Charles M. Thomas, *Thomas Riley Marshall*, 12–16.

2. Ibid., 27–28.

3. Ibid., 195.

4. Ibid., 22.

5. Ibid., 36.

6. Irving G. Williams, *The Rise of the Vice Presidency*, 98.

7. Thomas, *Thomas Riley Marshall*, 53–55.

8. McCombs, *Making Woodrow Wilson President*, 136–77.

9. Thomas, *Thomas Riley Marshall*, 133–34.

10. Ibid., 141.

11. Williams, *The Rise of the Vice Presidency*, 104.

12. Thomas, *Thomas Riley Marshall*, 144.

13. Bennett, *He Almost Changed the World*, 211.

14. Ibid., 200.

15. Thomas, *Thomas Riley Marshall*, 157–58.

16. Ibid., 175.

17. J. M. Cooper Jr., *Woodrow Wilson*, 339–41.

18. Ibid.

19. Ibid., 234.

20. Williams, *The Rise of the Vice Presidency*, 106.

21. Bennett, *He Almost Changed the World*, 208.

22. Ibid., 217.

23. Cooper, *Woodrow Wilson*, 356.

24. Bennett, *He Almost Changed the World*, 217.

25. Ibid., 218.

26. Thomas, *Thomas Riley Marshall*, 230–31.

27. Ibid., 178.

28. Ibid., 179; Ferrell, *The Presidency of Calvin Coolidge*, 18.

29. Williams, *The Rise of the Vice Presidency*, 108; Bennett, *He Almost Changed the World*, 235–36.

30. Thomas, *Thomas Riley Marshall*, 182.

31. Bennett, *He Almost Changed the World*, 249.

32. Ibid., 251.

33. Thomas, *Thomas Riley Marshall*, 223.

34. Ibid., 204.

35. Bennett, *He Almost Changed the World*, 276.

36. Ibid., 278.

37. Ibid., 279.

38. Ibid., 280.

39. Levin, *Edith and Woodrow*, 340.

40. Thomas, *Thomas Riley Marshall*, 224–25; Gene Smith, *When the Cheering Stopped*, 136.

41. Bennett, *He Almost Changed the World*, 281.

42. Witcover, *Crapshoot*, 64.

43. Thomas, *Thomas Riley Marshall*, 211.

44. Witcover, *Crapshoot*, 62.

45. Marshall, *Recollections of Thomas R. Marshall, Vice President and Hoosier Philosopher*, 368.

46. Levin, *Edith and Woodrow*, 342.

47. Ibid., 351.

48. Smith, *When the Cheering Stopped*, 124; Bennett, *He Almost Changed the World*, 296–97.

49. Bennett, *He Almost Changed the World*, 303.

29. CALVIN COOLIDGE

1. McKee, *Coolidge, Wit and Wisdom*, v.

2. Ibid., 43.

3. Ibid., 121.

4. Coolidge, *The Autobiography of Calvin Coolidge*, 145.

5. McCoy, "The Election of 1924," 2358.

6. Ferrell, *The Presidency of Calvin Coolidge*, 15.

7. Ibid., 16.

8. Ibid., 14.

9. Irving G. Williams, *The Rise of the Vice Presidency*, 118–19.

10. Ferrell, *The Presidency of Calvin Coolidge*, 4.

11. Coolidge, *The Autobiography of Calvin Coolidge*, 17.

12. Ibid., 93.

13. Ferrell, *The Presidency of Calvin Coolidge*, 10.

14. Gilbert, *The Tormented President*, 82–83.

15. William Allen White, *A Puritan in Babylon*, 151.

16. Ibid., 156.

17. Fuess, *Calvin Coolidge*, 217; White, *A Puritan in Babylon*, 158.

18. Sobel, *Coolidge*, 141.

19. Ibid., 142.

20. Ibid., 143.

21. Ibid., 144.

22 Ferrell, *The Presidency of Calvin Coolidge*, 15.

23. McCoy, *Calvin Coolidge*, 125.

24. Gilbert, *The Tormented President*, 105.

25. McCoy, "The Election of 1924," 2376.

26. Williams, *The Rise of the Vice Presidency*, 121.

27. Gilbert, *The Tormented President*, 106.

28. Ibid., 107.

29. Coolidge, *The Autobiography of Calvin Coolidge*, 159.

30. Ferrell, *The Presidency of Calvin Coolidge*, 18.

31. Coolidge, *The Autobiography of Calvin Coolidge*, 161.

32. Ferrell, *The Presidency of Calvin Coolidge*, 18.

33. Coolidge, *The Autobiography of Calvin Coolidge*, 173–76.

34. Fuess, *Calvin Coolidge*, 311.

35. Williams, *The Rise of the Vice Presidency*, 126.

36. White, *A Puritan in Babylon*, 345.

30. CHARLES G. DAWES

1. Timmons, *Portrait of an American*, 3–4.

2. Ibid., 9–10.

3. Ibid., 24–25.

4. Ibid., 26.

5. Ibid., 28.

6. Ibid., 54–55.

7. Ibid., 56.

8. Ibid., 65.

9. Dawes, *Notes as Vice President, 1928–1929*, 108.

10. Ibid., 183.

11. Ibid., 195.

12. Timmons, *Portrait of an American*, 201.

13. Ibid., 202.

14. Sobel, *Coolidge*, 291.

15. Leach, *That Man Dawes*, 192.

16. William Allen White, *A Puritan in Babylon*, 301.

17. Sobel, *Coolidge*, 303.

18. Ferrell, *The Presidency of Calvin Coolidge*, 59.

19. Gilbert, *The Tormented President*, 176.

20. Ibid., 176–77.

21. Ibid., 177.

22. Ibid., 136–39.

23. Sobel, *Coolidge*, 322–23; Timmons, *Portrait of an American*, 247.

24. White, *A Puritan in Babylon*, 322.

25. Ibid., 323.

26. Gilbert, *The Tormented President*, 179.

27. Dawes, *Notes as Vice President, 1928–1929*, 255.

28. Ibid., 299, 304, 316.

29. Ibid., 3–5.

31. CHARLES CURTIS

1. Ewy, *Charles Curtis of Kansas*, 5–9.

2. Unrau, *Mixed-Bloods and Tribal Dissolution*, 65.

3. Ibid., 45–49.

4. Seitz, *From Kaw Teepee to Capitol*, 18–19.

5. Ewy, *Charles Curtis of Kansas*, 9–10, 76.

6. Unrau, *Mixed-Bloods and Tribal Dissolution*, 72–74.

7. Ibid., 82.

8. Ewy, *Charles Curtis of Kansas*, 12.

9. Seitz, *From Kaw Teepee to Capitol*, 147–48.

10. Unrau, *Mixed-Bloods and Tribal Dissolution*, 85.

11. Ewy, *Charles Curtis of Kansas*, 14–15.

12. Ibid., 19; Seitz, *From Kaw Teepee to Capitol*, 161–62.

13. Unrau, *Mixed-Bloods and Tribal Dissolution*, 103.

14. Ibid., 172–73.

15. Ewy, *Charles Curtis of Kansas*, 23.

16. Ibid., 30–31.

17. Ibid., 37.

18. Hatfield, *Vice Presidents of the United States*, 379.

19. Fausold, *The Presidency of Herbert C. Hoover*, 84–85; Ewy, *Charles Curtis of Kansas*, 48–49.

20. Hatfield, *Vice Presidents of the United States*, 380–81.

21. Ibid., 381.

22. Ewy, *Charles Curtis of Kansas*, 57.

32. JOHN NANCE GARNER

1. Timmons, *Garner of Texas,* 1–5; Fisher, *Cactus Jack,* 2–3.
2. James, *Mr. Garner of Texas,* 12–17.
3. Timmons, *Garner of Texas,* 17.
4. Fisher, *Cactus Jack,* 11–12.
5. Ibid.; Irving G. Williams, *The Rise of the Vice Presidency,* 153–54.
6. Fisher, *Cactus Jack,* 15.
7. Ibid., 31.
8. Timmons, *Garner of Texas,* 42; James, *Mr. Garner of Texas,* 70.
9. Fisher, *Cactus Jack,* 68.
10. Timmons, *Garner of Texas,* 120–24.
11. James, *Mr. Garner of Texas,* 113.
12. Timmons, *Garner of Texas,* 137.
13. James, *Mr. Garner of Texas,* 126–27.
14. Timmons, *Garner of Texas,* 154.
15. Ibid., 157.
16. Ibid., 160.
17. Brands, *TR,* 247.
18. Fisher, *Cactus Jack,* 93; Timmons, *Garner of Texas,* 165.
19. Timmons, *Garner of Texas,* 168.
20. Fisher, *Cactus Jack,* 96.
21. Ibid.
22. Timmons, *Garner of Texas,* 177.
23. Fisher, *Cactus Jack,* 101.
24. Ibid., 111.
25. Timmons, *Garner of Texas,* 178–79.
26. Fisher, *Cactus Jack,* 114.
27. Ibid., 118.
28. Williams, *The Rise of the Vice Presidency,* 162.
29. Ibid., 160.
30. Ibid., 160–61.
31. Fisher, *Cactus Jack,* 128.
32. Timmons, *Garner of Texas,* 216.
33. Ibid., 216–17.
34. Fisher, *Cactus Jack,* 131.
35. Williams, *The Rise of the Vice Presidency,* 165; Farley, *Jim Farley's Story,* 84.
36. Ibid., 165–66.
37. Timmons, *Garner of Texas,* 222–23.
38. Farley, *Jim Farley's Story,* 84.
39. Blum et al., *The National Experience,* 712–13.
40. Timmons, *Garner of Texas,* 234.
41. Ibid., 139.
42. Fisher, *Cactus Jack,* 143.
43. Ibid.
44. Ibid., 143.
45. Ibid., 145.
46. Timmons, *Garner of Texas,* 267.
47. Nathan Miller, *FDR,* 450.
48. Fisher, *Cactus Jack,* 150.
49. Timmons, *Garner of Texas,* 278.

33. HENRY A. WALLACE

1. Irving G. Williams, *The Rise of the Vice Presidency,* 177–78.
2. Lord, *The Wallaces of Iowa,* 1–6.
3. Ibid., 10.
4. Ibid., 150.
5. Ibid., 159.
6. Culver and Hyde, *American Dreamer,* 49.
7. Ibid., 53–55.
8. Ibid., 90–91.
9. Ibid., 78.
10. Ibid., 107–8; Lord, *The Wallaces of Iowa,* 324.
11. Culver and Hyde, *American Dreamer,* 113.
12. Witcover, *Crapshoot,* 77.
13. Culver and Hyde, *American Dreamer,* 160.
14. White and Maze, *Henry A. Wallace,* 105–6.
15. Culver and Hyde, *American Dreamer,* 176.
16. Ibid., 210.
17. Farley, 254.
18. Tully, *FDR, My Boss,* xxx.
19. Culver and Hyde, *American Dreamer,* 220.

20. Rosenman, *Working with Roosevelt,* 215.

21. Ibid., 216; Nathan Miller, *FDR,* 452.

22. Culver and Hyde, *American Dreamer,* 218.

23. Ibid., 222.

24. Ibid., 223.

25. Brands, *TR,* 574.

26. Ibid., 266–68.

27. Ibid., 270.

28. Lord, *The Wallaces of Iowa,* 496–514; Culver and Hyde, *American Dreamer,* 309–10.

29. Culver and Hyde, *American Dreamer,* 310.

30. Flynn, *You're the Boss,* 181.

31. Culver and Hyde, *American Dreamer,* 349.

32. Ibid., 351.

33. Ibid., 351–52; Brands, *TR,* 768–69.

34. Culver and Hyde, *American Dreamer,* 352.

35. Witcover, *Crapshoot,* 96.

36. Ibid.

37. Culver and Hyde, *American Dreamer,* 362.

38. Ibid., 367.

39. Ibid., 369.

40. Ibid., 373.

34. HARRY S. TRUMAN

1. Daniels, *The Man of Independence,* 49–50.

2. Ibid., 51–52; McCullough, *Truman,* 42.

3. Truman, *The Autobiography of Harry S. Truman,* 52–53.

4. McCullough, *Truman,* 119–33.

5. Daniels, *The Man of Independence,* 103–4; Richard Lawrence Miller, *Truman,* 112, 149–50.

6. McCullough, *Truman,* 159–65.

7. Merle Miller, *Plain Speaking,* 159–63.

8. McCullough, *Truman,* 160.

9. Ibid., 184–85.

10. Hamby, *Man of the People,* 233; McCullough, *Truman,* 204.

11. Hamby, *Man of the People,* 233–47.

12. Ibid., 263.

13. Hamby, *Man of the People,* 233.

14. Allen, *Presidents Who Have Known Me,* 122.

15. Flynn, *You're the Boss,* 180.

16. Ibid., 181.

17. Culver and Hyde, *American Dreamer,* 348.

18. McCullough, *Truman,* 300–301.

19. Witcover, *Crapshoot,* 87.

20. Culver and Hyde, *American Dreamer,* 348–49.

21. Ibid., 349.

22. Byrnes, *All in One Lifetime,* 222.

23. Miller, *Plain Speaking,* 175.

24. Byrnes, *All in One Lifetime,* 226.

25. Miller, *Plain Speaking,* 192–93.

26. McCullough, *Truman,* 306; Culver and Hyde, *American Dreamer,* 353.

27. Tully, *FDR, My Boss,* 276–77.

28. Culver and Hyde, *American Dreamer,* 353.

29. Ibid., 359; McCullough, *Truman,* 314.

30. McCullough, *Truman,* 320.

31. Ibid., 330–31.

32. Hamby, *Man of the People,* 287.

33. McCullough, *Truman,* 336–37.

34. Ibid., 337.

35. Goodwin, *No Ordinary Time,* 604; McCullough, *Truman,* 342.

36. McCullough, *Truman,* 353.

37. Ibid., 376.

38. Ibid., 377.

35. ALBEN W. BARKLEY

1. Donovan, *Conflict and Crisis,* 405.

2. Barkley, *That Reminds Me,* 22.

3. Ibid., 27.

4. Ibid., 77.

5. Ibid., 79–80.

6. Ibid., 102.

7. Ibid., 110–11.

8. Ibid., 141.

9. Ibid., 139.

10. Ibid., 146.

11. Polly Ann Davis, *Alben W. Barkley*, 17.

12. Ibid., 30.

13. Ibid., 101–5.

14. Barkley, *That Reminds Me*, 157.

15. Ibid., 172.

16. Ibid., 172–73.

17. Davis, *Alben W. Barkley*, 143.

18. Barkley, *That Reminds Me*, 177.

19. Ibid., 180–81.

20. Ibid., 179.

21. Ibid., 178–79.

22. McCullough, *Truman*, 637.

23. Barkley, *That Reminds Me*, 201.

24. Ibid., 199.

25. Davis, *Alben W. Barkley*, 256.

26. Hamby, *Man of the People*, 450–51.

27. Ibid., 452.

28. Davis, *Alben W. Barkley*, 284–86.

29. Barkley, *That Reminds Me*, 209.

30. Ibid., 236–42; Hamby, *Man of the People*, 607–9.

31. Barkley, *That Reminds Me*, 21.

32. Davis, *Alben W. Barkley*, 314.

36. RICHARD M. NIXON

1. Roger Morris, *Richard Milhous Nixon*, 24–46.

2. Gellman, *The Contender*, 11.

3. Ibid., 20; Parment, *Richard Nixon and His America*, 85–88.

4. Morris, *Richard Milhous Nixon*, 317–34; Gellman, *The Contender*, 308.

5. Ibid., 468–69, 509–29.

6. Mitchell, *Tricky Dick and the Pink Lady*, 102; Gellman, *The Contender*, 308.

7. Morris, *Richard Milhous Nixon*, 606.

8. Klein, *Making It Perfectly Clear*, 79.

9. Ibid.; Morris, *Richard Milhous Nixon*, 632.

10. Morris, *Richard Milhous Nixon*, 668.

11. Ibid., 679.

12. Ibid., 694.

13. Ibid., 712.

14. Ibid., 726.

15. Ibid., 753.

16. Nixon, *Six Crises*, 81.

17. Mazo and Hess, *Nixon*, 102; Nixon, *Six Crises*, 83.

18. Ibid., 93.

19. Ibid., 115.

20. Ibid., 116–17.

21. Morris, *Richard Milhous Nixon*, 861–62.

22. Nixon, *RN*, 161.

23. Ibid., 164.

24. Witcover, *Crapshoot*, 127.

25. Ibid., 128.

26. Ambrose, *Nixon: The Education of a Politician*, 381.

27. Nixon, *Six Crises*, 160.

28. Ibid., 164.

29. Ambrose, *Nixon: The Education of a Politician*, 414–15.

30. Ibid., 421.

31. Ibid., 449.

32. Ibid., 452.

33. Nixon, *Six Crises*, 232–33.

34. Ibid., 250–58.

35. Ibid., 313–16; Ambrose, *Nixon: The Education of a Politician*, 551–53.

36. Ambrose, *Nixon: The Education of a Politician*, 559.

37. Ibid., 558–59.

38. Witcover, *The Resurrection of Richard Nixon*, 22.

37. LYNDON B. JOHNSON

1. Caro, *The Path to Power,* 6.
2. Unger and Unger, *LBJ,* 3–6.
3. Caro, *The Path to Power,* 74; Kearns, *Lyndon Johnson and the American Dream,* 36–37.
4. Caro, *The Path to Power,* 76.
5. Ibid., 99–103.
6. Ibid., 124–29.
7. Ibid., 153–60.
8. Caro, *The Path to Power,* 206–12; Dugger, *The Politician,* 125–26.
9. Caro, *The Path to Power,* 213–14; Dugger, *The Politician,* 127–29.
10. Dugger, *The Politician,* 170.
11. Ibid., 176–86.
12. Ibid., 201–3.
13. Caro, *The Path to Power,* 738–40.
14. Ibid., 757.
15. Dugger, *The Politician,* 239.
16. Ibid., 242.
17. Ibid., 244–50; Caidin and Hymoff, *The Mission,* 191.
18. Dugger, *The Politician,* 251.
19. Ibid., 319–32.
20. Ibid., 294.
21. Schlesinger, *Robert Kennedy and His Times,* 208.
22. Ibid., 210.
23. Evans and Novak, *Lyndon B. Johnson,* 303.
24. Ibid., 298.
25. Kearns, *Lyndon Johnson and the American Dream,* 161–62.
26. Evans and Novak, *Lyndon B. Johnson,* 319–21.
27. Merle Miller, *Lyndon,* 273.
28. Ibid., 275.
29. Ibid., 277; Caro, *The Years of Lyndon Johnson,* 168.
30. Evans and Novak, *Lyndon B. Johnson,* 326–27; Caro, *The Years of Lyndon Johnson,* 169–72.
31. Dallek, *Lone Star Rising,* 16–17.
32. Miller, *Lyndon,* 287–90.
33. Mooney, *The Lyndon Johnson Story,* 145.
34. Kennedy, *Thirteen Days,* 30.
35. Ibid., 110.
36. Shesol, *Mutual Contempt,* 97.
37. Leonard Baker, *The Johnson Eclipse,* 182.
38. Manchester, *The Death of a President,* 73.

38. HUBERT H. HUMPHREY

1. Griffith, *Humphrey,* 37, 44.
2. Ibid., 72.
3. Ibid., 73.
4. Ibid., 110–12.
5. Ibid., 112–13.
6. Ibid., 115.
7. Solberg, *Hubert Humphrey,* 114–15.
8. Griffith, *Humphrey,* 251–52.
9. Ibid., 158.
10. Humphrey, *Beyond Civil Rights,* 41–42.
11. Griffith, *Humphrey,* 160.
12. Humphrey, *The Education of a Public Man,* 188–89, 199.
13. Solberg, *Hubert Humphrey,* 209.
14. Humphrey, *The Education of a Public Man,* 475.
15. Solberg, *Hubert Humphrey,* 210.
16. Ibid., 276–87.
17. Ibid., 293.
18. McNamara, *In Retrospect,* 123.
19. Shesol, *Mutual Contempt,* 208.
20. Ibid., 208–9.
21. Humphrey, *The Education of a Public Man,* 300.
22. Eisele, *Almost to the Presidency,* 219.
23. Solberg, *Hubert Humphrey,* 263.
24. Eisele, *Almost to the Presidency,* 232.
25. Ibid., 224.
26. Solberg, *Hubert Humphrey,* 284.
27. Ibid., 290; Eisele, *Almost to the Presidency,* 244.

28. Eisele, *Almost to the Presidency*, 250.

29. Solberg, *Hubert Humphrey*, 317–18.

30. Witcover, *85 Days*, 28.

31. Witcover, *The Year the Dream Died*, 102.

32. Ibid., 142.

33. Witcover, *85 Days*, 290.

34. Eisele, *Almost to the Presidency*, 336.

35. Witcover, *The Year the Dream Died*, 321.

36. Ibid., 360.

37. Ibid., 372.

38. O'Brien, *No Final Victories*, 259–60.

39. Ibid., 261.

40. Humphrey, *The Education of a Public Man*, 403.

41. Califano, *The Triumph and Tragedy of Lyndon Johnson*, 325.

42. Witcover, *The Year the Dream Died*, 380.

43. Clifford, *Council to the President*, 582.

44. Ibid., 582.

45. Humphrey, *The Education of a Public Man*, 8–9.

46. Califano, *The Triumph and Tragedy of Lyndon Johnson*, 426.

47. Lyndon Baines Johnson, *The Vantage Point*, 437.

39. SPIRO T. AGNEW

1. Witcover, *White Knight*, 36–43.

2. Ibid., 64–74.

3. Ibid., 103.

4. Ibid., 123.

5. Lucas, *Agnew in Conflict*, 43.

6. Witcover, *White Knight*, 157–58.

7. Ibid., 155–56.

8. Ibid., 187.

9. Ibid., 5–6, 199.

10. Ibid., 11–17.

11. Ibid., 26.

12. Witcover, *The Resurrection of Richard Nixon*, 356.

13. Witcover, *White Knight*, 234.

14. Ibid., 241.

15. Ibid., 247–63.

16. Ibid., 293.

17. Ehrlichman, *Witness to Power*, 146.

18. Agnew, *Go Quietly . . . or Else*, 32.

19. Witcover, *White Knight*, 302–3.

20. Ibid., 305.

21. Ibid., 308.

22. Ibid., 311–13.

23. Ibid., 339.

24. Ehrlichman, *Witness to Power*, 150–52.

25. Ibid., 153.

26. Witcover, *White Knight*, 405.

27. Ibid., 405–7.

28. Ibid., 407.

29. Witcover, *Very Strange Bedfellows*, 163.

30. Ibid., 167.

31. Ibid., 179–80.

32. Ehrlichman, *Witness to Power*, 155.

33. Nixon Tapes, EOB 246–26, July 7, 1971, Nixon Collection, National Archives.

34. Ibid.

35. Nixon Tapes, OVAL 541–2, July 21, 1971, Nixon Collection, National Archives.

36. Ehrlichman, *Witness to Power*, 154–55, 261.

37. Nixon Tapes, OVAL 576–6, September 18, 1971, Nixon Collection, National Archives.

38. Witcover, *Very Strange Bedfellows*, 218.

39. Author interview with Patrick Buchanan, McLean, VA, August 15, 2005.

40. Ehrlichman, *Witness to Power*, 141–42.

41. Cohen and Witcover, *A Heartbeat Away*, 5.

42. Ibid.

43. Nixon Tapes, Abuse of Power,

E–255, 36–92, April 17, 1973, Nixon Collection, National Archives.

44. Ibid., E–257, 38–159, April 25, 1973.

45. Ehrlichman, *Witness to Power,* 143.

46. Haig, *Inner Circles,* 353

47. Agnew, *Go Quietly . . . or Else,* 103–4.

48. Cohen and Witcover, *A Heartbeat Away,* 348–50.

49. Nixon, *RN,* 1005.

50. Agnew, *Go Quietly . . . or Else,* 204.

51. Meyer and Schauble, "Agnew's Fee in Saudi Deal Related in Bankfuptcy Court," A3. 52. Witcover, *Very Strange Bedfellows,* 363.

53. Strober and Strober, *Nixon,* 432.

40. GERALD R. FORD JR.

1. Cannon, *Time and Chance,* 9.

2. Ibid., 14.

3. Brinkley, *Gerald R. Ford,* 7.

4. Ibid., 31–38.

5. Ibid., 18.

6. Ford, *A Time to Heal,* 73.

7. Ibid., 76.

8. Cannon, *Time and Chance,* 87–88.

9. Hatfield, *Vice Presidents of the United States,* 495.

10. Ford, *A Time to Heal,* 85.

11. Ibid., 86.

12. Ibid., 95.

13. Ehrlichman, *Witness to Power,* 197–98.

14. Brinkley, *Gerald R. Ford,* 39.

15. Haldeman, *The Haldeman Diaries,* 504.

16. Brinkley, *Gerald R. Ford,* 47.

17. Cannon, *Time and Chance,* 205.

18. Ford, *A Time to Heal,* 105.

19. Haig, *Inner Circles,* 419, 427.

20. Witcover, *Marathon,* 36–37.

21. Ibid., 38.

22. Ibid., 39–40.

23. Hartmann, *Palace Politics,* 120.

24. Ford, *A Time to Heal,* 4.

25. *Washington Post,* "Nixon Resigns," August 9, 1974.

26. Witcover, *Marathon,* 41.

27. Ibid., 43.

41. NELSON A. ROCKEFELLER

1. Reich, *The Life of Nelson A. Rockefeller,* xvii.

2. Ibid., 3.

3. Persico, *The Imperial Rockefeller,* 28–29.

4. Ibid., 30.

5. Ibid., 31.

6. Reich, *The Life of Nelson A. Rockefeller,* 167–69.

7. Ibid., 103–11.

8. Ibid., 144.

9. Ibid., 174–85.

10. Persico, *The Imperial Rockefeller,* 34.

11. Ibid., 35–36.

12. Ibid., 36.

13. Reich, *The Life of Nelson A. Rockefeller,* 688.

14. Ibid., 700–726.

15. Ibid., 765.

16. Joe Alex Morris, *Nelson Rockefeller,* 339.

17. Kramer and Roberts, *"I Never Wanted to Be Vice-President of Anything!"* 224–27.

18. Ibid.

19. Ibid., 233–34.

20. Desmond, *Nelson Rockefeller,* 287.

21. Kramer and Roberts, *"I Never Wanted to be Vice-President of Anything!"* 277.

22. Ibid.

23. Witcover, *The Resurrection of Richard Nixon,* 215.

24. Ibid., 219.

25. Kramer and Roberts, *"I Never Wanted to Be Vice-President of Anything!"* 368.

26. Ibid., 371.

27. Witcover, *Marathon,* 47–48.

28. Light, *Vice-Presidential Power,* 44.

29. Ibid., 45.

30. Kramer and Roberts, *"I Never Wanted to Be Vice-President of Anything!"* 372–75.

31. Witcover, *Marathon,* 51–52.

32. Ibid., 54.

33. Ibid.

34. Ibid., 55.

35. Ford, *A Time to Heal,* 328.

36. Cannon, *Time and Chance,* 407.

37. Witcover, *Marathon,* 83.

38. Ibid., 83–84.

42. WALTER F. MONDALE

1. Witcover, *Marathon,* 360–61.

2. Ibid., 365.

3. Ibid.

4. Lewis, *Mondale,* 34–36.

5. Ibid., 58–64.

6. Witcover, *Marathon,* 126.

7. Carter, *Keeping Faith,* 37.

8. Witcover, *Marathon,* 613.

9. Ibid., 613–14.

10. Ibid., 616.

11. Mondale, *The Good Fight,* 171.

12. Ibid., 172.

13. Carter, *Keeping Faith,* 40.

14. Shogan, *Promises to Keep,* 120.

15. Ibid., 206.

16. Mondale, *The Good Fight,* 183.

17. Gillon, *The Democrats' Dilemma,* 194.

18. Mondale, *The Good Fight,* 177–81.

19. Ibid., 184–85.

20. Ibid., 186–87.

21. Gillon, *The Democrats' Dilemma,* 200.

22. Ibid.

23. Carter, *Keeping Faith,* 370.

24. Mondale, *The Good Fight,* 205–11.

25. Ibid., 212–13.

26. Ibid., 233–35.

27. Ibid., 236.

28. Ibid., 238.

29. Carter, *Keeping Faith,* 464.

30. Clymer, *Edward M. Kennedy,* 299.

31. Ibid., 300.

32. Mondale, *The Good Fight,* 268.

33. Germond and Witcover, *Wake Us When It's Over,* 410.

34. Author telephone interview with Walter Mondale, Minneapolis, February 27, 2013.

35. Germond and Witcover, *Wake Us When It's Over,* 533.

43. GEORGE H. W. BUSH

1. Parmet, *George Bush,* 19.

2. Ibid., 23–24; Bush, *Looking Forward,* 23–24.

3. Parmet, *George Bush,* 24; Bush, *Looking Forward,* 28.

4. Bush, *Looking Forward,* 22–24; Parmet, *George Bush,* 24.

5. Bush, *Looking Forward,* 34–37, Hyams, *Flight of the Avenger,* 156.

6. Bush, *Looking Forward,* 79–86.

7. Ibid., 83–89; Naftali, *George H. W. Bush,* 11.

8. Bush, *Looking Forward,* 77.

9. Naftali, *George H. W. Bush,* 15.

10. Ibid., 18–19.

11. Parmet, *George Bush,* 161.

12. Haig, *Inner Circles,* 492–93.

13. Germond and Witcover, *Blue Smoke and Mirrors,* 169.

14. Witcover, *Crapshoot,* 307.

15. Author interview with Richard Cheney, McLean, VA, March 28, 2013.

16. Author interview with Ronald Reagan, Washington, March 25,

1981; Germond and Witcover, *Blue Smoke and Mirrors,* 183.

17. Ibid., 187.
18. Reagan, *An American Life,* 255–56.
19. Parmet, *George Bush,* 270.
20. Germond and Witcover, *Blue Smoke and Mirrors,* 326.
21. Witcover, *Crapshoot,* 326–27.
22. Parmet, *George Bush,* 281.
23. Witcover, *Crapshoot,* 329.
24. Green, *George Bush,* 228.
25. Witcover, *Crapshoot,* 419.

44. J. DANFORTH QUAYLE

1. Witcover, *Crapshoot,* 356.
2. Ibid., 361–62.
3. Ibid., 361.
4. Ibid., 365.
5. Ibid., 367–68.
6. Fenno, *The Making of a Senator,* 7–8.
7. Ibid., 12.
8. Ibid., 18.
9. Ibid., 22.
10. Witcover, *Crapshoot,* 376.
11. Broder and Woodward, *The Man Who Would Be President,* 21.
12. Germond and Witcover, *Whose Broad Stripes and Bright Stars?,* 386.
13. Quayle, *Standing Firm,* 9.
14. Germond and Witcover, *Whose Broad Stripes and Bright Stars?,* 388.
15. Ibid., 391.
16. Germond and Witcover, *Whose Broad Stripes and Bright Stars?,* 395
17. Witcover, *Crapshoot,* 347–48.
18. Germond and Witcover, *Whose Broad Stripes and Bright Stars?,* 440–41.
19. Quayle, *Standing Firm,* 63.
20. Germond and Witcover, *Whose Broad Stripes and Bright Stars?,* 441.
21. Quayle, *Standing Firm,* 66–67.
22. Witcover, *Crapshoot,* 380.

23. Ibid., 381–82.
24. Ibid., 383–84.
25. Ibid., 385.
26. Quayle, *Standing Firm,* 131.
27. Witcover, *Crapshoot,* 386.
28. Ibid., 387.
29. Quayle, *Standing Firm,* 138.
30. Powell, *My American Journey,* 440–44.
31. Witcover, *Crapshoot,* 388–89.
32. Ibid., 389–90.
33. Quayle, *Standing Firm,* 196–97.
34. Germond and Witcover, *Mad as Hell,* 393.
35. Broder and Woodward, *The Man Who Would Be President,* 125–26.
36. K. J. Cooper, "Divided House Bars Funds for Quayle Competitive Council." *Washington Post,* July 2, 1992.
37. Germond and Witcover, *Mad as Hell,* 395.
38. Ibid.
39. Germond and Witcover, *Mad as Hell,* 145.
40. Quayle, *Standing Firm,* 311.
41. Ibid., 400.
42. Germond and Witcover, *Mad as Hell,* 477.

45. ALBERT A. GORE JR.

1. Maraniss and Nakashima, *The Prince of Tennessee,* 54.
2. Ibid., 35.
3. Ibid., 106.
4. Ibid., 331–33.
5. Ibid., 383.
6. Turque, *Inventing Al Gore,* 262.
7. Ibid., 266–68.
8. Ibid., 272–73.
9. Ibid., 274.
10. Witcover, *Party of the People,* 675.
11. Ibid., 676–77.
12. Turque, *Inventing Al Gore,* 312–20.

13. Ibid., 322–24.

14. Ibid., 338.

15. Ibid., 348.

16. Ibid., 350.

17. Ibid., 356.

18. Witcover, *Party of the People,* 700–702.

19. Ibid., 705.

46. RICHARD B. CHENEY

1. Warshaw, *The Co-Presidency of Bush and Cheney,* 1–2.

2. Hayes, *Cheney,* 17.

3. Cheney, *In My Time,* 26.

4. Ibid., 27.

5. Ibid., 28.

6. Ibid., 30.

7. Savage, *Takeover,* 12.

8. Hayes, *Cheney,* 43.

9. Cheney, *In My Time,* 36.

10. Hayes, *Cheney,* 44.

11. Cheney, *In My Time,* 41–42.

12. Ibid., 59.

13. Ibid., 92.

14. Ibid.

15. Savage, *Takeover,* 53–56.

16. Ibid., 60–61.

17. Author interview with Richard Cheney, McLean, VA, March 28, 2013.

18. Ibid.

19. Ibid.

20. Cheney, *In My Time,* 254–55.

21. Ibid., 256.

22. Barton Gellman, *Angler,* 1–6.

23. Ibid., 6.

24. Cheney, *In My Time,* 257–58.

25. Ibid., 259.

26. Hayes, *Cheney,* 281.

27. Gellman, *Angler,* 7.

28. U.S. Constitution Amendment XXV, Section 4.

29. Cheney, *In My Time,* 320–22.

30. Gellman, *Angler,* 89.

31. Ibid., 92–93.

32. Ibid., 98.

33. Ibid., 104–7.

34. Cheney, *In My Time,* 318.

35. Gellman, *Angler,* 110.

36. Cheney, *In My Time,* 318–19; Gellman, *Angler,* 112.

37. Cheney, *In My Time,* 3.

38. Gellman, *Angler,* 120.

39. Cheney, *In My Time,* 3; Gellman, *Angler,* 124–25.

40. Cheney, *In My Time,* 334.

41. Mann, *Rise of the Vulcans,* 138; Warshaw, *The Co-Presidency of Bush and Cheney,* 161–62.

42. Cheney, *In My Time,* 335.

43. Gellman, *Angler,* 132.

44. Ibid., 135.

45. Ibid., 164–66.

46. Ibid., 176.

47. Savage, *Takeover,* 155.

48. Ibid., 393.

49. Cheney, *In My Time,* 402.

50. Savage, *Takeover,* 182, 219; Associated Press interview, September 8, 2005.

51. Savage, *Takeover,* 163.

52. Ibid., 163–65.

53. Ibid., 410.

54. Author interview with Richard Cheney, McLean, VA, March 28, 2013.

55. Cheney, *In My Time,* 408.

56. Gellman, *Angler,* 363.

57. Author interview with Richard Cheney, McLean, VA, March 28, 2013.

58. Cheney, *In My Time,* 418.

59. Savage, *Takeover,* 430.

60. Gellman, *Angler,* 329.

61. Cheney, *In My Time,* 434.

62. Gellman, *Angler,* 377.

47. JOSEPH R. BIDEN JR.

1. *Wilmington News Journal,* April 12, 2008.

2. *Newsweek,* November 13, 2008.

3. Ibid.

4. Author interview with Vice President Biden, Greenville, DE, December 21, 2009.

5. Biden, *Promises to Keep,* xi–xvi, 3–4, 9–11, 20–23.

6. Ibid., 24–34.

7. Ibid., 36–38.

8. Witcover, *Joe Biden,* 48–50.

9. *Dallas Morning News,* April 23, 1908, reprint of 1987 profile.

10. *Wilmington News Journal,* January 6, 1973.

11. *Wilmington News Journal,* August 13, 1980.

12. Witcover, *Joe Biden,* 215.

13. President George Bush, news conference, Kennebunkport, Maine, July 1, 1991.

14. Witcover, *Joe Biden,* 270; Senate Judiciary Committee, First Session, part 4, 5.

15. Witcover, *Joe Biden,* 273.

16. Ibid., 344.

17. Lott, *Herding Cats,* 238–41.

18. Witcover, *Joe Biden,* 347.

19. Author interview with Biden, December 21, 2009.

20. CNN, August 12, 2003.

21. Witcover, *Joe Biden,* 386.

22. *Wilmington News Journal,* January 5, 2008.

23. *New Yorker,* October 13, 2008.

24. Author interview with David Plouffe, Washington, December 7, 2009.

25. *Boston Globe,* August 24, 2008.

26. Biden, acceptance speech, Democratic National Convention, Denver, August, 27, 2008.

27. Heilemann and Halperin, *Game Change,* 413–14, 419.

28. President Barack Obama, e-mail response to written interview questions, March 1, 2010.

29. White House Press Office, February 7, 2009.

30. CNN, April 4, 2009.

31. Alter, *The Promise,* 389.

32. President Obama, e-mail response to written interview questions, March 1, 2010.

33. Author interview with Bruce Reed, Biden chief of staff, Washington, December 18, 2012.

34. Author interview with Biden, Washington, April 5, 2013.

35. Ibid.

36. Ibid.

37. Ibid.

48. THE EVOLVING ASSISTANT PRESIDENCY

1. Nathan Miller, *Theodore Roosevelt,* 342.

2. Witcover, *Crapshoot,* 404.

3. Author interview with George S. McGovern, Washington, 1973; Witcover, *Crapshoot,* 414.

4. Author telephone interview with Walter Mondale, Minneapolis, February 27, 2013.

5. Author interview with Gerald Ford, Washington, 1977.

6. Witcover, *Crapshoot,* 399.

7. Nelson, *A Heartbeat Away,* 45, 8.

8. Witcover, *Crapshoot,* 400.

9. Author interview with Joe Biden, Washington, April 5, 2013.

10. Author interview with Ford, Washington, 1977.

11. Author interview with Dick Cheney, McLean, VA, March 19, 2013.

12. Author interview with Biden, April 5, 2013.

13. Ibid.

14. Author interview with Ford, 1977.

15. Author telephone interview with Mondale, February 27, 2013.

16. Author interview with Cheney, March 19, 2013.

17. Author telephone interview with Mondale, February 27, 2013.

18. Ibid.

19. Author interview with Biden, April 5, 2013.

20. Author telephone interview with Mondale, February 27, 2013.

21. Ibid.

22. Author interview with Biden, April 5, 2013.

BIBLIOGRAPHY

Abbott, Richard H. *Cobbler in Congress: The Life of Henry Wilson, 1812–1875*. Lexington: University Press of Kentucky, 1972.

Ables, Jules. *In the Time of Silent Cal*. New York: G. P. Putnam's Sons, 1969.

Ackerman, Kenneth D. *Dark Horse: The Surprise Election and Political Murder of President James A. Garfield*. New York: Carroll and Graf Publishers, 2003.

Adams, Charles Francis. *The Works of John Adams*. Boston: Little, Brown, 1850–56.

Agnew, Spiro T. *Go Quietly . . . or Else*. New York: William Morrow, 1980.

Aitken, Jonathan. *Nixon: A Life*. London: Widened & Nicolson, 1993.

Albright, Joseph. *What Makes Spiro Run? The Life and Times of Spiro Agnew*. New York: Dodd, Mead, 1972.

Algeo, Matthew. *The President Is a Sick Man*. Chicago: Chicago Review Press, 2011.

Allen, George. *Presidents Who Have Known Me*. New York: Simon and Schuster, 1960.

Alter, Jonathan.

The Promise: President Obama, Year One. New York: Simon and Schuster, 2010.

Ambrose, Stephen E. *Nixon: The Education of a Politician, 1913–1962*. New York: Simon and Schuster, New York, 1987.

———. *Nixon: The Triumph of a Politician, 1962–1972*. New York: Simon and Schuster, 1989.

Ammon, Henry. *James Monroe: The Quest for National Identity*. New York: McGraw-Hill, 1971.

Anderson, Judith Icke. *William Howard Taft: An Intimate History*. New York: W. W. Norton, 1981.

Appleby, Joyce. *Thomas Jefferson*. New York: Times Books/Henry Holt, 2003.

Auchincloss, Louis. *Theodore Roosevelt*. New York: Times Books/Henry Holt, 2001.

Austin, James T. *The Life of Elbridge Gerry*. Boston: Wells and Lilly, 1829.

Baker, Jean H. *James Buchanan*. New York: Times Books/Henry Holt, 2004.

————. *The Stevensons: A Biography of an American Family*. New York: W. W. Norton, 1996.

Baker, Leonard. *The Johnson Eclipse*. New York: Macmillan, 1966.

Baker, Ray Stannard. *Woodrow Wilson: Life and Letters*. New York: Greenwood Press, 1968.

Barkley, Alben W. *That Reminds Me*. Garden City, NY: Doubleday, 1954.

Barry, David S. *Forty Years in Washington*. Boston: Little, Brown, 1924.

Bartlett, Irving H. *John C. Calhoun: A Biography*. New York: W. W. Norton, 1993.

Bauer, K. Jack. *Zachary Taylor: Soldier, Planter, Statesman of the Old Southwest*. Baton Rouge: Louisiana State University Press, 1985.

Belohlavek, John M. *George Mifflin Dallas: Jacksonian Patrician*. University Park: Pennsylvania State University Press, 1977.

Benedict, Michael Les. *The Impeachment and Trial of Andrew Johnson*. New York: W. W. Norton, 1973.

Bennett, David J. *He Almost Changed the World: The Life and Times of Thomas Riley Marshall*. Bloomington, IN: Authorhouse, 2007.

Bergeron, Paul H. *The Presidency of James K. Polk*. Lawrence: University of Kansas Press, 1987.

Berman, Edgar. *Hubert: The Triumph and Tragedy of the Humphrey I Knew*. New York: G. P. Putnam's Sons, 1979.

Bernstein, Irving. *Guns or Butter: The Presidency of Lyndon Johnson*. New York: Oxford University Press, 1996.

Beschloss, Michael R. *Taking Charge: The Johnson White House Tapes, 1963–1964*. New York: Simon and Schuster, 1997.

Biden, Joseph R., II. *Promises to Keep: On Life and Politics*. New York: Random House, 2007.

Billias, George Athan. *Elbridge Gerry: Founding Father and Republican Statesman*. New York: McGraw-Hill, 1976.

Binkley, Wilfred E. *American Political Parties: Their Natural History*. New York: Alfred A. Knopf, 1962.

Bishop, Jim. *The Day Kennedy Was Shot*. New York: Funk and Wagnalls, 1968.

————. *The Day Lincoln Was Shot*. New York: Harper and Row, 1955.

Blum, John M., William S. McFeeley, Edmund S. Morgan, Arthur M. Schlesinger Jr., Kenneth M. Stampp, and C. Vern Woodward. *The National Experience: A History of the United States*. 8th ed. New York: Harcourt Brace Jovanovich, 1993.

Bork, Robert H. *The Tempting of America: The Political Seduction of the Law*. New York: Free Press, 1990.

Borneman, Walter R. *Polk: The Man Who Transformed the Presidency and America*. New York: Random House, 2008.

Bowers, Claude G. *Jefferson and Hamilton: The Struggle for Democracy in America*. Boston: Houghton Mifflin, 1925.

————. *Jefferson in Power: The Death Struggle of the Federalists*. Boston: Houghton Mifflin, 1936.

————. *The Tragic Era: The Revolution after Lincoln.* New York: Blue Ribbon Books, 1929.

Brands, H. W. *TR: The Last Romantic.* New York: Basic Books, 1997.

Brant, Irving. *The Fourth President: A Life of James Madison.* Indianapolis: Bobbs-Merrill, 1970.

Brinkley, Douglas. *Gerald R. Ford.* New York: Times Books/Henry Holt, 2007

————. *The Unfinished Presidency: Jimmy Carter's Journey beyond the White House.* New York: Penguin Books, 1998.

Broder, David S., and Bob Woodward. *The Man Who Would Be President: Dan Quayle.* New York: Simon and Schuster, 1999.

Bunting, Josiah, III. *Ulysses S. Grant.* New York: Times Books/Henry Holt, 2004.

Bush, George. *All the Best: My Life in Letters and Other Writings.* New York: Lisa Drew/Scribner, 1999.

————. *Looking Forward: An Autobiography.* With Victor Gold. New York: Doubleday, 1987.

Byrnes, James F. *All in One Lifetime.* New York: Harper and Brothers, 1958.

————. *Speaking Frankly.* Westport, CT: Greenwood Press, 1947.

Caidin, Martin, and Edward Hymoff. *The Mission.* Philadelphia: Lippincott, 1964.

Califano, Joseph A. *The Triumph and Tragedy of Lyndon Johnson: The White House Years.* New York: Simon and Schuster, 1991.

Cannon, James. *Time and Chance: Gerald Ford's Appointment with History.* New York: HarperCollins, 1994.

Capers, Gerald M. *John C. Calhoun, Opportunist: A Reappraisal.* Gainesville: University Press of Florida, 1960.

Caro, Robert A. *The Path to Power: The Years of Lyndon Johnson.* New York: Alfred A. Knopf, 1982.

————. *The Years of Lyndon Johnson: The Passage of Power.* New York: Alfred A. Knopf, 2012.

Carter, Jimmy. *Keeping Faith: Memoirs of a President.* New York: Bantam Books, 1992.

Cheney, Richard B. *In My Time.* New York: Threshold Editions, 2011.

Chernow, Ron. *Alexander Hamilton.* New York: Penguin Books, 2005.

Chidsey, Donald Barr. *And Tyler Too.* Nashville: Thomas Nelson 1978.

Chitwood, Oliver Perry. *John Tyler: Champion of the Old South.* Reprint. Newtown, CT: American Political Biography Press, 1990.

Clifford, Clark, *Council to the President: Memoirs.* With Richard Holbrooke. New York: Random House, 1991.

Clymer, Adam. *Edward M. Kennedy: A Biography.* New York: William Morrow, 1999.

Cmiel, Kenneth. *Democratic Eloquence: The Fight over Popular Speech in the 19th Century.* New York: William Morrow, 1990.

Cohen, Richard M., and Jules Witcover. *A Heartbeat Away: The Investigation and Resignation of Vice President Spiro T. Agnew.* New York: Viking Press, 1974.

552 | BIBLIOGRAPHY

Cole, Donald B. *Martin Van Buren and the American Political System.* Princeton, NJ: Princeton University Press, 1984.

———. *President Martin Van Buren.* Princeton, NJ: Princeton University Press, 1984.

Coletta, Paolo E. *The Presidency of William Howard Taft.* Lawrence: University Press of Kansas, 1973.

Connolly, Michael J. "Vice President Garret A. Hobart and Nineteenth-Century Republican Business Politics." Abstract in New Jersey history. *Journal of the New Jersey Historical Society* 125 (2010).

Coolidge, Calvin. *The Autobiography of Calvin Coolidge.* New York: Academy Books, Cosmopolitan Books, 1984.

Cooper, John Milton, Jr. "The Election of 1900." In *Running for President: The Candidates and the Issues,* vol. 2, *1900–1992,* edited by Arthur M. Schlesinger, Fred L. Israel, and David Frent. New York: Simon and Schuster, 1994.

———. *Woodrow Wilson: A Biography.* New York: Alfred A. Knopf, 2009.

Cooper, Kenneth J. "Divided House Bars Funds for Quayle Competitive Council." *Washington Post,* July 2, 1992, A6.

Cornog, Evans. *Hats in the Ring.* New York: Random House, 2000.

Cramer, Richard Ben. *What It Takes: The Way to the White House.* New York: Vintage Books, 1993.

Crapol, Edward P. *John Tyler: The Accidental President.* Chapel Hill: University of North Carolina Press, 2006.

Culver, John C., and John Hyde. *American Dreamer: A Life of Henry A. Wallace.* New York: W. W. Norton, 2000.

Cunningham, Noble E., Jr. "The Election of 1800." In *Running for President: The Candidates and Their Images,* vol. 1, *1789–1896,* edited by Arthur M. Schlesinger Jr., Fred L. Israel, and David J. Frent. New York: Simon and Schuster, 1994.

———. *The Jeffersonian Republicans: The Formation of Party Organization, 1789–1801.* Chapel Hill: University of North Carolina Press, 1957.

———. *The Jeffersonian Republicans in Power: Party Operations, 1801–1809.* Chapel Hill: University of North Carolina Press, 1963.

Dalton, Kathleen. *Theodore Roosevelt: A Strenuous Life.* New York: Alfred A. Knopf, 2002.

Dallek, Robert. *Lone Star Rising: Lyndon Johnson and His Times, 1908–1960.* New York: Oxford University Press, 1991.

Daniels, Jonathan. *The Man of Independence.* Philadelphia: J. P. Lippincott, 1950.

Davis, Kenneth S. *The Politics of Honor: A Biography of Adlai E. Stevenson.* New York: G. P. Putnam's Sons, 1957.

Davis, Polly Ann. *Alben W. Barkley: Senate Majority Leader and Vice President.* New York: Garland Publishing, 1979.

Davis, William C. *Breckinridge: Statesman, Solder, Symbol.* Lexington: University Press of Kentucky, 2010.

Davison, Kenneth E. *The Presidency of Rutherford B. Hayes.* Westport, CT: Greenwood Press, 1972.

Dawes, Charles G. *Notes as Vice President, 1928–1929.* Boston: Little, Brown, 1935.

Depew, Chauncey. *My Eighty Years of Memories.* New York: Charles Scribner's Sons, 1922.

Desmond, James. *Nelson Rockefeller: A Political Biography.* New York: Macmillan, 1964.

Donovan, Robert J. *Conflict and Crisis: The Presidency of Harry S. Truman, 1945–1948.* New York: W. W. Norton: 1977.

Dugger, Ronnie. *The Politician: The Life and Times of Lyndon Johnson.* New York: W. W. Norton, 1982.

Ehrlichman, John. *Witness to Power: The Nixon Years.* New York: Simon and Schuster, 1982.

Eisele, Albert. *Almost to the Presidency: A Biography of Two American Politicians.* Blue Earth, MN: Piper Company, 1972.

Ellis, Joseph J. *American Sphinx: The Character of Thomas Jefferson.* New York: Alfred A. Knopf, 1997.

———. *First Family.* New York: Alfred A. Knopf, 2010.

———. *Founding Brothers.* New York: Alfred A. Knopf, 2000.

Engelmayer, Sheldon, and Robert J. Wagman. *Hubert Humphrey: The Man and His Dream, 1911–1978.* New York: Methuen, 1978.

Evans, Rowland, and Robert Novak. *Lyndon B. Johnson: The Exercise of Power.* New York: Signet Books, 1966.

Ewy, Marvin. *Charles Curtis of Kansas: Vice President of the United States, 1929–1933.* Emporia, KS: Emporia State Research Studies, Kansas State Teachers College, 1961.

Farley, James A. *Jim Farley's Story: The Roosevelt Years.* Westport, CT: Greenwood Press, 1984.

Fausold, Martin L. *The Presidency of Herbert C. Hoover.* Lawrence: University Press of Kansas, 1985.

Feller, David. "The Election of 1836." In *Running for President: The Candidates and Their Images,* vol. 1, edited by Arthur M. Schlesinger Jr., Fred L. Israel, and David J. Frent. New York: Simon and Schuster, 1994.

Fenno, Richard. *The Making of a Senator: Dan Quayle.* Washington DC: CQ Press, 1989.

Ferling, John. *Adams vs. Jefferson: The Tumultuous Election of 1800.* New York: Oxford University Press, 2004.

———. *John Adams: A Life.* Knoxville: University of Tennessee Press, 1992.

Ferrell, Robert H. *The Presidency of Calvin Coolidge.* Lawrence: University Press of Kansas, 1998.

Finkelman, Paul. *Millard Fillmore.* New York: Times Books/Henry Holt, 2011.

Fisher, O. C. *Cactus Jack.* Waco: Texan Press, 1978.

Flynn, Edward J. *You're the Boss: An Autobiography.* New York: Viking Press, 1947.

Foner, Eric. *The Fiery Trial: Abraham Lincoln and American Slavery.* New York: W. W. Norton, 2010.

Ford, Gerald R. *A Time to Heal: The Autobiography.* New York: Harper and Row, 1979.

Fuess, Claude M. *Calvin Coolidge: The Man from Vermont.* Hamden, CT: Archon Books, 1965.

Gellman, Barton. *Angler: The Cheney Presidency.* New York: Penguin Press, 2008.

Gellman, Irwin F. *The Contender: Richard Nixon, The Congress Years, 1946–1953.* New York: Free Press, 1999.

Germond, Jack W., and Jules Witcover. *Blue Smoke and Mirrors: How Reagan Won and Why Carter Lost the Election of 1980.* New York: Viking Press, 1981.

———. *Mad as Hell: Revolt at the Ballot Box, 1992.* New York: Warner Books, 1993.

———. *Wake Us When It's Over: Presidential Politics of 1984.* New York: Macmillan, 1985.

———. *Whose Broad Stripes and Bright Stars: The Trivial Pursuit of the Presidency, 1988.* New York: Warner Books, 1989.

Gilbert, Robert E. *The Tormented President: Calvin Coolidge, Death and Depression.* Westport, CT: Praeger, 2003.

Gillette, William. *Retreat from Reconstruction, 1869–1879.* Baton Rouge: Louisiana State University Press, 1979.

Gillon, Steven M. *The Democrats' Dilemma: Walter F. Mondale and the Liberal Legacy.* New York: Columbia University Press, 1992.

———. *The Kennedy Assassination: 24 Hours After.* New York: Basic Books, 2009.

Gittenstein, Mark. *Matters of Principle: An Insider's Account of America's Rejection of Robert Bork's Nomination to the Supreme Court.* New York: Simon and Schuster, 1992.

Goldstein, Joel K. *The Modern American Vice Presidency.* Princeton, NJ: Princeton University Press, 1982.

Goodwin, Doris Kearns. *No Ordinary Time: Franklin and Eleanor Roosevelt: The Homefront in World War II.* New York: Simon and Schuster, 1994.

Gordon-Reed, Annette. *Andrew Johnson.* New York: Times Books/Henry Holt, 2011.

Gould, Lewis L. *The Presidency of Theodore Roosevelt.* Lawrence: University Press of Kansas, 2011.

———. *The Presidency of William McKinley.* Lawrence: University Press of Kansas, 1980.

———. *The William Howard Taft Presidency.* Lawrence: University Press of Kansas, 2009.

Graff, Henry F. *Grover Cleveland.* New York: Times Books/Henry Holt, 2002.

Grant, U. S. *Personal Memoirs of U. S. Grant.* Cambridge: Da Capo Press, 2001.

Gray, Ralph D. *Indiana's Favorite Sons, 1840–1940.* Indianapolis: Indian Historical Society 1988.

———. "Thomas A. Hendricks: Spokesman for the Democracy." In *Gentlemen from Indiana: National Party Candidates, 1836–1940,* edited by Ralph D. Gray, 117–39. Indianapolis: Indiana Historical Bureau, 1977.

———, ed. *Gentlemen from Indiana: National Party Candidates, 1836–1940.* Indianapolis: Indiana Historical Bureau, 1977.

Grayson, Benson Lee. *The Unknown President: The Administration of President Millard Fillmore.* Washington DC: University Press of America, 1981.

Green, Fitzhugh. *George Bush: An Intimate Portrait.* New York: Hippocrene Books, 1989.

Greene, John Robert. *The Presidency of George Bush.* Lawrence: University of Kansas Press, 2000.

Griffith, Winthrop. *Humphrey: A Candid Biography.* New York: William Morrow, 1965.

Haig, Alexander M., Jr. *Inner Circles: How America Changed the World.* New York: Warner Books, 1992.

Haldeman, H. R. *The Haldeman Diaries: Inside the Nixon White House.* New York: G. P. Putnam's Sons, 1994.

Hamby, Alonzo L. *Man of the People: Harry S. Truman.* New York: Oxford University Press, 1995.

Hamlin, Charles Eugene. *The Life and Times of Hannibal Hamlin.* Port Washington, NY: Kennikat Press, 1899.

Harbaugh, William Henry. *Power and Responsibility: The Life and Times of Theodore Roosevelt.* New York: Farrar, Straus and Cudahy, 1961.

Hartmann, Robert T. *Palace Politics: An Inside Account of the Ford Years.* New York: McGraw-Hill, 1980.

Hatch, Alden. *Edith Bolling Wilson: First Lady Extraordinary.* New York: Dodd, Mead, 1961.

Hatfield, Mark O. *Vice Presidents of the United States, 1789–1993.* With the U.S. Senate Historical Office. Washington DC: U.S. Government Printing Office, 1997.

Hawthorne, Nathaniel. *The Life of Franklin Pierce.* Boston: Ticknor, Reed and Fields, 1852.

Hayes, Stephen. *Cheney: The Untold Story of America's Most Powerful and Controversial Vice President.* New York: Harper Collins, 2007.

Heck, Frank H. *Proud Kentuckian: John C. Breckinridge.* Lexington: University Press of Kentucky, 1976.

Heilemann, John, and Mark Halperin. *Game Change: Obama and the Clintons, McCain and Palin, and the Race of a Lifetime.* New York: HarperCollins, 2010.

Hensel, W. U. "A Biographical Sketch of Thomas A. Hendricks." In *Life and Public Services of Hon. Grover Cleveland,* edited by William Dorsheimer. New York, 1884.

Hirsch, Mark D. "Election of 1884." In *History of American Presidential Elections, 1789–2001,* vol. 4, edited by Arthur M. Schlesinger Jr. and Fred L. Israel. New York: Chelsea House, 2001.

Hobart, Jennie. *Memories.* New York: Carroll Hall, 1930.

Holcombe, John W., and Hubert M. Skinner. *Life and Public Services of Thomas A. Hendricks with Selected Speeches and Writings.* Indianapolis: Carlon and Hollenbeck, 1886.

Horsman, Reginald. "The Elections of 1789 and 1792." In *Running for President: The Candidates and Their Images,* vol. 1, edited by Arthur M. Schlesinger Jr., Fred L. Israel, and David J. Frent. New York: Simon and Schuster, 1994.

Howells, William D. *Sketch of the Life and Character of Rutherford B. Hayes; also a Biographical Sketch of William A. Wheeler.* Boston: Hurd and Houghton, 1876.

Humphrey, Hubert H. *Beyond Civil Rights: A New Day of Equality.* New York: Random House, 1968.

———. *The Education of a Public Man: My Life and Politics.* Garden City, NY: Doubleday, 1976.

Hunt, Gaillard. *John C. Calhoun.* Philadelphia: George W. Jacobs and Co., 1907.

Hunt, H. Draper. *Hannibal Hamlin of Maine: Lincoln's First Vice President.* Syracuse, NY: Syracuse University Press, 1969.

Hyams, Joe. *Flight of the Avenger: George Bush at War.* San Diego: Harcourt Brace Jovanovich, 1991.

Irwin, Ray W. *Daniel D. Tompkins: Governor of New York and Vice President of the United States.* New York: New York Historical Society, 1968.

Isenberg, Nancy. *Fallen Founder: The Life of Aaron Burr.* New York: Viking Press, 2007.

James, Mequis. *Mr. Garner of Texas.* Indianapolis: Bobbs-Merrill, 1939.

Johnson, Lyndon Baines. *The Vantage Point: Perspectives of the Presidency, 1963–1969.* New York: Holt, Rinehart and Winston, 1971.

Johnson, Sam Houston. *My Brother Lyndon.* New York: Cowles Book, 1970.

Jordan, David M. *Roscoe Conkling of New York: Voice in the Senate.* Ithaca, NY: Cornell University Press, 1971.

Kaminski, John. *George Clinton: Yeoman Politician of the New Republic.* Madison, WI: Madison House, 1993.

Karabell, Zachary. *Chester Alan Arthur.* New York: Times Books/Henry Holt, 2004.

Kaufman, Burton I. *The Presidency of James Earl Carter, Jr.* Lawrence: University Press of Kansas, 1993.

Kearns, Doris. *Lyndon Johnson and the American Dream.* New York: Harper and Row, 1976.

Kennedy, Robert F. *Thirteen Days: A Memoir of the Cuban Missile Crisis.* New York: W. W. Norton, 1969.

Kerber, Linda K. "The Federalist Party." In *History of the U.S. Political Parties,* vol. 1, edited by Arthur M. Schlesinger Jr. New York: Chelsea House, 1973.

Klein, Herbert G. *Making It Perfectly Clear: An Inside Account of Nixon's Love-Hate Relationship with the Media.* Garden City, NY: Doubleday, 1980.

Kramer, Michael, and Sam Roberts. *"I Never Wanted to Be Vice-President of Anything!": An Investigative Biography of Nelson Rockefeller.* New York: Basic Books, 1976.

Kurtz, Stephen G. *The Presidency of John Adams: The Collapse of Federalism, 1795–1800.* Philadelphia: University of Pennsylvania, 1957.

LaFeber, Walter. "The Election of 1900." In *History of American Presidential Elections,* vol. 3, edited by Arthur M. Schlesinger Jr. and Fred L. Israel. New York: Chelsea House, 1971.

Leach, Paul R. *That Man Dawes.* Chicago: Reilly and Lee, 1930.

Lee, John K. *George Clinton: Master Builder of the Empire State.* Syracuse, NY: Syracuse University Press, 2010.

Leech, Margaret. *In the Days of McKinley.* New York: Harper and Brothers, 1959.

Leech, Margaret, and Harry J. Brown. *The Garfield Orbit: The Life of President James A. Garfield.* New York: Harper and Row, 1978.

Levin, Phyllis Lee. *Edith and Woodrow: The Wilson White House.* New York: Scribner, 2001.

Lewis, Finley. *Mondale: Portrait of an American Politician.* New York: Harper and Row, 1980.

Light, Paul C. *Vice-Presidential Power: Advice and Influence in the White House.* Baltimore, MD: Johns Hopkins University Press, 1984.

Lippman, Theo, Jr. *Spiro Agnew's America: The Vice President and the Politics of Suburbia.* New York: W. W. Norton, 1972.

Lomask, Milton. *Aaron Burr: The Years from Princeton to Vice President, 1756–1805.* New York: Farrar Straus Giroux, 1979.

———. *Andrew Johnson: President on Trial.* New York: Octagon Books, 1973.

Lord, Russell. *The Wallaces of Iowa.* Boston: Houghton Mifflin, 1947.

Lott, Trent. *Herding Cats: A Life in Politics.* New York: Regan Books, 2005.

Lucas, Jim G. *Agnew in Conflict.* New York: Award Books, 1970.

Ludlow, Louis. *From Cornfield to Press Gallery: Adventures and Reminiscences of a Veteran Washington Correspondent.* Washington DC: R. F. Roberts, 1924.

Lyon, Walter Hastings. *The Constitution and the Men Who Made It: The Constitutional Convention 1787.* Boston: Houghton Mifflin, 1936.

Madison, James. *The Constitutional Convention.* New York: Modern Library, 2005.

Magie, David. *The Life of Garret Augustus Hobart, Twenty-Fourth Vice President of the United States.* New York: G. P. Putnam's Sons, 1910.

Manchester, William. *American Caesar: Douglas MacArthur.* Boston: Little, Brown, 1978.

———. *The Death of a President.* New York: Harper and Row, 1967.

Mann, James. *Rise of the Vulcans: The History of Bush's War Cabinet.* New York: Penguin Books, 2004.

Manners, William C. *TR and Will: A Friendship That Split the Republican Party.* New York: Harcourt, Brace and World, 1969.

Maraniss, David. *First in His Class: The Biography of Bill Clinton.* New York: Touchstone, 1995.

Maraniss, David, and Ellen Nakashima. *The Prince of Tennessee.* New York: Simon and Schuster, 2000.

Margolis, Jon. *The Last Innocent Year: America in 1964, the Beginning of the "Sixties."* New York: William Morrow, 1999.

Markowitz, Norman D. *The Rise and Fall of the People's Century: Henry A. Wallace and American Liberalism, 1941–1948.* London: Free Press, Collier-Macmillan, 1973.

Marshall, Thomas R. *Recollections of Thomas R. Marshall, Vice President and Hoosier Philosopher: A Hoosier Salad.* Indianapolis: Bobbs-Merrill, 1925.

Martin, John Bartlow. *Adlai Stevenson of Illinois.* Garden City, NY: Doubleday, 1976.

Mayer, Jane. *The Dark Side.* New York: Doubleday, 2008.

Mayer, Jane, and Jill Abramson. *Strange Justice: The Selling of Clarence Thomas.* Boston: Houghton Mifflin, 1994.

Mazo, Earl, and Stephen Hess. *Nixon: A Political Portrait.* New York: Harper and Row, 1968.

McCombs, William F. *Making Woodrow Wilson President.* New York: Fairview Publishing, 1921.

McCoy, Donald R. *Calvin Coolidge: The Quiet President.* New York: Macmillan, 1967.

———. "The Election of 1924." In *History of American Presidential Elections,* vol. 3, edited by Arthur M. Schlesinger Jr. and Fred L. Israel. New York: Chelsea House, 1971.

McCullough, David. *John Adams.* New York: Simon and Schuster, 2001.

———. *Truman.* New York: Simon and Schuster, 1992.

McElroy, Robert. *Grover Cleveland: The Man and the Statesman,* vols. 1 and 2. New York: Harper Brothers, 1923.

———. *Levi Parsons Morton: Banker, Diplomat and Statesman.* New York: G. P. Putnam's Sons, 1930.

McFeeley, William. "The Election of 1872." In *Running for President: The Candidates and Their Images,* vol. 1, *1789–1896,* edited by Arthur M. Schlesinger Jr., Fred L. Israel, and David J. Frent. New York: Simon and Schuster, 1994.

McKay, Ernest. *Henry Wilson, Practical Radical: Portrait of a Politician.* Port Washington, NY: Kennikat Press, 1971.

McKee, John Hiram. *Coolidge, Wit and Wisdom.* New York: Frederick A. Stokes Company, 1933.

McNamara, Robert S. *In Retrospect: The Tragedy and Lessons of Vietnam.* With Brian Van De Mark. New York: Vintage Books, 1995, 1996.

Merrill, Horace Samuel, and Marion Galbraith Merrill. *The Republican Command: 1897–1913.* Lexington: University Press of Kentucky, 1971.

Meyer, Eugene L., and Chris Schauble. "Agnew's Fee in Saudi Deal Related in Bankruptcy Court." *Washington Post,* April 4, 1978, A3.

Miller, Merle. *Lyndon: An Oral Biography.* New York: G. P. Putnam's Sons, 1980.

———. *Plain Speaking: An Oral Biography of Harry S. Truman.* New York: Berkeley Publishing, 1974.

Miller, Nathan. *FDR: An Intimate History.* Garden City, NY: Doubleday, 1983.

———. *Theodore Roosevelt.* New York: William Morrow, 1992.

Miller, Richard Lawrence. *Truman: The Rise to Power.* New York: McGraw-Hill, 1986.

Mitchell, Greg. *Tricky Dick and the Pink Lady.* New York: Random House, 1998.

Mondale, Walter F. *The Good Fight: A Life in Liberal Politics.* With David Hage. New York: Scribner, 2010.

Monroe, Dan. *The Republican Vision of John Tyler.* College Station: Texas A&M University Press, 2003.

Mooney, Booth. *LBJ: An Irreverent Chronicle.* New York: Thomas Y. Crowell, 1976.

———. *The Lyndon Johnson Story.* New York: Farrar, Straus, 1964.

Morgan, H. Wayne. "The Election of 1892." In *History of American Presidential Elections, 1789–2001*, vol. 5, edited by Arthur M. Schlesinger Jr. and Fred L. Israel. Philadelphia: Chelsea House, 2001.

Morris, Dick. *Behind the Oval Office: Winning the Presidency in the Nineties.* New York: Random House, 1997.

Morris, Edmund. *Theodore Rex.* New York: Random House, 2001.

———. *The Rise of Theodore Roosevelt.* New York: Ballantine Books, 1979.

Morris, Joe Alex. *Nelson Rockefeller: A Biography.* New York: Harper and Brothers, 1960.

Morris, Roger. *Richard Milhous Nixon: The Rise of an American Politician.* New York: Henry Holt, 1990.

Naftali, Timothy. *George H. W. Bush.* New York: Times Books/Henry Holt, 2007.

Nelson, Michael. *A Heartbeat Away: Report of the Twentieth Century Fund Task Force on the Vice Presidency.* New York: Priority Press Publications, 1988.

Nevins, Allan. Foreword to John F. Kennedy, *Profiles in Courage.* New York: Harper and Brothers, 1956.

———. *Grover Cleveland: A Study in Courage,* vol. 1. Norwalk, CT: Easton Press, 1932.

———, ed. *Polk: The Diary of a President, 1845–1849.* London: Longmans, Green, 1952.

Niven, John. *John C. Calhoun and the Price of Union.* Baton Rouge: Louisiana State University, 1988.

———. *Martin Van Buren: The Romantic Age of American Politics.* New York: Oxford University Press, 1983.

Nixon, Richard M. *RN: The Memoirs of Richard Nixon.* New York: Grosset and Dunlap, 1978.

———. *Six Crises.* Garden City, NY: Doubleday, 1962.

O'Brien, Lawrence F. *No Final Victories: A Life in Politics from John F. Kennedy to Watergate.* Garden City, NY: Doubleday, 1974.

Pancake, Thomas S. *Thomas Jefferson and Alexander Hamilton: Shapers of History.* Woodbury, NY: Barron's Educational Series, 1974.

Parmet, Herbert S. *George Bush: The Life of a Lone Star Yankee.* New York: Lisa Deew/Scribner, 1997.

———. *Richard Nixon and His America.* Boston: Little, Brown, 1990.

Pastan, Amy. *The Smithsonian Book of Presidential Trivia.* Washington DC: Smithsonian Books, 2013.

Perkins, Frances. *The Roosevelt I Knew.* New York: Viking Press, 1946.

Persico, Joseph E. *The Imperial Rockefeller: A Biography of Nelson A. Rockefeller.* New York: Simon and Schuster, 1982.

Peskin, Alan. *Garfield.* Kent, OH: Kent State University Press, 1978.

Peterson, Merrill. *The Great Triumvirate: Webster, Clay and Calhoun.* New York: Oxford University Press, 1987.

Peterson, Norma Lois. *The Presidencies of William Henry Harrison and John Tyler.* Lawrence: University Press of Kansas, 1989.

Phillips, Kevin. *William McKinley.* New York: Times Books/Henry Holt, 2003.

Plouffe, David. *The Audacity to Win: The Inside Story and Lessons of Barack Obama's Historic Victory.* New York: Viking, 2009.

Polakoff, Keith Ian. *The Politics of Inertia: The Election of 1876 and the End of Reconstruction.* Baton Rouge: Louisiana State University Press, 1973.

Powell, Colin L. *My American Journey.* With Joseph E. Persico. New York: Random House, 1995.

Pringle, Henry F. *The Life and Times of William Howard Taft.* Hamden, CT: Archon Books, 1964.

Quayle, Dan. *Standing Firm: A Vice Presidential Memoir.* New York: HarperCollins, 1994.

Rayback, Robert J. *Millard Fillmore: Biography of a President.* Newtown, CT: American Political Biography Press, 1959.

Reagan, Ronald. *An American Life: The Autobiography.* New York: Simon and Schuster, 1990.

Reedy, George. *Lyndon B. Johnson: A Memoir.* Kansas City, MO: Andrews and McMeel, 1983.

Reeves, Richard. *President Kennedy: Profile of Power.* New York: Touchstone Books, 1993.

Reeves, Thomas C. *Gentleman Boss: The Life of Chester Alan Arthur.* New York: Alfred A. Knopf, 1975.

Reich, Cary. *The Life of Nelson A. Rockefeller: Worlds to Conquer, 1908–1958.* New York: Doubleday, 1996.

Remini, Robert V. *Andrew Jackson and the Course of American Democracy, 1833–45.* New York: Harper and Row, 1984.

———. *Andrew Jackson and the Course of American Freedom, 1822–1832.* New York: Harper and Row, 1981.

———. "Election of 1828." In *History of American Presidential Elections, 1879–2001,* vol. 1, edited by Arthur M. Schlesinger Jr. and Fred L. Israel. Philadelphia: Chelsea House, 2001.

———. *Henry Clay: Statesman for the Union.* New York: W. W. Norton, 1991.

———. *Martin Van Buren and the Making of the Democratic Party.* New York: Columbia University Press, 1959.

Risjord, Norman K. "Election of 1812." In *Running for President: The Candidates and Their Images,* vol. 1, *1789–1896,* edited by Arthur M. Schlesinger Jr., Fred L. Israel, and David J. Frent, 65–73. New York: Simon and Schuster, 1994.

Roosevelt, Theodore. *The Autobiography of Theodore Roosevelt.* Edited by Wayne Andrews. New York: Charles Scribner's Sons, 1958.

———. *Rough Riders.* New York: Da Capo Press, 1990.

Roseboom, Eugene H. *A History of Presidential Elections.* New York: Macmillan, 1964.

Rosenman, Samuel I. *Working with Roosevelt.* New York: Da Capo Press, 1972.

Russell, Francis. *The Shadow of Blooming Grove: Warren G. Harding and His Times.* New York: McGraw-Hill, 1968.

Rutkow, Ira. *James A. Garfield.* New York: Times Books/Henry Holt, 2006.

Sandberg, Carl. *Abraham Lincoln: The War Years,* vol. 1. New York: Harcourt, Brace, 1936.

Savage, Charlie. *Takeover: The Return of the Imperial Presidency and Subversion of American Democracy.* Boston: Little, Brown, 2007.

Schachner, Nathan. *Thomas Jefferson: A Biography.* New York: Yosselof, 1957.

Schapsmeier, Edward L., and Frederick H. Schapsmeier. *Prophet in Politics: Henry Wallace and the War Years, 1940–1965.* Ames: Iowa State University Press, 1970.

Schieffer, Bob and Gary Paul Gates. *The Acting President.* New York: E. P. Dutton, 1989.

Schlesinger, Arthur M., Jr. *The Age of Jackson.* Boston: Little, Brown, 1945.

———. *Robert Kennedy and His Times.* Boston: Houghton Mifflin, 1978.

———. *A Thousand Days: John F. Kennedy in the White House.* Boston: Houghton Mifflin, 1965.

Schlesinger, Arthur M., Jr., and Fred L. Israel, eds. *History of American Presidential Elections, 1789–2001,* 11 vols. New York and Philadelphia: Chelsea House, 1971–2001.

Schlesinger, Arthur M., Jr., Fred L. Israel, and David J. Frent, eds. *Running for President: The Candidates and Their Images,* vol. 1, *1789–1896,* and vol. 2, *1900–1992.* New York: Simon and Schuster, 1994.

Scroop, Daniel. *Mr. Democrat: Jim Farley, the New Deal and the Making of Modern American Politics.* Ann Arbor: University of Michigan Press, 2006.

Seager, Robert, II. *And Tyler Too: A Biography of John and Julia Gardiner Tyler.* New York: McGraw-Hill, 1963.

Seigenthaler, John. *James K. Polk.* New York: Times Books/Henry Holt, 2004.

Seitz, Don C. *From Kaw Teepee to Capitol: The Life Story of Charles Curtis, Indian, Who Has Risen to High Estate.* New York: Frederick A. Stokes, 1928.

Shesol, Jeff. *Mutual Contempt: Lyndon Johnson, Robert Kennedy and the Feud That Defined a Decade.* New York: W. W. Norton, 1997.

Shogan, Robert. *Promises to Keep: Carter's First 100 Days.* New York: Thomas W. Crowell, 1977.

Silbey, Joel. "The Election of 1836." In *History of American Presidential Elections, 1789–2001,* vol. 2, edited by Arthur M. Schlesinger Jr. and Fred L. Israel. Philadelphia: Chelsea House, 2001.

Smelser, Marshall. *The Democratic Republic: 1801–1815.* New York: Harper and Row, 1968.

Smith, Elbert B. *The Presidencies of Zachary Taylor and Millard Fillmore.* Lawrence: University Press of Kansas, Lawrence, 1988.

Smith, Gene. *When the Cheering Stopped: The Last Years of Woodrow Wilson.* New York: Time, 1964.

Smith, Willard H. *Schuyler Colfax: The Changing Fortunes of a Political Idol.* Indianapolis: Indiana Historical Bureau, 1952.

Smith, William Henry. *The Life and Speeches of Charles Warren Fairbanks.* Indianapolis: Wm. B. Burford, Publisher, 1904.

Sobel, Robert. *Coolidge: An American Enigma.* Washington DC: Regnery Publishing, 1998.

Socolofsky, Homer E., and Allan B. Spetter. *The Presidency of Benjamin Harrison.* Lawrence: University Press of Kansas, 1987.

Solberg, Carl. *Hubert Humphrey: A Biography.* New York: W. W. Norton, 1984.

Spaulding, E. Wilder. *His Excellency George Clinton: Critic of the Constitution.* New York: Macmillan, 1938.

Stewart, David O. *Impeached: The Trial of Andrew Johnson and the Fight for Lincoln's Legacy.* New York: Simon and Schuster, 2009.

Stoddard, Henry L. *As I Knew Them: Presidents and Politics from Grant to Coolidge,* vol. 1. Port Washington, NY: Kennikat Press, 1927.

Strober, Gerald, and Deborah Hart Strober. *The Nixon Presidency: An Oral History of the Era.* New York: HarperCollins, 1994.

Summers, Mark Wahlgren. *The Era of Good Stealings.* New York: Oxford University Press, 1993.

Taylor, John M. *Garfield of Ohio: The Available Man.* New York: W. W. Norton, 1970.

Thomas, Charles M. *Thomas Riley Marshall: Hoosier Statesman.* Oxford, OH: Mississippi Valley Press, 1939.

Thomas, Lately. *The First President Johnson: The Three Lives of the Seventeenth President of the United States of America.* New York: William Morrow, 1968.

Thompson, Charles Willis. *Presidents I've Known and Two Near Presidents.* Indianapolis: Bobbs-Merrill, 1929.

Timmons, Bascom N. *Garner of Texas: A Personal History.* New York: Harper and Brothers, 1948.

———. *Portrait of an American: Charles G. Dawes.* New York: Henry Holt, 1953.

Trefousse, Hans L. *Andrew Johnson: A Biography.* New York: W. W. Norton, 1989.

———. *Impeachment of a President: Andrew Johnson, the Blacks and Reconstruction.* New York: Fordham University Press, 1999.

Troy, Gil. "The Election of 1848." In *Running for President: The Candidates and Their Images,* vol. 1, *1789–1896,* edited by Arthur M. Schlesinger Jr., Fred L. Israel, and David J. Frent. New York: Simon and Schuster, 1994.

Truman, Harry S. *The Autobiography of Harry S. Truman.* Edited by Robert H. Ferrell. Boulder: Colorado Associated University Press, 1980.

Tully, Grace G. *FDR, My Boss.* New York: Charles Scribner's Sons, 1949.

Turque, Bill. *Inventing Al Gore: A Biography.* Boston: Houghton Mifflin, 2000.

Unger, Irwin, and Debi Unger. *LBJ: A Life.* New York: John Wiley and Sons, 1999.

Unrau, William. *Mixed-Bloods and Tribal Dissolution: Charles Curtis and the Quest for Indian Identity.* Lawrence: University Press of Kansas, 1989.

Valenti, Jack. *A Very Human President.* New York: W. W. Norton, 1975.

Van Buren, Martin. *The Autobiography of Martin Van Buren.* Edited by John C. Fitzpatrick. New York: Da Capo Press, 1973.

Warshaw, Shirley Anne. *The Co-Presidency of Bush and Cheney.* Stanford, CA: Stanford Politics and Policy, 2009.

Watson, W. Marvin. *Chief of Staff: Lyndon Johnson and His Presidency.* With Sherman Markham. New York: Thomas Dunne Books/St. Martin's Press, 2004.

White, Graham, and John Maze. *Henry A. Wallace: The Search of a New World Order.* Chapel Hill: University of North Carolina Press, 1995.

White, Theodore H. *The Making of the President 1960.* New York: Signet Books, 1961.

———. *The Making of the President 1964.* New York: Signet Books, 1965.

White, William Allen. *A Puritan in Babylon: The Story of Calvin Coolidge.* New York: Macmillan Company, 1938.

Whitney, Henry Clay. *Life on the Circuit with Lincoln.* Caldwell, ID: Claxton Printers, 1940.

Wibberley, Leonard. *Man of Liberty: A Life of Thomas Jefferson.* New York: Farrar, Straus and Giroux, 1968.

Wicker, Tom. *George Herbert Walker Bush.* New York: Lipper/Viking, 2004.

Wilentz, Sean. *Andrew Jackson.* New York: Times Books/Henry Holt, 2005.

———. "The Election of 1840." In *Running for President: The Candidates and Their Images,* vol. 1, *1789–1896,* edited by Arthur M. Schlesinger Jr., Fred L. Israel, and David J. Frent. New York: Simon and Schuster, 1994.

Williams, Irving G. *The Rise of the Vice Presidency.* Washington DC: Public Affairs Press, 1956.

Williams, T. Harry, ed. *Hayes: Diary of a President, 1875–1881.* New York: David McKay Company, 1964.

Wills, Garry. *James Madison.* New York: Times Books/Henry Holt, 2002.

———. *Nixon Agonistes: The Crisis of the Self-Made Man.* Boston: Houghton Mifflin, 1970.

Wilmer, Ted. *Martin Van Buren.* New York: Times Books/Henry Holt, 2005.

Wiltse, Charles M. *John C. Calhoun: Nationalist, 1782–1828.* Indianapolis: Bobbs-Merrill, 1944.

———. *John C. Calhoun: Nullifier, 1829–1839.* Indianapolis: Bobbs-Merrill, 1949.

———. *John C. Calhoun: Sectionalist, 1840–1850.* Indianapolis: Bobbs-Merrill, 1951.

Witcover, Jules. *Crapshoot: Rolling the Dice on the Vice Presidency.* New York: Crown Publishers, 1992.

———. *85 Days: The Last Campaign of Robert Kennedy.* New York: G. P. Putnam's Sons, 1969.

———. *Joe Biden: A Life of Trial and Redemption.* New York: William Morrow, 2010.

———. *Marathon: The Pursuit of the Presidency, 1972–1976.* New York: Viking Press, 1976.

———. *Party of the People: A History of the Democrats.* New York: Random House, 2003.

———. *The Resurrection of Richard Nixon.* New York: G. P. Putnam's Sons, 1970.

———. *Very Strange Bedfellows: The Unhappy Marriage of Richard Nixon and Spiro Agnew.* Washington DC: Public Affairs Press, 2007.

———. *White Knight: The Rise of Spiro Agnew.* New York: Random House, 1972.

———. *The Year the Dream Died: Revisiting 1968 in America.* New York: Warner Books, 1997.

Woodward, Bob. *Plan of Attack.* New York: Simon and Schuster, 2004.

Young, Donald. *American Roulette: The History and Dilemma of the Vice Presidency.* New York: Viking Compass, 1974.

Also by the Author

85 Days: The Last Campaign of Robert Kennedy

The Resurrection of Richard Nixon

White Knight: The Rise of Spiro Agnew

A Heartbeat Away: The Investigation and Resigntion of Vice President Spiro T. Agnew
(with Richard M. Cohen)

Marathon: The Pursuit of the Presidency, 1972–1976

The Main Chanee (a novel)

Blue Smoke and Mirrors: Why Reagan Won and Carter Lost the Election of 1980 (with
Jack W. Germond)

Wake Us When It's Over: Presidential Politics of 1984 (with Germond)

Sabotage at Black Tom: Imperial Germany's Secret War in America, 1914–1917

Whose Broad Stripes and Bright Stars? The Trivial Pursuit of the Presidency, 1988 (with
Germond)

Crapshoot: Rolling the Dice on the Vice Presidency

Mad as Hell: Revolt at the Ballot Box, 1992 (with Germond)

The Year the Dream Died: Revisiting 1968 in America

*No Way to Pick a President: How Money and Hired Guns Have Debased American
Elections*

Party of the People: A History of the Democrats

The Making of an Ink-Stained Wretch: Half a Century Pounding the Political Beat

*Very Strange Bedfellows: The Short and Unhappy Marriage of Richard Nixon and Spiro
Agnew*

Joe Biden: A Life of Trial and Redemption

INDEX